The Book of Kells

Proceedings of a conference at
Trinity College Dublin
6-9 September 1992

The Book of Kells

Proceedings of a conference at
Trinity College Dublin
6-9 September 1992

edited by

Felicity O'Mahony

published for

TRINITY COLLEGE LIBRARY DUBLIN

by

SCOLAR PRESS 1994

Published by
SCOLAR PRESS
Gower House
Croft Road
Aldershot
Hants GU11 3HR
England

Ashgate Publishing Company
Old Post Road
Brookfield
Vermont 05036
U S A

Printed on acid free paper

British Library Cataloguing in Publication Data

Book of Kells: Proceedings of a Conference
at Trinity College, Dublin, 6-9 September
1992
I. O'Mahony, Felicity
091

ISBN 0-85967-967-5

Library of Congress Cataloging in Publication Data
applied for

Frontispiece: Book of Kells, folio 8r, detail

Printed in Great Britain at The University Press, Cambridge

Contents

Contributors

MICHELLE BROWN, Department of Manuscripts, British Library, London.
ANTHONY CAINS, Conservation Laboratory, Trinity College Library, Dublin.
ERIKA EISENLOHR, Eichendorffstrasse 1, 3550 Marburg/Lahn, Germany.
CAROL FARR, The University of Alabama in Huntsville, Huntsville, Alabama 35899.
IAN FISHER, RCAHMS, 16 Bernard Terrace, Edinburgh EH8 9NX, Scotland.
ROBERT FUCHS, Fachhochschule Köln, Ubierring 40, D-50678 Köln, Germany.
PETER HARBISON, 5 St Damian's, Loughshinny, Skerries, Co Dublin.
MÁIRE HERBERT, Department of Early and Medieval Irish, University College, Cork.
JOHN HIGGITT, Department of Fine Art, The University of Edinburgh, 19 George Square, Edinburgh EH8 9LD, Scotland.
EAMONN P KELLY, Irish Antiquities Division, National Museum of Ireland, Kildare Street, Dublin 2.
PATRICK MCGURK, 11 Ashdon Close, Woodford Green, Essex IG8 0EF, England.
DOUGLAS MAC LEAN, Department of Art, Lake Forest College, 555 North Sheridan Road, Lake Forest, Illinois 60045-2399, U S A.
MARTIN MCNAMARA, Woodview, 24 Mount Merrion Ave, Blackrock, Dublin.
BERNARD MEEHAN, Manuscripts Department, Trinity College Library, Dublin.
CHRISTIAN DE MÉRINDOL, 25 rue de la Republique, F 94220 Charenton, France.
NANCY NETZER, Director and Professor of Fine Art, Boston College, Museum of Art, Chestnut Hill, Massachusetts 02167-3809, U S A.
ÉAMONN Ó CARRAGÁIN, Department of English, University College, Cork.
DONNCHADH Ó CORRÁIN, Department of History, University College, Cork.
DORIS OLTROGGE, Fachhochschule Köln, Ubierring 40, D-50678 Köln, Germany.
JENNIFER O'REILLY, Department of Medieval History, University College, Cork.
WILLIAM O'SULLIVAN, c/o Manuscripts Department, Trinity College Library, Dublin.
MICHAEL RYAN, Chester Beatty Library, Shrewsbury Rd, Dublin 4.
ETIENNE RYNNE, Department of Archaeology, University College, Galway.
ROGER STALLEY, Department of History of Art, Trinity College, Dublin.
ROBERT STEVICK, Department of English, GN-30, University of Washington, Seattle, Washington 98195, U S A.
D L SWAN, 746 Howth Road, Dublin 5.
MARK VAN STONE, 3422 Southeast Grant Court, Portland, Oregan 97214, U S A.
MARTIN WERNER, Art History Department, Temple University, Ritter Annex, 13th & Cecil B Moore Ave, Room 857, Philadelphia 19122, U S A.

Preface

In 1992 Trinity College Dublin celebrated the quatercentenary of its foundation with a variety of academic and social events. It was appropriate that among many lectures, exhibitions and symposia covering a wide range of academic interests a conference should be devoted solely to the Book of Kells. This, the College's greatest treasure, has been in the care of the Library for over three hundred years.

The conference formed an adjunct to a series of international conferences on insular art held at Cork (1985) and Edinburgh (1991); the third in the series will be held in Belfast in 1994. The Book of Kells conference was unique in that it was devoted to a single manuscript, a fitting tribute to the supreme achievement of insular art. The analysis of this great gospel book has demanded the interdisciplinary skills of medieval historians, archaeologists, art historians, biblical scholars, scientists and calligraphers. The depth and range of scholarship evident in these papers is a measure of the continuing power of the Book of Kells to provoke fresh debate and stimulate new trends of study.

I am indebted to my colleagues Bernard Meehan and Stuart Ó Seanóir for advice; Jane Maxwell who devised the graphics used in the conference logo and John Higgitt's article; Peter Connell, Computer Laboratory, for technical support. John Kennedy of the Green Studio Ltd supplied photographs of College manuscripts. I wish to thank the following for kindly permitting the reproduction of photographs and drawings: Biblioteca Apostolica Vaticana, Vatican City; Bibliothèque Municipale, Amiens; Bibliothèque Nationale, Paris; Bodleian Library, Oxford; British Library, London; Cambridge University Library; Commissioners of Public Works in Ireland; Erzabtei St Peter, Salzburg; The Dean and Chapter of Durham Cathedral; Institut Royal du Patrimoine Artistique, Brussels; Musée des Monuments Français; National Museum of Ireland; Österreichische Nationalbibliothek, Vienna; Royal Commission on the Ancient and Historical Monuments of Scotland; Royal Irish Academy, Dublin; Universitätsbibliothek, Augsburg; University Library, Cambridge; Greta Byrne; Anthony Cains; Erika Eisenlohr; Robert Fuchs; Peter Harbison; Eamonn Kelly; Doris Oltrogge; I G Scott; Roger Stalley; Robert Stevick; D L Swan; Mark Van Stone.

The success of the conference was due largely to the work of the organising committee: Peter Fox, Librarian, TCD, Bernard Meehan, Keeper of Manuscripts, TCD, Michael Ryan, Director, Chester Beatty Library, Dublin, Roger Stalley, Professor of History of Art, TCD. The following sponsors of the conference are gratefully acknowledged: Aer Lingus, The British Council, Faksimile Verlag Luzern, The Green Studio Ltd, Lufthansa, TCD Quatercentenary Booksale.

An Taoiseach Albert Reynolds kindly hosted the official reception at Dublin Castle. Ms L Walsh of Bord Fáilte was very helpful in the organisation of the Mansion House reception hosted by the Lord Mayor Gay Mitchell TD. The conference was opened by the Vice Provost Professor T D Spearman.

My special thanks to Martine Gleeson who prepared the typescript for publication, remaining serene in the face of much provocation.

Felicity O'Mahony
Manuscripts Department
Trinity College Dublin

Abbreviated words

BL	British Library
BM	Bibliothèque Municipale
BN	Bibliothèque Nationale
c	circa
ch/s	chapter/s
col/s	column/s
ed	edited by
fig/s	figure/s
ill/s	illustrations
m	metre
MS/MSS	manuscript/s
n/n	notes/s
no/s	number/s
pl/s	plate/s
p/pp	pages/s
r	recto
repr	reprint
RIA	Royal Irish Academy
s.a.	sub anno
s.n.	sine numero
TCD	Trinity College Dublin
trans	translated
v	verso

Abbreviated titles

AFM	*Annals of the kingdom of Ireland by the Four Masters*, ed John O'Donovan, 7 vols (Dublin 1848-51)
Alexander, 'Illumination'	J J G Alexander, 'The illumination' in *Kells commentary*, 265-89.
Alexander, *Insular manuscripts*	J J G Alexander, *Insular manuscripts, sixth to the ninth century*, A survey of manuscripts illuminated in the British Isles 1 (London 1978)
Andrieu	Michel Andrieu, *Les ordines romani du haut moyen âge*, Spicilegium Sacrum Lovaniense 11, 23, 24, 28, 29 (Louvain 1931-61)
ATig	'Annals of Tigernach', ed Whitley Stokes, *Revue Celtique* 16 (1895) 374-419; 17 (1896) 6-33, 119-263, 337-420; 18 (1897) 9-59, 150-97, 267-303
AU	*Annals of Ulster*, ed W M Hennessy and B MacCarthy, 4 vols (Dublin 1887-1901)
AU²	*Annals of Ulster*, ed Seán Mac Airt and Gearóid Mac Niocaill (Dublin 1983)
Brown	T J Brown, 'Northumbria and the Book of Kells', *Anglo-Saxon England* 1 (Cambridge 1972) 219-46
CLA	*Codices latini antiquiores: a palaeographical guide to Latin manuscripts*, ed E A Lowe (Oxford 1934-72)
CCSL	Corpus Christianorum series latina (Turnhout 1953-)
Codex Cenannensis	*Evangeliorum quattuor codex Cenannensis*, ed E H Alton and Peter Meyer, 3 vols (Berne 1950-51)
CSEL	Corpus Scriptorum Ecclesiasticorum Latinorum (Vienna 1866-)

DACL

Dictionnaire d'archéologie chrétienne et de liturgie, ed F Cabrol and H Leclerq, 15 vols (Paris 1907-53)

DIL

Royal Irish Academy, *Dictionary of the Irish language based mainly on Old and Middle Irish materials* (Dublin 1913-75, repr Dublin 1983)

Dumville

Saint Patrick: AD 493-1993, ed D N Dumville, Studies in Celtic history 13 (Woodbridge 1993)

Farr, 'Lection'

Carol Farr, 'Lection and interpretation: the liturgical and exegetical background of the illustrations in the Book of Kells', unpublished PhD dissertation, University of Texas at Austin (1989)

Farr, 'Liturgical influences'

Carol Farr, 'Liturgical influences on the decoration of the Book of Kells' in *Studies in insular art and archaeology*, ed C Karkov, R T Farrell, American Early Medieval Studies 1 (Oxford, Ohio 1991) 127-41

Harbison

Peter Harbison, *The high crosses of Ireland: an iconographical and photographic survey*, Römisch-Germanisches Zentralmuseum, Forschungsinstitut für Vor- und Frühgeschichte, Monographien 17, 3 vols (Bonn 1992)

HBS

Henry Bradshaw Society for editing rare liturgical texts (London 1892-)

HE

Bede's Ecclesiastical history of the English people, ed Bertram Colgrave and R A B Mynors (Oxford 1969)

Henderson

George Henderson, *From Durrow to Kells: the Insular Gospel-books 650-800* (London 1987)

Henry

Françoise Henry, *The Book of Kells: reproductions from the manuscript in Trinity College Dublin, with a study of the manuscript by Françoise Henry* (London, New York 1974)

Herbert	Máire Herbert, *Iona, Kells and Derry: the history and hagiography of the monastic 'familia' of Columba* (Oxford 1988)
JRSAI	*Journal of the Royal Society of Antiquaries of Ireland*
Jungmann	J A Jungmann, *The Mass of the Roman rite: its origins and development*, trans Francis A Brunner, 2 vols (New York 1951-55; repr Westminster, MD 1986)
Kells commentary	*The Book of Kells, MS 58, Trinity College Library Dublin: commentary*, ed Peter Fox (Fine Art Facsimile Publishers of Switzerland/Faksimile Verlag, Luzern 1990)
Kells facsimile	*The Book of Kells, MS 58, Trinity College Library Dublin: facsimile* (Fine Art Facsimile Publishers of Switzerland/Faksimile Verlag, Luzern 1990)
LU	*Lebor na hUidre: Book of the Dun Cow*, ed R I Best and O Bergin (Dublin 1929)
McGurk, 'Gospel text'	Patrick McGurk, 'The gospel text' in *Kells commentary*, 59-152
McGurk, *Gospel books*	Patrick McGurk, *Latin gospel books from AD 400 to AD 800*, Les publications de Scriptorium 5 (Paris, Brussels, Amsterdam 1961)
McGurk, 'Texts'	Patrick McGurk, 'The texts at the opening of the book' in *Kells commentary*, 37-58
MacNiocaill, *Notitiae*	Gearóid Mac Niocaill, *Notitiae as Leabhar Cheanannais, 1033-1161* (Dublin 1961)
MacNiocaill, 'Charters'	Gearóid Mac Niocaill, 'The Irish "charters"' in *Kells commentary*, 153-65
Meehan	Bernard Meehan, 'The script' in *Kells commentary*, 245-56
PL	Patrologia Latina, ed J P Migne, 221 vols (Paris 1844-64)

PRIA   Proceedings of the Royal Irish Academy

Roosen-Runge/Werner   Heinz Roosen-Runge, AEA Werner, 'The
                                    pictorial technique of the Lindisfarne
                                    Gospels' in *Evangeliorum quattuor codex
                                    Lindisfarnensis*, ed TD Kendrick et al, 2 vols
                                    (Olten/Lausanne 1960) II, 263-77

Ryan   *Ireland and insular art AD 500-1200*, ed
                                    Michael Ryan (Dublin 1987)

Wordsworth-White   John Wordsworth and H J White, *Novum
                                    Testamentum domini nostri Iesu Christi
                                    latine, secundum editionem Sancti
                                    Hieronymi* (Oxford 1889-98)

The historical and cultural background of the Book of Kells

Donnchadh Ó Corráin

Pars etiam meriti meritum celebrare piorum

I begin with some assumptions. The first of these is that social and cultural background, in the broader sense of these terms, is relevant to the consideration of a major work of art, such as the Book of Kells. The second is a chronological and geographical assumption, namely, that the Book of Kells belongs very likely in the eighth century and within the broad area of Irish culture. I have no wish to join in the controversy about origins that has been going on for many years: whether the Book of Kells is Irish or Northumbrian or indeed the product of an unknown Pictish monastery.[1] The delusions of modern nationalisms have done, and continue to do, enough damage in these islands, and even what may appear to be soberer feelings of national pride should have no place in our proceedings. Rather, as citizens of the world, we should rejoice in great art as a triumph of the spirit, no matter where we find it, no matter when, no matter by whom.

Still, one may look at the historical possibilities of more exact localisation. The brilliant christian culture of Northumbria was established and brought to flower by the Irish mission from Iona which was dominant culturally until the 660s at least.[2] Northumbria was cross-fertilized and enriched by contact with the Roman mission in the south and by direct contact with Rome itself. Its position and connections made Northumbria a conduit, a re-distribution centre, that drew from and played back to its original source of inspiration, the Irish churches. These movements and cross-currents created an Irish-Northumbrian cultural landscape, a kind of single market with free movement of labour and services, segmented it is true, but sharing a remarkable christian Latin culture. It was segmented in language, Irish and English, but together these were unique in having the earliest western vernacular literatures — Irish first, and then English. It was segmented by certain usages, notably the date of Easter: the southern Irish churches were Roman in Easter

---

[1] F Masai, *Essai sur les origines de la miniature dite irlandaise*, Les Publications de Scriptorium 1 (Brussels and Antwerp 1947); idem, 'Il monachesimo irlandese nei suoi rapporti col continente (arte)', *Il monachesimo nell'alto medioevo e la formazione della civiltà occidentale*, Settimane di studi del Centro italiano di studi sull' alto Medioevo 4 (Spoleto 1957) 139-84; C Nordenfalk, 'Before the Book of Durrow', *Acta Archaeologica* 18 (1947) 141-74; Brown, 219-46; D Ó Cróinín, 'Pride and prejudice', *Peritia* 1 (1982) 352-62; idem, 'Rath Melsige, Willibrord, and the earliest Echternach manuscripts', *Peritia* 3 (1984) 17-49.

[2] T J Brown, 'An historical introduction to the use of Classical Latin authors in the British Isles from the fifth to the eleventh centuries', *La cultura nell'occidente latino dal VII all'XI secolo*, Sett Studi 22 (Spoleto 1972) 237-93 (pp 253-54).

reckoning (some since the 630s), Iona and its dependants 'Celtic' until 716, Northumbria undecided until the Synod of Whitby in 664, when it went Roman. The Book of Kells belongs to this variegated cultural landscape.

On balance, it seems to me to have been written in an Irish segment, Iona, a centre whose far-flung connections in both islands made it a cultural entrepôt and a point of broader contact. Interestingly enough for our argumentative contemporaries, Adomnán always thinks of Iona as being in *Britannia*; Bede claims political right over it for Britain (*ad ius quidem Britanniae pertinet*) but he usually says it is in *Scotia*. Perhaps the book was the centre-piece of a major celebration in the Columban church, some long-planned occasion on which large resources were splashed out — a memorial to a great event in the founder's life, perhaps even the bicentennial of his death (797). On these grounds, I try to justify an attempt to draw a broad (and necessarily gappy) sketch of the development of Irish culture and society down to the eighth century.

The beginnings are obscure. The evidence is scarce for fifth-century Ireland, and this is to be expected. It is a landscape lit by two quite different beams. The first is the report of the anti-Pelagian, Prosper Tiro (fl. AD 420-50) in his *Chronicle* for the year 431 that Palladius, probably a deacon at Auxerre, was 'ordained by pope Celestine and sent, as their first bishop, to the Irish who believe in Christ' — a mission that cannot be separated from that of Germanus, sent by the same pope, to extirpate Pelagianism in Britain. In his *Contra Collatorem*, dated to c434, Prosper says that Celestine had ordained a bishop for the Irish, kept the Roman island (ie Britain) orthodox, and made the barbarian island (ie Ireland) christian. Such christianization was still an aspiration, but here at least are dates, an ambitious papal policy of sending missions beyond the borders of the western empire, and an indication that the Irish christian community was mature enough to be involved in the Pelagian heresy.[3] The second great source, St Patrick's two letters, his *Confessio* and the *Letter to the soldiers of Coroticus*, provide no dates, and his evidence for the christianization of Ireland is difficult to interpret, though it is richly informative on the formidable character of Patrick himself and the cultural background from which he came.[4] A little can be wrung from later sources connected with Patrick. In 1986 Dr Ó Cróinín argued that the computus that Cummian believed to be that of St Patrick was the computus brought by Palladius 'that survived long enough to enter the record and pass to the southern churches'.[5] From the seventh-century Armagh dossier

[3]T M Charles-Edwards, 'Palladius, Prosper and Leo the Great: mission and primatial authority' in Dumville, 1-12; E A Thompson, *Who was saint Patrick?* (Woodbridge 1985) 51-65.
[4]'Libri epistolarum sancti Patricii episcopi', ed L Bieler, *Classica et Mediaevalia* 11 (1950) 1-150, 12 (1951) 79-214; L de Paor, *St Patrick's world* (Dublin 1993); R P C Hanson, *Saint Patrick: his origins and career* (Oxford 1968); D Howlett, 'Ex saliva scripturae meae' in *Sages, saints and storytellers: Celtic studies in honour of Professor James Carney*, ed D Ó Corráin, L Breatnach and K McCone (Maynooth 1989) 86-101.
[5]Dáibhí Ó Cróinín, 'New light on Palladius', *Peritia* 5 (1986) 276-83; D Dumville ('Bishop Palladius's computus?' in Dumville, 85-88) expresses reservations.

of St Patrick, it is possible to winnow the names of other missionaries thought to have been active in the fifth century — Auxilius, Iserninus, Cetiacus, Camelacus and others — and there are echoes of an older church order.[6] As far as datable and reliable contemporary sources go, the rest is virtual silence on most important matters until the sixth century.

Some three or more generations passed between the missionary period proper and the emergence of the Irish churches into the light of fairly detailed history. And in that period a powerful church establishment, episcopal and monastic, had come into being and its clergy had entrenched itself as the dominant culture-bearer and culture-maker. We do not know how this happened and we know almost nothing about the missionary church that brought it about. It is often said that the church was ruled by bishops in their dioceses, and some have held that there was a metropolitan. All this rests on doubtful evidence, or none.[7] What is clear is that monasticism made rapid strides in Ireland in the sixth century. Monastic churches of the seventh century and later looked back to founders in the sixth who are not associated with Patrick or Palladius or other early missionaries, but with the saints of the British church.[8] But the monastic church did not side-line the bishops and the organisation of the Irish church in the seventh century was a complicated one.

Historical sources are meagre. There are the annals that derive from entries made in the margins of 84-year Easter tables. Scholars have argued that these become contemporary records in the middle of the sixth century — and there is evidence, linguistic and historical, that supports that opinion.[9] Separating the good from the bad is the problem here, and in any case the pickings are thin before the time of Columbanus, apart from a strong and suspicious interest in dynastic history.

The evidence from church legislation is also thin: only two documents, the *Poenitentiale Vinniani* and the *Synodus Episcoporum* ('First Synod of St Patrick'), have been dated by some scholars to the sixth century. Kathleen Hughes made a case, regarded by many as persuasive, for taking the 'First Synod of St Patrick' 'as evidence for the government of the sixth-century

---

[6]Charles Doherty, 'The basilica in early Ireland', *Peritia* 3 (1984) 303-15; idem, 'The cult of St Patrick and the politics of Armagh in the seventh century' in *Ireland and northern France*, ed J-M Picard (Dublin 1991) 53-94; D Dumville, 'Auxilius, Iserninus, Secundinus, and Benignus' in Dumville, 89-105.
[7]See the critique by R Sharpe, 'Some problems concerning the organization of the church in early medieval Ireland', *Peritia* 3 (1984) 230-70; D N Dumville, 'Church government and the spread of christianity in Ireland' in Dumville, 179-81.
[8]D N Dumville, 'British missionary activity in Ireland' in Dumville, 133-45.
[9]T F O'Rahilly, *Early Irish history and mythology* (Dublin 1946) 235-59; F J Byrne, 'Seventh-century documents', *Irish Ecclesiastical Record* 108 (1967) 164-82; A P Smyth, 'The earliest Irish annals: their first contemporary entries and the earliest centres of recording', *PRIA (C)* 72 (1972) 1-48; D Ó Cróinín, 'Irish annals from Easter tables: a case restated', *Peritia* 2 (1983) 74-86.

church',[10] and as being earlier than the *Poenitentiale Vinniani* attributed to Vinnian.

But the 'First Synod of St Patrick' is very unlikely to be all early, and this is so for several reasons. The prominence of bishops is no help in dating (as Dr Hughes felt), for bishops were and remained prominent. The rule 'if a cleric has given surety for a pagan (*pro gentili homine*) in whatsoever amount and it so happens — as well it might — that the pagan by some ruse defaults upon the cleric, the cleric must pay the debt from his own means; should he contend with him in arms, let him be reckoned to be outside the church, as he deserves'[11] cannot bear the weight that Hughes puts on it. The word *gentilis* does not mean pagan; rather it means a lay kinsman, a member of one's *gens* (Irish *fine*). What is forbidden the cleric here is acting as a *naidm* or enforcing surety for a member of his kindred (sureties were normally of higher status than those they went surety for, and this is further evidence of the high rank of the clergy). In this case, when the principal defaulted, the surety was obliged to use physical force — up to wounding or killing — to enforce his bond, and this was most unsuitable activity for a cleric.[12] This canon is repeated in the *Hibernensis* (34:2; cf 34:8)[13] — the developed canon law of the Irish churches — and points not to the problems of a christian church in a largely pagan environment but to difficulties that arise from the close legal connections of clerics with their lay kindred in a mature christian community. Dr Hughes found another rule about dress and hair-cuts possibly sixth-century in tenor: 'Any cleric, from ostiary to priest, that is seen without a tunic and does not cover the shame and nakedness of his body, and whose hair is not shorn after the Roman custom, and whose wife goes about with head unveiled, shall both likewise be held in contempt by the laity and removed from the Church'.[14] This quaint figure is surely an early *clericus*

---

[10]A W Haddan and W Stubbs, *Councils and ecclesiastical documents* (Oxford 1873-78, repr 1964) II, 328-31 (text); Ludwig Bieler, *The Irish penitentials*, Scriptores Latini Hiberniae 5 (Dublin 1963) 54-59 (text and translation); *The bishops' synod*, ed M J Faris (Liverpool 1978). Kathleen Hughes, *The church in early Irish society* (London 1966) 44-63; eadem, *Early christian Ireland: introduction to the sources* (London 1972) 68-71; D A Binchy, 'St Patrick and his biographers: ancient and modern', *Studia Hibernica* 2 (1962) 45-49; idem, 'Patrick's "First Synod"', *Studia Hibernica* 8 (1968-69) 119-37. D N Dumville ('St Patrick at his "first synod"' in Dumville, 175-78) is agnostic and, depending on whether one thinks of it as a local or 'national' synod, will settle for a date between the fifth and seventh centuries.

[11]§8 Clericus si pro gentili homine fideiusor fuerit in quacumque quantitate et si contigerit, quod mirum non potest, per astutiam aliquam gentilis ille clerico fallat, rebus suis clericus ille soluat debitum. Nam si armis compugnauerit cum illo, merito extra ecclesiam conputetur.

[12]Binchy (1968-69, note 10 above) 51-53; idem, 'Celtic suretyship: a fossilized Indo-European institution?' in *Indo-European and Indo-Europeans: papers presented to the third Indo-European conference*, ed G Cardona (Philadelphia 1970) 335-67, repr *Irish Jurist* 7 (1972) 360-72.

[13]*Die irische Kanonensammlung*, ed Herrmann Wasserschleben, 2 edn (Leipzig 1885) 122, 124. (This text will henceforth be cited as *Hibernensis*, by book and chapter.)

[14]§6. Quicumque clericus ab hostiario usque ad sacerdotem sine tunica uisus fuerit atque turpitudinem uentris et nuditatem non tegat, et si non more Romano capilli eius tonsi sint, et uxor eius si non uelato capite ambulauerit, pariter a laicis contempnentur et ab ecclesia separentur. This text is echoed in *Hibernensis* 52:7 and

joculator, whose likes are condemned in the Gaulish councils,[15] rather than a non-conforming semi-barbarian of the missionary period. There may yet be some sixth-century material in this text, but it is difficult to identify.

The *Poenitentiale Vinniani*[16] seems to be the only piece of church legislation we can be tolerably sure is sixth-century. The identity of its author is uncertain, its date can only be established approximately, and one wonders what evidence proves that it is an Irish rather than a British text. Vinnian is generally thought to be Finnian of Clonard (died 549) or Finnian of Moville (died *c*579), and some would argue that the two are identical and represent a single British cleric working in Ireland.[17] The dating of the text must remain uncertain: what we do know is that it is anterior to the Penitential of St Columbanus (who cites it and this supplies a terminus ante quem of 591), and it is likely to lie within the period *c*540-590. According to Columbanus, this Vinniau was in correspondence with Gildas who sent 'a most polished reply' to his questions on monastic discipline.[18] Portions of this letter survive in Cambridge, Corpus Christi College, MS 279. Some of these were incorporated into the *Hibernensis*, and part reappears in Old-Irish translation in the vernacular laws.[19] Vinnian is not explicit about his sources (unknown for the most part) beyond saying that he 'followed the pronouncement of scripture and the opinion of some very learned men'. He echoes Cassian (§§28-29) and prescribes the Old Testament rule that a master may not sell a slave-concubine by whom he has had a child (§40). Vinnian urges a strict marriage ethic (§§41-47), differing notably on divorce from the later laws of the Old-Irish period proper, and ordained clerics must abstain from their wives (§27), echoed by Columbanus (epistle 1 §6). There is little detail about the institutional church (apart from a robust asceticism for cleric and lay person): a monastic establishment was in place and monks differed from secular clergy; there were monasteries that possessed at least some property (§30); a cleric served in a parish

---

occurs in full (with the rubric 'Canon Romanus') in Cambridge, Corpus Christi College, MS 265. Hughes (1966, note 10 above) 47-48.

[15] C Munier, *Concilia Galliae, a. 314-a. 506*, CCSL 148 (1963) 178; C de Clercq, *Concilia Galliae, a. 511-a. 695*, CCSL 148A (1963) 270; J Gaudemet, *Conciles gaulois du IVe siècle*, Sources Chrétiennes 241 (Paris 1977) 44, 48.

[16] Bieler (note 10 above) 74-95.

[17] L Fleuriot, 'Le "saint" breton Winniau et le pénitentiel dit "de Finiau"?', *Études Celtiques* 15 (1976-78) 607-17; Pádraig Ó Riain, 'Finnian or Winniau?' in *Irland und Europa; die Kirche im Frühmittelalter*, ed P Ní Chatháin and M Richter (Stuttgart 1984) 52-56; Richard Sharpe, 'Gildas as a father of the church' in *Gildas: new approaches*, ed M Lapidge and D Dumville, Studies in Celtic History 5 (Woodbridge, 1984) 198-202; D N Dumville, 'Gildas and Uinniau', ibid, 207-14.

[18] G S M Walker, *Sancti Columbani opera*, Scriptores Latini Hiberniae 2 (Dublin 1957) 8 (epistle 1 §7).

[19] Text: T Mommsen, *Monumenta Germaniae Historica Auctores Antiquissimi* 13 (1898), repr PL supplementum 4 (Paris 1969) 1255-58; Haddan and Stubbs (note 10 above) I, 108-13; M Winterbottom, *Gildas: the ruin of Britain and other works* (London 1978) 80-82, 143-45; Sharpe (note 17 above) 192-205; Liam Breatnach in D Ó Corráin, L Breatnach and A Breen, 'The laws of the Irish', *Peritia* 3 (1984) 382-438 (pp 418-20).

(*plebs*) and had to baptise (§§48-49); monks did not administer the sacraments to the laity and did not receive alms (§50); and clerics served the basilicas of the saints (*basilicis sanctorum ministrandum*), whether founders' churches or grave shrines (§33).[20]

Other documents cited in the sixth century have reference to the tangled problem of the computus and the calculation of the date of Easter: *Acta Concilii Caesareae (Epistola Philippi de Pascha)*, dated variously to AD 508 and *c*AD 550;[21] and Pseudo-Anatolius, *De ratione Paschae* (is it Irish?), cited twice by Columbanus (epistle 1 §2-4, 2 §5) and by Cummian in his Paschal Letter of *c*AD 632, and dated by Dr Walsh and Dr Ó Cróinín to the mid-sixth century.[22] These were amongst the authorities cited by the disputants of the seventh century. The documents of a liturgical nature, the Cathach of Columba and the Springmount Tablets, are too uncertain as to date and too controversial to be taken as sixth-century evidence.[23]

The evidence from hymnology is extremely difficult; there are serious and unsolved problems about authorship, sources, models, metrical forms and, above all, dating, and much remains to be done before the hymns can be used with any confidence as historical sources for the church culture of the fifth and sixth centuries. One thing is clear: the hymnody of christian Late Antiquity, and especially that of Gaul, was the inspiration of the Irish writers. The abecedarian hymn, 'Altus Prosator', attributed to Columba will illustrate some difficulties.[24] Kenney saw it as a christian cosmogony,[25] a kind of early Paradise Lost, ultimately based on Pseudo-Dionysius, *Celestial hierarchies* and the apocryphal *Book of Enoch*, rude and barbaric but vigorous and grammatically correct, and probably written by Columba. It has Hisperic words such as *iduma* 'hand',[26] *dodrans* 'flood

---

[20]cf M Herity, 'The tomb-shrine of the founder-saint' in *The age of migrating ideas: early medieval art in northern Britain and Ireland*, ed R M Spearman and J Higgitt (Edinburgh and Stroud 1993) 188-95.
[21]M Lapidge and R Sharpe, *A bibliography of Celtic-Latin literature, 400-1200* (Dublin 1985) §§317-19; James F Kenney, *The sources for the early history of Ireland: ecclesiastical* (New York 1929, repr New York 1966) §54; *A U*, IV, pp cxv-cxvii (p cxvii); Maura Walsh and D Ó Cróinín, *Cummian's Letter* De Controuersia Paschali *and the* De Ratione Conputandi (Toronto 1988) 35-37.
[22]Lapidge and Sharpe (note 21 above) §320; Kenney (note 21 above) §54iii. Ó Cróinín (1984, note 1 above) 26-28; Walsh and Ó Cróinín (note 21 above) 32-35; D Ó Cróinín, 'Early Echternach manuscript fragments with Old Irish glosses' in *Willibrord: Apostel der Niederlande Gründer der Abtei Echternach*, ed G Kiesel and Jean Schroeder (Luxembourg 1989) 135-43.
[23]Lapidge and Sharpe (note 21 above) §§505-06.
[24]Lapidge and Sharpe (note 21 above) §580; Kenney (note 21 above) 91. J H Bernard and R Atkinson, *The Irish Liber hymnorum*, 2 vols (London 1898) I, 62-83 (text), II, 150-53 (translation). E Coccia, 'La cultura irlandese precarolingia: miracolo o mito?', *Studi Medievali ser 3* 8 (1967) 299-302.
[25]This interest in cosmology and natural phenomena is present in *De mirabilibus*, in *De ordine creaturarum* and later in *Saltair na rann* (see John Carey, 'Cosmology in *Saltair na Rann*', *Celtica* 17 (1985) 33-52; idem, 'The heavenly city in *Saltair na Rann*', *Celtica* 18 (1986) 86-104; *Celtica* 20 (1988) 128-29).
[26]A Breen, 'Iduma (ιδουμα)', *Celtica* 21 (1990) 40-50.

of the sea', *tithis* 'sea' etc and there are seven or so examples of the use of the Vetus Latina, Old and New Testaments,[27] and this should at least point to a date not later than the middle of the seventh century, perhaps earlier. Simonetti sees 'no reason to doubt the attribution of this hymn to Columba', whilst Coccia dissents but thinks the hymn early.[28] Others agree that the Latin is barbarous and that there is no sign of classical literary influence.[29] For the rest, the hymn is undated and unprovenanced.

Professor Lapidge's identification of a hymn of Columbanus, on the other hand, is exemplary. The hymn 'Precamur patrem' (42 stanzas) is uniquely preserved in the Antiphonary of Bangor,[30] a liturgical common-place book written in Bangor *c*AD 700. This hymn was composed, as Lapidge has elegantly demonstrated,[31] by Columbanus before his departure for the continent *c*590. The proof is based on the quite unusual grecism *micrologus* (μικρολόγος) borrowed from Rufinus's translation into Latin of the *Orationes* of Gregory of Nazianzus, and understood in a peculiar way by Columbanus. Columbanus in his letter to Gregory the Great (epistle 1 §2) draws on Rufinus's translation of *Oratio* I and he is well aware of the play of words involved in *Oratio* III where Gregory uses the parallelism of the small dove (*parua columba*) and the μικρός or ineloquent rhetorician. This links 'Precamur patrem' to Columbanus when he was at Bangor and thus to the late sixth century. It is a hymn intended specifically for the vigil of Holy Saturday — its unified theme is the meaning of Easter day — wide-ranging, carefully controlled and tightly designed. There are many references to the Bible (in Vetus Latina form) and to apocrypha (*Gospel of Nicodemus*) and there are allusions to classical poets such as Virgil. There are references to patristic authors and especially Cassian, on whom Columbanus's 'Regula monachorum' depended heavily. In Lapidge's view, most of all he shows familiarity with the language and diction of late Latin hymnody, particularly with the hymns of Venantius Fortunatus, Prudentius and Caelius Sedulius. Evidently, the 'Old Hymnal' (apparently assembled by *c*540) was available at Bangor before 590. Here Columbanus depends on Venantius's 'Pange lingua' sung for the first time in November 569, but not in the 'Old Hymnal'.

There is no evidence here for a continuous classical tradition from antiquity, least of all in metrics.[32] The letter of an Irishman Colmán to his

---

[27]Bernard and Atkinson (note 24 above) II, 143-44; Bernard and Atkinson, II, 144-45) gives seven examples (ll.1, 21, 25, 33, 113, 117, 125).

[28]M Simonetti, 'Studi sull'innologia popolare cristiana dei primi secoli', *Atti della Accademia Nazionale dei Lincei, Memorie*, Classe di Scienze Morali, Storiche e Filologiche, ser. 8 4/6 (Rome 1952) 469; Coccia (note 24 above) 299-302.

[29]M Roger, *L'enseignement des lettres classiques d'Ausone à Alcuin* (Paris 1905) 230; Max Manitius, *Geschichte der lateinischen Literatur des Mittelalters*, 3 vols (Munich 1911-23) I, 10 ('noch in dem Hymnus Altus Prosator zeigt sich nicht die geringste Berührung mit der klassischen Literatur').

[30]Milan, Biblioteca Ambrosiana, C.5 inf. F E Warren, *The antiphonary of Bangor*, 2 vols (London 1893-95); M Curran, *The Antiphonary of Bangor* (Dublin 1984).

[31]Michael Lapidge, 'Columbanus and the Antiphonary of Bangor', *Peritia* 4 (1985) 104-16.

[32]Lapidge (note 31 above) 114-16.

'filius eruditissimus' Feradach, discussed by Bischoff and recently edited by Sharpe,[33] is relevant here. It is undated: it may belong to the seventh century, but it could be much later. Colmán tells Feradach that he has got many manuscripts from the Romani (Bischoff takes this to mean the Irish Romani — the southern clergy who followed Rome in the date of Easter — but this is not certain). From these manuscripts he has got to know many texts more accurately and more completely than had hitherto been available to him and to Feradach. He has a keen interest in textual quality.[34] Among the texts are Isidore's *De officiis ecclesiasticis* and 'the Chronicle'. But the greatest surprise was given them by the works of the christian poet Sedulius. They had only his *Carmen paschale* in a very corrupt text, while the *Opus paschale*, its re-elaboration in rhetorical prose, was quite unknown to them. And the first he gives to his 'eruditissimus filius', it appears, as an introduction to metrics and to the scansion of hexameters and pentameters. Bischoff's comment is fundamental: 'The necessity of such elementary instruction gives, in my view, the coup de grace to the widespread belief in the uninterrupted continuity of the classical tradition in the island'.[35] It is reasonable to believe that what Colmán did not know was equally unknown to his sixth-century predecessors. For all the range and bulk of the Hiberno-Latin texts the idea that Ireland was, in any real sense, the remote heir to classical learning must be rejected. Julian Brown puts it well: 'Not the more or less accidental inheritors of classical learning, the Irish were something much more laudable: the first of the three peoples who in the early Middle Ages went out and got what they could, by their own efforts, of the Christian and patristic learning of Late Antiquity ... . What little they knew of classical Latin literature came to them through patristic authors such as Jerome, through Isidore, through the Late Antique grammarians'.[36]

The sixth century and before is the British Period of the Irish churches. The extensive Irish settlements — in Cornwall, south Wales, Anglesey and, beyond the imperial *limes*, in western Scotland — brought some of the coastal kingdoms of southern and eastern and north-eastern Ireland (amongst others Uí Liatháin, Déisi, Laigin, Dál Riata and Airgialla) into close contact with Britain.[37] Settlement may have taken place in waves

---

[33]Bernhard Bischoff, 'Il monachesimo irlandese nei suoi rapporti col continente' in *Mittelalterliche Studien: Ausgewählte Aufsätze zur Schriftkunde und Literaturgeschichte*, 3 vols (Stuttgart 1966-67) I, 195-205 (p 199); Richard Sharpe, 'An Irish textual critic and the *Carmen paschale* of Sedulius: Colmán's letter to Feradach', *Journal of Medieval Latin* 2 (1992) 44-54.

[34]F Rädle, 'Die Kenntnis der antiken lateinischen Literatur bei den Iren in der Heimat und auf dem Kontinent' in *Die Iren und Europa im früheren Mittelalter*, ed H Löwe (Stuttgart 1982) 484-500 (p 490).

[35]Note 33 above, 199.

[36]Brown (note 2 above) 237-99 (pp 248-49).

[37]Kenneth Jackson, *Language and history in early Britain* (Edinburgh 1953) 149-87; M Richards, 'The Irish settlements in south-west Wales: a topographical approach', *JRSAI* 90 (1960) 133-52; C Thomas, 'Irish colonies in post-Roman Western Britain', *Journal of Royal Institution of Cornwall* ns 6 (1969-72) 251-74; John Bannerman, *Studies in the history of Dalriada* (Edinburgh 1974); M Miller, 'Date-guessing and Dyfed', *Studia Celtica* 12-13 (1977-78) 33-61; B Coplestone-Crowe, 'The dual nature

(christian as well as pre-christian) and it is likely that the colonies remained in close touch with the homeland and deepened relationships already long-established by raiding and trading in the Roman period. There may have been British settlements in Ireland from the fifth century: Professor Thompson argues cogently that the Coroticus denounced by St Patrick may have been a Romano-British leader in Ireland.[38] There may have been large bodies of refugees fleeing their Anglo-Saxon conquerors[39] — and these movements could have continued into the sixth century. Historical circumstances brought Ireland and Britain close: ecclesiastical connections gave them a single Hiberno-British religious culture, and the British quality of that culture is reflected in the form of Latin borrowings into Irish as in other matters.[40] The same is true of the discipline of penance: the earliest penitentials are those of Gildas, Vinnian and Columbanus, and penitentials as a genre began in the British church.[41] The successors of the Irish monastic founders of the sixth century claimed the monastic leaders of Britain as their masters. The Irish and British churches were agreed about the celebration of Easter.

In this relationship, Gildas, as a reformer urging monastic asceticism, is a nodal figure. As we have seen, he was the correspondent of the Vinnian who may have had a formative influence on Columba, the greatest of the Irish monastic founders. His letter to Vinnian was taken as a suitable prescription for the sixth-century Irish church (he alludes to the responsibilities of bishops and priests as well as those of monks), and it entered the Irish canonistic tradition.[42] Columbanus, a member of an Irish readership that appreciated his ornate and difficult Latin and one who had read his *De excidio*, cites him as an authority on church discipline in his remarkable letter to Gregory the Great (epistle 1 §§6-7), as if the pope should have known who Gildas was.[43] Provincialism or perversity? I should think both.

Columbanus is, in a sense, the best authority for the unity of the Hiberno-British churches. He quite naturally refers to his own writings as *occidentales apices de Pascha* 'Western letters about Easter' (epistle §5);

of the Irish colonization of Dyfed in the Dark Ages', *Studia Celtica* 16-17 (1981-82) 1-24; Tomás Ó Cathasaigh, 'The Déisi and Dyfed', *Éigse* 20 (1984) 1-33.

[38]Thompson (note 3 above) 126-37.

[39]E A Thompson, 'Gildas and the history of Britain', *Britannia* 10 (1979) 203-26.

[40]J Vendryes, *De hibernicis vocabulis quae a latina lingua originem duxerunt* (Paris 1902); E Mac Neill, 'Beginnings of Latin culture in Ireland', *Studies* (Dublin) 20 (1931) 39-48, 449-60; D McManus, 'A chronology of the Latin loan-words in early Irish', *Ériu* 34 (1983) 21-69; idem, 'The so-called *Cothrige* and *Pátraic* strata of Latin loan-words in early Irish' in Ní Chatháin and Richter (note 17 above) 179-96; idem, '*Linguarum diversitas*: Latin and the vernaculars in early medieval Britain', *Peritia* 3 (1984) 151-88; idem, 'On final syllables in the Latin loan-words in early Irish', *Ériu* 35 (1984) 137-62; A Harvey, 'Some significant points of early insular Celtic orthography' in Ó Corráin, Breatnach and McCone (note 4 above) 56-66.

[41]Kenney (note 21 above) 239-43; Bieler (note 10 above) 3-5 (comment), 60-107 (texts).

[42]Sharpe (note 17 above) 192-205.

[43]Joseph F Kelly, 'The letter of Columbanus to Gregory the Great', *Gregorio Magno e il suo tempo*, Studia Ephemeridis 'Augustianum' 33 (Rome 1991) 213-23.

he asks the pope's guidance (ironically?) on scriptural exegesis *ut tibi occidentalis in his gratias agat caecitas* 'so that in these matters Western blindness may thank you' (ibid §9); and in his challenge to the Gaulish bishops he writes *et videamus qualis verior sit traditio — vestra an fratrum vestrorum in Occidente. Omnes enim ecclesiae totius Occidentis ...* 'and let us see which is the truer tradition — yours or that of your brothers in the West. For all the churches of the entire West ...' (epistle 2 §5). Though he can mount a fiery defence of the Irish and their church (epistle §3), he sees the churches of the West (the British and the Irish) as an entity.[44] The bedrock of Irish christian culture in the fifth and sixth centuries is essentially British, with some Gaulish influence. What we do not know (and what we urgently need to know) is something of the literate and artistic culture of this founding period: what Latin literature was studied, what patristic, exegetical, legal, hymnological, grammatical and metrical texts were known, what texts were being written, what connections were there with continental Europe before the Irish church was overwhelmed by the transformations of the seventh and eighth centuries.

A most remarkable achievement of the sixth century was the creation of a literary vernacular — not merely a language developed to the point where it could be used for exegetical, homiletic, grammatical and various other discursive and analytical purposes as a medium of oral discussion, but as a written language with a fixed orthography. It was used for poetry and for prose. The earliest datable poem (*Amra Coluimb Chille*) is an elegy for St Columba, written in the year of his death (597), by a poet called Dallán Forgaill.[45] Writing of this poem, Gerard Murphy says: 'Parallel with the development of Latin metre by Irish churchmen ... goes similar experimentation with Irish metre. In the opening of Dallán Forgaill's *Amra* ... we have evidence for an Irish poet's experimentation with rime and stanzaic formation already by the end of the sixth century .... Here we have stanzaic structure and rime, borrowed from Latin hymns, joined to the native ornament of alliteration'.[46] Murphy's coyness about the nature of this poetry hides a lot. This cannot be the beginning of christian vernacular poetry in Ireland: it is metrically assured and lexically developed. Dallán Forgaill, whoever he may have been, was fully at home in ecclesiastical learning. As Professor Ó Néill has recently pointed out, the earliest explicit Irish reference to Cassian occurs in this text:

---

[44]Sharpe (note 17 above) 201-02.
[45]R Atkinson in Bernard and Atkinson (note 24 above) I, 162-83, II, 53-80, 223-35; 'The Bodleian Amra Choluimb Chille', ed and trans Whitley Stokes, *Revue Celtique* 20 (1899) 30-55, 132-83, 248-89, 400-37 (reference will be to the numbered sections of Stokes's edition); Vernam Hull, 'Amra Choluim Chille', *Zeitschrift für celtische Philologie* 28 (1960-61) 242-51. See also James Travis, 'Elegies attributed to Dallan Forgaill', *Speculum* 19 (1944) 89-103. The statement *is nu nad mair* 'it is lately he lives not' (§10-11) and the evident pathos of the opening lines (§§7-8) suggest that the poem was composed very shortly after Columba's death.
[46]Gerard Murphy, *Early Irish metrics* (Dublin 1961) 17-18.

Sluinnsius leig libru
libuir ut car Caisseoin
catha gulae gailais
libru Solman sexus

He made known books of law
books *ut* Cassian loved
he won the battles of *gula*
the books of Solomon he followed them

In this context, 'the books of law' may mean either the Pentateuch (in Irish usage *lex* often simply means the Pentateuch) or (much less likely) monastic rules. The battles of *gula* (note that the poem preserves the inflected Latin word) are against gluttony which Cassian (and he alone) places at the head of his list of the eight deadly sins. The last line of this citation refers to Columba's devotion to the sapiential books of the Old Testament (Proverbia, Ecclesiastes, and Sapientia).[47] Later, Basil is mentioned by name (*arbert Bassil bratha*, 180 §48), there are many Latin loanwords[48] and indeed purely Latin words occur in the text.[49] It has a developed vernacular religious vocabulary, extending to the functions of scholarship — religious study (§§27, 45, 48), teaching (§18), glossing (§53), exegesis (§54-55, 57, 59-60, 91), and computus (§§61-64). Binchy famously described it as 'an elaborate pastiche of traditional native and Christian-Latin elements'[50] but what can confidently be described as 'traditional native' is very uncertain: not the metre, not the heavily marked words, not the thought patterns. There was an appreciative readership and audience for the poem: it was preserved lovingly with a

---

[47]Pádraig P Ó Néill, 'The date and authorship of Apgitir Chrábaid: some internal evidence' in *Irland und die Christenheit*, ed P Ní Chatháin and M Richter (Stuttgart 1987) 203-15.

[48]§20 *abb* < abbas; §§32, 47, 123 *aingel* < angelus; §33 *archaingel* < archangelus; §112 *athfers* < versus; §§33, 47, 82 *axal* < apostolus (see D A Binchy, 'Old-Irish *axal*', *Ériu* 18 (1958) 164); §48 *Bassil* < Basilius; §119 *bennacht* < benedictio; §76 *cartoit* < caritas; §74-75 *cast* < castus; §74-75 *cath* < catus; §55 *Caisseoin* < Cassianus; §41 *celebrad* < celebrare; §§8, 20, 93 *cell* < cella; §30 *cléirech* < clericus; §83 *cléirchecht* < clericatus; §102 *corp* < corpus; §109 *credal* < credulus; §§92, 126, 131 *croch* < crux; §93 *custoid* < custodivit; §84 *díscrutain* < scrut- (as in scrutabilis, with Irish negative prefix *dí-* for Latin *in-*); §52 *ferb* < verbum; §§23, 127 *figlid* < vigilare; §59 *figuir* < figura; §53 *glúass* < glossa; §123 *grammatach* < grammatica; §123 *gréc* < graecus; §96 *héris* < haeresis; §94 *ídal* < idolum; §108 *ídlach* < idolum; §114 *iffern* < infernum; §§27, 55 (bis), 57, 59 *lebor* < liber; §§27, 55, 59 *léig, léigdocht* < lex; §81 *lien* < lenis; §35 *Móise* < Moyses; §4 *múr* < murus; §97 *oenid* < jejunare; §133 *leo* < leo; §139 *locharn* < lucerna; §93 *oiffrenn* < offerendum; §43 *robuist* < robustus; §35 *sacart* < sacerdos; §54 *salm* < psalmus; §60 *scoil* < schola; §60 *screptra* (gen) < scriptura; §§10, 140, *Sion* < Zion; §57 *Solman* < Salomon. There are two further loan-words that are perhaps a little doubtful: §122 *munter* < ? monasterium (see J Vendryes, *De hibernicis vocabulis* (Paris 1902) 157-58; idem, 'Notes étymologiques', *Zeitschrift für celtische Philologie* 9 (1913) 294-96; R Thurneysen, *Grammar of Old Irish* (Dublin 1946) 570 §919) and §80 *obeid?* < Ovidius (meaning a poet like Ovid) or < obediens (see Vendryes (note 40 above) 160.

[49]§132 *ecce*; §28 *Occidens*; §29 *Oriens*; §56 *gula*; §122 *magister*; §88 *manna*; §55 *ut*.

[50]D A Binchy, 'The background of early Irish literature', *Studia Hibernica* 1 (1961) 17-18.

cumulative apparatus of gloss, commentary and annotation that implies
an unbroken written tradition from the sixth century.

What of the environment of this poem? There are two main aspects, and
these are problematic: the development of vernacular literacy in Ireland
and the dating of the earliest Old-Irish verse. The first problem has
attracted considerable attention very recently, particularly from Dr
Harvey and Dr Stevenson.[51] These scholars argue that pre-christian
Ireland was heavily romanised, that the inventors of Ogam[52] (which was
parasitic on Latin) knew, spoke and wrote Latin, that a caste-limited
Latin literacy was never lost, that christianity gave a powerful impetus
to the development of a written literature but literacy pre-dated its
arrival, that the vernacular may have been written in the Roman
alphabet as early as AD 500, and that the later Ogam epigraphists and
the earliest manuscript scribes must have belonged to the same scholarly
milieu. All this is very likely. The dating of the earliest verse is more
problematic. This has been dealt with by Carney in four important and
controversial papers.[53] He claims that three pieces of verse survive from
the pagan period (ie before AD 450, in his terms), that there is another
from cAD 450, and that two others,[54] when shorn of later accretions, 'date
from the middle, or early part of the second half, of the fifth century'.[55]
Much of this seems to me very unlikely, and I have elsewhere given
reasons for believing that the latter poems — all Leinster dynastic poems
— date from the very early years of the seventh century[56] and I doubt
whether the others are any older. This is not, however, to deny the very
real possibility that these poems may contain much earlier materials. On
the contrary, this seems likely, but the poems, as they stand, have been
reworked for early seventh-century political purposes, and that reworking
may have removed earlier linguistic and historical features. Carney's

---

[51]Anthony Harvey, 'Early literacy in Ireland', *Cambridge Medieval Celtic Studies* 14
(1987) 1-15; Jane Stevenson, 'The beginnings of literacy in Ireland', *PRIA (C)* 89
(1989) 127-65; Anthony Harvey, 'Latin literacy and Celtic vernaculars around the
year 500' in *Celtic languages and Celtic peoples: proceedings of the second American
congress of Celtic studies*, ed C J Byrne, M Harry and P Ó Siadhail (Halifax NS 1992)
11-26.

[52]Anthony Harvey, 'The ogam inscriptions and their geminate consonant symbols',
Ériu 38 (1987) 45-71; D McManus, *A guide to ogam*, Maynooth Monographs 4
(Maynooth 1991).

[53]James Carney, 'Three Old Irish accentual poems', *Ériu* 22 (1971) 23-80; 'Aspects of
archaic Irish', *Éigse* 17 (1977-79) 416-35; 'The dating of early Irish verse texts', *Éigse*
19 (1982-83) 177-216; 'The dating of archaic Irish verse' in *Early Irish literature:
media and communications*, ed S T Tranter and H L C Tristram, ScriptOralia 10
(Tübingen 1989) 39-57.

[54]These are (1) 'Nuadu Necht ní dámair anblaith' stanzas 1-22 to which he would
splice the poem 'Nidu dír dermait' to make a poem of 44 stanzas in all and (2) 'Énde
Labraid lúad cáich', stanzas 1-21. These are edited and translated by Kuno Meyer,
'Über die älteste irische Dichtung', *Abh K Preuss Akad Wiss* 6, Jhg 1913 (Berlin 1913)
16-50, re-edited by M A O'Brien, *Corpus genealogiarum Hiberniae* (Dublin 1962) I, 1-
9.

[55]Carney (1989, note 53 above) 50-51.

[56]D Ó Corráin, 'Irish origin legends and genealogy: recurrent aetiologies' in *History
and heroic tale: a symposium*, ed Tore Nyberg, Iørn Piø, P M Sørensen and A Trommer
(Odense 1983) 58-63.

claim that some ten other pieces of verse date from the late sixth century and the first part of the seventh seem largely unobjectionable[57] and one can conclude that there was much literary activity (including metrical experimentation)[58] in the vernacular about AD 600 — and writing in the vernacular was no novelty but a well-established activity.

This extended to prose (and metrical prose) and I shall refer to two texts. The first is *Apgitir Chrábaid* ('The primer of piety'), attributed to Colmán moccu Béognae, abbot of Lann Elo (Lynally, co Offaly), who died in 611.[59] Thurneysen, Greene and Hull[60] are in agreement in dating the text to *c*AD 600. (Hull later doubted this and felt that 'this text is too sophisticated for an Irish monk of this period' — an unconvincing argument.) Its author is a monk writing a spiritual primer for his fellow-monks and for students. He refers to the fulfilling of the rule and the duty of the monk to reveal the minor faults of his brethren. The terminology for the monastic hierarchy is present: *manaig* 'monastic tenants'; *bráithre* 'brethren, fellow-monks'; *sruithi* (= seniores) 'elders of the community'; *secnap* 'prior, day-to-day admininistrator'; *airchinnech* 'monastic superior'; *érlam* 'patron saint, founder' (§§9-10). Most of these terms are guaranteed by the verse and if the text is as old as the linguists think (and Ó Néill cites highly convincing evidence in support of their date) it is a most valuable witness for the developed monasticism of the Irish church.

An interesting passage dealing with monastic discipline incidentally lists some of the monastic officials and will serve as an example of the style.

§10 *Cid as imgabthai do duine etail? Ní anse.*

   Írugud meinic
   mórtu cen dán {gloss: folud}

---

[57]There is one notable exception: 'Amra Senáin' which Carney dates to the sixth or early seventh century. In his recent edition of the text ('An edition of *Amra Senáin*' in Ó Corráin, Breatnach and McCone (note 4 above) 7-31) Liam Breatnach has shown that it is the work of Cormac mac Cuilennáin (died 908), king-bishop of Cashel.

[58]For a radical re-interpretation of early metrics see Liam Breatnach, 'Canon law and secular law in early Ireland: the significance of *Bretha Nemed*', *Peritia* 3 (1984) 439-59; idem, 'Zur Frage der "Roscada" im Irischen' in *Metrik und Medienwechsel*, ed H L C Tristram (Tübingen 1991) 197-205; idem, 'The caldron of poesy', *Ériu* 32 (1981) 435-93. Breatnach's work proves (amongst other things) that Irish poets in the eighth and ninth centuries and later (see, too, his edition of *Amra Senáin*, note 57 above) were masters of several registers (some of which, like *roscad*, appear ancient, and can be) and used a wide variety of metrical and literary techniques. These considerations are fundamental to the dating of poetic texts. In fact, they make the dating of texts on linguistic and prosodic grounds much more difficult.

[59]Vernam Hull, 'Aptigir Chrábaid: the alphabet of piety', *Celtica* 8 (1968) 44-89. Carney (1989, note 53 above, 425) suggests Fursu Cráibdech as the author of the text and dates it to *c* 640.

[60]R Thurneysen, 'Irisches. Altir. *ro-geinn* "hat Platz"', [*Kuhns*] *Z Vergleich Sprachforsch* 63 (1936) 114; V Hull, 'The date of Apgitir Crábaid', *Zeitschrift fur celtische Philologie* 25 (1956) 88-90; David Greene, 'Some linguistic evidence relating to the British church' in *Christianity in Britain 300-700*, ed W M Barley and R C P Hanson (Leicester 1968) 75-86 (pp 81-82); idem, 'Archaic Irish' in *Indogermanisch und Keltisch*, ed K H Schmidt (Wiesbaden 1977) 11-33 (pp 14-15).

díscre fri airchinnech
[ad]maille fri cloc
coicne fri antestai
imbeth forlúamno
fáitbe mbráithre
bríathra inglana
acairbe taithisc
toísam fri secnapaid
síthugud fri cúrsachad
comairb do manchaib
mence chestaigtho

What should a holy person avoid? Answer: growing angry frequently, haughtiness without accomplishment {gloss: without grounds}, unruliness towards the superior, slowness in answering the bell, plotting with wicked persons, excess of flightiness, derision of fellow-monks, impure words, asperity of reply, resistance to the prior, unruliness at reproof, strife with the monastic tenants, frequency of questioning.[61]

Ó Néill comments perceptively on the sources and the style. The most evident sources are Cassian's *Conlationes* and *Institutiones*, the fundamental works in the development of western monasticism. From Cassian the writer took the idea of monkish moderation as the prerequisite of sanctity, the notion that vices are cured by their opposites, and emphasis on temporal rewards for virtuous monks. Cassian figures prominently in the earliest Hiberno-Latin writers (Vinnian, Columbanus, Cummian) and, as we have seen, in the vernacular *Amra Coluimb Chille*.[62] So much for those who see the origins of Irish monasticism in the remote and exotic.[63] Ó Néill comments appositely on the style of *Apgitir Chrábaid*. It employs the techniques of Latin rhetoric: parallelism, *gradatio* (advancing term by term, repeating the previous term at each step (§§4-5, 18)) and asyndeton (parallel clauses not linked by conjunctions).[64] These characteristics (and the non-stanzaic verse) recur in vernacular legal texts over a century later (for example, *Bretha Nemed*).

---

[61]A few changes have been made to Hull's text and translation: *folud* is an obvious gloss and breaks the alliteration; *admaille* is substituted for the almost synonymous *maille* to restore the alliteration, and seems justified; *comairb do manchaib* must refer to strife with a category other than the *bráithre* 'fellow-monks', and the term must refer to the *manach* 'monastic tenant', familiar in the vernacular laws. For the rest, I have followed Hull's text and translation. Hull prints this passage as prose.

[62]Pádraig P Ó Néill (note 47 above) 206-08.

[63]Brendan Bradshaw, 'The wild and woolly west: early Irish christianity and Latin orthodoxy' in *Studies in church history* 25, ed W J Sheil and D Wood (Oxford 1989) 1-23.

[64]Ó Néill (note 47 above) 211-14.

The second of these texts is the somewhat later 'Cambrai Homily' (perhaps *c*630).[65] Ó Néill sees it as the earliest homily and one of the earliest extant pieces of continuous prose on a religious subject.[66] It is dependent on scripture and on Gregory the Great's *Homiliae in Evangelia* (written down in the last decade of the sixth century). The Old-Irish paraphrase assumes an audience that needed Latin explained to it — perhaps a monastic audience with lay people, penitents and people undergoing instruction,[67] the characteristic mix described in such eighth-century texts as the *Hibernensis* and *Bretha Nemed*.[68] Ó Néill thinks that it is 'evidence that the Irish church in the seventh century was well acquainted with the art of homiletics in the vernacular' for it displays a high level analysis of a long and discursive patristic source and a fine grasp of the craft of the homilist.[69]

Two developments delivered a sharp shock to the complacent confidence of the insular Hiberno-British church, wrenched it from its moorings, and pushed it off towards new and turbulent waters. The first was the mission of Columbanus to Europe, the second the mission of Augustine to England, and both brought the Irish church into contact with the erudite and energetic Gregory the Great and a resurgent papacy that directed its missionary activity towards the West.[70] I am not concerned with the effect of Columbanus — the short-term failure and ultimate triumph[71] — on Francia and Italia, but with the knowledge and influence that flowed back to Ireland on foot of the contacts he had established with continental European centres and his complex relationship with the papacy. Arrogant, prickly, independent-minded and self-assured, he encountered another and equally self-assured ecclesiastical organisation (and, besides, some Merovingian bishops who were learned) and he betrays, in his letter to Gregory the Great, at once the over-bearing self-confidence and insidious self-doubt of the provincial. The Easter question on which he argued with such passion was to be the dispute of the Insular churches for a century after his death, and the two-way traffic between Ireland and the Columbanian centres in continental Europe brought the attention of the Irish church to a wider world — its high culture, its learning, its texts and

---

[65]*Thesaurus palaeo-hibernicus*, ed Whitley Stokes and John Strachan (Cambridge 1903, repr Dublin 1985) II, 244-47; R Thurneysen, *Old Irish reader* (Dublin 1949) 35-36.

[66]Pádraig Ó Néill, 'The background to the Cambrai homily', *Ériu* 32 (1981) 137-47 (p 137).

[67]Any reader would have observed that Gregory's own *Homilia* were addressed to a mixed congregation of clergy and laity and a vernacular paraphrase would be in the spirit of Gregory's preaching: M Banniard, *Viva voce: communication écrite et communication orale du IVe au IXe siècle en occident latin* (Paris 1992) 156-72.

[68]H Wasserschleben, *Irische Kanonensammlung*, 161-62 (42: 1-4); *Bretha Nemed* §§3, 12 (L Breatnach, 'The first third of *Bretha Nemed*', *Ériu* 40 (1989) 8, 12-13; cf Breatnach (note 58 above) 445-47).

[69]Note 66 above, 147.

[70]Charles-Edwards suggests that the two missions may have been connected (note 3 above, 10-11).

[71]H B Clarke and M Brennan, *Columbanus and Merovingian monasticism*, British Archaeological Reports International Series 113 (Oxford 1981).

its debates — and drove a wedge between it and its more conservative elder sister, the British church.

The second development was the arrival of the Augustinian mission to Canterbury. Not long after its coming, there was direct contact between the Canterbury mission and Ireland. The letter of Laurentius, archbishop of Canterbury, Mellitus, bishop of London, and Justus, bishop of Rochester, to the bishops and abbots of Ireland is datable to the period 605-617, and may have been written c608. These Italian bishops complain that, while they had come with a high opinion of the holiness of the British and the Irish, they had now 'learned from bishop Dagan when he came to this island and from abbot Columbanus when he came to Gaul that the Irish did not differ from the British in their way of life. For when bishop Dagan came to us he refused to take food, not only with us but even in the house where we took our meals'.[72] Dagan's very presence in England may itself be a result of the Augustinian mission which had been dispatched by Gregory the Great less than a decade before. This letter and bishop Dagan's visit (and hostile attitude) are far from indicating a once-off contact and they are to be seen, as is evident from what Bede preserves of the letter, in the wider context of the Columbanian mission. Now that there was a Rome-inspired mission to England, the Irish church was inevitably in contact with it and with its teachings. This close contact — in Ireland as well as in England — continued throughout the seventh century and later, and the Theodorean mission, too, was to have an important influence in Ireland (a matter to which I hope to advert elsewhere).

A legal echo of this continued Irish contact with the Canterbury mission and with its influence may be found in a ruling about marriage incorporated in 'Synodus II Patricii'.[73] Gregory the Great in his letter of 601 to St Augustine of Canterbury, setting out the rules for the newly converted Anglo-Saxons and doubtless making concessions, absolutely rules out marriage of first cousins, but concedes that the Anglo-Saxons might marry their second and third cousins.[74] A statement on this matter, which rings of controversy, occurs in 'Synodus II S. Patricii':

De consanguinitate in conjugio. Intellege quod lex loquitur, non minos nec plus; quod autem observatur apud nos, ut quattuor genera diuidantur, nec uidisse dicunt nec legisse. 'Understand what the law says, neither less nor more: but what is observed amongst us, that they be separated by four degrees, they say they have neither seen nor read'.

---

[72]*HE*, II, 4; Kenney (note 21 above) 218-19 §56.
[73]Bieler (note 10 above) 184-97 (p 196 §28); K Hughes, 'Synodus II S. Patricii' in *Latin script and letters AD 400-900: Festschrift … Ludwig Bieler*, ed J J O'Meara and B Naumann (Leiden 1976) 141-47 (p 146). Hughes dates the synod to the second half of the sixth century — rather too early, I think.
[74]Haddan and Stubbs (note 10 above) III, 20-21.

The observers of this rule are the Irish Romani; 'those who have neither seen nor read' are the Irish conservatives. These rules of consanguinity would have played havoc with property transmission and conservation in Irish kindreds and it seems very likely that the conservatives had already arrived at that elegant solution to the consanguinity problem, based on Numbers 26: 28-34, 36:10-12 and set out in *Hibernensis* 32:20.[75] And the conservatives win on points, for they can cite the word of God against the word of Gregory the Great — perhaps making the row more acrimonious than it might otherwise have been.

The Irish church of the seventh century was riven with controversies (sometimes bitter in the extreme) over the date of Easter, tonsure, and related questions of discipline — matters on which the innovators encountered the stubborn resistance of conservatives who could point to a glorious past and the prospect of an uncertain and troubling future. The history of this conflict cannot be traced here but some of its effects can be adverted to. The debates, which arose from the new contacts with Rome (direct and indirect), set the Irish church and Irish learning off in new directions. Because of their intensity and because of the sheer energy and research devoted to their solution, they forced the churchmen to give deep thought to themselves and their institutions. This heightened consciousness was the pre-condition of subsequent developments in Irish culture, in the vernacular and in Latin. It led directly to a rapid — one might say urgent — cultivation of a higher learning, to writings of major significance in computistical, exegetical, grammatical and patristic scholarship and this was not driven by an academic pursuit of scholarship for its own sake (does this ever occur?), by the prospect of heavenly profit, or by the rewards of professional success in this life (though elements of all three will have been present), but by a pressing institutional need to know in order to solve problems that threatened the life of the church with disunity, even serious disorder. And the scholars really got to work: in the words of Bischoff, 'Irish production in the fields of exegesis and grammar, in the seventh and eighth centuries, exceeds in quantity all that was written in these fields in Spain, in England, in Italy'.[76] It is likely, too, that these debates forced the clergy to consider literature and culture in the broadest sense of these terms — to find and justify an attitude to the pagan past, to vernacular law, to the cultivation of a literature with an inherited caste of pagan kings and warriors. Indeed, their reading of the Fathers — Augustine, Jerome and Gregory the Great — would have forced them to consider just such questions. The resultant literary output is so large that only a few texts can be touched on here.

The controversies were between old and new — the Hiberno-British church that had come of age in the sixth century and the outward-looking, Rome-inspired reformers of the seventh, who are called (or did they call

[75]D Ó Corráin, 'Irish law and canon law' in Ní Chatháin and Richter (note 17 above) 157-61.
[76]Bischoff (note 33 above) 199.

themselves?) Romani. These were ardent believers in papal supremacy. For example, they saw the Roman tonsure of Gregory the Great as the Petrine one: the 'Celtic' as that of the father of heresy Simon Magus (Acts 8:9) or, worse still, that of the swineherd of the pagan king of Tara, Lóegaire mac Néill: the haircut tells the man.[77] They were preoccupied with the canonicity of the books of the Bible and the displacement of the Vetus Latina by the Vulgate is another aspect of this biblical concern. The Vulgate came to Ireland in the late sixth century: its widespread acceptance came in the seventh. The Romani were admirers of Gregory the Great. Cummian cites Gregory with high approval: 'etsi post omnes scripsit, tamen est merito omnibus praeferendus'.[78] The *Ecloga de Moralibus in Job* of Laidcend (died 667) is a digest dedicated to making Gregory's most important work known in Ireland.[79] The *Commentary on Catholic epistles* cites Gregory in third frequency after Jerome and Isidore: there are excerpts from all his major works.[80] The *Pseudo-Jerome commentary on Mark*, attributed to Cummian, has as its major source Gregory the Great's *Homiliae in Evangelia*. The Romani are the 'New Christians', the universalists who had come to be inspired by the new contact with Rome and the majesty of the see of Peter.

They sought texts everywhere, and especially from Visigothic Spain. In Dr Marina Smyth's view the most convincing hypothesis is that the high level of intellectual activity in Ireland was enabled by contact, probably by trade routes, with south-west Gaul and Visigothic Spain where the Roman tradition had been relatively well preserved. Either would explain the early availability in Ireland of the works of Isidore (died 636) and those of Gregory the Great (friend of Isidore's predecessor, Leander).[81] In a series of critically important papers, Professor Jocelyn Hillgarth has shown the indebtedness of the Irish to Isidore: Irish writers use *Etymologiae, De natura rerum, Differentiae, De ortu et obitu patrum, Allegoriae, Chronica, Synonyma, De officiis, Quaestiones in vetus testamentum*. The oldest surviving manuscript of *Etymologiae* (St Gall, MS 1399 a.1) was written in Ireland and it is dated by Julian Brown to the first half or middle of the seventh century.[82] Ireland received an African-Spanish collection of computistic tracts *c*630. Hillgarth adds significantly: 'It is possible that there is a connection between this group and the lawyers responsible for the Old Irish classical tracts of the

---

[77]Louis Trichet, *La tonsure* (Paris 1990) esp. 69-92; Louis Gougaud, *Christianity in Celtic lands* (London 1932, repr Dublin 1992) 201-06.

[78]Walsh and Ó Cróinín (note 21 above) 82-191.

[79]*Egloga ... de Moralibus Iob*, ed M Adriaen, CCSL 145 (1969); Lapidge and Sharpe (note 21 above) §293.

[80]R E McNally, *Scriptores Hiberniae minores*, CCSL 108B (1973) 3-50.

[81]Marina Smyth, 'The physical world in seventh-century Hiberno-Latin texts', *Peritia* 5 (1986) 201-34 (p 203). E James, 'Ireland and western Gaul in the Merovingian period' in *Ireland in early medieval Europe: studies in memory of Kathleen Hughes*, ed D Whitelock, R McKitterick and D Dumville (Cambridge 1982) 362-86.

[82]T J Brown, 'The Irish element in the insular system of scripts to circa AD 850' in Löwe (note 34 above) 101-19 (p 104).

seventh and eighth centuries: it has been suggested that the fondness for etymology which these authors display owes something to Isidore's example'.[83] Ó Cróinín has shown beyond doubt that *De natura rerum* and *Etymologiae* were known to the writer of an Irish computus before 658.[84] The *Hisperica famina*, which Professor Herren thinks were written in Ireland in the beginning of the second half of the seventh century, are strongly influenced, verbally, by Isidore's *Etymologiae*.[85] The eccentric grammarian, Virgilius Maro Grammaticus, who lived in Ireland in the middle of the seventh century, also uses Isidore,[86] and Virgilius, in turn, is cited in a computistical context that is firmly dated to AD 658.[87] The *lorica* of Laidcend (died *c*661) ('Suffragare trinitatis unitas') seems to use Isidore's *Etymologiae*, supplemented by an undetermined Graeco-Latin glossary or glossaries.[88] We can be certain, then, of the reception of works of Isidore in Ireland by the middle of the seventh century,[89] if not a little before.

I now refer very briefly to some of the well-known and important seventh-century texts that are attributed to the Romani. Cummian's *Paschal Letter* (which we now have in the excellent edition of Walsh and Ó Cróinín and dated to AD 632/33)[90] speaks of referring major matters in dispute 'ad caput urbium' ie to Rome, a principle enunciated by Innocent I in 404 and repeated by Dionysius Exiguus in his *Decreta*.[91] For Cummian, those who challenge the Roman Easter date challenge orthodoxy. Romani in seventh-century Ireland were those who followed Rome in Paschal dating (this was the diagnostic test) and they regarded that as a matter of loyalty: Cummian was one of them. Their position led naturally to a new openness to Roman influence, to foreign learning and to a deeper study of

[83]J N Hillgarth, 'Ireland and Spain in the seventh century', *Peritia* 3 (1984) 1-16 (p 10); idem, 'The east, Visgothic Spain and the Irish', *Studia Patristica* 6 (1961) 442-56; idem, 'Visgothic Spain and early christian Ireland', *PRIA (C)* 62 (1962) 167-94; idem, 'Old Ireland and Visgothic Spain' in *Old Ireland*, ed R McNally (Dublin 1965) 200-27. B Bischoff, 'Die europäische Verbreitung der Werke Isidors von Sevilla' in *Mittelalterliche Studien* (note 33 above) I, 171-94. M Herren, 'On the earliest Irish acquaintance with Isidore of Seville' in *Visgothic Spain: new approaches*, ed E James (Oxford 1980) 243-50.
[84]D Ó Cróinín, 'A seventh-century Irish computus from the circle of Cummian', *PRIA (C)* 82 (1982) 404-30.
[85]M Herren, *The Hisperica famina. I. the A-text* (Toronto 1974) 19-39.
[86]M Herren, 'Some new light on the life of Virgilius Maro Grammaticus', *PRIA (C)* 79 (1979) 27-71; cf idem (note 85 above) 27-32.
[87]D Ó Cróinín, 'The date, provenance, and earliest use of the works of Virgilius Maro Grammaticus' in *Tradition und Wertung: Festschrift Franz Brunhölzl*, ed G Bernt, F Rädle and G Silagi (Sigmaringen 1989) 13-22.
[88]M Herren, *The Hisperica famina II. Related poems* (Toronto 1987) 5-14, 39-45, 56-64; 76-89 (text); cf idem, 'The authorship, date of composition and provenance of the so-called *Lorica Gildae*', *Ériu* 24 (1973) 35-51.
[89]See the reservations (some questionable) of M Smyth, 'Isidore of Seville and early Irish cosmography', *Cambridge Medieval Celtic Studies* 14 (1987) 69-102.
[90]Walsh and Ó Cróinín (note 22 above); Maura Walsh, 'Some remarks on Cummian's Paschal letter and the Commentary on Mark ascribed to Cummian', Ní Chatháin and Richter (note 47 above) 216-29.
[91]Pádraig Ó Néill, 'Romani influence on seventh-century Hiberno Latin literature' in Ní Chatháin and Richter (note 17 above) 280-90.

patristics. Cummian composed his learned *Letter* in 632/33, in reply to an Iona charge of heresy. On balance, Cummian is the most likely to be identical with Cuimmíne Foto (died 662) *comarba Brénaind* ie abbot of Clonfert, author of a Penitential,[92] the poem 'Celebra Iuda',[93] 'De figuris apostolorum',[94] and a *Commentary on the Gospel of St Mark*.[95] His death is lamented in a poem by Colmán moccu Chluasaig, dated to the seventh century and defended convincingly as more or less contemporary by Professor Byrne.[96] Cummian's church of Clonfert had links with Iona. He had a good patristics library — 'solid if not exciting', says Walsh — including Jerome, *De exodo in vigilia paschae* and some of his letters; Cyprian; Origen, *Homilies on Leviticus*; Augustine; Ambrosiaster; Dionysius Exiguus; Pelagius (probably); and collections of church councils including good texts of the acta of the councils of Nice and Arles. Cummian's work is one of careful planning and rigorous scholarship and is founded upon a well-ordered archive of computistic and other texts.[97]

The Irish Augustine, in his *De mirabilibus sacrae scripturae*, finds his chief source and inspiration amongst the Fathers — Augustine, Basil of Caesarea, Eugippius, Gregory the Great, Jerome, Cassian, Orosius, Rufinus and Tertullian. The text dates to 655 (given by the author), but the author is unknown. He may have been writing in the Lower Shannon basin, perhaps Inis Cathaig.[98] Here is genuine and refreshing spirit of rational enquiry into natural phenomena that owes nothing much to ancient science, for the good reason that the Irish Augustine had no access to it. His work implies that he had adopted the cycle of Victorius and had, therefore, adopted the Roman Easter.[99] He shows no acquaintance with Isidore.[100]

In the case of another cosmological work, *De ordine creaturarum*, Professor Díaz y Díaz holds that 'an Insular setting is certain from the literary, doctrinal, biblical and lexicographical point of view'.[101] The first outside Spain to cite it is Defensor of Ligugé in his *Liber Scintillarum* of c700. The text must date after 655 for it depends on the Irish Augustine's *De mirabilibus sacrae scripturae* as the major source. It is also dependent on the remarkable and influential mid-seventh-century tract, *De XII*

---

[92]Bieler (note 10 above) 109-35.

[93]Lapidge and Sharpe (note 24 above) §582; Kenney (note 21 above) §92; Coccia (note 24 above) 294-96.

[94]D Ó Cróinín, 'Cummianus Longus and the iconography of Christ and the apostles in early Irish literature' in Ó Corráin, Breatnach and McCone (note 4 above) 265-79.

[95]J F Kelly, 'A catalogue of early medieval Hiberno-Latin biblical commentaries (II)', *Traditio* 45 (1989-90) 416-17; Walsh (note 90 above) 216-29.

[96]Francis John Byrne, 'The lament for Cummíne Foto', *Ériu* 31 (1980) 111-22.

[97]Walsh (note 90 above) 216-29.

[98]G McGinty, 'The Irish Augustine: De mirabilibus sacrae scripturae' in Ní Chatháin and Richter (note 47 above) 70-83.

[99]ibid, 73.

[100]ibid, 82. Smyth (note 89 above) 72-73.

[101]Manuel C Díaz y Díaz, *Liber de ordine creaturarum* (Santiago de Compostella 1972) 25.

abusivis saeculi.[102] More interesting still, it cites a credal formulation of the XI Council of Toledo (AD 675) and Díaz y Díaz is certain that this dependence is direct.[103] Therefore, it will date c675 X 700. The author knew Gregory the Great's *Homiliae in Evangelia*, his *Dialogi* and, of course, Isidore's *De differentiis uerborum* and *De officiis*. And he probably belonged to the circle of southern Romani.[104]

This, of course, was a culture of writing, consciously and expressly so, as we gather from the reflections of its makers and their preoccupation with grammar and language.[105] There is no room here for the cult of orality so beloved of latter-day romantics and primitivists and it is interesting to see how the ideology of book-culture is expressed in the literature. Many miracles in the earliest Irish hagiography are about books, the information technology of christian culture. This is evident in Adomnán's *Vita Columbae*: the boy carrying a book written by Columba dropped it in its book-satchel in a river where it remained from Christmas to Easter. It survived unharmed. A boy carrying books fell into the Boyne and was drowned; all the books were ruined except that a page 'written by the holy fingers of St Columba' was found dry, and not at all injured, 'as though it had been kept in a coffer' (II, 8-9). Muirchú, too, has an early example. Patrick and a druid engage in a miracle-working contest at Tara before king Lóegaire. The king suggests that both men place their books in water and he whose books come out dry will be the victor. Patrick is willing to undergo this ordeal but the druid refuses. What is interesting here is that a christian cleric of the late seventh century should imagine that druids had books,[106] that he cannot conceive of a clergy without written scriptures — striking evidence for the identification of the perceived role of the druid in the past with that of the christian cleric in the present, and the bookishness of that cleric.

Later Irish hagiography is full of miracles about books: their recovery from water unharmed, their miraculous writing and reading, their use to banish demons and monsters, and their wonderful interaction with animals: from Ciarán's use of a living antlered stag as a bookstand to the fly that walked along each line of Mochua's psalter as he read and remained as a living book-mark until he resumed reading. Similarly, there is a celebration of the acquisition of literacy — saints can read

---

[102]S Hellmann, *Pseudo-Cyprianus: De XII abusivis saeculi*, Texte u. Untersuchungen 34 (Leipzig 1909); H H Anton, 'Pseudo-Cyprian: *De duodecim abusivis saeculi* und sein Einfluß auf den Kontinent, inbesondere auf die karolingischen Fürstenspiegel' in Löwe (note 34 above) 568-617; A Breen, 'Pseudo-Cyprian *De duodecim abusivis saeculi* and the bible' in Ní Chatháin and Richter (note 47 above) 230-45; idem, 'The evidence of antique Irish exegesis in Pseudo-Cyprian, *De duodecim abusiuis saeculi*', *PRIA (C)* 87 (1987) 71-101.

[103]Note 101 above, 34.

[104]ibid, 21, 27.

[105]L Holtz, 'Irish grammarians and the continent in the seventh century' in Clarke and Brennan (note 71 above) 135-52; idem, *Donat et la tradition de l'enseignement grammatical: Étude sur l'Ars Donati et sa diffusion* (Paris 1982); Vivien Law, *The insular Latin grammarians*, Studies in Celtic History 3 (Woodbridge 1982).

[106]For a different interpretation, see Stevenson (note 51 above) 165.

without being taught, can read strange languages sight unseen, are taught
to read by angels — and of the craft of the scribe. Columba, without
having seen the scribe's copy, predicts that there will be a single mistake
— a given letter missing on a given page — and he is right (I, 23). All this
is a remarkable celebration of the technology of literacy.[107] As McNally
put it, '... the Irish Christians place a maximum emphasis on the written
word as a sacred sign, for the Christian God was himself the veritable
author of a Book'.[108]

There were two obvious results: the high artistic treatment of God's
ipsissima verba, particularly in the great illuminated gospel books, and
the production of very many biblical commentaries (some very elaborate)
that reveal many aspects of early Irish thought and reflection.[109] In *Liber
de numeris*, an eighth-century work,[110] the etymology of the Latin word
liber is given creatively:

> Book (*liber*) is thus named on the basis of three considerations, that is,
> reading (*legendo*), weighing (*librando*), freeing (*liberando*). Reading,
> that is, to read and understand the spiritual law; weighing, that is, to
> measure out punishment to the wicked and rewards to the perfect;
> freeing, that is, to release those who served and serve the devil and
> the world and sins.[111]

An exegete, writing in the seventh-century *Commentary on the catholic
epistle of Jude* offers an interesting reflection on the problem of textual
transmission:

> How is it called the Book of Enoch since he lived before the Flood and
> letters were not then given to mankind? Some say that he had written
> his book and that Noah took it with him in the ark or, as others
> think, that prophets wrote the book, inspired by the same spirit, so
> that they commemorated in writing in their times what he in his time
> had prophesied.[112]

The very successful construction of an Irish pre-history leading back
directly to Noah's Flood and beyond brought its problems to text-conscious

[107]J F Kelly, 'Books, learning and sanctity in early christian Ireland', *Thought* 54
(1979) 253-61.
[108]R McNally, *Old Ireland* (Dublin 1965) 122.
[109]B Bischoff, 'Wendepunkte in der Geschichte der lateinischen Exegese im
Frühmittelalter', *Sacris Erudiri* 6 (1954) 189-279, repr, *Mittelalterliche Studien*
(Stuttgart 1966) I, 205-73, trans 'Turning-points in the history of Latin exegesis in the
early middle ages' in *Biblical studies: the medieval Irish contribution*, ed M McNamara
(Dublin 1976) 74-160; J F Kelly, 'A catalogue of early medieval Hiberno-Latin
biblical commentaries (I-II)', *Traditio* 44 (1988) 537-71; 45 (1989-90) 393-434.
[110]R E McNally, *Der irische Liber de numeris: eine Quellenanalyse des ps-
isidorischen Liber de numeris* (Munich 1957).
[111]McNally (note 108 above) 129.
[112]R McNally, *Scriptores Hiberniae minores* CCSL 108B (1973) 49.51-57. D Ó
Corráin, 'Textuality and intertextuality: early medieval Irish literature' in *La storia di
Griselda in Europa*, ed R Morabito (L'Aquila 1987) 21-32.

literati, and occasions this exegetical explanation. A later tale was composed (*Suidugud Tellaig Temrach* 'the settling of the manor of Tara') to explain, amongst other things, how the Irish could have knowledge of their history before the Flood. In this aetiology of scholarship, its transmission was due to one Fintan son of Bochra son of Bith son of Noah who was a shape-shifter and who outlived the Flood and all later generations until the appropriate time when he taught history to all the historians of Ireland and received communion from the hands of bishop Erc. And the writer links him explicitly with Enoch:

> Is indemin immorro cía baile in rohadhnocht, acht is dóig leo is ina chorp chollaigi rucad i nnach ndíamair ndíada amail rucad Ele ₇ Enócc i pardus

> And the place where he [Fintan] is buried is uncertain however. But some think he was borne away in his mortal body to some secret place as Elijah and Enoch were borne into paradise.[113]

This environment of intense literary culture will have contributed something, too, to remarkable developments in hagiography. The purpose of hagiography was the glorification of the saint and so of the communities that claimed him or her as a founder.[114] The flourishing hagiography of the seventh century drew on scholarship, too, and based itself on models from early christianity. The main seventh-century texts are Cogitosus's *Vita Brigitae* (c650), the anonymous *Vita prima Brigitae*,[115] Muirchú, *Vita Patricii* (661 X 700), Tírechán, *Collectanea* (661 X 690),[116] and Adomnán's *Vita Columbae*.[117] These works were not the earliest: there was a corpus of the period 600-650 — material about Patrick, Columba, and earlier sources for Brigit. These Lives were replaced in the second half of the seventh century, and by then Irish hagiography was a well-established genre, mature in its conventions and with literary access to the best models. The following were all available to Adomnán: Sulpicius Severus, *Vita S. Martini*; Athanasius, *Vita S. Antonii* (in Evagrius's translation); *Acta S. Silvestri*; Constantius, *Vita S. Germani*; Gregory the Great, *Vita S. Benedicti* (in *Dialogi*). His *Vita S. Columbae* is written in the best tradition of European hagiography.

---

[113]R I Best, 'The settling of the manor of Tara', *Ériu* 4 (1910) 121-72 (p 161).

[114]J-M Picard, 'Structural patterns in early Hiberno-Latin hagiography', *Peritia* 4 (1985) 57-82.

[115]R Sharpe, 'Vitae S. Brigitae: the oldest texts', *Peritia* 1 (1982) 81-106; K McCone, 'Brigit in the seventh century: a saint with three lives?', ibid, 107-45; S Connolly and J-M Picard, 'Cogitosus: Life of St Brigit', *JRSAI* 117 (1987) 5-27; S Connolly, 'Vita prima sanctae Brigitae: background and historical value', *JRSAI* 119 (1989) 1-49.

[116]L Bieler, *The Patrician texts in the Book of Armagh*, Scriptores Latini Hiberniae 10 (Dublin 1979); R Sharpe, 'Palaeographical considerations in the study of the Patrician documents in the Book of Armagh', *Scriptorium* 36 (1982) 3-28.

[117]A O and M O Anderson *Adomnans Life of Columba* (Edinburgh 1961, 2nd ed Oxford 1991); J-M Picard, 'The purpose of Adomnán's *Vita Columbae*', *Peritia* 1 (1982) 160-77; idem, 'The Schaffhausen Adomnán — a unique witness to Hiberno-Latin', ibid, 216-49; idem, 'Structural patterns in early Hiberno-Latin hagiography', *Peritia* 3 (1984) 50-70.

The achievements of the first half and middle of the seventh century were an inheritance for the later seventh century and the eighth. One of the more notable achievements was the elaboration of a developed legal system based on lengthy legal texts in Hiberno-Latin and in the vernacular. The *Hibernensis* appears to be the compilatory work of Ruben (died 725) of Dairinis (near Lismore) and Cú Chuimne (died 747) of Iona — drawing on a rich archive of legal materials.[118] This text is a remarkable undertaking — nothing less, in fact, that an attempt to draw up, outside a Roman environment, a comprehensive legal framework for all aspects of christian life. As Fournier and Le Bras observe, 'no land made a more original or more abundant contribution to ecclesiastical law than the Insular christian communities'.[119] However, I shall confine myself to a few texts in the vernacular and I shall try to link them to the inheritance from Visigothic Spain and to the activities of the Romani. Vernacular texts are not to be seen in opposition to Hiberno-Latin ones: rather they complement one another, and together represent a single (though not necessarily unanimous) statement of the law for society as a whole by a single legal caste.

One of the more interesting of these is the fragmentarily-preserved 'Cáin Fhuithirbe', recently commented upon and translated by Breatnach.[120] The text is securely dated by Binchy to the years AD 678 X 683.[121] It records laws about the relationship of church and kings passed at a mixed council of clergy and kings, held near Killarney and presided over by the king of Munster. The ecclesiastical element is to the fore in the poem with which the text opens: *Mac Dé, ním dú dichell* 'It is not proper for me to neglect the son of God' and *fo rígaib rorath rom- ecailsi Muman -molsatar* 'under kings of great bounty the churches of Munster have recommended me'. These are the words of the clerical law-speaker.

The poem states the purpose of the assembly: it is, in effect, a mixed synod:

> *déraith dál inid comfocus Críst*
> *Cingiu dedáil i nderoll dílsi*
> *do lámaib lítho fer fíadun*
> an assembly of godly grace in which Christ is near

---

[118]R Thurneysen, 'Zur irischen Kanonensammlung', *Zeitschrift fur celtische Philologie* 6 (1907-09) 1-5; M P Sheehy, 'Influence of ancient Irish law on the *Collectio canonum Hibernensis*' in *Proceedings of the Third International Congress of Medieval Canon Law* (Vatican City 1971) 31-41; idem, 'The *Collectio canonum Hibernensis* — a Celtic phenomenon' in Löwe (note 34 above) 525-35; P Fournier and G Le Bras, *Histoire des collections canoniques en occident* (Paris 1931) I, 62-65; Hubert Mordek, *Kirchenrecht und Reform im Frankenreich* (Berlin 1975) 255-59.

[119]Note 118 above, 64.

[120]L Breatnach, 'The ecclesiastical element in the Old-Irish legal tract *Cáin Fhuithirbe*', *Peritia* 5 (1986) 36-52.

[121]D A Binchy, 'The date and provenance of the *Uraicecht Becc*', *Ériu* 18 (1958) 44-54 (pp 51-54). Seán Ó Coileáin, 'Mag Fuithirbe revisited', *Éigse* 23 (1989) 16-26 (I cannot quite follow the reasoning in this paper).

I approach a double assembly in which I may set apart rights
with the prosperous support of witnesses

Three clerics associated with the work of the synod are identifiable with
a high degree of confidence: Cuimmíne, is probably Cuimmíne Foto,
referred to above as Cummian, who died in 662, some seventeen to twenty-
two years before the promulgation of the law;[122] Díblíne who is either
Díblíne Elnai, abbot of Emly or Díblíne, abbot of Terryglass, both of whom
were signatories of *Cáin Adomnáin* in 697;[123] and Banbán is likely to be
the Bannbannus who appears as an authority on exegesis in the seventh-
century *Commentary on the catholic epistles*,[124] in the company of
Manchianus (died 652) of Min Droichit and Laidcend (died 661) of Cluain
Ferta Molua. These are some leading members in the circle of
distinguished southern Romani and their purpose in law-making is
evident. *Cáin Fhuithirbe* contains the explicit statement; *ro dílsiged le
dub in díchubus* 'that which is contrary to conscience has been made forfeit
by ink'. From this we can conclude that the aim of the legislators was to
provide written and coherent christian law for a christian people — an
aim which is evident elsewhere in the vernacular legal corpus.[125]

This leads to other questions. Were the Romani, then, a major spur to the
writing of vernacular Irish law? Probably. A fragment of *Cáin Fhuithirbe*
may even indicate that Banbán himself was seen as a jurist: *Ar-folmas a
mBanban brethaib* 'it was undertaken in the judgements of Banbán'.[126] Is
the mixed synod that issued *Cáin Fhuithirbe* modelled on the great
seventh-century Councils of Toledo? Possibly. We already know that the
author of *De ordine creaturarum* was familiar with the credal statement
of XI Council of Toledo (AD 675). It is reasonable to believe that a copy of
its *acta* reached Ireland and the *acta* of earlier Spanish councils may also
have come. I have not been able to find direct quotations from these in
Irish sources, but there are some suggestive similarities that might bear
further study. For example, the rules governing the division of property
between the ruler of a church and his heirs on the one hand and the church

---

[122]There is another link between Cummian and *Cáin Fhuithirbe*: Breatnach (note 120
above, 51) notes that the B-text of *Cáin Fhuithirbe* contained a version of the
Patrician legend, but Cummian's concern with Patrick is confirmed independently in
his *Paschal Letter* where he refers to him as 'sanctus Patricius papa noster' (Walsh
and Ó Cróinín (note 21 above) 84; Byrne (note 9 above) 174-75.

[123]Máirín Ní Dhonnchadha, 'The guarantor list of *Cáin Adomnáin, 697*', *Peritia* 1
(1982) 178-215 (pp 180, 186, 188).

[124]R E McNally, *Scriptores Hiberniae minores*, CCSL 108B, ix-x; A Holder,
'Altirische Namen im Reichenauer Codex CCXXXIII' in *Archiv für celtische
Lexikographie*, ed Whitley Stokes and Kuno Meyer (Halle a.S. 1907) III, 266-67; J F
Kelly (note 95 above) 430 §107.

[125]Ó Corráin, Breatnach and Breen (note 19 above) *Peritia* 3 (1984) 382-438; K
McCone, 'Dubhtach maccu Lugair and a matter of life and death in pseudo-historical
prologue to the *Senchas Már*', *Peritia* 5 (1986) 1-35; John Carey, 'The two laws in
Dubthach's judgement', *Cambridge Medieval Celtic Studies* 19 (1990) 1-18; D Ó
Corráin, 'Irish vernacular law and the Old Testament' in Ní Chatháin and Richter
(note 47 above) 284-307.

[126]Text and translation from Breatnach (note 120 above) 44-45.

on the other, as set out in the *acta* of IX Toledo (AD 655)[127] seem to be very close to those in the *Hibernensis* in the case of the parting of an abbot who was a *locum tenens* from his church.[128] The rules about the little local churches, very likely privately-owned ones, set out in the *acta* of the Council of Mérida (AD 666)[129] seem to be to be close enough to the rules governing the priests of the 'little churches of the *tuath*' in *Ríagail Phátraic*,[130] an episcopalian tract on church order in the vernacular, and dated to the early eighth century. Other Toledan usages — the chanting of the *Credo* at mass as prescribed by the III Council of Toledo (AD 589) and the doxology sanctioned by the IV Council of Toledo (AD 633) — also occur in Ireland.[131] It would not be at all surprising if the Toledan kind of mixed synod also made its appearance in Ireland under clerical influence, and precisely as a vehicle for wider legislation.

Seventh-century scholarship shaped the historical vision of the Irish for a millennium.[132] Acquaintance with Isidore changed their view of themselves for the Irish clergy adopted the Isidorian schema of the origins of the races, the descent of the European peoples from Japhet, and incorporated it into the higher levels of their genealogies, thus placing themselves within a grand vista of human history that traced man's ascent from the present to Adam and to God.[133] Isidore's listings of the races of the world was also a model: if a great christian scholar could devote himself to these things on the macro-scale, so could the Irish christian scholars on the micro-scale. Here is the justification for the histories and genealogies of the Irish dynasties and kingdoms — they called this learning *peritia* — and, after the model of Isidore, their need to link them together as a single people of God. These ideas complemented the clergy's practical need to know, to establish its title deeds to property and the dignity of its saints in a lineage society where church lineages (most often discards of the great dynasties) were major property holders. And if Isidore provided the schema, the Old Testament supplied the actual genealogical models (Numbers, Paralipomenon and 1 Esdras).[134]

---

[127]J Vives, *Concilios visigóticos e hispano-romanos*, España Cristiana 1 (Barcelona/Madrid 1963) 299-300 (§4. Quae de conquistis rebus inter ecclesiam et sacerdotis haeredes divisio fiat).

[128]*Hibernensis* 43:6; Ó Corráin (note 75 above) 161-64.

[129]Vives (note 127 above) 338.

[130]J G O'Keeffe, 'The rule of Patrick', *Ériu* 1 (1904) 216-24 (p 220 §§11-13) = D A Binchy, *Corpus Iuris Hibernici* (Dublin 1978) 2130.

[131]K Hughes, 'Irish monks and learning', *Los monjes et los estudios: IV semaña de estudios monasticos* (Poblet 1963) 67-68. The doxology appears on the Fahan Muru cross (in Greek uncials) and in the Antiphonary of Bangor: it does not necessarily come from Visigothic Spain (James, note 81 above, 372-73), but it may well do.

[132]For the development form of this 'history', see R Mark Scowcroft, '*Leabhar Gabhála* — part I: the growth of the text', *Ériu* 38 (1987) 81-142; '*Leabhar Gabhála* — part II: the growth of the tradition', *Ériu* 39 (1988) 1-66.

[133]This is earliest expressed in the higher levels of the Leinster dynastic poems that may date from the middle of the seventh century: Kuno Meyer, 'Über die älteste irische Dichtung', 16-50, re-edited by M A O'Brien, *Corpus genealogiarum Hiberniae*, I, 1-7.

[134]D Ó Corráin, 'An chléir agus an léann anallód: an ginealas', *Léachtaí Cholm Cille* 16 (Maynooth 1986) 71-86. I hope to deal with this matter in detail in my forthcoming Carroll Lecture.

Royal genealogy served the need of kings for glory and legitimacy, and king-lists created a comforting continuity across the centuries — even millennia — that guaranteed the present and assured the future. Like the historical books of the Old Testament, saga realised that past in dramatic form and functioned as political scripture, carefully crafted by the clergy.[135] Binchy's archaic sacral kings ringed with tabus, fossils from an ancient and imaginary Aryan past that Dr Wormald wittily described as 'priestly vegetables', are quite at odds with the evidence of the annals and genealogies and must be set aside, and his fainéant overkings must go the same way.[136] Kingship was about power, and kings waded in blood to get it and hold it, as they did in the Francia of Gregory of Tours, in Anglo-Saxon England, and throughout the rest of the barbarian world. In the seventh and eighth centuries, there was a hierarchy of kings but it is likely that this was not much different — terminology apart — from other areas of the barbarian West. The king of Tara, sometimes called *rex Hiberniae*, claimed precedence over all other kings and figures in the hagiography of Muirchú and Adomnán. These clerical witnesses are prescriptive as well as descriptive and therefore difficult to interpret, but in the kingship of Tara they found something real enough to use for their own ends.[137] The king, at whatever level, was responsible for the government and defence of his people and his was the final court of appeal. Inherited and exotic elements were mingled in the Irish idea of kingship. This is perhaps clear enough to historians but it was transparent to contemporaries. The metaphor of the sacred marriage of king and goddess and the related idea of the prince's truth and righteousness,[138] that made humans and animals fertile and the land prosperous, were dramatically reiterated in the sagas of early christian Ireland and skilfully integrated with christian concepts that derived mainly from the exegetes' reading of Old Testament kingship. Kingship, as in Merovingian Francia, was the property of the dynasty, not an impersonal *imperium*. Early, the clergy sought to christianise it. As royal confidants, they urged kings to rule justly as well as reign, to protect the church, the orphan and the poor, and they introduced the ceremony of royal ordination, based on

[135]D Ó Corráin, 'Historical need and literary narrative' in *Proceedings of the VII International Congress of Celtic Studies*, ed D E Evans, J G Griffith and E M Jope (Oxford 1986) 141-58.

[136]D A Binchy, *Celtic and Anglo-Saxon kingship* (Oxford 1970); P Wormald, 'Celtic and Anglo-Saxon kingship: some further thoughts' in *Sources of Anglo-Saxon culture*, ed Paul E Szarmach, Studies in Medieval Culture 20 (Kalamazoo MI 1986) 151-83.

[137]Francis John Byrne, *Irish kings and high-kings* (London 1973), esp 40-69.

[138]R A Breatnach, 'The lady and the king: a theme of Irish literature', *Studies* (Dublin) 42 (1953) 321-36; P Mac Cana, 'Aspects of the theme of king and goddess in Irish literature', *Études Celtiques* 7 (1955-57) 76-104, 8 (1958) 59-65; M Dillon, 'The Hindu act of truth in Celtic tradition', *Modern Philology* 44 (1947) 137-40; idem, 'The archaism of the Irish tradition' *Proceedings of the British Academy* 33 (1947) [1951]) 245-64; idem, 'The consecration of Irish kings', *Celtica* 10 (1973) 1-8; D Ó Corráin, 'Legend as critic' in *The writer as witness: literature as historical evidence*, ed T Dunne, Historical Studies 16 (Cork 1987) 23-38 (pp 31-35).

Samuel's anointing of Saul (1 Samuel 10): the ritual is set out in the *Hibernensis* and becomes narrative in Adomnán's *Vita Columbae*.[139]

Self-consciously, the literati saw the Irish as a people or *natio*, to be compared with the Germans, the Franks, or the peoples of classical antiquity.[140] In the seventh and eighth centuries the island was united culturally and linguistically, and the learned historical myth, biblical and Isidorian, derived its dynasties and peoples, by means of a complicated web of descent, from a single line. Place in that pecking order and not remote ethnic origins (which were only residually remembered) determined regional status. Royal and lordly power was in the hands of aggressive and confident hereditary upper class with a developed historical awareness, sharpened by the teachings of a clergy whose members belonged to the same class and were close kin of the rulers. The self-confidence of that clergy was one of birth as well as of learning and piety, and it was supported by great wealth, for the churches were amongst the largest landowners and lorded over a big dependent population.

When one turns to consider the mature church establishment, one is struck, in the first instance, by the deep impress of the christian church upon the toponomy of Ireland: it shaped and named the land to an extraordinary extent. It domesticated the landscape — mountains, islands, wells — and imposed thousands of its names and name-elements on the lands of settlement.

Recent revisionary work,[141] has clarified some institutional aspects of the Irish churches. The received idea that an episcopal missionary church was overwhelmed by a paruchially organised monastic church in which bishops were virtually made sacramental agents and abbots held jurisdiction almost exclusively has been effectively demolished. Like life, its replacement is neither as neat nor as simple. One must distinguish between ownership and management of church resources and spiritual jurisdiction: the first in many cases fell to the abbots and superiors of monasteries, the second remained always with the bishops. To the bishops first then.

Sharpe cites the powerfully episcopalian *Ríagail Phátraic*, issued from Armagh's sphere of influence in the first half of the eighth century, to buttress his arguments. Here the bishop has jurisdiction over churches of different kinds: proprietary churches, the 'little churches of the túath',

---

[139]'De regno', *Hibernensis* 25 (Wasserschleben, note 13 above, 76-84); M J Enright, 'Royal succession and abbatial prerogative in Adomnán's *Vita Columbae*', *Peritia* 4 (1985) 83-103.

[140]D Ó Corráin, 'Nationality and kingship in pre-Norman Ireland' in *Nationality and the pursuit of national independence*, ed T W Moody, Historical Studies 11 (Belfast 1978) 1-35.

[141]R Sharpe (note 7 above) 230-70; idem, 'Armagh and Rome in the seventh century' in Ní Chatháin and Richter (note 17 above) 58-71.

and churches ruled by *airchinnig*, often translated abbots but better monastic superiors:

> They shall have a principal bishop of every *túath* to ordain their clergy, to consecrate their churches, for spiritual guidance to their lords and the *airchinnig*, for saining and blessing their families after baptism. For any *túath* or any *cenél* that does not have a bishop for these functions, its rule of faith and belief dies. ... Every ordained cleric who has not the rule or the knowledge of the ministry of his order and who is not able to celebrate mass in the presence of king and bishop, he is not entitled to the status or honour-price of an ordained cleric in secular society or in church ... For the cause of disease and ailments upon the lineages ... is being without lawful baptism and confirmation at the proper times, for the fulness of the Holy Spirit does not come, no matter how zealously baptised he may be, unless he be confirmed after baptism. ... Every bishop whom the *túatha* and the churches have as bishop, he is the spiritual director of those in orders and he confers valid orders and he gives them help to meet their obligations in secular society and in church. He obliges every church to have its church building and graveyard clean, its altar always properly furnished for the ordained clergy.[142]

Not much wrong with that as episcopalianism.

Two other vernacular texts may be cited. The first is the difficult *Bretha Nemed*, the relevant portion of which is now available in the excellent edition and translation of Breatnach.[143] This text is all the more significant because it is a pedagogical one for use in the monastic schools as a primer of law and it belongs to the eighth century, the period of maturity in Irish church institutions. Two passages will serve to indicate the position of the bishop:

> *Iar n-ordaib cengair co h-epscop co secht n-grádaib*
> *comgrád Maic Dé Athar do doínib*
> *dóenacht do-ratai tlacht n-ecalso ord*

> By orders one advances to the bishop with seven orders; he of men who has the same orders as the Son of God the Father can confer on mankind the ornament of the orders of the church.

This is a statement to the effect that the bishop's orders are the highest and it is the bishop who ordains. The reference to Christ here has to do with the commonplace christian (and Irish belief) that Christ had all the orders of the church.[144]

---

[142]O'Keeffe (note 130 above) 218; Binchy (note 130 above) 2129.

[143]L Breatnach, 'The first third of Bretha Nemed toísech', *Ériu* 40 (1989) 1-40.

[144]A Wilmart, 'Les ordres du Christ', *Revue des Sciences Religieuses* 3 (1923) 305-27 (text repr in PL supplementum 4 (Paris 1968) 943-48); Roger E Reynolds, *The ordinals of Christ from their origins to the twelfth century*, Beiträge zur Geschichte und

*Tabair búaid / Dé do epscup/ .../ ro cethorcho blíadnae/ bélrai báin
bí/ biru is tresa eclais/ cach neimthiuso nár/*

Give divine excellence to the bishop who has forty years of the 'fair
language'; I adjudge that an ecclesiastic is more powerful than any
other noble one of privilege.

The second text is *Miadshlechta*,[145] a tract on social classes that belongs to
the first half of the eighth century.

*Cia neimhead is uaisle fil i talmain? Neimed n-eclasa. Cia neimed is
uaisliu fil a n-eclais? neimed n-easpuic. Is e espac as uaisliu dib-sidhe
easbuc ecalsa Peatair, ar is fo mam bite flaithe Rómhan. Ocas a n-
Eirind, cia dire as uaisle fil inde? Dire espuic oighe cona lanfoltaib
amail dlegar do.*

What dignity is the highest on earth? The dignity of the church.
What is the highest dignity in the church? The dignity of a bishop.
The most noble bishop of them is the bishop of the church of Peter, for
the rulers of the Romans are under his yoke. And in Ireland, what is
the highest honour-price? The honour-price of a celibate bishop who
has all the qualifications required of him.

The high status of the bishop is equally evident in the Latin laws.[146]

In Ireland there is, it is claimed, no formal episcopal hierarchy under a
metropolitan, though Armagh claimed primatial jurisdiction and
apostolic precedence — a claim that seems to have had the support of the
Munster Romani as early as the seventh century. There were, however,
grades of bishops and differing jurisidictions. There are at least four
references in the *Hibernensis* to a metropolitan. These are mostly in the
decrees of foreign synods, but they must have been seen as applicable, in at
least some circumstances, by the compilers of the *Hibernensis*.[147] The
'Canones Hibernenses' have reference to an 'episcopus episcoporum'[148] but

Quellenkunde des Mittelalters 7 (Berlin and New York 1978) 53-68 ('Early
Hibernian ordinals of Christ'); R McNally, *Der irische Liber de numeris* (Munich
1957) 118-19 (text and comment, Reynolds, op. cit. 66-67); *Hibernensis*, 8:1 (re-ed and
comment, Reynolds, op. cit. 61-63).

[145]Binchy (note 130 above) 588.

[146]'Canones Hibernenses', Bieler (note 10 above) 170 §§1-6, 9; 174 §7 = F W H
Wasserschleben, *Die Bußordnungen der abendländischen Kirche* (Halle 1851, repr
Graz 1958) 140-41 §§1-6, 9; 142 §§2, 9; *Hibernensis* 1:1-22; 2:4; 8:2; 21:1-2, 28; 42:22;
44:8; 45:12; 48:5; 59:3.

[147]For example: 1:4 (Sinodus Cartaginensis ait: Tunc consensu clericorum et laicorum
et totius provinciae episcoporum maximeque metropolitani vel epistola vel
auctoritate vel praesentia ordinetur episcopus), 20:3 (Quincunque causam habuerit,
apud suos judices judicetur et ne ad alienos causa vagandi et proterve despiciens
suam patriam transeat, sed apud metropolitanum episcopum suae provinciae
judicetur).

[148]Bieler (note 10 above) 174 §9; Wasserschleben (note 146 above) 142 §4.

it is not clear what this term means. There is some evidence for 'chorepiscopi'.[149] Such are the 'conepiscopi' mentioned in the copy of the *Hibernensis* in Paris, BN, lat. 3182 who are described as 'vicars of the bishops or of one *plebs*, ordained by one bishop'.[150] Elsewhere the canonists, in describing the ideal province, state that it has one bishop and other lesser ones[151] — and these can only be chorepiscopi who were, perhaps, the bishops of local communities (*túatha*).

Instead of a single hierarchical order, there was a diversity of structures and jurisdictions that we must be careful not to interpret as anarchy. It is quite unhistorical to postulate disorder just because order is not obvious to us, or conventional, or because it breaks down periodically, for example, in the inter-monastic battles of the eighth century. The churches were a major influence on society, they maintained themselves as highly effective institutions over many hundreds of years, and were the patrons of a learning and art that required continuous and extensive endowment. Therefore their rulers were institutionally capable and their management of resources effective. Hereditary succession (as distinct from kin succession) to the governance of monasteries had certainly begun by the seventh century and was common in the eighth. Clerical lineages can be traced in the annals and genealogies and they usually belong to discard segments of ruling secular dynasties.[152] The relationship is often close, as in Kildare in the seventh century and again in the ninth when the siblings of the king of Leinster were the rulers of the monastery. But hereditary succession does not necessarily make for bad government or bad morals or poor scholarship.

The governors of great monastic towns (Cork and Emly, for example) equalled the king of Munster in dignity and the rulers of Armagh, Kildare, Clonard, Clonmacnoise and other towns[153] were among the great political figures of the land, by law and by birth — more Medicis than abbots of monks and singers of matins. But there were others. The priests and superiors of the hundreds of tiny churches scattered throughout the countryside were no such grandees and rarely figure in the records of the

---

[149]*DACL*, III, 1423-52; W Smith and S Cheetham, *A dictionary of christian antiquities* (London 1875) I, 353-55.

[150]Wasserschleben (note 13 above) 5 note (i).

[151]*Hibernensis* 20:2: Certa provincia est, quae decem civitates habet et unum regem et tres minores potestates sub se, et unum episcopum aliosque minores, decem judices, ad quorum judicium omnes causae civitatum referuntur, et si causae difficiles oriantur, ad omnium judicium decem judicum referendae sunt. Cf *Hibernensis* 42.23. De majore episcopo dividente et minore eligente. Sinodus Romana: Episcopus major dividat, et minor elegat, quia Abraham divisit, Loth tantum elegit. On structures see T Charles-Edwards, 'The pastoral role of the church in the early Irish laws' in *Pastoral care before the parish*, ed J Blair and R Sharpe (Leicester 1992); R Sharpe, 'Churches and communities in early medieval Ireland', ibid, 81-109.

[152]D Ó Corráin, 'The early Irish churches: some aspects of organisation' in *Irish antiquity: essays and studies presented to Professor M J O'Kelly*, ed D Ó Corráin (Cork 1981) 327-41.

[153]Charles Doherty, 'The monastic town in early medieval Ireland' *The comparative history of urban origins in non-Roman Europe*, ed H B Clarke and A Simms, British Archaeological Reports International Series 255 (Oxford 1985) 45-75.

great and the good. These small churches — some monastic, some not —
were at least as plentiful as parish churches now are. They served a local
community — if they served one at all — and were very different from
bustling towns like Lismore or Trim with their workshops and markets,
schools and scriptoria. Many of these small foundations were proprietary
churches owned by a clerical branch of the local gentry. Some were royal
property, some were owned by great monasteries, some were free. Not all
could maintain a religious life, and the law-tracts talk of churches that
lose their status and thus are failed churches:

> *Ceall o neitcither cach richt, ceall dia ndentar uaim tadhut, ceall dia
> ndentar loch peca, ceall a mbi airchindech laich cin cairiuga do abuid,
> cell o teit cloc 7 salm cin dlige cin fuidell, ceall a mbid aircindech
> doairngair a bithdenma et etarsca fri cach claen nabi fir noch tindta
> fri peacad aitherrach, ceall ocna frithairither tratha, ceall bis fas*[154]

a church that refuses everybody hospitality, a church that becomes a
den of thieves, a church that is made into a place of sin, a church
where there is a lay superior unreproved by an abbot, a church from
which bell and psalm have gone without right without judgement, a
church in which there is a superior who vows perpetual chastity and
the avoidance of all evil, but this is not true for he falls into sin again,
a church where the canonical hours are not observed, a deserted
church.

There were shortages of clergy and the more powerful monasteries
encroached upon the independent churches and channelled their resources
into the maintenance of the great church institutions of the land. Over
this diversity of churches, however managed and however owned, the
bishops exercised pastoral jurisdiction.

There were worldly and opulent prince-abbots with aristocratic wives,
great administrators and political clerics, rigorist anchorites like Colcu
who gave most of his food to the poor because he doubted the purity of the
monks who provided it, poor country parsons, and a cultivated clergy that
maintained a high level of scholarship, produced fine art, and a
literature of distinction. The great monastery-towns that had deep
pockets and high aspirations carried this cultural activity as long as they
had the resources to do so. The Book of Kells is the finest monument to
their kind.[155]

---

[154]Binchy (note 130 above) 1-2, 1229, 1881-82.
[155]I wish to thank Fidelma Maguire, Damian Bracken, Elva Johnston, Dáibhí Ó
Cróinín, and Richard Sharpe for thier helpful comments and corrections. I have
adopted many, but not all, of their suggestions.

The monastery of Iona in the eighth century

Ian Fisher

Soiscelae mor Coluim Cille; 'the great gospel-book of St Columba'. The annalist who recorded the theft from Kells in 1007 of an enshrined manuscript, which is surely to be identified with the Book of Kells, was in no doubt of its association with the greatest of Irish monastic founders. The modern Gaelic names of the island of Iona, Irish *I Cholm Cille* and Scottish *I Chaluim Chille*, similarly associate the saint with the Hebridean island where he spent the last thirty-four years before his death in 597.[1]

It is one of the many paradoxes of Columba's character and career that his principal foundation was not in his native land, where his royal status gave him such authority, but on a small peripheral island of the Irish colony in north Britain. However, as Donnchadh Ó Corráin emphasized in the opening lecture of this conference, modern political divisions are irrelevant to the art and history of the early christian period. Culturally, Iona was as Irish as any monastery in the five fifths of Ireland, and those abbots whose pedigrees have been preserved were without exception from mainland Ireland rather than Scottish *Dál Riata*. At the same time, its situation in north Britain, where each of Bede's four modern languages of Britain was spoken, and its own historical connections with Pictland and Northumbria as well as Ireland, made Iona particularly receptive to artistic and other influences from Britain and further afield, and capable of disseminating new ideas through its position as a centre of pilgrimage.

The eighth century was a momentous period in the history of Columba's principal foundation. Adomnán, the second of the island's great saints, died in 704, among his own monks but at odds with the majority of them over his acceptance of the Roman Easter.[2] That protracted dispute was resolved twelve years later through the persuasiveness of the Northumbrian Ecgbert, whose sanctity and long exile in Ireland are a recurrent theme in the last three books of Bede's *Historia Ecclesiastica*. His earlier achievements, as first organiser of the mission to Frisia and as head of a community in Ireland which has been proposed as the home of some of the finest insular

---

[1]For a full historical narrative and a detailed illustrated description of the monastic archaeology and sculpture of Iona (of which the present writer was principal author and joint editor) see Royal Commission on the Ancient and Historical Monuments of Scotland, [RCAHMS], *Argyll: an inventory of the monuments*, vol 4, *Iona* (Edinburgh 1982) (hereafter cited as *Iona Inventory*). This includes full references to the main historical sources, including the various editions of Adomnán and Bede. Important subsequent literature is noted below, but special attention may be drawn here to M O Anderson's revision (Oxford 1991) of *Adomnan's Life of Columba*, ed A O and M O Anderson.
[2]See articles on Adomnán by J M Picard, *Peritia* 1 (1982) 160-77, 216-49; 3 (1984) 50-70; A Smyth, *Warlords and holy men: Scotland, AD 80-1000* (London 1984); Herbert.

manuscripts,[3] surely had a strong influence on the monks of Iona among whom he died on Easter day, 729. In particular, they may have inspired the career as missionary and scholar of Virgil (Fergil), bishop of Salzburg and abbot of a monastery there whose confraternity-book includes a complete list of the abbots of Iona (pl 59), kept up-to-date until shortly before his own death in 784.[4]

The continuing influence of Iona in mainland Ireland was reinforced by the enactment of the *cana*, or laws, of Adomnán in 727-30 (with explicit mention in the annals of the circuit of his relics), and of Columba himself in 753, 757 and 778. These prestigious and profitable exercises no doubt strengthened the attraction of Iona as a place for the 'pilgrimage and penitence' of great men such as Niall Frossach (died 778), king of the Cenél nEógain, and Artgal son of Cathal, king of Connaught (died 791), who each spent their last years there. Recorded contacts with Northumbria in this century are rare, but a fortuitous reference in a manuscript of Nennius preserves evidence of a visit by abbot Sleibine (752-67) to the former Irish foundation at Ripon.

Other historical problems deserve further research, including the overlapping periods of office and varying titles recorded in the annals for the heads of the community of Iona; the associated question of bishops, and their pastoral roles;[5] and the reality of the monastic *paruchia* at this period. What was the true significance of the apparent expulsion of Columban monks from Pictland in 717? How close was the relationship between Iona and the Irish foundations of Columba and his successors, such as Durrow and Lambay? Were there continuing links with the monastery founded (*c*665) by Colman on Inishbofin after he left Lindisfarne and consulted the *seniores* of Iona, or with his second foundation at Mayo 'of the Saxons', a major site whose eight-hectare enclosure is comparable in scale with that at Iona itself?[6] However, the main concerns of this paper are the physical environment and remains of the Columban mother-house, as revealed by

[3] D Ó Cróinín, 'Rath Melsigi, Willibrord, and the earliest Echternach manuscripts', *Peritia* 3 (1984) 17-49; but it is not certain that Ecgbert's base in the 690s was still *Rath Melsigi*, identified as Clonmelsh, county Carlow (T Fanning, 'Some field monuments in the townlands of Clonmelsh and Garryhundon, county Carlow', ibid, 43-49), where Bede (*Historia Ecclesiastica*, book 3, ch 27) places the beginning of his Irish career thirty years earlier.

[4] *Virgil von Salzburg: Missionar und Gelehrter*, ed H Dopsch and R Juffinger (Salzburg 1985). See especially the paper by T Ó Fiaich (pp 17-26) corroborating my arguments that Virgil was an Iona monk (*Iona Inventory*, 47, 270 n 108), against the previous objections of P Grosjean.

[5] For mainland Ireland see now R Sharpe, 'Some problems concerning the organization of the church in early medieval Ireland', *Peritia* 3 (1984) 230-70.

[6] Sketch-plan by D L Swan in *Landscape archaeology in Ireland*, ed T Reeves-Smyth and F Hamond (Oxford 1983) 272. I am grateful to Jim Higgins for joining me in one of my visits in 1991, when we identified several additional fragments of early christian graveslabs. For the scanty surviving remains on Inishbofin, see M Gibbons, *Inis Bó Finne: a guide to the natural history and archaeology* (Cleggan 1991).

recent field-survey, excavation and detailed recording of its early sculpture.[7]

The geographical setting of the island is of great interest. The view from Dùn I, its highest summit, embraces the Hebrides from Islay north to Rum and Skye, and out to Coll and Tiree, as well as the distant mainland of Argyll. Adomnán records constant voyaging in skin-covered or wooden boats, with Columba himself visiting Skye and Ardnamurchan, as well as Ireland and the Inverness area of Pictland. Large timbers for buildings and boat building were transported in the late seventh century from the mainland, a distance of at least 75km, and the massive slabs of schist required for St John's and St Martin's Crosses were brought a similar distance from the Loch Sween area in the following century.[8] Despite the recorded drownings of monks of Iona and of Applecross 'in the depth of the sea' (*in profundo pilagi*),[9] the island was ideally placed for its regional and international roles, yet safely removed from the centres of political power and warfare in Dál Riata.[10]

The Hebrides also offered opportunities, rivalled only in western Ireland, for the establishment of dependent houses and hermitages, and major foundations such as Iona, Eigg and Inishbofin may be classed not merely as 'island monasteries' but rather 'archipelago monasteries'. This is attested by Adomnán's numerous references to dependencies of Iona, and by the survival throughout the Hebrides, from the south coast of Islay to the remote outliers of St Kilda and North Rona, of enclosed sites or carved stones in situations where secular settlement was unlikely.[11] Iona's natural surroundings reinforced the ascetic tradition bequeathed by its founder, and it is significant that Cilléne Droichtech (died 752), the first abbot who can be considered as a possible patron of the Book of Kells, was himself an anchorite.

The western bay below the Machair or *campulus occidentalis* is *Camus Cùil an t-Saimh*, 'the Bay at the back of the Ocean', and Iona is as truly an Atlantic island as Tory, Inismurray or Inishbofin. The jibe that the Irish, and particularly the Columban monks, occupied 'the remotest corner of the world' was frequently repeated during the controversies of the seventh century, and Bede represents Adomnán as accepting its truth during a visit

---

[7] *Iona Inventory,* passim; excavation reports cited in note 19 below

[8] For the probable quarry source of St John's Cross at Doide on the east shore of Loch Sween, see RCAHMS (note 1 above) vol 7, Mid Argyll & Cowal, no 236.

[9] *AU*[2], 190-91, s.a. 736/7.

[10] I do not accept the arguments of J Bannerman ('appendix' to K Hughes, 'The church and the world in early christian Ireland', *Irish Historical Studies* 13 (1962) 99-116 (pp 113-16) for major secular political interference at Iona in the eighth century.

[11] RCAHMS (note 1 above) vols 1-7 passim. This subject will be discussed by the writer in a chapter of *The prehistory of Argyll,* ed J N G Ritchie (forthcoming), and in the introduction to I Fisher, *Early medieval sculpture in the West Highlands* (RCAHMS, forthcoming).

to Northumbria.[12] Yet Adomnán's own book on Arculf's visit to the Holy Places, Virgil's missionary work on the eastern frontier of Europe, and other indications of the cosmological interests of Iona scholars, suggest that awareness of their position on the western limit of the christian world enhanced their interest in other parts of that world. Moreover the visions of demons seen by Columba himself above the island of Tiree, or by other monks voyaging in the ocean, and the constant location of Columban monasteries and churches on islands, suggest that they perceived themselves as guarding the frontier of Christendom against the demonic forces of the ocean; those ancient powers which, in the folk-tradition of Glencolumcille in his native Donegal, were driven from the land by Columba himself.[13]

Iona measures only 5.5km from north to south by 2.5km in greatest width and 1.5km across the low-lying central belt, yet it includes a great variety of terrain in its 800 hectares. The 100m summit of Dùn I, which overlooks the monastic site, may be identified with Adomnán's *munitio magna*, suggesting an original local name, *Dùn Mór*. Over half of the island's area is composed of two blocks of rocky outcrops and heather moorland, intersected by many steep-sided gullies containing grass. There is thus abundant rough grazing for cattle, which have always been important in the island's economy. In the late nineteenth century the cattle stock numbered about two hundred and fifty, with six hundred sheep, although the imbalance at the present day is greater. The provision of winter fodder, however, must always have been difficult, and turning surplus calves into vellum would be an attractive alternative for monastic landlords. Midden material from the monastic site shows that cattle of prime age were regularly used for food, but the paucity of sheep bones confirms the negative evidence of Adomnán. If there is any historical basis for the story of the ship-load of wool sent from Iona to St Samthann (died 739),[14] it is unlikely that much of it was produced on the island itself. Other natural resources attested in the middens include red deer, numerous varieties of fish, and seals, which as well as providing meat and oil may have been valued for their skins. The magnificent furry sealskin binding of the Oxford manuscript of Manus O'Donnell's mid-sixteenth-century Irish Life of Columba suggests a possible literary application.

At the present day only about a tenth of the island's area is under arable cultivation, mainly on the glacial soils of the east coastal plain. Until the nineteenth century, however, the white shell-sand of the western bay and the north end were also in tillage. Pollen analysis of deposits from the monastic area indicates that cereals were being grown on the eastern plain

---

[12]Bede (note 3 above) book 2, ch 19 (Pope Honorius to the Irish, 634), book 3, ch 25 (Wilfrid at Whitby, *c* 664), book 5, ch 15 (Northumbrians to Adomnán, 686); *Cummian's letter* De Controversia Paschali *and the* De Ratione Conputandi, ed M Walsh and D Ó Cróinín (Toronto 1988) 72-73.

[13]S Ó hEochaidh, 'Colm Cille sa tSeanchas' in *Irisleabhar Muighe Nuadh*, 1963; idem, 'Folach Eireann' in *Oidhreacht Ghleann Cholm Cille*, ed S Watson (1989) 31-48 (p 32).

[14]*Vitae Sanctorum Hiberniae*, ed C Plummer, 2 vols (Oxford 1910) II, 259-60.

in the seventh and eighth centuries.[15] However, it is clear from Adomnán's account that the main cultivation area in Columban times was the 'little western plain' or *campulus occidentalis*, which still retains its equivalent Gaelic designation, 'the Machair'. Its light soil was susceptible to spring and early summer droughts, one of which, in the 680s, was ended by a miraculous downpour following a monastic procession to Columba's *colliculus angelorum*, the (natural) mound of Sithean ('Fairy Hill'), bearing relics of the saint including books written in his own hand. Here and elsewhere in the Hebrides, however, the abundant supplies of seaweed as natural fertiliser compensated for the lightness of the soil.[16] The rocks along this shore and elsewhere on the island bear lichens which for many centuries were an important natural resource for dyeing textiles, and which may be relevant in considering the purple dyes of the Book of Kells.

Port na Curaich, a small bay at the extreme south end of Iona, is the traditional site of Columba's arrival from Ireland in 563, and a series of cairns on the adjacent shingle beach may witness to pilgrimage in the medieval period or even earlier. The monastery itself was laid out on the eastern plain that slopes gently to the Sound of Iona and is traversed by Sruth a' Mhuilinn (pl 60). This 'mill stream' flows out of the Lochan Mór, a loch below the south slope of Dùn I, which before drainage in the eighteenth century measured about eight hectares and which is bounded on the south-west by an ancient earthwork *tochar* or causeway. In early times, when other valleys to the south-west were occupied by lochs, this was probably one of the best means of access to the cultivated area on the west coast. The south-west part of the monastic enclosure included a rocky hillock, Cnoc nan Càrnan, whose eastern cliff may have sheltered the oak and ash trees represented in the pollen record from the earliest monastic phase. A smaller outcrop, Tòrr an Aba, situated immediately west of the medieval abbey, may be the eminence from which Columba pronounced his final blessing on the monastery, and it was marked by a cross, probably of medieval date, which like others in the literary and archaeological record had a millstone for its (surviving) base. The eastern edge of the monastic area was marked by a steeper fall to a rough foreshore littered with erratic granite boulders, but sheltering several small 'ports', tiny sandy beaches or narrow gullies into which a currach or small boat could be drawn. One of these inlets is Port an Dìsirt, situated about 450m north-east of the abbey and close to Cladh an Dìsirt, 'the burial-ground of the hermitage', where the footings of a chapel suggest continuing use in the eleventh or twelfth century, at the same period as the charter references to the *disert* at Kells. A smaller building of clay-mortared stone, excavated in 1992 some 400m south of the abbey under Teampull Ronaig, the Romanesque parish church of the island, is similar to the smallest of the rural chapels found in Islay and elsewhere in Argyll, and when dating-evidence is available it may cast light

[15] J W Barber, 'Excavations on Iona, 1979', *Proceedings of the Society of Antiquaries of Scotland* [hereafter *PSAS*] 111 (1981) 282-380 (pp 347-48).

[16] A ritual offering to the sea of *am brochan mór* ('the great porridge'), designed to secure abundant kelp and fertile crops, continued to be made in this bay during Easter week until the middle of the nineteenth century (*Iona Inventory*, 265 n 22).

on the problem of whether there was a lay population on Iona in Columban times.[17]

Adomnán's Life of Columba is one of the principal literary sources for the layout of early Irish monasteries, describing a wide range of domestic buildings and workshops, churches and oratories, burial-places, crosses and open spaces, all surrounded by the *vallum monasterii* (rampart of the monastery).[18] Parts of the vallum at Iona, to the north-west and west, are indeed massive upstanding earthworks associated with partly infilled ditches, while elsewhere the lines of buried ditches (and other artificial disturbances) can be identified by aerial photography or by measuring variations in the magnetism and resistivity of the soil. Although there is much scope for further research of this kind, as well as excavation, it is clear that the earthworks of the Columban monastery enclosed an area of eight hectares or more and were of great complexity.[19] Recent excavation has indicated the possibility that part of the western vallum is of pre-Columban date,[20] and the obvious overlapping lines or internal divisions reflect the growth so vividly described in the preface to the *Martyrology of Oengus*, whereby small monastic settlements became 'Romes with multitudes, with hundreds, with thousands'. However it is likely that the enclosed area reached its greatest extent, some 360m from north to south and 200m to 300m from east to west, in or shortly before the eighth century.

The most detailed excavation of the vallum, conducted by John Barber for the Scottish Office's Central Excavation Unit in 1979 in advance of burial-ground extension, examined a 15m length of ditch, about 5m wide and 3m deep, which ran north-west to south-east immediately outside the north-east boundary wall of the burial-ground, Reilig Odhráin. At the north-west the ditch terminated in a causeway (later followed by a medieval boulder-paved road), beyond which it presumably continued south-west to meet the eastern cliff of Cnoc nan Càrnan below an upstanding earthen rampart. Peat began to form to a substantial depth in the ditch as soon as it was completed, probably early in the seventh century, and by the eighth century it was a wide but shallow feature which may by then have marked the boundary of the burial-ground. Surviving plant-remains indicate that it was bounded by a hedge containing elder, hawthorn and holly which, if a later poem 'attributed' to Columba is to be believed, was a possible source of

---

[17]I am grateful to the excavator, Jerry O'Sullivan, and to John Barber, director of AOC (Scotland), Ltd, for access to the excavation and for permission to refer to it in advance of full publication. The building measured about 4.5m by 3.3m within walls 0.8m thick.

[18]*Adomnan* (note 1 above) passim; *Iona Inventory*, 12-13, 31-45; A D S Macdonald, 'Aspects of the monastery and monastic life in Adomnán's Life of Columba', *Peritia* 3 (1984) 271-302.

[19]M Redknap, 'Excavation at Iona Abbey, 1976', *PSAS* 108 (1976-77) 228-53; R Reece, *Excavations in Iona 1964 to 1974* (London 1981); Barber (note 15 above) passim; E and P J Fowler, 'Excavations on Tòrr an Aba, Iona, Argyll', *PSAS* 118 (1988) 181-201; A M Haggarty, 'Iona: some results from recent work', *PSAS* 118 (1988) 203-13. See also A Hamlin, 'Iona: a view from Ireland', *PSAS* 117 (1987) 17-22.

[20]F McCormick in Historic Scotland, Archaeological Operations & Conservation, *Annual Report 1989*, 28-30.

ink.[21] The question of whether a rampart was associated with this ditch, and if so whether it lay to north or south of it, is a contentious one, but the writer believes that the ditch was the south boundary of the monastery in the seventh century.[22] Geophysical evidence shows that it continues east across the adjacent field, and that a curving ditch to the south enclosed an annexe including Reilig Odhráin, while the same survey indicates a presumably later arrangement with an annexe (whose ditch was excavated in the grounds of the St Columba Hotel in 1974) attached to another buried ditch running north-west to south-east across the field. The continuation of this last ditch north-west across Reilig Odhráin would reach the cliff-face of Cnoc nan Càrnan at the same point as the early seventh-century ditch, below the earthwork on the higher level, and this alignment coincides with a massive granite cross-base in Reilig Odhráin which may have marked an entrance through the vallum.

The peat that formed in the lower part of the excavated seventh-century ditch contained quantities of worked wood, waste cores from the manufacture of alder-wood bowls on a pole-lathe, and leatherwork including shoes with decorative vents and tongues identical to those shown in the Books of Durrow and Mulling. This waste material suggests that workshops for these crafts were situated close to the ditch in the first half of the seventh century, while evidence of metal- and glass-working was identified in 1979 in a pit a few metres north of it.[23] Other craft-material, including moulds for glass studs (pl 62),[24] was found about 90m to the north, close to a small lime-kiln, but no associated workshop structures have been identified in either area.

The worked wood from the ditch includes a pole with a withy twisted round it and a square-section oak timber, 1.1m in length and grooved on two faces, which was probably used as a vertical post with timber panels or wickerwork slotted into it. These finds, and the excavated remains of buildings, fully support the evidence of Bede and Adomnán that timber was the normal material of Irish monastic buildings. In the area north of the excavated ditch the west end of a circular or round-ended building was identified in 1979. Its inner ring of post-holes, whose timbers had been renewed more than once, measured about 13m across, while an outer ring containing slighter posts showed no signs of re-use and had presumably held a verandah, or perhaps buttresses which were not essential to the

---

[21]*Early Irish lyrics*, ed G Murphy (Oxford 1956) 70-71; verse translation by F O'Brien, *The hair of the dogma* (London 1987) 4-5.

[22]The discussion and sketch-plans in Barber (note 15 above) 361-64, do not adequately represent the results of the RCAHMS field-survey or of the geophysical survey carried out by the Ancient Monuments Laboratory in 1977.

[23]The contents of this pit, and of others in the same area, had already been excavated in 1959 by Professor Charles Thomas, whose excavation-finds from Iona include lidded crucibles and other craft-working material, and a cast bronze male head. The importance of this unpublished material has been enhanced by the more recent excavations.

[24]Report by J Graham-Campbell in Reece (note 19 above) 24-25; *Iona Inventory*, fig 15H.

stability of the main structure. While circular stone buildings are common in small monastic settlements in western Ireland and Scotland, timber ones are rare, although smaller ones have been excavated in secular contexts such as Deer Park Farms (county Antrim) and Moynagh Lough Crannog (county Meath). This structure invites comparison with the *monasterium rotundum* mentioned by Adomnán as existing at Durrow in Columba's time. Material from a pit underlying the building suggests a date later than the middle of the seventh century, and it evidently remained in use for a considerable period. A short distance to the west, and just south of Tòrr an Aba, a trench for one wall of what was presumably a rectangular building, about 10m in length and with adjacent buttress-pits, was identified in 1959. No report has yet been published, and it is not certain whether any dating evidence was recovered, but it has been suggested that the building technique was the same as that of 'style IV' at the Northumbrian royal palace of Yeavering (Northumberland), with continuous vertically-set planks in a trench about 0.3m wide. Both of these buildings seem appropriate for the communal structures, such as the refectory and guest-house, mentioned by Adomnán, or the *magna domus* for which timber was imported from the mainland in his own time. Further evidence of timber building was identified in 1967 under the medieval bakehouse west of the abbey, in the form of a mass of post-holes, but once again dating was uncertain and no individual building-plans could be identified. Excavation in other areas, including east of the abbey, has shown hearths and other evidence of occupation, but no buildings have been recognised.[25]

Adomnán seems to indicate a single church (*ecclesia, oratorium*) in Columba's monastery, large enough to contain the monks and with an attached chamber or *exedra*. The area immediately west of the medieval abbey church was evidently a major liturgical focus in the eighth century and later, marked by St John's and St Matthew's Crosses, and it is probable that an early church underlies the medieval nave, although it is impossible to say whether the building of Columba's time occupied that position. The medieval church and the eighth-century crosses are orientated about twenty-three degrees south of true east (unlike a number of outlying medieval chapels and other buildings, which have sometimes wrongly been identified as preserving a pre-Benedictine layout), and this suggests that the crosses were associated with a church large enough to follow the slope of the site rather than run obliquely across it. It may be assumed that by the eighth century the principal church on Iona would have rivalled the scale and elaboration of that at Kildare described by Cogitosus. Close to the north-west angle of the nave, and separated from St John's Cross by a small enclosure containing early graveslabs, there is a tiny chapel, rebuilt in 1962 on its original wall-footings. Measuring only 3.2m by 2.2m internally and with projecting buttresses or antae flanking the narrow west doorway, it is to be compared with the very smallest Irish oratories, such as Teampull Diarmada, Inchcleraun (county Longford), Teampull Benen, Inis Mór (Aran Islands), and those on Skellig Michael (county Kerry) and North Rona

---

[25]Reece (note 15 above) passim; Haggarty (note 19 above) passim.

(Lewis),[26] rather than with chapels such as that below St Ronan's Church (see above) and elsewhere in Argyll. Excavation outside the south wall found no trace of a timber predecessor, but the retention of this humble structure indicates its great antiquity and sanctity. Indeed, the traveller Martin Martin in the last decade of the seventeenth century reported that 'in a little cell lies Columbus's tomb ... This gave me occasion to cite the distich, asserting that Columbus was buried in Ireland, at which the natives of Iona seemed very much displeased, and affirmed that the Irish who said so were impudent liars'.[27] This patriotism (so very different from the spirit of the Book of Kells Conference!) may nevertheless have a basis of truth, and it is possible that the chapel and St John's Cross mark the site of the original burial-place from which Columba's remains were translated, probably in the second half of the eighth century (see below).

The question of burial-grounds on Iona in the Columban period suffers, as on many Irish sites, from the continuing use of Reilig Odhráin for burial up to the present, and the lack of visible remains at the several other burial-places remembered in local tradition. As indicated above, the probable alignment of the vallum in the eighth century appears to bisect Reilig Odhráin (whose present enclosure dates only from the eighteenth century except on the north), and it may have developed in or after that period as a site for aristocratic lay burials, a function which it retained until the end of the medieval period. The monastic cemetery, which presumably included Columba's grave, marked by the stone that he had used as a pillow, may well have been in the area west of the medieval abbey where several burials have been identified. The major crosses in this area are likely to have been visited during processions, and Adomnán mentions a cross marking an incident in the last few days of Columba's life, which in his own time still stood in a millstone base beside a roadway. It is probable that an early path followed the shingle ridge on which a medieval cobbled road was laid out, running south-west from the abbey to Reilig Odhráin and crossing the original causeway through the excavated vallum ditch. The probable location of a major cross (perhaps St Oran's) beside a subsequent vallum gateway about 30m further south has already been mentioned. The shingle ridge carrying the medieval road is still liable to collect surface-water after heavy rainfall, and in this and other excavated areas there were numerous stone-built drains of early christian and later date.

The most obvious relics of the Columban monastery are the carved stones, about one hundred in number (almost a quarter of the total from western Scotland), and ranging from small gravemarkers with simple incised crosses to some of the largest of Irish high crosses.[28] While some stones display

---

[26]H G Leask, *Irish churches and monastic buildings*, 3 vols (Dundalk 1955-60) I, figs 2, 3, 23-24; H C Nisbet and R A Gailey, 'A survey of the antiquities of North Rona', *Archaeological Journal* 117 (1962) 88-115 (pp 103-08, 111).

[27]M Martin, *A description of the Western Islands of Scotland*, new edn (Stirling 1934), 287-88.

[28]About three hundred stones from Argyll are illustrated and described in *Inventory of Argyll*, vols 1-7. A further one hundred and fifty in the area extending from the

Scandinavian influence, and the simpler ones cannot be readily dated, it is likely that a high proportion of them are of seventh- and eighth-century date, and it would be interesting to compare the collection with large Irish ones such as Clonmacnoise if the later stones at each site could be separated out. Many of the simple stones resemble those found at small monastic sites, hermitages and burial-grounds from Skellig Michael to North Rona, but there are also a number of large recumbent graveslabs, mostly bearing ringed crosses, of a type that does not occur elsewhere in the West Highlands and only rarely in western Ireland. Seven of these graveslabs bear Irish names or inscriptions, mostly using the formulae OR(OIT) DO X or OR(OIT) AR ANMAIN X ('A prayer for [Fergus; Loingsechan; Mael-Phadraig]'; 'a prayer for the soul of [Eoghan; Flann]'), although Latin appears on a wedge-shaped gravemarker which is inscribed on the top edge LAPIS ECHODI ('the stone of Echoid'). However, the small number of inscriptions in one of the most literate of Irish monasteries, and the amateur character of the lettering and design of most of the carved stones, suggest that personal commemoration was a low priority in eighth-century Iona, in contrast to the splendour of the high crosses. The stone of Echoid, whose name is represented in modern Irish O hEochaidh (Haughey), is probably of the seventh century and bears a simple but elegant compass-drawn Chi Rho cross. The difference between its ornament and that of St John's Cross is comparable with the gulf between the Cathach and the Book of Kells, but the contrast in both cases was one of function as well as chronology.

The major crosses of Iona — St Oran's, St John's and St Martin's — were fully described and illustrated in the Royal Commission's Iona inventory of 1982, and the related Kildalton Cross in the Islay volume (1984), so the discussion here will deal mainly with points relevant to the Book of Kells. They were described as 'an early and experimental group, and not derived from any established tradition of stone-carving', and there is no reason to alter this judgement. Adomnán himself refers to three crosses on Iona in or soon after Columba's lifetime, and these were presumably of timber, like the one erected by the Iona-educated Oswald before the battle of Heavenfield c635. Despite this long tradition, which by the eighth century is likely to have produced timber crosses of considerable scale and ornamental elaboration, the decision to produce monumental crosses in stone, equalling the largest Northumbrian ones in height and far exceeding them in span, was a bold one in an area where there was no tradition of stone architecture and where memorial stones were, as has been described, of the simplest character. The close relationships between the individual crosses are established by certain shared motifs, notably snake-and-boss and a specific pattern of spiral ornament, but their great differences in design and ornamental treatment show the constraints imposed by the shortage of suitable stone for carving, and the difficulties faced by the stonecarvers (presumably imported from an area with a longer tradition and better

Clyde islands to the Outer Isles will be catalogued, and the entire corpus illustrated and re-assessed in the light of comparative material in Ireland and elsewhere, in Fisher (note 11 above).

sources of stone) in identifying and exploiting this material.[29] If the eighth-century date proposed for the crosses is correct, it is as unlikely that expert carvers could be found in mainland Ireland as in Dál Riata, and the suggestion that Pictish carvers were imported (from an area with excellent freestone and a tradition of design and craftsmanship displayed in superb cross-slabs from the early eighth century onwards) may be repeated. Certain stylistic features, such as the lack of framing in the figure-carving on the west face of St Martin's Cross, support this argument, but for the most part the carvers would be mere executants, working under the direction of monks with their own traditions of manuscript and metalwork design, which are very obvious in the ornamental repertoire of the crosses. It may be that this hypothesis does injustice to the adaptability of Irish woodworkers or graveslab-incisers, or that Irish craftsmen had already been sent abroad to learn new skills, but the question of how long is required to establish a tradition of sophisticated relief-carving *de novo* deserves more serious consideration than it has so far received.

The Commission's interpretation of the Iona crosses built upon the analysis of their structure published by the late Robert Stevenson in 1956,[30] and benefited from his perceptive observations as the original fragments of St John's Cross were freed in 1980 from the concrete of Macalister's and later restorations. Geologically and structurally the earliest of the group is the ringless St Oran's Cross, three massive but incomplete pieces of coarse mica-schist from Mull fitted together by mortice-and-tenon joints cut into a horizonal arm 1.99m across. It has large rounded armpits, and its ornament combines snake-and-boss and interlinked bossed spirals, of surprising sophistication in such intractable material, with small figure-scenes or paired beasts in the constrictions around the cross-head. The carving of the Virgin and Child between two angels, at the top of the one surviving face of the cross-shaft (**fig 1a; pl 63**), has many analogies with the illustration in the Book of Kells although the Virgin is seated frontally rather than in profile.

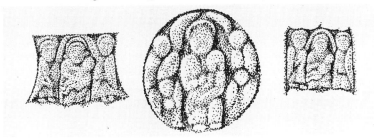

Fig 1 Virgin and Child carvings (*scale* 1:15; *drawing, I G Scott*)
      (a) St Oran's Cross   (b) St Martin's Cross   (c) Kildalton Cross

[29]The comments in D Kelly, 'The heart of the matter: models for Irish high crosses', *JRSAI* 121 (1991) 105-45 (pp 122-24) fail to appreciate the acute difficulty of finding stone suitable for such large crosses in an area where no local tradition of monumental stone-carving existed.

[30]R B K Stevenson, 'The chronology and relationships of some Irish and Scottish crosses', *JRSAI* 86 (1956) 84-96.

The flanking angels raise their inner wings to form a canopy, a motif found in Egyptian and Armenian representations and reflected in the Book of Kells, and the Child raises an arm to touch the Virgin's breast.[31]

St John's Cross, whose damaged but magnificent original stonework was returned to Iona in 1990 for display in the Abbey Museum (pl 64), measured at least 5.3m in height and 2.17m in span, the widest cross in these islands except for the extraordinary cross at Ray in north Donegal.[32] In its final complete form it comprised four main pieces (one of them lost), and four ring-segments of which only a single fragment has been recovered, all linked by mortice-and-tenon joints. The shaft and the greater part of the cross-head, which was jointed behind its bossed centre, are of green chlorite-schist from the distant Argyll mainland, and the top of the upper arm (including a zoomorphic finial which is paralleled only at Mayo Abbey)[33] and the ring-fragment are of mica-schist from the Ross of Mull. On the basis of visible damage to the base of the cross, the structural inefficiency of its construction, and the way in which these joints cut across panels of complex ornament, it was suggested in 1982 that the pieces of local mica-schist were additions and repairs to an original ringless cross, which probably began with a single joint at the centre of the cross-head. In this form, and with its double-curved arms, it would have resembled (but with a much greater span) such Northumbrian crosses as Ruthwell, or the metal-plated Rupertus Cross which was probably produced by an Anglo-Saxon craftsmen for Virgil of Salzburg.[34] Whether or not the designer was consciously emulating Northumbrian models, his ornamental language was purely Irish, and in the realm of books exactly the same is true of the Book of Kells. In the new technology of stone-carving, however, Iona lacked the experience or the materials to realise the ambitions of the abbot who commissioned St John's Cross, and it is likely that it was damaged in an early fall. The repairs described above may thus have created for the first time in stone one of the world's most celebrated monumental forms, the 'Celtic' ringed cross.

The ornamental repertoire of St John's Cross is an extension of that of St Oran's with many varieties of snake-and-boss and spiral ornament in panels

---

[31]D Mac Lean, 'Iona, Armenia and Italy in the early medieval period', *Atti del quinto simposio internazionale di arte Armena, 1988*, ed B L Zekiyan (Venice 1992) 559-68; M Werner, 'The *Madonna and Child* miniature in the Book of Kells', *Art Bulletin* 54 (1972) 1-23, 129-39.

[32]A Graham, 'An Irish millstone cross', *PSAS* 87 (1952-53) 187-91; B Lacy, *Archaeological survey of county Donegal* (Lifford 1983) 287-88.

[33]This unringed cross-head, whose lower part is cemented into a modern grave-surround, has short ringless arms and is decorated with interlace and key-patterns. On the top surface of the upper arm there is a lean quadruped with arching body. Although stylistically different from and later than St John's Cross, this carving (and also the high-relief lion on the east face of the Drumcliff Cross, reminiscent of those at Kildalton) may reflect continuing contacts between Iona and Columban monasteries in Connaught..

[34]*The making of England: Anglo-Saxon art and culture AD 600-900*, ed L Webster and J Backhouse (London 1991) 170-73; colour illustrations in Dopsch and Juffinger (note 4 above) pls 13-17.

framed by slightly-sunken interlace, well described by Macalister as being of 'painful minuteness'.[35] His comparison with manuscript ornament, and particularly the Chi Rho page of the Book of Kells, is valid, but the main influence on this new three-dimensional style is that of metalwork, seen in the multitude of small interlinked spirals and the granule-like pellets in the 'bird's nest' bosses. The cruciform groups of large bosses, repeated on all of the Iona crosses, resemble those on the later shrine of St Manchan, and it was suggested by Smith that the Steeple Bumpstead boss came from such a setting.[36] The spiral-ornamented flange of this magnificent gilt-bronze piece finds a close parallel in the circular surround of the recessed centre of the west face of the head of St John's Cross. This hollow itself probably held a metal boss giving greater relief than was allowed by the thickness of the stone, and the central boss of the east face of the Kildalton Cross may preserve its form — a boss with four creatures climbing up the outside, in a manner very reminiscent of Steeple Bumpstead, and snakes emerging from a hollow centre.

The most significant metalwork parallels are with the snake-and-boss ornament of St John's Cross, where lizard-like creatures are attacked by fierce dragon-heads attached to snakes' bodies which spiral out of the principal bosses.[37] This motif is closely paralleled in the gilt-bronze plaques now at St Germain-en-Laye, which John Hunt convincingly identified as the finials of a great house-shaped shrine.[38] The late Egil Bakka drew attention to similar fragments in a ninth-century grave at Gausel near Stavanger, which he thought had been cast in identical moulds.[39] In considering a context for the dispersal of these high-quality pieces, we may note the poem by Walafrid Strabo (died 849) on the Iona monk Blathmac, who was martyred by 'Danes' in 825 after refusing to divulge the hiding-place of 'the precious metals wherein lie the holy bones of St Columba'. The close links of the St Germain/Gausel finials with the Book of Kells (discussed by Michael Ryan in this volume) and with the panel of snake-and-boss ornament on the great Pictish cross-slab at Nigg make an Iona provenance likely. While the shrines of other Columban saints, notably Adomnán, may also have remained on Iona for part of the ninth century, these artistic links suggest that the snake-and-boss motif was associated with Columba himself, who intervened to save his companions from monsters, and whose final blessing of his island secured its people and cattle from the venom of snakes 'so long

[35]R A S Macalister, 'The cross of St John, Iona', *Antiquity* 3 (1929) 215-17 (p 216).
[36]R A Smith, *Proceedings of the Society of Antiquaries of London*, 2nd series, 28 (1915-16) 87-95; see now S Youngs, 'The Steeple Bumpstead boss' in *The age of migrating ideas*, ed R M Spearman and J Higgitt (Edinburgh 1993) 143-50.
[37]The Commission's identification of these very weathered details has been followed in I Henderson, 'The Book of Kells and the snake-boss motif on Pictish cross-slabs and the Iona crosses' in Ryan, 56-65, and by D Mac Lean, 'Snake-bosses and redemption at Iona and in Pictland' in Spearman and Higgitt (note 36 above) 245-53.
[38]J Hunt, 'On two "D"-shaped bronze objects in the St. Germain Museum', *PRIA* 57C (1956) 153-57; *The work of angels: masterpieces of Celtic metalwork, 6th-9th centuries AD*, ed S Youngs (London 1989) no 138; see now M Ryan (this volume).
[39]E Bakka, 'Some decorated Anglo-Saxon and Irish metalwork found in Norwegian Viking graves' in *The Fourth Viking Congress*, ed A Small (Edinburgh 1965) 32-40 (pp 39-40).

as its inhabitants keep Christ's commands'. Its diffusion to Pictland may have been through pilgrims rather than stone-carvers, for the Nigg cross-slab shares with the finials passages of interlace to which the serpentine bodies are linked, but it lacks the fierce biting heads of St John's Cross.

The Kildalton and St Martin's Crosses, which were both designed with monolithic rings and still stand in their original positions, have many points of ornamental and iconographic interest. Discussion here will be confined to their Virgin and Child panels (fig 1), which raise the same questions regarding creative use of models as folio 7v of the Book of Kells itself. At Kildalton, where the abstract ornament shows astonishing virtuosity in intractable local epidiorite, the Virgin and Child with two angels occupy the top of the east face of the shaft, as on St Oran's Cross (pl 63), and the representation is a simplified version of that carving. St Martin's Cross, 4.3m high but only 1.19m in span, places the same scene in the centre of the west face of the cross-head, above an Old Testament series (Daniel, Abraham and Isaac, and David as harper with another musician). Here there are four angels, diminutive in relation to the Virgin unlike those on St Oran's Cross, although the wings of the upper two form a similar canopy. Was a completely different model used, or is this roughly-executed carving a skilful adaptation of the Book of Kells archetype to a circular format?

The placing of these Virgin and Child panels in dominant positions on three of the crosses of the Iona group, and the repetition on both faces of the top arm of St John's Cross of what appear to be miniature 'Mother and Child' groups, are consistent with the special role accorded to Mary in the Columban *paruchia* from the seventh century onwards. The most discussed example is the drawing incised on the wooden coffin of St Cuthbert in 698,[40] but a few years earlier Adomnán had recorded the story of a miraculous icon of 'the holy Mary ever Virgin' seen by Arculf in Constantinople.[41] Closer in date to the Iona crosses and the Book of Kells there is the celebrated hymn *Cantemus in Omni Die* by the Iona monk and canon-law scholar, Cu-chuimne (died 747).[42] Its references to the liturgical praise of *Maria de tribu Iude* seem particularly apposite to St Martin's Cross, with its image of Christ and his Mother set above the most significant figures in their genealogy and facing an ancient processional way.[43]

What then of the relationship between Iona, Kells and the 'great gospel-book of Columba'? Despite the catastrophic nature of the Norse raids of 802 and 806, the poem of Walafrid Strabo shows that monastic life continued

[40]E Kitzinger, 'The coffin-reliquary' in *The relics of St Cuthbert*, ed C F Battiscombe (London 1956) 248-65; Werner (note 31 above) 1-23, 129-39.
[41]*Adamnan's De locis sanctis*, ed D Meehan (Dublin 1958) 118-19.
[42]*The Irish Liber Hymnorum*, ed J H Bernard and R Atkinson, 2 vols (London 1898) I, 32-34.
[43]Cf the vernacular *de thriub Iuda* in an ?eighth-century poem on the Virgin (*The Poems of Blathmac, son of Cú Brettan*, ed J Carney (Dublin 1964) 110-11). A middle Irish poem published by K Meyer (*Zeitschrift für Celtische Philologie* 12 (1918) 394) records that Mary regularly visited Reilig Odhráin.

and that the founder's shrine was still on Iona in 825, although Blathmac was not the abbot of the community. Relics of Columba passed in both directions between Iona and Ireland until about 849, when some were taken to Kells and others to Kenneth MacAlpine's new church in eastern Scotland, probably at Dunkeld which preserved an enshrined staff (the *Cathbuaidh*) until the Reformation.[44] In theory then the Book could have been made on Iona during the early ninth century, and Françoise Henry suggested a possible connection with the bicentenary in 797 of Columba's death, when the scribe Connachtach was abbot.[45] My own preference, however, is for an earlier period, the middle of the eighth century, when it is likely that the bodily remains of Columba were translated, before the enactment of the *Cáin* in 753, into the rich shrine described by Walafrid Strabo.[46] The creation of a great gospel book on this occasion would correspond to the relationship between the translation of Cuthbert in 698 and the production of the Lindisfarne Gospels, as suggested by Brown and Bruce-Mitford, but with far greater probability. Iona at this period was rich and prosperous, already surely the owner of many of the land-holdings named in the papal confirmation to its Benedictine successor in 1203,[47] and with its wealth and prestige enhanced by the three year tour of Adomnán's relics in 727-30. The celebration of Columba's enshrinement by the creation of a gospel book and stone crosses of unprecedented splendour and technical audacity would seem in any other context to verge on megalomania. To the abbot of Iona, it would seem no more than the honour due to his patron, that overwhelming confidence in their 'most reverend father Columba' that led Colman from Lindisfarne to Inishbofin and Mayo, inspired Cumméne and Adomnán to their hagiographical labours, and was to bring Blathmac to a martyr's death while preserving the relics of one of the chief saints of the western world.

Acknowledgements: The survey and research on which this paper is based were carried out for the Royal Commission on the Ancient and Historical Monuments of Scotland, and I am indebted to the Commission for permission to use copyright illustrations. I owe a particular debt to Ian G Scott and Geoffrey B Quick, the Commission's former illustrator and photographer, for their technical skills and dedication to the highest standards of recording. Innumerable friends in Britain, Ireland and beyond, many of whom attended the Dublin conference, have contributed to this paper by their past advice, encouragement and criticism. My greatest inspiration was the friendship and scholarship of Robert B K Stevenson who died shortly before the conference and whose widow Elizabeth represented him there. I dedicate this paper to them, as a small token of gratitude.

---

[44]A O Anderson, *Early sources of Scottish history, AD 500 to 1286*, 2 vols (Edinburgh 1922) I, 279, 407-08; Henderson, 190-91.

[45]Henry, 221.

[46]This hypothesis was suggested independently by P Meyvaert, 'The Book of Kells and Iona', *Art Bulletin* 71 (1989) 6-19, apparently in ignorance of the present writer's brief discussion of 1982 (*Iona Inventory*, 47). The subject is also treated, with due acknowledgement, in Henderson, 194, and in *Kells commentary*, 289 n 144.

[47]See map and list in *Iona Inventory*, 145-47. The fertile islands of Canna, Islay and Tiree, included in the 1203 confirmation, also have Columban church dedications and significant early sculpture.

Kells and its Book

D L Swan

The 'Book of Kells' is the title universally attributed to the great gospel book which for the past thousand years or so has been associated with Colum Cille and with Kells, and Kells is the historic setting in which this great treasure is first encountered. In this paper an analysis will be attempted of the physical surroundings which Kells presented in the period prior to the establishment of the Columban foundation as well as during its subsequent development as head of the *paruchia* of Colum Cille.

In a sense, it can be said that Iona died in the early ninth century. After the first, devastating Norse raid in AD 795, it was again pillaged in 802 and 806.[1] Although it continued to function in some measure, and even maintained a notional primacy in the Columban *paruchia*,[2] Iona's fortunes were in irreversible decline, and the death of Flan Mac Maile Duin in 891 witnessed the end of any direct link between Iona and the holder of the office of abbot.[3] From the initiation of this process, Kells emerged as the contender most likely to replace Iona, and thereafter, rapidly developed to a position of unrivalled pre-eminence within the whole family of Columban foundations. However, in order to trace the ecclesiastical history of Kells from its earliest origins, it will be necessary to review the somewhat scanty evidence for the prehistoric and early historic period.

That Kells was already a site of some significance, whose importance was recognised in the prehistoric period, may be inferred from the entry in the *Annals of the Four Masters* under the year 1207 BC. Here there is reference to the doubtless mythical incident of the establishment by Fiacha Finnailches, king of Ireland, of his chief residence, or *Ceanannus*, at a place previously referred to as *Dun-Chuile-Sibrinne*, or the Fortress of the Corner of the Adulterers, coyly rendered by O'Donovan as *arx anguli adulterii*.[4] The element *dún* in such place-names generally indicates the existence of a stronghold, a fortification, or a royal residence.[5] This interpretation is perhaps strengthened by the admittedly late references in the Book of Lismore, the Martyrology of Donegal and Manus O'Donnell's *Life of Colmcille*, which identify Kells as the *dún* or royal residence of Diarmait

[1] James F Kenney, *The sources for the early history of Ireland: ecclesiastical* (New York 1966).
[2] Herbert, 72-74.
[3] Herbert, 75.
[4] AFM, I, 57.
[5] P W Joyce, *The origins and history of Irish names of places*, 6th edn, 3 vols (Dublin 1891) I, 277.

MacCerbaill, later to become king of Tara in the mid-sixth century.[6] An additional hint of a prehistoric connection is detailed by Joyce, in his analysis of the name 'Suffolk', which still survives as a street name in present-day Kells.[7] That it is of early origin can scarcely be in doubt since it is mentioned in one of the charters transcribed into the Book of Kells, referred to above, as well as in the *Annals of the Four Masters* at AD 1156, which record that 'Kells was burned ... from the cross of the portico gate to Siofioc'. This term is interpreted by Joyce as referring to a prehistoric burial mound, *Sitheog*, the linguistic equivalent of *Sidhean* a place-name term which is by no means unusual in similar contexts. The possible site of such a mound was known, and indeed pointed out, by local residents until recently built over and destroyed.

Cenannus also figures in the dynastic struggles of the sixth century, and appears to have been particularly associated with the figure of Diarmait mac Cerbaill, who according to Byrne, was the last to hold 'the sacral kingship of Tara', as well as having some right to be ranked as 'the first Christian high king of Ireland'.[8] There are indications in the annalistic records that like his legendary ancestor, Cormac mac Airt, he too had his residence at Kells before moving on to the more prestigious kingship of Tara.[9] Here, it is claimed that he was visited by Colum Cille, who foresaw that Kells was to become the most glorious of all his foundations, thus setting out a suitably early claim for a Columban possession as well as a retrospective record of a self-fulfilling prophecy. The seventh-century compilation sometimes known as the *Collectanea* of Tirechan also refers to Kells in terms of a place which is readily recognisable (and widely known), when identifying the location of *Ath da loarc*, where Patrick spent the second day of Easter, as *Vadum Duarum Furcarum, id est Dá Loarcc iuxta Cenondas*.[10]

In the early eight century, two battles are recorded in the *Annals of Ulster* as having taken place here or hereabouts, in the years AD 718 and 742. The first of these references records *Bellum Ceninnso*, with a list of those killed, and the second refers to *Bellum Serethmaighe, la Domnall mc Murchadha .i. i Ceanannas*.[11] These were part of the on-going dynastic struggles which apparently had continued from the sixth century or earlier, and represented the consolidation of the grip of the southern Ui Neill, in particular the Clann Cholmain, descendants of Diarmait mac Cerbhail, on these territories.

---

[6]Gearóid Mac Niocaill, *Ireland before the Vikings*, Gill History of Ireland 1 (Dublin 1972) 19.
[7]Joyce (note 5 above) III, 396-97.
[8]Francis John Byrne, *Irish kings and high-kings* (London and New York 1973) 104-05.
[9]Anngret Simms with Katherine Simms, *Kells*, ed J Andrews and A Simms, Irish historic towns atlas 4 (RIA Dublin 1990) 1; Kim McCone, *Pagan past and christian present in early Irish literature* (Maynooth 1990) 159.
[10]*The Patrician texts in the Book of Armagh*, ed and trans Ludwig Bieler, Scriptores Latini Hiberniae 10 (Dublin 1979) 146.
[11]*AU²*, 172-73 and 196-97.

Another early reference to ecclesiastical activity in this area is to be found in
the late eight or early ninth-century compilation known as the *Felire
Oengusso Celi De*. The reference is found as a note to the entry under
December 1st, and refers to the saint whose feast is commemorated on that
date. He is identified as *epscop mac Cainde ó Ath da loarcc i tóeb Chenansa*, or
'bishop Mac Cainde of Ath da loarc beside Kells'.[12] As has already been
noted, this site is also mentioned in Tireachan's compilation. A detailed
analysis of such references by O'Connell, identifies *Ath-da-laarc* as the now
obsolete place-name, the 'Ford of the Two Forks', applied to a site on the
river Blackwater, a short distance to the north-east of Kells, where the river
widening out into an oxbow lake, forms with its islands, two natural river-
forks.[13]

There is a sufficient number of references to support the supposition that
there was indeed here an early christian foundation, associated with if not
actually founded by Patrick. Both the *Vita Tripartita* and the Collections of
Tireachan in the Book of Armagh refer to this foundation and the putative
Patrician connection. That the foundation continued its existence into the
late eleventh century is indicated by an entry in one of the charters
contained in the Book of Kells referring to Moenach O Cinetha, erenagh of
Ath-da-loarg. This was also the general location of another lost site,
established it would appear in the Anglo-Norman period, and dedicated to
Mary Magdalene. The dedication still survives in the name 'Maudlin Bridge'
which crosses over the Blackwater at a point approximately 1km north-east
from the town, and likewise, obviously gave its name to the Maudlin Gate
which is marked on the maps of the Down Survey.[14] Even though the
precise location of these two ecclesiastical sites — the one early christian
and the other Anglo-Norman — has never been pin-pointed, it is not
unreasonable to suggest that in fact we are here dealing with a single
location, where the later Anglo-Norman foundation merely took over the
earlier site, continuing the ecclesiastical tradition under the new
dispensation, with a not unusual change in dedication.

There is no mention of a church, ruinous or otherwise, in the
documentation, nor has any tradition of a burial-ground survived in this
area, but the lands hereabout remained church property and in the Civil
Survey are shown as part of the properties of the archdeacon of Meath. In
addition, the lands on either bank of the river still indicate the ecclesiastical
connection: the name of the townland to the south being Archdeaconry
Glebe, while that to the north is still called Maudlin. There is one further
element which may point towards an early christian, perhaps even a
Patrician connection. In the village of Carlanstown about 2.5 km to the
north there is a holy well, still much revered by the people of the locality,
dedicated to St Patrick.

---

[12]Whitley Stokes, *The Martyrology of Oengus the Culdee*, HBS 29 (London 1905) 256-57.
[13]Philip O'Connell, 'Loughan and Dulane', *Riocht na Midhe* 1 (1958) 14-32.
[14]Simms and Simms (note 9 above) 3, fig 2.

Thus, it is manifest, that in the period preceding the arrival of the community from Iona, there was here both a secular, royal or quasi-royal fort or *dún*, as well as an ecclesiastical foundation. The latter was located on the banks of the Blackwater, a short distance to the north-east of the town, while established precedent would have placed the former on, or close to, the summit of the ridge, more or less centrally located within the present-day street pattern.[15] One can only speculate as to the morphological details of the ecclesiastical site of Ath-da-Laarc, in the absence of more precise knowledge as to its location. Nevertheless, it is likely that it would have conformed to the established pattern of such sites which have been studied in detail in many parts of the country.[16] The standard layout for these sites would have consisted of a circular, enclosing earthen bank with outer ditch, having a defended entrance probably towards the east, and containing one or more church buildings. Also within there would have been a number of other features, the most important of which would have been a burial ground, some small circular huts, workshops, and open-air working areas. They did not differ significantly from the layout and format of the contemporary, secular ringforts, except for the presence of the church (or churches) and of the burial ground, and in as much as they tended to be somewhat larger in size.

The secular settlement of Ceanannus is usually identified as having been located on the summit of the ridge in a naturally defensive position, where in contrast with the ecclesiastical sites, the major secular sites were frequently positioned.[17] The somewhat meagre evidence referring to this site from between the fifth and ninth centuries provides a picture of a royal residence or stronghold, which might most easily be equated with the type of archaeological site known as a hillfort, rather than the more plebeian and ubiquitous ringfort. In seeking suitable examples from the excavation records two sites in particular suggest themselves as providing possible comparisons, bearing in mind that the paucity of detailed information invites a considerable degree of speculation. Since it is already linked with Ceanannus in the documentary evidence, a brief examination of Tara is instructive. Deserted in the mid-sixth century, according to the annals,[18] and apparently never since occupied, the main focus of the earthworks at Tara consists of the large, sub-circular hillfort known as Rath na Riogh, defined by the remains of an earthen bank and ditch almost 300m in diameter, enclosing within a pair of smaller, conjoined enclosures and at least one prehistoric burial mound, the Mound of the Hostages, which has been excavated (**pl 65**).

---

[15]ibid, 1.
[16]Vincent Hurley, 'The early church in the south-west of Ireland: settlement and organisation' in *The early church in western Britain and Ireland: studies presented to C A Ralegh Radford*, ed S M Pearce (Oxford 1982) 320-32; D L Swan, 'Enclosed ecclesiastical sites and their relevance to settlement patterns of the first millennium AD' in *Landscape archaeology in Ireland*, ed T Reeves-Smyth and Fred Hammond (Oxford 1983) 269-80.
[17]Máire and Liam de Paor, *Early christian Ireland*, Ancient peoples and places 8 (London 1964) 8.
[18]Byrne (note 8 above) 95.

More detailed evidence is forthcoming from Freestone Hill, a hillfort in Kilkenny which was excavated by Gerhard Bersu in 1948-49, the results of which were published by Raftery.[19] Here, a burial cairn of the Early Bronze Age had been enclosed within a surrounding outer oval rampart formed by a quarry-ditch and inner bank. The total area contained within the enclosing bank was over five acres in extent. The burial cairn had been almost completely destroyed and subsequently formed the main focus for habitation within the great enclosure. The habitation area had also been enclosed within a small circular enclosure, less than 40m in diameter, consisting of a stone rampart with inturned entrance to the south-east. This small enclosure occupied the summit of the hill, not quite centrally located within the outer rampart, and although no house sites survived there was ample evidence of human occupation in the hearths and the artefacts which were recovered. Raftery suggests the probable occurrence of five or six structures within the shelter of the enclosing wall. The occupational evidence within its bi-vallate defences was dated to the fourth century AD, and it appears to have been in use for a relatively short period of time.

These two hillforts may be said to be fairly typical of the series, consisting of a large outer vallum, more or less circular or oval in plan, located below the summit of a hill or ridge, and following fairly closely the natural contours of the topography. This vallum encloses a much smaller, more nearly circular enclosure, centrally located on, or close to the summit. In almost all cases there is evidence of prehistoric activity, dating to the Neolithic or Early Bronze Age, and frequently this will be identified as a prehistoric burial site. Although Rath na Riogh at Tara can be seen to have a double internal enclosure — nevertheless, the more eccentrically positioned earthwork known as An Forradh, is manifestly later, clearly cutting through the south-eastern sector of the earlier, centrally located Teach Cormaic — it too originally conformed to the general pattern. It is not however to be understood that the inner enclosure was necessarily part of the original layout and therefore contemporaneous with the outer vallum, Clogher in county Tyrone being a case in point.[20] Most hillforts have been shown by excavation to have been multi-period sites, subjected to much adaptation and modification over extremely long periods of time.

Unlike the examples mentioned above, Kells has had continuous and probably intensive occupation from at least the ninth century onwards, as a result of which the original topography has been overlain by medieval and subsequent activity, thus perhaps obliterating, or at least concealing, significant evidence. Without extensive excavation it is unlikely that a definitive picture will emerge. Nonetheless, in many respects Kells can be said to conform to the general pattern detailed in respect of the hillforts cited above: the probable existence here of a royal site; prehistoric activity

[19]Barry Raftery, 'Freestone Hill, County Kilkenny: an Iron Age hillfort and Bronze Age cairn', PRIA 68 C (1969) 1-108.
[20]Richard Warner, 'Clogher demesne hillfort' in *Excavations 1972*, ed T G Delaney (Belfast 1973) 2.

likely to have been associated with an early burial mound, and a large enclosure reflected in the great curve of the present-day street pattern closely following the line of the natural contours of the ridge.[21]

Firstly, from the documentary evidence, there is ample evidence that this was a royal or quasi-royal site of the late prehistoric/early historic period. Secondly, there is an indication of early activity, in this case, most likely to have resulted from the existence here of a prehistoric burial place. Thirdly, the present-day layout of the town is dominated by the great arc of a circle described by the street pattern where it curves around from the north-west to the south-east, following the 75m contour fairly closely for most of its course. It has been argued elsewhere that where such topographical features occur they are most likely to reflect the outlines of early enclosures, now surviving in fossilised form as street, or road patterns or property boundaries. Morphologically, at least, this feature corresponds in some measure to the large, circular or sub-circular enclosures which so strikingly characterise the type of hillfort under consideration. The aerial photograph of Kells (pl 66) clearly illustrates the relationship between the circular street pattern and the natural topography of the landscape.

The historical settlement of Kells must however be dated from the early ninth century, when the community of Iona decided to transfer back to Ireland as a result of the Viking attacks over the previous decade or so. The late and somewhat enigmatic interpolation apparently referring to this event in the *Annals of Ulster* for the year 804 states that 'Kells was given without battle to the melodious Colum Cille in this year'.[22] Curiously, there seems here to be an echo of a reference to an earlier period of the history of Kells, found in the *Corpus genealogiarum Hiberniae*, noting how Cathair Mar and Conn Cetcathach were contemporary, 'Cathair in Tara and Conn in Kells, without battle or war between them'.[23]

It is possible from an analysis of certain key surviving elements to postulate a reconstruction of a typical early Irish monastic establishment. These elements usually include a burial ground, a church or church ruin, evidence for the monastic enclosure, an indication of the location of the entrance, evidence for a round tower, carved stone crosses or cross slabs or both, the occurrence of a holy well and a souterrain.[24] In the case of Kells each of these elements is either extant or can be shown to have existed.

In a manner similar to Armagh, Kildare, Duleek, Lusk, and many other comparable sites, Kells too has been shown to reflect its monastic origins in

---

[21]D L Swan, 'Monastic proto-towns in early medieval Ireland: the evidence of aerial photography, plan analysis and survey' in *The comparative history of urban origins in non-Roman Europe*, ed H B Clarke and Ánngret Simms (Oxford 1985) 77-102.
[22]Herbert, 69.
[23]McCone (note 9 above) 159.
[24]Hurley (note 16 above) 314-26; Swan (note 21 above) 77-102.

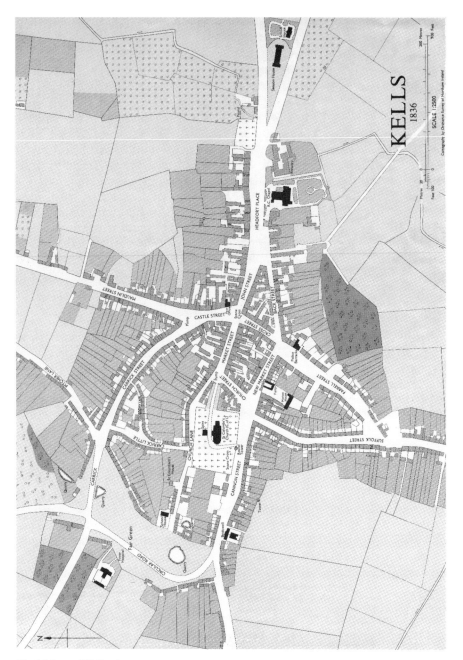

Fig 1 Map of Kells showing street plan (*Royal Irish Academy*)

its present-day street pattern.[25] This may be clearly seen in **fig 1** where the curve described by the street pattern can be traced from Carrick Street in the north, to Castle Street and Cross Street in the east, and around towards Suffolk Street in the south. This curve is complemented to the west by the line of property boundaries lying just west from the dotted line of the new Circular Road. The line to the south-west is less clear, but is most likely to have continued the curve suggested above from the west towards Suffolk Street, intersecting the present line of that street about half way along its length where it bends noticeably, south-west from the Market House. From here it would have curved towards the north-east, to join up with Cross Street north of the Police Barracks. This would have left a sub-triangular or 'D- shaped' feature formed by the area between Suffolk Street and Farrell Street protruding from the line of the enclosure towards the south. This appears to have been the result of a deliberate plan, since a similar feature may be seen in approximately the same position in the street plans of Kildare, Duleek and Armagh, and may be suggested to have occurred in a number of instances elsewhere. In the case of Armagh, this feature appears to be represented on Bartlett's map dating from the beginning of the seventeenth century, and has been tentatively identified by Henry as lying between Trian Mór to the south and Trian Masain to the east, and is thus perhaps an indication of an early 'suburb' extending outside of the main enclosure.[26]

Again, based on the analogy of Armagh where Bartlett marks the entrance to the east, and where the Cross of the Gate of the Rath (*Crois Dorais ratha*) still stood until the eighteenth century,[27] Kells, too, should have had its gateway somewhere in this sector. Under the entry for the year 1156 it is recorded that Kells was burned from the Cross of the Gate of the Portico to Siofoc, *crois dorais urdoim co Siofoicc*.[28] This would seem to indicate that there was here a somewhat elaborate gateway, perhaps comparable to that which still survives at Glendalough, marked by a cross nearby. It is scarcely coincidental that both Armagh and Kells are recorded as having had crosses mark their entrances and indeed there are sufficient indications from elsewhere that the entrance cross was probably a standard feature of these sites. Nor is it likely to be a coincidence that these crosses, and the area in which they stood, later became identified with market functions.[29] It can be argued that the entrance cross at Kells can be identified as the so-called Market Cross, which now stands at the junctions of Cross Street, Castle Street and Market Street. If this be accepted, then this must have been the original entrance to the monastic enclosure, and Market Street, leading directly towards the core of the settlement, marks the line of the original main thoroughfare.

---

[25]Francoise Henry, *Irish art during the Viking invasions (800-1020 AD)* (London 1967) 42-45; E R Norman and J K S St Joseph, *The early development of Irish society: the evidence of aerial photography* (Cambridge 1969) 117-18; Swan (note 21 above) 84-85.
[26]Henry (note 25 above) 41.
[27]*AFM* (AD 1166) I, 1157.
[28]*AFM*, I, 1119.
[29]Swan (note 21 above) 99-100.

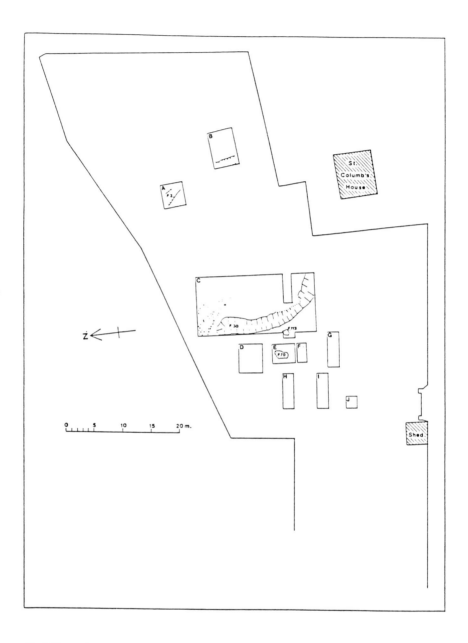

Fig 2 Plan of excavation cuttings and features (*Greta Byrne*)

In all examples studied, the church and burial ground form the core of these sites, and here too Kells is no exception. The suggested outline of the enclosure pattern clearly focuses on the church and churchyard, with the surrounding concentration of crosses, cross slabs and other early stone-work, the round tower and the early stone structure known as Teach Colm Cille or Colm Cille's House. It is virtually certain that the principal church of the early monastery would have stood here or hereabouts, even though no trace survives overground. Nonetheless, it has been established that the position of the modern church is a useful indication as to where this most important building would have been located, since churches replacing their predecessors tended to be located more or less on the same site. Likewise, the position of the round towers help to determine the position of the principal church, since the doorway of the round tower generally faces towards the doorway of this church.[30] Since the early churches conformed strongly to a standard pattern of design, being aligned along an east-west axis, with the altar always towards the east and the doorway to the west, it is probable that the original church would have occupied much the same position as that of the present church within the churchyard.

A major site such as Kells would be likely to have had a number of churches, and based on the available evidence, not all of these would necessarily have been located within an inner enclosure. The inner enclosure also seems to have been more or less standard in the monastic sites, and in many examples it is possible to suggest its general outline from the existing street pattern or the surviving walls and property boundaries. The street pattern in Kells, however, is not very much help in this matter. Nevertheless, this enclosure would have been focused on the precinct of the church and churchyard. The curve of the line of Church Lane to the north of the churchyard may provide a hint and since these tended to have been located close to the boundary of the inner enclosure, the position of the round tower may provide another clue. It is very likely that the entrance to the inner enclosure would have been to the east, probably at the intersection of Market Street and Church Street.

Recent excavations within the large enclosure have contributed further to our understanding of the development of Kells in this period. These were carried out on a recently cleared site to the north-west of Teach Colm Cille by Ms Greta Byrne, who kindly gave permission for this as yet unpublished material to be used. The plan of the excavated cuttings (**fig 2**) shows their position in relation to the early structure and summarizes the most significant results. In the largest of these cuttings, identified as Cutting C, part of the curving line of a ditch was revealed. The ditch terminates towards the north end of the cutting where a concentration of post-holes, appearing on the plan as small black dots, may be seen. This was interpreted as part of the outer ditch of a destroyed circular enclosure, probably of the ringfort type, which would have been between 20 and 30m

---

[30]George Lennox Barrow, *The round towers of Ireland: a study and gazetteer* (Dublin 1979) 26.

in diameter. The entrance was towards the north-west, and consisted of some kind of formal or perhaps defended gateway, probably reconstructed on a number of occasions, now marked by the concentration of post-holes shown on the plan. The ditch contained material and artefacts commonly associated with such sites and for the most part not closely dateable. It is fairly clear however, that originally this feature would have extended underneath or very close to the site of the early church, so much so that it can be deduced that the church is manifestly later than the ringfort. The evidence from the ditch-fill clearly showed that it had been opened for some considerable period of time. Layers of natural silting at the base contained remarkably little occupation debris, while the central layers had relatively enormous concentrations of domestic refuse. Directly overlying these central layers was material which derived from the collapse or destruction of the inner bank, and finally, in the upper levels there appeared to be deliberate infilling of what still remained of the ditch. It is possible that this infilling took place in connection with a change in use of this area of the site, perhaps to prepare the surface for new construction. Most of the materials and artefacts recovered showed evidence of industrial and domestic activity, while the animal bones and charcoal samples will ultimately yield a great deal of environmental evidence as well as throwing light on the butchering techniques and dietary habits of the occupants.

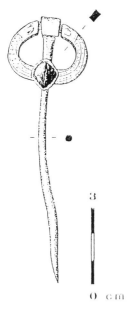

Fig 3 Bronze brooch from Kells excavations (*Greta Byrne*)

The most striking artefact recovered in the course of these excavations however, was a bronze brooch, which was found in the layers just above the primary silting of the ditch. This object (**fig 3**) belongs to a type of personal ornament known as a brooch pin, usually dated to the eighth or ninth century.[31] If the deposition of this object can be associated with the deliberate infilling of the ditch, this would most likely have taken place sometime after the beginning of the ninth century. Likewise, the construction of the early church is unlikely to have been undertaken until sometime after the backfilling had been completed. It is not impossible that these activities may be related to the occupation of Kells by the community from Iona, when major changes of use within the area of the enclosure would be expected. The completely secular character of the artefacts recovered from within and around the ringfort, and the complete absence of any burial evidence from this area, would seem to point towards normal occupational activity which

---

[31]Raghnall Ó Floinn, 'Secular metalwork in the eighth and ninth centuries' in *The work of angels: masterpieces of celtic metalwork, sixth to ninth centuries AD*, ed Susan Youngs (London 1989) 104-06.

was deliberately terminated by backfilling the enclosing ditch and levelling the surrounding area. At some subsequent period the stone church was constructed. Since this building is unlikely to date to a period earlier than the twelfth century,[32] it is not inconceivable that it may well have replaced an earlier structure occupying approximately the same position.

An entry in the *Annals of Ulster* states that in the year 814 the building of the church of Cenannus was completed,[33] and the same annals record that in 831 and 849 the Iona abbots travelled to Ireland with the reliquaries of Colum Cille.[34] Could these have included the Great Gospel of Colum Cille (*Soiscel Mor Cholaim Chille*) and could the archaeological evidence revealed in the area of the early stone church relate to preparations for these events?

Acknowledgement: I wish to acknowledge my sincere gratitude to Ms Greta Byrne, MA, of Ballycastle, county Mayo, for allowing me access to her report on the excavations which she carried out at Kells, and for allowing me to refer in detail to her findings. The interpretations and conclusions are, however, entirely my own responsibility. I also wish to express my indebtedness for Ms Byrne's kind permission to reproduce her excavation plan and the drawing of her bronze brooch.

---

[32] Peter Harbison, 'St Doulagh's Church', *Studies* (Dublin) 7 (spring 1982) 27-42.
[33] *AU*², 271.
[34] Herbert, 71.

Charter material from Kells

Máire Herbert

There is no historical evidence available to us at present which can establish when or how the Book of Kells came to be in that monastery.[1] It is generally held that the 'Great Gospel of Colum Cille' reported stolen from the monastery of Kells and subsequently recovered in the year 1007 is the manuscript which we now know as the Book of Kells.[2] Yet if we are to have documentary evidence rather than inference, the association of manuscript with monastery is conclusively attested only from the late eleventh century. From that period, and for about eighty years thereafter, records of property transactions were entered in blank leaves and empty spaces of the Book. These records, moreover, do more than witness to the history of the manuscript. They are themselves valuable sources of historical evidence.

At present, seven such entries in the Irish language survive in the Book of Kells. Thanks to the work of Gearóid Mac Niocaill, further records of Kells transactions now missing from the manuscript have been identified in a seventeenth-century copy.[3] When did the leaves containing these additional records become detached from the gospel book? A seventeenth-century transcript of Kells vernacular entries made for Archbishop Ussher is incomplete as far as the surviving texts are concerned, and so is inconclusive as evidence of contemporary content of the manuscript.[4] A transcript of the vernacular entries made in the year 1826, however, indicates that at that time the manuscript contained only the material which now survives.[5]

A copy of one of the now-missing entries is found in a late eighteenth-century manuscript of Charles O'Conor.[6] Did O'Conor discover its exemplar

---

[1]There has, of course, been a great deal of unwarranted inference, drawn mainly from ninth-century annals.

[2]*AU²*, s.a. 1007. However, eleventh-century usage indicates that the annal term *soiscélae* could apply to any sacred volume, and does not specifically denote a gospel. See *ATig*, s.a. 1090: this annal records the bringing of two 'gospel-books' to Kells, one of which seems to have been the *Cathach*, a copy of the psalms. See Herbert 92-93.

[3]BL, MS Add. 4791 folios 119-22. See Mac Niocaill's edition of texts in *Notitiae* and his new edition, with translation, 'Charters' in *Kells commentary*, 153-65.

[4]Transcript in TCD MS 580 folios 59v-61r. See T K Abbott and E J Gwynn, *Catalogue of the Irish manuscripts in the Library of Trinity College Dublin* (Dublin 1921) 3. On Ussher's association with the Book of Kells, see Aubrey Gwynn, 'Some notes on the history of the Book of Kells', *Irish Historical Studies* 9 (1954-55) 131-61 (p 149).

[5] Dublin, National Library of Ireland, MS G 583. See Pádraig Ó Macháin, *Catalogue of Irish manuscripts in the National Library of Ireland*, fasc XI (Dublin 1990) 11-12.

[6]Dublin, RIA, MS 934 (A v 3) p[d]. See Mac Niocaill, 'Charters', 154.

in the course of his researches in the Library of Trinity College, Dublin?[7] Did he single out this entry because its subject, Ua Ruairc, was of particular interest to him?[8] Were other Kells entries in O'Conor's exemplar left uncopied? Perhaps some answers may yet be found.

In the interim, we are indebted to Mac Niocaill for his identification of the copies of the texts now lost from the gospel book, and for his edition of all the known corpus of Kells materials. This provides a basis on which commentary may proceed. A fundamental question is that of the status of these texts. How are we to assess the information which they contain?

It is Mac Niocaill's view that the Kells texts are copies of earlier records, which were transcribed into the gospel book around the third quarter of the twelfth century, in preparation for a confirmation of monastic properties.[9] However, there are no palaeographical criteria which would conclusively assign the manuscript entries to the late twelfth century rather than to the period of which they testify. The inference that the records are not contemporary seems to be largely founded on the conclusion that the two texts on folio 27r, one dated to 1161, the other dated 1114-17, are in the same hand.[10] This, however, is not the case.[11] In fact, all seven of the Book of Kells entries are in different hands. It seems a mistaken enterprise, moreover, to look for any synchrony between the order of the manuscript and the order of the entries. It is clear that the scribes move forward or backward in the codex, entering their records in whatever blank spaces were nearest to hand.

There are reasons other than palaeographical for taking issue with the view that the Kells entries are copied records. The transactions (entered by seven different people) do not seem at all the kind of materials which might be purposefully assembled as evidence of monastic property-holding. Certainly, there are records of grants received. But there is nothing like a comprehensive documentation of properties. Several of the entries deal with small-scale transactions of only immediate significance. They concern individuals rather than the Kells monastic community, and they detail the minutiae of their purchases, the prices paid, and the guarantors of the deal. This material is evidently of contemporary importance only to the interested parties, and has no direct relevance to monastic property-holding at any time. That it would have been transcribed into the gospel book about a century after its initial recording is difficult to envisage. If there had been an effort to register monastic property claims, this would surely have

---

[7]See CC and RE Ward, *The letters of Charles O'Conor of Belangare*, 2 vols (Michigan 1980) I, 205-06, 214, 221.

[8]Ward (note 7 above) I, 7 n3, 257-59.

[9]Mac Niocaill, *Notitiae*, 1-2; 'Charters', 153.

[10]ibid.

[11]I am very grateful to Jane Bulfin of University College Cork for palaeographical and calligraphical advice concerning the hands on folio 27r.

assembled a more substantial record than the present miscellaneous collection.[12]

I suggest that, with one exception, all of the surviving texts in the Book of Kells are contemporary testimonies of the transactions which they narrate. While we do not have the same immediate access to the texts which survive only in later copies, I think it reasonable to infer that they, too, were contemporaneous entries. As for the Kells originals, I believe that the earliest entries are those on folio 6v, which continue on folio 7r (pls 7-8). These are datable to the late eleventh century. Following on, at line 14 of folio 7r, is the only entry which I hold to be retrospective. This concerns a grant datable between the years 1033 and 1049. The text has obvious signs of transcription and edition. Interlinear glosses, giving the names of those who had originally been designated only by their office, have been added. An omitted line is also inserted interlineally.

In my opinion, the Kells texts thereafter are again contemporaneous. The next entry is probably that found at the end of folio 27r, dated between the years 1114-1117. Then, in a small cramped script, the remainder of folio 7r (lines 32-38) is filled, sometime between 1117 and 1133. Following that, on 11 November 1133 is an entry begun at the end of folio 6r, and continued at the end of folio 5v. The latest of the entries surviving in the codex is that on the top of folio 27r, concerning the freedom of Ardbraccan, datable to 1161. The now-missing texts are all datable prior to 1161. Where in the manuscript they were entered, and whether entered consecutively or in the random order of the surviving texts, we cannot now say.

What are the characteristics of these Kells entries? Features of a Celtic charter tradition have been set out by Wendy Davies.[13] A distinctive characteristic is the retrospective nature of the records. The Kells entries accord with this pattern, as they are narrative accounts of transactions which have been performed. They are evidentiary rather than dispositive, a permanent testimony that actions have taken place, that certain consequences are to follow, and that named guarantors are to oversee the fulfilment of the process.[14]

---

[12]On specific problems concerning the proposed confirmation of properties in the late twelfth century, see below pp 74-75.

[13]W Davies, 'The Latin charter tradition in western Britain, Brittany and Ireland in the early medieval period' in *Ireland in early medieval Europe; essays in memory of Kathleen Hughes*, ed D Whitelock, R McKitterick, and D Dumville (Cambridge 1982) 258-80.

[14]See Davies (note 13 above) 262-66. On general matters related to charter material I am indebted throughout to the work of Pierre Chaplais, collected in *Prisca munimenta: studies in archival and administrative history presented to Dr AEJ Hollaender*, ed Felicity Ranger (London 1973) 29-107; to Patrick Wormald, *Bede and the conversion of England: the charter evidence* (Jarrow Lecture 1984), itself a source of considerable bibliographical material, and to other works of Wendy Davies, in particular, *An early Welsh microcosm: studies in the Llandaff Charters* (London 1978), and *Small worlds: the village community in early medieval Brittany* (London 1988).

In speaking of the constituents of the documents we must take account of their different purposes as well as of their general similarity of intent. We have records of five grants, along with eight purchases, one dispute settlement, and one entry which concerns the immunity of the monastery of Ardbraccan. The records of grant contain the disposition, which may include a statement of the extent of the property granted or the conditions attached. Fundamental also to these records is a list of sureties, and in three cases there is a sanction. In the case of purchases, we get the disposition, which in almost all instances sets out the extent and boundaries of the property in question. The price paid is always included, as is the list of sureties. Only in two instances is there a sanction. In the case of dispute settlement, there is a brief account of the matter at issue, the settlement reached, the payment involved, and the list of sureties. One each of the documents of grant and of purchases is preceded by the pictorial invocation of a cross.[15]

It is evident that the Kells texts are all intended as comprehensive evidence of transactions. The fact that many lack sanctions, and that most lack initial invocations does not diminish their testimonial status.[16] They are detailed in the essential matters, what property has changed hands, what conditions are involved, and, in particular, who the sureties are. The record of matters of ownership and finance, moreover, is enshrined in a holy book, which in itself confers authenticity as well as security. The cumulative evidence suggests, therefore, that the texts offer valuable contemporary insight into the practice of property transfers, and into the social, political, economic, and ecclesiastical worlds in which they are situated. The very existence of these materials in the Book of Kells raises important preliminary questions about the keeping of records of property transactions in early Ireland.

The practice of written documentation of property transactions in the Celtic areas has been shown to have its origins in the late Roman world, and was probably first adopted by christian clerics in Britain in the fifth century. In the early stages of Irish christianization, ecclesiastical legislation was already seeking the introduction of land contracts *more Romanorum*. By the eighth century we have evidence both of legal stipulation and of practice. The *additamenta* which follow Tírechan's account of Patrick in the Book of Armagh contain detailed records of transactions, and though they lack formal charter features such as witnesses or surety lists, their general character testifies to a charter-writing tradition in the Irish church by that time.[17] Indeed, this is also borne out by texts concerned with ecclesiastical legislation and dues. Both *Cáin Adomnáin* and *Cáin Éimíne Báin* have been

---

[15]Folio 6r, and folio 27r, line 15.

[16] In the case of transactions lacking final sanction clauses, in some instances, at least, the omission may simply result from the fact that they are written in rather confined spaces at the ends of pages, as on folio 7r, lines 32-38, and on folio 27r, lines 15-25.

[17]Davies (note 13 above) 269-80; Jane Stevenson, 'Literacy in Ireland: the evidence of the Patrick dossier in the Book of Armagh' in *The uses of literacy in early medieval Europe*, ed Rosamund McKitterick (Cambridge 1990) 11-35 (pp 27-32).

shown to preserve contemporary lists of sureties, as well as other features of content which point to the written recording of formal contracts in the late seventh and early eighth centuries.[18]

It is the case, however, that despite this commitment on the part of the early church to written documentation, secular Irish law and practice remains largely outside of a literate framework? Furthermore, does ecclesiastical documentation itself subsequently become attenuated in Ireland after the eighth century? Conclusions to date about these matters have been essayed on the basis of a narrow range of material.[19]

Yet as far as Irish secular society is concerned, we are still far from being in a position to draw firm conclusions. It is difficult to ascertain with any degree of assurance the extent to which land could be, and was, granted, bought and sold at particular periods. Thus, the extent of possible record-keeping is not clear. The suggestion that secular society remained largely impervious to the use of written testimony, however, at least invites some scepticism. Even in the eighth century, references in vernacular law texts cite writing as a means by which perpetual possession is proven, as an instrument in dispute resolution, and as evidence of a bequest.[20] We must allow for ecclesiastical influence on the written redaction of the secular laws. Yet we note that the prescriptions concerning writing in a secular context are not identical to those specifically addressed to contemporary churchmen, and written testimony is not allowed an exclusive role in any of these instances.[21] It is a particular difficulty that there has been scant diachronic investigation of legal theory and practice in Irish secular society during the period between the eighth and eleventh centuries. Yet we know that this was a period of increasing territorialization of royal power, and of ever-closer church-state relationships. Contemporary sources may yet yield up more information.

If we are prepared to recognise a degree of verisimilitude in literary texts, for instance, we may note the depiction of coexistent oral and written modes of testimony in an Irish tale compiled from earlier materials in the eleventh or twelfth century. Here, in a purely secular setting, ownership of a sword is falsely asserted on the evidence of a name clandestinely inscribed on it.[22] What is significant is the assumption that a debate about the

---

[18]Máirín Ní Dhonnchadha, 'The guarantor list of *Cáin Adomnáin, 697*', *Peritia* 1 (1982) 178-215; Erich Poppe, 'A new edition of *Cáin Éimíne Báin*', *Celtica* 18 (1986) 35-52, and 'The list of sureties in *Cáin Éimíne*', *Celtica* 21 (1990) 588-92.

[19]Stevenson (note 17 above) 32-33, 35; Richard Sharpe, 'Dispute settlement in medieval Ireland: a preliminary enquiry' in *The settlement of disputes in early medieval Europe*, ed Wendy Davies and Paul Fouracre (Cambridge 1986) 169-89.

[20]Sources cited by Mac Niocaill, *Notitiae*, 7 and 'Charters', 1. See also Fergus Kelly, *A guide to early Irish law* (Dublin 1988) 163, 204.

[21]See H Wasserschleben, *Die irische Kanonensammlung*, 2nd ed (Leipzig 1885) 123, 163, and Mac Niocaill, *Notitiae*, 6, 'Charters', 1.

[22]See J F Nagy, 'Sword as *Audacht*' in *Celtic language, Celtic culture*, ed A T E Matonis and D F Melia (Van Nuys, California 1990) 131-36; John Carey, 'The testament of the dead', *Éigse* 26 (1992) 1-12.

acceptability of evidence in a property issue should involve reference to writing.

Whatever the role of documentation in secular Irish society, in the Irish ecclesiastical sphere written records of property transactions were very specifically legislated for, and were, indeed, in use in the eighth century. But is it the case that the Armagh documents which we have noted earlier represent 'an isolated experiment' within the Irish church?[23] Is there a fall-off thereafter in the use of charters until the late eleventh century, when we find the documents in the Book of Kells, along with a contemporaneous transaction in the Book of Durrow?[24] Do these documents represent a short-lived revival of charter writing, possibly confined to Columban churches?[25] These are some of the matters which will now be addressed.

In the Book of Armagh, we find not only texts which specifically note property transactions, but also a seventh-century hagiographical work largely concerned with matters of ecclesiastical ownership. Tírechan's account of Patrick's mission uses charter terminology to record grants and offerings made to the saint, but his material is entirely set in a narrative framework. It has been suggested that this methodology actually represents a move away from charter-like documents towards an appeal to memory and story, and that this was a compromise forced on the church by the secular legal tradition.[26] But hagiography and the use of charters are not mutually exclusive ecclesiastical statements. Rather, they may be complementary.[27] In Ireland, as elsewhere, a church's claims to ownership might at times be more effectively proclaimed by reference to a fake hagiographical charter set in the founder's era than by the production of contemporary legal records. But this does not mean that conventional charters necessarily became supplanted. In fact, on occasions they may have served as the basis of the hagiographer's work.

Many Irish hagiographical texts, both Latin and vernacular, from the centuries after Tírechan retain the formal terminology of grant.[28] This is a

---

[23]Stevenson (note 17 above) 32.

[24]Since my concern is with Irish evidence, I do not propose to discuss the Scottish property records from the Columban monastery of Deer, for which see *The Gaelic notes in the Book of Deer*, ed Kenneth Jackson (Cambridge 1972).

[25]Sharpe (note 19 above) 173-74.

[26]Stevenson (note 17 above) 32.

[27]See Baudouin de Gaiffier, 'Les revendications de biens dans quelques documents hagiographiques du XIe siècle', *Analecta Bollandiana* 50 (1932) 123-30; Wendy Davies, 'Property rights and property claims in Welsh *Vitae* of the eleventh century' in *Hagiographie, cultures et sociétés: IVe-XIIe siècles*, ed E Patlagean, P Riché, M Sot (Paris 1981) 515-33.

[28]See, for instance, *Vitae sanctorum Hiberniae: ex codice olim Salmanticensi nunc Bruxellensi*, ed WW Heist (Brussels 1965) 129 §46, 251 §14, 268 §27; *Vitae sanctorum Hiberniae*, ed Charles Plummer, 2 vols (Oxford 1910, repr 1968) I, 184 §xxix, II, 66 §xiii, 231 §xiii; *Bethada Náem nÉrenn: lives of Irish saints*, ed Charles Plummer, 2 vols (Oxford 1922, repr 1968) I, 13 §13; 16 §28-29; 26-27 §20-23; 35 §60; II, 202 §41, 211-12 §73. *Betha Colmáin Maic Luacháin: life of Colmán son of Luachán*, ed Kuno Meyer (Dublin 1911) 18-19 §19, 38-39 §39, 76-77 §73-74.

further indication that the practice of written notification of property transactions did not fall entirely into abeyance after the eighth century. In fact, we find echoes of charter formulae, not only in hagiographical texts, but also in literary compositions and in annal notices.[29] While the majority of these texts date from the period of the eleventh and twelfth centuries, their use of formulae does not appear to be explicable by reference to outside influence at that time.[30] Rather, it is indicative of continuity. Moreover, since charter language occurs in different types of text, the continuity cannot readily be explained away as conventional literary repetition. I do not think it reasonable to expect to find the full range of charter constituents such as witness lists and sanction clauses in narrative or annal contexts.[31] It is more logical to expect the material to be tailored to suit its particular setting.

How frequently monastic establishments might have been involved in significant property transactions, especially in the unsettled period of the Viking wars in the ninth and tenth centuries, is difficult to estimate, as is consequently the amount of documentation which might have been lost. It seems to me, however, that a general paucity of surviving documents in the period from the late eighth century, and a greater level of survival from the eleventh and twelfth centuries, probably best explain the present clustering of Irish charter materials. As charters independent of secondary contexts may have included single-leaf records, it should not be surprising that such have not survived.[32]

Overall, I believe that the sum of evidence points to a level of continuity of written property records in the Irish church. I am not persuaded that eleventh and twelfth-century records represent a revival of the practice. Furthermore, while the surviving gospel book records are all of Columban provenance, charter formulae occur in texts associated with several different Irish monastic establishments.[33] Therefore, there does not appear to be good reason for viewing the later evidence in terms of a specifically Columban phenomenon.

The eleventh and twelfth-century Irish property records preserved independently of narrative contexts are, as we know, entered in the gospel books of Kells and of Durrow.[34] Whether there were other such records in

---

[29]For an instance in the tale *Cath Cairn Chonaill*, in *Lebor na hUidre: Book of the Dun Cow*, ed R I Best and O Bergin (Dublin 1929, repr. 1970) (hereafter *LU*) 288, lines 9592-9600. For annal examples of transactions and terminology comparable to those from Kells see *Chronicon Scotorum*, ed WM Hennessy (Dublin 1866) s.a. 1089; *ATig*, s.a. 1127, 1143; *AFM*, s.a. 1044, 1072, 1076, 1089, 1161, 1162, 1176.
[30]See also Davies (note 13 above) 266-69.
[31]*Pace* Charles Doherty, 'Some aspects of hagiography as a source for Irish economic history', *Peritia* 1 (1982) 300-28 (p 306).
[32]Note, for instance, the use of *chirographum* in an early eighth-century source, cited by Mac Niocaill, 'Charters', 1.
[33]*AFM*, s.a. 1044, 1089 refer to Clonmacnoise, *ATig*, s.a. 1127 to Tuam.
[34]For the Durrow text, see R I Best, 'An early monastic grant in the Book of Durrow', *Ériu* 10 (1928) 135-42.

now-lost manuscripts we cannot say. The practice of recording transactions in holy books is attested on the Continent, but it appears to be mainly an insular phenomenon in the period from about the ninth century onward.[35] In general, a need for greater security in an era of societal instability may have motivated the procedure, given the perceived status of the holy book as a protective and inviolable relic. Anglo-Saxon evidence indicates that it may have been early practice to place single-sheet charters in reliquaries, and hence also to place them inside the covers of sacred books.[36] The transition to a closer and safer attachment by incorporation into the books themselves is readily understandable.

Yet while the general context is clear, there were, of course, specific circumstances which impelled charter-writing in particular gospel books. As far as the Book of Kells entries are concerned, we need to examine the texts themselves in more detail. As we have noted already, they fit the broad category of property documentation, but their specific preoccupations are various. The earliest of the contemporary entries concerns a grant of the *dísert* or retreat of Colum Cille in Kells 'to God and to pious pilgrims forever'.[37] We note that the grant is made jointly by the local magnate, Máel Sechnaill, king of Tara, and the abbot and community of Kells. May we deduce anything further about this? The emphasis is on the endowment of a site consecrated to piety within the larger framework of the monastic community. The occasion is evidently solemn, and perhaps unusual, in that king and abbot are acting jointly. If, as seems likely, the grant was made in response to particular circumstances, a possible context is suggested by the Irish annals. In the year 1076, a claimant to the kingship of Tara was slain in the bell-tower of Kells.[38] As the monastery had been made the site of secular affray, we may, perhaps, envisage a joint action by king and abbot as an act of reparation, and as a reassertion of the role of the religious within the community.

The entry is fulsome, spread over the greater part of a page in the Book of Kells, and it uniquely includes the name of the scribe. All of this contributes to the view that it is the first of its kind. It may well be that the ceremony which it commemorates took place before the altar of the monastic church, and that the grant was solemnly sworn on the gospel book, the revered relic of Colum Cille. Was the event recorded in the gospel book because of the attendant circumstances? We can only speculate.

What we do know is that the practice of recording in the book is continued thereafter. The next entry is made within a decade or two, and concerns a

---

[35]See Dafydd Jenkins and Morfydd E Owen, 'The Welsh marginalia in the Lichfield Gospels: (part 1)', *Cambridge Medieval Celtic Studies* 5 (Summer 1983) 37-66 (pp 64-65).
[36]See, for instance, M Clanchy, *From memory to written record: England 1066-1307* (London 1979) 125-27.
[37]Mac Niocaill, *Notitiae* II, 12-16; 'Charters' (no 2) 155-56. (In future, citation will refer to the numeration of the text in each of the edited versions (abbreviated *N* and 'C'). Where relevant, line references in *N* will be added.
[38]Entry in *AU*.

purchase of land by the priest of Kells and his kin.[39] In the manuscript, an endnote is subsequently added to the effect that no tribute was due from the land before it was bought, and none was due thereafter.[40] Then a grant made about half a century previously is entered. An opening narrative details a breach of sanctuary by Conchobor Ua Máel Sechnaill, king of Tara, in which he seized and blinded an opponent who had been under the protection of the Kells community. As compensation for this outrage, the king granted Kildalkey 'to God and Colum Cille'.[41]

Why is it thought necessary to enter this past grant retrospectively? The scribe seems particularly concerned with the question of immunity of ecclesiastically owned lands. This is the substance of the addendum to the late eleventh-century entry, and the subsequent transcript is headed *Do Saíre Cille Delga inso* 'This concerns the immunity of Kildalkey'. The purpose of the retrospective entry, therefore, is not so much reiteration of the grant itself as assertion of the status of the property. In an era when church freedom from secular imposition was an issue of much contention, it would appear that the Kells writer is responding to perceived threat. In the case of Kildalkey, he is insisting that the immunity of a possession given in the reign of Conchobar Ua Máel Sechnaill should be honoured by subsequent rulers.[42]

The contemporary entries resume with two more purchases, one of land, the other of a building or enclosure, both datable to the early twelfth century.[43] Though the abbot and members of the ecclesiastical hierarchy of Kells are among the sureties, in both cases what we have are transactions between individuals rather than involvement at community level. One of the purchasers belongs to the family which dominated the office of priest in Kells, and he buys from a craftsman apparently resident in the monastic settlement.[44]

In the next entry the *dísert* or retreat is once more the beneficiary of a grant from the larger monastic community, though this time there is no royal participation.[45] The circumstances are implicit in the text. The grant 'to God and Colum Cille' is made at a time of economic disaster, in the year when 'the cattle and pigs of Ireland perished'. The bequest by the larger community from its own resources must have been motivated, in some degree at least, by its perceived need in crisis to ensure the prayers of the pious, and to restate a commitment to matters spiritual.[46] It is a measure of the secularisation of the monastic settlement of Kells, however, that the

---

[39]*N* III, 'C' 3.
[40]Folio 7r, line 13.
[41]*N* I, 'C' 4.
[42]Compare the entry of *ATig* for the year 1108, in which the clerics of Clonmacnoise fast against the Ua Máel Sechnaill king of Tara to obtain the immunity of Cell Mór.
[43]In probable order of entry these are *N* V = 'C' 7, *N* VI = 'C' 5.
[44]*N* VI, 'C' 5. See Herbert, 99, 103, 105.
[45]*N* IX, 'C' 1.
[46]Herbert, 104.

grants reveal the abbot and his officials designating the *dísert* as the locus of religious life, while they themselves act as its patrons much as worldy lords.

Hereafter, our view of the property affairs of Kells comes from the records which survive only in later copies.[47] We no longer have the advantage of being able to see the original manuscript setting of the entries, but otherwise there is a strong thread of continuity in content with what has preceded. A grant datable within the first half of the twelfth century is made to the main monastic settlement of Kells by its new secular overlord, Tigernán Ua Ruairc.[48] But as well as bequeathing this land 'as a perpetual alienation to God and Colum Cille', Ua Ruairc also makes a bequest to the specifically religious of the community, to support the newly-consecrated church of *int Edhnén*, which appears to have been associated with the *dísert*.[49] The evidence of our texts, therefore, cumulatively establishes a distinction between the main Kells foundation, rich in resources, and governed by property-owning officials, and the community dedicated to piety within its precincts.

The remaining documents further illuminate this distinction, for they detail the transactions of particular individuals, in the main identifiable as Kells monastic officials, who are increasing their private holdings by further purchases.[50] The priest of Kells buys land for his sons from the community of the *dísert* who had received it as a bequest.[51] The abbot, the *comarba* of Colum Cille, Muiredach Ua Clucáin, makes three purchases in the period between 1133 and 1154. In one instance, the land which he buys belonged to the community itself, in another case, it was 'a field in contention'.[52]

While detailed specifications of what is bought, of prices paid, and of the lists of sureties minimize the possibility of disruptive dispute, it is evident, nevertheless, that such did happen. We do not know whether the abbot's purchase of disputed land was part of a settlement procedure. Another Kells text, however, is more explicit. We learn that the *fosairchinnech* or lay administrator was party to a dispute, and had driven his opponent's cows to the market of Kells. It is not clear whether the legal process of distraint is invoked here.[53] In any case, the act seems to have hastened a settlement.

---

[47]The one remaining contemporary record in the Book is that concerning the freedom of the neighbouring foundation of Ardbraccan in 1161. See p 76 below.
[48]*N* VII [2], 'C' 8 [2].
[49]*N* VII [1], 'C' 8 [1]. See Herbert, 99. The term *eidhnén* literally 'ivied' (church) seems to be used in connection with various monastic establishments. Sites of that name seem to have been associated with both Clonard and Glenn Uissen. (See *Ériu* 10, pp 138-40). In Munster there is *Eidhnén Molaga* (E Hogan, *Onomasticon Goedelicum* (Dublin and London 1910). For a possible Clonmacnoise example, see *AFM*, s.a. 1024.
[50]The principals in the transaction printed as *N* VIII and 'C' 9 are not designated by office but the fact that the abbot of Kells is among their guarantors indicates that they lived within monastic jurisdiction.
[51]*N* XI, 'C' 10.
[52]*N* X, 'C' 11. The purchase from the community is [1] of the published texts, that of *acath incosnoma* is [2].
[53]On distraint see Kelly (note 20 above) 177-89.

Terms are then set out. A payment for right of full possession of the land is agreed and a list of sureties guarantees the outcome.[54] Records of Irish dispute settlement in action are rare. Yet this explicit example was not cited in a recent discussion of the topic.[55] An interesting parallel to the Kells text is the ninth-century Welsh record of dispute settlement, the so-called *Surexit* memorandum.[56]

Overall, the Kells documents offer a view of the operation of legal procedures in a variety of transactions. In all cases, the mechanism for ensuring the fulfilment of obligations lies, not in an external agency, but in a system in which the security of the transaction is guaranteed by named sureties. Such suretyship is not an exclusively Irish phenomenon, but rather a feature of late Roman practice adapted in northern Europe.[57] Our texts indicate that the sureties who guaranteed the actions of the principals were, like the principals, subject to divine sanction. Indeed, in one instance the sureties are singled out as subject to blessing or curse for the manner in which they fulfil their obligations.[58]

Furthermore, the presence of clerical sureties carrying the relics or insignia of their patron saints indicates the significance of spiritual sanctions in securing the legal agreements.[59] But there are also lay sureties, evidently chosen on account of their status and position, since they include kings and lesser lords. Does this indicate that these are seen to be in a position to compel compliance, if necessary? It is interesting to note in one instance that an exiled claimant to the kingship of Cashel is named as witness to a transaction, not as a surety.[60] This seems to indicate that he was not considered qualified to act in the latter capacity.

The early Irish secular tracts testify to a system in which different kinds of surety could be called on as different circumstances demanded.[61] We must beware, however, of basing our reading of eleventh and twelfth-century practice on this eighth-century theoretical model. Even the terminology shows changes. While the early term *rátha*, originally 'paying sureties', occurs in three instances, the most common term for sureties is *slána*, occasionally with the synonyms *commairche* or *dílsi*. All of these words have connotations of safeguard and security, and they may imply that the

---

[54]*N* IV, 'C' 12.

[55]Sharpe (note 19 above, p 170) indicates that the Book of Durrow entry (for which a dispute has to be assumed) is 'the only documentary record, such as it is, of an actual case'.

[56]Jenkins and Owen (part 1, note 35 above) and part 2, 'The *Surexit* memorandum', *Cambridge Medieval Celtic Studies* 7 (summer 1984) 91-120.

[57]See Wendy Davies 'Suretyship in the *Cartulaire de Redon*' in *Lawyers and laymen*, ed T M Charles-Edwards, Morfydd E Owen and D B Walters (Cardiff 1986) 72-91 (p 86). On the historical background, see D B Walters, 'The general features of archaic European suretyship', ibid, 92-116; D A Binchy, 'Celtic suretyship, a fossilized Indo-European institution?' *Irish Jurist* 7 (1972) 360-72; Kelly (note 20 above) 176-73.

[58]*N* III lines 30-32, 'C' 3.

[59]*N* I lines13-15, 'C' 4; *N* III lines 17-19, 'C' 3; *N* VII line 11, 'C' 8.

[60]*N* II, 'C' 2.

[61]Kelly (note 20 above) 167-73.

primary function of the sureties at this time was one of overseeing that the provisions of grants, sales, or agreements were fully implemented.[62] Indeed, in most cases the texts state that what was guaranteed was *dílse* or full possession of an acquired property against any claims by the previous owners.[63]

As has been noted already, the written account of transactions in the manuscript represents subsequent confirmation of what had taken place in a public ceremonial. There is evidence that in Ireland, as elsewhere in northern Europe, a sod of earth or some other substitute was handed over or placed on the altar at a public gathering to symbolize the conveyance.[64] In one of the Kells records we are told that the named sureties had proceeded around the land and to the centre of the land. This indicates a ceremony *in situ*, to ensure that all who guaranteed the contract were aware of the accurate extent of the property in question.[65] The identification of the personnel of the surety lists may be a guide to the location of the initial transaction. Grants to Kells by Tigernán Ua Ruairc, for instance, may first have been formalized in the areas in which the properties were situated, for both lay and clerical sureties came from his Bréifne lordship.[66] For the most part, however, the participants in the transactions came from the immediate vicinity of Kells, and the probable site of the transferred properties may be deduced from the presence among the sureties of local worthies. In one instance there are representatives from the monasteries of Dulane and of Donaghpatrick north-east and east of Kells,[67] in another, representatives from Girley and Kilskyre, south of Kells.[68] It is probable that the transactions involving the whole panoply of officials of the Kells monastic community were solemnised before the altar and thereafter recorded in the gospel book.[69] The overall picture is one in which lay and clerical interests co-operate closely, and are evidently closely enmeshed. The charter material falls within a politically eventful period in Meath history. The chief secular patrons of Kells in the eleventh-century records, the Ua Máel Sechnaill kings, were forced to concede their premier position in the Irish midlands in the early twelfth century. The community of Kells reveals itself as adapting to the prevailing circumstances, insofar as twelfth-century gospel-book entries depict the new power in the area, Ua Ruairc, in the role of royal benefactor and guarantor which had previously belonged to the Ua Máel Sechnaill kings.[70] Indeed, the Kells sources, in revealing Ua Ruairc's strategy of seeking ecclesiastical favour in the area, extend the view provided by the

---

[62]See *DIL*, s.v. *slán, commairge, dílse*.

[63]For example *N* V lines 11-3, 'C' 7.

[64]On the general topic, see Paul Vinogradoff, 'The transfer of land in Old English law' in *The collected papers of Paul Vinogradoff* (Oxford 1928) I, 149-67. For an Irish example see *Cath Cairn Chonaill* in *LU*, lines 9595-9597, which refers to an offering *amal fód for altóir* 'as a sod on the altar'.

[65]*N* III lines 18-20, 'C' 3.

[66]*N* VII, 'C' 8.

[67]*N* X [2], 'C' 10 [2].

[68]*N* III, 'C' 3.

[69]For example *N* II, V, VI, IX, XI = 'C' 2, 7, 5, 10.

[70]See Herbert, 96-97, 106-07.

contemporary annals, which document only his military offensives against
local rulers.

Moreover, we find information complementary to that of the annals
concerning these offensives of Ua Ruairc. As regards the minor kingdom of
the Gailenga in the immediate locality of Kells, the annals record the killing
of its king in battle against Ua Ruairc in 1130.[71] In Kells transactions datable
to the 1130s, Ua Ruairc's ally, Gafraid Ua Ragallaig, is referred to as ruler of
the plain of Gaileng, and has evidently been placed as resident deputy in
the area.[72]

Is Ua Ragallaig's role as guarantor of Kells transactions in this period an
indication of his acceptance by the neighbouring community? The
cumulative evidence reflects some ambivalence. As a wealthy land-owning
corporation, and as a corporation of individually wealthy landowners, the
security of Kells rested on co-operation with ambitious overlords. But the
evidence from the guarantor lists points to engagement with political
macrocosm and microcosm. The corporate community deals with the major
secular powers like Ua Ruairc and Ua Ragallaig,[73] but its members appear
to be more locally oriented in their personal transactions.[74] Indeed, a
network of relationships with both secular and ecclesiastical neighbours is
revealed by the guarantor lists. The lists, moreover, allow us to monitor
both survival and change in local power over the decades. They indicate
that at least some families and individuals maintain their position despite
political upheavals.[75] Like Kells itself, these appear to accommodate to, but
to resist full assimilation with, the new rulerships.

As the Kells monastic *seniores* are depicted both in their public capacities
and in their private property-owning roles, what were the boundaries
between the ecclesiastical and secular domains in the monastic settlement?
The evidence of the Kells documents combined with that of the annals
indicates that important positions in the monastic hierarchy became the
preserve of particular families. Succession to office was thus linked with
control of its property benefits.[76] It is evident also that the incumbents of
senior offices in Kells had the material resources to allow them to purchase
additional properties.[77] Ultimately, it is their corporate role which
distinguishes them from lay magnates. The Book of Kells documents reveal
the monastic officials maintaining collectively the structures of a
community united in allegiance to its patron, Colum Cille. The abbot of

---

[71]*AU, ATig.*
[72]*N* IX lines 11-12, 'C' 1; *N* XI line 23, 'C' 10.
[73]For example *N* IX, 'C' 1.
[74]*N* V, VIII, 'C' 7, 9.
[75]For example, representatives of the family of Ua Máelscíre maintain themselves in
Sogan in the twelfth century (*N* V, XI, 'C' 7, 10), and Uí Chaindelbáin rulers remain
prominent (*N* I, XII, 'C' 4, 6).
[76]See Herbert, 98-103.
[77]*N* III, X, XI = 'C' 3, 11, 10.

Kells continues to be styled as the saint's *comarba* or successor, and grants to the community are made 'to God and Colum Cille'.[78]

Moreover, while there is scant evidence of religious qualification for office among the hereditary property-owning monastic hierarchy, yet there is ample evidence of continued support for such central monastic functions as learning and hospitality.[79] The guarantor-lists indicate that the office of *fer léiginn*, probably best rendered as 'chief scholar', was of particular importance. This office is complemented by the existence of a separate office of student-master. Thus, it would appear that Kells's reputation for learning, attested in the annals in the eleventh century, was being maintained even in the more turbulent and secularized decades which followed.[80] Indeed, in a property-sale dated between 1114 and 1117 the education of the vendor's son is included as part of a deal conducted with a Kells official.[81]

As the guarantor lists generally maintain a distinction between clerical and lay sureties, it is evident that monastic officials are legally accounted as clergy, though they may be neither in holy orders nor celibate. Yet one category shift is observable. The holder of the office of *fosairchinnech* 'resident superior/administrator' of Kells, is usually accounted along with his fellow clerical officials. However, he is designated as a lay surety in a transaction datable sometime between the 1130s and 1154.[82] Moreover, in the same period the holders of the title of *airchennach* 'administrator/superior' of the monasteries of Dulane, Donaghpatrick, and Ráth Lugdach are accounted as laity, though previously such personnel were numbered among the clergy.[83] Such change may imply acknowledgement that those specifically concerned with the practical regulation of a monastic settlement could no longer be considered to have other than a purely secular role.

There certainly are indications in the records that twelfth-century Kells had developed into a more complex institution than that which had been founded in the early ninth century. It had acquired urban characteristics, having a market, and numbering among its inhabitants, not only a monastic community, but also property-holders legally capable of incurring liability.[84] Silver bullion circulated as the chief medium of exchange, and property prices were linked to economic circumstances.[85] The extent of administration was not bounded by the monastic enclosure for Kells evidently possessed substantial outlying properties. This is indicated, not only by the records of grant to the monastic settlement, but also by the

---

[78]*N* I, VII, 'C' 4, 8.
[79]The office of guest master is mentioned in *N* VI, 'C' 5; For the full listing of office-holders associated with scholarship and teaching, see Herbert, 98-100.
[80]*AU*, s.a. 1050, 1070.
[81]*N* V lines 4-5, 'C' 7.
[82]*N* X [1], 'C' 11 [1].
[83]*N* X [2], 'C' 11 [2].
[84]*N* IV lines 3-4, VI lines 1-2, VIII line 3 = 'C' 12, 5, 9.
[85]See Herbert, 104.

amount of property, including two mills, which the monastic settlement itself was in a position to bestow on the *dísert*.[86]

The range of transactions recorded in the Book of Kells thus reflects the contemporary monastic context. There is an urbanized settlement, which, nevertheless, is ecclesiastical in status. Yet the practice of religious life appears to be largely confined to the dedicated of the *dísert*. Members of the Kells hierarchy are propertied magnates, though collectively they maintain the institutions of a monastic establishment. The boundaries between clerics and laity, and between monastic settlement and neighbouring minor lordships, often appear indeterminate. Yet overall, the records suggest a tolerantly pluralist community, more affirmative of common bonds than of divisive factors.

The manner of preservation of the records reveals the Kells gospel book as a unifying sacred space in which items of concern to community and to individual members, to the main settlement and to the *dísert*, are given place. There is a diversity of interests involved, but common assent is given to the status of the holy book. It is itself a surety which safeguards all transactions within it, a relic, guaranteeing as it were, on oath, the veracity of the records inscribed in it. It is, moreover, a visible component of the legacy of Colum Cille, whose commemoration still united cleric and layman, and still gave Kells its identity and communal outlook up to the mid-twelfth century.

From the mid-twelfth century, just when contemporary recording of property transactions ceases, historical sources reveal changes in the ecclesiastical institutions of Kells. Much remains unclear, however, about the process and consequences of these changes. Do our records of Kells transactions over about eighty years cast any light on the matter? Despite the formulaic character and narrow range of reference of the documents, I believe that they do supplement other sources and do provide insight into the later history of the monastic settlement.

It is evident that the recorded activities of the monastic hierarchy, the *comarba* of Colum Cille, and his officials, reveal the extent of the secularization of the original Columban foundation. Thus the annal report of the year 1150 indicating that Derry had taken over from Kells as the head of the Columban churches is hardly surprising, given the northern monastery's adherence to the contemporary ecclesiastical reform movement.[87]

But what of the survival of monastic life in Kells? As indicated previously, Mac Niocaill held that the charter documents were copied into the gospel book in preparation for a confirmation of Kells possessions sought and obtained from Hugh de Lacy between 1175 and 1186. But it is evident from

---

[86]*N* IX, 'C' 1.
[87]See Herbert, 106-18.

the text of the confirmation that the possessions in question are not those of the Columban monastery of Kells, but those of St Mary's in Kells, which was a house of Augustinian canons.[88] The problem of the relationship of this foundation to the original Columban monastery is not addressed by Mac Niocaill. Aubrey Gwynn suggested that St Mary's Abbey was 'an entirely separate establishment from the early monastery of St. Columcille'.[89] Yet Maurice Sheehy's examination of the text of de Lacy's confirmation led him to the view that there was a connection between St Mary's and the older monastery. He pointed out that certain properties confirmed to the house of canons are mentioned in the Book of Kells records.[90]

But the properties common to the Kells records and to the Norman confirmation, those of *Ard Min* and *Ros Mindig*, had been granted, not to the Columban monastery, as Sheehy asserts, but for the support of the church of *Int Edhnén*, and, implicitly, the community of the *dísert*.[91] We have already noted the co-existence of this religious community alongside the main Columban establishment in Kells. In an era of reform in the Irish church, it seems very likely that the religious of the *dísert*, seeking to maintain a structured monastic life, adopted the rule of the canons regular of St Augustine as did many other Irish communities. This would then explain the transfer of their properties to the new institution.

It is not clear precisely when the change-over might have happened. Many Irish foundations appear to have adopted Augustinian rule in the 1140s.[92] There are grounds for thinking that the Kells move might have come towards the end of that decade. Máel Ciaráin mac Mengáin, consecrator of the church of *Int Eidhnén*, and probable head of the *dísert*, died in the year 1148. In the year 1150 the abbot of Derry had replaced the Kells abbot as the head of the Columban monasteries.[93] It seems reasonable to speculate that a change of leadership among the dedicated religious of Kells might have been the catalyst for change to the new rule. Furthermore, the separation of the religious from the larger secularized institution in Kells might have been another precipitating factor in the replacement of Kells by the reform-minded community of Derry in the leadership of the Columban monastic federation.

The church reform movement was to have further impact on Kells in the mid-twelfth century. In the year 1152 the movement towards organisational reform culminated in the establishment of diocesan structures. The political influence of Tigernán Ua Ruairc seems to have ensured the creation of a

---

[88]Text of confirmation published by Mac Niocaill, *Notitiae*, 38.
[89]A Gwynn and R N Hadcock, *Medieval religious houses: Ireland* (London 1970) 181.
[90]*Pontificia Hibernica: medieval papal chancery documents concerning Ireland, 640-1261*, ed M Sheehy, 2 vols (Dublin 1962-5) II, 106-7, n 267.
[91]*N* VII [1], 'C' 8 [1]. Other identifications of properties made by Sheehy are not convincing.
[92]R N Hadcock, 'The origin of the Augustinian order in Meath', *Ríocht na Midhe* 3 (1964) 124-31.
[93]Both dates from *AFM*.

bishopric for his Uí Briúin territories, with Kells nominated as its episcopal see.[94] Thus, the monastic church of Colum Cille in Kells must have been designated as a cathedral church, so that it retained its importance despite the changed circumstances of the Columban foundation which it had originally served. Moreover, the church which had been the repository of the Gospel book of Colum Cille continued to maintain guardianship of this valued relic.

Indeed, the latest transaction entered in the Book of Kells testifies to continuity as well as change in the immediate aftermath of reform. In the year 1161 it was recorded that the church of Ardbraccan was to be immune from secular imposition after payment had been made to the king of Lóegaire for the ensuing loss of his dues. This arrangement was guaranteed by leading ecclesiastical and secular sureties.[95] The initiative for the keeping of the record must have come from the community of Ardbraccan, a few miles south-east of Kells. There were no monastic officials of Kells listed among the sureties of the transaction. The status of the foundation undoubtedly had changed. Yet Kells, and particularly its gospel book, were still honoured by the principals in the proclamation of Ardbraccan's freedom, including the successor of Patrick, Gilla Meic Liag, a former Columban abbot, and the king of Ireland, Muirchertach mac Lochlainn.

It is noteworthy, however, that there is no mention of a bishop of Kells in the 1161 document, though the bishop of Meath, based at Clonard, is listed as a surety. Is the omission of a Kells bishop significant? It may be linked with the absence from the guarantor list of any secular magnates associated with Ua Ruairc. In fact, the annals report the killing of Ua Ragallaig, Ua Ruairc's lieutenant in the Kells area, in the year 1161.[96] The gospel book entry of that year appears to witness to a reassertion of local Meath interests in the locality after Ua Ragallaig's death. Is there an implication that Kells was being claimed for Meath, and detached from the Uí Briúin diocese? Did it subsequently come under Uí Briúin influence again? The title of bishop of Kells is still used sporadically thereafter in the short-lived period of the survival of the Uí Briúin diocese, but our present state of information does not extend further.[97] It is evident, however, that the presence or otherwise of a resident bishop did not ultimately affect the continuation in use of the church of Kells, nor its guardianship of the gospel book of Colum Cille, which was maintained until the mid-seventeenth century.[98]

While the great relic of the saint continued to repose in Kells, however, the surrounding world underwent great change. Shortly after the date of the latest Kells entry the Norman incursion into Meath brought the first of the

---

[94]For a summary of these developments see Gwynn and Hadcock (note 89 above) 82, 88.

[95]N XII, 'C' 6.

[96]ATig records that he was killed in Kells by a son of Ua Ruairc.

[97]Gwynn and Hadcock (note 89 above) 82.

[98]Gwynn (note 4 above) 157-60; William O'Sullivan, 'Medieval Meath manuscripts', Ríocht na Midhe 7 (1985-6) 3-21 (pp 16-17).

major upheavals which would seriously affect the social, political, and ecclesiastical life of the region. The records preserved by the gospel book, therefore, document an important closing phase in Irish history. They provide a unique insight into the life of the monastic settlement in which they were preserved, and they also afford a window on to a microcosm of Irish society on the eve of the Norman conquest. They come from a world aware that it is in a state of internal transformation, but unaware that external transforming forces are imminent. They speak directly to us of the practicalities of business and legal arrangements, and of the interactions of secular and clerical institutions. The information thereby provided complements other contemporary sources in a manner which the present survey has by no means exhausted. The Book of Kells is, indeed, a monument of Irish history, but it is also a medium of transmission of a further valuable part of that history.

Irish gospel texts, Amb. I.61 sup., Bible text and date of Kells

Martin McNamara, MSC

'To the textual scholar, the quality of the Gospel text of the Book of Kells does not match its artistic exuberance and virtuosity, but the book was not made to be read or studied but presumably for a practical sacred purpose'. Thus writes Dr Patrick McGurk in the most recent and the most authoritative examination of the biblical text of the Book of Kells.[1] Yet despite the shortcomings of the biblical texts of Kells when compared with the illumination, we can hardly forget that everything in this codex is really there by reason of some connection with the biblical text and out of respect for it, and is intended for the better understanding of the text, whether it be the prefatory material (gospel prefaces, chapter lists, lists of Hebrew names, canon tables) or the illumination. The various component parts of the Book of Kells lead us into so many aspects of the world and the culture that gave it birth. An examination of the biblical text helps us understand a very important part, in fact the central point, of the monastic life of early Irish monasteries. Such a study will also take us into the history of the Latin Bible itself, from its origins, through various recensions down through the middle ages. In this essay I intend to treat first of the Latin biblical texts, and the problems involved in situating individual manuscripts in context. I illustrate this by the examples of the biblical text of a manuscript written by Irish scribes hitherto not given much attention. I then go on to say something of the text of the Book of Kells (*siglum* Q) and what implications this might conceivably have on the date to be assigned to the work.

Manuscripts of the Latin Bible

Manuscripts of the Latin gospels, particularly of the Vulgate, are numerous, especially from the tenth century onwards. The oldest versions seem to have been made from the second century onwards independently of one another. By Jerome's day these Old Latin versions (*Vetus Latina*) circulated in widely different forms, but within two large groupings, the African (*Afra*) and the European (*Itala*). In Jerome's words there were then current almost as many Latin forms of the gospel text as there were manuscripts. Pope Damasus wished to remedy matters and in 383 he asked Jerome to make a revision of the gospel text against the Greek. This Jerome did and presented it to Damasus a few years later, with the covering letter on the question, beginning *Novum opus*. We do not know what kind of Old Latin (*Vetus Latina*) text Jerome revised nor the Greek manuscripts against which he made the revision. Some scholars think the Old Latin text was of the *b* (Veronensis) type. The Greek texts he used seem to have been of the Koine or Byzantine type. Jerome's translation (to become the Vulgate, official text

---

[1] McGurk, 'Gospel text', 68.

of the church) did not end the proliferation of gospel texts. The Old Latin continued to be copied down to the thirteenth century at least: VL *c*, *Colbertinus* (Paris, BN, lat. 254) probably southern France, is twelfth century, and *gig*, *Codex Gigas* (Stockholm, Royal Library, s.n.) is thirteenth century, from Bohemia. Together with Old Latin and Vulgate texts there now emerged mixed types of text, Old Latin contaminated by the Vulgate and Vulgate contaminated by the Old Latin.

A task confronting scholars is how to arrange the manuscripts of the Latin gospels. True Old Latin texts could be separated from genuine Vulgate texts easily enough. Two distinct families of the Old Latin version were also isolated, the *Afra* and the *Itala* or European *Vetus Latina*. Matters were less easy with regard to the bulk of the gospel manuscripts which were Vulgate or of a mixed text. In their critical edition of the Vulgate Wordsworth and White divided the Vulgate manuscripts into two large groups: class 1 (with five sub-groups) connected with Italy, and class 2 with three sub-groups DELQR (the Celtic family), BG, *codex Beneventanus* (BL, Add 5463, (Gaul)), and CT (Spain). The Celtic family of texts was in the process of being isolated over the previous decades since examination of the available material was first seriously studied by B F Westcott in 1863.[2]

Samuel Berger[3] popularised the view that the European mixed text was due to the influence of Irish manuscripts brought to the Continent by missionaries. This opinion was accepted by Wordsworth and White,[4] even though it was severely criticised as not responding to the facts by Peter Corssen in 1894.[5] The issue was taken up again by Dom Bonifatius Fischer, O.S.B. who has devoted the greater part of his scholarly life to the study of the Latin gospel texts. His view, now shared by most scholars, is that the position of Berger, too hastily and uncritically accepted by Wordsworth and White, does not correspond to the facts. He notes that from the sixth to the ninth century we have evidence for the existence throughout Europe of a rich variety of mixed text (of Vulgate and Old Latin readings). He believes that at the basis of this text stands an Italian edition from the sixth century at the latest. This edition, in his view, has its chief witness in the BL, MS Harley 1775 (given the *siglum* Z). The different European mixed texts are but variants of this Z-type.[6] In an 1972 essay Fischer has also expressed the

[2]B F Westcott, 'Vulgate, The (Latin Versions of the Bible)', in *A dictionary of the Bible*, ed William Smith (London 1863, 2nd edn 1893) III, 1688-1718.

[3]S Berger, *Histoire de la Vulgate pendant les premiers siècles du moyen age* (Paris 1893, repr New York 1961).

[4]Wordsworth-White, especially in *Pars Prior, Epilogus* (1898) 651-779. See also a summary of this research by M McNamara, *Studies on texts of early Irish Latin gospels (AD 600-1200)*, Instrumenta Patristica 20 (Steenbruge/Dordrecht 1990) 1-12.

[5]P Corssen, in his review of S Berger's work in *Göttingische gelehrte Anzeigen* 2 (1894) 855-75 (pp 862-66).

[6]Bonifatius Fischer, 'Bibelausgaben des frühen Mittelalters' in *La Bibbia nell'alto medieva*. Settimane di studio del centro italiano di studi sull'alto medievo 10 (Spoleto 1963) 519-600 (pp 524-25) (= B Fischer, *Lateinische Bibelhandschriften im frühen Mittelalter*. Aus der Geschichte der lateinischen Bibel 11 (Freiburg 1985) 54-55; Fischer, 'Das Neue Testament in lateinischer Sprache: der gegenwärtige Stand seiner Erforschung und seine Bedeutung für die griechische Textgeschichte' in *Die alten*

opinion that in the Split manuscript of the Chapter Library (now Split, Chapter Archives, MS 621), given the *siglum* P in the Stuttgart Vulgate, we have the bridge between Z and E of the Celtic/Irish group.[7] In the course of the same 1972 essay[8] he noted that in this matter of Latin gospel texts further progress could not be made by random tests, but only by systematic and major research.

When Fischer makes his next public appearance it is to announce the completion of his own major researches in the text of the Latin gospels. At the age of 71 in 1986 at a colloquium at Louvain-la-Neuve he announced the completion of his major work on the text of the Latin gospels, of the reason for it, and the principles behind it.[9] This work he published in four yearly volumes between 1988 and 1991.[10] After decades of study Fischer reveals the immensity of the task confronting us in the study of the text of the Latin gospels. He expresses reservations on Wordsworth-White's division into two large classes, and this on the basis of some thirty manuscripts. In the introduction to this new work he notes that no genuine progress can be made until the task is properly confronted. We cannot speak of text type or text relationship until this has been done. The only classification permitted at the moment, in his view, is a geographical one — according to the areas of composition or transcription. Codicological examination is of course permitted. The question of textual affiliations, however, can only be undertaken when a new study of the manuscripts has been completed. And in this manuscript study a cut-off point is necessary. This he takes to be the beginning of the tenth century with the multiplication of manuscripts in the Ottonian age. All indirect transmission through citations is also excluded.

In the introduction to the volumes Fischer expresses himself as follows:

> The critical text recension of the Gospels in the 'manual edition' (Handausgabe) of the Stuttgart Vulgate rests on sure foundations. And with this the certainty ends. With regard to the transmission of the text positions are put forward as certain which are really only assumptions. The researcher must venture forth unprejudiced, without map, into unknown territory and must himself outline his own plans, which may serve as a landmark, possibly even as a coordinate system, for future researchers. This in practice means that one can not select out a definite number of passages in the Gospels in which the manuscripts differ from

Übersetzungen des Neuen Testaments, die Kirchenväterzitate und Lektionare, ed Kurt Aland (Berlin, New York 1972) 1-92 (pp 37, 39, 53).

[7]B Fischer (1972, note 6 above) 37-39, 53, 55-56.

[8]ibid, p 8.

[9]B Fischer, 'Zur Überlieferung des lateinischen Textes der Evangelien' in *Recherches sur l'histoire de la Bible latine,* ed R Gryson and P M Bogaert, Cahiers de la Revue théologique de Louvain 1 (Louvain-la-Neuve 1967) 51-104.

[10]B Fischer, *Die lateinischen Evangelien bis zum 10. Jahrhundert,* I, *Varianten zu Matthäus,* II, *Varianten zu Markus,* III, *Varianten zu Lukas,* IV, *Varianten zu Johannes,* Aus der Geschichte der lateinischen Bibel 13, 15, 17, 18 (Freiburg 1988, 1989, 1990, 1991).

one another in a characteristic manner, for the purpose of bringing together for these texts the readings found in all the witnesses.[11]

Fischer's approach in the four volumes is to choose four test pericopes (*Probeabschnitte*) from each of the four gospels, amounting to about one tenth of the whole. In each of these sixteen pericopes there are about three hundred texts (*Stellen*) in which manuscripts differ: for Matthew and Mark together 2848 places, and for all four gospels 5690 places. For the study of these pericopes and texts Fischer makes an exhaustive examination of some four hundred and sixty-six pre-tenth-century manuscripts. These he divides into twenty-nine groups according to Old Latin text and geographical origin of the manuscripts: eg X (Old Latin, twenty-one/twenty-two MSS), Italy (J; twenty-six MSS, including Amb. I. 61 sup), Northumbria (N, nine), England (E, fifteen), Hibernia (Ireland-Wales-Scotland) (H, twenty-two MSS); Brittany (B, twenty-six), Gaul before Charlemagne (G, sixteen MSS, including Echternach Gospels, Ge), etc. He notes nine manuscripts with mixed texts and assigns them to the appropriate groups, eg the *codex Usserianus secundus* (r^2) as Hg and mull (I, thirty-five, Mulling) as Hm Hn, and gat. (Gatianum; thirty) as Bt.

It is obvious that the material presented by Fischer requires analysis and interpretation, and it is doubtful if anyone but Fr Fischer himself is capable of doing this. He is scheduled to provide this analysis in two forthcoming volumes in the same series, under the title: *Untersuchung und Auswertung des vorgelegten Materials aus den lateinischen Evangelien.*[12]

A question arising from Fischer's monumental work is whether any further study or classification or collation of Latin gospel manuscripts is indicated or even permissible until the implications of his exhaustive collation of one tenth of the gospel material has been assessed.

We know of twenty-nine Irish gospel texts, to which we can add four other related ones: Lichfield Gospels, Lichfield Cathedral Library, MS 1 (L); the related text of Hereford, Cathedral Library, P.I.2; Egerton Gospels, BL, MS Egerton 609 (E); Augsburg Gospels, Augsburg, Universitätsbibliothek MS I.2.4° 2.[13] Of these twenty-nine texts, one (r^1, *codex Usserianus primus*, TCD, MS 55) has a genuine Old Latin text; one is true Vulgate (Book of Durrow, TCD, MS 57); others have the mixed text (DLQR, Ep[mg], Oxford, Bodleian, MS Rawlinson G. 167), and others have not been properly studied, collated or classified. While questions remain about the existence of an Irish mixed family of texts in any meaningful sense of the word, the fact is that Irish texts do present a certain combination of non-Vulgate readings which must be taken account of. It is also a fact that this peculiar combination of

---

[11]Fischer (note 10 above) I, 7-8.
[12]See reviews of B Fischer's work by J K Elliott in *Journal of Theological Studies* NS 41 (1990) 637-40; 42 (1991) 282-82, 663-64; 43 (1992) 633-35.
[13]On the Augsburg Gospels see now Dáibhí Ó Cróinín, *Evangeliorum Epternacense* (*Universitätsbibliothek Augsburg, Cod. I.2.4° 2*): *a colour microfiche edition* (Munich 1988) 30-34 for biblical text and preliminaries.

readings is strongly attested in the glosses of the Echternach Gospels (Paris, BN, lat. 9389) from about AD 700. From this it would seem to follow that the mixed texts in question were known in Irish circles in Northumbria, and presumably in Iona, and in Ireland during the seventh century.

A certain amount of work on the collation of these Irish manuscripts has been done. The texts of DELQR and Ep have been collated for the Wordsworth-White edition of the Vulgate (D by John Gwynn; E by G M Youngman; Ep by H J White; L by F H A Scrivener; Q by T K Abbott[14] and R by I S J Johnson and G M Youngman). T K Abbott also collated *Usserianus secundus* (r^2), a collation which Hoskier also wrote on.[15] C Verey has collated the Durham Gospels,[16] with readings in places related to that of Irish gospel texts. H J Lawlor[17] and P Doyle[18] have collated part of the text of Mulling. Other scholars are working on the collation of Oxford, Bodleian, MS Auct. D.2.19 (Mac Regol or Rushworth Gospels) and Rawlinson G. 167.

The most thorough collation of any Irish text in modern times is that of Q (the Book of Kells) done by Patrick McGurk for the 1990 facsimile edition of this manuscript. In this work Dr McGurk tells us that for this collation he has made a fresh study, whether in microfilm or manuscript, of DELQR, of Ho (Rawlinson G. 167) and Ep (Paris, BN, MS lat. 9389).[19] We trust that he shall publish as much as possible of this material.

In 1986 and later the present writer gave a brief survey of the study of the Irish gospel text and put forward a plan for a study of the subject which, taking account of the work already done, would work towards a systematic examination, complete collation and, if needs be, edition of all the known manuscripts.[20]

---

[14]T K Abbott, *Evangeliorum versio antehieronymiana ex Codice Usseriano (Dublinensi), adjecta collatione Codicis Usseriani Alterius: accedit Versio Vulgata Sec. Cod. Amiatinum, cum varietate Cod. Kenanensis (Book of Kells) et Cod. Durmachensis (Book of Durrow)* (Dublin 1884).

[15]H C Hoskier, *The text of Codex Usserianus 2, r_2 ('Garland of Howth'): with critical notes to supplement and correct the collation of the late T K Abbott*, Old Latin biblical texts (London 1919).

[16]C D Verey, 'A collation of the gospel texts contained in Durham, Cathedral MSS A.II.10, A.II.16 and A.II.17' (unpublished MA thesis, University of Durham, 1969); idem, 'Notes on the gospel text', 'Inventory and textual collation of the Durham Gospels' in *The Durham Gospels*, ed C D Verey, T Julian Brown, E Coatsworth, Early English Manuscripts in Facsimile 20 (Copenhagen 1980) 68-76; 76-105; 'The gospel texts at the time of St Cuthbert' in *St Cuthbert, his cult and his community to AD 1200*, ed G Bonner, D Rollason and C Stancliffe (Woodbridge 1989) 142-50.

[17]H J Lawlor, *Chapters on the Book of Mulling* (Edinburgh 1897).

[18]Peter Doyle, 'A study of the text of St Matthew's Gospel in the Book of Mulling and the palaeography of the whole manuscript' (unpublished PhD dissertation, National University of Ireland, 1967); Doyle, 'The text of St Luke's Gospel in the Book of Mulling', PRIA (C) 73 (1973) 177-200.

[19]McGurk, 'Gospel Text', 59-152 (pp 62-63).

[20]Martin McNamara, 'The text of the Irish Latin gospels', in *Folio*, the Newsletter for the Ancient Biblical Manuscript Center for Preservation and Research, Claremont, CA, 6 (Fall 1986); McNamara, *Studies on texts of early Irish Latin gospels (AD 600 - 1200)*, Instrumenta Patristica 20 (Steenbruge-Dordrecht 1990) 8-11.

After the publication of Bonifatius Fischer's four volumes the question arises whether such an approach is permitted and whether given the problems involved it is likely to lead anywhere. Invaluable as Fischer's monumental work is, I do not believe it dispenses with the desirability (indeed the necessity) of complete collation of individual manuscripts. Each individual manuscript does have a personality, an individuality, all its own which is not revealed when reduced to the status of a cipher in a large collection, not to speak of a collection totalling four hundred and sixty-six manuscripts. While the exhaustive analysis of the sixteen pericopes from the gospels put before us by B Fischer opens up new vistas for gospel study and permits us to situate any particular reading within the complete context as known to us, I think that there remains a number of aspects of individual gospel texts which this evidence does not reveal. To illustrate by a few examples from Irish or Irish-related gospel texts: the Echternach Gospels (Ge in Fischer's list) appear to have at least one hundred non-Vulgate readings which agree with the MacDurnan Gospels (London, Lambeth Palace Library, MS 1370) and with other gospel texts of Armagh provenance.[21] Seventeen of these occur in the pericopes collated fully by Fischer, where they are shown to be rare readings. In his introduction to the four volumes (p 6*) Fischer notes that Hs (the Irish Gospels in Sankt Gallen, Stiftsbibliothek 51) in his section 11 (Matthew 2:19-4:17) is found to be as far removed from the Vulgate as the Latin text of *Codex Bezae* and scarcely less removed than the Old Latin *Codex Bobiensis*. With regard to this one must observe that while this is true for the earlier chapters of Matthew, there are many 'Irish' readings in the later chapters of codex 51, and throughout St John there is an altogether extraordinarily close correspondence between Hs and the Irish texts D (the Book of Armagh) and R (the Mac Regol or Rushworth Gospels).[22]

While a new era in the study of the Latin gospels has probably been ushered in by the painstaking researches of Bonifatius Fischer in his four-volume *magnum opus*, there still remains a place for collation of individual manuscripts. However, any collation against the limited evidence of Wordsworth-White will now have to bear in mind the exhaustive collation of Fischer for the select pericopes. A full collation against this critical edition of Wordsworth-White will have to guard against the pitfalls of such an exercise. One danger is that in the consideration of the agreement of variant readings of a particular manuscript with the 'Irish' or DELQR group, the researcher may ignore the quality of this agreement and also the many disagreements that may exist in other readings. Some of the agreements may be merely orthographical, or in the form of personal and place names. What seems indicated in the present state of research is that the interested person carry out a full collation of individual manuscripts against the Stuttgart critical edition and the apparatus of Wordsworth-White and then

---

[21]See Martin McNamara, 'The Echternach and Mac Durnan Gospels: some common readings and their significance', *Peritia* 6-7 (1987-88) 217-22 (in slightly revised form in McNamara (note 4 above) 102-11.
[22]See McNamara (note 4 above) 113-60, 244-45.

test provisional conclusions deriving from this against the full collation for select pericopes of Fischer. This I have done for the gospel of Matthew in Codex Ambrosiana I.61 sup.

Collation of Milan, Biblioteca Ambrosiana, MS I. 61 sup. : Matthew
Cod. Amb. I. 61 sup. (now S. P. 10, 21) came to the Ambrosian Library, Milan, from the monastery of Bobbio and has a fifteenth-century Bobbio ex-libris. It is a work that has received relatively little attention. Samuel Berger examined its text for his history of the Vulgate.[23] He notes that it does not have the large Irish interpolations although Irish readings abound in it. He expresses the view that it was not at all impossible that the manuscript was copied at Bobbio itself (rather than in Ireland). E A Lowe gives a rather detailed description of the manuscript:[24]

> Irish majuscule, saec. VII[2] ... The typical Insular abbreviations are lacking in the text (but the *autem*-symbol) ɧ occurs in additions by scribe and early corrections ...Spelling shows confusion between **e** and **i** but not the Irish misuse of **s** for **ss**... the **Q** at the beginning of Luke (fol. 46) shows the fish motif and fringe-like finial strongly redolent of North Italy. Parchment prepared in the Irish manner and rough to the touch, except for foll. 69-74, 77-82, 86-87, prepared in the Continental manner. Script is an Irish majuscule by more than one hand... Marginal entries in early uncial (fol. 2), in cursive (foll. 1v ...) and in various Irish hands (fol. 15 etc.). ... Written by Irish scribes, probably at Bobbio.

Bonifatius Fischer has included the codex in his study of the Latin gospels and has completely collated sixteen passages from it, four for each gospel: for Matthew (1) 2:19-4:17; (2) 8:2-9:6; (3) 16:9-17-7; (4) 26:39-58; 27:29-46. He includes it among the twenty six manuscripts of his Italian group of texts (J) and assigns it the *siglum* Ji and dates it as from the first half of the seventh century.[25]

The manuscript Amb. I.61 sup. has been noted in the more recent studies of insular and continental parchment and the early history of the Bobbio Scriptorium.[26] It is regarded by Di Majo, Federici and Palma as belonging to a group with a characteristic mixture of insular and continental parchment, who assign a date (in a general way) to the second half of the eighth century.[27] They also note that according to Engelbert[28] and Brown[29] the

[23]S Berger (note 3 above) 58-59.
[24]*CLA* (1938) III, no 350
[25]Fischer (note 10 above) 14*.
[26]E G Anna Di Majo, Carlo Federici and Marco Palma, 'Indagini sulla pergamena insulare (secoli VII-XVI)', *Scriptorium* 42 (1988) 131-39; P Engelbert, 'Zur Frühgeschichte des Bobbieser Skriptoriums', *Revue Bénédictine* 78 (1968) 220-60.
[27]Di Majo (note 26 above) 136. Thus also Englebert, p 243 and n 4.
[28]Engelbert (note 26 above) 243, n 4.
[29]T J Brown, 'The Irish element in the insular system of scripts to circa AD 800' in *Die Iren und Europa im früheren Mittelalter*, ed H Löwe (Stuttgart 1982) 109. The parchment, they also note, is described as 'vellum', except for folios 69-74, 77-82, 86-87.

manuscript is of Bobbio origin. In his treatment of the matter Engelbert cites G Mercati's words on the Irish at Bobbio after Columbanus: *La documentazione della presenza d'Irlandesi a Bobbio dopo S. Columbano è nulla per il secolo VII, minima per l'VIII e il IX.*[30]

The biblical text of the manuscript has never been fully examined. On the presumption that it was written in Bobbio, rather than in Ireland, one might assume that it represents an Italian rather than the mixed Irish text. The present writer has undertaken a full collation of its text and has completed it for Matthew's gospel.[31] The collation was based on the Stuttgart edition of the Vulgate. Variants from this amounted to eight hundred and forty-four. As a first stage these were compared with the critical apparatus of the critical edition of Wordsworth-White (from about thirty manuscripts). A computer analysis of this admittedly limited collation indicated a very strong affiliation with the 'Irish' group, DELQR, Ep. The affiliations were as follows:

1. Amb agrees with L in four hundred and sixty four variants.
2. Amb agrees with R in three hundred and seventy variants.
3. Amb agrees with E in three hundred variants.
4. Amb agrees with D in two hundred and ninety-nine variants.
5. Amb agrees with Q in two hundred and four variants.
6. Amb agrees with Ep in one hundred and ninety-five variants (Ep[1] 8; Ep[mg] 33).

The agreement of Amb with multiple DELQR texts out of eight hundred and forty-four is as follows: with DE one hundred and nineteen times; with DEL twelve; with DELQ five; with DELQR four; with DE Ep sixty-three; with EL one hundred and twenty-seven; with ELQ four; with LQ sixty-six; with LQR forty-nine; with LR seventy-eight; with DLR ten; with DL three; with QR thirty-two.

It might appear from this evidence that the text of Amb. I. 61 sup. is to be regarded as Irish rather than Italian. Any such conclusion, however, would be unwarranted without situating the text in the fuller tradition as put before us by Bonifatius Fischer. As a second stage of the investigation I compared the variants with the full Italian (J) and Celtic (H: Ireland, Scotland, Wales) evidence as presented by Fischer for the four pericopes of Matthew. This showed the complexity of the situation, and indicated that no such conclusion as to marked Irish affiliations could be drawn. The evidence which seems to emerge from this fuller collation is that the variants of Amb. I.61 sup. are well attested both in the Italian (J) and Irish

---

[30]Engelbert (note 26 above) 243, with reference to G Mercati, *De fatis bibliothecae monasterii S. Columbani Bobiensis* ... (Città del Vaticano 1934) 24.

[31]M McNamara, 'Non-Vulgate readings of Codex Amb. I.61 sup. I. The Gospel of Matthew', *Sacris Erudiri* 33 (1992) 183-257. The *Vetus Latina* readings are examined in an essay of the same heading in *Philologia Sacra. Biblische und patristische Studien für Hermann J Frede und Walter Thiele zu ihrem siebzigsten Geburtstag*, I, ed Roger Gryson, Aus der Geschichte der lateinischen Bibel 24/1(Freiburg i. Br. 1993)177-92.

(H) group of texts, sometimes more strongly in one than in the other.[32] A more detailed analysis of the Amb readings which are attested in no known Vulgate manuscript (and hence presumably *Vetus Latina*) revealed nothing spectacular. No affiliation with any particular *Vetus Latina* manuscript (whether Irish, r[1] or Italian) became apparent. What conclusions will emerge for this manuscript from Bonifatius Fischer's work I cannot say. As illustration of the method involved I give here an example of both collations, against the apparatus of Wordsworth-White, and then against the Italian (J), Irish (H) and *Vetus Latina* (X) texts as presented in the last section of Fischer's fourth pericope for Matthew, ie Matthew 27:29-46.

Matthew 27:29-46 collated against Wordsworth-White's apparatus

27:29	capud *(caput)*	=BRT
27:29	arundinem *(harundinem)*	=θJLORTW
27:29	in dexteram eius *(in dextera eius)*	-am DθJKLQR
27:29	aue *(haue)*	=DθJK MTr RVW
27:30	acciperunt arundinem *(acceperunt harund.)*	acciperunt DE Ep LO* arund- Ep θJKLORTW
27:30	capud *(caput)*	=BERWY
27:30	clamidem *(clamydem)*	=BE Ep FOR^c
27:31	induerunt uestimentis eius *(induerunt eum uest. eius)*	om. eum E
27:32	inuenerunt hominem Cyreneum uenientem obuiam sibi nomine Symonem hunc angarazauerunt ut tolleret *(inuenerunt hominem Cyreneum* *nomine Simonem hunc* *angariauerunt)*	+uenientem obuiam (obiam X²) sibi, B Ep^mg ILO*^sax RX*², Y^cz; illis E; uenientem in obiam sibi Q Symonem, CDEJWX*; angarizauerunt

---

[32] It is also worth noting that the readings of Amb. I.61 sup. do not coincide with the gospel of Matthew used by Columbanus; for this see G S M Walker, *Sancti Columbani Opera*, Scriptores Latini Hiberniae 11 (Dublin 1970) 216-20 (pp 217-18 for Matthew's gospel) and McNamara (1992, note 31 above) 195-96.

Matthew

		DE Ep^{1} LQR; angariszau-E; -garaz- unique
27:34	(cum felle) mixto *(cum f. mixtum)*	=J
27:35	diuiserunt sibi uestimenta *(diuiserunt uestimenta)*	=BQX
27:35	et (puncta *above and below*) sorte mittentes *(sortem mittentes)*	sorte VL f
27:35	(mittentes) ut inpler- etur quod dictum est per profetam dicentem diuiserunt sibi uestimenta (mea interl.) et super uestem meam miserunt sortem. Et sedentes *(mittentes. Et sedentes)*	=*(with minor variants, in* W/W) ABE Ep^{mg} H^{c} θKMTr O*QWXYZ
27:37	capud *(caput)*	=BR
27:40	(dicentes) ua qui distruebas templum Dei et in triduo illud reaedificabas *(dicentes qui destruit templum* *et in triduo illud reaedificat)*	ua BD Ep^{mg} ILO^{c} QR distruebas ... reaedificabas Ep^{mg} QRX*; VL MSS
27:40	(si filius Dei es) et discende (*si filius Dei es descende*)	+ et VL *a b c d h*
27:41	inludentes eum cum scribis (*inl. cum scribis*)	+ eum E; VL *c f* ff^{2} *h q* r^{2}
27:41	cum scribis et fariseis (*cum scribis et senioribus*)	Pharisaeis θ, VL *a b* ff^{2} *q*
27:42	discendat *(descendat)*	= D Ep LO^{c} R
27:42	et credimus *(et credemus)*	credimus Vg W/W

Matthew

27:43   credat in Deo   credat unique
        (confidet in Deo)

27:44   qui crucifixi erant   crucifixi Vg W/W
        (qui fixi erant)

27:46   lama zabathani   =W; lamasbatha L
        (lema sabacthani)

27:46   Deus Deus meus   om. Deus 1° JQX*
        (Deus meus Deus meus)

27:46   quare me dereliquisti   quare ERT
        (ut quid dereliquisti me)   > me d. EJLOg¹ RT

Matthew 27:29-46 in B Fischer's complete collation (J in italics; H in bold type).

27:29   capud   =BRT
        caput)

27:29   arundinem   =θJLORTW
        (harundinem)

27:29   in dexteram eius   -am Fischer 1418Oh:
        (in dextera eius)   Xbf*r?ho *Jf*gji* Ed Ge
                                         Hflhwsrmgqd² iebxyz

27:29   aue   Fischer 14185w: Xclo
        (haue)   *Jivuet* Ed
                                         Hsrmngqdabxz

27:30   acciperunt arundinem   acciperunt Fischer
        (acceperunt harund.)   14188v: *Jyo* Ed
                                         Hlhwsmngqdabyz
                                         Be Ge
                                         arund- Ep θJKLORTW

27:30   capud   =BERWY
        (caput)

27:30   clamidem   =BE Ep FORᶜ (et multi)
        (clamydem)

27:31   induerunt uestimentis eius   om. eum, Fischer 14198b:
        (induerunt eum uest. eius)   *Ji* **Hw** Bekx*v Uz* Oe Ze
                                         CO Iz*

Matthew

27:32 inuenerunt hominem
       Cyreneum uenientem obuiam
       sibi nomine Symonem hunc
       angarazauerunt ut tolleret
       (inuenerunt hominem Cyreneum
       nomine Simonem hunc
       angariauerunt)

+uenientem obuiam
sibi nomine simonem
(vel sim.), Fischer 14205z:
Xcaf*r?h *Jwziqo*^{2}x*. $^3d^2$ *blvt*
Hlhwsrmngqiexz Be Ge^2
Symonem Fischer 14208i:
*Jriyx*lt* **Hd Be**
angarazau- unique, Fischer
14209t; angarizauerunt Nr
Ear Be Ge^2
Hflhwrmngqdie*abxyz*

27:34 (cum felle) mixto
       (cum f. mixtum)

Fischer 14218i: *Jji*
Sdm Gb*t Th* Fgq Ld*

27:35 diuiserunt sibi uestimenta
       (diuiserunt uestimenta)

+ sibi, Fischer 14226h:
Xdcabhql *Jyix?* Ebc
Hqie*xyz

27:35 et (puncta *above and below*)
       sorte mittentes
       (sortem mittentes)

sorte Fischer
14229 *Ji* (no **H**)

27:35 (mittentes) ut inpler-
       etur quod dictum est per
       profetam dicentum diuiserunt
       sibi uestimenta (mea interl.) et
       super uestem meam miserunt
       sorte. Et sedentes
       (mittentes. Et sedentes)

add. with minor variants,
Fischer 14230w: Xabrhq;
*Jwziqo*xd^{2}blvu* Be
Hsm*gqex
Ep^{mg}

27:37 capud
       (caput)

=BR

27:40 (dicentes) ua qui
       distruebas templum Dei et
       in triduo illud reaedificabas
       (dicentes qui destruit templum
       et in triduo illud reaedificat)

+ua Fischer 14259v:
Xdcabfrhgl
Jrfwyio^{2}xd^2 *bvu** Ee
Hflhwsrmgqdie*by Ge^2
(=Ep^{mg})
distruebas, Fischer
14261h Xbho *Ji* Ee
Hlhwsrm*qix Bt^1 el*
reaedificabas, Fischer
14265h: Xbho *Ji* Ee
Hlhwsrm*qi Bt^{1}e
Ep^{mg} (=Ge^2)

Matthew

27:40   (si filius Dei es) et   + et, Fischer 14267h
        discende   (+t): Xdcabrh *Ji* Ec
        (si filius Dei es descende)   **Hg** (+**Hb**, om. si) Bek*

27:41   inludentes eum cum scribis   +eum, Fischer
        (inl. cum scribis)   14276h: Xcr?hqo *Jgiq*
                                                  Hfm²gqia Be

27:41   cum scribis et fariseis   pharisaeis. Fischer
        (cum scribis et senioribus)   14279g: Xdcabfrhq *Ji*
                                                  Ee **Hgx**

27:42   discendat   =D Ep LO^cR (et multi;
                                                  Fischer *(descendat)*
                                                  14287v)

27:42   et credimus   credimus Vg W/W;
        (et credemus)   Fischer 14289w:
                                                  Xcabfrhglo
                                                  Jrwmjzyiqoxdblvuetk
                                                  Hflwsrgexyz* Ge

27:43   credat in Deo   credat unique;
        (confidet in Deo)   Fischer 12493r

27:44   qui crucifixi erant   crucifixi Vg W/W;
        (qui fixi erant)   Fischer 14302w:
                                                  Xcabfho *Jw²mg jz²* iobvuetk
                                                  Hhmq²dieabxyz Be

27:46   lama zabathani   lama, Fischer
        (lema sabacthani)   14316w: Xdbfh *Jyix²*
                                                  Ed **Hlwsrmdeabyz**
                                                  zabathani, Fischer
                                                  14317h: *Ji* Ee **Hm*** Uv²
                                                  Zy*Fy²

27:46   Deus Deus meus   om. Deus 1°, Fischer
        (Deus meus Deus meus)   14219s: Xhqlo
                                                  *Js*ji*x** Ev **Hwsm*q**

27:46   quare me dereliquisti   quare. Fischer
        (ut quid dereliquisti me)   14320h: *Jv* **Hrgq** Be
                                                  (also Stu Wdes Gk Vh² Qb)
                                                  > me d. Fischer 14321s:
                                                  Xdcabfhglo *Jswgo²x*vt*
                                                  Hlhwsrmgqdieabxyz Be

The text of the Book of Kells

The Book of Kells has fared better than most biblical Irish gospel manuscripts with regard to the study of its text. It has been collated by T K Abbott,[33] and this work has been published by Wordsworth and White.[34] Dr G O Simms collated the entire manuscript against the critical edition of Wordsworth-White, and these variants with the corresponding Vulgate text were published in the first facsimile edition of Kells.[35] Christopher Verey studied the text of Q in his collation of the Durham Gospels (Durham, Cathedral Library, MS A. II. 17). He notes that John and Mark in Durham are almost certainly derived from a text closely akin to that of O (Oxford, Bodleian, MS Auct. D. 2. 14 (s. VII ?; written possibly in Rome; in Fischer Jo) and Luke quite possibly so.[36] He also notes that the readings shared with O provide indications of certain other relationships. In John over 90% of O (X) readings are also found in Q (as far as John 17:13, where Q ends). A much smaller proportion, some 50%, are also found in other members of the so-called 'Irish' group, but not consistently in any one. This altogether close relationship of Durham Gospels with Q might be explained by direct descent of Q from the Durham Gospels and with very few intermediaries, or they could be very close relatives descended from a common archetype. He gives twenty-two readings of Durham (John) found also only in Q.[37] The relationship of Q with Durham (which extends through Mark and Luke but nowhere to the same degree as in John) raises the question whether Durham is an Irish text. The influence of Italian gospel books (such as is O) in Anglo-Saxon England is an accepted fact. But together with the Italian mission in England there was also the Irish one from Iona and Irish missionaries could also have introduced gospel books which are likely to have been copied in England. It is thus conceivable that the Durham Gospels could derive from an archetype of Irish descent, of which same archetype Q was a parallel, but later, descendant.[38]

He goes on to note, however, that the question of the origin of Q is complex, and Q does not appear to show distinct indications of Northumbrian influence. In the first place the close relationship (of Durham) with Q does not extend to other members of the so-called Irish family, DELR and Ep[mg]. The list of readings shared with O (X; X = S. Augustini; Cambridge, CCCol 286; end of s. VI; Rome? Jx) shows that while many are also found in Q, few are found in DELR and Ep[mg]. Overall only about half of the all variants shared with Q are also found in DELR and Ep[mg]. In this context Verey further notes that the differences in levels of agreement reflects the fact that

---

[33] Abbott (note 14 above).
[34] Wordsworth-White (note 4 above).
[35] *Codex Cenannensis*.
[36] Verey (1980, note 16 above) 72.
[37] ibid, 73. They are at John 1:23; 3:14 (collated in Fischer); 4:17; 5:6; 6:19; 8:7 (collated in Fischer); 8:19; 8:25; 8:46; 9:28; 9:40; 11:33; 11:39; 11:44; 13:29; 15:18; 15:22; 16:4; 16:22; 16:25; 16:33 (Q ends at 17:13). Unfortunately only two of these texts (3:14; 8:7) are in the four pericopes for John (John 2:18-3:31; 7:28-8:16; 12:17-13:6; 20:1-21:4) analysed by Fischer (note 10 above) vol 4. See further below.
[38] Verey (1980, note 16 above) 73.

DELQREp^{mg} differ significantly between themselves. For reasons he has referred to earlier there are doubts as to whether one can talk about an 'Irish' textual family.[39] Much of the common stock of these manuscripts reflects a shared attitude towards the text which is also found in many books from Anglo-Saxon England.

There is no *a priori* reason, in Verey's view, why the relationship of Durham and Q, which was written possibly up to a generation later, should be presumed to derive from an early type imported in Northumbria from Ireland. The most probable conclusion to be drawn from the evidence is that Durham derives from a text-type close to O (or possibly O itself), imported from Italy, and that the same type was followed in Q John and that the link between the O(X) and Q goes through, or very close by, Durham itself. With the exception of the Hebrew names, nothing in the prefatory matter of Durham appears to derive from the Irish in Northumbria.

Non-Vulgate readings of Q compared with Bonifatius Fischer's collation
The most thorough examination of the text of Q made to date is by Patrick McGurk for the recent facsimile edition.[40] McGurk was unable to use Fischer's analysis (published in 1991) for his examination of the biblical text of Q John, of which he has given a full collation. I here give the fuller evidence for the Q variants in the pericopes fully collated by Fischer (ie John 2:18-3:31; 7:28-8:16; 12:17-13:6). I believe the new evidence tends to corroborate the conclusions arrived at by Verey on the special relationship of Q with the text of the Durham Gospels (Fischer's Ef). Before the Q reading I give that of the Stuttgart Vulgate in brackets.
Note: Hu=St Gallen, Stiftsbibliothek 60 (St John's gospel); Jo=O of Wordsworth-White: Oxford, Bodleian, MS Auct. D.2.14 ('Gospels of St Augustine'); Jy=Split, Chapter Library s.n.; E (English group; Ef: Durham, Cathedral Library, MS A.II.17); Ge=Paris, BN, lat. 9389 (Echternach Gospels).

John

2:19   (respondit) respondens, *only in* Hqzw Fm Lmr.

2:22   (resurrexisset) surrexisset, X1 Ns Ef Hrt^{2}qc Btr Sb Tt1*b Uv^{2}lad Oh*k* Ze Cz Qk Ycr.

3:1   (Nicodemus nomine) nomine Nicodemus (vel sim), Xbf1 Jju Evc Huq Btwes*cg Wceo Gmrt^2 Dw*. (*The orthography* nicodimus *is common in Irish texts; also in* Jio^2, *and some others.*)

[39]ibid, 70.
[40]McGurk, 'Gospel text', 59-102.

John

3:2   (Deus) Dominus, Xc Jjz^{2}qox^{2}hluek Edhrb Hfhosrmtqdacxy Bbkalmods*z G(5 *MSS*) A(11) T(19) U(8) O(9)m V(6) Z(12) P(11) C(11) Q(2) R(4) K(10) Y(12) M(4) D(3) F(10) L(8) I(3).

3:3   (denuo) de nouo Ji Nr* Edh* Hfhosr (de nauo) mtuqdiacyz Gert*.

3:4   (iterato) rursus Hqcz Efrco J(7 MSS) B(8) T(20) *and some other texts.*

3:4   (nasci) renasci. *In* H *only* Hq; *also in* Xeabfr?j?ql Jriol Nr Bbams^{2}c^2 *and some other texts.*

3:5   (spiritu) + sancto Xafr? Jw* Nr Efhva Hfhosrmtuqdiabyz B(11, *including* Be) S(5) W(3) G(7) *and other texts.*

3:6   (caro est) + quia de carne natum est (*vel sim.*) Xeabfrjq*; Jz*oxt Nr Efb Huq Bw, *and nine other texts.*

3:6   (spiritu spiritus est) + quia Deus spiritus est et ex Deo natus est Xaj? Jz*ob Nr Efb Hq Sdm*? Gr^{2}t^{2}u* Ta*? Oh^{2}mf* Vm Zw Kh Ye*f Mc*k. (*All* H *witnesses, apart from* Hq, *have the ed. cr. reading.*)

3:7   (denuo) de nouo, Ji Nr* Efdh* Hfhosrmtuqdiabyz Ger^{2}t^2.

3:8   (spirat) aspirat, Jqoh Efc* Hqzw.

3:10   (magister) + in, Xca Jwj^{2}ziqoxbvdk Nr*fr Efhvarbc^{2}o Hfhsrmuqdiabxyz, *and several other texts.*

3:12   (credetis) creditis Xfl Jw^{2}yq*hv* Nfr Ehab*c Hosrqy Bwhamoxy Sx Weso Gkd*f*hm*ru* Tt Oh*k*p* Zw Pb*kf*t*w, *and twenty other texts.*

3:13   (in caelum) in caelo, Xq Ef*f Hqac Wbo Gg. (*The other Irish,* H, *texts have* in caelum, *as has* Be.)

3:14   (Moses exaltauit) exaltauit Moyses; *inversion only* in Ef Hoqb.

3:16   (Deus) + hunc, Xa?r?jq Jcg Nr Efhv Hformtqdiacbyz Btek*a*eg Ge^{2}mrt Kc^{2}Dw*.

3:20   (mala) male, *most texts* (*ed. cr.* Huax), *including* Jio, Ef, Hfhosrmtqdicbyz, Be.

3:23   (Iohannes) Iohannis, Xel^2 Jio Nr Efdghc Hhosrmuqab Btwec Sh Gd*gh*e^{2}t*u* Pb Ce* Mc* Dw* Fm (Iohannes Hfticxyz).

John

3:23 (adueniebant) + multi, Xr?j Jwk² Efhvac Hfsrmtuqdicb Bts* Gmrt
Aq² Zs² Pa*?b² k Dw Fgke; (+ multi ad eum, Hhz; *ed. cr. includes*
Horxy Jio Ed).

3:24 (Iohannes) Iohannis, Xebfrj Jio Efdghac Hhosrtuqdiabyz* Btwe
Ggh*e²u* Pb* Ce* Ke* Mc*t Fmr*.

3:27 (Iohannes) Iohannis Xbfq Jiq*o Nr Efdghv*ac Hbosrtuqaz Btwes*
Ggh*e²u* Aj Pb* ce* Fmi*h Lt*.

3:28 (mihi testimonium) testimonium mihi, Xa?bf Ef Hqabyz Tp Ve Ze
Ca² Qi Kg; (*ed. cr. includes* Jo Hfhsrtudicx Be).

3:29 (eum) + et, Xer? Jy nr² Ef Hfqb Bs* Gu Of*t Zb Pp*.

7:29 (ego) + autem, Xdcbfr Jg Efc Hq Be Zvz Pa² Ch² Kl. (*other H texts,*
Hfhosrmndlacbxyz, *and* Jio *have* Vg *reading*).

7:29 (scio eum) + et si dixero quia nescio eum ero similis uobis mendax
et scio eum. *This, or similar words, added in* Jwzodblouk Nr Efvak
Be (*of* B *with* 10 MSS), Wes G(6) A(2) T(7) U(7) O(7) V(2) z(4)
P(11) C(6) Qx Ri³ K(4) Y(2) D(3) F(7) L(6); of H only Hq.

7:34, (quaeretis) quaeritis, *in several MSS:* X(7) J(18, *including* Jio) N(5)
36 E(7), Hfhosrmuqdiacbxyz, etc. *In general* quaeritis *outnumbers*
quaeretis *in these verses by ratio of about 6:4 and 5:4.*

7:35 (se) semet; *witnesses for* semet (*with* Homqx, Jio etc) *outweigh* se (*with*
Hfhsudiacbyz) *by ratio of* 6.5:1.5.

7:35 (inueniemus) inuenimus (eum), Nr Ef* Hhosrqa Bik*aqns* Sx* We
Ta*k* Ud Oh* Vrb² Rnw* Kl Fiv Lb*. (Inueniemus, *ed. cr. includes*
Jio Hfudcbxy.)

7:36 (ego) + uos; uos MSS (*including* Jio Hfosmqdabx Be) *outweigh ed. cr.*
(*including* Hhruicyz) *by approximate ratio of* 6.5:1.5.

7:39 (non) nondum; *MSS with* nondum (*including* Hqx *only of* H, Jio)
outweigh ed. cr. (*including* Hfhosrmudiacbyz) *by approximate ratio of*
5.5:3.5.

7:39 (spiritus) + datus. *MSS with* + datus (*including* Jio
Hhosrmqdiacbxyz Be) *far outweigh those with the ed. cr.* (ie Xz
Jsrfcz*h Nys*f Gg Pg).

7:45 (ergo) igitur, (*only in*) Efd Hrtuqc Ge².

John

7:46   (hic homo) homo loquitur (om. hic; + loquitur), Hq Zw* Kl; hic
       homo loquitur Ef etc. Ji.

7:51   (ab ipso prius) prius ab ipso (Fischer, vol 4, 42244h): primum ab
       ipso vel sim., Xdafg Efdc Hrtuqc Btes*g Gt* Rvxz Kc* Fmq.

7:52   (scrutari) + scripturas, Hq, Jio Er; + scripturas et uide, *many MSS
       including* Hfosrmtudicbxyz, Be.

8:6   (autem, 2°) om. *only* Hq Bn*.

8:6   (terra) terram, Xdf Jzyioblk Nr Efd Hfhormtuqdiacyz B(11,
       including Be) Schx Wde² Gige Ta² Uc Otk Zq²xv Pgq Cfg Kl Dw*j*x
       Lamt*b Iz.

8:7   (primus) primum, Jy Ef Hsq*a Bm Sb Co.

8:10   (erigens autem se) erigens se autem, Jy Ef Hq St We.

8:10   (sunt) + qui te accusant, Jw*jax*l Nv Ea Hft (accussant) q Be Gt* Of*
       Kl Fpf Izsct; *most MSS (including* Hhosrmugd²iacbyz) *have* qui te
       accusabant.

8:12   (eis) omits. Xr? Hftuqi Bt* Sx Ua Os Vw Kl.

8:12   (lucem) lumen Xecbrl Jgu*k Efa*o Hfhosrmtuqdiacbyxz;
       Btebhi*jkaqmnos*xycvzg² So (*and sixty-nine other MSS from
       different groups*). Jio, *as most MSS, have* lucem. Also Htuk.

8:14   (unde uenio) unde unde ueniam, *only* Hq; unde ueniam Xe
       Jwjzoxhblk Efaro Ba¹Sd*m*x T(19) U(6) O(7) Vb Pqw Cep Kl Ybs
       Mc*?k Dj*? Ffgke Ltd*.

8:14   (uado) uadam, *many texts, including* Xa, Efaro Hq (*only text in* H)
       T(19) U(6) (8).

8:16   (iudicium), iudicium corr. ex iudicioum, Hq *alone.*

12:19 (ergo) autem, Xcfrl Jgji*e Efdrc Hfhrtuqiabyz Bte Get Te Kw*?.

12:21 (accesserunt), *omits. Not registered in Fischer.*

12:22 (andreae) andrae, Htuqi Btbmc* Ge* Tt Cw Kb Lg. (*Many Irish, H,
       texts have* andriae, Hfhmby.)

12:24 (uobis) + quia, Rf, Hrqc *only.*

John

12:27   (saluifica me) saluum me fac, *many MSS including* J (9, *including* Jo),
         Efarc*o Hq Bkrnds*z Sdm*x Wes Grt²u* T(20) U(7) O(5) Vb Zaw
         P(3) C(4) Qi R(3) Kl Yb Djm F(2) Lt Iz.

12:27   (ex hora hac) ex hac hora (vel sim.; *many MSS*), Xecabfrl Jrgx*e Nr*
         Efa*bc Hfsmqcbyz B(12), *and about fifty more MSS from different
         groups. (Ed. cr.* Xdz Hhortudiox Jio Be.)

In Q, John 12:28-13:20 is missing and the text of John ends defectively at
John 17:13 on folio 339v. Fischer's two final pericopes are John 12:17-13:6;
20:1-21:4.

Q John, Durham A.II.17 and the date of the Book of Kells

There is little, if anything, that can be added to what Patrick McGurk has
written on the biblical text of Q, apart from what may be implications of the
relationship of the Q text of John to that of Durham A.II.17. Before we come
to this we must first treat of certain more general questions of Kells, which
seem preliminary to any fuller consideration of the biblical text. These are
the book's structure (gatherings etc), the illumination and its relation to the
text, the scribes and the presumed date of the work.

It is theoretically possible that individual gospels in a gospel book may once
have had independent existence and have had separate transmission
histories. This is the case in the Book of Mulling.[41] This, however, is not the
case with Kells. The gatherings show that it was designed from the
beginning as one book. This, of course, does not mean that all its gospels
had the same history of composition or transmission.

It appears that the work's biblical text must be studied in conjunction with
the illumination, not independent of it. The two have been planned to go
together. We cannot quite exclude the possibility that a particular 'biblical'
reading was chosen by reason of an accompanying illumination page. Thus,
for instance, the otherwise unattested addition in folio 113v *quod confringitur
pro saeculi vita* to *Hoc est corpus meum* at Matthew 26:26.[42] This stands
opposite the picture of what appears to be the arrest of Christ.

The hands of Kells have been studied in detail by Bernard Meehan in the
companion volume to the 1990 facsimile edition.[43] The subject is also
discussed in detail in other papers in this volume. The prevailing view

---

[41]See J F Kenney, *Sources for the early history of Ireland: ecclesiastical* (Columbia
University Press 1929) 632.
[42]No corresponding text has been identified in Greek manuscripts. For Matthew
26:26 see S C E Legg, *Nouum Testamentum secundum textum Wescotto-Hortianum.
Euangelium secundum Matthaeum cum apparatu critico nouo plenissimo* (Oxford 1940).
At Matthew 26:26 the *Vetus Latina ff¹* adds *quod pro uobis tradetur* to *Hoc est corpus
meum,* and at the corresponding text in Mark 14:22) the *Vetus Latina a (Codex
Vercellensis)* adds *quod pro multis confringitur in remissionem peccatorum.*
[43]Meehan, 245-56.

today is that the Book of Kells was written at Iona. In 1978 J J G Alexander wrote[44] : '... neither its date, nor the place of its origin, nor the sources of its style and iconography are established. Older scholarship dated it to the early eighth century'.[45] Friend, he notes,[46] argued for a later date at the turn of the eighth/ninth century. Recently Brown[47] has reopened the question and argued for an earlier date in the second half or even the middle of the century. Françoise Henry[48] argues for a date at the end of the eighth century, giving 797, the second centenary of the death of St Columba, as a possible occasion for the undertaking. P Meyvaert[49] proposes a date of mid-eighth century. In his more recent study J J G Alexander,[50] while acknowledging the difficulties and uncertainties involved, says that such few comparisons as are available with other illuminated manuscripts tend, in his opinion, to support the until recently accepted date of late eighth to early ninth century:

> The Canon tables, the figure scenes, the ornamental use of plant scroll and human figure decoration all set the Book of Kells apart, and moreover they all suggest not just a later stage than the Lindisfarne Gospels or the Lichfield Gospels, but a different conceptual and creative purpose, not merely different models but a different use of those models in terms of transformation and creativity.[51]

An argument in favour of an earlier dating comes from the comparison of Kells with the Gospels of Lindisfarne, the Durham Gospels (MS A.II.17) and the Echternach Gospels — all assigned to *c* AD 700. The main arguments for the later dating come principally from the illumination, especially in the canon tables.

Here one can ask whether the arguments from the illumination are really such as to require a mid- or late eighth-century date, given that there appear to be strong arguments favouring an earlier date, even a late seventh-century one, a date roughly contemporary with the Durham Gospels (late

---

[44]Alexander, *Insular manuscripts*, 73.

[45]With reference to E H Zimmermann, *Vorkarolingische Miniaturen* (Berlin 1916-18).

[46]With reference to A M Friend, 'The canon tables of the Book of Kells' in *Medieval studies in memory of Arthur Kingsley Porter*, ed W R W Koehler (Cambridge, Mass. 1939) II, 611-41.

[47]T J Brown, 'Northumbria and the Book of Kells' in *Anglo-Saxon England* (Cambridge 1972) I, 219-46.

[48]Henry, 221.

[49]P Meyvaert, 'The Book of Kells and Iona', *Art Bulletin* 71 (1981) 6-19.

[50]J J G Alexander, 'The illumination', 265-89.

[51]ibid, 289. (A date of about 698 is generally accepted for the Lindisfarne Gospels; the Lichfield Gospels date from the first quarter of the eighth century.) I may note that Gertrud Schiller, *Iconography of christian art*, vol 2, *The Passion of Jesus Christ*, trans by Janet Seligman (London 1972), in her treatment of Christ, both in the text (p 53) and at the corresponding plate (fig 167) for Kells gives the date AD 700-710, but without any supporting arguments. I thank Dr Witold Witakowski (Upplands Väsby, Sweden) for this reference, and also his wife who points out that this is an early iconographic type, without Judas kissing Christ, to be found in Ravenna (Schiller, fig 159) and also in Ethiopian miniature painting which generally preserves early Christian iconographic types

seventh or early eighth century). To begin with we have the evidence from John's gospel. It seems clear that for John the scribe of Kells changed exemplar. While the text of Matthew, Mark and Luke can be classed as belonging to the mixed 'Irish' group of texts, that of John belongs to another tradition. The text is strikingly similar to the text of Durham MS A.II.17 and the Vulgate O, as Dr Christopher Verey has demonstrated. Another very interesting piece of evidence is that Hand A, the most clearly recognisable of the hands of Kells, is practically confined to the gospel of John, and has written all the text of John. This is also the hand in Kells that is closest to the hand of the Durham Gospels.[52] The simplest explanation of these facts would seem to be contemporaneity, and origin in the same living tradition.

There does not appear to be any argument against a late-seventh-century date in the mixed text of the first three gospels in Kells. The marginal glosses of the Echternach Gospels show that by AD 700 this mixed text was an accepted standard of comparison, and must have been established in Northumbria (and Ireland) during the seventh century.

The models used by the painter(s) or decorator(s) of the book should also be considered in this context. Almost all scholars stress dependence of the illumination in the Book of Kells on some models from the Mediterranean area and some are even convinced that the book depends on models originating in Coptic Egypt.[53] Neither this dependence, nor the availability of models for artists, has been clarified. The likelihood would seem to be through imported objects. In this context mention tends to be made of those which Bede says Biscop took from Rome to Wearmouth-Jarrow. Another example given is that of Bishop Arculf who according to Adomnán, abbot of Iona, depicted for him the shape of the church of the Holy Sepulchre on wax tablets, which Adomnán later transferred to parchment. The importance of this example is the use of wax tablets for making representations of works of art coupled with the fact that Arculf came to Iona after a journey back from the Holy Land, Egypt and Constantinople. The text of Adomnán and the general historical context merit consideration. 'At Iona', Adomnán says, 'he (he uses the plural 'we') questioned Arculf carefully concerning holy places in Jerusalem, especially concerning the sepulchre of the Lord and the church built over it, the shape of which Arculf himself depicted for me on a waxed tablet' (*cuius mihi formulam in tabula cerata Arculfus ipse depinxit*).[54] I believe we are entitled to presume that what Arculf did for Adomnán was

---

[52]Meehan, 250.

[53]Alexander, 'The illumination', 287-88. On the larger question of Egyptian influences, see Jean Doresse, *Des hiéroglyphes à la Croix. Ce que le passé pharaonique a légué au christianisme* (Istanbul: Nederlands Historisch-Archaeologische Instituut in het Nabije Oosten 1960) 24ff for the use of the 'ankh'-sign by the Copts. For the question of Eastern influences on Ireland (especially in book illumination), see Piotr Ó Scholz, 'Christlicher Orient und Irland' in *Nubia et Oriens Christianus*. Festschrift für C Detlef G Müller zum 60. Geburtstag, ed P O Scholz and R Reinhard Stempel (Bibliotheca Nubica 1, Verlag Jürgen Dinter 1987) 387-433. I owe these last two references to Dr Witold Witakowski.

[54]*Adamnan's 'De locis sanctis,'* ed Denis Meehan, Scriptores Latini Hiberniae 3, (Dublin 1958) 42-43 (Book I, ch 2).

not to copy from memory but from a wax tablet or some other representation brought with him from Jerusalem. Wax tablets may have been in more or less general use for models for drawings or pictures. Another example is the Book of Kildare mentioned by Giraldus Cambrensis in AD 1185.[55] The book which was believed to have originated in the time of St Brigid, was a gospel book, 'where for every page there are different designs, distinguished by varied colours'. Henderson[56] believes 'that the Book of Kildare was a product of one and the same scriptorium and painters' workshop as the Book of Kells itself; that is, of Iona'. According to the tradition known to Giraldus, the scribe copied his designs from drawings made on tablets shown him by an angel (*figuram quandam tabulae quam manu praeferebat impressam*).[57]

Arculfus was a Frankish bishop probably from Neustria in western Gaul. From the evidence available the dates of his pilgrimage and visit to Iona can be precisely determined. It was during the abbacy of Adomnán (679-704) who seems to have completed the composition of *De locis sanctis* by 686. Arculf would seem to have spent his nine months of pilgrimage in Jerusalem, visiting Palestine and Syria in 679-680, and to have sailed from Joppe to Alexandria in Egypt in 680. From there he sailed to Constantinople and was in that city from Easter to Christmas either in 680 or 681.[58] He journeyed from there to Sicily, and possibly Rome, probably in the spring of 682.[59] His arrival at Iona could hardly have been before 683.

These were important years for the church in Northumbria, Ireland, and in both East and West. In 664 Wilfrid had won the day for the Roman party at Whitby; Bishop Colman resigned and with his followers withdrew to Iona and later to the island of Inishboffin off the Mayo coast in western Ireland. Later the Anglo-Saxon monks of this group would found their own monastery nearby in Muigeo in 667.[60] By 664, Bede notes, English monks were studying in Ireland and among these a special mission to the Continent and Germany was being planned.[61] Bede also notes the presence of Egbert and others in the Irish monastery of Rathmelsigi (exact location still uncertain). The mission actually took place when, after completion of his course of studies and priestly ordination in Ireland in 690, Willibrord with twelve companions sailed directly from Ireland to the Continent.[62]

---

[55]*Topographia Hibernica*, ch 38, in *Giraldi Cambrensis Opera*, ed J F Dimock, Rolls Series (London 1867) v, 123-24. See also Giraldus Cambrensis (Gerald of Wales), *The history and topography of Ireland [Topographia Hiberniae]*, trans by John J O'Meara, revised edn (Mountrath 1982). For a discussion of the importance of Giraldus's text see Henderson, 195-96.

[56]Henderson, 195.

[57]Thus for the scribe's first drawing. The angel did likewise the following night: *eandem figuram aliasque multas ei praesentans*.

[58]Meehan (note 54 above) Book V, ch 9.

[59]ibid, Book VI, ch 3.

[60]*HE*, Book III, ch 25; Book IV, ch 4.

[61]*HE*, Book III, ch 27.

[62]*HE*, Book V, chs 9-10.

In these years Britain, Northumbria, Iona and Ireland were not isolated from the church in Rome and the East. In an attempt to unite the monophysites and Chalcedonians in Egypt and elsewhere, a doctrine of a single operation and will in Christ (monotheletism) was put forward by the Emperor Heraclius in 624. This gave rise to discussions over the next decades. In the East the chief opponent of the doctrine was Maximus the Confessor (c 580-662).[63] A synod on the matter was held in Rome in 680, at which Wilfrid (since 664 made bishop) was present. In England a synod on the same matter was held at Hatfield (Haethfeld) that same year.[64] The faith of the English or Celtic church on the matter was not in doubt. A general council on the same issue took place in Constantinople (the Sixth General Council; Constantinople III) in 680-681.

It seems likely that Arculf was in Constantinople during this Council (which began in November 680) and may even have sailed westwards with the Roman delegates to the Council in 682. Present at the Council also were delegates from Alexandria and Antioch. In 675 the Eleventh Council of Toledo took place. The Acts of this Council seem to have been known in Ireland, or in Irish circles on the Continent, since they are a source for the Hiberno-Latin (Pseudo-Isidorian) *Liber de ordine creaturarum*,[65] composed between 680 and 700. Councils XIII and XIV of Toledo were held in 683 and 684, and before the closure of the latter Pope Leo II had forwarded to them the essential points of the Sixth Ecumenical Council. A matter exercising the minds of christian artists during the sixth century and earlier was the manner of representing Christ in art — whether by portraits, 'in the flesh', or through allegorical figures such as the lamb and the shepherd. By the middle of the sixth century, most christians were no longer mistrustful of images. On the eve of the iconoclastic controversy (conventionally regarded as beginning in 726), Byzantine authorities took two actions confirming their acceptance of the christian cult of images. The so-called synod In Trullo (*Quinisext*) which met at Constantinople in 692, prescribed (canon 82) that the portrait of Christ 'in the flesh' replace the earlier christian allegorical image of the lamb, and this with the avowed purpose of reaffirming the reality of Christ's incarnation. Almost about the same time, the Emperor Justinian II (685-695, 705-711) placed the portrait of Christ on the coinage of the empire.[66]

---

[63]On the earlier development of this controversy and the central role of Maximus up to his death (in 662), see F M Léhiel, *Théologie de l'Agonie du Christ. La Liberté humaine du Fils de Dieu et son importance sotériologique mises en lumière par Saint Maxime le Confesseur* (Paris 1979), (I wish to thank Fr Ray Maloney, SJ for his reference.) Central to this discussion of the human will and the freedom of Christ was the Gethsemane (Olivet) scene and the texts of Mark 14:36 ('... not what I will but what you will'; *non quod ego uolo sed quod tu*) (=Matthew 26:39); cf also John 5:30. It may be that the portrait of Christ in Kells, folio 114r (under the heading *et ymno dicto exierunt in montem Oliueti*, Matthew 26:30) should be interpreted against some such background.

[64]*HE*, Book IV, chs 17-18.

[65]*Liber de ordine creaturarum. Un anónimo irlandés del siglo VII*, ed Manuel C Díaz, Estudio y edición crítica (Santiago de Compostela 1972) 26-28 for author and date.

[66]See Robert Grigg, 'Iconoclasm, Christian' in *Dictionary of the Middle Ages*, ed Joseph R Strayer (New York 1985)VI, 400.

Some of those events may have little or no bearing on the art or events of late seventh-century Northumbria, Iona or Ireland. On the other hand they may well have had. We do not know Arculf's itinerary between Sicily and Iona, the port from which his ship set sail nor the intended destination before Iona. We are fortunate that we know what little we do. Further analysis of the evidence may conceivably show no weak links between Europe, the Mediterranean, the Near East and Northumbria, Iona, Ireland during the late seventh century, links that may explain some of the mysteries of the Book of Kells.

An edition of the abbreviated and selective set of Hebrew names found in the Book of Kells

Patrick McGurk

Around AD 389/91, St Jerome was working on his *Hebrew names* or *Onomasticon*, an etymological guide to biblical proper names, which he arranged alphabetically under separate books.[1] The subject of the present edition is an abbreviated and selective set, which was almost certainly based on those in Jerome's dictionaries for the gospels, and which is found, apparently with only one exception, in gospel books either of insular origin or with insular connections. The distinctiveness of the names for the gospel of Mark was first noted by Verey, and further comment was made more recently in the commentary volume which accompanied the colour facsimile of the Book of Kells.[2] A full edition of this set should make plain its peculiarities and corruptions. The set appears in the gospel books listed below.

The following signs are used:

x   shows the presence of a list

*   means that the list is either incomplete or mutilated

-    indicates that the list seems to have been deliberately omitted

()   records the absence of evidence through loss or mutilation.

(The possible date and origins of the manuscripts are indicated in the list of *sigla codicum* below at the opening of the edition.)

---

[1]Paul Lagarde's edition of Jerome's *Hebrew names* in the gospels has been reprinted in *S Hieronimi opera*, Part I, *Opera exegetica*, CCSL 72, 134-42. His edition of the Lactantius genealogical text in which etymologies are embedded was published in the *Abhandlungen der Königlichen Gesellschaft der Wissenschaften zu Göttingen* 38 (1892) 5-44. F Wutz, *Onomastica sacra*, Texte und Untersuchungen 41 (1914) considers the background to Jerome's etymologies in detail.

[2]*The Durham Gospels*, ed C D Verey, T J Brown and E D Coatsworth, Early English manuscripts in facsimile 20 (Copenhagen 1980) 23-24. McGurk, 'Texts', 47-52.

Manuscript	Matthew MT	Mark MK	Luke LK	John JN
Cambridge, Corpus Christi College Library, MS 197b (pp 245-316) and London, BL MS Cotton Otho C.V.	( )	x	( )	( )
TCD, MS 52	x	x	x	x
TCD, MS 55	( )	( )	x*	( )
TCD, MS 57	x	( )	x	x
TCD, MS 58	x*	-	x*	-
Durham, Cathedral Library, MS A.II.17	( )	x	( )	( )
London, BL, MS Harl. 1802	x	-	-	-
Paris, BN, MS lat. 9389	x	x	x	x
Poitiers, BM, MS 17	x	x	x	x
Stuttgart, Württembergische Landesbibliothek, MS Bibl. 2° 44	x	-	-	-
Vatican, Biblioteca Apostolica Vaticana, MS Barb. lat. 570	x	-	-	x

(The last manuscript has a colophon for Mark's Hebrew names but these have been omitted.)

The witnesses are datable to the seventh- to early ninth- centuries with the exceptions of the eleventh-century Stuttgart volume and of the British Library Harleian codex which is datable to 1138. They are written in an insular script again with two exceptions: the Poitiers codex, which had insular features, including a poem on the canons by the seventh-century Irish writer, Aileran the Wise; and the Stuttgart manuscript, which alone has no demonstrable insular links.[3]

---

[3]TCD, MS 52 is described and completely transcribed in *Liber Ardmachanus: the Book of Armagh*, ed J Gwynn (Dublin 1913). TCD, MSS 55, 57, 58, Durham, Cathedral Library, MS A.II.17, Paris, BN, MS lat. 9389, Poitiers, BM, MS 17, and Vatican, MS Barb. lat. 570 are respectively nos 83bis, 87, 13, 2, 59, 64 and 137 in McGurk, *Gospel books*. BL, MS Harl. 1802 has Irish additions which are described in S O'Grady and Robin Flower, *A catalogue of Irish manuscripts in the British Museum*, 2 vols (London 1926) II, 428-32. There is no catalogue description of the eleventh-century continental manuscript at Stuttgart, though for a recent discussion of some of its gospel prefaces see J Regul, *Die antimarcionitischen Evangelienprologe*, Aus der Geschichte der

They differ from Jerome's list for the gospels in many ways. They quite often abbreviate, or extract from, Jerome's interpretations: thus, for instance, Jerome's 'discretus siue seiunctus uel conuertit siue conuoluit me' for 'Neptalim' (Matthew 78) becomes 'seiunctus', and his interpretation for 'Zaccheus' (Matthew 103) 'iustificatus aut iustus uel iustificandus. Syrum est, non hebraeum' is rendered simply 'iustificatus siue iustificandus'. Jerome's shorter glosses are often fully reproduced: thus, for instance, Matthew 42 'Fares diuisio' or Mark 7 'Tyro angustiae' or Luke 75 'Salman pax'. Occasionally there is an apparent rephrasing: thus Luke 30 'Fase' rendered as 'transitus siue transgressio, pro quo nostri pascha legunt' becomes 'transitus quod nos dicimus pascha'. It is, of course, possible that some of the readings in the abbreviated set come from variants not recorded in Lagarde's edition or from witnesses which he did not consult, though it would be surprising if a significant number of them do.[4]

The set is selective. In Matthew, for instance, all sixteen names beginning with A, and the first entry with B, are omitted, and only one out of the three items under T appear. In Mark five out of eleven names are omitted. The pruning of names is neither even nor regular: in Luke, for instance, seven of the eighteen entries under S are left out, six of the eight under N, but only three of the twelve under A.

Nor is the order of Jerome's names always followed. Jerome's names are usually arranged in the order of their appearance in a gospel, but this order is not always followed in our shorter set: thus the Matthew I names 52-67, for instance, or the Matthew R names 81-88 are arranged differently.[5] It is perhaps worth noting that the names in the fuller Hebrew names lists printed anonymously by De Bruyne sometimes show a different word order under a particular letter from that printed in Lagarde's edition, and the explanation for our set's differences might again be sought in earlier witnesses which are either lost or unpublished.[6]

---

lateinischen Bibel 6 (Freiburg 1969) 19, 35, 71, 73, 99. It is of course possible that other witnesses of this abbreviated set survive.

[4]The critical apparatus below occasionally notes readings for the Lagarde witnesses BFH when the abbreviated set agrees with one or other of them (eg Matthew 24[c d], 33[b], John 5[c]).

[5]In Luke the P and R names keep to the order of Jerome, but in some witnesses the two R names begin with P; thus 'Ram' is rendered 'Pam', and 'Ros', 'Phas' or 'Phos'. This could have arisen from a misreading in an archetype of R as P, which is just possible in insular script.

[6]De Bruyne Préfaces de la Bible latine (Namur 1920) 188-191 gives an edition of these names based on three manuscripts in the Paris, BN, MS lat. 268, 9389 and 11959, and on Stuttgart, Württembergische Landesbibliothek MS Bibl. 2°. 44. There is a different order from Jerome's in the I and P names in Matthew and the order of the two A names of Mark is reversed. It is also worth noting that De Bruyne's witnesses omit two names (Matthew 'Amen', Mark 'Tyrus'), place Mark 'Israhel' towards the end of the list before 'Fetha' and 'Trachonitidis', and add seven names, Matthew 'Achim', 'Ezechias', 'Iesse', Ozias', Mark 'Fetha', Luke 'Abia', 'Zorababel'. The additional names are found in the gospels concerned, and suggest that the tradition of separate Hebrew name lists (at least in the gospels) is more complex than the Lagarde edition indicates. The omisions in the De Bruyne witnesses are of course, not as extensive as those in our set, which at points is very different.

Other differences might go back to a single disordered archetype. It was suggested in the Kells facsimile commentary volume that the arbitrary opening of the Matthew list with the second B name 'Bartholomeus' after the omission of the first sixteen A names may have been caused by a defective exemplar in which the first leaf was either lost or mutilated.[7] There are more striking differences. The Mark list, which, as has been already noted, was selective, ends with two additional entries: first 'Setha aperi' (certainly a corruption of 'Aeffeta adaperire'), which was placed in the Lagarde edition at the opening of Luke, and second a comment on 'Paulus', which is obviously inappropriate to a gospel text. It is possible that the first addition ('Setha') could be explained by a gliding together of a Mark and a Luke list, but this will clearly not explain the addition of 'Paulus'. It is worth noting that this first addition ('Aeffeta') refers to a word which only appears in the gospel of Mark, and is therefore inappropriate for Luke. Thus an alternative explanation for the appearance of 'Setha' under Mark (though not that of Paul) might be an earlier list in which 'Aeffeta' was included under Mark, though the presence of a name beginning with A or E at the end of a putative Mark list ending with five T names would still demand an explanation.[8] The contents of the John list are not so easily explicable. It begins with nine of Jerome's fifteen names; follows with two names not from Jerome's John list, that is 'Agios' (John 16), a name completely unknown in the Jerome *Onomasticon* and an 'Osanna' (John 17), a name already found under Matthew; and concludes with a repeat of the selective Mark list where two comments on 'Israhel' follow upon the already noted anomalous 'Paulus'. It is difficult to make sense of this disorder. It could be suggested that a John and a Mark list were unintentionally merged. This might indicate an archetype which followed a non-Vulgate order of the gospels where Mark followed John.[9] There are other anomalies in the abbreviated list, such as the insertion of a comment on 'Sabaoth' (a word which does not appear in the gospels) between 'Golgotha' (Matthew 47) and 'Iesus' (Matthew 49). A complete explanation for the peculiar selectiveness and distinctive order and additions of this abbreviated set is very hard to find, but the possibility that the archetype was made up of lists written down on small single scraps or sheets with some marginal jottings, with the lists themselves not very clearly separated from each other, must be seriously considered. Such a list could have been kept apart from the gospels and may have come to be added fitfully and patchily to their accessory texts.

---

[7] McGurk, 'Texts', 48.

[8] The uncertain position of 'Aeffeta' is made clear in the apparatus to Lagarde's edition (note 1 above) 139. An anomaly in Jerome's names for the gospels as printed by Lagarde should be noted. The names glossed in a particluar gospel list are not always found in that gospel, eg Matthew 'Thare' occurs, not in Matthew, but in Luke 3:34, Zachaeus' in Luke 19:2 and John's 'Banereem/Boanerges', 'Barsemia' and 'Beelzebub' come from Mark 3:17, 10:46 and Luke 11:15 respectively.

[9] This is on the assumption that the sequence of the lists corresponded to that of the gospels which they may have accompanied.

There are many changes and some corruptions in this shorter set. In Mark 6 the gloss on 'Salome' is expanded from 'pacifica' to 'pax siue pacifica'. Luke 34's 'volutabilis' for 'Galilaea' becomes 'uolubilitas' in all except three witnesses.[10] Under Luke 55 for 'Martha' the explanation 'inritans, prouocans. Sermone autem syro domina interpretatur uel dominans' becomes 'prouocans deum'. Under John/Mark 21 for 'Israhel' 'uir uidens deum' becomes 'anima uidens deum'. Paul Meyvaert has drawn attention to the reading 'salus bona' for 'surbana' under Luke 35 'Gerasenorum' and to 'Iori' for 'Ioni' under Luke 38.[11] Under Matthew 32 'latine' is added after 'grece' in some witnesses, and in this way Jerome's gloss on 'diabolus' is misunderstood. Some of these changes and corruptions could go back to unpublished variants in the Jerome tradition but they became a firm part of this shorter set.

The lists were more naturally laid out in two columns like glossaries, and such a layout could account for particular errors in witnesses. A misreading of entries in imperfectly aligned or awkwardly separated columns could explain both the

Erui   gilans

for 'Er uigilans' in Luke 26 in *codex Usserianus primus* (TCD, MS 55) and the blended entries for Luke 55-62 in the Book of Durrow (TCD, MS 57) 'Marthanaa provocans deum pulchra' which should have been separated on two lines as:

Martha   provocans deum
Naa   pulchra

A faulty reading in a list written continuously in long lines could lie behind TCD, MS 52's 'Sichar conclussio siue missus' for John/Mark's 14-15 'Sichar conclusio' and 'Syloe missus'. It has been recently argued that the significant misplacing in the Luke list in the Book of Kells of the entry for 'Satan' (85) between those for 'Galilea' (34) and 'Gerasenorum' (35) suggests that Kells' exemplar was written in two columns since the eye could have moved erroneously from 'Galilea' in one column to a 'Satan' which might have adjoined it in the next.[12] It is likely that these lists were relatively late additions in the history of early Latin gospel books. They may have been inserted haphazardly rather in the way the Luke list was written down in fairly cramped columns on a blank recto in the Book of Durrow and such almost random additions together with their putative origins in jottings on single scraps or leaves could explain their disorder and some at least of their misreadings.

The critical apparatus shows that the disorder of the Mark and John lists was paralleled by corrupt readings in the whole set. These are so many and shifting that it is not possible for a stemma to be constructed, but at least three separate strands may be detected. The eleventh-century continental gospels at Stuttgart, which will be further discussed below, unfortunately

---

[10]The witnesses which keep Jerome's 'uolutabilis' are *HqEdXr*.
[11]P Meyvaert, 'The Book of Kells and Iona' in *Art Bulletin* 71 (1989) 8-9.
[12]Meyvaert (note 11 above) 8.

only preserves the names for Matthew, but its failure to insert the misplaced and odd 'Sabaoth' between 47 and 49, and some minor variants set it apart from the others. Its readings 'uomens ore' (25^c), 'iudicat' (34^b) and 'pinguedinum' (46^b) agree with Jerome against the other witnesses and so it is here closer to the Jerome glosses.[13] It has distinctive mistakes but it clearly goes back to an early stage in the abbreviated set's transmission.

The Book of Armagh (TCD, MS 52) has some marked differences from the others. It gives correct or quite different readings: thus Matthew 44 'principum' for 'principium', Mark 12 'Effeta' for 'Feta', Luke 14 'Cyrinus' for 'Caereneu', Luke 38 'Iona' for 'Iori', and John/Mark 3 'Bonarches' for 'Banereem'. The last difference is worth noting. Boanerges, and not Banereem, is the name which appears in the gospel of John. Armagh might represent an informed effort at making the name match that in the gospel text or it could suggest access to the full comment of Jerome which reads 'Banereem filii tonitrui, quod conrupte Boanerges usus optinuit'. At Matthew 48 it omits the words apparently added to Jerome's text and found in nearly all our witnesses: 'angelorum; alii omnipotens'. Under John/Mark the Book of Armagh omits six names: nos 17, 18, 20 and 28-30. It is difficult to decide whether the 'better' readings and the omissions in this witness are the result of editing or go back to an archetype. The particular omission of six names in the John/Mark list could have been caused by scribal error in omitting a line or two. The continued presence of many demonstrably wrong readings shows that it shared some of the corruptions of the other witnesses. There are also other readings exclusive to it (eg Luke 12^b, 45^b). If the differences in Armagh had been in part the result of the editing of a corrupt text, this could not have been thorough. Armagh might therefore be regarded as preserving the better readings of an archetype which had already however been much corrupted.

The remaining witnesses form an amorphous group. They share with Armagh the insertion of the gloss on 'Sabaoth' (Matthew 48), but they all expand that gloss. The expansion of Matthew 48 and the reading 'Elia deus meus' for 'Elia deus dominus' (Matthew 40) are their two most obvious distinguishing features.[14] The Barberini Gospels (Vatican, MS Barb. lat. 570) has a strikingly large number of errors, though its omission of the unnecessary 'latine' in the gloss on 'Diabulus' (Matthew 32) brings it closer here to Jerome than even Armagh. The Books of Kells and Durrow have long been known to have a distinctive package of accessory texts, and particular errors in the few names which the fragmentary Matthew and

---

[13]It also omits the nonsensical 'latine' at 32^d (like three other witnesses), and has 'dominus' for 'meus' (like Jerome and Armagh) at 40^b.

[14]The most likely explanation for 'Elia deus meus' as against 'Elia deus dominus' is the eye skipping from the entries immediately above or below 'Elia' where 'deus meus' is to be found, but it is possible that the mistake arose in a common archetype of this amorphous group.

Luke Kells lists share with Durrow provide some weak confirmation of their interconnections.[15]

Particular errors in the earliest surviving witness, the so-called *codex Usserianus primus* (TCD, MS 55) which has only a mutilated Luke list, show that it was not the archetype and that this must therefore go back to at least the first half of the seventh century.[16] The Stuttgart witness (Württembergische Landesbibliothek, MS Bibl. 2° 44), only has the Matthew names, but it has prologues for Mark, Luke and John of great antiquity. These form a distinctive family with the prologues in the ninth-century Munich, Staatsbibliothek, MS Clm 6212, a manuscript whose colophon links it to a sixth-century Ravenna exemplar.[17] It has no preface for Matthew. If its abbreviated and selective Matthew Hebrew names were part of the same package of accessory texts as the prologues to the last three gospels then the history of these shorter lists could be extended back to the sixth century. This is impossible to prove and Stuttgart's differences from the other witnesses must be simply noted. They could represent a transmission of the set with a history independent of those which circulated in these islands.

The earliest and the latest of the witnesses were written in Ireland, and the Books of Durrow, Kells and Armagh confirm the strong Irish associations of the set.[18] The continental eighth-century book in which it appears, Poitiers, BM, MS 17 has, as has already been noted, the poem on the canons by the seventh-century Irish writer Aileran, and this strengthens the Irish connections of its accessory texts. It is reasonable to assume that the presence of the set in the other insular manuscripts reflects Irish influence. Their appearance in the package of accessory texts common to the Books of Durrow and Kells which include Old Latin chapter lists as well as excellent texts of the ancient gospel prefaces could point to their antiquity.[19] It is very likely that they were known in Ireland at a very early date though their presence in the Stuttgart codex could rule out their first confection in that island.[20]

---

[15]See the critical apparatus for Luke at 5[a], 15[a], 16[a], 34[b], but note that there are differences. At 34[b] their 'uolutabilis' has the support of Lagarde's Jerome against 'volubilitas' of the other witnesses. The last reading has the support of F, one of the Jerome witnesses used by Lagarde, and it is not surprising that the Poitiers witness conflates 'uolubilitas uolubilis'.

[16]See the critical apparatus for Luke at 32[b], 45[b] and 81[b].

[17]The most recent discussion is in Regul (note 3 above) 19, 73. This group of manuscripts has the rare Cy family of chapter lists for Mark, Luke and John. The colophon of the ninth-century Munich manuscript points to an archetype corrected for Archbishop Ecclesius of Ravenna (521-532).

[18]If it is true that opinions are still divided on the origins of the Books of Durrow and Kells, the Irish connections of their accessory texts have not been questioned.

[19]See McGurk, 'Texts', 37-58.

[20]I am grateful to Paul Meyvaert for reading an earlier draft; and to Olivier Szerwiniack for a most careful reading of the edition and for drawing attention to many errors. I alone am responsible for the mistakes which remain and for the views expressed.

Sigla Codicum

Xr   TCD, MS 55 (*Codex Usserianus primus*). Ireland, VII[med].

Hd   TCD, MS 52 (Book of Armagh). Armagh, *c* AD 807.

Hq   TCD, MS 58 (Book of Kells). Iona, VIII-IX.

Hz   London, BL, MS Harl. 1802. Armagh, 1138.

Ed   TCD, MS 57 (Book of Durrow). ?Columban centre, VII[2].

Ef   Durham, Cathedral Library, MS A.II.17, folios 2-102. Northumbria, VII-VIII.

Eg   Cambridge, Corpus Christi College Library, MS 197, pp 245-316 and London, BL, MS Cotton Otho C.V. ?Northumbria, VIII.

Ev   Vatican, Biblioteca Apostolica Vaticana, MS Barb. lat. 570 (Barberini Gospels). England, VIII.

Ge   Paris, BN, MS 9389 (Echternach Gospels). ?Northumbria, VII-VIII.

Pa   Poitiers, BM, MS 17. Amiens, VIII[ex].

C   Stuttgart, Württembergische Landesbibliothek, MS Bibl. 2° 44. XI, at Comburg in the early sixteenth century.

The readings of the witnesses used in Lagarde's edition of Jerome's *Onomasticon* are given when they might be of interest. They are

(B)   *codex Berolinus*. Berlin, Deutsche Staatsbibliothek, MS theol. folio 353. XI.

(F)   *codex Monacensis*. Munich, Bayerische Staatsbibliothek, MS Clm. 6228. IX.

(H)   *codex Bambergensis*. Bamberg, Staatliche Bibl., MS Bibl. 154* (B.iv.19). IX[ex].

An asterisk before a name in the abbreviated set (eg Matthew 52 or 53) indicates that it is not placed in the same order as that of Jerome.

Jerome's entries are in the left column. The Jerome text is not given where there is no corresponding entry in the abbreviated set (eg Matthew 1-17). It was not possible to take one witness as the base manuscript.
[1,2] suprascript after *sigla* indicates first scribe, second scribe.

Lists of Hebrew names

Matthew

Jerome	*Abbreviated set* (Witnesses *HdzEdvGePa C Hq* (93-103 only)
1. Abraham.	-
2. Aminadab.	-
3. Abia.	-
4. Asa.	-
5. Aazia.	-
6. Aaz.	-
7. Amon.	-
8. Abiu.	-
9. Azor.	-
10. Archelaus.	-
11 Amen.	-
12. Andreas.	-
13. Alphaeus.	-
14. Amora.	-
15. Abel.	-
16. Acheldemach.	-
17. Booz.	-

Matthew

18. Bartholomaeus filius
suspendentis aquas uel me.
Syrum est, non hebraeum.

Bartholomeus syrum[a]
filius suspendentis[b] aquas.

19. Bethsaida domus frugum
uel domus uenatorum.

Bethsaida[a] domus frugum siue
uenatorum.[b]

20. Bariona filius columbae.
Syrum est pariter et hebraeum.
Bar quippe lingua syra filius,
et iona columba utroque
sermone dicitur.

Bariona[a] syrum[b] filius
columbae.

21. Bethfage domus oris uallium
vel domus bucae. Syrum est,
non hebraeum. Quidam putant
domum maxillarum uocari.

Bethfage[a] syrum[b] domus
uallium uel[c] domus buccae[d].

22. Bethania domus adflictionis
eius uel domus oboedientiae.

Bethania domus adflictionis[a]
uel domus oboedientiae[b].

23. Barachia uel benedictus
dominus uel benedictio
domini.

Barachia benedictus dominus[a]
[b]uel benedictio[b] domini.

Matthew critical apparatus

The names open with these incipits in the following manuscripts: Hd incipit interpretatio ebreorum nominum secundum Matheum; Ge incipit interpraetatio cata matheum hebreorum nominum atque verborum interpraetatio; EvPa cata Matheum hebreorum nominum adque (Pa atque) verborum interpraetatio; Hz de interpretatione ebreorum nominum.

The lists are arranged in separate columns of names and glosses except in EdvC which are in long lines.

18.   [a] syrum] sirum *HdEv*, sirum id est *Hz*
    [b] suspendentis] suspendentes C (*H*)
19.   [a] Bethsaida] Betzaida *Hd*, Betsaida C
    [b] uenatorum] natorum *Ed*
20.   [a] Bariona] Hebariona C
    [b] syrum] sirum *HdzEv*
21.   [a] Bethfage] Bethphage *Pa*
    [b] syrum] sirum *HdzEv*
    [c] uel] siue *HzPa*
    [d] buccae] boccae *Hd*, buccellae *Pa*, bucae *Hz*
22.   [a] adflictionis] afflictionis *Pa*
    [b] oboedientiae] obaedientiae *Edv*, oboedentiae *Hd*, obodientiae *Hz*
23.   [a] dominus] deus *Ev*
    [b-b] uel benedictio] siue benedictus *Pa*

Matthew

24.	Barrabban filium magistri eorum. Syrum est, non hebraeum.	Barabban[a] syrum[b] filius[c] magistri nostri[d].
25.	Caifas inuestigator uel sagax. Sed melius uomens ore.	Caifas[a] inuestigator[b] siue uomens[c].
26.	Codrantes.	-
27.	Corbana oblatio.	Corban[a] oblatio
28.	Cananaeus possidens siue possessio.	Cannaneus[a] possidens[b] siue[c] possessio[d].
29.	Chanani.	-
30.	Chorozaim.	-
31.	Chananaei.	-
32.	Diabolus defluens. Graece uere dicitur criminator.	Diabulus[a] [b]defluens[c]. Grece[bd] [e]uero dicitur[e] criminator [f].
33.	Dauid desiderabilis aut fortis manu.	Dauid desiderabilis[a] uel[b] fortis manu.
34.	Danihel iudicium dei uel iudicat me deus.	Daniel[a] iudicium dei uel iudicans[b] me deus[c].

---

24.   [a] Barabban] Baraban *Hz*
    [b] syrum] sirum *HdzEv, omits C*
    [c] filius] filius *(F)*
    [d] nostri] nostri *(FH)*

25.   [a] Caifas] Caifan *Ev*, Caefas *Hd*, Caiphas *Pa*, Caiphan *Hz*, Caifa *EdGeC (F)*
    [b] inuestigator] inuestigatur *Hz*, inuestigatus *C*
    [c] uomens] euomens *Ev*, uomens ore *C*

27.   [a] Corban] Corbanan *Pa*

28.   [a] Cannaneus] Channaneus *Pa*, Cananeus *C*
    [b] possidens] possedens *HdzGe*
    [c] siue] uel *Hz*
    [d] possessio] possedio *Ev*, possesio *Hz*

32.   [a] Diabulus] Deabulus *Ev[1]*, Diabolus *PaC*
    [b-b] defluens. Grece] grece defluens *Hd*, deorsum fluens grece *Ev*
    [c] defluens] deffluens *Ed*
    [d] Grece] *adds* latine *HdGePa*
    [e-e] uero dicitur] *Hd omits*, dicitur *Ed*, vero dicitur *(F)*
    [f] criminator] creminosus *Ev*, creminator *HdzEd*

33.   [a] desiderabilis] dissiderabilis *Hd*
    [b] uel] uel *(FH)*

34.   [a] Daniel] Danihel *HdPaC*

Matthew

35.	Esrom sagittam uidit siue atrium eorum.	Esrom[a] sagittam uidit.
36.	Essai insulae libatio. Sed melius incensum.	Esaia[a] incensum.
37.	Eliacim dei resurrectio uel deus resuscitans uel deus suscitauit.	Eliachim[a] dei[b] resurrectio siue[c] deus resuscitans.
38.	Eliu deus meus iste uel dei mei istius.	Eliu[a] deus meus iste[b].
39.	Eliezer deus meus adiutor.	Eliezer[a] deus meus adiutor[b].
40.	Elia deus dominus.	Elia[a] deus dominus[b].
41.	Eli eli lama sabactani deus meus, deus meus, quare me dereliquisti?	[a]Elii elii[a] lama[b] sabachtani[c] deus meus[d], [e]deus meus[e], quare [f]dereliquisti[g] me[f]?
42.	Fares diuisio.	Fares[a] diuisio[b].
43.	Farisaei diuidentes uel diuisi.	Farisaei[a] [b]diuidentes siue diuisi[b].

---

   [b] iudicans] iudicat *C*

   [c] deus] dominus *Ev*

35.   [a] Esrom] Esron *C*

36.   [a] Esaia] Essaias *Hd*, Essaia *Ev*, Esia *Ed*, Esai *C*

37.   [a] Eliachim] Heliacim *Pa*, Eliacim *HdEd*

   [b] dei] domini *Ev (F)*

   [c] siue] uel *Hd*

38.   [a] Eliu] Heliu *Pa*, Elu *C*

   [b] iste] istae *Ed*

39.   [a] Eliezer] Elezer *Hd*, Heliezer *Pa*

   [b] adiutor] adiutor *with* deus meus *interlined Pa*

40.   [a] Elia] Helia *Pa*, Eliam *C*

   [b] dominus] meus *HzEdvGePa*

41.   [a-a] Elii Elii] Eli Eli *HdEvC*, Heli Heli *Pa*

   [b] lama] laba *Ev*, lema *C*

   [c] sabachtani] sabathani *Hd*, sabachthani *Ge*, samabastani *Ev*, sabactani *Pa*, sabactanai *Hz*, sabachtani *C*

   [d] meus] *omits HdzEdC*

   [e-e] deus meus] *omits EvGe*,

   [f-f] dereliquisti me] me diriliquisti *Hd*, me dereliquisti *EvC*, me dereliquisti me *Hz*

   [g] dereliquisti] diriliquisti *HdGe*, direliquisti *Ed*

42.   [a] Fares] Phares *Pa*

   [b] diuisio] diuissio *Hd*

43.   [a] Farisaei] Farissei *Hd*, Farisei *EvC*, Farisai *Hz*, Pharisaei *Pa*

   [b-b] diuidentes ... diuisi] diuissi uel diuidentes *Hd*

Matthew

44.	Gennesar hortus principum.	Genesar[a] ortus[b] principum[c].
45.	Gehennam de ualle sunt siue uallis gratuita.	Gehennam[a] uallis gratuita.
46.	Gethsemani uallis pinguedinum.	Gesamani[a] uallis pinguidinis[b].
47.	Golgotha caluaria. Syrum est non hebraeum.	Golgotha caluaria.
48.	-	Sabaoth[a] exercituum siue uirtutum[b].
49.	Iesus saluator uel saluaturus.	Iesus saluator.
50.	Isaac.	-
51.	Iacob.	-
52.	Iudas confitens uel glorificans.	*Iudas[a] confitens.
53.	Iosafat ipse iudicans. Sed melius dominus iudicauit.	*Iosafat[a] domini iudicium[b].

---

44.   [a] Genesar] Genezar *Hdz*, Gennesar *EdC*, Genessar *Ev*
        [b] ortus] hortus *HdC*
        [c] principum] principium *HzEv[1]GePaC (BF)*
45.   [a] Gehennam] Gehenna *HdPaC*, Gegennam *Hz*, Gehennan *Ev*
46.   *added in the margin by the scribe with a* signe de renuoi *Ge*
        [a] Gesamani] Gezamani *Hd*, Gessamani *EdC*, Gethsamini *Pa*, Gessimani *Hz[1]*,
        Gessemani *EvHz[2]*, Gesemani *Ge (FH)*
        [b] pinguidinis] pinguitudinis *Hd*, pingidinis *Hz*, pinguedinis *EdPa*,
        pinguedinum *C*
48.   *C omits like Jerome a name unknown in the gospels. Lagarde gives the following
        glosses on 'Sabaoth' (page references are to the text printed in the CCSL):* 'virtutum
        siue exercituum' *(De epistola Pauli ad Romanos, p 153, De epistola Iacobi, p 150);*
        exercituum siue uirtutum' *(Primi libri Regum, p 105) and* 'exercituum siue
        uirtutum uel militiarum' *(De Isaia propheta, p 120). Wutz (note 1 above) 38
        quotes Ambrose's comment:* 'Sabaoth interpres alicubi Dominum uirtutum,
        alicubi regem, alicubi omnipotentem interpretati sunt'.
        [a] Sabaoth] Sabahot *Ev*
        [b] uirtutum] *adds* angelorum *Ed, adds* angelorum. Alii (Ali *followed by an erasure
        Ge*) omnipotens *HzEvGePa*
52-67. *The abbreviated set follows the following order: 53, 52, 66, 61, 62, 64, 67*
52.   *C merges 53 and 52 by its erroneous omission of 52[a]*
        [a] Iudas] *omits C*
53.   [a] Iosafat] Iosaphat *HdEv*, Iosaphath *HzPa*
        [b] iudicium] *adds* confitens *C but see 52[a]*

Matthew

54.	Ioram.	-
55.	Ionatham.	-
56.	Iezechia.	-
57.	Iosia.	-
58.	Ioachim.	-
59.	Iechonias.	-
60.	Ioachim.	
61.	Ioseph adposuit siue adponens.	*Ioseph[a] adponens[b].
62.	Ierusalem uisio pacis uel timebit perfecte.	*Hyerusalem[a] uisio[b] pacis.
63.	Ieremias.	-
64.	Iohannan cui est gratia uel domini gratia.	*Iohannan[a] cui est gratia domini[b].
65.	Isaia.	-
66.	Iscarioth memoriale domini. Quod si uoluerimus Issacharioth legere, interpretatur est merces eius. Potest autem dici et memoria mortis.	*Iscarioth[a] memoriale[b] domini.
67.	Iericho odor eius siue luna.	*Hiericho[a] odor eius[b] siue luna.
68.	Lebbaeus.	-

---

61. [a] Ioseph] Iosep *Ev*, Iosafat *C*
     [b] adponens] ponens *C*
62. [a] Hyerusalem] Ierusalem *HdHz²*, Hierusalem *EvGeHz¹PaC*
     [b] uisio] uissio *Hd*
64. [a] Iohannan] Ioanna *Hd*, Iohanna *Pa*, Iohannis *C*, Iohannan (*H*)
     [b] domini] dei *Pa*
66   [a] Iscarioth] Scarioth *GePaHzC*, Isecharioth *Hd*
     [b] memoriale] memorale *HzEdv*
67. [a] Hiericho] Iericho *HdHz²*, Hiricho *Ev*, Hierycho *Pa*, Hyericho *Ed*
     [b] eius] *?adds* est *Ed*

Matthew

69. Manasses.   -

70. Matthan.   -

71. Mariam plerique aestimant   Maria stella[a] maris.
    interpretari inluminant me isti
    uel inluminatrix uel zmyrna
    maris. Sed mihi nequaquam
    uidetur. Melius est autem ut
    dicamus sonare eam stillam
    maris siue amarum mare.
    Sciendumque quod Maria
    sermone domina nuncupatur.

72. Matthaeus donatus quondam.   Mattheus[a] donatus.

73. Magedda.

74. Magdalene turris. Sed melius   Magdalena[a] turris[b].
    sicut a monte Montanus, ita
    Turrensis a turre dicatur.

75. Naason quidam putant   Naason[a] augurans[b].
    requietum sonitum interpretari.
    Sed uerius est augurans siue
    serpens.
76. Nazareth flos aut uirgultum   Nazareth[a] flos munditiae [b]aut
    eius uel munditiae aut separata   uirgultum[b].
    uel custodita.

77. Nazaraeus mundus.   Nazareus[a] mundus[b].

78. Neptalim discretus siue   Neptalim seiunctus[a].
    seiunctus uel conuertit siue
    conuoluit me.

---

71.   [a] stella] stilla *HdEdPa*, zella *Hz*
72.   [a] Mattheus] Matheus *HdzEvC*
74.   [a] Magdalena] Magdalenae *HzEdvC*
      [b] turris] turralis *GePa*
75.   [a] Naason] Nasson *Hdz*, Naasson *EdPaC*
      [b] augurans] augorians *Hd*, augurians *GePa*, coangustans *Ev*
76.   [a] Nazareth] Nazareth siue *C*
      [b-b] aut uirgultum] *omits Pa, but see* 77[b]
77.   [a] Nazareus] Nazoreus *Ed*, Nazarenus *Hz*
      [b] mundus] mundus aut uirgultum *Pa, but see* 76[b]
78.   [a] seiunctus] seunctus *Hd*

Matthew

79.	Obed seruiens.	Obet[a] seruiens.
80.	Osanna saluifica, quod graece dicitur σωσον δη. Utrumque autem nomen per O extensam litteram legendam.	Osanna[a] saluifica[b].
81.	Raab lata siue dilatata.	*Rab[a] dilatata[b].
82.	Rachab.	-
83.	Ruth festinans.	*Ruth festinans[a].
84.	Roboam.	-
85.	Rachel ouis uel uidens deum.	*Rachel[a] ouis uidens deum.
86.	Rama excelsa siue exaltata.	*Rama[a] excelsa[b].
87.	Racha uanus.	*Racha[a] uanus.
88.	Rabbi magister meus. Syrum est.	*Rabbi syrum[a] magister.
89.	Ramatham.	-
90.	Salman sensibilis uel sensus.	Salman[a] sensibilis[b].
91.	Salomon pacificus siue pacatus erit.	Salomon[a] pacificus.
92.	Salathihel petitio mea deus.	Salathiel[a] petitio mea deus[b].

---

79. [a] Obet] Obeth *HdzPaC*, Obeht *Ev*
80. [a] Osanna] Ossanna *HdzEd*
 [b] saluifica] saluiuica *Hz*
81-88. *The abbreviated set follows the following order: 86, 85, 81, 83, 87, 88.*
81. [a] Rab] Raab *EdvGePaC*
 [b] dilatata] delatata *Hd*, dilectata *Hz*, dilat *C*
83. [a] festinans] festinat *C*
85. [a] Rachel] Rahel *HdGe*
86. [a] Rama] Ram *Hz*
 [b] excelsa] excaelsa *EdGe*
87. [a] Racha] Raha *Ge*, Raca *Pa*
88. [a] syrum] sirum *HdEv, omits Hz*
90. [a] Salman] Salmon *Hdz*
 [b] sensibilis] sensibiles *Ev*
91. [a] Salomon] Salemon *Hdz*
92. [a] Salathiel] Salatiel *Ed*, Salathel *Hz*
 [b] deus] dominus *HdEvC, omits Hz*

Matthew

93. Sadoc iustificatus siue iustus.   Saddoc[a] iustificatus.

94. Sidon uenatio.   Sidon[a] uenatio.

95. Thamar.   -

96. Thomas abyssus uel geminus,   Thomas abyssus[a].
     unde et graece Διδυμος
     adpellatur.

97. Thare.   -

98. Zara.   -

99. Zorobabel ipse magister   Zorobabel[a] ipse[b] magister
     Babylonis, id est confusionis.   Babylonis[c].

100. Zabulon habitaculum. Potest   Zabulon[a] habitaculum[b].
     et habitaculi substantia
     nuncupari.

101. Zebedaeus.   -

102. Zacharia.   -

103. Zacchaeus iustificatus aut   Zaccheus[a] iustificatus siue
     iustus uel iustificandus.   iustificandus.
     Syrum est, non hebraeum.

---

93. *Hq starts its imperfect Matthew names here*
     [a] Saddoc] Sadoch *Hd*, Sadoc *HqzEdvPaC*
94. [a] Sidon] Sydon *Hd*, Sadon *C*
96. [a] abyssus] abisus *EvGe*, abysus *HqzEd*
99. [a] Zorobabel] Sorobabel *Hd*, Zorobbabel *Ge*
     [b] ipse] iste *HdGePa*
     [c] Babylonis] Babilonis *EdvHqzC*, Babyllonis *Pa*
100. *C omits* 100
     [a] Zabulon] Sabulon *Hd*
     [b] habitaculum] habitaculum eorum *Hz* (*just possibly altered from*
        habitaculum)
103. [a] Zaccheus] Zacheus *HzEvC*, Sacheus *Hd*

The end of these names is announced thus in the following witnesses: Hd finit finit amen *Ge*
explicit interpraetatio nominum ebreorum; *Pa* finiunt nomina ebreorum euangelii
matthei.

Mark

Jerome	*Abbreviated set* (Witnesses *HdEfgGePa*)
1. Abba pater. Syrum, est non hebraeum.	Abba[a] syrum[b] pater.
2. Arimathia.	-
3. Idumaea rufa siue terrena.	Idumea rossa[a] siue terrena.
4. Israhel uir uidens deum. Sed melius rectus domini.	-
5. Cenna.	-
6. Salome pacifica.	Salome[a] pax[b] siue pacifica.
7. Tyro angustiae.	Tyro angustiae.
8. Tyrus.	-
9. Tiberius.	-
10. Talithacumi puella surge. Syrum est.	Thabithacumi[a] syrum[b] puella surge.
11. Trachonitidis negotiatio tristitiae.	Traconitidis negotiatio tristitiae.

Mark critical apparatus

The names are announced thus in the following witnesses: Hd incipit interpretatio ebreorum nominum secundum Marcum; *EfPa* incipit interpraetatio nominum ebreorum (*Pa* hebreorum); *Eg* cata marcum; *Ge* incipit interpraetatio nominum eiusdem.

The lists are arranged in separate columns of names and glosses except in Efg which are in long lines

1. [a] Abba] Abbas *Eg*
    [b] syrum] sirum *HdEgGe, omits Pa*
3   [a] rossa] rosa *EfgPa*
6. [a] Salome] Solome *HdEf*, Salone *Eg*, Salomae *Pa*
    [b] pax] *omits Efg*
10. [a] Thabitacumi] Thabithacommi *Hd*, Thabithacum *Eg*, Tabitha *Pa*
    [b] syrum] siri *Ge*, syris *Eg*, syre *Pa, omits HdEf*

Mark

12. (Aeffeta adaperire.)   Setha^a aperi^b.

13. (Paulus mirabilis siue   Paulus mirabilis siue electus^a
     electus).   pacificus.

---

12. *This is printed under Luke Hebrew names in Lagarde's edition, though the word glossed occurs at Mark 7:34*
     ^a Setha] Effeta *Hd*, Fheta *(H)*
     ^b aperi] aperi (F)
13. *Jerome has this under Paul's epistle to the Romans.*
     ^a electus] *omits Pa*

*The end of these names is announced thus in the following witnesses:*Hd finiunt hae interpretationes horum nominum; *Ef* finit interpretatio nominum; *Ev* (finit *but no names*) finit interpraetatio nominum; *Pa* explicit interpraetatio nominum hebreorum.

Luke

Jerome	Abbreviated set (Witnesses *HdEdGePaXrHq* (2-44, 85 only)
1. Aeffeta adaperire.	-
2. Augusti sollemniter stantis aut sollemnitatem additam.	Agusti[a] sollempniter[b] stantes[c].
3. Abiline.	-
4. Aaron mons eorum.	Aaron[a] mons eorum.
5. Anna gratia eius.	Anna[a] gratia eius.
6. Aser beatus aut beatus erit.	[a] Aser[b] beatus[a].
7. Amos onerans aut onerauit.	Amos[a] onerans[b].
8. Agge.	-
9. Addai robustus. Violenter figuratum nomen ab eo quod dicitur saddai.	Addai[a] robustus[b].

Luke critical apparatus

*For Xr, reliance has been placed on *Evangeliorum versio antehieronymiana ex codice Usseriano*, ed TK Abbott (Dublin 1884) I, 378.

The names are announced thus in the following witnesses: Hd incipit interpretatio ebreorum nominum secundum Lucanum; *GePa* incipit interpraetatio nominum eiusdem (*Pa* hebreorum)
The lists are arranged in separate columns of names and glosses.

1. *The abbreviated set has this under Mark 12*
2. [a] Agusti] Agustus *Hd*, Augusti *Pa*, [......] *Xr*
   [b] sollempniter] sollemniter *EdPa*, sollenniter *Xr*
   [c] stantes] stans *Hd*, [..]te[.] *Xr*
4. [a] Aaron] [....]n *Xr*
5. *Ge places 6 before 5*
   [a] Anna] Ana *HqEd*, [...]a *Xr*
6. [a-a] Aser beatus] Asser benedictus beatus *Hd*
   [b] Aser] [..]ser *Xr*
7. [a] Amos] [.]mons *Xr*
   [b] onerans] honerans *HdGeXr*
9. [a] Addai] [..]dai *Xr*
   [b] robustus] rubustus *Hd*

Luke

10.	Arfaxad sanans depopulationem.	Arfaxat[a] sanans[b] depopulatione[c].
11.	Adam homo aut terrenus siue indigena.	Adam[a] homo[b] terrenus.
12.	Ammaus populus abiectus.	Ammaus[a] populus abiectus[b].
13.	Caesar possessio principalis.	Caesar[a] possessio principalis.
14.	Cyrinus heres, qui apud nos melius effertur et uerius per Q litteram, ut dicatur Quirinus.	Cyrinus[a] heredes[b].
15.	Cosam diuinans.	Cossam[a] diuinans[b].
16.	Cainam luctus aut lugens.	Cainan[a] luctus.
17.	Cafarnaum ager uel uilla consolationis.	Cafarnaum[a] ager consulationis[b].
18.	Eseli.	-
19.	Eber transitus.	Cheber[a] transitus.
20.	Enoch.	-
21.	Enos.	-
22.	Erodes pelliceus gloriosus.	Herodis[a] pellicius.

---

10. [a] Arfaxat] Arfaxad *Hd*, Arfaxath *Pa*, [.]rfaxat *Xr*
     [b] sanans] sanans uel *Hd*, sonans *Pa*
     [c] depopulatione] de populo *Hd*
11. [a] Adam] [.]dam *Xr*
     [b] homo] homo siue *Hd*
12. [a] Ammaus] Amaus *Ge*, [.]mmaius *Xr*
     [b] abiectus] subiectus *Hd*
13. [a] Caesar] Cessar *Hd*, [.]esar *Xr*
14. [a] Cyrinus] Caereneu *HqEd*, Cereneu *GePa*, [.]ereneu *Xr*
     [b] heredes] heredes siue heres *Hd*, heredis (*H*)
15. [a] Cossam] Cosam *HqEdXr*
     [b] diuinans] ?[.]dinans *Xr*
16. [a] Cainan] Cinam *HqEd*, Cainam *Ge*, [.]enam *Xr*
17. [a] Cafarnaum] Capharnaum *GePa*, Cafarnau *HqEd*, [.]afarnau *Xr*
     [b] consulationis] consolationis *Pa*
19. [a] Cheber] Cedar *Hd*, Heber *Pa*, [.]heber *Xr*
22. [a] Herodis] Herodes *Pa*

Luke

23. Elisabeth dei mei saturitas   Elisabeth[a] dei mei saturitas.
    uel dei mei iuramentum aut
    septimus.

24. Eli adscendens.   Heli[a] ascendens.

25. Elmadai dei mei mensura.   Elmadadi[a] dei[b] mensura.

26. Er uigilans aut uigilia.   Er[a] uigilans[b].

27. Enam oculus eorum.   Enam[a] oculus eorum.

28. Elisaeus dei salus.   Helise[a] dei salus.

29. Fanuhel facies dei.   Fanuel[a] facies dei.

30. Fase transitus siue trans-   Fasse[a] transitus quod nos
    gressio, pro quo nostri   dicimus pascha[b].
    pascha legunt.

31. Falec.   -

32. Filippus os lampadis uel   Filippus[a] os[b] lampadis.
    os manuum.

33. Gabrihel confortauit me   Gabriel[a] fortitudo dei siue
    deus aut fortitudo dei uel   [b]confortatio dei[b].
    uirtus mea deus.

---

23. [a] Elisabeth] Elizapheth *Hd*, Helizabeth *Ge*, ?Aelisabeth *Hq*, Helisabeth *Pa*,
     Elisabeth *Xr*
24. [a] Heli] [.]eli *Xr*
25. *Ed places 25 and 26 erroneously on one line, with* Elmadadi Er *in the column for*
     names and dei mensura uigilans *in the column for their interpretation*
     [a] Elmadadi] Helmadadi *HdXr*, Helimadadi *Ge*, Helimadach *Pa*, Elmadadi (*FH*)
     [b] dei] *omits Hd*
26. [a] Er] Her *HdGePa*, [.]r *Xr*
     [b] uigilans] *stop after* ui *which is mistakenly placed in the column for names after* Er
     with gilans *entered in the column for their interpretation* Xr, uigelans *Hd*
27. [a] Enam] Henam *HdPa* [.]nam *Xr*
28. [a] Helise] Helisae *Ed*, Helesseus *Hd*, Heliseus *Pa*, [.]elisae *Xr*, Elisae *Hq (FH)*
29. [a] Fanuel] Phanuhel *Pa*
30. [a] Fasse] Phasec *Ge*, Fasec *HqEdXr*, Phasee *Pa*
     [b] pascha] pasca *Hd*
32. [a] Filippus] Philippus *GePa*
     [b] os] *apparently omitted but it may have been added in the now mutilated margin* Xr
33. [a] Gabriel] Gabrihel *Pa*
     [b-b]confortatio dei] dei confortatio *HdPa*

Luke

34. Galilaea uolutabilis aut   Galilea[a] uolubilitas[b].
    transmigratio perpetrata.

35. Gerasenorum suburbana aut   Gerasenorum[a] salus bona.
    coloni ibidem.

36. Ituraeae montanae. Syrum est.   Itureae[a] montanae[b].

37. Iordanis descensio eorum   Iordanis[a] discensus[b].
    aut adprehensio eorum uel
    uidens iudicium.

38. Ioni columba mea.   Iori[a] columba[b] mea.

39. Iannai.   -

40. Ioiarim dominus exaltans uel   Ioiarim[a] dominus exultans[b].
    est exaltans.

41. Iared.   -

42. Iona.   -

43. Iohanna dominus gratia eius   [a]Iohanna dominus gratia eius[a].
    uel dominus misericors.

44. Iairus inluminans uel   Iairus[a] inluminans.
    inluminatus.

45. Lysania natiuitas tenta-   Lisania[a] natiuitas
    tationis. Sed nimium   temptationis[b].
    uiolenter.

---

34.   [a] Galilea] Galilia *Hd*, Galilaea *Ed* (*twice with second* Galilaea *expunctuated*) *PaXr*
      [b] uolubilitas] uolutabilis *HqEdXr*, uolubilitas uolubilis *Pa*, uolubilitas *(F)*
35.   *Hq places 85 between 34 and 35*
      [a] Gerasenorum] Gerasinorum *Xr*, Gerassinorum *Hd*, Gerasearum *Hq*
36.   [a] Itureae] Iturae *HdGePa*, [.]turae *Xr*
      [b] montanae] montandae *Ed*, montaneae *Xr*
37.   [a] Iordanis] [..]rdanis *Xr*, Iordanes *Pa*
      [b] discensus] descensus *(FH)*
38.   [a] Iori] Iona *Hd*, [....] *Xr*
      [b] columba] culumba *Hq*
40.   [a] Ioiarim] Iotharim *Hd*, Iotarim *EdGe*, Ioarim *Pa*, Itarim *Hq*, [...] *Xr*
      [b] exultans] exsultans *HqEdXr*
43.   [a-a]Iohanna ...eius] [....] dominus [....] eius *Xr*
44.   *Xr's entry apparently lost, Hq's Luke names stop with 44*
      [a] Iairus] Iarus dominus *Hd*, Iairius *Ed[1]*
45.   [a] Lisania] Lissaniae *Hd*, Lisaniae *EdXr*
      [b] temptationis] tempestatum *Hd*, *?omits Xr*

Luke

46. Leui.   -

47. Lamech humilis. Quidam   Lamech[a] humilis.
putant percutientem siue
percussum posse resonare.

48. Lot.   -

49. Lazarus adiutus.   Lazarus[a] adiutus[b].

50. Moyses.   -

51. Mathathia donum dei aut   Mathathia[a] donum[b] dei.
aliquando.

52. Melchi rex meus.   Melchi rex meus.

53. Mathusale mortuus est et   Mathusala[a] mortuus est et
misit.   misit[b].

54. Maalelehel laudatus dei uel   Malaliel[a] laudans deum.
laudans deum.

55. Martha inritans, prouocans.   Martha prouocans deum.
Sermone autem syro domina
interpretatur uel dominans.

56. Naason.   -

57. Naum.   -

58. Neri.   -

59. Nathan.   -

60. Nachor.   -

---

47.   [a] Lamech] Lamec *Ed*
49.   [a] Lazarus] Latzarus *Hd*
      [b] adiutus] adiutor *Pa*
51.   [a] Mathathia] Matthatia *EdXr*, Mathatia *GePa*
      [b] donum] domus *Hd*, domum *Ed*
53.   [a] Mathusala] Mathusale *Hd*, Muthusalam *Pa*, Matusala *(FH)*
      [b] misit] missit *Hd*, m[....] *Xr*
54.   [a] Malaliel] Malaliae *Hd*, Malaliæl *Ed*, Malalehel *Pa*
55.   *Ed writes* 55 *and* 62 *erroneously on one line, placing a continuously written* Marthanaa *in the column for names and* prouocans deum pulchra *in the column for their interpretation*

Luke

61. Noe.   -

62. Naa pulchra.   Naa[a] pulchra[b].

63. Niniuitae natiuitas   Niniuitae[a] nati[b] speciosi[c].
    pulchritudinis aut speciosi.

64. Petrus agnoscens.   Petrus agnoscens.

65. Pontius declinans consilium.   Pontius declinans consilium[a].

66. Pilatus os malleatoris.   Pylatus[a] os malleatoris[b].
    Sed sciendum est quod apud
    Hebraeos P littera non
    habetur nec ullum nomen est
    quod hoc elementum sonet.
    Abusiue igitur accipienda
    quasi per F Litteram scripta
    sint.

67. Ros caput.   Ros[a] caput[b].

68. Ram sublimis.   Pam sublimis.

69. Reu.   -

70. Sicera ebrietas. Omne   Sicera[a] ebrietas[b].
    enim quod inebriare
    potest, apud Hebraeos
    sicera dicitur.

71. Symeon.   -

72. Sedi.   -

73. Semi.   -

---

62. [a] Naa] Naar *GePa*
     [b] pulchra] pulcra *Hd*
63. [a] Niniuitae] Nineuitae *GePa*, Niniuitae *Hd*, Niniuite *Xr*
     [b] nati] natis *Ed*
     [c] speciosi] speciossi *Hd*, specios[.] *Xr*
65. [a] consilium] con[...] *Xr*
66. [a] Pylatus] Pilatus *PaXr*
     [b] malleatoris] malliatoris *HdGePa*, malleator [..] *Xr*
67. [a]Ros] Phos *HdGePa*
     [b] caput] capud *EdXr*
70. [a] Sicera] Sicer *Ge*
     [b] ebrietas] aebrietas *Ge*, ebreitas *Hd*

Luke

74. Salathiel.   -

75. Salman pax.   Salman[a] pax.

76. Seruch.   -

77. Sale misit.   Salem misit[a].

78. Sem nomen   Sem nomen.

79. Seth.   -

80. Sarepta incensa siue   Sareptha[a] incensa siue
    angustia panis. Nomen   [b]angustia panis[b].
    ex hebraeo syroque
    conpositum.

81. Simon pone moerorem   Simon[a] pone[b] merorem[c].
    uel audi tristitiam.

82. Susanna lilium aut gratia   Susanna[a] lilium.
    eius. Sed melius si femininum
    nomen figuretur a lilio.

83. Samaritae custodes.   Samaritae[a] custodes[b].

84. Sodoma.   -

85. Satan aduersarius siue   Satan[a] aduersarius siue
    transgressor.   transgressor[b].

86. Saba captiuitas.   Saba[a] captiuitas.

---

75. [a] Salman] Salmon *Hd*, Saliman *Pa*, Salmaman *Xr*[1]
77. *Ge (which arranges the names in columns) writes* 77 *on the same line as* 75
     [a] misit] missit *Hd*
80. [a] Sareptha] Serepta *Hd*, Sarepta *Ed (written first before* 78 *but expunctuated)*
     [b-b] angustia panis] an[......] *Xr*
81. [a] Simon] Semeon *HdGe*
     [b] pone] pane *Xr*
     [c] merorem] merrorem *Ed*, memor [..] *Xr*
82. [a] Susanna] Sussanna *HdEd*, Subsanna *Xr*
83. [a] Samaritae] Samarite *Xr*
     [b] custodes] custodis *Xr*
85. *Hq places this between* 34 *and* 35
     [a] Satan] Satanan *Hd*
     [b] transgressor] transgresor *Hq*, transgessor *Ge*
86. [a] Saba] Sabaa *HdGePa*

Luke

87.   Sadducaei iustificati.   Sadducaei[a] iustificati.

---

87.   [a] Sadducaei] Saducei *Hd*, Sadducei *Xr*

The end of the names is announced thus in the following witnesses: *Hd* finit amen (amen *in Greek letters*); *Pa* finiunt nomina hebreorum.

John

Jerome	*Abbreviated set* (Witnesses *HdEdvGePa*)
1. Aenon oculus aut fons eorum.	Enom[a] fons.
2. Anani.	-
3. Banereem filii tonitrui, quod conrupte Boanerges usus optinuit.	Banerem[a] filii[b] tonitrui.
4. Barsemia.	-
5. Beelzebub habens muscas aut uir muscarum. In fine ergo nominis B littera legenda est, non L. Musca enim zebub uocatur.	Beelzebub[a] habens muscas aut[b] [c] deuorans aut uir muscarum[cd].
6. Barabbas filius patris.	Barabba[a] filius patris.
7. Cephas Petrus. Syrum est.	Cephas[a] Petrus.
8. Cana.	-

John critical apparatus

The names are announced thus in the following witnesses: Hd incipit interpretatio ebreorum nominum secundum Iohannem; *Ge* incipit interpraetatio nominum eiusdem; *Pa* incipit interpretatio hebreorum nominum secundum Iohannem.

The lists are arranged in separate columns of names and glosses except in Edv which are in long lines

1.   [a] Enom] Ennon *Hd*, Aenom *(F)*
3.   [a] Banerem] Bonarches *Hd*, Benarcem *Pa*
         [b] filii] fili *Ev*
         [c] tonitrui] thonitrui *Ed*
5.   [a] Beelzebub] Belzebub *HdEdPa*, Beelzebul *Ge*
         [b] aut] uel *Hd*
         [c-c] deuorans …muscarum] deuorans muscas aut uir muscarum *(H)*
         [d] muscarum] muscarius *Ed*
6.   [a] Barabba] Barabban *Hd*, Barabba *(FH)*
7.   [a] Cephas] Caephas *Hd*, Chephas *Ge*, Cefas *Ev*

John

9.	Efraim fertilis siue auctus, quem nos possumus ab augendo Augentium dicere.	Effraim[a] fertilis.
10.	Messias unctus, id est Christus.	Messia[a] unctus, id est Christus.
11.	Manna.	-
12.	Nazareth.	-
13.	Salim.	-
14.	Sichar conclusio siue ramus. Conrupte autem pro Sichem (quae transfertur in umeros) ut Sichar legeretur, usus optinuit.	Sichar conclusio[a].
15.	Siloe missus.	Syloe[a] missus[b].

(two extra names)

16.	-	Agios[a] sine terra.
17.	(Osanna saluifica, quod graece dicitur οωσον δη.)	Osanna[a] saluifica.

(repeated Mark names)

18.	Abba pater. Syrum est non hebraeum.	Abba sirum[a] pater.
19.	Arimathia.	-

---

9.   [a] Effraim] Effrem *Hd*
10.   [a] Messia] Missias *Hd*, Mesia *Ed*, Messia *(FH)*
14.   [a] conclusio] conclussio *Hd*
15.   *Hd merges* 14 *with* 15, *having an erroneous reading for* 15[a]
      [a] syloe] Siloe *EvGePa*, siue *Hd*
      [b] missus] misus *EdvGe*
16.   [a] Agios] Ageus *Hd*
17.   [a] Osanna] Ossanna *Ed*
17, 18 and 20. *omits Hd*
18.   [a] Sirum] Syrum *EdPa*

John

20.	Idumea rufa siue terrena.	Idumea[a] rosa[b] siue terrena.
21.	Israhel uir uidens deum. Sed melius rectus domini.	*Israhel anima uidens deum.
22.	Cenna.	-
23.	Salome pacifica.	Salome[a] pax siue pacifica.
24.	Tyro angustiae.	Tyro[a] angustiae.
25.	Tyrus.	-
26.	Tiberius.	-
27.	Talithacumi puella surge. Syrum est.	Thabithacum[a] syrum[b] puella surge.
28.	Trachonitidis negotiatio tristitiae.	Traconitidis[a] negotiatio angustiae.
29.	(Aeffeta adaperire).	Setha aperi.
30.	(Paulus mirabilis siue electus).	Paulus mirabilis siue electus[a] pacificus.
31.	-	Israhel[a] princeps cum domino[b].

---

20. [a]Idumea] Idumiea *Ed*
  [b] rosa] rossa *Ge*
21. *The abbreviated set places this before* 31 *below.*
23. [a] Salome] Solome *Hd*, Salomae *EdPa*
24. [a] Tyro] Tiro *Ev*
27 [a] Thabithacum] Tabithacommi *Hd*, Thabitacum *Ev*, Tabithacum *Pa*
  [b] syrum] *omits Hd*, sirum *Ev*
28-30. *Not found in Hd*
28. [a] Traconitidis] Traconitis *Ev*
30. *Jerome has this under the names for Paul's epistle to the Romans. It is not found in Hd*
  [a] electus] *omits EdvPa*
31. 21 *is placed before* 31 *in the abbreviated set*
  [a] Israhel] Istrahel *GePa*, Israel *Ed*
  [b] domino] deo *HdPa*

The end of the names is announced thus in the following witnesses: Hd finit; *Pa* finiunt nomina hebreorum.

Errata in McGurk, 'Texts at the opening of the Book of Kells: lists of Hebrew Names' in *The Book of Kells, MS 58, Trinity College Library Dublin: commentary*, ed P K Fox (Luzerne 1990) 37-58

p 49, n 32, line 1: delete *'Amos' (Luke 7) is spelt '(A)mous' and*
p 49, n 33, line 2: for *'Caerenen'* read *'Caereneu'*

The Stuttgart Matthew names were omitted from the witnesses considered and the following consequential changes become necessary.
p 47, col ii, after line 12: *Stuttgart, Württembergische*
Landesbibliothek MS 2°44 should be added with a / under Matthew and - under Mark, Luke and John.
line 16: for *exception* read *exceptions of the eleventh-century Stuttgart witness and*
line 17, for *They all* read *With the exception of the Stuttgart witness, they*
p 48, n 26,   line 1: for *four* read *on the Stuttgart manuscript and three*
line 3: for *the only one in our selective insular list, and three* read *two*
line 4: delete *163,*

Colour material and painting technique in the Book of Kells

Robert Fuchs and Doris Oltrogge

Observations and conclusions from a technical analysis of some of the pages.[1]

I. Methods of analysis

In 1991 and 1992 we had the opportunity to investigate the colour materials and painting technique of a number of pages in the Book of Kells.[2] The non-destructive analysis could be carried out with portable machines only: the binocular microscope and the colour spectrometer (**pls 147-48**). With these instruments a number of medieval colour materials can be identified with certainty and others can be determined with some probability. Only very few materials show identifiable structures under a microscope. The curves of the colour spectrometer give more conclusive results. This instrument illuminates for half a second a small spot of about 3 mm on the surface of the miniature.[3] Each coloured material absorbs parts of the white light and reflects other parts. The reflected light is analysed in the apparatus and forms a curve which is characteristic for different materials.[4] It has proved helpful for the interpretation of the colour curves to calculate their first derivation.[5] The combination of the results of microscopic analysis and colour measurement allows us to identify most colour materials. Some can be identified only with a certain probability, if, for example, they show characteristic deterioration. A few materials cannot be analysed with portable machines but would need non-destructive methods which could be used only in the laboratory in Cologne.[6] If materials have suffered too much change because of environmental influences or inappropriate preservation treatment analysis becomes extremely complicated and sometimes impossible.

---

[1]We should like to thank Christopher de Hamel for reading our text in English.
[2]We should like to thank P Fox and B Meehan, Trinity College Library, for giving us the (nearly unique) opportunity of analysing the Book of Kells. Many thanks are also due to F O'Mahony and S Ó Seanóir for their patience in turning pages. Our research was facilitated by a generous grant from Trinity College Library, Dublin.
[3]The light corresponds with daylight.
[4]Robert Fuchs, 'Zerstörungsfreie Untersuchungen an mittelalterlicher Buchmalerei' in *Zerstörungsfreie Prüfung von Kunstwerken*, Deutsche Gesellschaft für Zerstörungsfreie Prüfung, Berichtsband 13 (Berlin 1990) 120-27.
[5]See below (II.B.1) and fig 1a.
[6]Non-portable instruments are the XR-diffractometer, and the infra red-spectrometer; both instruments have been modified especially for our laboratory to allow non-destructive analysis of manuscripts. See Fuchs (note 4 above) 120-27.

In the first part of this paper we would like to present results of our analysis of the materials of the Book of Kells, which will be compared with materials in other insular manuscripts. Then we shall discuss the question of later additions and peculiarities of the painting technique.

II. Writing and painting materials

A. Materials of the Book of Kells

The manuscript is written with iron gall ink. Additional writing materials are red lead, orpiment, red ochre and a pink-mauve-coloured mixture made from a purple-coloured dye[7] and chalk. The palette used for the illumination is extraordinarily rich[8]:

yellow:
- orpiment
- yellow ochre

red:
- red lead
- red ochre

green:
- green copper pigment
- *vergaut* made from orpiment and indigo
- sap green
- green-brown mixture made from yellow-brown ochre and sap green

purple:
- purple-coloured dye
- pink mixture made from purple-coloured dye and chalk

blue:
- indigo
- blue mixture made from lapis lazuli (?), indigo and chalk (in a darker and a brighter variant)
- dark blue mixture made from lapis lazuli (?), indigo, chalk and purple-coloured dye (?)

---

[7] The same dye was used in the paintings, see below.
[8] Previous analysis of the colour material has been made by Roosen-Runge and Werner and by Cains with the microscope. Due to the limitations of this method a number of materials could not be identified. See Roosen-Runge/Werner, 263-77 (pp 273-74); Anthony Cains, 'The pigment and organic colours' in *Kells commentary*, 211-27. For a synopsis of these results, see Cains, 225-27.

brown:
- brown ochre
- iron gall ink
- *vergaut* mixed with iron gall ink

black:
- iron gall ink

white:
- chalk

B. Interpretation

1. *Yellow*[9]

The most important yellow and one of the main pigments of the Book of Kells is orpiment (**pl 150**). Very often orpiment can be identified even under the microscope because of its characteristic pigment structure. The pigment grains often look like fatty glittery scales, a form not found for instance in lead yellow. Also distinctive is the curve of the colour spectrometer (**fig 1a**) The spectral reflectance curves show the reflected parts of the visible (rainbow) colours. The curves show wavelengths versus intensity of the reflected light from left (violet, 380 nm) to right (red, 730 nm). The curve of pure orpiment shows that this pigment absorbs blue and green light and reflects yellow and red. The most important characteristic of the shape of the curve is its turning point. This can be seen more precisely in the first derivation of the curve printed here as a dotted line. Comparing the curve of a known sample of orpiment with the curve of the yellow in the Book of Kells (**fig 1b**), the similarity of both spectra is obvious, especially at the turning point. The orpiment in the Book of Kells has sometimes lost its very bright yellow hue; on some pages it has been turned white or brown by light, humidity and dirt which can on occasion disturb the measurement.[10]

2. *Red*[11]

The main red colour is the inorganic pigment red lead (**pl 154**). The bright orange-red hue is very typical for this material. Conclusive for the identification is the curve of the colour measurement; the curve of red lead (**fig 2a**) is significantly different from curves of vermilion (**fig 2b**) and red ochre (**fig 2c**), and this gives absolute proof that the red pigment in the Book of Kells is red lead (**fig 2d**).[12]

---

[9]For the interpretation of yellow ochre, see below (6/7 brown, black).

[10]For the deterioration of orpiment in manuscripts, see Robert Fuchs, Doris Oltrogge, 'Kontaktkorrosion', *Maltechnik* (forthcoming).

[11]For the interpretation of red ochre, see below (6/7 brown, black).

[12]One of the arguments of Roosen-Runge/Werner for the identification of the red pigment as red lead was a supposed reaction of red lead with orpiment to black lead sulfide (p 273). But in the Book of Kells the red lead is only seldom corroded. This mislead Cains (note 8 above) 212-13, to refute the identification and to propose

3. Green

One of the main green materials in the Book of Kells is a copper pigment (**pl 149**). The mineral malachite, for instance, is a natural green copper pigment. Furthermore, in antiquity and the middle ages artificial green copper pigments were also produced. The reconstruction of different recipes proves that this so-called 'verdigris' is normally a mixture of several green or blue-green copper pigments and that it can even include malachite.[13] These different compounds can be identified in medieval manuscripts with non-destructive (but non-portable) measurements.[14] Portable equipment allows the identification of green copper pigments in general but not the exact differentiation between all possible chemical compounds.

The colour curves of the very brilliant green in the Book of Kells show more similarities with malachite than with copper acetate. Therefore it may well be an artificial copper green in a mixture of copper carbonate, mixed with a smaller portion of copper acetate, and perhaps other compounds. An exact identification of these different compounds would only be possible with X-Ray-diffractometry.[15]

Another important green colour material in the Book of Kells is the dull *vergaut* (**pl 152**) mixed from yellow orpiment and blue indigo. The orpiment can mostly be identified by the microscope because of its crystalline structure; indigo can be identified by the colour curve (**fig 3**).

---

vermilion as the material of the main red pigment. But it should be noted that the chemical reaction of red lead and orpiment is not very common. Experiments have proved that red lead does not react easily with orpiment, especially when embedded with much medium. Even under bad conditions, as for example humidity, a reaction of red lead with orpiment does not necessarily occur. More dangerous seem to be environmental gases (hydrogen sulfide, H_2S) which can react in rather humid conditions with red lead to form black lead sulfide; but even here red lead is considerably more stable than lead white. Thus, if in the Book of Kells there are very few black corrosions of red lead, this is no conclusive argument against the identification of the red pigment as red lead. The red lead is always painted with much medium and is thus quite well preserved. The curves of the colour spectrometer show very distinctive differences between the medieval red pigments: red lead, vermilion and red ochre. The turning points clearly differ in their position. Thus, in this case the colour measurement is a conclusive argument for the identification of the main red pigment in Kells as red lead. It is interesting that so far in no early medieval manuscript could vermilion be found.

[13] Oskar Glemser, Gudrun Koltermann, et al, 'Über Grünspan, hergestellt nach mittelalterlichen Vorschriften', *Naturwissenschaftliche Rundschau* 46 (1993) 222-27.

[14] R Fuchs, D Oltrogge, 'Utilisation d'un livre de modèles pour la reconstitution de la peinture de manuscrits; aspects historiques et physico-chimiques' in *Pigments et Colorants*, Actes du Colloque International, Orléans 1988 (Paris 1990) 309-23 (pp 320-22).

[15] Green copper pigments are opaque pigments but 'verdigris' is water-soluble and can thus be dissolved in a very liquid medium. In this case it appears almost translucent even if under the microscope a few pigment grains nearly always remain visible. Depending on the liquidity of the medium, 'verdigris' can be painted as a translucent or as an opaque colour; a white 'body' (Cains, note 8 above, 214) is thus not necessary to produce an opaque 'verdigris' colour.

The greenish garment of St John on folio 291v (**pl 153**) is painted with a mixture of yellow brown ochre with sap green; the drawing of the folds is added in pure dark sap green.[16] Medieval recipes mention a number of green plant dyes for book illumination, for example the sap of rue,[17] cabbage, leeks or lilies.[18] It is not possible to distinguish these plant juices with portable machines because sap greens are very sensitive to environmental influences which can change their colour.

4. *Purple/pink*

Of great interest are the purple and pink colours which were extensively used in the illumination and in the script of the Book of Kells. Portable instruments do not allow an exact identification of the purple-coloured dye (**pls 158-59**). But the colour spectra show some characteristics which help at least to limit the number of possible candidates. Three different shades of the purple-coloured dye can be found in the Book of Kells: brownish purple, deep red purple and bluish purple;[19] the red and bluish purples were also mixed with white[20] to obtain a pink or mauve hue.[21] The spectra of these different hues are nearly identical and prove that the same dye was always used (**fig 4**).[22] Different kinds of preparation produced variations of purple hues.[23]

What sort of dye was this? In antique and medieval recipes the following purple colours are mentioned: true purple from purple shellfish,[24] *folium*

---

[16]Sap green seems to be used very seldom in the Book of Kells; with the exception of folio 291v we could detect the mixture of yellow brown ochre and sap green only on folio 202v in some greenish hairs.

[17]Göttingen Model Book, folio 5v, see Doris Oltrogge, Robert Fuchs, Solange Michon, 'Laubwerk - Zur Texttradition einer Anleitung für Buchmaler aus dem 15. Jahrhundert', *Würzburger medizinhistorische Mitteilungen* 7 (1989) 179-213 (p 201).

[18]Green colour produced from the sap of cabbage, leeks and lilies is described for example by Theophilus I, 32, see *Theophilus. De diversis artibus. The various arts*, ed Charles R Dodwell (London 1961) 30.

[19]The bluish purple (identified by Roosen-Runge/Werner, 273 as *Folium saphireum*) was occasionally used, for instance, on folio 13.

[20]The white 'body' was presumably chalk; see below.

[21]The mauve colour which was produced with the bluish purple dye seems to be used more often than pure bluish purple dye (for instance on folio 290v).

[22]Depending on the hue, the last turning point shifts somewhat towards the red or the blue; but such small variations are due only to the difference in hue, and the nearly identical form of curves and derivation prove the identity of the material.

[23]Although the Book of Kells has suffered heavily, the different hues are not produced by corrosion but have been prepared deliberately by the painters (even the brownish purple). This can clearly be observed on one of the rather better preserved pages, folio 290v, where in a rich play of colour all three variations of purple dye, together with the pink and the mauve mixture, were used.

[24]Purple dye from shellfish is often mentioned in antiquity, for example in Pliny IX, 125-38, see *C. Plinius Secundus d. Ä., Naturalis Historiae Libri XXXVII*, ed Roderich König (Darmstadt 1979ff) 92-103; Vitruvius VII, 13, see *Vitruvii de architectura libri decem*, ed Curt Fensterbusch, 4th edn (Darmstadt 1987) 350-51. An eighth-century recipe is found in the Lucca manuscript, T 22-27, see *Compositiones ad Tingenda Musiva*, ed Hjalmar Hedfors (Uppsala 1932) 172. Bede mentions the dyeing of cloths with purple shellfish from the Irish Sea in *HE* I, see *Bedae opera historica*, ed C Plummer (Oxford 1956) 2.

from Crozophora tinctoria Juss.,[25] purple dye from elderberries, dwarf elder, blueberries,[26] brazil wood[27] and papaver.[28] As a local purple dye Cains proposed various lichens,[29] materials which so far have not been identified in medieval recipes.

Comparing the spectra of the Kells purple and pink colours with those of the dyestuffs just mentioned, some prove to be extremely different. Thus the true purple shows a significantly different curve, and even more distinctive is the first derivation which defines the turning points of the curve. Therefore we can exclude the true purple dye from shellfish. Very different also are the curves of elderberry, blueberry, brazil wood, papaver, and madder (**fig 5**).

On the other hand there seems to be a certain conformity with the spectra of alcanna, of *folium* from the Crozophora tinctoria Juss. and of cudbear lichen (Ochrolechia tartaria L.) (**fig 6**).[30] The characteristic form of the curves in particular and the form of the first derivation show great similarities, but not complete identity. Agreement is not conclusive enough to determine exactly which of the three materials is that used in the Book of Kells, but these three dyestuffs remain the most likely candidates for the identification.[31] For the decision further analysis with other non-destructive methods would be necessary.

---

[25]A good description of the production of the purple dye from folium is found in Theophilus I (note 18 above, 30-31). For other recipes and the identification of folium with Crozophora tinctoria Juss., see R Fuchs, D Oltrogge, 'Das Blau in der mittelalterlichen Buchmalerei - Quellenschriften als Basis naturwissenschaftlicher Farbuntersuchungen' in *Blau - Farbe der Ferne* (Exhibition catalogue Heidelberg März bis Juni 1990) 104-30 (pp 118-19). Folium was proposed by Roosen-Runge/Werner, 273 as the purple dye in the Lindisfarne Gospels and the Book of Kells.

[26]Purple dye produced from blueberries is already mentioned by Vitruvius VII, 14 (note 24 above, 352-53). *Sucus sambuci* from elderberries is known from Theophilus I, 14 (note 18 above, 12). The Mappae Clavicula 97, see 'Mappae Clavicula', ed Cyril Stanley Smith, John G Hawthorne, *Transactions of the American Philosophical Society*, ns, 64, 4 (1974) 3-128 (p 41) describes a purple dye produced from dwarf elder. Recipes for the use of berries for the production of purple dye became very common in the late middle ages; see Fuchs, Oltrogge (note 25 above) 121-24.

[27]The earliest known recipe for a colour material produced from brazil wood is the eleventh-century Heraclius III, 34, see *Heraclius. Von den Farben und Künsten der Römer*, ed Albert Ilg (Wien 1873) 76-77. But the use of brazil wood as colour material can be proved already in Roman antiquity, for instance in the Quedlinburg Itala from about 400, see Robert Fuchs, Doris Oltrogge, Gertrud Schenk, Renate van Issem, 'Glas oder Kunststoff? Zur Konservierung der Italafragmente der Deutschen Staatsbibliothek in Berlin (DDR)', *Restauro* 96.4 (1988) 285-91 (p 288).

[28]A recipe is found for instance in the fifteenth-century Strassburg Manuscript, see *Das Straßburger Manuskript. Handbuch für Maler des Mittelalters*, ed and trans Viola and Rosamund Borradaile, 3rd edn (München 1982) 36-37.

[29]Cains (note 8 above) 216-17, for example the Ochrolechia tartaria.

[30]We should like to thank Anthony Cains for the opportunity of measuring one of his samples produced from cudbear lichen, chalk water and ammonia. For a description of the preparation of these samples, see Cains (note 8 above) 216-17.

[31]It is not yet clear if it is possible to produce the bluish purple shade from alcanna or lichen. Our experiments with alcanna have so far failed; lichen was prepared by Cains who got only brownish and red purple shades.

5. *Blue*

Four different shades of blue are used in the Book of Kells: very light blue, azure, dark blue and very greenish blue. The greenish blue contains no pigment grains; the colour curves prove it to be indigo. This colour material could be obtained from the *Indigofera tinctoria* L. plant or from woad (*Isatis tinctoria* L.). It is not possible to distinguish the plant source since the dyestuff is, in both cases, indigo and thus chemically identical. The indigo found in the Book of Kells often looks very greenish (**pl 160**) because, due to the method of production, residues of chlorophyll remained in the pigment.

The three other shades (**pls 160, 164-65, 186**) just mentioned always contain pigment grains: a white body (presumably chalk)[32] and small bright blue crystals. The colour curves of all three mixtures are very similar, the difference in the hue seems to be due only to the addition of chalk. The curves of the dark blue show some smaller differences which seem to indicate a mixture with a third material.

How can this blue be identified? In all curves the characteristics of indigo are predominant in the form of curve and derivation (**figs 7** and **3b**). Thus indigo is an important ingredient of the mixture.[33] But there are always some minor differences which seem to be due to the blue pigment which can be detected under the microscope. Form and colour of these bright blue crystals could be an indication of lapis lazuli; the characteristics of the colour curve does not contradict this identification.[34] A conclusive proof is not possible with colour measurement; this would be achieved only with XR-diffractometry.

For the brilliant dark blue another material was added to the mixture of lapis lazuli, indigo, and chalk, which seems to be the purple dye. Indications of this can be found on folios 2v and 7v. Here the dark blue is partly lost, and the parchment beneath is coloured purplish. The most satisfactory explanation is that the dark blue was mixed with the purple dye. This has coloured the medium, and with the medium, also the parchment.[35] This should be distinguished from another technique, the glazing of blue with purple dye, which we will discuss later.

---

[32]For the identification of chalk, see below.

[33]Indigo cannot be identified with certainty under the microscope; in mixtures it is often not possible to detect it at all. Therefore Roosen-Runge/Werner, 273, and Cains (note 8 above, 214) could only detect the blue pigment, which they interpreted as pure lapis lazuli.

[34]The other candidate for identification would be azurite; but mixed with indigo it remains more dominant in the colour measurement even if only a little azurite is added to the indigo.

[35]Also the colour curve suggests an addition of purple dye to the dark blue.

6. Brown/
7. Black

Occasionally different shades of yellow, brown, red and red-brown ochre are used for hairs and beards[36] (pls 151, 155) and for frames.[37] Finely ground red-brown ochre painted with much medium is also the material of the nearly transparent garments of the two men 'arresting' Christ on folio 114v (pl 161).

A red-brown translucent material was also used for the filling of interlace ornaments (pl 157) or as a glaze on red lead and orpiment (pl 156).[38] Painted with much medium it has a pasty lacquer-like structure. Under the microscope pigment grains could not be found; it could thus be either an organic dye or an extremely finely ground pigment. The very small lines of less than 1 mm allowed only few measurements with the colour spectrometer (fig 8). At first sight the curve looks very unspecific because the spot is so small that the parchment and the black ink contour are also measured. But in the first derivation the turning point (dotted line) can be determined precisely indicating that the red glaze must contain red-brown ochre (fig 2c). This pigment can be pulverised so much that it is nearly impossible to detect pigment grains under a binocular even with our highest magnification (factor 128). The interpretation of the colour curves cannot totally exclude the possibility that a second organic material was mixed with the ochre; but this cannot be proved with portable instruments. At the very least we can say that red-brown ochre is the main material of the brown interlace fillings and glazes.

The drawing material varies between black and black-brown; a light translucent yellowish brown ink was also used as a glaze on copper green. This ink could be either a buckthorn ink or the brown component of iron gall ink.[39] The black and brown-black material can be identified as iron-gall ink. Carbon seems to have been used only very occasionally.

The identification of iron gall ink is proved by its hue (pl 163) and its structure under the microscope. Iron gall ink does not form a perfect solution; the black iron-gallate compound, which is not soluble in water, results from a reaction with oxygen from the air and it creates flakes of colour.[40] In the inkpot these black compounds often settle to the bottom after some time. The painter or scribe would find a lighter brown liquid in

---

[36]Yellow ochre is used for instance on folios 28v, 291v, red-brown ochre on folio 114.

[37]For instance the red-brown frames on folio 290v.

[38]This material was described as 'kermes' by Roosen-Runge/Werner, 273.

[39]Roosen-Runge/Werner, 273 identified this material with oxgall. This seems improbable because of the brownish hue, whereas oxgall tends to be more greenish. An exact identification with portable instruments is not possible.

[40]This is very different in structure from the grains of carbon or lamp black, an identification proposed for the very black lines by Cains (note 8 above) passim. Normally the painters of the Book of Kells used iron gall ink for their black lines.

the upper part of the pot and the black iron-gallate complex at the bottom. This explains the changes of hue from brown to black of writing ink and drawing material. The intensive black material also belongs to iron gall ink.[41]

A unique 'black' was used for the devil in the Temptation (pl 162); it is a mixture from *vergaut* with iron gall ink on which even 'blacker' lines were drawn, this time probably with carbon or lamp black.

8. White

The identification of white pigments with the portable colour spectrometer is restricted because white has no colour or, if we may say so, has all colours. But the way that the white of the Book of Kells has survived gives some good indications for the identification of the painted white. The two possible white materials of the middle ages were lead white[42] and chalk. Lead white is sensitive to environmental influences. Very often it reacts with the hydrogen sulfide (H_2S) of the air or with orpiment and the surface of the lead white blackens to lead sulfide. This deterioration occurs also with red lead. In the Book of Kells only the red lead sometimes shows this effect but not the white (pl 166) or its mixtures.[43] Chalk on the other hand is much more stable which would explain the good condition of the white and its mixtures. Chalk could either be found as mineral or produced from bones or from ground shells.[44]

9. Binding media

The analysis of binding media is very complicated; even with 'destructive' methods of analysis it is not always possible to identify the substances exactly. With portable instruments an exact identification of media is impossible. Only the characteristic bubbles are a good indication for the use of egg white — such bubbles are found in the red lead and in the pink mixture of the Book of Kells. But due to the different characteristics of painting materials the illuminators often used different media for different colour materials. Therefore the possible use of egg white for the pink

---

[41]The exact identification of different inks is now possible with IR-reflectography, a method which was not yet available during our research work in Dublin.

[42]This is the material proposed for the Book of Kells' white by Roosen-Runge/Werner, 273 and Cains (note 8 above) 214-15.

[43]As mentioned before (note 12 above) lead white is very much more sensitive to environmental influences than red lead which makes it even more improbable that the very well preserved white in the Book of Kells could be lead white. But it should be noted that the portable colour spectrometer and microscope do not allow a conclusive proof for lead white or chalk. It is now possible to identify both white materials with IR-reflectography, a portable method, which was not yet available during our research work in Dublin.

[44]Heraclius II, 40 (bones) (note 27 above, 80-81); Mappae Clavicula 174A (shells) (note 26 above, 52).

mixture gives no information about the media for the other pigments and dyes.

C. The question of later changes in the canon table on folio 2v and in some parts of the text: the technological aspect

On some pages the possibility of later changes has been discussed. The smaller columns on folio 2v are clearly painted after the writing of the text (**pls 167-68**). The question is only whether this was done immediately, perhaps by the scribe himself to separate the different text columns more clearly, or — as was suggested by Friend[45] — whether it was done some years later to complete an unfinished manuscript. The possibility of a later addition to an unfinished manuscript has also been suggested for the striking break in the framing of the canon tables on folios 5v and 6.[46] Furthermore, there are some pages on which text is repeated in another script, and, as Meehan argues, also by a scribe whose hand can only be found in such 'additions'.[47] Alexander[48] and Meehan suggested that a scientific analysis of the materials could perhaps help to solve the question.

Dating of pigments and dyes is not normally possible (except for falsifications with modern material). What can be done with colour measurement is a comparison of colour materials. Thus, if there are doubts of the homogeneity of script or painting of a manuscript, one can compare the materials throughout the manuscript. This can give some indication about the production of the manuscript but it should always be interpreted together with analysis of painting technique, text and style.

For reasons of time we analysed only the canon tables on folios 2v, 5v, 6 and the questionable script on folios 13, 22, 24, 26, 114, 183 and 203.[49] The script is written and ornamented with iron gall ink, red lead, orpiment, purple-coloured dye and pink; the columns on folio 2v are painted with purple-coloured dye, and the contours of one capital are drawn with iron gall ink. Purple-coloured dye in different shades from brown to red purple is also the material for the grid canon tables on folios 5v and 6. Iron gall ink, red lead and orpiment are the most common colour materials in insular scriptoria and are used ubiquitously. Thus, these materials are irrelevant for the question of homogeneity or of later additions. Only the organic purple

---

[45]A M Friend, 'The canon tables of the Book of Kells' in *Medieval studies in memory of Arthur Kingsley Porter*, ed W R W Koehler (Cambridge, Mass 1939) II, 611-41 (p 615).
[46]ibid, 615. Patrick McGurk, 'Two notes on the Book of Kells and its relation to other insular gospel books', *Scriptorium* 9 (1955) 105-07 has shown that a similar break in framing occurs in BL, MS Royal 7. C. xii and has argued that a common model with the Royal manuscript, and not a break in the working process, should be responsible for the different framing forms in Kells.
[47]See Meehan, 245-56. Hand B is found for instance on folios 114, 183, 249v.
[48]Alexander, 'Illumination', 271.
[49]The analysis of folios 5v, 6, 13 and 114 was carried out only after the conference in September 1992 and was not included in the lecture. But the results confirm the conclusions drawn from the analysis of folios 2v, 22, 24, 26, 183 and 203.

dye and the purple dye mixed with white to obtain a pink colour can be more specific, because this colour can be prepared from a number of different sources.

The curve of the purple-coloured dye used for the small columns on folio 2v is identical with the curves of other purple-coloured dyes found in the manuscript, for example in the capital on folio 3 (**pl 169**) or in the garment of Christ on folio 114 (**pl 171**). The same characteristics are found in the colour curves of the purple-coloured dye on folio 6. The spectrum of the brownish purple of folio 6 for instance is identical with that of the brownish garment of Christ on folio 32v (**fig 9**). The pink and mauve mixtures in the script on folios 24 and 26 are also clearly made from the same material. If we compare the curves of pink mixtures used for example in the picture of the Virgin we always detect the same characteristic turning points and a very similar form of the curve and of the first derivation (**fig 10**). Therefore, we can conclude that it is very likely that the purple dye and thus also the pink mixture are always the same materials throughout the manuscript.

The next question is whether this material was common or not. We can compare the Book of Kells purple-coloured dye with some other insular manuscripts: Cambridge, Corpus Christi College, MS 179B,[50] the Book of Mulling,[51] Durham, MS A.II.17,[52] the Durham Cassiodorus,[53] the Barberini Gospels (**pl 172**),[54] the St Gall Gospels[55] and the Stockholm *Codex Aureus* (**pl 170**).[56] The colour curves of the purple and pink in these manuscripts are very similar to the curves of the Book of Kells' purple and pink (**fig 11**). Even if the material cannot be identified with certainty this striking conformity is an indication that probably the same material was used in all these manuscripts. It is not impossible that the same dye was also used in continental book illumination, since the curve of the purple-coloured dye in the *Codex Argenteus* in Uppsala shows the same characteristics found in insular manuscripts.

The purple dye in the Book of Kells is thus most probably a well-known material in insular scriptoria of different times and places. When considering the question of later changes, this means that the material for the pink and purple colours alone is not conclusive for, or against, a time-lap of some years or even another scriptorium. We have thus to consider all aspects on folios 2v, 5v and 6: that is working process, layout of the page and material.[57] The script on folio 2v was clearly written before the painting of the smaller columns, even if the layout of the architectural frame must

---

[50]Alexander, *Insular manuscripts* 44, no 12 (hereafter cited as Alexander).
[51]TCD, MS 60; Alexander, 67-68, no 45.
[52]Durham, Chapter Library, MS A.II.17; Alexander, 40-42, no 10.
[53]Durham, Chapter Library, MS B.II.30; Alexander, 46, no 17.
[54]Rome, Bibl. Vat., Barb. lat. 570; Alexander, 61-62, no 36.
[55]St Gall, Stiftsbibliothek, MS 51; Alexander, 66-67, no 44.
[56]Stockholm, Kungliga Bibl., MS A. 135; Alexander, 56-57, no 30.
[57]For a summary of the different problems of layout and decoration of the canon tables, see Alexander, 'Illumination', 268-73.

have been designed before. It is also possible that the painting of the
architectural frame was completed before the writing, as was clearly done
on folio 3. But it should be remarked that conclusive proof for the same
working process is missing on folio 2v and that for the scribe the
preliminary drawing would have been sufficient for his layout.[58] He filled
the three spaces between the four larger columns with six columns of text
for which an additional separation would seem more than logical.[59] The
material for these smaller stripes is identical with the purple dye of the
painting, for example in the base of the outer columns and also in the script
in some of the letters. Even if this material was known for a long time in
insular scriptoria there seems to be no reason to assume that the stripes
were added at a later time. It is possible either that the whole painting of the
page was done after the script or that the scribe who used the same purple
dye to emphasize some of the letters added them as an attempt to achieve a
clearer layout.[60]

D. The materials of the Book of Kells and materials in other insular and in continental book illumination of the early middle ages

We have already mentioned that the purple dye and pink mixture were also
used in other insular manuscripts. We should now ask how common the
other materials of the Book of Kells were in early medieval, and especially
in insular, book illumination. Up to now we have had the opportunity of
analysing the following insular manuscripts:[61]

-        Cambridge CCC 179B[62]

-        Book of Armagh[63]

---

[58]There seem to be no general rules for the working process in the Book of Kells. On
folio 3 the architectural framing was completely painted before the numbers were
written since they overlap the painting in some places. On folio 5v first the layout of
the grid canon table was drawn, then the numbers were written, and finally the
purple dye was filled in (and sometimes overlaps the script). On the other hand we
have some pages with completed text but unfinished painting, for instance folios 30-
31, where only orpiment and mauve were filled in.

[59]Folio 3 also contains two columns of numbers between two columns of the
architectural frame, but here the numbers are often so long that a separation would
have been impossible. This is perhaps the reason why on this page the painter or
scribe decided against one.

[60]The question of folios 5v and 6 is more complicated because of the enigmatic
change in the layout. Considering the material it would seem very likely that the
grid canon tables were written and painted in the same working period as the mn-
canon tables and the rest of the manuscript, even if the materials could also have
been available at a later period or even in another scriptorium.

[61]We should like to thank those responsible in the Corpus Christi College Library,
Cambridge, Trinity College Library, Dublin, the Chapter Library, Durham, the
Stiftsbibliothek, St Gall, the Royal Library, Stockholm, the Biblioteca Apostolica
Vaticana for their generous assistance in our investigation.

[62]See note 50 above.

[63]TCD, MS 52; Alexander, 76-77, no 53.

- Garland of Howth[64]

- Book of Durrow[65]

- Book of Dimma[66]

- Book of Mulling[67]

- Durham: earlier gospel fragment[68]

- Durham: later gospel fragment[69]

- Durham Cassiodorus[70]

- St Gall Irish Gospels[71]

- Stockholm *Codex Aureus* of Canterbury[72]

- Barberini Gospels[73]

For a broader comparison with late antique and early medieval book illumination we can use our results from the analysis of the late-antique Quedlinburg Itala,[74] of some Merovingian[75] and Carolingian manuscripts[76] and of a number of Ottonian[77] manuscripts. Two of the main colour

---

[64]TCD, MS 56; Alexander, 80, no 59.
[65]TCD, MS 57; Alexander, 30-32, no 6.
[66]TCD, MS 59; Alexander, 69, no 48.
[67]See note 51 above.
[68]Durham, Chapter Library, MS A.II.10; Alexander, 29-30, no 5.
[69]See note 52 above. Early English manuscripts in facsimile 20, ed C D Verey, T J Brown, E Coatsworth (Copenhagen 1980).
[70]See note 53 above.
[71]See note 55 above.
[72]See note 56 above.
[73]See note 54 above.
[74]Berlin, Staatsbibliothek, theol. lat. fol 485; Fuchs, Oltrogge, Schenk, van Issem (note 27 above) 288.
[75]Missale Gothicum (Vat. Reg. lat. 317), *Vaticana. Liturgie und Andacht im Mittelalter* (Ausstellungskatalog Erzbischöfliches Diözesanmuseum Köln 1992) 62, no 2; Sacramentarium Gelasianum (Vat. Reg. lat. 316), *Vaticana*, 64-65, no 3; Missale Gallicanum Vetus (Vat. Pal. lat. 493), *Vaticana*, 68, no 4.
[76]Lorsch Gospels (Vat. Pal. lat. 50), *Vaticana* (note 75 above) 74-75, no 6; Fulda Gospels (Würzburg, Universitätsbibliothek, M.p.th.f.65), Gottfried Mälzer, Hans Thurn, *Kostbare Handschriften der Universitätsbibliothek Würzburg* (Wiesbaden 1982) 66, no 26; Folchart Psalter (St Gall Cod. 23), *Der Folchart-Psalter aus der Stiftsbibliothek St Gallen*, ed P Ochsenbein, B v. Scarpatetti (Freiburg, Basel, Wien 1987); Wolfcoz Psalter (St Gall Cod. 20), Alfred Merton, *Die Buchmalerei in St Gallen vom 9. bis zum 11. Jh.* (Leipzig 1923) 17-27; Golden Psalter (St Gall Cod. 22), Christoph Eggenberger, *Psalterium Aureum Sancti Galli* (Sigmaringen 1987); Wandalbert of Prüm (Vat. Reg. lat. 438), *Vaticana* (note 75 above) 82, no 8.
[77]A broad survey of materials and techniques of Ottonian book illumination is in progress; a number of important manuscripts from Reichenau, Trier, Echternach, Regensburg, and Hildesheim have already been analysed. For preliminary reports, see R Fuchs, D Oltrogge, 'Kerald und Heribert. Zur Entstehung des Widmungsbildes

materials of the Book of Kells are also two of the most important colour materials of early medieval book production in general: red lead and orpiment.[78] Thus, we have found in nearly all insular manuscripts so far analysed that red lead and orpiment are the main red and yellow colour materials respectively.[79] Both pigments are also well documented in antique and medieval recipe texts.[80] The use of iron gall ink as the main black and brown-black colour material for writing and drawing is also typical for all insular manuscripts which we have been able to analyse.

Well-known in insular and other early medieval book illumination, as well as in antique and medieval recipe texts,[81] are the copper green pigments. Copper green is the only green colour material in the Book of Durrow, in the later gospel fragment in Durham, in Cambridge CCC 179B and in the Durham Cassiodorus. In the Barberini Gospels a copper green pigment and *vergaut* were used. 'Verdigris', ie copper green pigment, and *vergaut* were also found by Roosen-Runge/Werner in the Lindisfarne Gospels.[82] In the other insular manuscripts so far analysed, *vergaut* is the only green colour material. This mixture is quite common in early medieval book illumination. In insular manuscripts we have found it in the Irish Gospels in St Gall, the earlier gospel fragment in Durham (**pl 173**),[83] the Book of Mulling, the Book of Dimma, the Garland of Howth and the Stockholm *Codex Aureus*. An early medieval recipe is known only from Heraclius.[84] He describes two *vergaut* mixtures, one made from orpiment and indigo, and the other from orpiment and lapis lazuli. In the early medieval manuscripts analysed so far the mixture from orpiment and indigo proves to be more common.[85]

---

im Codex Egberti', *Kurtrierisches Jahrbuch* 29 (1989) 65-86; idem, 'Naturwissenschaft und Stilkritik — Handschriften aus dem Umkreis des Registrum-Meisters', *Kunsthistoriker* Jg. VIII (Sondernummer 1991) 96-104.

[78]A synopsis of all colour materials of the insular manuscripts cited is found in fig 13.

[79]In the Garland of Howth we analysed only the miniature on folio 1 and the incipit of Mark on folio 22, where only red ochre was used. Since we were not able to check the whole manuscript it cannot be excluded that on the text pages red lead was used.

[80]The production of red lead is already described by Pliny xxxv, 38, 39 (note 24 above, 36-41) and Vitruvius VII, 12 (note 24 above, 348-51). Medieval recipes are found for instance in Mappae Clavicula VII, (note 26 above, 27), Heraclius III, 36 (note 27 above, 76-79), Theophilus I, 37 (note 18 above, 33). Orpiment is mentioned for instance by Vitruvius VII, 7 (note 24 above, 338-41). Red lead and orpiment are also very common in Merovingian and Carolingian book illumination.

[81]The earliest recipes for artificial green copper pigments are Theophrastos, Peri lithôn 57, see *Theophrastus on stones*, ed Earl R Caley, John F C Richards (Columbus, Ohio 1956) 191-93, Vitruvius VII, 12 (note 24 above, 348-49), Pliny xxxiv, 110, 111 (note 24 above, 80-83). In the middle ages recipes for artificial green copper pigments can be found in nearly every recipe collection.

[82]Roosen-Runge, Werner, 263-72.

[83]Here it is a mixture from a blue pigment (presumably lapis lazuli), indigo and orpiment which is very uncommon in insular book illumination; the normal insular *vergaut* seems to be a mixture from indigo and orpiment.

[84]Heraclius III, 56, 14 (note 27 above, 92-93); the *azurium* in this case probably means lapis lazuli.

[85]For instance in Carolingian manuscripts such as the Fulda Gospels in Würzburg, the Wolfcoz and the Folchard Psalters in St Gall.

Less common in insular book illumination are blue and purple colours which are omitted in a number of manuscripts.[86] Indigo is a wide-spread material in early medieval book illumination; it seems to have been generally known. Insular manuscripts using indigo are the Book of Armagh, the Book of Dimma,[87] the Book of Mulling, the Garland of Howth, the Barberini Gospels and the Stockholm *Codex Aureus*. Roosen-Runge/Werner found it also in the Lindisfarne Gospels.[88] The greenish hue which is characteristic of indigo in the Book of Kells can be compared with the Book of Armagh, the Garland of Howth and the Barberini Gospels.[89] In the *Codex Aureus* only rather dark blue indigo and deep blue indigo mixed with white are found.

Less familiar in early medieval scriptoria is the use of a blue pigment. We have been able to prove it only in the earlier Durham Gospels (pl 173), in the Book of Dimma,[90] in the Book of Mulling, in the Barberini Gospels and the Irish Gospels in St Gall (pl 174).[91] The curves are very similar to the curves of the Kells blue mixture which would suggest a mixture with indigo (fig 12). Furthermore, in the Book of Kells, as in all these insular manuscripts, a white body, presumably chalk, is added to the mixture of indigo and blue pigment. The pigment cannot be identified with certainty, but, as in the Book of Kells, there are certain indications in form and colour of the pigment crystals and in some characteristics of the colour curve that the pigment might be lapis lazuli. If this identification is correct, these manuscripts would be among the earliest examples of the use of lapis lazuli for book illumination. In antiquity lapis lazuli was not used as a pigment but only as a stone. Therefore it is not found in antique book illumination; for example in the late antique Quedlinburg Itala (*c*400 AD) the material for the blue colour is indigo.[92] In the early middle ages we find the earliest

---

[86]Purple is missing in the earlier Durham Gospels, in Durrow, Armagh and Dimma. Blue is missing in Durrow, Cambridge, the later Durham Gospels and the Durham Cassiodorus.

[87]In the miniatures and initials in Matthew, Mark and Luke; in John only a mixture made from a blue pigment (presumably lapis lazuli), indigo and chalk can be found.

[88]Roosen-Runge, Werner, 263-72. They mention also a greenish hue.

[89]This could be an indication for woad, since the greenish hue is obtained during the preparation as an inferior colour material; see R Fuchs, S Michon, 'Memento manuscriptorum ornatorum. Überlegungen zur Erhaltung mittelalterlicher Buchmalerei - Untersuchungen zur Technik illuminierter Handschriften am Beispiel des Pfäferser Liber Viventium', *Unsere Kunstdenkmäler — Nos monuments d'art et d'histoire — I nostri monumenti storici* (Mitteilungsblatt für die Mitglieder der Gesellschaft für Schweizerische Kunstgeschichte) 37.4 (1986) 354-68. Woad and imported indigo were already used in Roman antiquity as Vitruvius VII, 9 and VII, 14 prove (note 24 above, 344-45; 352-53). As mentioned before, the colour material of both indigo and woad is chemically identical, and so they cannot be distinguished with certainty.

[90]Only in the John miniature; in the other miniatures only indigo is used.

[91]A blue pigment was found by Roosen-Runge/Werner, 263-72, also in the Lindisfarne Gospels; they identified it as lapis lazuli. Because they were only able to make their analysis with a microscope the question of a mixture with indigo remains open. This problem could only be solved with a colour spectrometer.

[92]Fuchs, Oltrogge, Schenk, van Issem (note 27 above) 288. In wall painting the earliest examples of lapis lazuli pigment have been found in the wall paintings in Kyzil (Central Asia, presumably third century); see Josef Riederer, 'Technik und

examples of lapis lazuli use as pigment: the insular manuscripts mentioned and some Carolingian codices.[93] But up to the tenth century, even in luxury manuscripts such as the Codex Aureus from Canterbury, other blue materials such as indigo and azurite are often used rather than lapis lazuli.[94] Only in the Ottonian book illumination did lapis lazuli become the most important blue colour material. Perhaps this is due to the difficulties of preparing a beautiful blue pigment from lapis lazuli. Lapis lazuli contains much waste rock which is very hard to separate from the blue material. Therefore, the ground lapis lazuli looks very greyish. The earliest examples of lapis lazuli in manuscripts have a rather dull azure hue, as in the Book of Kells, and they are mostly mixed with indigo. Only in the late tenth century do we find a deep blue pure lapis lazuli pigment[95] obtained by a complicated method which seems to have been invented in the ninth or tenth century in Arabia.[96] Before the fifteenth century the refining process of lapis lazuli seems to have been almost unknown to Europeans, and the one recipe of the Mappae Clavicula[97] may be an echo of Arabian techniques; presumably European painters imported the refined pigment and not the stone material. The western treatises describe only the preparation of blue pigment for actual painting, ie the grinding and mixture with media or other materials.

As mentioned before, in some other insular manuscripts purple dyes and pink mixtures made from purple dye and white pigment can be found which seem to be the same material as in the Book of Kells.[98] For a comparison of the purple dye and the pink in the Lindisfarne Gospels an analysis with the colour spectrometer would be necessary.[99]

Farbstoffe der frühmittelalterlichen Wandmalereien Ostturkestans', Veröffentlich-ungen des Museums für Indische Kunst Berlin 4 (1977) 353-423. In late antique and early medieval European wall-painting lapis lazuli pigment seems not to have been used; blue pigment up to Carolingian times is mostly Egyptian blue.

[93]In the Wolfcoz Psalter (c 800) and the Folchard Psalter (c 870) at St Gall and in the Lorsch Gospels (c 810).

[94]In the Codex Aureus only indigo is used (pure and in different mixtures with white). In the Fulda Gospels in Würzburg indigo and azurite could be proved.

[95]One of the earliest manuscripts to use a very deep blue lapis pigment is the Petershausen Sacramentary, illuminated c980 at Reichenau (Heidelberg, Universitätsbibliothek Cod. Sal. IX.b; see Fuchs, Oltrogge (note 25 above, 128).

[96]Robert Fuchs, Doris Oltrogge, 'Farbherstellung' in Europäische Technik im Mittelalter, 800-1400, ed U Lindgren (1993). The earliest known recipe is Al-Muaizz Ibn Badis (1007-1061), Umdat al-kuttab wa'uddat dhawi al-albab ... (The book of the scribe's stick ...), 'Chemical Technology in medieval arabic bookmaking', ed Martin Levey, Transactions of the American Philosophical Society, ns 52.4 (1962) 3-74.

[97]Mappae Clavicula 288 (note 26 above, 71).

[98]Insular manuscripts with purple dye are the Cambridge Gospels, the later Durham Gospels, the Durham Cassiodorus, the Book of Mulling, the St Gall Gospels, the Barberini Gospels, the Codex Aureus. In the Durham Cassiodorus, the Book of Mulling, the Barberini Gospels and the Codex Aureus pink mixtures were also used. Purple dye and pink mixtures were also found in the Lindisfarne Gospels (Roosen-Runge/Werner, 263-72).

[99]Roosen-Runge/Werner were only able to analyse the material with a microscope which does not allow the identification. They propose folium as the material (pp 263-72).

The variants of ochre are only occasionally used in insular book illumination, generally only as minor pigments.[100] Sap green could only be found in a mixture with yellow ochre in the Barberini Gospels.[101]

Conclusions

Looking at the materials we can conclude that there is no pigment or dye which is totally unknown to other insular scriptoria. Only the richness of the palette is exceptional and the selection of the materials used (**fig 13**). The palette of insular manuscripts is often rather restricted; in most of them only few colour materials are used and we seldom find more than one hue for blue, purple, green, yellow, brown or black.

The painters of the Book of Kells used nearly every material known (and available) in insular scriptoria. This can only be paralleled with few other manuscripts, the Stockholm *Codex Aureus*, the Barberini Gospels and the Lindisfarne Gospels. In the *Codex Aureus* and in the Barberini Gospels the selection of the materials is not identical, but in the Barberini it is rather similar. Following the analysis of Roosen-Runge and Werner, there seem to be a number of conformities with the Lindisfarne Gospels,[102] but since our results for the Book of Kells disagree in some cases with those made only by microscopic analysis by Roosen-Runge and Werner, it would be necessary to analyse the Lindisfarne Gospels with the more precise spectroscopic method. The small number of surviving insular manuscripts does not allow judgements as to whether there were any workshop characteristics in insular scriptoria,[103] and we can only conclude that the scriptorium of the Book of Kells had access to the whole range of materials available on the British Isles.[104]

---

[100] Red, brown and yellow ochre were used fairly extensively in the Barberini Gospels, and to a lesser extent also in the *Codex Aureus*. Red ochre is an important pigment in the St Gall Gospels and the Garland of Howth; in the Book of Dimma it is only used in John. Red and yellow ochre were also found in the Book of Mulling.

[101] Also in continental manuscripts sap green is only found occasionally, for instance in the Wolfcoz and the Folchard Psalters from St Gall. Most often sap green is only used in mixtures, for instance with copper green pigments or yellow ochre, or it is used for the modelling of green garments or of faces.

[102] Roosen-Runge/Werner concluded a nearly complete agreement between both manuscripts except for the use of gold ink which occurs only in the Lindisfarne Gospels. Their list of painting materials of the Lindisfarne Gospels and the Book of Kells contains red lead, kermes, orpiment, yellow and brown ochre, oxgall, ultramarine, indigo, blue, red and purple folium, verdigris, *vergaut* made from orpiment and indigo, a pink mixture made from folium and lead white, brown ink with charcoal, and lead white.

[103] This was proposed by Brown, 230, who concluded from the similarities in material in the Lindisfarne Gospels and the Book of Kells a continuity of scriptoria (in this case not necessarily Lindisfarne, but a monastery with strong Lindisfarne connections). In the later middle ages occasionally workshops used a specific palette, see R Fuchs, D Oltrogge, 'Untersuchungen rheinischer Buchmalerei des 15. Jhs.: historische, kunsthistorische, naturwissenschaftliche und konservatorische Aspekte', *Imprimatur* 14 (1991) 55-80. But it seems that most often the selection of colour materials is only characteristic of certain times and areas and not of specific scriptoria.

[104] Our knowledge about the trade and production of colour materials in the early middle ages is extremely limited. There are a few notes, for instance the letter of

III. Painting technique

Whereas the variety of materials of the Book of Kells can be compared with other luxury manuscripts such as the Lindisfarne Gospels, the Stockholm *Codex Aureus* or the Barberini Gospels, the use of these materials in the Book of Kells and the coloristic effects achieved with these colours seem to be unique. It has been observed before that these colours were often not painted simply in single layers but that 'glazes' were sometimes used.[105] But the various forms of these 'glazes', their purpose and their models have not yet been discussed.

First we have to define the term 'glaze'. Normally, this term means the overpainting of an opaque colour material with a translucent dye. In the Book of Kells we find not only this true glaze but also another form of overpainting: here an opaque colour material is overpainted with another opaque material, the second layer being painted very liquid and uneven so that the first layer shows through, a technique which I would like to call 'semi-glaze'. This technique must be distinguished from *pentimenti*, ie coloristic corrections which should totally cover the first layer.

The Christ miniature (folio 32v)

How were these glazes and semi-glazes applied and what was their purpose? If we examine the Christ miniature on folio 32v (**pl 175**) we can observe some different forms of overpainting. Like all miniatures, initials and ornaments, the picture was prepared by drawing with iron gall ink. Then the different colour materials were filled in. The drawing is usually not covered and supplies the major outlines of the completed painting. Additional lines in blue, orpiment, red lead and ink were drawn on the figures, animals and borders. Most of the colours were applied in single layers, only with a drawing on top, but there are also a number of glazes, semi-glazes and overpaintings. The border of the square 'capitals' was first painted in orpiment. Then, it was completely overpainted with red lead, which again was completely covered with the pink mixture on which lines in red lead were drawn. The different layers can only be seen in places were the upper layers are cracked (**pl 180**). Thus this superimposition of three layers can only be interpreted as *pentimento*. A similar *pentimento* can be found in the pink-coloured border just at the top of the arch, with the same sequence of colours as in the 'capitals'.

Bishop Frother of Toul who at the beginning of the ninth century asks the English Abbot Aglemar for some pigments for wall painting, see Julius Schlosser, *Schriftquellen zur Geschichte der karolingischen Kunst* (Wien 1892) 310, no 896. These pigments are orpiment (*auripigmentum*), red lead (*minium*) and probably green earth (*prusinum*); furthermore Frothar asks for two blue colours which cannot be identified with certainty: *folium indicum* (indigo/woad? or folium) and *lazur* (azurite, lapis lazuli?).

[105]Françoise Henry, *Irish art during the Viking invasions: 800-1020 AD* (London 1967) 75-76; Roosen-Runge/Werner, 273; Cains (note 8 above) 213.

More complicated is the interpretation of superimposed colour layers in the feathers of the peacocks. In the completed form the coloristic appearance of both birds is nearly identical; but the first version of the painting was asymmetrical (**pls 177-78**). Only the left peacock had a blue body ornamented with ink lines and red dots; the body of the right peacock was green. On the other hand the rich sequence of green, blue, yellow, and purple fields in the tail feathers of this peacock were planned from the beginning, whereas in the tail feathers of his pendant there were only alternating triangles of yellow and green, the blue being painted only as a 'correction' over some of the green fields. But the superimposition of a second layer is not always caused by a search for the 'right' coloristic appearance of the picture. Thus, the blue triangles in the tail feathers of both peacocks are always glazed with the transparent purple-coloured dye. This glaze is intended to produce a very dark blue which contrasts with the brighter non-glazed blue, for instance, in the tunic of Christ. This use of purple glaze on blue is very common throughout the whole manuscript and was used to enhance the painters' palette. But the purple-coloured dye did not always completely cover the blue layer. Each peacock has one leg which is unevenly glazed only with purple-coloured dye, whereas the other leg is overpainted with the opaque pink mixture. The pink is also unevenly painted over the blue, so that it cannot be a *pentimento*. The striking difference between the glaze and semi-glaze of both legs seems to indicate that the painter was trying to imitate an illusionistic painting with the lighter leg in the foreground and the darker leg in the background. Whereas this 'modelling' seems rather unrealistic, the more logical use of purple shades in the vases reflects more clearly the formal inspiration of an illusionistic model (**pl 176**). But, in general, the illuminator of the Christ miniature preferred the unrealistic form of 'modelling' seen in the peacocks' legs. This is found for example in the blue mantle of the upper angel at the right, which is unevenly glazed with opaque pink; the tunic of the angel below and the mantle of the upper angel at the left are unevenly glazed with purple dye (**pl 179**).

Thus, the superimposition of two or more colour layers on folio 32v could be a *pentimento* or a form of unrealistic modelling. Perhaps a third effect of glazes or semi-glazes was intended in the zoomorphic ornaments of the broad border. They are coloured red (red lead), blue-green (indigo), yellow (orpiment), blue (blue mixture), pink (pink mixture), purple (purple-coloured dye) and green (green copper pigment). Some of the bands are ornamented with thick dots in different colours. Only the green bands are frequently nearly completely overpainted with an opaque blue layer, which has often flaked off. The decay has obscured the original effect of these double layers, but the upper layer always seems to leave a small margin, so that originally the opaque blue would have appeared as a relief over the green margin (**pl 183**). A similar effect can be observed on other pages, for instance on folio 2 where it is better preserved. If this effect was really intended also on folio 32v, the double-layer technique in the border would be neither a *pentimento* nor a modelling, but an uncommon coloristic and plastic effect.[106]

Form and function of the double-layer technique on other pages

These three different functions of the double-layer technique can also be observed on other pages. *Pentimenti* seem to be not very common; they are found only on few places.[107] In general the superimposition of colour layers is deliberately used for modelling or for coloristic effects; and often both functions are found together on the same page (**pl 185**). Thus the blue garment of the angel on folio 27v is 'modelled' with an unevenly painted semi-glaze of the pink mixture; a similar unrealistic 'modelling' in pink is laid on the blue body of the lion.[108] The blue calf's body is unevenly glazed with purple dye. On the other hand, the pink semi-glaze on the blue borders of the frame cannot have been intended as 'modelling'. Here the iridescent changing between blue and pink was only used for its coloristic effect. Furthermore, different glazes enhanced the palette of the miniature: in the yellow borders and in the cross of the angel bright yellow alternates with a reddish yellow, produced by a red ochre glaze on orpiment. Two different red shades were obtained by alternating pure red lead with glazed red lead.[109]

Also on folio 290v, pigments applied purely alternate with pigments glazed with a transparent layer or unevenly glazed with an opaque layer. The coloristic appearance is even richer than on folio 27v; all colour materials of the Book of Kells are used in the miniature and we find even such strange combinations as the iridescent semi-glaze of pink and mauve on green (**pl 189**). In the tips of the angel's feathers three colours are set one upon the other in irregular pasty dots: first copper green, then mauve and finally red lead, each dot being slightly smaller than the dot below (**pl 190**). Since the

---

[106]The three dimensional appearance is usually lost due to the pressing of the manuscript. Margins can be found with each of the mentioned colour combinations but they occur most often with a green (copper green) ground layer and a dark blue or azure semi-glaze. Sometimes the blue can be painted even opaque on the green so that it only appears as a relief over the green margin without iridescent effects, see for example folio 2 or folio 114v. An inverse relief effect can be observed in the pink-blue circles on folio 2v. The contours were first drawn with iron gall ink, then the outer circles were filled with indigo, the inner circle with the blue mixture. In both cases the drawn stripe was not totally filled but a small margin was left on both sides. Afterwards all three circles were covered with an unevenly painted semi-glaze of pink mixture, this time the stripe was totally filled. Thus, the stripes got a relief-like structure with a thicker and darker stripe between small margins; furthermore the appearance of the dark bluish appearance of this stripe varied between a darker blue-pink appearance in the outer and a lighter appearance in the inner circles.

[107]For instance on folio 3v, where green figures are changed into red figures.

[108]Here the painting is quite well preserved so that it is very clear that the iridescent effect of pink and blue is neither a *pentimento* nor a deterioration, since even the top layer with its final drawing with red lead is completely preserved.

[109]The glaze is again red ochre.

structure has not been much disturbed by pressing, the rich coloristic variety and the strong three-dimensional appearance remain visible.[110]

The coloristic effects of the Book of Kells - some considerations on their purpose and models

To convey the richness of coloristic effects we have compiled a list of all possible combinations of glazes, semi-glazes and small multicoloured spots.

First layer: blue mixtures (light blue/azure/dark blue)
Second layer:

- pink (**pl 185**)
- mauve
- purple-coloured dye (**pls 184, 187**)
- indigo
- red lead
- orpiment

First layer: copper green pigment
Second layer:

- pink
- mauve
- purple-coloured dye
- blue mixture (**pl 183**)
- indigo
- red lead
- honey-coloured dye
- orpiment

First layer: pink/mauve
Second layer:

- blue mixture
- purple-coloured dye

First layer: purple-coloured dye
Second layer:

- orpiment

---

[110]Today most of the plastic effects are only partly visible because they have mostly been lost under pressure during treatment, which has also often destroyed the iridescent appearance of the semi-glazes. The superimposition of different dots can be found on only a few pages; usually the three-dimensional effect has been destroyed. On folio 290v it is quite well preserved; it is found not only in the angel's wing but also in the shamrock ornaments of the calf. Here the circles of the shamrock were first filled in with the blue mixture, on which a pasty spot of mauve was painted which then received a small red dot. Also on folio 7v, the three-dimensional structure has been preserved in the wings of the angel standing below at the right. Here on green feathers pasty blue strokes are painted, on which a thick pink dot was set.

First layer: red lead
Second layer
- blue mixture
- translucent glaze with red ochre

First layer: orpiment
Second layer:
- translucent glaze with red ochre

First layer: indigo
Second layer:
- pink

Multicoloured spots (**pls 182, 190**)
- copper green pigment - indigo - blue - pink
- copper green pigment - blue - pink
- copper green pigment - mauve - red lead
- blue - pink

The painter of folio 290v used the whole range of these effects to produce an extremely rich and sophisticated coloristic appearance. Other illuminators preferred a more serene and harmonious selection, as for example the artist of folio 27v which is dominated by blue-purple-pink hues. On other pages the use of colours and glazes is restricted even more or totally missing. A comparison of the coloristic methods and preferences throughout the manuscript would be a valuable help in distinguishing the different illuminators, a problem which is not the subject of this paper.

Here we should consider only the question of models for this painting technique. In comparison with other insular book illumination, this technique and coloristic appearance stands unique. Normally, insular illuminators prepared their representations with preliminary ink drawings which remained visible in the completed painting. In the spaces between the ink lines, colours were filled in single paint layers, a technique which can be compared with the appearance of cloisonnée enamel.[111] On these paint layers linear ornaments or little dots can be drawn. Only in very few cases are two colour layers found, for example in the Cambridge Gospel fragment (Cambridge, Corpus Christi College 179B) where the eagle's head is painted in a pink mixture, which is then partly covered with a purple glaze. Smaller colour layers are often painted with three-dimensional effect, for example the eagle's feathers in the Book of Durrow, but the use of superimposed multicoloured spots in the Book of Kells seems to be unique.

Only in the *Codex Aureus* in Stockholm and in the Barberini Gospels do we find superimposed washes, but here they are clearly part of the painterly technique of modelling. Modelling with washes of different colours, which

---

[111]This technique is also predominantly used in the Book of Kells; it is only enriched by the double-layer technique.

was common in the classical tradition of painting, was in some places applied in the Book of Kells, for instance in the peacocks and the angels' garments of the Christ miniature. Here it is clearly inspired by the Mediterranean model, even if the application seems somewhat unrealistic.[112]

But more often the purpose of the double-layer technique of the Book of Kells was coloristic. For this, we have no direct precedents in book illumination. So far, we have traced no models or patterns for the techniques and artistic interests of the illuminators of the Book of Kells. Perhaps in the Lichfield Gospels some previous stages can be found, but the descriptions of Roosen-Runge and Werner[113] are not sufficient for judgement on the extent of the connection. Perhaps, this could give an indication of the relationship of both manuscripts and of their position in insular book illumination.

One reason for the 'invention' of the unusual technique was apparently the search for an even richer palette (**pls 186-87**). The alternation of pure orpiment and glazed orpiment, of pure red lead etc, enhanced the number of different shades of yellow, red etc. The semi-glazes also enhance the palette, but the appearance of a range of iridescence of for instance blue and pink, or green and pink, is clearly different (**184-85**). The same is true for the multicoloured spots. In book illumination only distant models can be found. First, there is a certain similarity in the painting of backgrounds in illusionistic late-antique manuscripts and in manuscripts painted in the classical tradition. Rather common is a blue background with washes in darker blue and pink.[114] There is also some resemblance of the iridescent effects with the imitation of marble and other illusionistic effects in the representation of architecture in late-antique, Byzantine and Carolingian manuscripts. But the appearance of the semi-glazes in the Book of Kells, for example in the frames of folio 27v or in the initials on folio 130 and 188, is clearly different, since no illusionistic landscape or architectural painting was intended but an abstract coloristic effect. Furthermore, the Classical paintings do not explain all effects, in particular the multicoloured spots or the three-dimensional effects have no parallels. Because the Book of Kells lacks both direct precedents and successors in book illumination, we might ask whether the illuminators had models of different materials. The

---

[112]The coloristic appearance of the page may also be in some parts a reflection of this model, for example in the otherwise unused purple background or in the yellow drawing on the garment of the angel standing below at the left. Normally, the drawing is made with iron gall ink or red lead, but sometimes also with the dark blue mixture. The yellow orpiment which is used for the lines of the blue angel's garment on folio 32v seems to be a reflection of the gold highlights often found in late antique (for instance in the Quedlinburg Itala or the Cotton Genesis), Byzantine or Carolingian book illumination. The imitation of this chrysography with orpiment is not uncommon: it is found for example also in the Matthew miniature of the Barberini Gospels.

[113]Roosen-Runge/Werner, 276-77.

[114]For instance in the *Vergilius Vaticanus* or the Quedlinburg Itala; see the colour reproduction in Kurt Weitzmann, *Spätantike und frühchristliche Buchmalerei* (München 1977) pls 1, 5.

multicoloured spots show many similarities with a form of glass bead on which differently coloured plastic spots are set one upon another (**pls 182, 190-91**).[115] Comparable plastic effects and also some likeness with the iridescent effects show some of the Sutton Hoo escutcheons with red enamel, on which blue or green enamel and millefiori ornaments are set.[116] Even more comparable is the appearance of red-green marbled glass used for luxury vessels in the Roman and early medieval periods.[117] Because of the difference in technique the illumination does not imitate glass or enamel; but there may be visual inspirations for some of the coloristic effects of the miniatures. The coloristic appearance and the structure of the paint layers are thus perhaps inspired not only by paintings but also by works of very different materials and techniques. As far as we can judge from the surviving manuscripts these were unique 'experiments' by the illuminators of the Book of Kells.

Conclusions

We may conclude that we can now determine most of the materials of the Book of Kells; in few cases further research with non-portable methods would be necessary for an exact identification. The analysis has proved that the materials of the Book of Kells were all known in early medieval insular scriptoria, but that the richness and variety of the palette can be paralleled only with very few luxury manuscripts. The unique use of these materials by the painters of the Book of Kells has resulted in extraordinary coloristic effects.

---

[115]See for example the findings in seventh-century graves in Eichstätten (Baden-Württemberg), Barbara Sasse, *Leben am Kaiserstuhl im Frühmittelalter* (Stuttgart 1989) 26, fig 11, colour plate front cover.

[116]Mavis Bimson, 'Aspects of the technology of glass and copper alloys' in *Sutton Hoo*, ed R L S Bruce-Mitford (London 1983) III, part 2, 924-44, colour plates, III, part 1, between 408 and 409.

[117]Vera I Evison, 'Bichrome glass vessels of the seventh and eighth centuries', *Studien zur Sachsenforschung* 3 (1982) 7-21; for good colour reproductions see Erwin Baumgartner, Ingeborg Krueger, *Phönix aus Sand und Asche. Glas des Mittelalters*, Ausstellungskatalog Bonn, Basel 1988 (München 1988) 71, no 14, 72, no 16. Red marbled glass was found on the continent and in England; for English examples, see *The making of England: Anglo-Saxon art and culture, AD 600-900*, ed Leslie Webster and Janet Backhouse (London 1991) 87, no 66(v).

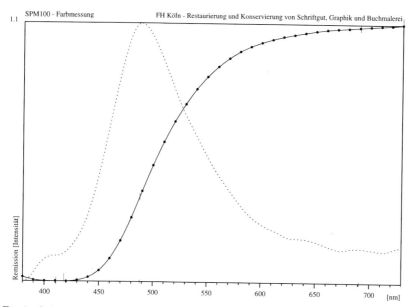

Fig 1a Colour curve of orpiment

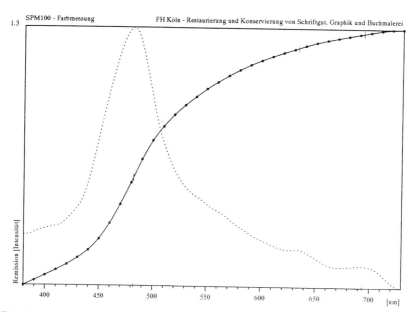

Fig 1b Colour curve of yellow pigment in the Book of Kells

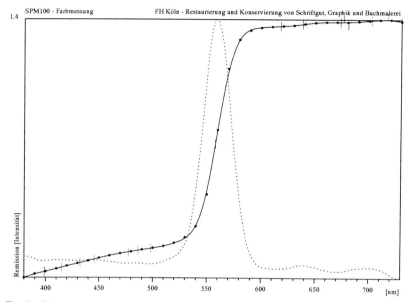

Fig 2a Colour curve of red lead

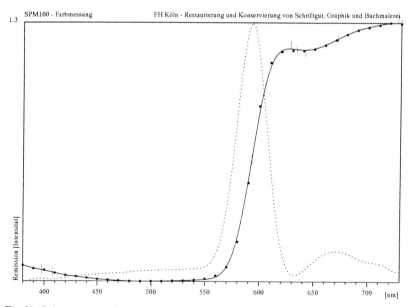

Fig 2b Colour curve of vermilion

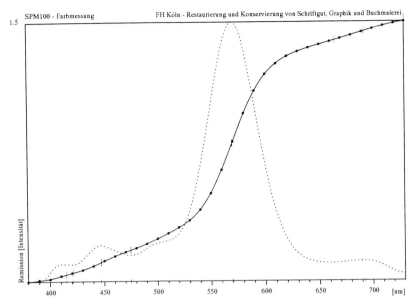

Fig 2c Colour curve of red ochre

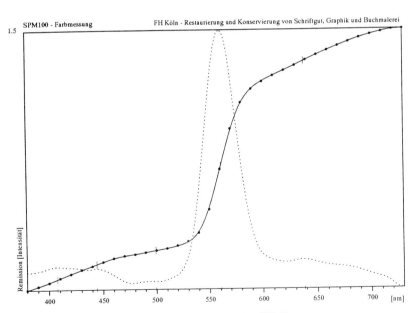

Fig 2d Colour curve of red pigment in the Book of Kells

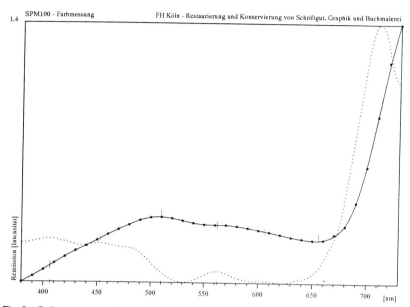

Fig 3a Colour curve of *vergaut* in the Book of Kells

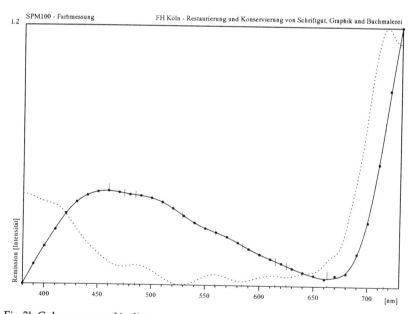

Fig 3b Colour curve of indigo

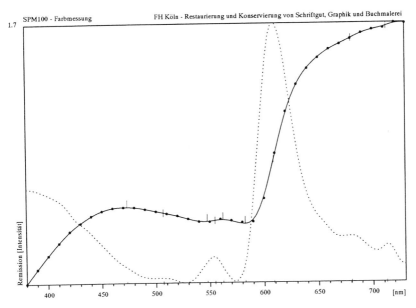

Fig 4a Colour curve of red purple in the Book of Kells

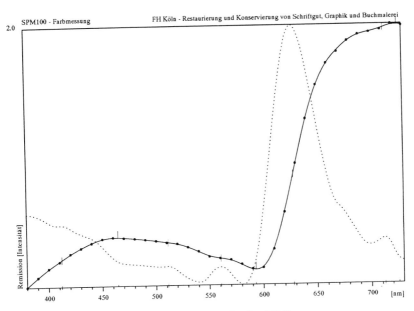

Fig 4b Colour curve of bluish purple in the Book of Kells

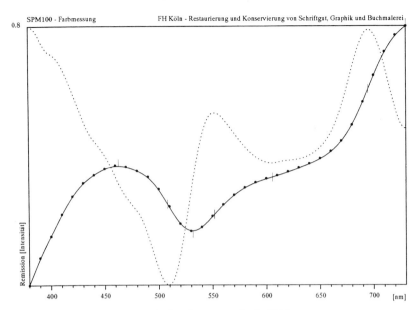

Fig 5a Colour curve of purple dye from purple shellfish

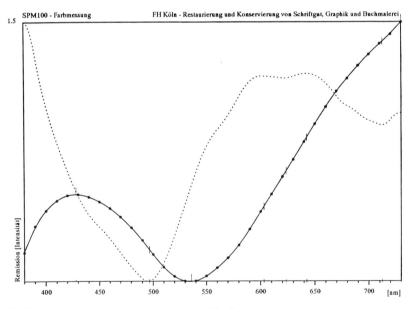

Fig 5b Colour curve of purple dye from blueberries

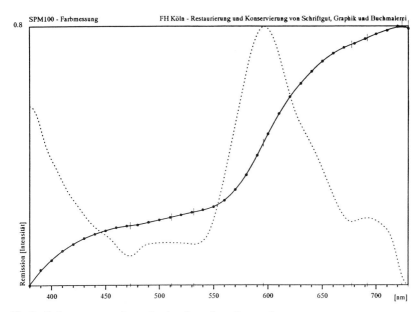

Fig 5c Colour curve of purple dye from brazil wood

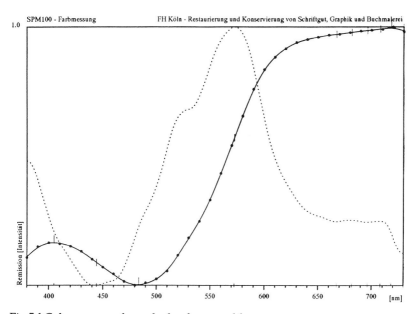

Fig 5d Colour curve of purple dye from madder

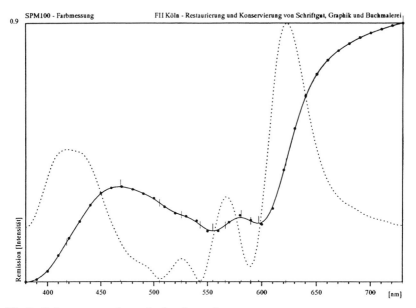

Fig 6a Colour curve of purple dye from alcanna

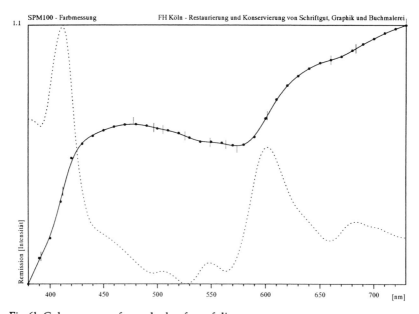

Fig 6b Colour curve of purple dye from folium

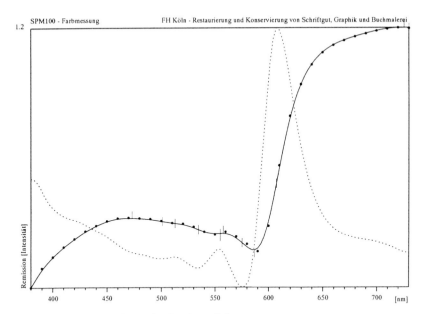

Fig 6c Colour curve of purple dye from lichen

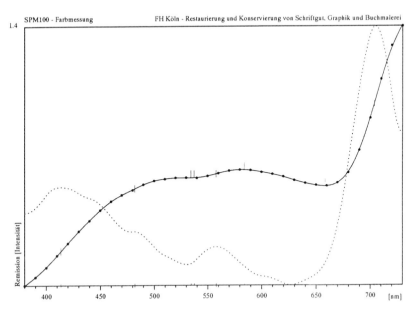

Fig 7 Colour curve of blue mixture in the Book of Kells

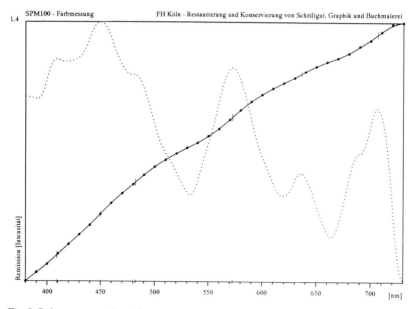

Fig 8 Colour curve of red-brown interlace in the Book of Kells

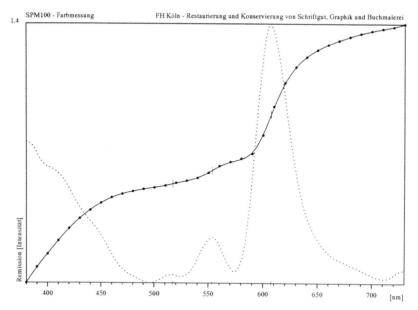

Fig 9a Colour curve of purple dye in the grid canon tables on folio 6

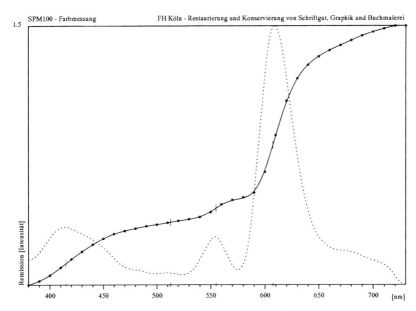

Fig 9b Colour curve of the garment of Christ on folio 32v

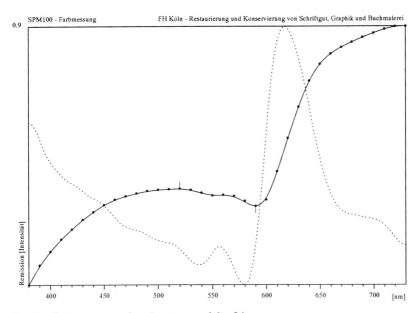

Fig 10a Colour curve of pink script on folio 26

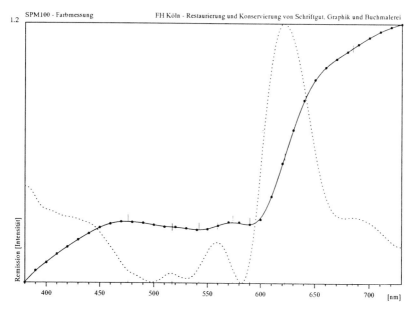

Fig 10b Colour curve of the pink garment of the Virgin on folio 7v

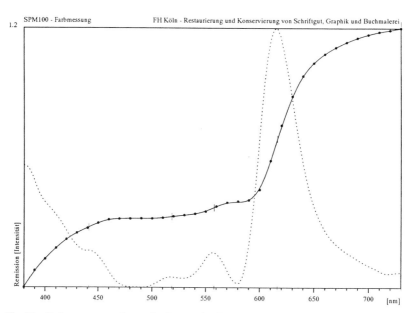

Fig 11a Colour curve of purple dye in the Barberini Gospels

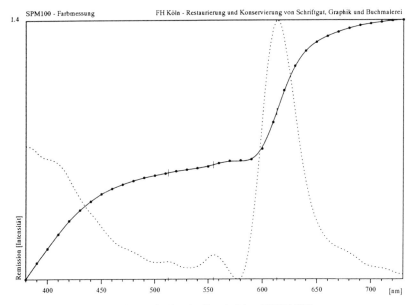

Fig 11b Colour curve of purple dye in Cambridge CCC 179B

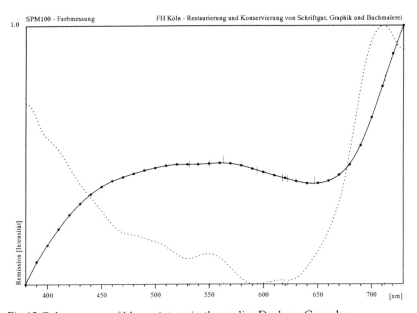

Fig 12 Colour curve of blue mixture in the earlier Durham Gospels

Fig 13 Colour materials in insular book illumination

CCC	Cambridge Corpus Christi College 179B
ARM	Book of Armagh
GH	Garland of Howth
DUR	Book of Durrow
DIM	Book of Dimma
MUL	Book of Mulling
DEG	Durham, earlier Gospels
DLG	Durham, later Gospels
CAS	Durham Cassiodorus
BARB	Barberini Gospels
SGAL	St Gall, Irish Gospels
CAUR	Stockholm, *Codex Aureus*
KEL	Book of Kells

	yellow	red	blue	purple
CCC	orpiment yellow dye	red lead	-	purple dye
ARM	orpiment	red lead red ochre	indigo	-
GH	orpiment	red ochre	indigo	-
DUR	orpiment	red lead	-	-
DIM	orpiment	red lead red ochre	blue mixture	-
MUL	orpiment yellow ochre yellow dye	red lead red ochre	blue mixture indigo	purple dye pink mixture
DEG	orpiment	red lead	blue mixture	-
DLG	orpiment	red lead	-	purple dye
CAS	orpiment	red lead	-	purple dye pink mixture
BARB	orpiment yellow ochre yellow dye	red lead red ochre	blue mixture indigo	purple dye pink mixture
SGAL	orpiment yellow dye	red lead red ochre	blue mixture indigo	purple dye
CAUR	orpiment yellow ochre yellow dye	red lead red ochre	indigo	purple dye pink mixture
KEL	orpiment yellow ochre	red lead red ochre	blue mixture indigo	purple dye pink mixture

Fig 13 Colour materials in insular book illumination   *contd*

	green	brown	black	white
CCC	copper green	iron gall ink	iron gall ink	-
ARM	-	iron gall ink	iron gall ink	chalk?
GH	*vergaut*	buckthorn ink	iron gall ink	chalk?
DUR	copper green	iorn gall ink	iron gall ink	-
DIM	*vergaut*	buckthorn ink	iron gall ink	-
MUL	*vergaut*	brown ochre	iron gall ink	white
DEG	*vergaut*	iron gall ink	iron gall ink	-
DLG	copper green	iron gall ink	iron gall ink	-
CAS	copper green	iron gall ink	iron gall ink	
BARB	copper green *vergaut* ochre + sap green	iron gall ink brown ochre	iron gall ink	white
SGAL	*vergaut*	iron-gall ink	iron gall ink	white
CAUR	*vergaut*	buckthorn ink brown ochre	iron gall ink	white
KEL	copper green *vergaut* ochre + sap green sap green	buckthorn ink brown ochre	iron gall ink	chalk

The surface examination of skin: a binder's note on the identification of animal species used in the making of parchment

Anthony Cains

The basis of the method of examination is to compare the subject material with samples of recently produced skins of parchment, the species of which are clearly identified, and the skin of other early manuscripts or covers that have been identified with the aid of modern samples.[1] A subject can be identified by hair side features, such as follicle pockets, or if this is lacking, then flesh side features, such as gland pockets and veining which, generally speaking, are the least disturbed by the vellum makers' and scribes' preparation treatment. In the first instance the hair and flesh sides must be distinguished; the first obvious clue here is the tendency of the skin to curl towards the hair side even if it has been heavily pounced; the second clue is the difference in colour and texture. The new comparative material should be from as wide a selection of animal species and age groups as possible. This means in the case of goat a range of skins from fine kid of approximately three square feet to billy goat of ten or twelve square feet. The animals I have are sheep, goat and calf. (I would like deer, which I only have as a vegetable tanned skin).[2] I have exotic examples such as kangaroo which has no relevance and pigskin which I have never seen or recognised as a writing material. The sample skins should be obtained from as many vellum makers as possible because of the difference in processing technique. I have material from Cowley of Newport Pagnell, Buckinghamshire, Band (formerly of Brentford, Middlesex, now part of Cowley's), Elzas of Celbridge, county Kildare, Vorst (formerly of north London), Gentilli of Rome, and La Pergamena of Verona, Italy. We have also prepared a complete calfskin in TCD Conservation Laboratory; a messy business but it gives one a greater understanding of the process even if the product turns out to be a poor thing as ours did. A fragment is not as useful as a skin, particularly if the area whence it came is not known. Skins can be further scraped and pounced to replicate the scribes' treatment of the material and to note what detail survives such treatment.

Perhaps a linen glass will serve, but a binocular microscope with a cold light fibre optic illumination is best for the examination. Although one will find it convenient to search and study detail at various magnifications one must settle on a specific magnification (eg x10) when comparing materials

---

[1]This is written as a supplement to my article 'The vellum' in *Kells commentary*, 177-81, to illustrate my methods of identifying animal skin type by visual examination.
[2]Christopher Clarkson of the Edward James Foundation, West Dean College, Chichester, tells me that skins were prepared for an Imperial College London project in the late 1960s, but he has no sample. I believe Dr Reed's sample noted below is from this batch.

so that the relative proportion of detail between species and age group can be kept in the mind's eye: look at calf at too high a relative magnification and one might call it goat. The problem with modern processing is that it frequently produces a skin that is translucent and gelatinous, making detail difficult to see. This can be overcome to some extent by staining with leather dye. The vellum maker often stains or tones the skin for cosmetic purposes or chooses skins that have residual blood pigment remaining in the vein system for 'antique' covering vellum. This is artificial in a sense, because manuscript skins do not as a rule display this colour (although I have detected some in the Book of Kells), but the vein system of calf is clear to see in Kells and can be compared to the modern 'antique' vellum vein pattern. Old manuscript parchment was often used by binders for covers, spine and joint linings and inner fold guards for paper texts. These can provide samples for both skin and pigment, but I do not advocate their unnecessary removal.

The skin types most usually found as covers (depending on production area) are calf, sheep and less frequently, goat. Calfskin (on bindings) is roughly speaking characterised by its smooth creamy surface, almost featureless at first glance (**pls 132-40**). In the case of a seventeenth-century Dutch large-format atlas, the skin is of good substance over its entire area and some follicle pockets and colour remain in the spine area; fine veining can also be discerned. The animal spine runs fore-edge to spine which gives an idea of the original size of the skin. A comparable cover (nearly a full skin) in sheepskin will show the pronounced follicle grain of the axilla (armpit/belly) area of the skin blending into the finer overall grain. In some examples of goat and sheep, the grain is clouded by areas of the residual epidermal layer (*stratum corneum*) — which shows the follicle pattern and grain more clearly to the naked eye. The sheepskin tends to more yellow on the hair side compared to calf and goat (**pls 141-43**). Goatskin will display a similar but more pronounced pattern but the contrast of the grain and follicle spacing of the axilla and the general follicle pattern is not so great (**pls 144-46**). Goatskin often displays a pronounced spine colour — a light brown compared to the pale buff or creamy colour of the flanks — not the rather yellow tone of old sheepskin.

In the case of an Italian twelfth-century manuscript, at first sight it appeared a fine, beautifully prepared, slunk (uterine) calf, but at closer view was seen to be kidskin, the grain replicating in miniature all the features on a modern example of the mature animal of six to eight square feet. I also have full (meaning unsplit) wool lambskins of about three square feet which again display the same characteristics found on early texts and covers. The skin is very greasy and has got progressively more yellow over the years (it was made in 1968 by La Pergamena). It is interesting that the wool follicle pattern of this skin is so very fine that, in the absence of the axilla, one could think it calf. There is a distinct vein pattern surviving in the spine area which could be confused with the overall network that survives in calf. The general recognition by scholars of the contrasting yellow tone of the hair and flesh side of sheepskin has led one historian to identify the Cathach

(Dublin, RIA, 12.R.33, a Vulgate text of psalms written in Irish half-uncial in the sixth or seventh century) as having been written on sheepskin,[3] but clear areas of calf follicle and hair deny this. A characteristic difference between a bland almost featureless sheepskin, such as modern document repair parchment, from flesh splits can be noted by the look-through, which is rather wild and blotchy compared to calf. If thin fine skins have been heavily pounced to give a napped suede-like surface, a regular even texture would indicate the more compact nature of calf and kidskin. Sheepskin does not entirely lend itself to this treatment, giving a rather irregular texture, coarse in the belly/axilla area and fine along the spine and central flank area.

In the case of a complete manuscript of clearly the same type of skin a single leaf may not reveal clear, irrefutable evidence of the species, but examination of its companion leaves and gatherings will reveal an accumulation of evidence. For example one leaf may show surviving hair around scar tissue, another the axilla grain, or unabraded areas revealing a clear grain pattern. For most manuscripts the business of identification is straightforward and becomes easier the more one handles them. The eye gets trained into recognising and interpreting detail; but after a long period on other unrelated work one loses confidence so that the importance of a study collection will be realised.

Reference to my rather incomplete collection is essential particularly when one's identification is challenged. In a recent examination of the Book of Kells, a visiting scientist noted that some leaves are goatskin and sheepskin. This I cannot support. I lack a sample of deerskin parchment and I feel there is a possibility that it may be a candidate for closer scientific analysis. Dr Ron Reed illustrates the grain pattern of modern deerskin parchment[4] but it is rather a poor reproduction. The sample collection also follows his recommendation.[5] He says: 'The grain pattern of cattle is similar to that of calf but on a coarser scale since the blood vessels are larger and the hairs are thicker. Veals and kips are intermediate between these two extreme patterns of grain surface'.[6] He defines the flayed weight of 'hide' as 30-90 lb; of 'veal' as 14-25 lb and 'calf' as 4-12 lb. 'Kips' are small Indian hides of 20-50 lb. I believe that the heavy hair follicle pattern seen on some heavy gauge folios in Kells is the product of a 'veal' age skin and not the grain pattern of the axilla, remembering that the Book of Kells is a large-format text.[7]

---

[3]See note 1 above.
[4]R Reed, *Ancient skins, parchment and leathers* (London 1972) 294. I have rarely found the reproduction of photomicrographs to be useful as a sole means of identifying skin types and Dr Reed's illustration is a case in point.
[5]ibid, 282-324.
[6]ibid, 41.
[7]See also W T Roddy, 'Histology of animal skins' in *The chemistry and technology of leather*, ed F O'Flaherty et al (New York 1956) I, 1-40.

The palaeographical background to the Book of Kells

William O'Sullivan

The oldest surviving Irish manuscript is generally taken to be the copy of the Old Latin version of the gospels in Trinity College Library (TCD, MS 55; *CLA* (1972) II, no 271). In his edition of the text in 1884 the then librarian, T K Abbott, gave it the name *Usserianus* on the grounds that it was kept with Archbishop Ussher's manuscripts.[1] There is however no evidence that it ever belonged to the archbishop. From the damage it has suffered, it clearly spent the middle ages rattling about in a box shrine as the relic of an Irish saint in constant demand for oath taking and talismanic purposes. All margins have been lost and the remains of the leaves at the beginning and end are very small, those in the middle being the largest. There is plenty of green staining from the copper plates of the shrine.

In April 1681 the Trinity professor of divinity, William Palliser, whose splendid library is now housed in the Long Room and, as his will directed, next to that of Archbishop Ussher, wrote to the learned Henry Dodwell, later Camden professor of history at Oxford.[2] After a reference to Bishop Henry Jones's gift of the Books of Durrow and Kells to the Library he goes on: 'S. Brigit's Testament, I fear is lost, for I have sought for it several times, and so hath the library keeper too, and could not find it', clearly implying that the manuscript had been in the Library. Dodwell entered the College in 1655 and became a fellow in 1662 and, because of his theological and historical tastes, must have been familiar with the collection of manuscripts. The first catalogue,[3] made about 1670, omitted the unbound manuscripts and contains no reference to the *codex Usserianus primus*. Samuel Foley, the compiler of the second and much fuller catalogue,[4] wrote in February 1681/2 'the great confusion of all the manuscripts and the untoward character of some and imperfections of others may excuse his having yet done but about half'.[5] In such a situation, it is not surprising that Palliser in the previous year should have failed to find one that was at best in some kind of box, but perhaps more likely wrapped up in a parcel in a larger box with the great mass of other unbound manuscripts. By the time Foley had

---

[1]TCD, MS 55, *CLA* (1972) II, no 271. T K Abbott, *Evangeliorum versio antehieronymiana ex codice Usseriano (Dublinensi), adjecta collatione codicis Usseriani alterius. Accedit versio vulgata sec. cod. Amiatinum, cum varietate Cod. Kenanensis (Book of Kells), et Cod. Durmachensis (Book of Durrow)* (Dublin 1884) iii.
[2]C MacNeill, *The Tanner letters: original documents and notices of Irish affairs in the sixteenth and seventeenth centuries, extracted from the collection in the Bodleian* (Dublin 1943) 440. *Dictionary of national biography* for Palliser and Dodwell.
[3]TCD, MS 7/2.
[4]TCD, MS 7/1, 3.
[5]McNeill (note 2 above) 462.

completed his work, the gospel book had a brief description and a shelfmark[6] and must by then have acquired a box of its own. The description however contains no reference to St Brigid and provides no provenance of any kind, but then Foley entered the College ten years after Dodwell's departure and if, as seems most probable, the manuscript was shaken out of its shrine in Cromwellian times and reached the library then, or shortly after, Dodwell was in a position to know. There is always the intriguing possibility that the reference is to the Book of Kildare which, as described by Giraldus Cambrensis,[7] seems to have been very like the Book of Kells. However, if that was ever here it never turned up again. *Usserianus primus* need not have come from St Brigid's headquarters in Kildare. There are more than fourteen parishes called Kilbride, besides thirty-five townlands, and of course there are many other possibilities, including Kilbreedy in county Limerick, a main Munster centre of her cult. Ussher's seeming unacquaintance with it suggests that it may have belonged to the southern half of the country. However, until another reference to the existence of such a manuscript, or at least to a likely lost shrine of St Brigid turns up, it will have to continue to bear his name. Had he known it, he would certainly have included this, now the only known Irish Old Latin example, among his collations of Irish gospel texts, but these were unhappily lost when he was attacked as he fled from Cardiff in 1646.[8]

Although I shall be rejecting his conclusions, I should like to mark the very great esteem in which I have always held Julian Brown, the late professor of palaeography in the University of London and the outstanding worker in the field of insular script in our time, by dedicating this lecture to his memory. Strong friendship, tempered by sometimes strong disagreement in matters of palaeography, characterised our long acquaintance. I first met him in 1953, when I was sent to the Department of Manuscripts at the British Museum to learn my trade and, with the kindness for which he is well remembered, he immediately took me under his wing. He had just completed what must have been one of the most daunting tasks ever undertaken by a librarian, the organisation in eighteen volumes of the manuscript of *Finnegans Wake*.[9] More importantly, he was just then beginning the studies that were to see the light in 1961 in the commentary volume of the Urs Graf facsimile of the Lindisfarne Gospels,[10] which set the course of his future career in insular palaeography. Starting as he did with such a magnificent subject, to which he was to do full justice, it is easy to understand how Northumbria in general and Lindisfarne in particular

---

[6]These were printed in Edward Bernard, *Catalogi librorum manuscriptorium Angliae et Hiberniae* (Oxoniae 1697) II, part 2, p 28, no 412/272.

[7]Giraldus Cambrensis, *Topographia Hibernica*, ed J F Dimock, *Giraldi Cambrensis Opera*, Rolls Series (London 1867) V, 123-24; Gerald of Wales, *The history and topography of Ireland*, translated by J J O'Meara, revised edition (Portlaoise 1982) 84.

[8]Richard Parr, *The life of James Ussher, archbishop of Armagh; with a collection of three hundred letters between him and his contemporaries* (London 1686) 171.

[9]British Library, *Catalogue of additions to the manuscripts, 1951-55* (London 1982) I, 5-10.

[10]*Evangeliorum quattuor codex Lindisfarnensis*, ed T D Kendrick et al, 2 vols (Olten and Lausanne 1960) II, 17-104.

came, in my view, to loom inordinately in his work. His concept of the Lindisfarne scriptorium, drawing to itself so many manuscripts for such unsubstantial reasons, I have not been able to accept. Indeed I remember at an early stage in the development suggesting to him, not then altogether seriously, that the gospels would fit much better into a Wearmouth-Jarrow milieu. The importance of his work in his chosen field cannot be exaggerated and although not moving in the same direction, this lecture is clearly dependent on the trail that he has broken.

In a splendid article on Irish script, entitled 'The oldest Irish manuscripts and their late antique background', he writes[11] :

> I conclude that the system of scripts used in the British and Irish Churches in the fifth and sixth centuries descended from the personal, unofficial end of the Later Roman script system ... rustic capitals, uncials and formal half-uncials were excluded. Included were three main elements: *scrittura di base*; a literary cursive, comparable to the script of the Springmount Bog tablets [CLA (1971) Suppl. no 1684], which could be formalised to produce a kind of half-uncial suitable for liturgical use, as in the 'Ussher' Gospels [CLA (1972) II, no 271]; and a documentary cursive, some traces of which can be detected in the fragment of Isidore from St. Gallen [CLA (1956) VII, no 995] and in the last ten lines of Mark in Durham A.II.10 [CLA (1972) II, no 147], but which has left a clearer impression of itself in the oldest known Anglo-Saxon minuscule, some from Northumbria and some from the South West, and in the small Irish minuscule of the grammar texts written at Bobbio, of 'pocket Gospel-books' such as *Mulling*, and of the Book of Armagh.

Elsewhere he writes[12]:

> If you take literary cursive, as found in the Springmount Bog tablets, remove most of the ligatures, change the ductus from cursive to set and transform loops into wedges, the result is bound to be a kind of half-uncial, such as we find in the 'Ussher' Gospels.

Earlier he had written[13]:

> Most primitive in script, and so perhaps earliest in date, are the set of waxed tablets ... and the Gospel book generally known — mistakenly — as codex Usserianus primus. The handwriting of the tablets is mature and expert (to write well on wax was not easy) ... The Gospel book is also a mature performance ...

---

[11]T J Brown, 'The oldest Irish manuscripts and their late antique background' in *Irland und Europa: die Kirche im Frühmittelalter*, ed Próinséas Ní Chatháin and Michael Richter (Stuttgart 1984) 311-27 (p 321).
[12]ibid, 320.
[13]ibid, 312.

Brown's literary cursive is the equivalent of Bischoff's cursive half-uncial[14] and of Lowe's quarter-uncial,[15] a script mixing uncial and half-uncial letter forms and mostly found as an annotating hand in late antique manuscripts but also used for copying whole texts in the fifth century. Some of these few are grammatical and were formerly at Bobbio (*CLA* (1972) II, nos 397a, 398; III (1938) no 462), probably a mark of the Irish interest in that subject. One example, however, the Bodleian offset of *Arator* dating from the sixth century, would suggest the persistence of the script in Italy or France (*CLA* (1971) Suppl., no 1740). Because of its use of mixed or alternative letter forms, this script has been proposed as the origin of insular majuscule.

When we examine the scripts of *Usserianus primus* and the Springmount tablets (the latter has been studied in detail by Bella Schauman[16]) we find not the true looping of early cursive in either case but an approach stroke to the verticals such as produced clubbing in early half-uncial and which in the gospels sometimes opens in certain conditions of the pen and ink to suggest a small loop, but never as Brown implies a wedge or triangular serif. In Springmount this stroke is normally a hook. The same script and even the same degree of formality is present in both examples and such differences as they present — like the occasional pinched top to the *a* in the tablets, which may account for its unfortunate description as minuscule — is clearly the result of the stylus and wax medium. Contrary to what Brown implies, neither uses a cursive ductus, both are true half-uncials, with numerous pen or stylus lifts. I believe that we have here survivors of the half-uncial that reached Ireland in the fifth century and continued to be practised until the invention of insular. They are totally unlike the seventh-century half-uncial of the Continent, which is the current, perhaps improbable, date ascribed to *Usserianus primus*. The half-uncial script is generally believed to have developed out of the Roman cursive in North Africa in the third century, but reached its canonical phase only during the course of the sixth century in Italy. It continued to be known to the Irish as the African script.[17] Failure to recognise the Irish form for what it is, is the result of comparing it with sixth-century types and forgetting the much greater fluidity that prevailed in the fifth century, when it reached Ireland. The relative isolation of the early Irish church can thus be seen not only to have led to the continued preference for an older way of calculating the date of Easter, but to the continuing use of an early form of half-uncial. However, we cannot yet certainly date either of the two surviving examples, though Brown pinned his hopes of dating *Usserianus primus* on the use of the cross with 'suspended' *alpha* and *omega*, which marks the colophon of Mark's gospel and such designs are noted to occur in a sixth-century manuscript of Avitus of Vienne now in Paris (*CLA* (1950) V, no 573).

---

[14]B Bischoff, *Latin palaeography: antiquity and the middle ages*, trans D Ó Cróinín and D Ganz (Cambridge 1990) 76.

[15]*CLA* (1947) IV, p xvi.

[16]B T Schauman, 'The emergence and progress of Irish script to the year 700' (thesis submitted to the University of Toronto in 1974) 308-10.

[17]Bischoff (note 14 above) 86, n 23.

Usserianus primus lacks the special characteristics of the insular majuscule: the triangular serifs, the alternative letter forms and the diminuendo. I prefer Lowe's name, majuscule, for the script rather than half-uncial, particularly as I believe we have a true Irish half-uncial in *Usserianus primus*. The invention of the majuscule is commonly believed to have been triggered by familiarity with uncial books as a result of renewed contact with the Continent in the second half of the sixth century. While failure to imitate so many aspects of uncial makes this hard to establish, the greater solemnity of uncial may have influenced the result. It is easy to see that Irish half-uncial must have served as the model towards which a putative native cursive with alternative letter forms was upgraded as a result of increased demand for writing in the second half of the sixth century. The use of the term majuscule preserves the distinction between the two scripts.

The script of the manuscript and tablets, apart from the occasional minuscule *n*, is innocent of alternatives. The alternative forms, uncial, half-unical or minuscule, of *d, n, r* and *s* have been seen to point to the script Lowe called quarter-uncial, which I have referred to above, as the type that the Irish up-graded. However, to complicate matters, the Irish at Bobbio when writing one of their grammars scrubbed out a fine half-uncial, late fifth- or early-sixth-century copy of the Old Latin version of Acts and Epistles, now at Naples, which had uncial *d, r* and *s* as occasional alternatives (*CLA* (1938) III, no 395). Being an out-of-date version may have sealed its fate. *Usserianus primus* was probably saved from a similar fate by an early association with a saint. The Naples manuscript also has its colophons in uncial, a feature of several of the early half-uncials, like the oldest copy of the Vulgate gospels, dating from Jerome's lifetime (*CLA* (1956) VII, no 984). The scribe of *Usserianus primus* seems to have set out to write the Marcan colophon (folio 149v) in uncials, but his knowledge of the script or that of his model was clearly defective. The preceding 'Amen' shows him familiar with the uncial *a* with the long spiked bow, which reappears in the Cathach (*CLA* (1972) II, no 266). The colophon includes the only occurrences of uncial *m* and *s*. Besides those here, I have noticed a very rare uncial *d* in the text, and this is also used by the corrector and the glossator. It is not used in the tablets. Uncial *g* I have found once. The use of red and the framing of the colophon in a border of pothooks and dots is paralleled in a half-uncial script in Sulpicius Severus's Life of St Martin copied in 517.[18]

Two scribes worked on *Usserianus primus*: the first writing Matthew and John, and the second Luke and Mark (**pls 68-69**). The first scribe writes the opening words of sections in red, another early feature, and the black ink of the second is brought into conformity by covering it with red dots. The *g* readily serves to distinguish the scribes, the first man's being totally angular, the second's having a more rounded tail. They both use the special Irish version with the tucked-in tail, which persists in Irish insular majuscule until the tenth century. The top of the *g*, unlike that in the tablets,

---

[18]M B Parkes, *Pause and effect* (Aldershot 1992) pl 4.

is one-sided, on the right, and readily becomes s-shaped, as in the fifth-century type ligatures with following *n* and *r*, another feature that will persist in the insular. The right-sided top reappears in the Bobbio Orosius (*CLA* (1938) III, no 328) and the Mulling John (*CLA* (1972) II, no 276), and occasionally in the Cathach. The other gospels in Mulling, the Book of Armagh (*CLA* (1972) II, no 270) and the Boniface hand[19] use a left-sided top. The *c* and *e* are generally tall as in some early half-uncial like the oldest copy of the Vulgate (*CLA* (1956) VII, no 984), and the tall *e* in ligature is paralleled in an early sixth-century half-uncial manuscript of Gallican canons (*CLA* (1950) V, no 619). The *a* and *o* are normal size, not smaller as in the oldest manuscript of the Vulgate. The hasta of the *f* is high, as commonly in half-uncial, whereas in the majuscule manuscripts, with the single exception of the Bobbio Orosius, it is on the line, perhaps in imitation of the uncial. Curiously enough, the only other candidate for Irish half-uncial or pre-insular majuscule status, the Bobbio Basilius (*CLA* (1938) III, no 312) has it at the half-way point. This manuscript has, however, one very important difference. Unlike *Usserianus primus* and the tablets, where spacing is used only for punctuation, it is not written in *scriptio continua*. Malcolm Parkes, the authority on punctuation, credits the Irish with the introduction of word division and dates it to the seventh century.[20] The Irish also developed the use of initials to improve legibility, hence the diminuendo, where the opening letters of a section diminish gradually from a large initial to text size. Both *Usserianus primus* and tablets lack this development, which again marks their earliness, but so does the Basilius, which must remain a puzzle. Ascenders are on the whole short, looking forward towards the majuscule. The descender of the *q* turns to the left as in some early manuscripts like the Berlin *Computus* (*CLA* (1959) VIII, no 1053), in uncial, dated by Lowe to AD 447, and this form reappears in Kells with the help of an extra hair stroke. There is little contrast of thick and thin, but the script is often thin in the horizontal tops of *t* and *g* and always in the narrow loop at the top of the *et* ligature. This ligature, which is the basis of so much splendid decoration in Kells, was current in Italy in the fifth century. The final stroke of *m* often curves inwards as in some early Italian half-uncial. The bow of the *p* is flattened, as in the Bobbio Orosius and Durham A.II.10, whose text, though Vulgate, shows the influence of *Usserianus primus* according to Verey.[21] What most clearly sets the Irish half-uncial script and all its majuscule descendants apart is the flat topped *t*, which is already disappearing in sixth-century Italy. Henceforth all continental half-uncial *t*s are contaminated by the curl to the left. This clearly seems to rule out the possibility, suggested by David Wright, that the insular majuscule was

---

[19] M B Parkes, 'The handwriting of St Boniface: a reassessment of the problems' in *Beiträge zur Geschichte der deutschen Sprache und Literatur* 98 (1976) 161-69; reprinted in M B Parkes, *Scribes, scripts and readers* (London 1991) 121-42.
[20] Parkes (note 18 above) 23-25.
[21] C D Verey, 'The gospel texts at Lindisfarne at the time of St Cuthbert' in *St Cuthbert, his cult and his community to AD 1200*, ed G Bonner, D Rollason, C Stancliffe (Woodbridge 1989) 143-50 (p 145).

invented in Bobbio.[22] The half-uncial written there — some perhaps by Irishmen, as Bella Schauman[23] claims in the case of part of Jerome's commentary on Isaiah — which is certainly decorated in an early insular way (*CLA* (1938) III, no 365), is always marked by the left curl to the *t* top. If such a scribe was not an Italian under Irish influence, then he may have been an Irishman writing Italian style script in the interests of local legibility, as seems to have often been their custom later when working on the Continent.

My second point concerns the script referred to by Brown as Anglo-Saxon minuscule phase I A (Northumbrian). Besides corrections noticed above Durham A.II.10 and the *Usserianus primus* also share an occasional *h* whose ascender leans backwards, a feature found in later Burgundian minuscule. The relationships between Irish and French scripts badly need serious investigation and in neglecting the latter, Brown has, I think, been led astray. The Merovingian horned *o*, found in the final lines of the Durham manuscript and in the Book of Armagh, may indeed be a vestige of New Roman cursive as written in Ireland, as he proposes, but it might more probably derive from contemporary scripts used in France. This must certainly be the case with the split stems of *f*, *p* and *s* in Irish scripts, which is so characteristic of Luxeuil. Françoise Henry's juxtaposition of the opening page of the Bobbio Orosius and a later Luxeuil manuscript[24] is impressive, especially as the destruction of the Luxeuil library by the Moors has deprived us of earlier and probably more telling examples. A late-seventh-century Luxeuil Augustine on papyrus, partly in uncial and partly in half-uncial (*CLA* (1950) V, no 614), uses insular wedge serifs on the verticals of the latter script, so the influence was certainly working both ways.

Brown's reference, quoted above, to 'the oldest known Anglo-Saxon minuscule, some from Northumbria' is to one of the scripts of the Palatine Paulinus (*CLA* (1934) I, no 87) with a probable Lorsch provenance, of which a facsimile under his editorship appeared posthumously (**pl 70**).[25] He found the minuscule (Phase I A) in two Echternach manuscripts, Jerome on Isaiah and Augustine on the Trinity (*CLA* (1950) V, nos 584, 588), which share a single scribe. He believed all three manuscripts were written in Northumbria some time before the reform of the Anglo-Saxon minuscule, which Malcolm Parkes places in the second decade of the eighth century at Wearmouth-Jarrow.[26] Nancy Netzer, in her recent study of the Echternach

[22]A Dold, L Eizenhöfer, D H Wright, *Das irische Palimpsestsakramentar im Clm 14429 der Staatsbibliothek München*. Texte und Arbeiten 53-54 (Beuron 1964) 36.

[23]B T Schauman, 'The Irish script of the MS Milan, Biblioteca Ambrosiana, S.45 Sup.', *Scriptorium* 32 (1978) 3-18.

[24]F Henry, 'Les débuts de la miniature irlandaise' reprinted in *Studies in early christian art and medieval Irish art*, ed Françoise Henry and Geneviève Marsh-Micheli (London 1984) II, 18-19.

[25]Brown (note 11 above) 314; *Codex Vaticanus, Palatinus latinus 235*, ed T J Brown and T W Mackay, Armarium codicum insignium 4 (Turnhout 1988).

[26]M B Parkes, 'The scriptorium of Wearmouth-Jarrow' in *Scribes, scripts and readers* (London 1991) 93-120.

scriptorium, considers Brown's proposal to be improbable in the case of the manuscripts which share a common scribe.[27] Being in Paris in 1991 I took another look at the manuscript (*CLA* (1950) V, nos 605, 606b) that now combines Willibrord's Calendar and Martyrology as well as other items and found that the copy of the letter from Pope Honorius to King Edwin was in the same script (**pl 71**). Written partly on the manuscript of the Calendar and partly on that of the Martyrology it must therefore be later than the binding together of these two, perhaps towards the middle of the eighth century. This shows the hand was certainly in use in Echternach, and besides would seem to undermine Brown's re-dating to *c*700 and favour a date in the middle of the eighth century and a continental rather than a Northumbrian source for all these manuscripts, including the Cologne Canons (*CLA* (1959) VIII, no 1163), which shares the hand type, and which Nancy Netzer would also prefer to attribute to Echternach. The date I propose would be closer to Lowe's original suggestion for the two Echternach manuscripts, even if his 'VIIIex' for the Paulinus may be a bit late. Lowe also gave this date to the Jena Charisius (*CLA* (1959) VIII, no 1227) and a manuscript of *Grammatica* at Würzburg (*CLA* (1959) IX, no 1399), written in a closely related script which, however, he labelled Irish minuscule. He attributed both, mistakenly I believe, to a single scribe because of a curious break at the tops of the stems of *f, p, s*, but this also occurs in the Stowe Missal (*CLA* (1972) II, no 268) and must not be seen as personal. The hands otherwise seem to be different. Such notable features of the script as the looped *d* and *q*, the characteristic long narrow closed bowl to the *g* and reversed *e* must surely point towards Merovingian influence on insular scribes working on the Continent.

---

[27]N Netzer, 'The early scriptorium at Echternach: the state of the question' in *Willibrord Apostel der Niederlande Gründer der Abtei Echternach ...* ed G Kiesel, J Schroeder (Echternach 1990) 132.

The division of hands in the Book of Kells[1]

Bernard Meehan

Since Françoise Henry's 1974 study of the Book of Kells, the idea that more than one artist was responsible for the major pages of the manuscript has become a standard one. Henry personified these artists as 'the Goldsmith', 'the Illustrator' and 'the Portrait Painter'. Her work on the text pages has been less prominent, and, understandably, there has been less inclination to refer to such intangible personalities as scribes A, B and C. There has been no published disagreement, so far as I am aware, with Henry's division of hands, and little consideration of the question of whether, and how far, scribe and artist were one in the Book of Kells.

Before considering these questions, it is necessary first to set the background. In 1935, E A Lowe expressed the opinion that the Book of Kells was 'written by several scribes'.[2] He maintained this view in the second edition of his work published in 1972, but did not indicate in either edition where he felt the divisions fell.[3] In 1950, Peter Meyer suggested that there was only one scribe, but a scribe who was capable of two different styles. He characterised these scripts as the standard half-uncial of the text pages, and the cursive minuscule used occasionally at the foot of pages. He felt that what he termed 'transitions', such as on folios 20v-26v or 125v-129r, 'show that both scripts are by the same hand'. Meyer did not seem to allow his scribe any involvement in the more artistic side of the book's production, or so he infers in his assertion that the interlinear, space-filling 'fleurons', or decorative devices mainly in red throughout the manuscript 'are clearly not by the hand that wrote the text'.[4]

Disagreeing with E A Lowe, Julian Brown claimed the Book of Kells as the work of 'one great scribe'[5] employing different styles in different parts of the manuscript. The gospels, in his view, are written 'mostly in a large, somewhat exuberant majuscule', while folios 29v-31v and 292v-339v are written in 'a plainer, slightly smaller majuscule', and the opening pages of the prefaces (folios 8v-20v) are in a majuscule 'plainer and smaller still'. The remaining prefatory material (folios 20v-26v) and the gospels at

---

[1] I am grateful to Mr Urs Düggelin for permission to reprint this article, in a revised form, from *The Book of Kells, MS 58, Trinity College Library Dublin: commentary*, ed Peter Fox (Fine Art Facsimile Publishers of Switzerland/Faksimile Verlag Luzern 1990)
[2] *CLA* (1935) II, 43.
[3] *CLA* (1972) II, 43. Several updatings to Lowe are necessary: the division of gatherings was established by Roger Powell; the manuscript did not belong to Ussher; the first folios are no longer kept separately.
[4] *Codex Cenannensis*, III, 28, 33.
[5] Brown, 230.

folios 127v-129v are in 'a highly decorative script best described as minuscule ... majuscule **a** is used, but the angle of the pen is slanted, not straight'.[6] While conceding to Lowe that the manuscript exhibits 'obvious differences in script', Brown pointed to 'a background of impressive consistency in minor details' in support of his view that the manuscript was the work of a single scribe. He cited, as 'a small sample', the following conventions used at line ends: 'the many variant forms of **a** designed to save space; the tall, narrow form of uncial **d**; the curled final stroke of **m**; the compressed forms of uncial **r** and of uncial **s**; the flourished final strokes of **a, e,** half-uncial **r** and **s,** and **t**; the various vertical, current forms of **m** and **n**; suprascript letters (especially **u**) and subscript letters (especially **i**); the **s**-like stroke used for final **m**; and the **mo** ligature'.[7]

Françoise Henry agreed with Lowe that there was more than one scribe. She felt able to distinguish 'at least three different hands, very close to each other and at times nearly merging into each other',[8] but, whereas Brown had argued that differences in script employed in different parts of the manuscript meant that the solitary scribe had simply chosen to use different styles for different sections, Henry observed that the similarities of the scripts, both in letter forms and in punctuation, pointed not to an identity of scribe but rather to training and practice in the same scriptorium.

Henry's 'Hand A' appears in the preliminaries (folios 1r, 8v-19v) and in the gospel of John (folios 292v-339v).[9] Hand A used brown ink made from iron-gall. Henry characterised Hand A as 'the most massive and compact' of the scripts, with letters lower in height than the other scribes, using more majuscule and fewer superscribed letters. The prefaces are ruled for nineteen lines, the gospel of John for eighteen lines, except for folio 312r/v, where a nineteen-line format is again used.

Henry contrasted the 'sedate and careful' approach of Hand A with the 'extrovert' character of Hand B. Whereas Hand A had made only occasional use of purple ink for the titles of *Breves causae* a n d *Argumenta*,[10] Hand B made prolific use of purple, red and carbon black to write text as well as titles. There are more minuscule letter forms than occur in Hand A, with many end lines 'in a compressed writing suggestive of the appearance of minuscule and sometimes including minuscule as well as majuscule A. These lines have very ornamental flourishes of the lower

---

[6]Brown, 230-31.

[7]Brown, 231.

[8]Henry, 154.

[9]Presumably by a proofreading slip, Hands 'A' and 'C' are transposed in the collation diagram in Henry, 225. Other slips in her diagram include the following: p 223 'HANDS' column, for folio 29r read folio 29v; for '12 lines' folios 30r-31r read 13 lines; p 224 'HANDS' column at 124v: for '12 lines' read 16 lines.

[10]Henry may have meant a faded organic red (perhaps kermes) rather than organic purple, which was not used by A for text.

limbs of letters'.[11] B has no consistency in the number of lines to the page, using sometimes seventeen, sometimes eighteen and sometimes nineteen lines. Hand B appears, Henry said, only on folios 20r-26v, 127v-129r.[12] On folios 127v-129r the scribe had not used inks of different colours, in the way he had done on folios 20r-26v, but the identity with the scribe of folios 20r-26v is suggested, in Henry's view, by, as before, a tendency towards the use of minuscule in end lines, and by the fact that the elaborated opening words *Uespere autem* at the top of the page seem to be in the same hand as the *I* on folio 24r and the *A* on folio 26r. She thought that 188v might possibly be the work of Hand B, 'carefully disguised' to resemble Hand C.

The bulk of the manuscript (folios 29v-127r, 131r-187r, 189r-289r) is the work, in Henry's scheme, of Hand C. Like A, this hand used only brown iron-gall ink, though Henry observed 'something freer'[13] in the work of C than of A, with perhaps more use made of occasional minuscule letters, but only 'one or two' minuscule end lines. The letter forms of C seemed to Henry slightly higher than those of A, except between folios 260r and 289r, where the format of the pages changed from seventeen lines to sixteen, and where she felt there were changes in the heights of letters from the earlier part of C, though no further change of hand.

Neither Brown's scheme nor Henry's for the breakdown of scripts or hands is entirely satisfactory in detail, though Lowe and Henry must surely be correct in supposing the manuscript to have been the work of more than one scribe. While it is not impossible that a major manuscript like the Book of Kells could have been the work of a single scribe, since it is arguable that the Lindisfarne Gospels and the MacRegol Gospels were such productions, a division of labour seems observable. The consistency in line endings, noted by Brown throughout the manuscript, can be attributed simply to scriptorium practice. The resources moreover, both in vellum and in pigments, enjoyed by the scriptorium which produced the Book of Kells make it unlikely that such a major project need have been entrusted to a single scribe even if the scribe were a master of several different styles.

Henry's study is a little schematic and incomplete, giving, for example, no indication of where the canon tables (folios 1v-6r) or folio 290r are to be placed. But it must be stressed that the modifications suggested below to her scheme form only another working hypothesis, and that further study of the manuscript will probably indicate further refinements. It seems hazardous to bring to a manuscript so full of caprice any sense of absolute certainty, since it is unusually difficult in the case of the Book of Kells to point to the kind of sustained and unequivocal distinctions in the

---

[11]Henry, 155.

[12]It is not clear whether Henry intended to include 129r, since she did not include it specifically, citing these pages as '124 ff': see p 155. Brown did include 129r, which presumably he intended to cite rather than 129v, where there is no script.
[13]Henry, 155.

formation and size of letters, or the spacing between letters or lines, or the format of the page, which in other manuscripts indicate unmistakably the work of different scribes. An additional difficulty is that hands do not customarily seem to change at the beginnings of new gatherings. As Henry remarked, different styles seem to merge into each other, making the division between scribes extraordinarily difficult to discern, and seeming to point to a high degree of skill on the part of the scribes in effecting as smooth a transition as possible. This may be noticeable at, for example, folio 88, a change of scribe probably coming at the recto, as a change in the form of stabbing shows, rather than the verso, though little can be inferred with certainty from the rather anonymous script of 88r.

Hand A is characterised by letters generally smaller than the other scribes; by a greater compactness; by lines of text slightly longer than the other scribes; by a more upright *s*; by the distinctive use of a rounded form of initial *N* (as in folio 8v line 8: *Non[no] venit*; or folio 303r line 4: *IN hiis*) (pl 26); by shorter ascenders; by, in general, a more sober and conservative quality of script and decoration, making it the hand closest in style to that of the Durham Gospels.

I agree with Henry that Hand A is on folios 1r, 8v-19v and 292v-339v. Hand A can also be seen in folios 130v-140v (gospel of Mark). Here, the lines of text are, like the preliminaries and John, slightly longer than those of the other scribes. The eighteen-line format used by A for St John's gospel was pricked for folios 130v, 131 and 132 but the bottom line was not used, presumably in order to bring Mark into line with the format already established for Matthew. Here, too, the script generally has A's sobriety, with few flourishes or spaces left for ornament, spaces left at the ends of lines often being filled with a 'rosette' form of interline ornament not exclusive to A but used by him a great deal in the preliminaries. There is a tendency in folios 130v-140v for the last lines of sections to begin at the left margin, as is the practice in St John's gospel, rather than near the middle of the line[14] (pl 30). The script seems to change to that of C on folio 141r, where the lines of text return to a slightly shorter format than the immediately preceding pages; and where stabbing replaces pricking. At this point too, more use is made of elongated letters and there is more embellishment of the script. A bold, interlinear quadruped is introduced on 145v; there is an elaborate correction at the foot of 146v (though perhaps by another hand); and geometric initials are introduced on 147v.

Scribe A may perhaps have had some involvement in the design of the canon tables (1v-6r), folios over which there has been much debate. That there was a certain lack of coordination in the execution of the canon tables is indicated by peculiarities in their ruling and pricking. In the middle of the arcades on folios 3r and 3v, rulings were drawn for secondary pillars in the manner of those painted in organic purple and white on 2v, but these rulings were subsequently ignored. Folios 5 and 6 were both

---

[14]I owe this last observation to Patrick McGurk.

pricked for nineteen lines of single-column text, in the format used by Hand A in the preliminaries, but this marking was superseded by a grid pattern, almost like graph paper, superimposed on folios 5v and 6r. Whether A's involvement in the canon tables extended beyond — or even as far as — this pricking is not possible to quantify.

Further discussion of the canon tables is necessary at this point. The canon tables display no overall uniformity in the priority of script and decoration. In the first column of 1v, there seems no doubt that script followed decoration, since the final digit of *xiiii* intrudes on the head of the crouching figure at the top of the column. At the foot of the first column of 2r, on the other hand, script seems to have come first, judging by a break in the ornament. At the top of the second, third and fourth columns of 2r, script seems to have been in place before the yellow orpiment of the arcades was added, the orpiment being painted around the numbers.[15] The lines were in place before the numbers were added, though at the top of column two a second line was drawn after the numbers. Similarly, the second pillar in purple was painted around the third column of figures on 2v. On 3r, however, script can be seen over decoration at the foot of columns one and three, indicating that script came second. On 3v, the columns are headed in iron-gall ink which intrudes on the thin red line beneath the symbols. On 5v, the order of work seems to have been that the grid pattern established by ruling was used to paint the internal boxes in orpiment and organic purple mixed with white (though not the border, which was painted in a dilute wash of purple over white). The script was then added — this being seen from the intrusion of script on ornament at the foot of the second column — followed by the thin red line of decoration, the flourish from the final *e* of *propriae* going under the red in the final column (third box from top), and the red lines being interrupted to accommodate script at the foot of the second column and around the middle of the final column (fourth box from the top). The border, being painted around the script in this box, and going over script in two places higher up the same column, seems to have been the final element in the design. The dilute purple used for this border was repeated for the third vertical line (the first three boxes) of folio 6r.

On folio 6r, the order of work seems to have been that the thin ink lines of the frame were drawn first, followed by the thin red lines which complete the frame and which go over the ink lines to the right of the first column of numbers; the canon numbers were then added, *xxxuiiii* going over a red line in the third column; and finally the frames were filled with yellow and purple pigment, the yellow partially obscuring the lower parts of the same number *xxxuiiii* in the third column. On 5v, squares of the frame left uncoloured between the bars of yellow and purple were filled with ornament, and further ornament was supplied at the top and bottom of the frame. Folio 6r has by contrast a slightly unfinished look, with three of

---

[15]This may have been an unusual sequence of work, to judge from folio 30r, where orpiment was the first pigment laid down.

the squares in the frame left uncoloured, and no additional ornament supplied outside the frame.

Without attempting to identify the artist or artists responsible for the decoration of 1v-5r, the hand which added the columns of numbers and rubrics on those pages, and which effected both script and decoration of 5v-6r, seems to have been that of scribe B. He is to be identified by his distinctive use of organic purple, organic red, orange-red (red lead) and yellow orpiment for script on 20r-26v — though on folios 5v-6r he used iron-gall ink rather than black carbon ink — and by the resemblance of the incipits and explicits of the canon tables to the minuscule of 20r-26v. On folios 3r-4r, he used an organic purple, now largely faded or washed out, for some numbers. As on folios 114v and 183r,[16] he filled space in the final column of 5v with an unnecessary repetition of rubrics.[17]

B copied the final pages of the prefaces (to folio 26v) in a highly decorative script with strong elements of display minuscule (reminiscent of pages of the Book of Armagh) which seems to begin, *pace* Brown, at 20r rather than 20v, and probably at the beginning of the page, where a now-faded organic red was used. On these folios, B began the lines of script, not, as in the common practice of the manuscript, more or less tight on the pricking, but around 9 mm to the right of the prickings. B was probably the scribe who supplied rubrics using faded organic red in spaces left by A on folios 13r, 15v, 16v and 18r for decorated bands of display capitals and rubrics. Space left near the top of folio 19v was not filled, which suggests that A had left both rubrics and display capitals to be done later by another scribe.[18] The integration of display capitals and rubrics, taken together with the palette used, suggests that B was responsible for the display capitals on 13r, 15v and 16v, though perhaps not those on 18r, and a different scribe probably supplied those on 19v.

B supplied another extended portion of text between folio 125v line 11 (*et terra*) and folio 129r, with an endline in minuscule on 125v. It seems doubtful that this hand begins at 127v, as both Henry and Brown have it, the change more probably coming at the point (*et terra*) where a black carbon ink was used. It might be thought that the change is at the top of 127v, despite the identity of inks, a change being heralded by rows of red decorated lines at the foot of 127r; but against this it can be argued that gathering 15 (folios 125-28) was constructed as one designed simply for the completion of St Matthew's gospel. With only four leaves, it was ruled, like the previous gathering, for a line of text several millimetres shorter

---

[16]See p 190.

[17]I owe this point to Patrick McGurk.

[18]Patrick McGurk has pointed out to me that the scribe would probably have left a space for rubrics even when, as in this case, there was no rubric in his textual exemplar, the Book of Durrow or its clone.

than the norm.[19] Taking over this task on 125v, scribe B may have felt
that, with more than three leaves remaining to bring the text to its end,
he could afford to fill space decoratively at the foot of 127r in order to
begin the next page with an elaborate *Uespere autem*. In the event, he
miscalculated, completing the text on the single leaf folio 129r at the
beginning of a new gathering and on the reverse of a major decorated page.
Here, B used iron-gall ink, perhaps because he was writing after an
interval, but he continued to employ minuscule letter forms and
embellished the page with his usual pigments: orange-red, yellow
orpiment and an organic purple (mixed with white). He also supplied the
rubric for the gospel of St Mark (*Secundum Marcum*) in orange-red with
fillers of purple mixed with white.

Further rubrics in orange-red seem to have been added by B on folios 11v
(the end of the *Breves causae* of Matthew and beginning of the
Argumentum of Mark): *finiunt braeues causae / euangelii secundum
matheum / Incipit argumentum euangelii / secundum matheum*. That this
is a different hand from the rest of 11v is indicated by an increased size of
letter; by the 'shivered' line 11 which, as with the minuscule endlines on
folio 12v, had been intended to act as an end line; and by the greater verve
of the scribe, seen for instance in such tricks as the placing of the *a* of
Matheum within the second arch of the *M* (line 13) (**pl 11**). B also supplied
the same style of rubrics on folio 290r for the end of St Luke's gospel and
beginning of St John's (*Explicit euan/gelium secun/dum Lucam / Explicit
euangelium / secundum Lucam / Incipit secundum / Iohannem*); and
perhaps the intruded word *Initium* on 327v line 8. It was probably Hand B
who began, on folios 292v-293r, but did not complete, the addition of canon
numbers to St John's gospel.

B's palette of organic red, orange-red, organic purple, orpiment and carbon
black, used for the text pages 20r-26v, was not followed by any other
scribe, though some further use of carbon black was made for a few lines on
folios 166v and 167r. These may have been replacement passages by B of
text which had failed to adhere properly to the vellum.[20] It may be noted
that organic purple and orpiment also dominate the decorative scheme of
the *Liber* page (29r), the Eight-Circle Cross page (33r), and the Chi-Rho
page (34r), prompting the tentative suggestion that these major pages too
might be ascribed to B. The hand which wrote *autem generatio* on 34r was
surely that responsible for the rest of the page. There is a resemblance
here to the hand of B, especially in the shape of the *g* of *generatio*, which
is close to the *g* of 126v line 10 (*magda[/linae]*). The cat standing on its

---

[19]Gathering 14's lines are slightly (1 or 2 mm) longer than those of gathering 15. Folio
187r is also ruled for a slightly shorter line, since little text remained to bring St
Mark's gospel to an end.

[20]On 166v, carbon ink was used for the end of the bar of the final *t* on line 3, as well
as the triple point punctuation sign to its right, and for lines 4-5 (*Et ... uobis*). Here,
there are signs that the carbon ink was used to reinforce the same text in iron-gall ink,
but there are no signs of iron-gall ink beneath the carbon ink of folio 167r lines 1, 2
(*nec pater ... uestra*).

hind legs on 34v is close in style to that of 24r and the range of pigments used is also similar. Hand B may thus be seen as both scribe and decorator of 34v, and responsible for recto and verso of the single leaf, folio 34.[21] Henry speculated that the *Quoniam* page (folio 188r), which 'does not fit in at all with the other Introductory pages', may have been the work of B.[22] Henry's feeling that 188v might be from the hand of B seems to be confirmed by the endline in minuscule. Like 188r, but unlike 29r, 33r or 34r, the *Initium* page (folio 130r) makes extensive use of blue from lapis lazuli, but there are resemblances between the display initials of this page and those on 13r, 15v, 16v, and 18r, in particular the *G* on 130r and 15v, and the *EU* of 130r and 18r. In addition to differences in palette, however, stylistic differences between pages like 188r and 29r seem to make it unlikely that they are the work of the same man. Orpiment and organic purple were also used for minor initials on 38r-40r, 42v, 43r/v and 49r (perhaps executed by B after the page had been written by a different scribe) as well as a number of other initials such as those on 89v, 184r, 192r, 194r or 255r, though clearly it would be stretching the argument to suggest that B was at work every time these two pigments were used in tandem, especially as folio 255r/v is in a section which, it is argued below, was written by another scribe.[23] The palette of B also occurs on the unfinished pages 29v-31v, the spirals on 30v and 31r echoing those of 29r and 34r, but the hand seems to be that of C. Folio 31v is, however, ruled for eighteen lines, a format used by B on a number of pages, as well as by A for the gospel of John, but one not otherwise used by C.

For effect, B added unnecessary, repetitious lines of text (as on folio 290r) to fill space on the decorated text pages 114v and 183r, again in his familiar orange-red, with fillers, as on 129r, of organic purple mixed with white. On 114v, he repeated the text drawn in display capitals: *Tunc dicit illis Ih̄s omnes / uos scan[dalum]*, while he lifted line 14 from folio 182v and repeated it at the foot of 183r: *Et crucifigentes / eum / diuise[runt]*. These additions and rubrics by B seem to have been made without the aid of pricking or ruling, confirming that they did not form part of the original plan of the manuscript.[24] It seems likely that B also added the head and feet which appear to the top right and lower left of folio 183r, and the words *angelus d(omi)ni* to 187v, along with the rest of the orange-red on that page.

The main difficulty in agreeing with Henry that the bulk of the manuscript (folios 29v-127r, 131r-187r, 189r-289r) is the work of a single scribe, C, is that many of the pages of script and initials within these folios are strikingly different from each other, not in basic letter forms or

---

[21]The artists may, on the other hand, have been copying a model. Other cats, similar to those on 34v and 24r, though not as close in style, appear on 87r, 116r and 257v.

[22]Henry, 211-12.

[23]This problem may be answered by Erika Eisenlohr's suggestion (in this volume p 198) that Hand B may have been responsible for longer passages in the second half of Luke.

[24]It seems possible that B was also the correcting hand using red on 39r and 218v.

even in scribal techniques — since the manuscript was produced in a single, coordinated scriptorium — but in the general appearance of the page due either to the size of the individual letters and the number of them used on a page, or to the decoration and ornament of a text page and the relation of script and decoration to each other. Taken as a more or less random sample, folios 67r and 89r (chosen since they are examples of text hand reproduced in Alexander, *Insular manuscripts*, pls 258-59) do not impress on examination as the work of the same scribe. In certain sections of the manuscript (including folio 89r) there is, I suggest, a fourth major scribe, D, who wrote a large, confident, slightly more angular hand than C, which often fitted marginally less text to the page, using longer ascenders — with a difference of around 2 mm in the height of *b* and *d* — and a more oval *o*; made more use of elongated letters, particularly at the ends of lines; often had a distinctive flick or serif at the beginning of *s*, meeting or coming close to meeting the diagonal downstroke of the letter; employed the occasional greatly flourished letter, such as the *h* of *huc* (165r line 1) (**pl 31**); and often preferred a slightly darker ink. It may be suggested that scribe D's work can be observed on folios 88r-125v, 164r-187v, and 243v-289r, while C is on folios 29v-31v, 35r-87v, 141r-163v, 189r-202r, 203v-243v. It is extraordinarily difficult to be certain where the change occurs in St Luke's gospel. There may be significance in the fact that folios 234 and 235 were stabbed as well as pricked, but I am inclined to suggest, tentatively, that D took over from C at 243v line 13 (*non dico*), where there is a change of ink, and from which point, beginning with *peribitis* (line 15), the final lines of verses and other sections are generally not placed at the left margin but are indented to varying degrees.

The relationship of scribe and artist is important in the context of the division of hands, different scribes having a different approach to decoration. Scribe A tended to leave spaces in his copying of the text on, for example, folio 15v, for the addition of ornamented script. That A may have had a certain indifference to the insertion of decorated initials is seen on folios 292v-295r, where only a minimum of indentation was provided for their insertion, and on 296v, where the need for initials was disregarded, forcing the artist to add an ornamental *R* in the margin.[25] Scribe B tended to use the script itself as a decorative device. There are places in the canon tables (to which attention has been drawn above) where Hand B inserted script after decoration (decoration not necessarily of his own creation), but generally B left the further ornamentation of his page until the text was completed. This can be seen on folio 24r, for example, where the claws of his cat impinge on the *g* and *n* of *agnus* (line 4). That this particular decoration was planned by B is suggested by his ruling of the page for eighteen lines but leaving the top line free.

In the case of Hand C and Hand D, it is necessary to look more closely at the relationship between scribe and artist, and to examine Françoise Henry's observations on the matter. Folios 62v and 193r are examples of

---

[25]The two lower *R*s are later additions.

pages where, to judge from spaces not satisfactorily filled, there appears to be some discrepancy between the intentions of the scribe as expressed in his layout and the execution of ornament by the artist (pl 36).[26] In other areas of the manuscript, a letter or two after the initial, generally a modest one, seems to have been executed by the artist, and in a style of script so close to that of the rest of the page as to point towards both script and ornament as being the work of the same man. Examples are 35v (*Tunc*) and 43r, where the *Ite* of *Iterum* seem to be in the hand of an artist who has also 'reinforced' the first stroke of *r*. Folio 44r line 5 (*Ego*) also seems to show this extremely close relationship, while on 250r line 14, *Aut q* has been reinforced in this way. There are three further such examples on 122r. On folio 40r line 13, and on 64r (final line) only the outline and base colour of the initials were drawn, with artistic elaboration remaining to be added. On 74r line 9, the bar of an initial *T* is linked to an *x* in the line above. These examples seem to leave open the question of the relationship between scribe and artist, but they point to the likelihood that the scribe of these pages was at least capable of providing the outline of initials. Henry expressed the view that the unfinished pages 29v-31v show scribe and artist working in 'close accord'. Here, the frame for decoration was drawn first, then script was added, and after that orpiment was used, followed by organic purple and orange-red. She concluded that 'the man who traced these schematic indications was probably the scribe himself'. Despite this, her expectation, based on 'a common habit of medieval scribes', was that the scribe would have left a space for decoration to be added later. In her view, folio 91r conformed to this expectation, while 111r did not do so entirely, since on this page 'the scribe may have traced the heavy black outlines of the first five initials, leaving the painter to add colour embellishments to them'.[27] There are a great many examples in the manuscript of this style of initial, which, as Henry noted, is more than simply a matter of the artist supplying the initial. Further examples are on folios 83r, 84v, 85v, 87r. On 87v, an *s* is formed around a quadruped, while on 281v (*Iterum*), the *I* and the bar of the *t* are composed, almost certainly by the scribe, from zoomorphic ornament of a highly accomplished kind. There are occasional examples of the artist supplying letters other than initials, as on folio 45r line 1, where the final *s* of *hominibus* was painted rather than written. Frequently, the relationship is extremely close, as on folio 200r, between the final *h* of *maath* and the foot of the warrior in the bottom right corner, with the foot appearing to be drawn around the letter.

Both C and D should, I conclude, be regarded as artist-scribes, with some clear similarities in technique. In their preparation of the page, both C and D seem to have preferred stabbing to pricking, and both wrote lines of

---

[26] As a caveat, the Cathach (Dublin, RIA, MS 12 R 33) might however be useful to bear in mind. Here, script and ornament are certainly by the one hand which did not always feel it necessary to fill all the available space; see for instance folio 12v. As a further caveat, a failure to fill space may also be observed in folio 177r, a page which I am inclined on other grounds to ascribe to Hand D.
[27] Henry, 212.

roughly the same length. Hand D, however, displays the confidence to integrate script and decoration to a greater extent than does Hand C. There are examples of different kinds, such as on folio 255v lines 3-4, where the serif of the final minim of the *m* of *unum* is wittily extended to form the tonsure of the rider; or 110r, where a parallel layout of display initials boldly dictates the decorative scheme of the page. Another example is folio 273r. The layout here is unusual, with the text at the foot of the page indented in a way which left spacing for two decorated initials, a design which involved close planning of the page. On 253v, the word *Audiebant* is prefixed by a decorative, though redundant, initial *A*, but this seems to indicate a slip by Hand D rather than an artist following the scribe. It can be demonstrated for other pages that the penwork at least of decorated initials, if not necessarily the pigment, was in place before all the lines of script were written. On 244r, *eorum* (line 14) was split to accommodate the tail of a long ornamental *R* on the line above. On 249r, *aedificare* (line 5) was similarly split to accommodate the tail of the *Q* of *Quis* from the line above. It seems impossible to explain this in any way other than that the *Q* was drawn first by the scribe of the page. It does not seem likely that the scribe left a space after *aedifi* knowing that *Q* would be placed there, since the tail of a conventional *Q*, like that on 248v line 12, would have been to the left of the space left free (pl 44). Most strikingly, on folio 255r, the *b* of *[inpos]sibile* (line 16) had to be written in two parts, to avoid a paw already in place from the decorative *Et* ligature in the line above. Examination under binocular microscope reveals no disturbance of the continuity of the texture of the vellum which would indicate the possibility that the top of the ascender of *b* was scraped away to allow the paw to be drawn (pl 48). There is a similar example of this by Hand C on folio 206v line 9, where the word *multis* is split to accommodate the *x* of *exibant* from the line above. Such divisions in the middle of words are an abnormal occurrence, it being more common for words to be run together. There is an example at folio 39r line 8 (*pro fetam*), but signs of erasure are clear. On folio 36*v *uoc abit* (line 4) has the appearance of a word split by mistake, decoration being added after the page of script was completed.

A close examination of pigment supports the view of an identity between scribe and artist. Occasionally, pigment intrudes on script. On folio 49r line 5 [Hand C], yellow orpiment was brushed over the shaft of the initial letter of *fructibus*, and similarly on 50r line 14 [Hand C], white pigment used for the cat's tongue was brushed over the *d* of *[qui]dam*. This is not unexpected, given the conventional sequence of work, but on other pages, script can be seen, with the aid of a binocular microscope, to impinge on areas of pigment. On 70v [Hand C], the first letter (*U* of *Unde*) is written partially over the green of a quadruped's leg. This need not necessarily demonstrate anything more than the artist supplying the first letter, though the hand of *Unde* has all the appearance of the hand of the rest of the page; but there is the same occurrence of ordinary text (as opposed to initial letters) written over pigment on at least another two pages, showing conclusively the scribe following decoration. On folio 122r [Hand

D], the *u* of the word *Tunc* on lines 8 and 11 was in each case written over the ornamental zoomorphic initial *T*. On folio 249v [Hand D], the tail of the *q* of *quem* (final line) was written over the pigment of the decoration, as was the *u* of *unam* on 250r (line 16) [Hand D] (**pl 45**).

A predictable sequence of work was not always followed in the Book of Kells. On folio 114r the text in the tympanum was written after the drawing of the design of the page, but before the application of all the pigment. At *dicto*, the line of the arch can be seen by binocular microscope to go under the *o*, while the letter is skirted by the red pigment. The final point of the triple-point punctuation after *oliueti* is written unmistakably over the blue pigment of the spray. Contrary to what might be thought the logical sequence of work, on folio 285r the line of text at the top of the frame was written first: the sprays from the mane of the lion can clearly be seen under binocular microscope to go over the word *secundum*.

Considerable caution is necessary in attempting to demarcate the hands. As Patrick McGurk has pointed out, greater opportunities for decoration presented themselves in those sections of the text which had more Eusebian concordances than others, so that conclusions about script cannot be argued solely from styles of decoration. Hands C and D are in places so lacking in uniformity in such matters as the style of pricking that further examination may well reveal the existence of more than four major scribes. Even the apparently uniform script of A contains features more common in other sections of the manuscript. On 328r (line 17), the bowl of the second letter, *b*, is broken by a foreleg protruding from the zoomorphic *A* before it. It may be that D completed the initial and second letters of the line in a space left by A. On folios 309r-311v and 335r, spaces were left for decoration which were filled zoomorphically in a style which does not seem typical of A. Here may be the work of the artist whom Henry saw as responsible for the 'host of little wandering animals' which meander through the manuscript, the script itself not seeming to betray any change of style. This artist may perhaps be D, since so many other examples of the style occur in his pages, and since on 174v it may have been he who had the freedom to paint the feathers of an eagle over his own script. It is possible too that a minor artist or artists went through the manuscript adding such embellishments as, for example, the hare on folio 131r line 15, or the cat on 171v line 13, completing at the same time the colouring of such pages.

Other parallels between features of the script pages and the decorated pages make it possible to speculate that the major artists of the Book of Kells may also have been its scribes. There is a resemblance between the capital bands of 19v and the *Natiuitas* line of 8r, as well as the letters *RINCI* of the *In principio* page (folio 292r), and some resemblance to the *Ma* initial of 191v. The tilted head and shoulders of folio 95r line 6 may relate to the Matthew symbol of folio 5r. But much work remains to be done on the decoration as well as on the script and on the relation of one to the other. In this area of the study of the Book of Kells, as in other areas, we are handicapped by not knowing to what extent the manuscript was completed in one location or two, and to what extent, if at all, its execution was interrupted for a significant period.

In summary, Hand A appears to be the scribe who had some involvement in the canon tables, began the preliminaries, was responsible for St John's gospel and began St Mark's gospel. Scribe B completed the canon tables, the preliminaries, and St Matthew's gospel, as well as supplying rubrics and other additions, possibly including major decorated pages, throughout the manuscript. Hands C and D are separate scribes, though in places it is difficult to distinguish the division between them. Hands C and D copied the bulk of Matthew, Mark and Luke. There is, however, little that is certain about the Book of Kells, and the following breakdown of hands is presented as a provisional one.

Folio	Hand	Folio	Hand
1r	A	130r	B?
1v-6r	B	130v-140v	A
7v, 8r	?	141r-163v	C
8v-19v (11v, 13r, 15v, 16v, 18r rubrics by B)	A	164r-187v (166v, 167r, 183r, additions by B)	D
20r-26v	B	188r	B?
27v, 28v	?	188v	B
29r	B?	189-202r	C
29v-31v	C?	202v, 203r	?
32v	?	203v-243v?	C
33r	B?	243v?-289r	D
34r	B?	290r	B
34v	B?	292v-339v (327v, addition by B)	A
35r-87v	C		
88r-125v (114v, addition by B)	D		
125v-129r	B		

The puzzle of the scribes: some palaeographical observations

Erika Eisenlohr

Elias Avery Lowe wrote in 1935 that the Book of Kells was written by more than one hand and reconfirmed his view in 1972.[1] In the same year 1972 Julian Brown thought that one great scribe had written the manuscript but used different styles: mostly an exuberant majuscule for the main passages, a somewhat smaller and less elaborate hand for parts of the preliminary texts and the beginning of the Matthew and John gospels, and another still simpler and less elaborate hand for the pages with the *argumenta* and *capitula*.[2] Against apparent graphic differences he argued that other details were continuous throughout the manuscript. In 1974 Françoise Henry supported Lowe and proposed several scribes.[3] She argued that the similarities of the scripts were not different styles of one scribe but the marks of one scriptorium[4] with scribes who had been trained in the same way and 'worked in some kind of accord'. She suggested 'at least three different hands, working very close to each other and at times nearly merging into each other', and three miniaturists.[5] In the *Commentary* to the 1990 facsimile edition of the Book of Kells Bernard Meehan suggested, provisionally, four hands, and stressed that 'the relationship of scribe and artist seems crucial in the context of the division of hands'.[6]

The similarity or dissimilarity of hands has so far mainly been based on more general impressions of the scripts. My aim is to focus attention on some specific features which were singled out to pursue the consistency of scribal habits and I shall discuss details of letter forms which seem to have passed unnoticed over the length of six hundred and seventy-eight pages. Like any palaeographer, I am well aware that a simple stroke of pen may alter the form of a letter, but I think that a proficient scribe will revert to his habitual form of writing. Shades of ink, pricking techniques and lengths of lines, the size of initials, their ornamentation, colour schemes and marginal decorations will not be considered.

Fig 1 presents the collation of the entire Book of Kells and the order of the

---

[1]*CLA* (1972) II, no 274; in der deutschen Fassung des *Kommentarbandes*, hg. v. Anton von Euw und Peter Fox (Luzern 1990), 'Die Schrift', übers. v. Erika Eisenlohr, S. 261-74.
[2]Brown, 219-46 (p 230) for discussion of folios 29v-31v and 292-339, folios 8v-20v.
[3]Henry, 154-57.
[4]With regard to house styles see Malcolm B Parkes, 'Introduction' in *The role of the book in medieval culture*, ed P G Ganz, Bibliologia, elementa ad librorum studia pertinentia 3 (Turnhout 1986) 11-16.
[5]Henry, 154-57.
[6]Meehan, 245-56.

preliminary texts, the gospels, and the placement of the miniature and initial pages in the gatherings.[7] The quire number is given along the left margin. The regular quire is the quinio[8] with five bifolia numbered one to ten at the top of the collation frame and gathered graphically at the bottom. Blank double squares divided by a dotted line represent the recto and verso side of each folio.[9] The squares for single leaves — often the major decorated pages — are dotted. A gathering of five bifolia shows folios 1 and 10 on the outer edges, folios 2 and 9, 3 and 8, 4 and 7 converging on the centre, where the main fold of the innermost bifolium 5 and 6 is marked by a thick black line. The impression is that the present collation is more irregular than regular. The smallest gathering of three single leaves, quire 1, contains the extant prefatory material. About ten leaves are considered lost. The most voluminous gathering is quire 5 with 13 leaves, that is, five double leaves telling the gospel *secundum matheum* and three single leaves with miniatures and decorated pages. Black squares represent the missing leaves in quires 4, 15, 21, 22 or at the end of St John's gospel. The folio number is always entered in the left corner of each double square. A diagonal stroke through a square indicates an originally blank page. The fine or heavy top line of each square stands for the hair (thick bar) or flesh side (thin line) of each parchment.[10]

The division of Hands A, B, C and D was entered into the squares as proposed by Françoise Henry and Bernard Meehan:[11] one letter per box signifies agreement between the two authors, two letters two opinions. Henry's version, being the older one, is entered first (left letter in cases of two), Meehan's second (right letter).[12] It is evident that both authors agree for the greater part of the manuscript. Hand A wrote the glossary, the preliminary texts, had some share in quire 16, the first gathering of Mark and copied the entire gospel of John in quires 34 to 38. Hand B

---

[7] The idea of dismembering a quire and spreading the leaves onto a plane was developed by Peter Rück. Frank M Bischoff added the information on parchment and programmed the layout for computer use. The diagram was first published by Peter Rück, 'Die Schriften' in *Das Evangeliar Heinrichs des Löwen. Kommentar zum Faksimile*, ed Dietrich Kötzsche (Frankfurt am Main 1989) 122-54, fig 1; see also Frank M Bischoff, 'Methoden der Lagenbeschreibung', *Scriptorium* 46 (1992) 3-27. Bischoff adapted his programme for the Book of Kells data as given in the quire diagram; I would like to thank him for his great help.

[8] Brown, 219-46 (p 229).

[9] The arrangement differs from B Meehan, 'Summaries of text' in *Kells commentary*, 333-54 where the text reads from the beginning of the verso side, top left corner, down to the recto side, bottom right corner. Frank M Bischoff, 'Systematische Lagenbrüche. Kodikologische Untersuchungen zur Herstellung und zum Aufbau mittelalterlicher Evangeliare' in *Elementa Diplomatica*, ed Peter Rück (Potsdam 1994) (in preparation).

[10] Instead of Meehan's letters 'h' (hair) and 'f' (flesh) sides which always label the recto side of the vellum, the determinant here is the hair side. The heavy black bar across the top of any square marks the hair side and signifies recto or verso of a particular folio. As to the difference between vellum and parchment see the different aspects covered in *Pergament. Geschichte - Struktur - Restaurierung - Herstellung*, ed Peter Rück, Historische Hilfswissenschaften 2 (Sigmaringen 1991).

[11] The diagram transposes the data given by Meehan, 'Collation', in *Kells commentary*, 185-92, and idem, 'Dimensions and original number of leaves', ibid, 175-76.

[12] Henry, 223-25; Meehan, 256.

Key to fig 1	
	Ten or more leaves lost before
Quire 1:	folios 1-3 Preliminary text
	folio 1r: Glossary of Hebrew names, folios 1v-3v: Canon tables I-IV
Quire 2:	folios 4-12 Preliminary text
	folios 4r-6r: Canon tables IV-VI
	folios 6v-74: originally blank (twelfth-century copies of charters)
	folio 7v: The Virgin and Child
	folio 8r: *Natiuitas*
	folios 8v-11v: *Breves causae* of Matthew
	folios 12r-12v: *Argumentum* to Matthew
Quire 3:	folios 13-22 Preliminary text
	folio 13r: *Argumentum* to Matthew, *Breves causae* of Mark
	folios 13v-15v: *Breves causae* of Mark, *Argumentum* to Mark
	folio 16v: *Argumentum* to Mark, *Argumentum* to Luke
	folios 17r-18r: *Argumentum* to Luke, *Argumentum* to John
	folio 19v: *Argumentum* to John, *Breves causae* of Luke
Quire 4:	folios 23-28 Preliminary text
	folios 23r-23v: *Breves causae* of Luke
	folios 24r-25v: *Breves causae* of John
	folios 26r-26v: Glossary of Hebrew names to Luke
	one leaf lost between folios 26 and 27
	folio 27r: originally blank (twelfth-century copies of charters)
	folio 27v: Symbols of the four evangelists
	folio 28r: blank
	folio 28v: Portrait of St Matthew
Quires 5-15:	folios 29-129: Gospel of St Matthew
quire 5	folio 29r: *Liber generationis*
	folios 29v-31v: Genealogy of Christ
	folio 32r: blank
	folio 32v: Portrait of Christ
	folio 33r: Eight-Circle Cross
	folio 33v: blank
	folio 34r: Chi Rho
quire 13	folio 114r: Arrest of Christ
	folio 114v: *Tunc dicit illis*
quire 14	folio 124r: *Tunc crucifixerant*
quire 15	folio 129v: Symbols of the four evangelists
	one leaf missing between folios 129 and 130 ?
Quires 16-21:	folios 130-87: Gospel of St Mark
quire 16	folio 130r: *Initium evangelii*
	one leaf missing between folios 177 and 178
quire 21	folio 183r: *Erat autem hora tertia*
	folio 187v: Symbols of the four evangelists (incomplete)
Quires 22-33:	folios 188-290: Gospel of St Luke
	Portrait and symbols page missing ?
quire 22	folio 188r: *Quoniam*
quire 23	folios 200r-202r: Genealogy of Christ
	folio 202v: Temptation
	folio 203: *Iesus autem plenus*
quire 27:	one leaf missing between folios 239 and 240
quire 32	folio 285r: *Una autem sabbati*
quire 33	folio 290r: Explicit Luke, incipit John
	folio 290v: Symbols of the four evangelists
Quires 34-38:	folios 291- 339: Gospel of St John
quire ?	folio 291r: blank
	folio 291v: Portrait of St John
quire 34	folio 292r: *In principio erat uerbum*
quire 37	three leaves missing between folios 330 and 331
quires:	about ten leaves missing after folio 339

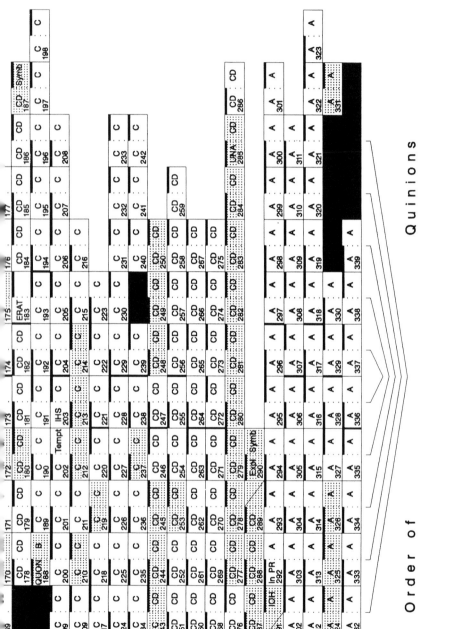

Fig 1 Description of collation diagram with contents of quires and major decorated pages

Book of Kells: Collation diagram

Legend:

empty page — Canon tables

Folio

leaf missing

single leaf

hair side / flesh side / fold

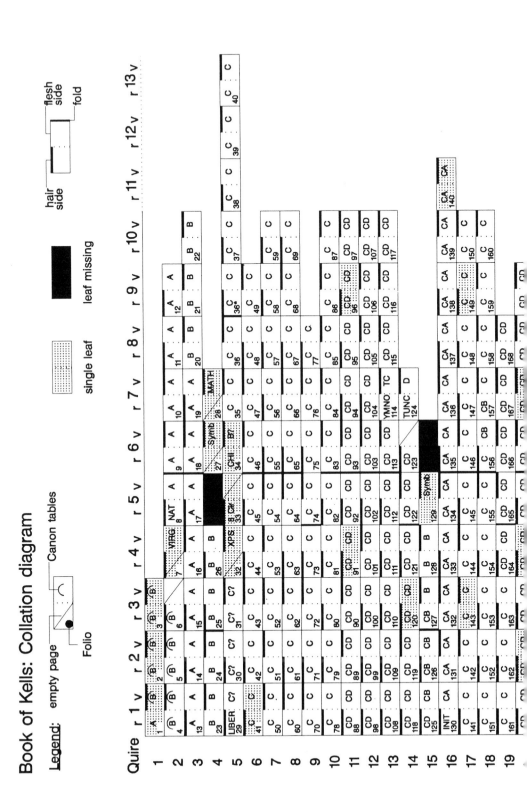

appears here and there but neither author views him as a main writer of text. In Henry's view scribe C wrote the bulk of the gospels. Meehan subdivides between scribes C and D for the synoptic gospels and, consequently, two letters dominate in quires 11-15, 19-21 and 28-33. Meehan's subdivision for the gospel of Luke is supported by Anton von Euw, who also divides between folios 189v-243v (quires 22-27) and folios 243v-289r (quires 28-33).[13] Meehan attributes the major part of quire 16 to scribe A, where Henry's option is not explicit.[14]

To illustrate the differences between the four main hands, some sample lines of each hand were selected and arranged side by side for easy comparison (pls 54a-b and 55a-b). The verso side of the *Natiuitas* page (pl 54a; folio 8v) beginning with the *Breves causae* to Matthew was written by Hand A which in Henry's words is 'the most massive and compact' of scripts.[15] She describes the hand as 'slightly archaic' compared with Hands B and C which seem more up to date.[16] The carefully written individual letters are even and well placed. The left bows of *a, c* and *e* are leaning towards the left. Due to short ascenders and descenders in relation to minim letters the lines of script run across the page like ornamental bands in the style of epigraphic inscriptions. They create comparatively wide interlinear spaces which make the letters seem a little stiff and static.

According to Henry and Meehan the *Breves causae* to Luke (pl 54b; folio 21r) were written by Hand B. The script has an elongated and somewhat angular appearance. In comparison to the 'sedate and careful' Hand A, Henry calls Hand B, aptly, an 'extrovert' script.[17] It seems much more lively and not quite as regular. The ascenders and descenders are tall compared to the width and the oversized open *e* resembles a letter that might be found in charters. Letters joining to form a word stand close together, spaces between words are clearly marked. I am not sure whether scribe B could not also be responsible for longer passages in different script in the second half of Luke's gospel.

The sample lines from the gospel of St Matthew (pl 55a; folio 85r) were written by scribe C, to whom Henry attributed the greater part of the Book of Kells.[18] The letter forms are even and elegant. They create the 'subtle rhythm' which has so often been admired in the Book of Kells. The ascenders and descenders of varying length contribute to the flow of script

---

[13] Anton von Euw, *Irland und das Book of Kells. Vorgeschichte, Rundgang und Kurzbeschreibung, Ausstellung in der Galerie* 'le point' *am Hauptsitz der Schweizerischen Kreditanstalt* (Zürich 1990) 22.

[14] Henry, 224.

[15] Henry, 154.

[16] Henry, 155, 220-21: he uses brown iron-gall ink and the lines of text are slightly longer than those of the other scribes.

[17] Meehan, 249-50: The scribe uses black carbon ink to write text and titles and is not consistent in the number of lines.

[18] Henry, 155: he uses brown iron-gall ink.

in long, even lines. Where word separation is intended it is marked by a space or medial dot. If words are joined to provide reading aids,[19] *t*-tongues along the head line or *a*-tails along the base line conduct the eye to the following word. The *t* -bars — meticulously straight and horizontal — touch the *e* in perfect balance just below the cupula (**pl 55a**; line 2: *sunt eum*), connect *i* and *e* (line 3: *saei temp*). The exit strokes of *&*-ligatures point exactly to minim height (line 5: *& homini*). The inside shapes of the letters match the outside form to perfection. This scribe's harmonious and beautiful calligraphy can only be admired and marvelled at.

The following sample lines, also taken from the gospel of St Matthew (**pl 55b**; folio 94r), are from the quire following that in **pl 55a**, written by Hand D (see **fig 1**). Meehan describes it as a large, confident, slightly more angular hand. The ascenders are longer, a more oval *o* is used and there is often a distinctive flick or serif at the beginning of *s*.[20] Hand D writes the tallest letters and the flow of script seems more often interrupted by an ascending *l* and *b* or a descending *p* and *q* reaching out far into the interlinear space. The individual forms are not quite as regular, the inner shapes often somewhat elongated. Connecting tongues between words are less frequent and word separation not as clearly marked. The rhythm of writing is not as pronounced nor as exact as with Hand C.

The impression of any script is influenced by the proportion of ascenders and descenders to minim height. The name of the holy city *Jerusalem* is used to exemplify the height and width and variety of form among the scribes (**pl 56**).[21] The first syllable may either be spelt with *y* or *i*. Both forms of *y* are practiced by all scribes and must have been part and parcel of the canon of letters. Whether an *a* or *o* before and an *i* or *e* after the *l* was preferred by a scribe, or transferred from an exemplar, is irrelevant in this context — the choice of form is the point. The eight samples by Hand D — three of which occur on the same page — demonstrate the writing rhythm of the scribe as each individual letter has the same width and shape. Scribe D seems to delight in writing the minuscule *l*: The pointed triangular head and the long and elegant slope recall the head of a bird and its long graceful neck (see **pls 55a-b** and **56**). It seems a little doubtful whether the *hyerusalem* on folio 282 was written by the same hand considering the rather nondescript *l*, the wide space between *a* and *l*, the narrow, longish form of *u*, and the round lower bend of the *y*. The nine letters in Hand A's much smaller script use roughly 1 cm less line space than the same nine letters written by Hand D.[22] The number of letters per page could be calculated and compared if the text were not broken by so many smaller or larger initials to mark a new Eusebian section. Checking and counting about two hundred lines did not really bring determinative

[19]Paul Saenger, 'The separation of words and the order of words: the genesis of medieval reading', *Scrittura e Civiltà* 14 (1990) 49-74.

[20]Meehan, 254: Hand D often seems to use a slightly darker ink.

[21]The samples were cut out of photocopied pages and mounted in columns.

[22]In original size 49 mm against 59 mm.

results. The many enlarged majuscule and (punctuation) spaces within the text, used to indicate the commencement of a new *kolon*,[23] and the spreading or cramming of words to finish a clause or a section at the end of a line, seemed to distort the calculation. A single text line without irregularities has between twenty-six and thirty-six letters, on average between thirty to thirty-three letters. This is somewhat surprising: in antiquity thirty to thirty-five letters to the line — corresponding to a *stiché*, the length of a hexameter verse — served as basis for scribal pay, and even during the thirteenth century when the *pecia* system developed and quires were distributed for copying, the rule was thirty-two letters to the line.[24]

To demonstrate the difference between the main hands, the width of *autem* was measured for tests on a small scale. The homogeneous group of five curved and four straight strokes of regular minim height occurs on almost every page. It was found that a scribe — if not hampered by lack of space — adhered to a regular rhythm. If well written the first three letters *a u t* form an entity which is difficult to read and separate.[25] Possibly this very common adverb may be illustrative of where a word was not deciphered letter by letter, but recognised visually by the shape of its word picture. Not measuring the *autems* at line ends the letters stretch between 26 to 37 mm, that is more than a centimetre difference for five letters. Generally speaking, Hand A needs around 26 to 30 mm line space, Hand C 29 to 31 mm and Hand D more than 30 mm. Fluctuations of 1 or 2 mm occur on the same page, but if there is a jump of 3 mm or more, it needs a closer look.

On the basis of this experiment minim letters *m*, ascenders *d* and descenders *p* were measured at intervals throughout the manuscript to determine the typical proportions for each hand. Scribe A averages 4:6:6 mm in height and 7:5:5 mm in width, that is, *m* measures about 4 mm, *d* and *p* 6 mm in height and about 7:5:5 mm in width. Ascenders and descenders of scribe A are about the same length. Scribe C writes a minim of approximately 5 mm, the ascenders and descenders are relatively shorter. Scribe D averages a minim height of 5-6 mm and writes with proportions of 6:9:10 mm for the tallest and 8:6:7 mm for the broadest letters. The interlinear space, which seems widest for scribe A with relatively small letters, contributes to the impression of a massive and compact script. Considering that D writes letters that measure about one and a half times the size of A onto the same seventeen lines, the interlinear space shrinks and the script gains in monumentality. To sum up: the script measuring

---

[23]Erika Eisenlohr, 'Kola und Kommata - Von Hieronymus zum Evangeliar Heinrichs des Löwen' in *Mabillons Spur*, ed Peter Rück (Marburg an der Lahn 1992) 105-32.

[24]Stephan Beissel, *Geschichte der Evangelienbücher in der ersten Hälfte des Mittelalters*, Ergänzungshefte zu 'Stimmen aus Maria Laach' 92/93 (Freiburg im Breisgau 1906) 12, 17-18. Richard Rouse and Mary Rouse, 'The Dissemination of texts in *pecia* at Bologna and Paris' in Rück (note 9 above).

[25]There is none on the sample pages, compare *autem* on folios 51v, 93v, 127v, 141v, etc.

4:6:6 occurs mainly on folios 8v-19v, 130v-46v, 292v-306v and some pages in quire 38. All sections were ascribed to Hand A with some uncertainties in St John's gospel. The proportions of 5:7/8:7/8 coincide with passages written by Hand C. The passages attributed to Hand D average proportions of 5/6: 8/9: 8/9. Henry noted the difference in the height of letters but hesitated to attribute them to a different hand — as Meehan did — because, in her opinion, the letters were treated in the same way.[26] The problem of hand identification lies in the transitional zones where one scribe takes over from another without apparent change in height, width and shape.

Left-hand bows add verticality to a script when the swelling runs parallel to the downward stroke of the pen, thereby causing the inner oval to stand upright. If the swelling is broadest in the lower half of the bow, the letter leans to the left. Thus the o -forms of Hand A and, to a lesser degree, of Hand C are inclined towards the left. The o -forms of Hands B and D appear vertical in comparison. The more roundish or oblong shapes of the o, d and p also offer an indication as to the width of a script (**pls 54a-b** to **58a-b**).

The many thousands of very similar letter forms make it difficult to spot variations and assess their significance. Several graphic details such as the length and decorative serifs of descenders q or g and the plain or boxed horizontal f -bars were registered. The varieties were defined by shape, each shape given a number code, fed into the computer and evaluated by sorting and grouping. The results, however, were disappointing and did not lead to the hoped-for identification of hands. Either the question was put the wrong way, or the definition of form had not been precise enough to yield results, or this particular feature was in common use in the scriptorium and could not be attributed to the peculiarity of a scribe. The plain f in *cafarnaum* (**pl 54a**, line 2) differs notably from the boxed f in *fieri* (**pl 54b**, line 13) or the f in *farissaei* (**pl 55a**, line 3) or in *aedificauit* (**pl 55b**, line 1) where the two letters *fi* are ligatured. The boxed and plain f appears in quires 6-10, 16-20, 26 until the end, but is found less in quires 11-15, 21-25, 34 and sections of 35.

Descending letters such as f, p, g and q show varying length of the perpendicular stem and form of foot. They may stand tiptoe or flat-footed, be naked, or decorated with shorter or longer triangular or forked serifs and embellished with additional dots. Hand C on folio 81v or Hand D on folio 282 write long descenders, Hand A on 309v a very short one. But these varieties occur in most passages and are difficult to tie to one hand. The use of serifs is not consistent. A more elaborate serif such as a flower spray is sometimes added to decorate the bottom lines of pages.[27] Descenders p and f remain bare.

---

[26]Henry, 155; Meehan, 254.
[27]So far I have not been able to detect a system as to when, where and why they were used.

The minuscule *r* with an elongated horizontal terminal in *saequatur* (**pl 54b**, line 9) contains a decorative element which is mainly used at the end of lines to reach the margin or — within the text block — to emphasize the last word of a Eusebian section. The letter occurs most often in quires 3, 5, 11-13, 20, 22-23, 29, 31 and 34, but is almost absent in quires 6-11, 14-21, 24-28, 32, 37-38. As all scribes use the form at least occasionally it must be included in the canon of letters, although B seems particularly fond of using it,[28] followed by D, whereas C uses the form sparingly. Again there are no clear boundaries but a puzzling overlapping of forms.

The height of two letters could be indicative for the hand who shaped them: long-*s* ligatured with *t* and elongated *e* bending down to join the horizontal bars of *t* and *g* (see **pls 57a-b**). The long *s* — already having moved up from the interlinear space and resting its foot on the base line — differs in thickness of stroke and height and length of the bow. Hand A writes a curve ending just short of the *t* -stem. He prefers the round *s* but uses its long counterpart on the first folios occasionally and more often in the gospel of John. The *s* -form of Hand B is characterised by its broad lower stem and thinnish upper stroke making the letter look unbalanced. Hand C writes a longish flat curve hovering over the main stroke of *t* in the same fashion as the elongated *e* aims to join the *g*. Similar to Hand A, Hand D writes a fairly high and thin stem but a shorter curve. The tall *e* with open or closed bow occurs most frequently when it descends on the *t* in the name of *Petrus* or in combination with *g* as in *regnum*. The straight or rounded back may grow to almost double minim height as with Hands B and C (**pl 54b**). The eye of the *e* is open or closed. Comparing the letter form with the long-*s*, it is interesting to note that scribe C actually joins the *e*-bow with the *g* stroke whereas the other scribes rest the bow on the horizontal bar. The origins of the elongated *e* could possibly go back to the later Roman cursive of the fifth and sixth centuries when a tall *e* formed a ligature with *g* or *t*.[29] When the letters were aligned, the use of the ancient ligature could only be continued, if the *e* was extended like an ascending letter.

It is common that a number of letters are expressed in several forms. The fairly rare *y* or *z* appear in two versions throughout the manuscript (see **pl 56**), although the half-uncial insular form is more common. The choice of letter forms becomes a puzzle in those cases, where the ligatured *st* is given preference on one page and the round-*s* and *t* on the next.[30] It seems doubtful that a scribe would go so far as to copy the shape of a letter from his exemplar. A change could be interpreted as the whim of the scribe, if

---

[28]Folios 20-26.

[29]Jan-Olof Tjäder, *Die nicht-literarischen lateinischen Papyri Italiens aus der Zeit 445-700*, Skrifter utgivna av Svenska Institutet i Rom, 4o XIX/ 1-3 (Stockholm 1955-82) I, 101-10.

[30]Relation of *st*-ligature to round-*s* *t*: folio 169v: 0 to 3; folio 170r: 5 to 5; folio 170v: 0 to 2; folio 171v: 3 to 0.

letter forms did not change so abruptly in some places.[31] Alerted to the alternating frequency of form for one letter, capital N and minuscule n, as well as uncial d and Carolingian d, were counted to prove the point. Some scribes seem to prefer the capital N to the minuscule n.[32] It does happen that the round uncial d is more frequently used than the straight Carolingian d in some pages and not in others, as counts on some forty random pages suggest.[33] The choice of certain letter forms — palaeographical 'time signals' such as the length of the descender r, round or straight d, long or round s — could be interpreted in twelfth-century charters from Aachen as conservatism or progressivity of a scribe or a scriptorium.[34] It would hardly be applicable to the Book of Kells, the greater part of which was probably written in one scriptorium within a few years. It could mean that more scribes, perhaps assistants, were at work to write gospel text between initials of Eusebian sections or that scribes and miniaturists took turns in some passages of the manuscript. In her recent studies on the division of work in a scriptorium Aliza Cohen maintains that a quire was the work unit for a scribe and the bifolium the unit for the miniaturist.[35] The division of labour might explain frequent changes. So far the working procedure for the Book of Kells has not been worked out or explained satisfactorily. As no obvious changes in script are apparent, it would also mean that the manuscript would have to be written in a scriptorium where a considerable number of expert scribes with the same training and proficiency were available. It is generally accepted that one aim of the Carolingian script reform was to reduce the variety of letter forms to one only for each letter. If so, the reform may not have greatly influenced the scribes of the Book of Kells. Choice of form, suprascript letters m and u and subscript i, all tend to indicate that they were perpetuating traditions of the later Roman cursive and still enjoyed the freedom of choosing what seemed to fit best. The aesthetic aspect and/or the facilities to provide reading aids would also play a part. As long as writing was a different task from reading, scribe and reciter/reader were dependent upon each other and could not be separated. Script may then be understood as the effort of the scribe to harmonize contrary

---

[31] Relation of st-ligature to round-s t: folio 179r: 1 to 4 ; folio 180r: 1 to 0; folio 180v: 6 to 2.

[32] Relation of capital N to minuscule n: folio 87r: 11 to14; folio 87v:11 to13 (end quire 10); (beginning quire 11) folio 88r: 22 to11: folio 88v: 27 to 11; folio 89r: 17 to 7, but folio 90r: 5 to 21.

[33] Relation of straightbacked d to uncial d: folio 87r: 12 to 6; folio 87v: 6 to 2 (end quire 10); (beginning quire 11) folio 88r: 9 to 9; folio 88v: 5 to 7; folio 89r: 13 to 14, but folio 90r: 15 to 5.

[34] Erika Eisenlohr, 'Paläographische Untersuchungen zum Tafelgüterverzeichnis des römischen Königs (Hs. Bonn UB S. 1559). Schreibgewohnheiten des Aachener Marienstifts in der zweiten Hälfte des 12. Jahrhunderts', Zeitschrift des Aachener Geschichtsvereins 92 (1985) 5-74 (pp 42-43).

[35] Aliza Cohen-Mushlin, The making of a manuscript: the Worms Bible of 1148 (British Library, Harley 2803-2804), Wolfenbütteler Forschungen 25 (Wiesbaden 1983) 147-55; idem, 'The division of labour in the production of a twelfth-century manuscript' in Rück (note 9 above). For matters relating to a school of scribes and working procedures see idem, A medieval scriptorium: Sancta Maria Magdalena de Frankendal, Wolfenbüttler Mittelalter-Studien 3 (Wiesbaden 1990) 53ff.

intentions: economize work and facilitate reading.[36] There are instances
when the consonant *d* is doubled as in frequent verb forms of *reddere*. The
letters are chosen in such manner that the first uncial *d* bends over the *e*,
perhaps to signal the end of the prefix, whereas the second,
straightbacked *d* is to introduce the conjugated ending, or the other way
round so that minuscule *d* is used for the prefix and uncial *d* for the ending
(see *d*-forms in **pls 54a-b** and **55a-b**).[37] The capital *N* with vertical strokes
gives more stability to the script and is easier to detect between rounded
forms. Could it be that the choice is not random but conveys a specific
meaning?[38]

Vertical and suprascript end-*m* at right margins constitutes one of the
features Julian Brown pointed out as running all the way through the
manuscript and led him to assume that there was only one scribe.[39] A
closer look, however, reveals a variety of forms which speak in favour of
several scribes (**pl 58a**). They range from three round bows (nos 2, 6) to
those where the last stroke is curled in (nos 1, 12), or drawn out (no 5),
pointed (nos 3, 7, 11), or bent to the right (no 10). Different again are those
which show one or two zigzags instead of a second curved stroke (nos 4, 8,
9). As a rule the end-*m* is joined at the top of the preceding vocal of the
female or male accusative. Samples of *m* pending from the lower end of *e*
are rare (no 12). The rounded forms occur mainly in quires 5-10, 22-29, the
pointed forms in quires 12-14, 20-21 and the zigzag forms in quires 30-33.
The forms with prolonged bows turned to the left or right appear in quires
34-38. In most parts of the manuscript the forms cannot be strictly
separated but overlap as in quires 16-19. In quires 1-4 vertical end-*m* is
rarely used. The question is how diversified the repertory of a scribe may
be and when a line between him and the next scribe is to be drawn.

A second graphic device for the accusative *m*-ending is the suprascript *s*
joined to the marginal side of the preceding letter (**pl 58b**). The difference
of form lies in the flat (nos 6-8) or half-raised position (nos 1, 9) and the
pointed or flattened tips of the upper bow as an indicator as to how the
pen was held (nos 1, 9). Suprascript *m* occurs throughout the manuscript but
more so in the sections attributed to scribe C. He makes liberal use of the
device and uses it in combination with all the vowels, whereas scribe D
uses it sparingly and almost exclusively in the combination of *u-m*.

A marginal letter which must have formed part of the canon of letter
forms, is the suprascript *u*. It resembles a minuscule *c* with a drawn out
terminal stroke. The form goes back to the later Roman cursive where the *u*
form could be written above the line 'in a large size and often with a

---

[36]Jean Irigoin, 'De l'alpha à l'omega. Quelques remarques sur l'évolution de l'écriture
grecque', *Scrittura e Civiltà* 10 (1986) 1-19.
[37]See folio 10v, line 6: *reddere*.
[38]The idea of looking at the 'graphic neighbourhood' of single letters I owe to
Professor Peter Rück and discussions in our Seminar. I started work along these lines
recently and cannot present any results yet.
[39]Brown, 231.

wave-like appearance', or in a small size high up on the line, or as a large *u* turned 'to the right and connected with the following letter by a stroke running downwards'.[40] The suprascript *u* is found in all parts of the manuscript, but seems to be fairly regularly used by Hand C. Apart from suprascript *m* and *u* belonging to the canon of letter forms, word endings or even words are written above and below the line on many of the pages of the gospels, but seldom on the preliminary text pages. They are often encased by an ornament or animal shape and Henry suggests that they may have been used as excuses for embellishment.[41] Subscript *i* is also a relic of the later Roman cursive scripts. The graphically insignificant letter *i* carries no mark of distinction and has to be employed in certain stroke combinations so as not to be overlooked. To differentiate between the two letters of short *i* and long *l* the scribes of later Roman cursives let the short *i* descend into the interlinear space. The letter could be ligatured with the letter from the left, but could never be continued on the right. The subscript form with the stem pending free into interlinear space is still present in the Book of Kells, although far more minuscule *i*s are positioned between minuscule letters on the base line.

Palaeographers consider the form of the *e caudata* one feature contributing to the identification of a scribe, because the almost insignificant flick of the pen below the base line hardly influences the impression of the script as a whole. Triangular and drop-like shapes of varying length are in use (pl 54a).[42] Rounded forms occur most frequently, though not exclusively, in quires 5-9 and 34-38, and pointed forms in quires 10-14 and 28-32. In the gospels of Mark and first half of Luke a curious mixture of forms prevails. Only one scribe seems to specialize in the rare ligatured *ae*.

The *nomina sacra* are contracted with single or double horizontal bars above the letters. On some pages the double bars are filled with tiny dot or stroke patterns, sometimes drawn in red. It seems hardly possible to assign a particular form to one scribe because some original single bars seem to have been doubled or decorated at a later stage by a corrector or miniaturist using a red pen. Abbreviations are sometimes used for the end syllables *-bus* and *-que*. They vary in form from two squarish dots to two or three round dots. Occasionally commata are used which joined together resemble the arabic numeral 3. This abbreviation sign seems to be connected with Hand B occuring on pages assigned to him, but it is also found sporadically on odd pages throughout the book. The one abbreviation used by all scribes is *autem* written in insular fashion. Thin diagonal strokes or apices[43] over certain words seem to appear in clusters on some pages, are absent in others, and return at irregular intervals without apparent reason. They may be written as double lines, one line

---

[40]Jan-Olof Tjäder, 'Some ancient letter-forms in the later Roman cursive and early mediaeval script and the script of the *notarii' Scrittura e Civiltà* 6 (1982) 5-21 (pp 8-9, 13-15, cited pp 14-15 with fig 7). The 'large *u*' is not used by the Book of Kells scribes.
[41]Henry, 155.
[42]Only the pointed form is represented on the sample sheets.
[43]Saenger (note 19 above) 49-74.

with a dot, or one line only. They are difficult to tie to different hands, because they could — at least in some instances — have also been added later. The apices have the function to stress personal pronouns like *sé*, *té* and *eís* and supply reading aids for single syllables such as *ádeo* or *ámen*. They also indicate the length of *i* or double *ii* vowels as in *discipulis suis*, the most frequently accentuated phrase. The idea of lengthening *i*-vowels leaps to mind in those cases where only one *i* is actually written and the second replaced by a diagonal stroke as in *hiis* or *variis*.

One intriguing feature in the Book of Kells is the joining and separation of words and groups of words and the punctuation of clauses or parts of speech.[44] Words belonging to a phrase or unit of thought (*sensus*) are linked by extending horizontal *t*-strokes, *e*-tongues or *et*-ligatures, by using marks of punctuation such as single points at medium height or three points arranged in triangular form, by enlarging minuscule or majuscule letters, or by means of blobs of colour or red dots or a combination of several features. The idea is to draw attention and give aid to the reader. Not considering the preliminary text each Eusebian section begins with an initial and ends with a space; in the majority of cases spaces are filled with a sign of punctuation, an ornament or just leaving a blank space. Hand A is the most meticulous and, as a rule, uses the three dot triangle to mark the end of a Eusebian section. It would be open for discussion if rules for the layout of the gospel texts were given; if so, Hands C and D do not seem to follow them in all aspects.

To conclude: based on the hypothesis of one against several scribes and the present state of work, palaeographical evidence speaks in favour of several hands. I agree with Bernard Meehan that four main scribes wrote most of the Book of Kells. They may have been helped by assistants who wrote certain passages or even lines in some Eusebian sections, or scribes and miniaturists may have taken turns. The problem of hand identification lies in the joint achievement of a harmony of scripts which negates individuality. Although this report discusses some palaeographical details — proportions of ascenders and descenders to minim height, scribal rhythm and width of writing, variation and distribution of letter forms, suprascript and subscript letters as relics of an ancient heritage, abbreviations and apices — the puzzle of the scribes remains unsolved. Work has to continue before a synthesis may be proposed. Although initials were not considered, changes in script sometimes seem to go with an obvious change of initials and it was easier if the initials so closely linked with the script were analysed and a working procedure established. The 'inseparable unity' between artist and scribe, which is the precondition for perfect planning and execution of most pages,[45] is also its greatest hindrance for analysis.

---

[44]M B Parkes, *Pause and effect: an introduction to the history of punctuation in the West* (Aldershot 1992), does not refer to the Book of Kells specifically; for the effect of punctuation in the Gospels of Henry the Lion (twelfth century) see Eisenlohr (note 23 above) 128-30 and figs 1-2, 4-6.
[45]Von Euw (note 13 above) 15.

The display script of the Book of Kells and the tradition of insular decorative capitals

John Higgitt

The display script of the Book of Kells shows the same inventive variety as do the decoration and the script of the text. Within the variety it is nevertheless possible to see some consistency, if not uniformity. The display script with which this paper is concerned appears in the one or more bands following the major initials that mark the openings of the four gospels, of the *Breves causae* and *Argumenta* that precede them and of seven selected passages within the gospels of Matthew, Mark and Luke (three of which relate to the Passion, two to the Resurrection and one to the Temptation of Christ and one of which marks the second opening of Luke).[1] The purposes of this paper are to examine the use of this display script and to analyse the style and letter forms of the 'insular decorative capitals' that are used for most of the display script in Kells.[2] The aim of this analysis is to show how the Kells capitals relate to those in other insular manuscripts and in insular inscriptions.

The display script serves as a transition between the decorative exuberance of the initials and the clarity and comparative sobriety of the text. Although some of the lettering is relatively plain and legible, most of the openings present the reader with some difficulty — and in one case (on folio 114v), which is by no means the most obscure, the words have been repeated below in red in half-uncial text script, perhaps as an aid to the reader. The convoluted treatment of much of the lettering of course links the display script visually with the surrounding decoration but it is tempting to think that it was deliberately designed in some cases as a kind of puzzle that demanded some effort of the reader. Although most of the patterning of the display script seems to have been simply decorative or riddling in intention, the arrangement of four short sections of lettering to form a chi in the middle of the Crucifixion narrative in Matthew (**pl 29**) is surely more than a coincidence and, as Suzanne Lewis suggests, the design was presumably used because of its associations with the Cross and with the name of Christ.[3]

---

[1] Gospel openings (folios 29r, 130r, 188r, 292r); *Breves causae* (except for John) and *Argumenta* (folios 8r, 12r, 13r, 15v, 16v, 18r, 19v); gospel passages (folios 114v, 124r, 127v, 183r, 188v, 203r, 285r). For the tradition of emphasizing certain gospel passages see McGurk, *Gospel books*, 117-19. The one or two display capitals that follow some of the minor text initials, for example on folios 48v and 74v, are omitted from this discussion.

[2] For 'insular decorative capitals' see fig 2 and Appendix below.

[3] Suzanne Lewis, 'Sacred calligraphy: the Chi Rho page in the Book of Kells', *Traditio* 36 (1980) 139-59 (p 144); O K Werckmeister, *Irisch-northumbrische Buchmalerei des 8. Jahrhunderts und monastiche Spiritualität* (Berlin 1967) 152; Jennifer O'Reilly, 'The Book of Kells, folio 114r: a mystery revealed yet concealed' in *The age of migrating ideas:*

Whilst it is perfectly possible that the symbolic arrangement was invented by the designer of the page, the idea was perhaps suggested, directly or indirectly, by the square picture-poems incorporating verses in the shape of the Chi Rho monogram, a sort of sacred crossword puzzle, by the fourth-century Publilius Optatianus Porfyrius, whose works were known to Bede and, as Carl Nordenfalk has argued, probably lie behind the design of some pages of the Stockholm *Codex Aureus* (Royal Library, MS A. 135).[4]

In spite of the great variety in treatment and detail the Kells display script consists of two principal types: (i) freer curvilinear lettering that is coloured and usually zoomorphic in form; and (ii) the more rigid, calligraphic, and frequently angular, capitals which are usually executed in dark ink, although a few are coloured. The two types can be used hierarchically, as at the opening of the *Breves causae* of Matthew, with the coloured curvilinear lettering being the higher grade, a distinction that already appears after the initial to Matthew in the Lindisfarne Gospels.[5] As might be expected, this hierarchy is not strictly followed in Kells.

The second, more calligraphic type of display script in the Book of Kells belongs to the tradition of insular decorative capitals, an inventive, sometimes fantastic, and far from uniform script, used both as a manuscript display script and in some inscriptions, but the Kells capitals include a higher proportion of angular and rectangular forms than the early stage represented by the Lindisfarne Gospels. Julian Brown's description of the Lindisfarne decorative capitals as being made up of 'a mixture of enlarged text letters [that is insular half-uncial forms] and text letters made rectangular, with a few forms apparently derived from Roman capitals' would apply equally well to the Book of Kells (see **fig 2** and Appendix) and indeed to insular decorative capitals in general.[6] This repertoire which mixes forms based on half-uncial letters of Irish origin with others based on Roman and Roman-derived capitals is found in many Northumbrian manuscripts and inscriptions and is as genuinely 'Hiberno-Saxon' as the

---

early medieval art in northern Britain and Ireland, ed R M Spearman, J Higgitt (Edinburgh and Stroud 1993) 106-14 (pp 108-09).
[4] *Publilii Optatiani Porfyrii Carmina*, ed I Polara (Torino 1973) 32-36, 57-60, 72-75, 93-96; Carl Nordenfalk, *Die spätantiken Zierbuchstaben* (Stockholm 1970) 57-61 and pl 12; Otto Homburger, *Die illustrierten Handschriften der Burgerbibliothek Bern* (Bern 1962) 162-63 (Cod 212), pl 147; Bede, 'De Arte Metrica et de Schematibus et Tropis' in *Bedae Venerabilis Opera*, Pars VI, *Opera Didascalica*, 1, CCSL 123A, ed C W Jones (Turnhout 1975) 138.
[5] Alexander, *Insular manuscripts*, pl 39 (folio 27r).
[6] T J Brown in *Evangeliorum quattuor codex Lindisfarnensis*, ed TD Kendrick et al, 2 vols (Olten and Lausanne 1956) II, 93. See also pp 75-77, 93-94, 99 for Brown's fundamental analysis and discussion of the decorative capitals in the Lindisfarne Gospels. For insular decorative capitals in inscriptions see J Higgitt, 'The Pictish Latin inscription at Tarbat in Ross-shire', *Proceedings of the Society of Antiquaries of Scotland* 112 (1982) 300-21 (pp 314-15); and idem, 'The stone-cutter and the scriptorium' in *Epigraphik 1988: Fachtagung für mittelalterliche und neuzeitliche Epigraphik, Graz, 10-14 Mai 1988*, ed W Koch, Österreichische Akademie der Wissenschaften Philosophisch-historische Klasse Denkschriften 213 (Wien 1990) 149-62 (pp 155-7).

mingling of Celtic and Anglo-Saxon patterns in the decoration of manuscripts such as Lindisfarne and Kells.

The character of the insular decorative capitals in the Book of Kells is strongly affected by the way that they are set on the page. On initial pages they appear in bands and are strictly governed by a head-line and a foot-line. These bands are further unified by the repeated verticals and by the infilling of the background with decoration or areas of colour. Most of the bands are contained within some sort of frame. The letters are normally set off from their backgrounds by very fine framing strips of apparently bare vellum.

A comparison of the beginning of the *Breves causae* of Matthew in Kells with the opening to John in the Lindisfarne Gospels brings out the kinship as well as some differences in treatment (**pls 10 and 72**). In both books the letters are tall and laterally compressed, although the angularity and grid-like treatment is more marked in the slightly heavier letters in Kells. Again in both the lines of lettering obey ruled head and foot-lines. In Lindisfarne the letters float with some freedom between lines of red dots; in Kells letters are held rigidly in place by the frames. Tops and bottoms of verticals are strictly horizontal and are finished flush with the frames in Kells in contrast to the slightly concave and lightly sloping terminations seen in Lindisfarne. Both use wedge serifs especially to tops of verticals (projecting to the left) and to horizontals and finish off the feet of verticals with a rather more gradual flaring out. Throughout Lindisfarne and on two folios of Kells (folios 8r and 15v) the thin strips of bare vellum that separate letters from areas of colour (in Lindisfarne inside the letters only) swell out into trumpets at half height (**pls 10 and 72**). Display capitals with 'trumpet linings' of this sort are found in only four insular manuscripts (the Lindisfarne and Lichfield Gospels and the Books of Kells and Armagh (**pls 14 and 74**)); Lichfield and Kells are the only two in which these linings appear both inside and outside the letters.[7] Small triangles of uninked vellum are left in the horizontals of *T* in line 3 of the Lindisfarne John opening and *D* in line 3 of the *Breves causae* to Matthew in Kells (**pls 10 and 72**).[8] In Kells pattern governs more of the decisions. On this folio the lines alternate large and small, rather than starting large and then reducing in size, and the placing of the three smaller letters in line 5 is dictated by symmetry and the desire to provide a visual link with lines of smaller lettering above and below rather than by a need to save space.

The display capitals in Kells are embellished in a number of other ways. As is normal with insular decorative capitals, most letters appear in a variety of forms. The lettering is so fluid and inventive that it is not always easy to decide when minor variations should be classified as separate letter forms.

---

[7] Wendy Stein, *The Lichfield Gospels* (D Phil thesis, University of California, Berkeley 1980) 56; Alexander, *Insular manuscripts*, pl 76 (Lichfield, p 5).
[8] Similar triangles appear in the display script on folio 15v of Kells and comparable uninked disks on folio 114v.

This is illustrated by the double-barred *M* (Appendix **M2** and **M3**; **fig 2**), which appears with straight bars, with lentoid bars (eg folio 8r, line 2; **pl 10**), with delicate box-like features set into the angles (eg folio 8r, line 2; **pl 10**) and with curved bars with angle boxes (folio 124r; **pl 29**). These angle boxes seem to be unique to the decorative capitals of the Book of Kells; they probably derive from the work of one or more of the text scribes who sometimes used similar boxes on the letters *F* (eg folios 9v, 43r, 44r, 282v) and *N* (eg folios 111v, 174v).[9] The stem of the *M* on line 3 of folio 8r is split, a trick that can already be seen in initials to the *Cathach* of St Columba (Dublin, RIA, MS 12 R 33).[10] Other decorative embellishments include: serifed loops to the tops of the verticals of some of the half-uncial *Bs* and *Hs* (eg folios 8r and 13r; Appendix **B2** and **H2** and **fig 2**); lentoid treatment of bars in *M* and *N* (eg folio 8r; **pl 10**); variations in the form of the central bar of *E* and *F* (folio 124r; **pl 29**); and strokes with rectangular indentations (eg V on folio 124r; **pl 29**).

Some enrichments are applied to groups of letters rather than to individual letters. Letters are made to overlap on folios 12r, 183r and 203r and in addition on folio 12r they are subjected to a series of angular breaks, while on folio 183r letter strokes are drawn out into a series of interlacing patterns.

Most of the bands of display capitals in Kells are broadly similar to those on folio 8r (**pl 10**), although the effect varies with height and spacing from the small, tight-packed sections of lettering on the *In principio* page (folio 292r; **pl 52**) to the tall and slender grid on folio 114v. Most could be the work of a single scribe or artist. The display script of the *Argumentum* of Matthew (folio 12r) in which the angular letters overlap and interlock in a dense overall pattern is probably better explained as a device for emphasizing the first gospel rather than indicating the work of a new scribe. The interlacing display script on folio 183r is so similar to a number of the minor initials in Luke (eg folios 244v-246v, 261v, 263v-265v) that they could be the work of the same hand. A clearer case of a distinct hand can be seen in the looser design and overlapping letters on folio 203r which lack the tautness of most of the display script. The rather dumpy coloured letters at the opening of Matthew's gospel (folio 29r), which Peter Meyer saw as similar in character to those in the St Gall Gospels, also seem less sharp than most of the capitals.[11]

Whilst the scribes of the display script were not particularly concerned with textual accuracy, the two or three garblings and slips are no worse than those in the text.[12] The obscure letters at the bottom of the *In principio* page

---

[9]Examples of both letters can be seen on line 9 of folio 77r (Henry, pl 37).
[10]See for example Alexander, *Insular manuscripts*, pls 5, 9.
[11]Johannes Duft and Peter Meyer, *The Irish miniatures in the Abbey Library of St Gall* (Olten, Bern and Lausanne 1954) 130-31. For illustrations of the display script on folios 12r, 29r, 183r and 203r of Kells see Henry, pls 12, 23, 55 and 69.
[12]The garbled texts are on folio 124r (TUNC CRUCIFIXERANT XRI CUM EO DUO LATRONES for Matthew 27:38), on folio 203r (IHS AUTEM PLENUS SPS SCO for Luke 4:1) and on folio 292r (which is discussed below).

(folio 292r; **pl 52**) are probably the result of the scribe or artist failing to follow the stylus sketch of the lettering accurately. (Such stylus sketches have been noticed by Julian Brown under some of the rubrics in the Lindisfarne Gospels).[13] The last three words should have read *verbum et verbum* and the present *UERBU*, followed by a third rectangular *U/V* and a vertical with a short horizontal stroke to the top left and then a monogram of *UER* followed by another two rectangular *Us*, can be explained by supposing that the verticals were all correctly followed from the sketch but that some of the horizontal linking strokes were missed or wrongly placed. The diagram (**fig 1**) shows what was perhaps intended: *UERBUM* with *U* and *M* in ligature followed by the Tironian sign for *et*, and then *UERBU* with a mark of contraction above the *U*.[14]

Fig 1 Last line of display script on folio 292r (diagrams):
(a) as executed
(b) as perhaps intended (suggested reconstruction of stylus sketch)

In spite of some differences of treatment and the probable involvement of more than one hand the underlying forms of the insular decorative capitals in the Book of Kells are consistent enough to allow comparison with other insular manuscripts. An analysis of the letter forms used in the Kells decorative capitals (see Appendix and **fig 2**) shows a close kinship with those of the Lindisfarne Gospels, which include around twenty-four of these forms, a higher proportion than any other manuscript. One or two other of the Kells capitals could be accounted for as derivatives of the Lindisfarne capitals. Three other insular manuscripts which also contain early examples of insular decorative capitals, the Corpus Christi College Gospels with its largely incinerated other half, Cotton Otho C.V, Durham, Cathedral Library, MS A.II.17 and the Echternach Gospels match roughly eighteen, thirteen

---

[13]Brown in Kendrick et al (note 6 above) 75 and pl 1e.
[14]For the Tironian sign for *et* see below (pp 215 and 233) and fig 2.

and thirteen forms respectively. The Kells *P* with a lower loop illustrates these relationships clearly (see Appendix and **fig 2**). It first appears in display script in the Book of Durrow, which is not yet in fully developed insular decorative capitals, and is otherwise only found in the Lindisfarne Gospels, Durham A.II.17, Cotton Otho C.V and the Freiburg-im-Breisgau Gospels. From the evidence of surviving manuscripts it is clear that many of the decorative capitals that appear in Kells were being used in manuscripts in Lindisfarne and perhaps elsewhere in Northumbria and in Echternach around the year 700. The Kells alphabet, however, includes more angular and fewer rounded forms than the lettering in these manuscripts of the Lindisfarne generation.

The use of an angular form of the Greek letter omega for O on the initial page to Luke (folio 188r) also shows Kells following in the footsteps of Durrow, Lindisfarne, Echternach, Durham A.II.17 and the Corpus Christi Gospels, which all make occasional use of Greek letters in display script, as do some later manuscripts such as the Mac Regol Gospels.[15]

It is time now to turn to some of the Kells letter forms that do not appear in the Lindisfarne Gospels (see Appendix and **fig 2** for details).[16] The strange *O* (**O2**) that looks like a Roman capital *D* is peculiar to Kells. The *G* is an angular version of the half-uncial letter and is again apparently unique, but there are comparable angular forms in the Lindisfarne, Lichfield and Mac Regol Gospels and the Garland of Howth. The *M* (**M2** and **M3**) that consists of three verticals and two horizontals is a development from the form with a single horizontal that first appears in insular display script in the Lindisfarne and Corpus Gospels. I have only found the Kells two-horizontal form in three other manuscripts (the Lichfield Gospels, St Gall 51 and the Mac Regol Gospels) and on the Ardagh chalice. There is also a variant in the Garland of Howth. The form of *N* (**N2**) that looks like a capital *H* may again be a somewhat later form that was developed to fit in with a taste for rectilinear and right-angled forms. The only other examples that I have found are in three manuscripts of the later eighth or early ninth centuries (St Gall 1395, the Mac Regol Gospels and a gospel book in Paris (BN, nouv. acq. lat. 1587) that may have been written in Brittany). Similar parallels can be provided for the two rectilinear and right-angled forms of *S*. The version with horizontals at the ends of the vertical (**S3**) is used in St Gall 1395 and the version with horizontals that branch off short of the ends of the vertical (**S4**) appears in the Freiburg, Lichfield, Rawlinson and Mac Regol Gospels

---

[15]E Sullivan, *The Book of Kells* (London 1920) 19-20; Alexander, *Insular manuscripts*, pls 19, 39, 49, 70, 148 and 269. See also J Higgitt in J Lang, *York and Eastern Yorkshire*, Corpus of Anglo-Saxon stone sculpture (Oxford 1991) III, 44-45, 65.

[16]For illustrations and discussions of the parallels discussed below see Alexander, *Insular manuscripts*, nos 9 (Lindisfarne), 12 (Corpus Christi), 21 (Lichfield), 25 (Freiburg), 43 (Rawlinson), 44 (St Gall 51), 54 (Mac Regol), 56 (Paris, BN, nouv. acq. lat. 1587), 57 (St Gall 1395), 59 (Howth); Earl of Dunraven, 'On an ancient chalice and brooches lately found at Ardagh, in the County of Limerick', *Transactions of the Royal Irish Academy* 24 (1874) 433-54; E Okasha, 'A new inscription from Ramsey Island', *Archaeologia Cambrensis* 119 (1970) 68-70; E Okasha, *Hand-list of Anglo-Saxon non-runic inscriptions* (Cambridge 1971) pl 23.

and the perhaps Breton gospel book in Paris, as well as on inscriptions on Ramsey Island, in Carlisle and (in reverse) on the Ardagh chalice.

The oddly runic-looking capital used for N on folio 8r in Kells (N4; pl 10) also appears in the Lichfield Gospels but there it is used for M. The normal transliteration of the Anglo-Saxon rune of this form is d, but it is also similar to runic m. Two or three of the capitals in the Lichfield Gospels resemble runes. Wendy Stein sees these as evidence for 'a visual although illiterate acquaintance with runic forms' and they are accepted by Ray Page as borrowings of 'individual runic graphs, sometimes correctly used, sometimes not'.[17] The Kells N could, of course, simply have been an independent geometric variation on the capital form rather than a runic borrowing. Another, perhaps coincidental, correspondence with runic forms can be seen in Kells U/V4 (see Appendix). Whether or not the Kells scribes borrowed specific runic forms, familiarity with runes no doubt contributed in a more general way to the taste for rectilinearity and angularity in insular decorative capitals.

The parallels for the rectilinear and right-angled forms discussed in the last two paragraphs are to be found in manuscripts of later phases than the Lindisfarne Gospels. Most of these manuscripts incidentally set their capitals within the same kind of rigid framed bands as Kells.[18] Apart from Lichfield, whose origins are uncertain, these manuscripts were probably written either in Ireland or on the Continent.[19] The Mac Regol Gospels show that these rectilinear forms were in use in Ireland, probably in the monastery of Birr, early in the ninth century but the display script in this book is ponderous, unimaginative and unremittingly rectilinear and looks like a later reflexion of the Kells phase.[20] The display capitals following the initial to the Apocalypse in the Book of Armagh, which was written by Ferdomnach at Armagh in about 807, demonstrate that a rectilinear type of insular decorative capitals was in use in at least one other scriptorium in early ninth-century Ireland (pl 74).[21]

If I am right that the Tironian sign for et was intended in the garbled passage of display script at the foot of the initial page to St John's Gospel in Kells on folio 292r (see above p 213), the sign would have been a borrowing from the stock of abbreviations used most commonly in manuscripts written in insular minuscule. Several of the insular gospel books in half-

---

[17]Alexander, *Insular manuscripts*, pls 50 and 78 (Lichfield, pp 143 and 221); Stein (note 7 above) 58-59; R I Page, 'Roman and runic on St Cuthbert's Coffin' in *St Cuthbert, his cult and his community to AD 1200*, ed G Bonner, D Rollason and C Stancliffe (Woodbridge 1989) 257-65 (p 258).

[18]See for example Alexander, *Insular manuscripts*, pls 50, 76, 78 (Lichfield), 196 (Rawlinson), 261 (St Gall 1395), 266-69 (Mac Regol), 270-72 (Paris), 274-75 (Howth). St Gall 51 sets its capitals equally rigidly but between ruled lines rather than within framing strips (Alexander, pl 201).

[19]Alexander, *Insular manuscripts*, references cited in note 16 above.

[20]Alexander, *Insular manuscripts*, pls 266-69.

[21]Reproductions in John Gwynn, *Liber Ardmachensis: the Book of Armagh* (Dublin 1913) 315; and E H Zimmermann, *Vorkarolingische Miniaturen* (Berlin 1916) pl 207b.

uncial make use of some of these symbols; the scribes of Kells used four of them (those for *autem, enim, est* and *quae*) in the text and the symbol for *autem* appears among the display capitals on folio 127v. The Tironian *et*, however, seems not to have been taken up in half-uncial liturgical manuscripts in the same way, although it was used amongst the half-uncials of the Corpus Glossary as well as in Irish gospel books in minuscule.[22] The form fits with the repeated verticals of the rectilinear style of decorative capital but the probable Tironian *et* in Kells seems to be the only example amongst surviving insular decorative capitals.

The formation of the insular decorative capital display script in manuscripts like the Lindisfarne Gospels probably owed something to epigraphic lettering, as Julian Brown suggested,[23] and in some centres decorative capitals came themselves to be used in inscriptions on metal and on stone. They were used on metal objects found in central Ireland, southern Northumbria, Lindsey and East Anglia (the Ardagh chalice, the York helmet, a lead tablet from Flixborough in South Humberside and the Brandon plaque), although there is no certainty that they were made at or near where they were found.[24] The inscription on the chalice resembles the Kells capitals in style, for example in the taste for rectilinear and right-angled forms. The chalice and the manuscript also share some thirteen individual letter forms (see Appendix).

Inscriptions on stone give more definite information on the distribution of insular decorative capitals. Outside Northumbria their use on stone seems to have been very exceptional.[25] In Ireland there are two examples at Toureen Peakaun and an obscure inscription from Nendrum which may show knowledge of decorative capitals.[26] They are absent from Wales with the exception of one offshore example on Ramsey Island.[27] The small corpus of inscriptions in Latin lettering from Pictland includes two in decorative

---

[22]W M Lindsay, *Notae latinae; an account of abbreviation in Latin manuscripts of the early minuscule period (c 700-850)* (Cambridge 1915) 74-77. For insular abbreviations in half-uncial manuscripts see *CLA* (1972) II, for example nos 125, 138, 148b, 149, 159, 187, 214, 231, 256, 269, 272, 274 (= Kells). For Tironian *et* see for example *CLA* (1972) II, nos 122 (Corpus Glossary), 133, 235, 241, 267, 270, 275-7.

[23]Brown in Kendrick et al (note 16 above) 75.

[24]Dunraven (note 16 above); L S Gogan, *The Ardagh Chalice* (Dublin 1971) 47-50; E Okasha, 'The inscriptions: transliteration, translation and epigraphy' in *The Anglian helmet from 16-22 Coppergate*, ed D Tweddle, The archaeology of York: the small finds 17/8 (York 1992) 1012-15 and illustrations; *The making of England: Anglo-Saxon art and culture AD 600-900*, ed L Webster and J Backhouse (London 1991) 82-83, 94-95; E Okasha, 'A second supplement to *Hand-List of Anglo-Saxon non-runic inscriptions*', *Anglo-Saxon England* 21 (1992) 46-47, 58-60.

[25]For discussions of decorative capitals in insular inscriptions see Higgitt (note 6 above).

[26]Harbison, I, 174, 364-65, III, fig 1021; M Moloney, 'Beccan's Hermitage in Aherlow: the riddle of the slabs', *North Munster Antiquaries Journal* 9 (1964) 99-107 (figs 1 and 2); Government of Northern Ireland, Ministry of Finance, *An archaeological survey of county Down*, Archaeological Survey of Northern Ireland (Belfast 1966) 102, 292, pl 81.

[27]E Okasha, 'A new inscription from Ramsey Island', *Archaeologia Cambrensis* 119 (1970) 68-70.

capitals (at Tarbat and Lethnot).[28] Insular decorative capitals also appear in at least one inscription in Brittany (from Lanrivoaré and now in the museum at Landevennec).[29] In England, outside Northumbria, there is only the lost inscription from Caistor in Lincolnshire, which incidentally is only some twenty miles from Flixborough, where decorative capitals have been found on a lead tablet (see above). In Northumbria there are inscriptions that can be classed as being in insular decorative capitals at Carlisle, Hartlepool, Jarrow, Lindisfarne, Ruthwell, Thornhill, Wensley, Whitby and York. Some of those at Lindisfarne are particularly reminiscent of manuscript display script, one representing an extreme and elongated form of the rectilinear fashion.[30]

It is interesting that none of the early medieval inscriptions on Iona — or for that matter at Kells — is in insular decorative capitals but, given the scale of losses, that is not a fatal objection to either hypothesis for the origin of the book.[31] Nor is it necessary to assume for the centre that produced the Book of Kells the same kind of close contacts between the designers of manuscript display script and epigraphic lettering as can be inferred for Lindisfarne.

None of the insular inscriptions is similar enough to help in locating the precise origin of the Kells decorative capitals and none is closely datable but their distribution shows Northumbria as the region with by far the largest number of inscriptions in insular decorative capitals. The examples in Ireland, Pictland, Ramsey Island, Lindsey and Brittany look like outliers. Taken on its own the distribution of the inscriptions would point to a Northumbrian origin for insular decorative capitals. The presence amongst them of Roman capital forms and the possible influence of runic angularity are also more easily explained in Northumbria than elsewhere. The evidence from the manuscripts suggests that the Kells capitals are descended from the sort seen in the Northumbrian Lindisfarne Gospels and the inscriptions fill in the predominantly Northumbrian background against which they can be seen. The Kells capitals look as if they belong to an early and creative phase in the geometricization of insular decorative capitals. The capitals in Irish manuscripts such as the early ninth-century Mac Regol Gospels and Book of Armagh on the other hand could be derivatives of those in Kells.[32] The decorative capitals of the Book of Kells seem then to

[28]Higgitt (note 6 above, 1982); E Okasha, 'The non-Ogam inscriptions of Pictland', *Cambridge Medieval Celtic Studies* 9 (1985) 43-69.

[29]P-R Giot, 'Glanes protohistoriques, II, Quelques stèles gauloises gravées ou inscrites', *Annales de Bretagnes* 59 (1952) 213-20 (pl I.2, pp 218-20); G Bernier, *Les chrétientés bretonnes continentales depuis les origines jusqu'au IXème siècle*, Équipe de Recherche N° 27 du CNRS, Université de Rennes (Rennes 1982) 166, 170, 184 (a reference that I owe to Dr Elisabeth Okasha).

[30]For illustrations of some of the clearer examples from England see E Okasha (note 16 above, 1971) pls 18, 22-24, 44-47, 49, 62, 75-78, 80 (rectilinear style), 83, 105, 120-21, 133-34, 151. On Lindisfarne see also Higgitt (note 6 above, 1990) 149-50, 156-57.

[31]Royal Commission on the Ancient and Historical Monuments of Scotland, *Argyll: an inventory of the monuments*, vol 4, *Iona* (Edinburgh 1982) 181-82, 184-87, 189; Harbison, I, 361-62, II, figs 345, 347, III, fig 1019; R A S Macalister, *Corpus Inscriptionum Insularum Celticarum*, 2 vols (Dublin 1945-9) II, 33-34, pl XLIII.

[32]See notes 20 and 21 above.

belong typologically between the early Northumbrian phase of *c*700 and the early ninth-century phase exemplified by Mac Regol. This analysis has not revealed the scriptorium in which the Kells display script was written, but it has shown that the calligraphers of the Book of Kells participated in and contributed to a highly distinctive tradition of insular lettering which probably originated in Northumbria. Later examples of the rectilinear and right-angled style of the Book of Kells seem mostly to have come from scriptoria in Ireland or on the Continent. An examination of the decorative capitals of the Book of Kells throws some light on their ancestry and on some possible descendants but the ecclesiastical centre in which they were designed remains elusive.

Fig 2 Insular decorative capitals in the display script of the Book of Kells: computer-drawn diagrams of the principal forms

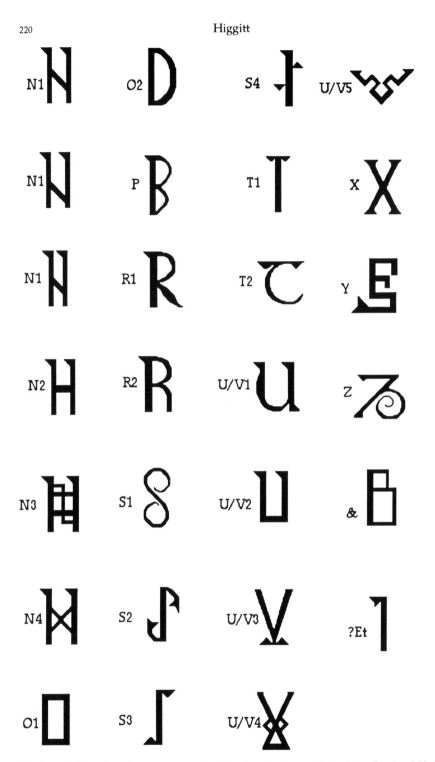

Fig 2 *contd* Insular decorative capitals in the display script of the Book of Kells:
computer-drawn diagrams of the principal forms

APPENDIX

Insular decorative capitals in the display script of the Book of Kells: an analysis of the principal forms

The forms discussed here are illustrated in **fig 2**. The search for comparative material has been limited to insular decorative capitals used in manuscript display script and in inscriptions. The parallels with the Lindisfarne Gospels are placed first before those in other manuscripts in order to highlight the relationship between the Lindisfarne Gospels and the Book of Kells.

Key to abbreviated titles of manuscripts cited below

(Manuscript numbers are followed by the catalogue number in J J G Alexander, *Insular manuscripts, sixth to the ninth century* (London 1978). See E H Zimmermann, *Vorkarolingische Miniature* (Berlin 1916) and G Henderson, *From Durrow to Kells: the insular gospel books 650-800* (London 1987) for further illustrations.)

Armagh (TCD MS 52; Alexander no 53)

Augsburg (formerly Schloss Harburg; Universitätsbibliothek, Cod. I.2.4°.2; Alexander no 24)

CCCC 197B (Cambridge, Corpus Christi College, MS 197B; Alexander no 12)

Cologne (Cologne, Dombibliothek, Cod. 213; Alexander no 13)

Cotton Otho C.V (London, BL, Cotton Otho C.V; Alexander no 12. See also the eighteenth-century facsimile of display script from this manuscript in BL, Stowe 1061, folio 36r).[33]

Durham A.II.10 (Durham, Cathedral Library, MS A.II.10; Alexander no 5)

Durham A.II.17 (Durham, Cathedral Library, MS A.II.17; Alexander no 10)

Durrow (TCD, MS 57; Alexander no 6)

Echternach (Paris, BN, MS lat. 9389; Alexander no 11)

Freiburg (Freiburg-im-Breisgau, Universitätsbibliothek, MS 702; Alexander no 25)

Hereford (Hereford, Cathedral Library, MS P.I.2; Alexander no 38)

Howth ('Garland of Howth', TCD, MS 56; Alexander no 59)

---

[33]Webster and Backhouse (note 24 above) 117, 119.

Leningrad (St Petersburg, Public Library, Cod. F.v.I.8; Alexander no 39)

Lichfield (Book of St Chad, Lichfield, Cathedral Library; Alexander no 21)

Lindisfarne (London, BL, MS Cotton Nero D.IV; Alexander no 9)

Macdurnan (London, Lambeth Palace, MS 1370; Alexander no 70)

Mac Regol (Oxford, Bodleian Library, MS Auct. D.2.19; Alexander no 54)

Mulling (TCD, MS 60; Alexander no 45)

Paris, BN, lat. 2 ('Second Bible of Charles the Bald', fol 416r, illustrated in G L Micheli, *L'enluminure du haut moyen âge et les influences irlandaises* (Brussels 1939) pl 201)

Paris, BN, n.a. lat. 1587 (Paris, BN, nouv. acq. lat. 1587; Alexander no 56)

Rawlinson (Oxford, Bodleian Library, MS Rawlinson G. 167; Alexander no 43)

St Gall 51 (St Gall, Stiftsbibliothek, MS 51; Alexander no 44)

St Gall 60 (St Gall, Stiftsbibliothek, MS 60; Alexander no 60)

St Gall 1395 (St Gall, Stiftsbibliothek, MS 1395; Alexander no 57)

Stowe 1061 (eighteenth-century facsimile of display script from partially destroyed Cotton Otho C.V (see above))

Trier 61 (Trier, Domschatz, MS 61; Alexander no 26)

Epigraphic parallels cited below

(References to Okasha numbers below are to the catalogue in E Okasha, *Hand-list of Anglo-Saxon non-runic inscriptions* (Cambridge 1971)).

Ardagh Chalice (notes 16 and 24 above).

Caistor (Okasha no 18)

Carlisle I (Okasha no 23)

Hartlepool O (Okasha no 44)

Hartlepool IV (Okasha no 46)

Hartlepool V (Okasha no 47)

Jarrow II (Okasha no 62)

Lanrivoaré (note 29 above).

Lethnot (E Okasha, *Cambridge Medieval Celtic Studies* 9 (1985) 43-69, no 3)

Lindisfarne O (Okasha no 74)

Lindisfarne VII (Okasha no 80)

Lindisfarne X (Okasha no 83)

Lindisfarne XIV (Okasha no 84)

Ramsey Island (E Okasha, *Archaeologia Cambrensis* 119 (1970) 68-70)

Ruthwell (Okasha no 105. For photographs see *The Ruthwell Cross: Papers from the colloquium sponsored by the Index of Christian Art, Princeton University, 8 December 1989*, ed B Cassidy (Princeton 1992)).

Tarbat (E Okasha, *Cambridge Medieval Celtic Studies* 9 (1985) 43-69, no 8; J Higgitt, *Proceedings of the Society of Antiquaries of Scotland*, 112 (1982) 300-21)

Thornhill (Okasha no 116)

Toureen Peakaun (note 26 above).

Wensley I (Okasha no 120)

Wensley II (Okasha no 121)

Whitby DCCXXXII (Okasha no 133)

Whitby DCCXXXIII (Okasha no 134)

York VI (Okasha no 151)

A1   (folios 8r, 13r, 16v, 18r, 29r, 114v, 285r, 292r)
The Roman capital form with a straight bar across the top.
Manuscripts:
        Lindisfarne, folio 11r, 25v, 93v, 137v, 139r, 209v.
        Augsburg folio 83r; Freiburg, folio 1r; Lichfield, p 221;
        Rawlinson, folio 1r.
Inscriptions:
        Ruthwell

A2   (folio 124r)
As A1 with pendant serifs at ends of top bar.
No parallels found.

A3   (folio 8r)
The Roman capital with a split lentoid form used for the cross-bar and
surmounted by two horizontal split lentoids and a vertical lentoid.
No parallels found.

A4   (folio 18r)
As A1 except that the cross-bar is curved.
No parallels found.

A5(i)   (folios 8r, 12r, 15v, 16v, 124r, 183r, 285r)
A form of the Roman capital with an angular cross-bar and a straight bar
across the top.
Manuscripts:
>   Lindisfarne, folios 3r, 11r, 29r, 90r, 91r, 139r, 211r.
>   Howth, folio 1r; Leningrad, folio 78r; Macdurnan, folio 5r.

Inscriptions:
>   Hartlepool IV; Lanrivoaré; Wensley II.

A5(ii)   (folio 13r)
A variant of A5(i) in which the angular cross-bar is set well above the base
line.
Manuscripts:
>   Cotton Otho C.V (copy in Stowe 1061)

Inscriptions:
>   Lanrivoaré; Lindisfarne X; Ruthwell; Whitby DCCXXXII.

A6   (folio 13r)
A variant of A5 in which the angular bar is developed into an angled loop.
Manuscripts:
>   Paris, BN, n.a. lat. 1587, folios 2v, 85v.

A7   (folio 8r)
Combines curved cross-bar of A4 and angular cross-bar of A5.
No parallels found.

A8   (folio 13r)
The insular half-uncial letter.
Manuscripts:
>   Lindisfarne, folios 29r, 95r.
>   Augsburg, folios 52v, 53v; Cotton Otho C.V (copy in Stowe 1061);
>   Durrow, folios 14r, 15r, 17r, 18r, 86r, 126r, 193r; Echternach, folios 19r,
>   115v, 116r.

Inscriptions:
>   Tarbat.

A9   (folio 130r)
Probably the uncial letter with the righthand stroke treated as a vertical because of the ligature with *N*. If the eighteenth-century copy in Stowe 1061 is to be trusted, there was a very similar letter in Cotton Otho C.V.
Manuscripts:
>   Lindisfarne, folio 27r.
>   Cotton Otho C.V (copy in Stowe 1061)

B1   (folios 13r, 188v, 285r, 292r)
A rectangular version of the insular half-uncial letter. The example on folio 188v is decorated with small 'boxes' in the internal angles.
Manuscripts:
>   Lindisfarne, folio 27r.
>   Mac Regol, folios 1r, 127r.
Inscriptions:
>   Ardagh Chalice.

B2   (folios 8r, 285r)
As B1 with the addition of a loop to the top right of the ascender (cf H2).
Manuscripts:
>   Lindisfarne, folios 8r, 95r, 139v, 211r.
>   Durham A.II.17, folios 2r, 38⁴r; Echternach, folio 177r.
Inscriptions:
>   Ramsey Island.

C   (folios 8r, 15v, 16v, 18r, 114v, 124r, 203r)
A narrow rectangular version of the capital.
Manuscripts:
>   Lindisfarne, folios 3r, 29r, 93v, 95r, 137v, 131r, 139r.
>   Armagh, folio 160r; Cotton Otho C.V (copy in Stowe 1061); Durham A.II.17, folio 2r; Echternach, fol 177r; Freiburg, folio 1r; Leningrad, folio 78r; Lichfield, pp 5, 143, 221; Macdurnan, folio 5r; Mac Regol, folios 52r, 85r, 127r; Rawlinson, folio 1r; St Gall 60, p 5; St Gall 1395, p 426; Trier 61, folio 9r.
Inscriptions:
>   Ardagh Chalice; Jarrow II; Ruthwell; Tarbat.

D   (folios 8r, 124r, 188v, 285r)
A rectangular version of the uncial-derived letter used as an alternative in insular half-uncial script.
Manuscripts:
>   Lindisfarne, folio 27r.
>   Lichfield, p 221; Mac Regol, folio 1r; Rawlinson, fol 1r.
Inscriptions:
>   Carlisle I. (Lindisfarne X has a version in which the 'bow' is left slightly open at the top left. This also appears on p 143 of Lichfield).

E1 (folios 8r, 12r, 13r, 15v, 18r, 48v, 114v, 124r, 130r, 188v, 203r, 285v, 292r)

A narrow version of the Roman capital with the middle bar usually somewhat above the centre of the letter.

Manuscripts:

Lindisfarne, folios 3r, 8r, 27r, 29r, 91r, 139r.

Augsburg, folio 16r; CCCC 197B, folio 2; Durham A.II.17, folio 38⁴r; Freiburg, fol 1r; Leningrad, folio 78r; Lichfield, pp 5, 143; Mac Regol, folio 1r; Paris, BN n.a. lat. 1587, folio 2v; St Gall 51, pp 3, 7; Trier 61, folio 9r.

Inscriptions:

Ardagh Chalice; Ruthwell; Tarbat; York VI.

E2 (folios 8r, 12r)

A rectangular version of the half-uncial letter, or alternatively, the Roman capital with the ends of the top and bottom horizontals turning inwards at right angles.

Manuscripts:

Cotton Otho C.V (copy in Stowe 1061); Durham A.II.17, folios 2r, 38⁴r; Echternach, folios 19r, 20r, 176v.

Inscriptions:

Caistor (now lost; form shown in early engraving); Thornhill (?).

F1 (folio 8r)

The insular half-uncial letter with arched upper stroke.

Manuscripts:

Lindisfarne, folios 3r, 11r, 27r, 95r.

Cotton Otho C.V (copy in Stowe 1061); Leningrad, folio 78r.

Inscriptions:

Lethnot; Ruthwell (?); Wensley I; Whitby DCCXXXII (?)

F2 (folios 8r, 124r)

The Roman capital (with a straight upper horizontal stroke), or perhaps a rectangular version of F1. Folio 8r shows a variety of decorative treatments of the lower horizontal.

Manuscripts:

Lichfield, p 143; Mac Regol, folios 1r, 52r.

Inscriptions:

No parallels found.

G (folios 8r, 15v, 29r, 130r)

A rectangular form derived from the insular half-uncial letter. It is comparable to rectangular forms in Lindisfarne (folio 3r), Howth (folio 1r), Lichfield (p 143) and Mac Regol (folio 1r). I have found no exact parallels. Howth, which has the only other example with a short lower horizontal stroke on the left side of the vertical, comes closest to the Kells form.

H1   (folios 8r, 13r (=) eta; 188v)
A rectangular form of the insular half-uncial letter. Used for both *H* and eta
in the *nomen sacrum* for *Iesus* etc.
Manuscripts:
> Lindisfarne, folios 11r, 25v.
> Cotton Otho C.V (copy in Stowe 1061); Lichfield, p 143; Mac Regol,
> folio 1r, 52r; Paris, BN, n.a. lat. 1587, folio 32v; St Gall 51, p 3.
Inscriptions:
> Ardagh Chalice; Lindisfarne X.

H2   (folios 13r, 18r, 114v (= eta), 130r (= eta))
As H1 with the addition of a loop to the top right of the ascender (cf B2).
Manuscripts:
> Lindisfarne, folio 10r, 209v.
> Durham A.II.17, folio 38[4]r.
Inscriptions:
> No parallels found.

H3   (folio 12r)
An angular rather than rectangular variant of the looped form found in H2.
Alternatively an angular version of the uncial letter with a loop. (The uncial
form underlies the *H* with a zoomorphic terminal on folio 183r and is also
found in Augsburg, folio 53v, and Leningrad, folio 78r).
No exact parallel found.

I   (folios 8r, 12r, 13r, 15v, 18r, 114v, 124r, 130r, 188v, 285r, 292r)
The simple vertical capital. As this is the standard form in other
manuscripts and in inscriptions, no lists of occurrences are given.

L   (folios 8r, 15v, 114v, 124r, 130r, 203r, 285r)
A narrow version of the Roman capital form.
Manuscripts:
> Lindisfarne, folios 3r, 27r, 95r, 137v, 139r.
> Echternach, folio 115v, Leningrad, folio 78r; Mac Regol, folios 1r, 52r,
> 85r; Trier 61, folio 9r.
Inscriptions:
> Lindisfarne O (?); Lindisfarne XIV[34]; Ruthwell; York VI.

M1   (folio 8r)
A broad letter that looks like a hybrid that derives its left half from the
uncial and its right half from the insular half-uncial form.
No parallels found.

M2   (folios 8r, 13r, 114v, 130r, 285r)
A rectangular capital consisting of three verticals linked by two horizontal
cross-bars. There are decorative variations of the basic form: with cross-bars

---

[34]R Cramp, *County Durham and Northumberland*, Corpus of Anglo-Saxon Stone
Sculpture (Oxford 1984) I, 202 and 36 for Lindisfarne O and XIV.

formed of lentoid or spindle-like forms (folios 8r, 13r); with box-like forms set in the angles, hollow on folio 8r and solid on folio 285r. This form is presumably a development of the simpler and commoner insular form with a single cross-bar which is found, for example, in the Lindisfarne Gospels (folios 3r, 93v, 95r).

Manuscripts:
> Lichfield, p 5; Mac Regol, folios 1r, 52r, 127r; St Gall 51, pp 7, 129. A variant in which the cross-bars extend beyond the verticals was used in Howth (folios 1r, 22r).

Inscriptions:
> Ardagh Chalice.

M3   (folio 124r)
A variant of M2 in which the cross-bars are curved. There are hollow box-like forms in the angles.
No parallels found.

N1   (folios 8r, 13r, 18r, 48v, 114v, 124r, 130r, 188v, 203r)
Forms derived probably from the insular half-uncial N. The shallow diagonal is set in varying positions from near the bottom of the verticals to around mid-height. Lentoid or spindle-like diagonals are used on folio 8r and hollow box-like features decorate the angles on folios 15v and 188v.

Manuscripts:
> Lindisfarne, folios 27r, 29r, 95r, 139r, 209v, 211r.
> Augsburg, folio 83r; Cologne, folio 1r; Cotton Otho C.V (copy in Stowe 1061); Durham A.II.17, folio 38[4]r; Echternach, folio 19r, 20r etc; Freiburg, folio 1r; Howth, folio 1r; Lichfield, pp 5, 143, 221; Macdurnan, folio 5r; Paris, BN, n. a. lat. 1587, folio 32v, 52v; Rawlinson, folio 1r; St Gall 51, pp 3, 7, 79; St Gall 60, p 5; Trier 61, folio 9r, 19r.

Inscriptions:
> Ardagh Chalice; Lindisfarne VII; Ramsey Island; Tarbat; Wensley I; Whitby DCCXXXII (?).

N2   (folios 13r, 16v, 18r)
A form with a horizontal cross-bar that resembles Roman capital H. This comparatively uncommon form was probably suggested in the insular context by the form of M with three verticals and one or two horizontals, although it is also found occasionally in Late Antique and early medieval inscriptions on the Continent.[35]

Manuscripts:
> Mac Regol, folios 1r, 127r; Paris, BN, n.a. lat. 1587, folio 32v; St Gall 1395, p 426.

Inscriptions:
> York VI (?)[36]

---

[35]E Le Blant, 'Paléographie des inscriptions latines du IIIe siècle à la fin du VIIe', *Revue archéologique* (3rd series) 30 (1897) 35-36.
[36]Higgitt (note 15 above) 63.

N3 (folio 8r)

A fanciful rectangular development of the capital in which the two verticals are linked by two horizontals and a 'diagonal' with two right-angle breaks. I have found no exact parallel but the same 'diagonal' can be seen in CCCC 197B, folio 2r. The intersection of the horizontals and the 'diagonal' form small 'boxes'.

N4 (folio 8r)

The connection between the verticals is effected by two intersecting diagonal strokes that create an X. The form could have been invented as another geometric variation but it might equally have been suggested by the identical runic form. If so, the borrowing was runically illiterate since the rune represents *d*. The same form is used in Lichfield for both *P* (p 143) and *M* (p 221).[37]

O1 (folios 8r, 13r, 18r, 114v, 124r)

A rectangular version of the capital.

Manuscripts:

Lindisfarne, folios 11r, 17v, 131v.

Armagh, folio 160r; Augsburg, folio 83r; CCCC 197B, folio 2r; Lichfield, pp 5, 221; Macdurnan, folio 5r; Mac Regol, folios 85r, 127r; Rawlinson, folio 1r; St Gall 51, pp 3, 7 129; St Gall 60, p 5.

Inscriptions:

Ardagh Chalice; Hartlepool IV and V; Ruthwell (?); Toureen Peakaun; York VI.

O2 (folios 8r, 114v, 124r, 188v, 203r, 292r)

An odd form identical with Roman capital *D*, perhaps a synthesis of the Roman capital and the rectangular versions of *O*. I have found no parallels in insular manuscripts or inscriptions.

P (folios 8r (= rho), 13r, 130r (= rho), 203r, 292r)

An insular display script form resembling the Roman capital with the addition of a loop hanging below the bow. It is used both for the letter *P* and for the Greek rho in the *nomen sacrum* for *Christus* etc.

Manuscripts:

Lindisfarne, folios 3r, 8r, 17v, 27r, 29r, 95r, 221r.

Durrow, folios 4r, 86r, 193r; Durham A.II.17, folio 2r; Freiburg, folio 1r; Cotton Otho C.V (copy in Stowe 1061)

Inscriptions:

No parallels found.

R1 (folio 8r)

The common capital (or uncial) form with a diagonal leg. It is similar to the more frequent form of *R* used in the text scripts.

Manuscripts:

---

[37]See note 17 above.

Lindisfarne, folios 3r, 5v, 17v, 27r, 29r, 90r, 95r, 131r, 139r, 211r.
Augsburg, folios 3r, 16r, 52v, 53v, 127r; CCCC 197B, folio 2; Cotton
Otho C.V (copying Stowe 1061); Durham A.II.17, folio 2r; Durrow,
folio 17r, 22r, 39r, 126r, 193r; Echternach, folios 19r, 20r, 177r;
Leningrad, folio 78r; Lichfield, pp 143, 221; Macdurnan, folio 5r;
Rawlinson, folio 1r; St Gall 51, p 3; St Gall 60, p 5; St Gall 1395; p 426;
Trier 61, folio 19r.

Inscriptions:
    Ardagh Chalice; Ramsey Island.

R2   (folios 8r, 13r, 16v, 124r, 183r, 188v, 292r)
An unusual variant of the Roman capital form (or of the uncial) with a more
or less vertical right leg.

Manuscripts:
    CCCC 197B, folio 2r; Cotton Otho C.V (copy in Stowe 1061).

Inscriptions:
    No parallels found.

S1   (folios 8r, 13r, 203r)
The Roman capital (or uncial) form, which is also the more frequent form of
S used in the text script. In the Kells display script the upper and lower
curves are continued to create more or less closed circles.

Manuscripts:
    Lindisfarne, folios 5v, 29r, 90r, 91r, 95r.
    Cotton Otho C.V (copy in Stowe 1061); Durrow, folios 17r, 126r, 193r;
    Echternach, folios 18v, 19r, 20r; Freiburg, folio 1r; Trier 61, folios 18v,
    19r.

Inscriptions:
    Ardagh Chalice.

S2   (folio 124r)
The central section of the capital is straightened out into a vertical; the
terminals remain curved. I have found no parallels.

S3   (folios 8r, 12r, 13r, 16v, 18r, 29r, 114v, 188v, 285r)
A rectangular treatment of the capital with a central vertical and generally
short horizontal terminals.

Manuscripts:
    St Gall 1395, p 426.

Inscriptions:
    No parallels found.

S4   (folio 15v)
A rectangular variant of the capital with a central vertical and short
horizontals branching off to left and right somewhat short of the ends. This
letter is analogous to angular forms of C and E found in one or two insular

manuscripts and inscriptions in which short horizontals branch off a vertical somewhat short of the ends.[38]
Manuscripts:

>Freiburg, folio 1r; Lichfield, p 221; Mac Regol, folios 52r, 85r; Paris, BN, n.a. lat. 1587, folio 52v; Rawlinson, folio 1r.

Inscriptions:

>Ardagh Chalice (reversed); Carlisle I; Ramsey Island.

T1   (folios 8r, 12r, 13r, 114v, 124r, 183r, 188v, 285r, 292r)
A narrow version of the Roman capital.
Manuscripts:

>Lindisfarne, folios 3r, 27r, 29r.
>Augsburg, folio 55r; CCCC 197B, folio 2r; Cotton Otho C.V, folio 28r; Durham A.II.17, folios 2r, 2v, 38[4]r; Echternach, folios 115v, 177r; Leningrad, folio 78r; Lichfield, p 221; Macdurnan, folios 5r, 172r; Mac Regol, folios 52r, 85r, 127r; Paris, BN, n.a. lat. 1587, folio 2v; Rawlinson, folio 1r; Trier 61, folios 9r, 19r.

Inscriptions:

>Ardagh Chalice; Carlisle I; Hartlepool O; Hartlepool IV; Hartlepool V; Jarrow II; Ramsey Island; Ruthwell; Wensley II; Whitby DCCXXXII

T2   (folios 8r, 13r)
The insular half-uncial letter. The form is quite common in insular manuscript display script but in insular inscriptions it appears mainly in half-uncial scripts (eg Kilnasaggart and many other inscriptions in Ireland; Billingham, Dewsbury I, Falstone, Hartlepool VI and Yarm in England; St Vigeans and Barnakill in Scotland; Llangadwaladr and other Welsh inscriptions).[39]
Manuscripts:

>Lindisfarne, folios 29r, 211r.
>Cotton Otho C.V (copy in Stowe 1061); Durham A.II.10, folio 2r; Durham A.II.17, folio 72v; Durrow, folios 23r, 86r, 126r, 193r; Echternach, folios 19r, 116r; Hereford, folio 102r, Trier 61, folio 18v.

Inscriptions:

>Ruthwell (with sinuous top).

U/V1   (folios 200v-201r)
The half-uncial letter used in the continuation lettering following the initials in the genealogy of Luke.
Manuscripts:

>Lindisfarne, folios 3r, 5v, 8r, 29r, 90r, 95r, 131r, 139r, 211r.
>Cotton Otho C.V (copy in Stowe 1061); Durham A.II.10, folio 2r; Durham A.II.17, folios 2r, 2v, 38[2]v, 69r, 72v; Durrow, folios 4r, 17r,

---

[38]Stein (note 7 above) 57 and n 70; Higgitt (note 6 above, 1982) 315.
[39]F Henry, *Irish art in the early christian period (to 800 AD)* (London 1965) pl 49; Okasha (note 16 above, 1971) nos 9, 30, 39, 48, 145; Okasha (note 28 above) 43-69; V E Nash-Williams, *The early christian monuments of Wales* (Cardiff 1950) 55-57.

23r, 86r, 126r, 193r; Echternach, folios 115v, 116r, 177r; Freiburg, folio
1r; Paris, BN, n.a. lat. 1587, folio 2v.
Inscriptions:
    Hartlepool IV; Lanrivoaré; Ruthwell (?).

U/V2   (folios 8r, 12r, 15v, 18r, 114v, 124r, 130r, 188v, 285r, 292r)
A rectangular form probably derived from the half-uncial letter.
Manuscripts:
    Lindisfarne, folios 3r, 25v, 27r, 93r, 95r, 137v.
    Armagh, folios 109r, 123r; Augsburg, folios 55r, 83r; CCCC 197B, folio
    2r; Cologne, folio 1r; Cotton Otho C.V (copy in Stowe 1061); Howth,
    folios 1r, 22r; Echternach, folio 19r; Freiburg, folio 1r; Lichfield, pp 5,
    143, 221; Mac Regol, folios 1r, 52r, 85r, 123r; Rawlinson, folio 1r; St
    Gall 51, pp 7, 79, 129; St Gall 1395, p 426.
Inscriptions:
    Ardagh Chalice; Caistor (?); Tarbat.

U/V3   (folios 13r, 15v, 16v, 200r, 201v, 202r, 203r, 285r)
The Roman capital form with a serifed cross-bar at the base. This cross-bar
could have developed from *V* with wedge serifs at its base, a form that
appears in line 3 of the display script on folio 29r of the Lindisfarne Gospels.
The form is also analogous to the lozenge-shaped *O* with upper and lower
cross-bars seen on the same page.
Manuscripts:
    Armagh, folio 215r; Leningrad, folio 78r.
Inscriptions:
    Ardagh Chalice.

U/V4   (folio 188v)
A form of the capital in which the diagonals intersect above the base. The
resultant lower angle is closed by a horizontal stroke at the bottom. The
Kells letter seems to be unique in adding small angular embellishments on
either side of the intersection. These additions are strikingly similar,
although perhaps coincidentally, to those on two runic forms (for *k/c* and *g*)
used only locally in northern and north-western England.[40]
Manuscripts:
    Durham A.II.17, folio 2r; Lichfield, pp 143, 221; Mulling, folio 36r;
    Paris, BN, lat. 2, folio 416r; Paris, BN, n.a. lat. 1587, folio 32v.
Inscriptions:
    Ramsey Island; Whitby DCCXXXIII.

U/V5   (folio 124r)

A geometric variation on the Roman capital in which each of the two
diagonals is embellished with a rectangular indentation. I have found no
exact parallels. The simple Roman capital is comparatively rare among

---

[40]R I Page, *An introduction to English runes* (London 1973) 46; idem, *Runes* (London,
1987) 19-20.

insular decorative capitals. Manuscript examples include Augsburg, folios 5r, 52v, Durham A.II.17, folio 39r, Echternach, folios 76r, 115v and Macdurnan, folios 5r, 172r. It is also used in the following inscriptions: Lindisfarne III (?); Ramsey Island; Ruthwell; and Whitby DCCXXXII. The simple Roman form also appears as a painted capital within the initial on folio 188r of Kells.

X   (folios 8r (= chi), 124r, 130r (= chi))
The straight-lined Roman capital used both for X and for chi in the *nomen sacrum* for *Christus* etc.
Manuscripts:
        Lindisfarne, folios 3r, 27r, 95r.
Inscriptions:
        Whitby DCCXXXII.

Y   (folio 16v)
A rectangular version of the half-uncial text letter. I have found no parallels for the rectangular version but the half-uncial form is used in its simple form in display script in Lindisfarne, folio 131r and Freiburg, folio 1r.

Z   (folio 13r)
A form based presumably on the half-uncial text letter. The undulating base stroke of the text letter has been turned downwards into an incipient spiral. Initials following this form and that of the text letter can be seen at the end of the list of Hebrew names on folio 1r of Kells. As Z appears only rarely, the lack of parallels is not significant.

&   (folios 8r, 13r)
A simplified rectangular version of the *et* ligature. Slightly more complex forms, in which the cross-bar of the T is still vestigially present, can be seen in Lindisfarne, folio 29r; in Cotton Otho C.V (copy in Stowe 1061) and in Durham A.II.17, folio 2r.

⌐   (fol 292r)
It is suggested above (p 213) that this form should be read as the Tironian sign for *et*. It does not seem to appear elsewhere in insular display script or in inscriptions in insular decorated capitals but the use of the *autem* sign in the painted display capitals on folio 127v would be a comparable use of an insular abbreviation symbol.

Ornamental techniques in Kells and its kin

Mark Van Stone

Insular art comprises an eclectic stew of European and Near Eastern motifs brewed in Irish monasteries and their British colonies. Those motifs most peculiar to it are:

- The script itself, originating in North Italy

- Display script, inspired by letterforms in Byzantine monuments and teutonic runes

- Animal interlace, or zoomorphs, from Teutonic art

- Heraldic animals, from Pictish art

- Knotwork, braidwork, abstract interlace from various sources; simple Roman braidwork found in mosaics from Syria to Britain and more complex knotwork found in early christian Mediterranean art — Italy, Byzantium, perhaps Coptic

- Fretwork or Key patterns: who knows their immediate source? Presumably they originate in Classical Greece, but there are 'Greek' key-patterns on the first-century Celtic Turoe Stone in county Galway

- Finally, native Celtic spirals, usually called La Tène spirals

The craftsmen who executed the Book of Kells and its family were uncommonly brilliant and persevering, but they were not angels. Several scholars have analysed the layout and construction of various Hiberno-Saxon ornamental pages, and many have noted the striking simplicity of the principles underlying their construction. In the words of Jacques Guilmain, writing in *Art Bulletin* (December 1985, p 544), 'Once the design as a whole had been planned … the artist could proceed to complete any section of the work at any time, knowing that the whole would come out correctly in the end'. As usual in the analysis of awe-inspiring accomplishments of our less technologically 'advanced' forebears, they made up for their lack of sophisticated technology with brilliantly simple design. An understanding of their techniques inspires our appreciation of both their cleverness and humanity. The very 'additive' aspect of their abstract ornamental motifs allowed a major work like the Book of Kells or the Durham Gospels to proceed at a human pace. The work, like that on a cathedral, is eminently interruptible, and it would be quite impossible if it were not so.

In the 1960 Lindisfarne facsimile commentary, Rupert Bruce-Mitford noted a compulsive dependence on compasses in the ornament of the Lindisfarne Gospels. The Echternach eagle is clumsy due to an overdependence on the compass — a rare weakness which Bruce-Mitford and Julian Brown count as evidence that the scribe-artist was under unusual time-pressure from his client. As a professional graphic artist, I have complete sympathy.

Françoise Henry inferred a more skilful use of curved templates or 'French curves' in constructing say, the X-form in the Chi Rho page of Kells. The hurried artist of Echternach gave us a clear tracing of one of his 'French curves — dozens of times — in the mane of the rampant Lion (**pl 75**). It is the same classic shape as today's French curve. The body is covered with outlines of a smaller one, and the legs, a still smaller one.

As an artist, I can also sympathise with an artist developing his style in the course of a single ambitious work. This has also been frequently noted, as in the Lindisfarne or Durrow incipits. In Durrow, the artist uses two kinds of interlace: that framing the Man-symbol is very difficult to design, like later Coptic interlace. In the Lion, he uses two bands of the difficult stuff and two of the much easier Roman braidwork. On the frames of the Calf and Eagle his knots are progressively easier to execute, and the interlace round the Eagle actually mimics the circular knots of the more difficult knotwork around Matthew — an effect as pleasing without all the work. It is as if he discarded the more complex Mediterranean knots for the simpler stuff — we shall see just how much simpler — and indeed, the clumsy interlace is not present in any other (presumably later) insular manuscript. If one based art history on a Darwinian view of interlace one could conclude that Durrow is earlier than its fellows (not a very controversial point) and that the symbol pages were executed in the Jeromian order: Man, Lion, Calf, Eagle. That conclusion might be a bit more controversial.

The actual tools they used are still an open question, and there is no surviving physical evidence to help us. The most important aspect of these techniques is what goes on inside the head. They, like all great inventors, designers, artists, developed tools to achieve what they dreamed up. Their work is utterly different from the continental painterly work, not because they had sharper tools, but because they dreamed different dreams. Their dreams drove them to invent sharper tools. In a particular manuscript, each dog-head is drawn according to a formula (**fig 1**).

Fig 1 Technique for drawing animal-heads

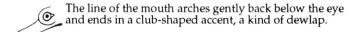 Circular eye, centred pupil (and later, forward-looking pupil).

Brow concentric with eye.

The snout is nearly always this distinctive shape with a little curled nose.

The line of the mouth arches gently back below the eye and ends in a club-shaped accent, a kind of dewlap.

The lower jaw is parallel to the mouth-line and curls round parallel to the corner of the mouth to connect to the brow.

Sometimes this line is broken, allowing the jaw to connect to the outline of the neck.

The brow continues up and back to the ear, from which the back of the neck issues. This is the generic dog-head.

The bird-head is exactly the same except for the treatment of the end of the nose.

A cat is the same except for bigger ears and a shorter snout.

A lion is a cat with a mane.

Fig 1 *contd*

The neck stays the same thickness no matter how long or knotted it becomes.

The shoulder swells a little, and the upper leg emerges like a drumstick.

There is usually some indication of an elbow,
and the toes — one, two or three according to the artist's taste and how much room he has — are thin at the base with swollen pads and sharp claws.
The chest tapers into a waist the same thickness as the neck, following the same rules of interlacement as the neck,
and then terminates in the hind haunch. The hind leg is much like a larger version of the foreleg, with the same toes.
Leave a gap for the tail to connect. The tail's job is to wind about elegantly filling all the rest of the available space.

The design of a beast-panel was not formulaic. One must underdraw at least the position of the various body parts inside the frame — and these stylus-underdrawings are frequently still visible, even in clumsy manuscripts like the MacRegol Gospels. The real artistry of the insular beasts lay in how they were arranged inside the box. It is no accident that beast panels do not exist outside the insular mileu — the layout technique can only be learned during a long apprenticeship — but that the formulaic beast heads are quite common in Franco-Saxon and Romanesque art in later centuries.

Until Kells, a beast ornament was almost always confined to a framed box. Lindisfarne beasts, for instance, tightly filled their space. Eadfrith had no qualms about drawing a beast with one foreleg and one hind leg, or one front leg and two hind legs, or a fully ambulatory dog with two of each, in order to fit his animals in neatly. He was the same about his distribution of toes. If there was no room for more than one toe, that was all the dog or bird got. The artists of Lichfield and Kells, on the other hand, cared so much about their animals' organic integrity that they consistently gave their quadrupeds a full complement of limbs and toes.

The Lichfield beasts do not fill their spaces quite as neatly, and it has been remarked how much more lively they seem, how much more appealing and modern the designs are, with their irregular negative spaces. I am not claiming that every beast in every manuscript is drawn exactly this way. This is sort of a generic beast, rather like the Lindisfarne animal. The Durham Gospels have more duck-like snouts and fin-like feet, and even more primitive beasts, as in Durrow, have rubber lips and rubber flippers; their snouts and limbs can tie in knots like strings. In mature insular manuscripts, animals have more organic integrity; only those body parts with vertebrae or no bones at all — neck, waist, tail, ear, tongue — can knot like ropes. Rigid body-parts like heads and legs stay rigid. Every artist had somewhat different style animals, but within a manuscript, a style was quite consistent.

Romilly Allen inferred a formula for drawing insular fret-patterns which apparently cannot be improved upon:

Fig 2

You begin with a framed panel, marking the corners of squares along the edge.

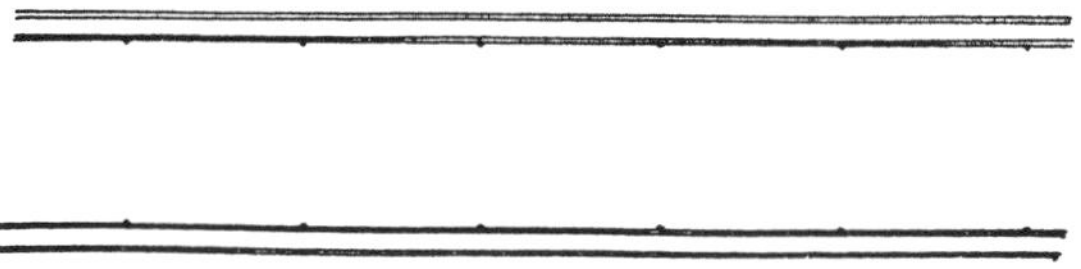

With a ruler, draw diagonals between adjacent corner-marks, leaving gaps in the middle or at the ends thus

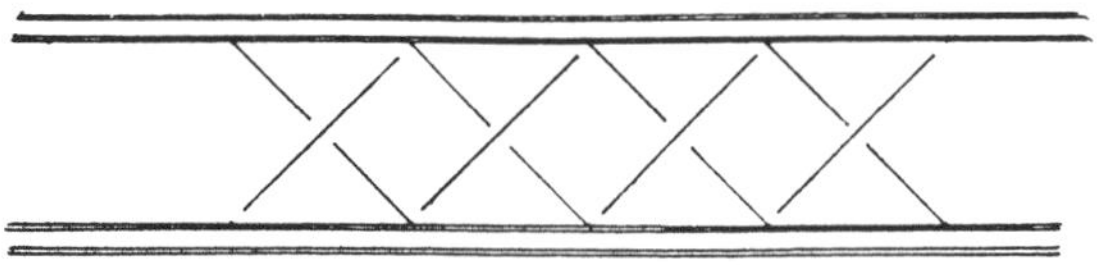

Then from the gapped ends extend lines parallel to the walls

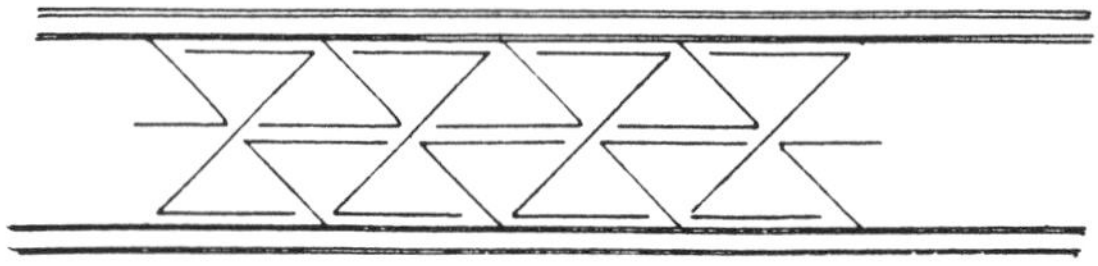

Fig 2 *contd*

and parallel to the diagonals.

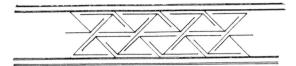

All that is left is to connect the pathways into one zigzag maze,

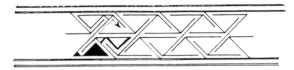

which insular artists did with great variety and invention.

This is one long narrow, complex path — a major theme in insular art. This prominent aesthetic aspect relates fretwork to the interlaced animals, and to virtually every other motif in this art.

Spiral ornament began simply with curlicues which appear in all early christian initial ornament, and indeed, doodles that spring instinctively from the pens of nearly everyone. Once the spirals suggested La Tène ornament to the Celtic artists, they were off and running. The artists kept their spirals as circular as possible by drawing them — perhaps with graduated curve-templates — over a stylus-impressed compass-drawn circle. The telltale compass prick, and usually its impressed circle, is still visible in every insular manuscript, such as in the *D* in *DEIOHANNE* IN DURHAM A.II.17, folio 38⁴r (pl 77), from whose unfinished spiral disks the compass-prick glares out. You can also see them easily in the unfinished spirals on Kells *Quoniam* page (pl 34), and on Kells *Liber* page (pl 19), except where the disks have been disfigured by the clumsy later artist with a fat red pen who went through Kells to 'finish it' — I call him the 'Master of the Felt Marker', and his work clearly dates from an age whose standards were not so high. These compass-drawn circles even underlie the stifled lumpy spirals of the MacRegol Gospels, though Mac Regol more or less ignored them. In the worn *Quoniam* page of Bodleian Ms Rawlinson G. 167, the ink is frequently worn off so completely that the compass-disks are all that is left. Spiral ornament sank without a trace after the insular Golden Age. It had no visible effect on later art; I think because its aesthetic was so purely Celtic and alien to mainstream European art. There is no simple way to execute it, and its visual grammar is subtle and complex — like animal-interlace layout, it takes a long apprenticeship to master it. Like the

similarly alien, complex and fluid art of the Amerindians of the Northwest
Pacific Coast, you have to grow up with it, drenched with it, to understand
it (or even to *like* it).

Knotwork, on the other hand, had a far-flung effect in European art, and
this is mainly because it has a simple formula. As with frets and beasts, you
begin with a frame. Any frame which can be broken into small unit squares
can be filled with interlace. See **fig 3** for a step-by-step construction of a
simple knot which shows how quickly this pattern can proceed when one
knows the secret method.

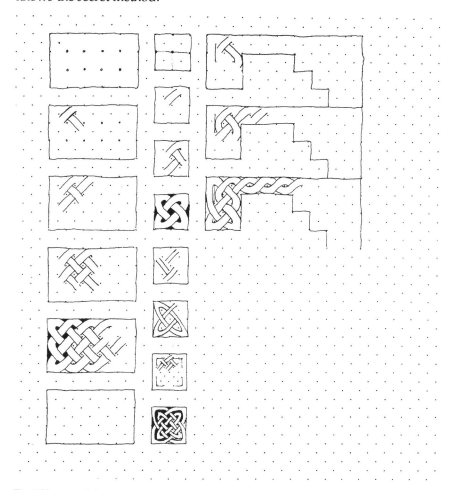

Fig 3 Knotwork by steps

Seeing the interlace technique demonstrated shows how an artist like Mac
Regol of Birr could draw such embarassing animal and human figures, such
illegible display letters and clumsy spirals, and such crystalline, beautiful
interlace. At the end of Matthew in Durham A.II.10, folio 3v, we have a case
of an artist beginning at the bottom with a simple braid, inserting breaks
parallel to the walls for a more interesting middle frame, then inserting L-

shaped breaks for a very interesting pattern for the top frame. Either that, or he began at the top very ambitious, and ran out of time as he went down. Interestingly, exactly the same three break-patterns appear in the interlace of the Mark initial of Durrow. I have no doubt that artists carried about pattern-books, showing dot-grids and break-patterns, with an example of the knot which results from each.

In the Durrow Calf (pl 78) the frame across the bottom is twenty unit squares wide, which the artist has divided with breaks to produce a pattern of ten tulip-shaped knots. I do not think he used a ruler to measure the dots' spacing because across the top frame, which is the same size, he laid out only nineteen squares, producing a pattern of nine and a half tulips. You can see the degenerate tulip here, just to right of top centre. This is not an isolated incident. Layout mistakes in other manuscripts suggest that the squares were improvised, laid out by eye. This supports Robert Stevick's suggestion that the layout of decorated pages was accomplished entirely with compass and straightedge, without the aid of measuring rulers.

Plates accompanying this article include a carpet-page and initial *SI TE DOLOR* (pls 79 and 80), which I did for a film in 1978, to demonstrate insular technique. Both together took me eight days, about one hundred and twenty hours all told. I used no templates, except a straightedge. Had I used French curves or spiral-curve templates, the time might have been increased by about 50%, and the curves would have been a bit cleaner. I used no magnification, just rested my chin two inches above the work. I am nearsighted, and (with correction) I have sharp vision — about 20/15, which my optometrist tells me is true of about one out of five Americans — and I have no doubt that sharp-eyed myopes got the manuscript jobs in insular scriptoria.

However, rock-crystal magnifying lenses existed in seventh-century Ireland — there is one on the bottom of the Ardagh Chalice — and I suspect that some future archaeologist or art historian will find a lenticular magnifier which could have been used as a loupe. So far, all the early christian magnifiers I have seen are cabochons — flat on the bottom, and domed on the top, unsuitable for scribal aids. But they were aware of some optics, and at most were just one step away from inventing the loupe.

Of course the artists were human. Of course they were brilliant. Their drawings were partly improvised and partly formula, and relied as little as possible on underdrawing. Where underdrawing is necessary, as in animal interlace or spirals or curved knots, it is still visible.

Thanks to Romilly Allen and George Bain for paving the way for me, even though many of their methods were not those actually used. I discovered insular knotwork technique in 1972 — a dot-grid showing clearly through the interstices of a badly-drawn knot in the Stowe St John in the Royal Irish Academy, while I was still an undergraduate (fig 4).

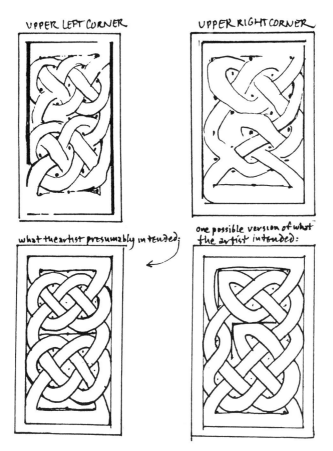

UPPER LEFT CORNER   UPPER RIGHT CORNER

what the artist presumably intended;   one possible version of what the artist intended:

Fig 4 Stowe St John portrait knot-panels

Thereafter, wherever I looked for dots, I found them: from the entire corpus of insular manuscripts to Roman mosaics, to Coptic manuscripts to Persian Qur'an borders from the sixteenth-century, to interlace in Leonardo's notebooks. Later, I found that I had been scooped by Dr Joseph Thiele of Germany, who published the same technique in 1968; he had found it in St Gall MS 24, which has a border containing an unfinished band of interlace. It begins whole, drops to just a dot-grid, then the dot-grid peters out just before the end of the frame-panel. Apparently our artist left his work unfinished when the lunch bell rang, and never got back to it. Though it is possible to enjoy and analyse music without being able to play it, I think no one would argue that a musician has a more intimate understanding of, say, J S Bach, than a non-musician. You can learn to execute most of these designs with little effort, and by doing so you will learn something important that you can learn in no other way.

Page design of some illuminations in the Book of Kells

Robert D Stevick

Although it seems never to have been noted, commodulation is characteristic of the designs in the full-page illuminations in the Book of Kells, just as it is in illuminations of most other gospel books in the early Irish-Northumbrian tradition. In this paper I shall first illustrate how commodular design can be created; then I will explain fundamental commodular features in some of the Kells designs; in addition, I shall try to characterise the use of commodulation in the Book of Kells in relation to its use in other manuscript illumination within the same tradition.

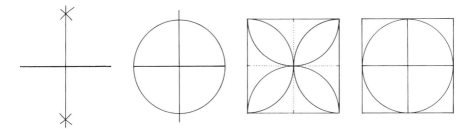

Fig 1 A common method for constructing concentric cross, circle and square on a given linear measure

All the designs that I will describe — or even mention — can be developed readily from the figure of a circle and cross (**fig 1**). The cross is created by bisecting a line of a given length. The circle proceeds from that given length as its diameter, its centre at the intersection of the cross. For designs adapted to leaves of a codex, there will also be need to construct accurate rectangles in relation to the circle and cross. With the compass still set equal to the radius of the circle, it is a simple matter to plot the corners of a contiguous square (which is a 'perfect' rectangle) having the same centre as the cross and the circle (which are also 'perfect' figures). From the unity of a single given measure — that of the initial line — the dimensions and proportions of the cross, circle, and square are thus derived. Symmetrical extensions of the square will then produce other accurate rectangles.

My initial illustration of commodular construction reproduces the layout of the main face of Soiscél Molaise (**fig 2a**).[1]

---

[1]National Museum of Ireland, R. 4006. This is described in *Treasures of early Irish art, 1500 BC to 1500 AD*, catalogue of exhibition at the Metropolitan Museum of Art (1977), and dated to the eighth century, with additions from the eleventh and fifteenth centuries (pp 182-83).

Fig 2a The main face of Soiscél Molaise (*National Museum of Ireland R. 4006*)

This portion of the bookshrine is valuable to test a construction procedure against; because the basic rectangular design is wrought in a single sheet of metal it will not have shrunk or warped as parchment may do. It is especially instructive because the plan itself embodies a circle and a cross. The plan in fact evolves with utmost simplicity from comparable geometrical figures serving as its source (**fig 2b**).

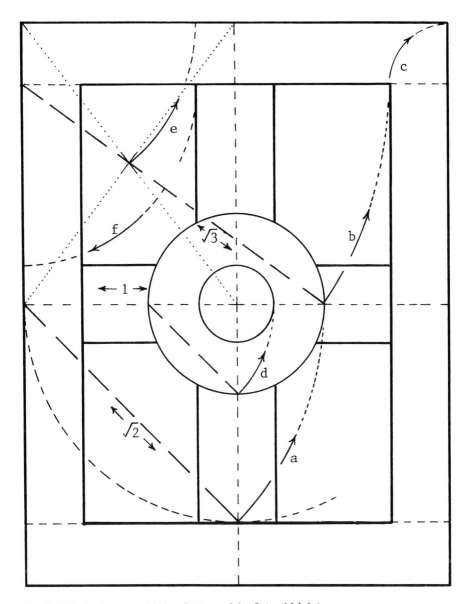

Fig 2b Principal commodular relations of the Soiscél Molaise

From within the underlying figures of square and circle quartered by the cross will be selected two diagonal measures, and from these measures and figures together the full layout can be generated. One measure is the diagonal of a quadrant of the square; this is also the measure of the chord of a quadrant of the underlying circle. In either case, if 1 is the measure of the side of a quadrant of either circle or square, the measure of the diagonal or chord is √2 (in modern notation). If this measure is copied (*a*) to mark a point along one of the cross arms, the second diagonal measure is the distance between an opposite corner of the square and the point just marked; this measure (in modern notation) is √3.

Now if one copies (b) this second measure from each corner of the large square to mark points along the upper and lower sides of that square, this operation will set the corners of the inner panel. For the outer framing rectangle the width is that of the underlying square; the height is set by copying symmetrically (c) the difference between the widths of the panel and the square.[2]

Next, the circular design. Its centre is at the centre of the underlying circle, cross, and square, and the radius of the larger circle is defined by the point that was marked along the cross using the first diagonal measure. The inner circle is derived (d) from the last circle by repeating the procedure that set the larger radius.[3]

Now the cross design. Diagonals in each quadrant of the outer frame bisect each other: starting from each corner of the frame, use their half-length to set the vertical lines, as illustrated (e); then starting from each corner of the underlying square use that same measure to set the horizontal lines of the cross (f).

It should be mentioned at this point, perhaps, that the construction method just illustrated produces a homologous model so precise and simple that it is difficult to imagine the design being created without employing the same principles of constructive geometry.

The rest of the layout can be reconstructed in similar fashion and with equal precision, but this will be far enough to illustrate the essential points about this kind of design. The operations that produce it, carried out with only compass and straight-edge, are indeed simple, ideally suited to drafting rectangular and circular designs. They do not depend on use of a scale or a ruler, hence they do not depend on numbers or numerical computation. Nonetheless, they produce a complete commodulation of measures. The most obvious example of this lies in the two circles and the frame: the ratio of the diameter of the smaller circle to that of the larger one is equivalent to the ratio of the larger diameter to the width of the frame (which is to say, to the diameter of the initial, underlying circle); in algebraic notation, they have the relation $a: b:: b: c$. Here is not an equivalence of ratios which lie in equal measures — something found in the bilateral symmetry of the design. Rather, it is equivalence of ratios among *unequal* measures. This is a basic

---

[2]In black-and-white photographs the outline of the principal rectangle may be difficult to trace, because of the silver tubing binding the upper, right, and lower sides of the face, and the underlying material showing along the left side. The form I shall be describing is the decorated plane having circular 'nailheads' still in place at three of its four corners.

[3]This procedure is accurate for the diameter measured vertically; the inner circle is not true (though the outer one is), presumably having been modified to fit a jewel or precious stone.

aspect of commodulation: the proportionality found in recurring ratios among differing measures.

Most commodulation will necessarily be less obvious, though it is not less palpable. It lies essentially in setting the measure of each new element in a design by drawing on a simple proportion already implicit in it. Sometimes it copies a part of the rectangular form itself, as was shown in setting the height of the frame and the horizontal lines of the cross. Sometimes it uses length of the chord of a quadrant, as was shown twice. Typically it appropriates a diagonal measure within a rectangular configuration, as was shown in setting the width of the inner panel and (by extension) the height of the outer frame. The operational linking of the measures in such a process of constructing the design is a physical analog to a conceptual integration; it is this linking and integration, I think, that are the sources of an aesthetic unity produced by commodular design.[4]

The St John page in the Book of Kells, folio 291v (pl 51), is ostensibly the most complex in design among the portrait pages, yet it too answers readily and thoroughly to commodular analysis.[5] The ratio embodied in its fundamental rectangular outline is derived by another process of extending one dimension of the underlying square. If the width is once again taken as the given dimension, the height in a model can be set by one of the methods shown in fig 3: it depends crucially on just one of the 'geometrical' measures ($\sqrt{3}$) that informed the Soiscél Molaise design. The derivation shown first (figs 3a-b) develops the shape of the frame more simply. The second derivation (fig 3c) is the one I shall posit for its being symmetrically developed from the underlying square (it follows exactly the same method as the first, extending in two directions instead of one, but at half the scale of the other).

Unlike the other portrait pages, with their constant and uniform thickness of the four sides of the frame, the inner area on this page is not outlined by

---

[4]It may be added that the unity of the design embraces the whole book shrine. Its third dimension (for depth of the box) is related to the width of the face as $(1/\sqrt{2})$: 1, derivable directly again from circle, cross, and square.

[5]According to Bernard Meehan, 'Collation' in Kells commentary, 185-92, this page was prepared on a single leaf which was then inserted into its gathering of bifolia; so were the other pages discussed in this paper (folios 7, 28, 32, 33), with one exception (folio 114). The size of the St John portrait is considerably greater than the others, and it appears in some respects to be slightly irregular. The left side bows outward along its outer band (outside the fairly straight dark line separating the two continuous bands of colour); the right side also bows outward (including the dark line). The overall measures of the width reflect this bowing of both sides: they are 195 and 194.5 mm at the top and bottom corners, nearly 196mm in the middle. The bottom outline lies along a fairly straight line, but the top is not at all straight: measurements for height range from 265 (left) to 267.5 mm (right). On the other hand, the picture-area within the frame is almost perfectly regular: width varies only as 114-114.5mm, height is constant at 157mm, diagonals are within a millimetre of being equal. Whatever caused the irregularities of the outer structure of the frame, it is a fair inference from the dimensions alone that the underlying plan was conceived in accurate rectangular (and circular) configurations. The relations among the principal structural lines, to be shown next, will support this inference.

the sides of a simple rectangle. When the plan is analysed for a plausible procedure that will replicate the shape, neither the outer set nor the inner set of parallel lines turns out to be the fundamental shape for the framing.

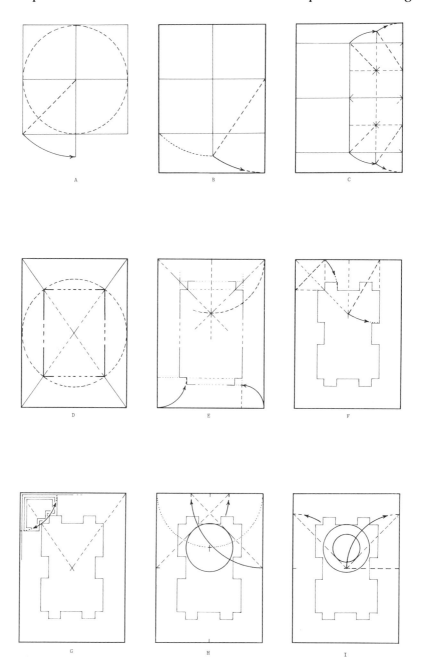

Fig 3 The principal commodular relations of the St John portrait, Book of Kells, folio 291v

Instead, it is the greater width and lesser height that define the fundamental rectangle of the inner area — one whose corners lie along the diagonals of the overall frame. The clue to this lies in the equivalence of the outer width of the frame (measured at the corners) and the diagonal measure of the inner picture panel. Accordingly, construction requires only that the fixed foot of dividers be set at the centre, the moving foot at the side boundary of the frame, in order to sketch the path of a circle: where this circle intersects the diagonals of the outer rectangle will be the corners of an inner rectangle (**fig 3d**). These two rectangles thus constructed will have sides with equivalent ratios, but without sharing any dimension. Obviously, this kind of commodular relation is quite easy to create; it is also easy to appreciate before — or entirely apart from — understanding the mathematical relations entailed.

The symmetrical 'notching' at the four corners and along the four sides of the picture-panel is no less commodular than the elements described thus far. The corners of the inner rectangle just designated are at unequal distances from the nearest sides of the outer rectangle — at distances, obviously, in the same relations as are the unequal sides of each rectangle of the frame. It is those unequal measures that are then copied (**fig 3e**) to set the paths of lines defining the ostensive insets at the corners; diagonal measures are then copied to set the inner limits of the inner square devices at the midpoints of all four sides (**fig 3f**). The remaining structure points for drawing the mid-side configurations within the picture panel are already in place, so that from them the extrusive elements of the frame take their shape, forming the cross-like devices at the midpoints of all four sides (not illustrated). In effect, the picture-area is defined by neither the innermost nor the outermost sets of parallel lines, nor is it the area of the initially derived inner rectangle. It is rather an area complexly defined by commodular measures all of which are related by their direct derivation from the dimensions of the outer rectangle of the frame.

The corner cells of interlace seem to have had their sizes set as is shown the next panel (**fig 3g**).

So far, the St John page layout uses no kinds of measure other than the kinds also found in the initial layout stages of the Soiscél Molaise design; it only combines and orders them differently. Such is the constancy of elementary features in an assured and well disciplined tradition of art.

Finally, the halo has its centre on the vertical axis of the painting, at a distance half the width of the frame from the top (**fig 3h** illustrates one way to locate it). Down the vertical axis, the distance to the centre of the halo and the distance to the centre of the frame, of course, will have the same ratio as do the unequal sides of the frame itself. Locating a prominent design element with its centre just here extends the commodular relations of the design, while for the first time breaking its vertical symmetry.

Setting the measures of the inner and outer circles of the halo provides an especially open demonstration of commodular ties — just as did the circles at the centre of the Soiscél Molaise design. The outer circle was not drawn at a size just to fill the available area within the picture panel, and in fact it doesn't quite fit there, given its centre and circumference. It overlaps slightly the top of the inner rectangle, and it misses slightly the insets on either side of the frame. Rather, its measure is yet another derivation from the fundamental ratio of the frame. Its radius can be set by tangents, using lines set at 45° from left and right midpoints of the sides. One obvious procedure (if a 45° drafting tool was not available) is to copy the half-height dimension along the top, measured from either corner; then connect the points thus marked to the midpoints of the sides. These connecting lines function as tangents that determine the size of the outer circle (**fig 3h**). Size of the inner circle follows from a complementary method. In each of the upper two quadrants, run lines from the centre of the frame at 45° to left and right of the centreline (these are diagonals of the upper two quadrants of the underlying square). They will set the radius of the inner circle by acting as tangents to it. An obvious procedure for this echoes the procedure just used for the outer circle: copy the half-width dimension along each side, measured from the middle of the frame's sides; then connect the points thus marked to the centre of the frame. The connecting lines are the tangents determining the size of the inner circle (**fig 3i**). For both inner and outer circles of the halo, then, basic measures inherent in the shape of the rectangular frame are re-used in deriving their sizes relative to each other, and relative to the frame itself. Ultimately, *all* principal structural lines will be found to embody measures related one to another by elementary geometrical ratios. Not only that: the simple ratio laid down initially in the unequal sides of the frame is a function of *all* the major proportionalities for this page. That is the essence of the finest commodular designs.

While the design of the St John page is unique, it has some affinities to designs in other early gospel books as well as to others within the Book of Kells itself. Most significantly, the ratio of the dimensions of its basic rectangular area is the same as that in the frames of one page in the Echternach Gospels, one leaf in the Durham Gospels, and three pages in the St Gall Gospels.[6] The first two of these provide a striking comparison to the St John page (**fig 4**). Their frames differ from that of the Kells page by having uniform thickness on all four sides. On the other hand, all three frames are alike in having not only identically proportioned rectangular outlines, but also in having inset elements in the middle of all four sides of the inner panel. The dimensions of the insets for the Durham Gospels design are derived from the underlying square (**figs 4a-c**).

---

[6]These are respectively the *imago hominis* page, Paris, BN, MS lat. 9389, folio 18v; the framed text (recto) and the Crucifixion miniature (verso) — these two being in perfect registration front-to-back on the leaf — in Durham, Cathedral Library, MS A.II.10, folio 38³; and the cross-page (p 6), the Crucifixion (p 266), and the Last Judgement (p 267) in St Gallen, Stiftsbibliothek, Cod. Sang. 51. I have described their commodular structures in detail in separate essays: *Peritia* 5 (1989) 284-308 and *Scriptorium* 44 (1990) 161-92.

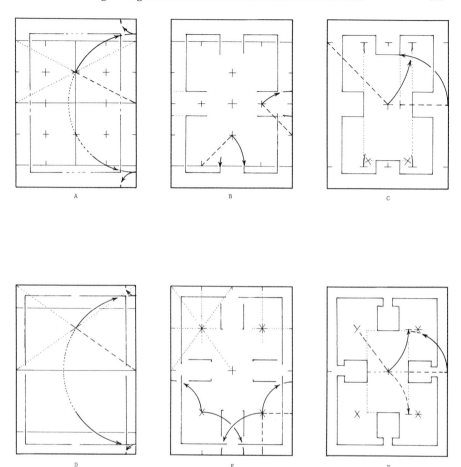

Fig 4 Two other frames with 'notched' inner panels, Echternach Gospels *imago hominis* page, folio 18v, and the framed text of Durham, Cathedral Library, MS A.II.10, folio 38³r

Those of the Echternach design are derived from the rectangular outline (**figs 4d-f**) — in this respect much closer to the Kells plan. The compass work represented in the second panel for the Echternach design is very similar to part of the construction method shown earlier for the St John page. The point of this comparison is that, while the design of the St John page is unique, it shares a frame-type, the ratio in its outer rectangle, and several specific commodular features with illuminations in other insular gospels. It is only the elaborateness of the frame for the St John portrait, requiring the fuller development of the governing ratio of its design, that distinguishes this frame configuration from the others.

The other rectangular illuminations in the Book of Kells have frames made with concentric rectangles so as to have uniform thickness of their four sides, even when they are evolved in disparate steps. They too share configurations and commodular features with frame designs in other books.

In fact, nearly every ratio of measures for the rectangular outlines in Kells can be found at least once in the rectangular frames in other codices. I have space for no more than brief mention of the main ones.

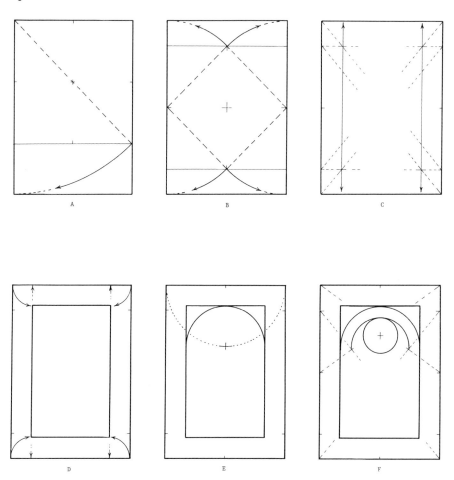

Fig 5 Commodular aspects of the St Matthew portrait, Book of Kells, folio 28v

The design of the St Matthew page, on folio 28v (**pl 18**), has the same proportioning for its outline and employs the same governing ratio as do the illuminations of the *David Rex* page in the Durham Cassiodorus and the St Matthew page in the Book of Mulling, and the decorated binding of the St Cuthbert Gospel of St John.[7] It is a simple $\sqrt{2}$:1.[8] The principal commodular

---

[7]Durham, Cathedral Library, MS B.II.30, folio 81v; Dublin, TCD, MS 60, folio 12v (formerly p 189); the Stonyhurst Gospel, on loan to the British Library. I have described their commodular structures in detail in separate essays: *Durham Archaeological Journal* 5 (1989) 43-54, *JRSAI* 121 (1991) 27-44, *Artibus et Historiae* 15 (1987) 9-19.
[8]The Book of Kells itself may well be an example of this ratio being used for the shape of the leaves of a codex (and the whole area of two leaves viewed together when the book is opened flat). Although the original measurements are uncertain because of 'substantial cropping in 1821 and perhaps earlier', Françoise Henry

relations are illustrated in **fig 5.** It should be noted that the centre of the arcade is located in exactly the same relation to the upper portion of the frame as is the halo for St John.[9] The shape of the rectangular outline of the famous Kells cross page, folio 33r (**pl 21**), is identical to that of the cross-page and two portrait pages in the Lichfield Gospels,[10] as well as to those for two evangelist portraits in the St Gall Gospels[11] (and others). It is a simple numerical 4:3.[12]

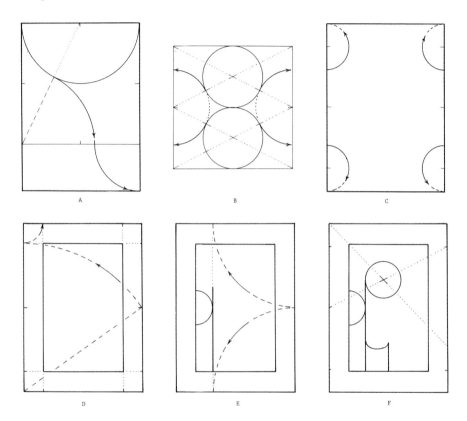

Fig 6 A method of constructing the rectangular shape for Book of Kells, folios 32v and 7v, with further illustration of commodular relations on 7v

estimated an original leaf size of around 370 x 260mm (Meehan, 175, n 5), which is a *very* close approximation of this ratio. The Lindisfarne Gospels are another apparent instance of a codex with leaves in the same shape: according to T J Brown 'the leaves measure about 340mm x 240mm', and they have had minimal cropping (*Evangelium quattuor codex Lindisfarnensis*, ed T D Kendrick et al, 2 vols (Olten & Lausanne 1956, 1960) II, 63.
[9]One way to locate it was shown earlier. Another way is this: copy the width of the frame along the sides, measured from the top corners, and connect the points thus marked. Where the lines cross will mark the centre for the arcade.
[10]Pp 220 (cross), 142 (St Mark), 218 (St Luke).
[11]Those of St Mark (p 78) and St John (p 208).
[12]The relation between the Kells double-arm cross and that of the Book of Durrow has been commented on a number of times. I will only note here that their governing ratios and their schemes of commodular relations are very different indeed, the Durrow page employing $\sqrt{2}:1$ in a way that is unique among the surviving miniatures $((1 + \sqrt{2}/2):1)$.

The outline for the portrait on folio 32v (**pl 20**), Christ attended by angels, has the same proportioning and governing ratio that is employed for the St Matthew and St Lukes pages in the St Gall Gospels.[13] Alternate methods for setting the governing ratio in the rectangular outline are illustrated (**figs 6a and 6b-c**); the inner rectangle of the panel can be constructed from it as shown in **fig 6d**. For that matter, this ratio is used as well for the Madonna and Child portrait in the Book of Kells, folio 7v (**pl 9**); not only that, the relation of the picture panel outline to the outline of the overall frame is exactly that which is found on folio 32v.[14] I will mention only two further particulars of the commodular structure on this other page (**figs 6e-f**). The back of the throne upon which the Virgin sits is placed at a distance from the right border of the frame exactly equal to half the height of the frame. The placement of the halo is then especially revealing. Since it does not lie along the centreline of the frame, it cannot be at the intersection of equal diagonal lines, like the halo for St John and the arcade for St Matthew. It is nonetheless exactly defined by the intersection of two fundamental diagonals: the one starting from the upper left corner is like those on the other pages just mentioned, a 45° diagonal; the one starting from the upper right corner is a diagonal of the upper half of the centred underlying square. The measure of the halo for the Virgin is determined by its centre together with the back of the throne, to which it is tangent. When the page is analysed fully, every structural element in this design, too, will be found to be controlled by a commodular chain of relations.

One other pair of miniatures deserves brief mention, because they draw on the same scheme for depiction of an event — the Arrest of Christ — and for ornamental text: they are on opposite sides of a single leaf (folio 114), in registration one with the other.

The frame for folio 114r (**pl 28**), depicting the Arrest, differs in several conspicuous ways from the inner- and outer-rectangle pattern of the other pages already described. The sides are irregularly segmented columns, each with a stepped base, the bottom is left open, and the top is a semicircular arch. As different as the plan is in these ways, though, the repertory of construction procedures is limited, and it is clearly related to those employed for the portrait pages. The frame in fact fits within a rectangular outline much as the others do. In this instance the rectangle is partially recognisable from the shine-through on the left side, above, from the frame for ornamented text on the verso of the leaf. That frame follows a rectangular outline but leaves one corner open. The dependence of the frames on both sides of the leaf on the same rectangular outline is made

---

[13]The overall rectangular area of the frame is a function of the golden section ratio (this ratio along with $\sqrt{2}:1$ make up 'the two true measures of geometry'). In algebraic notation it is $1 + (1 - 1/\phi):1$, equivalent to $3-\phi:1$.

[14]The dimensions — measured from the new facsimile — differ while the ratios remain identical, implying that each of these portraits was laid out separately but with the same methods up to this point. Similarly, two of the evangelist symbol pages, folio 27v and folio 129v, have dimensions differing slightly but with identical ratios in the measures of their vertical and horizontal (and diagonal) extensions.

obvious by the shine-through to the verso of the cross-shaped devices level with the head of Christ (recto), and the discoloration at the base of the frame from the lowest extensions of the stepped base of the columns on the recto. Some drypoint rulings, visible in several places on the Arrest page, show the same thing. In the facsimile edition widths of the frames vary as 167-68mm, for one, 169mm and less for the other.

The nature of the underlying pattern for both pages is clearest in the plan on the verso. The lower part follows the outline of a square, the upper part being in the nature of an extension of that square. The height of the frame (on the right side) measures approximately 245m (it is not quite straight). The ratio of height to width cannot have been planned as, say, 3:2 (requiring height of 252-53mm), and it cannot have been planned as √2:1 (requiring height of 237-38mm), and it does not match any common integer ratio that can be traced in the underlying structure of the rest of the plan. In fact there seems to be no structural feature of the frame for the ornamented text that will account for the specific proportioning that the frame exhibits. Rather, it is in the plan on the recto that the clue to the proportioning lies. The procedure that will generate the basic shape for both pages shows little in the way of logic, in the sense that the others show a kind of practical logic. It does, though, resemble the other procedures in an unmistakable way. This is how I believe the plan was laid out.

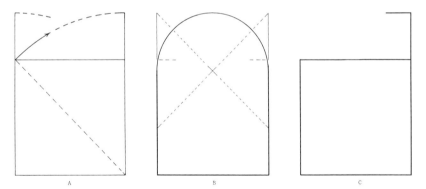

Fig 7 Derivation of commodular relations within the designs on Book of Kells, folio 114r

As usual, begin with a quartered square with sides equal to the measure to be the width. From the square derive a rectangle in the ratio √2:1 by a single extension above the square (fig 7a, which is merely the inverse of fig 5a). (It may be noted in passing that the elongated forearms of Christ lie along diagonals of the underlying square). Then from the midpoint of each side of the square sketch a diagonal line to the opposite corner at the top of the rectangle: where these lines intersect marks the center of the arch (fig 7b); radius is the distance to the side of the figure. For the frame on folio 114r, the basic outline is now complete. For the frame on the verso it remains to copy along upper extensions of the sides the measure along the centre line from the top of the arch to the top of the initial square: this sets the corners for the underlying rectangle (**fig 7c**). In short, the simple √2:1 shape has been used this time to generate a slightly more complex shape, using a technique similar to that which located the centres of arcades on folios 28v and 32v, and here used to locate the centre of the arch that forms the top of the frame.

All in all, the illuminations exhibiting rectangular frames in the Book of Kells seem to be thoroughly commodular in design. Further, I have found no elements of commodular form in these pages that cannot be found elsewhere within the same tradition; most of them in fact can be found a number of times, entwined in other unique designs. What has struck me most about these designs in general is that they imply a very clear and well articulated tradition — not articulated in extant documents describing their assumptions, or methods, or purposes, but articulated unmistakably in the designs themselves. Each design is unique (why make *another* one of those, if you already *have* one? why *imitate* a painting rather than create a *new* one?). Yet each is developed from the same small, well defined repertory of relational concepts. The result is a rich variety of designs, all of them binding their parts by a commodular linking, all of the designs growing from the shared rules that are part of the definition of a truly great tradition.

Finally, *if* one were to take degree of complexity as a concomitant of relative chronology, the designs in the Book of Kells that I have described would seem to represent the end of a brilliant tradition, that final stage when polish and perfection of detail have reached highest development, when layers of allusions have accumulated, when knowledge of the traditional methods of creating commodular plans has produced a collection of formulae, when elaboration is the rule and radical innovation is at an end.[15]

---

[15]This assessment is consistent, I believe, with the assertion by Alexander, 'Illumination', 289, n 5, that 'The Canon tables, the figure scenes, the ornamental use of plant scroll and human figure decoration all set the Book of Kells apart, and moreover they all suggest not just a later stage, but a different conceptual and creative purpose, not merely different models but a different use of those models in terms of transformation and amplification'.

Scribe and mason: the Book of Kells and the Irish high crosses

Roger Stalley

Just over a century ago, the distinguished antiquarian, Romilly Allen, drew attention to some of the remarkable parallels that exist between Pictish carving and the Book of Kells.[1] He was particularly struck by the way in which the superbly modelled cross slab at Nigg, on the northern shores of the Moray Firth, seemed to reflect the ornamental pages of the insular gospel books, as if a folio of the Book of Kells had been enlarged and transformed into stone (pl 81). On the carving at Nigg the Pictish sculptors even followed the illuminators' practice of filling the main motif — in this case a cross — with animal interlace, which in turn was set against a background of curvilinear or bossed decoration, as on the Chi Rho page of the Book of Kells.

The relationship between Kells and Pictish sculpture has recently been explored at length by Dr Isabel Henderson in two important papers.[2] The analogies she found are numerous and striking. They include a wide range of ornamental as well as figural motifs: the fashion for entangled men, seen on one of the carvings at Meigle, for example; or the individual horsemen moving purposefully, either along the text or across the surface of the stone.[3] As everyone now recognises, during the eighth and ninth centuries the sculptors of Pictland somehow acquired an understanding of the art of the great gospel books. Dr Henderson's evidence has considerable implications for students of the manuscript, for her analogies appeared to leave open the possibility of a provenance for Kells either in Pictland or in mainland Scotland.

Unfortunately there is no equivalent study of the relationship between the Book of Kells and the Irish high crosses to set beside Dr Henderson's work. The literature on Irish sculpture is studded with references to the book, usually parallels for individual decorative motifs, but they have never been gathered together in any systematic or meaningful way. Isolated parallels are not hard to find. The evangelist symbols at Duleek, for example, recall

---

[1] J Romilly Allen, 'Report on the sculptured stones earlier than AD 1100', *Proceedings of the Society of Antiquaries of Scotland* 74 (1890-91) 426.
[2] I Henderson, 'Pictish art and the Book of Kells' in *Ireland in early medieval Europe, studies in memory of Kathleen Hughes* (Cambridge 1982) 79-105; idem, 'The Book of Kells and the snake boss motif on Pictish cross-slabs and the Iona crosses' in Ryan, 56-65.
[3] The entangled men appear on Meigle stone ECM 26, illustrated in Henderson (1982, note 2 above) pl XIId; analogies can be found on folios 5r, 27v, 130r and 188r of the Book of Kells. A typical Pictish rider is carved on Meigle stone ECM 3, which can be compared with riders on folios 89r and 255v in the Book of Kells.

those in the manuscript, and the crouching warriors on the base of the
Market Cross at Kells, with their round shields and distinctive spears, have
many allies within the folios.[4] For these, and dozens of other images, the
manuscript has long been exploited as a convenient quarry. But what
exactly does it all mean?

There is a general assumption that the sculptors of the crosses merely
copied what they saw in the books, though nobody has given much thought
to the practicalities of this. Did the sculptors have direct access to the
precious, illuminated texts and was it really possible to copy the minute
designs? Even with the splendid new facsimile, it is difficult enough and, in
the age before photography, attempts to reproduce the folios reduced artists
to despair.[5] What the masons needed were not copies but large scale
drawings which they could trace on to the stone, drawings prepared of
course by someone proficient in the systems of insular ornament — not
necessarily the mason himself.[6]

In the past the Book has been linked, both with a group of crosses from the
Clonmacnois region, and more specifically with the Tower Cross at Kells
itself.[7] This latter cross has a particular relevance to the study of the
manuscript, for it is located within a few yards of the site of the great church
at Kells, where the gospel book spent so much of its life. If one wants to
come to a better understanding about the relationship between sculpture
and illumination, this is a good place to start. Many scholars have been
convinced that the Tower Cross and the Book of Kells were joint products of
a great 'flowering of the arts' within the Columban federation — to use a
favourite cliché — and produced within a few years of each other. In
addition, the Tower Cross is thought to be one of the first of the scripture
crosses, setting a pattern to be followed and developed by many of the later
monuments.[8] If the carving on the cross is really linked to the decoration in

---

[4]The upright position of the symbol of St Luke, on the south side of the cross head at
Duleek, is especially reminiscent of the equivalent symbol on folio 27v of the
manuscript. The Duleek sculpture is illustrated in Harbison, II, pl 242. For
illustrations of the base of the Market Cross at Kells see Harbison, II, pl 338. There is
a good comparison for the warriors in the Book of Kells, at the bottom right of folio
200r. A more intriguing link between crosses and manuscripts can be found in the
eagle depicted in the Last Judgement scene of Muiredach's Cross at Monasterboice.
The bird raises one wing in a manner reminiscent of St John's symbol set in the
spandrels of the canon table on folio 5r.
[5]Kells commentary, 17.
[6]The nature of the models that the sculptors had in front of them as they carved has
long been a controversial question. Drawings on parchment are one possibility. In
the later middle ages masons sometimes recorded architectural mouldings on cloth
or canvas, L F Salzman, Building in England down to 1540, 2nd edn (Oxford 1967) 22.
It is conceivable that such methods were used in early Ireland, as Mary Ann Gelly
has suggested to me.
[7]The links between the Clonmacnois crosses and the Book of Kells are discussed by
Carola Hicks, 'A Clonmacnois workshop in stone', JRSAI 110 (1980) 5-35.
[8]See for example H Richardson and J Scarry, An introduction to Irish high crosses (Cork
1990) 17; J A Calvert, The early development of Irish high crosses and their relationship to
Scottish sculpture in the ninth and tenth centuries (PhD dissertation, University of
California 1978) 165-66, 295-96, 303; and N Edwards, 'The South Cross, Clonmacnois'

the book, this would indeed be a powerful argument in favour of Kells as a provenance for the manuscript.

The Tower Cross is not an easy monument to study, for its sandstone surfaces are badly abraded and most of the angle mouldings have, at some stage in its history, been deliberately hacked off (pl 82). While this has deprived the cross of its visual quality, the major subjects are not difficult to identify. The shaft and cross head are cut from a single block of stone and decorated with a mixture of christian iconography and ornamental motifs. The east face contains four Old Testament scenes: Adam and Eve placed together with Cain and Abel, the three Hebrews in the furnace, Daniel in the lions' den and the sacrifice of Isaac. The right arm depicts St Paul and St Anthony being fed by the raven, with the feeding of the five thousand in the upper arm.[9] The left arm contains a carving of the sacrifice of Isaac. The mixture of hagiography with Old and New Testament subjects might at first sight seem arbitrary, but, as Professor Ó Carragáin has shown in a brilliant paper, the subjects around the cross head are ingeniously united through their eucharistic symbolism.[10] The opposite, western face has only two major christian subjects: the Crucifixion on the shaft and above it a rather ambiguous image of Christ (pls 83 and 84). With the exception of this latter carving, most of the iconography follows the conventions found on other scripture crosses.

Both Françoise Henry and Helen Roe were convinced that links existed between the Tower Cross and the manuscript. Dr Henry based her opinion on the supposed presence of the four evangelist symbols, concluding that 'It is striking that the Cross of the Tower of Kells, which probably belongs to the early ninth century, is the only one of the Irish high crosses to have the symbols of the Evangelists ... In any case, the symbols are there and they link the Cross and the Book'.[11] It is however far from certain that the symbols are there (pl 84). What Françoise Henry regarded as a depiction of the *Majestas Domini* is an unorthodox image and quite unlike any in the Book. The eagle of St John seems more closely associated with the

---

in *Early medieval sculpture in Britain and Ireland*, ed J Higgitt, British Archaeological Reports, British Series, 152 (1986) 31.

[9]The iconography is described by H Roe, *The high crosses of Kells* (Dundalk 1975) 10-25, and by Harbison, I, 108-111. Harbison rejects the generally accepted interpretation of the sculptures on the eastern cross head. Instead of the multiplication of the loaves and fishes, with David and his harp filling the space alongside, he prefers an identification of David playing before Saul. This is unsatisfactory for a number of reasons. It destroys the eucharistic symbolism which, as Ó Carragáin (see note 10) has shown, unites the subjects at the top of the cross; it fails to explain the large number of heads at the top of the panel; and it leaves the two fishes below isolated and meaningless. While the carving of David playing his harp may seem out of place, the author of the psalms was a mobile figure on the crosses: he occurs in a similar format within the Last Judgement scenes at Monasterboice (Muiredach's Cross) and Durrow.

[10]E Ó Carragáin, 'The meeting of St Paul and St Anthony: visual and literary uses of a eucharistic motif' in *Keimelia: studies in medieval archaeology and history in memory of Tom Delany*, ed G MacNiocaill and P Wallace (Galway 1989) 15-20.

[11]Henry, 218.

Crucifixion below[12] and St Matthew is shown as an angel lifting a medallion containing the *agnus dei*. This latter carving is surely derived from early christian images of angels, like that in the vault of S. Vitale at Ravenna, and has no counterpart in the Book of Kells. While the sculpture of the cross head could be read as a *Majestas*, it can equally well be seen as an image of Christ between two beasts, following the text of the canticle of Habakkuk: 'In the midst of two animals you will be revealed'. As Professor Ó Carragáin has stressed, in the Roman office this canticle was sung every Friday morning at lauds.[13] It is worth noting that on the Ruthwell Cross the image of Christ between the beasts is depicted immediately below the *agnus dei*. A further complexity comes with the attributes carried by Christ, the cross and the flowering rod.

Elsewhere in Irish sculpture, these attributes help to define Christ as Judge, as at Monasterboice and Durrow.[14] Anyone familiar with Irish carving would immediately make the association with the Last Judgement, though that is not how the cross head has been interpreted by most commentators. The composition at Kells is thus unusual and ingenious — a conflation of the Last Judgement with the Apocalyptic Vision. Almost deliberately, the sculptor appears to have left open a range of possible meanings and symbolic allusions. It calls to mind the words of the Irish biblical scholar, Diarmait, who warned that he would leave 'opportunities for greater understanding to the readers themselves, if they wish to add things'.[15] The ambiguity and mystery of the image — particularly the way it is formulated — invite comparison with some of the complex pictures in the Book of Kells, though it must be stressed that the iconography itself has no obvious counterpart in the manuscript.

Helen Roe had different reasons for connecting the sculpture and the Book, describing the Tower Cross as a 'manuscript cross' on account of the profusion of its surface decoration and the similarity of many of the ornamental patterns.[16] While she did not specify the parallels she had in mind, she was probably referring to examples like the four interlocked men on the west face or a panel on the south side, where a section of interlace is stretched between pairs of animals. There is no doubt that these do find echoes in the book, but even here the analogies are far from precise. What is

---

[12]A bird is associated with the Crucifixion on a number of other crosses: it appears at the foot of Christ at Monasterboice (Muiredach's Cross) and at Clonmacnois (Cross of the scriptures), and above Christ's head at Durrow (both crosses) and Termonfechin, Harbison, I, 275, 280. Citing Visser, Harbison suggests it was meant to be an eagle, representing the Resurrection.

[13]Ó Carragáin (note 10 above) 4-5.

[14]Christ is shown in Last Judgement scenes with the cross and flowering rod at Arboe, Armagh, Donaghmore (Down), Durrow, Clonmacnois (Cross of the Scriptures), Monasterboice (Muiredach's Cross), and Termonfechin. The most recent discussion of the iconography of the cross head at Kells can be found in Harbison, I, 110-11 and 299. He describes it as a *Majestas Domini* with elements from the Last Judgement.

[15]Cited by K Hughes, *Early christian Ireland: introduction to the sources* (London 1972) 199.

[16]Roe (note 9 above) 10-11.

far more striking are the *differences* between the sculpture and the painted decoration: nowhere in Irish sculpture can one find the lithe, agile cats which fill the pages of the manuscript, and the bewildered birds are very rare.[17] It was not until the twelfth century, at Annaghdown (Galway) that Irish sculptors began to transform mouldings or borders into monstrous, elongated beasts, as happens so often in the Book of Kells.[18] Most noticeable, however, is the fact that the christian iconography on the crosses draws on a completely different set of images from those found in the gospel books. This of course reflects the very different functions of sculpture and illumination: one intimately related to a text and reserved for an exclusive audience; the other a public declaration of christian beliefs.

One of the main reasons why historians have been tempted to compare the cross and the book is their supposed similarity in date. It has been taken for granted that the Tower Cross is the earliest of those surviving at Kells, the assumption being that it was carved not long after the monastery's foundation in 804/7.[19] Françoise Henry had no doubt about this, declaring confidently in her 1967 book that 'the monastery of Kells shows from the start a vigorous artistic activity'.[20] She had the Tower Cross very much in mind. But as far as sculpture is concerned, confirmation of this 'vigorous artistic activity' is hard to find.

The Latin inscription on the base of the cross, recording the names of St Patrick and St Columba, has been taken as one of the signs of an 'early' date. Françoise Henry and Liam de Paor both argued that the inscription specifically refers to the unusual circumstances of the founding of Kells. While a dedication to St Columba is to be expected, the joint dedication with St Patrick is surprising. As the founding saint of Armagh, Patrick was of course the champion of the rival *paruchia*, which was seeking to impose its authority throughout the country, to some extent at the expense of Kells and Iona. Françoise Henry adopted a 'charitable' interpretation of this evidence, seeing the foundation of Kells as an act of benevolence, with Armagh providing a place of refuge for the Columban monks as they tried to escape the Vikings. The inscription, she suggested, 'would then appear as

---

[17]Some of the animals depicted on the Clonmacnois group of crosses come closest to those in the Book of Kells: the cross fragment discovered in 1955 (Harbison, I, catalogue no 57), decorated with two enormous affronted lions, can be compared with the cats at the top left of folio 29r in the Book of Kells. I am sure Hicks (note 7 above, 16) was right to include this fragment with the early sculptures from Clonmacnois. A recent attempt to attribute it to the Romanesque era is not convincing, N Edwards, 'Two sculptural fragments from Clonmacnois', *JRSAI* 114 (1984) 59-60.

[18]H G Leask, *Irish churches and monastic buildings* (Dundalk 1955) I, 157-58.

[19]F Henry, *Irish high crosses* (Dublin 1964) 60; F Henry, *Irish art during the Viking invasions (800-1020)* (London 1967) 151; Roe (note 9 above) 8; Calvert (note 8 above) 295-96; N Edwards (note 8 above) 31; L de Paor, 'The high crosses of Tech Theille (Tihilly), Kinnitty, and related sculpture' in *Figures from the past: studies on figurative art in christian Ireland in honour of Helen M Roe*, ed E Rynne (Dublin 1987) 147-48; Richardson and Scarry (note 8 above) 18, 39-40.

[20]Henry (1967, note 19 above) 70.

commemorating this gift'.[21] Liam de Paor has interpreted the inscription in more prosaic and political terms, regarding it as a 'document of compromise', in which Armagh's primacy was formally acknowledged in return for recognition of the new Columban house.[22]

There is however no proof that the inscription refers to the foundation of the monastery at all. It is known that Armagh had a cross dedicated to St Columba and nobody has felt the need to adduce a political explanation for this.[23] And even if the inscription does have political overtones, there are other periods in the history of Kells when such an inscription might be equally explicable: the reign of abbot Máel Brigte mac Tornáin for example, who was already abbot of Armagh, when appointed to Kells in 891.[24] A joint dedication to Patrick and Columba would have been singularly appropriate during his abbacy.

Some scholars have turned to arguments involving form and design to try to confirm a date in the first half of the ninth century. The location of the Crucifixion on the shaft, rather than within the cross head, has for example been seen as an 'early' feature (pl 83). It is an arrangement that is also found at Clonmacnois (South Cross). One recent commentator has suggested that 'its position on the shaft indicates that these crosses belong to a period before it was customary to place it on the crosshead'.[25] It is hard to follow this reasoning, which reflects a Darwinian insistence that things must evolve in an orderly sequence. One glance at the Tower Cross indicates that the arrangement was devised as a way of devoting more space to the Crucifixion and giving it greater prominence. This particular iconography of the Crucifixion, which is related to a series of metal plaques, could not have been fitted into the cross head without doing great violence to the design.[26] The location of the subject is better explained in visual and religious terms, rather than by evolutionary patterns.

If one forgets old assumptions and looks with an unjaundiced eye at the sculpture, it soon becomes apparent that the Tower Cross belongs with the midland scripture crosses — Monasterboice, Durrow, Clonmacnois and the Market cross at Kells, as argued by Macalister long ago.[27] These crosses

---

[21]Henry (1967, note 19 above) 20, 138.

[22]de Paor (note 19 above) 146-47.

[23]A Hamlin, 'Crosses in early Ireland: the evidence from the written sources' in Ryan, 138-40.

[24]Herbert, 74-77.

[25]Edwards (note 8 above) 25. A similar view was put forward by Henry (1967, note 19 above) 151.

[26]The relationship between the Crucifixions at Kells and Clonmacnois (south) are discussed by D Kelly, 'Crucifixion plaques in stone at Clonmacnois and Kells', *Irish Arts Review Yearbook, 1990-1* (Dublin) 204-09.

[27]R A S Macalister, *Muiredach abbot of Monasterboice, AD 890-923* (Dublin 1914) 21. It is not possible in this context to give a complete list of all the connections between the Tower Cross and the crosses at Monasterboice, Clonmacnois (Cross of the Scriptures) and Durrow. It is however worth noting that the winged beasts either side of Christ as Judge at Kells are very similar to those depicted within the vinescroll on the south side of Muiredach's Cross. Moreover, the striped drapery

were products of a single sculptural workshop — a workshop I like to call Muiredach's workshop, after the great cross at Monasterboice. Most of the christian subjects on the Tower Cross are repeated almost exactly elsewhere in the group, sometimes with precisely the same iconographical arrangements. On the Market Cross for example, one can see the same awkward squeezing of Abraham and Isaac into the south arm of the cross and an almost identical depiction of David and the lion on the southern end. The scene with the three Hebrews in the furnace, with the soldiers stoking faggots on the fire, reproduces that on the west cross at Monasterboice.[28] The *agnus dei* recurs at Durrow. There is no doubt that the sculptors of the Tower Cross had access to the same iconographical models as Muiredach's workshop.

The style of the carving on the Tower Cross appears to be flatter than that on the midland scripture crosses, but this is because the surfaces are badly decayed. In the few places where the carving is well preserved, as in the face and body of Christ the Judge (pl 84), one encounters the same distinctive, rounded modelling. Even the circular-shaped face of Christ, adorned with curly hair, recalls the cheerful chubby faces of Muiredach's Cross (pl 87). Without wanting to get too Morellian in approach, it is also worth noticing that the sculptor uses exactly the same trick of curving the hemline up across the thigh — a trick which was ultimately borrowed from the illuminators.[29]

I hope I have said enough to show that however one looks at the Tower Cross — whether on the basis of iconography, style or technique — it is difficult to believe that many years separate it from the great series of scripture crosses. But what significance does this have for the Book of Kells? It confirms — if confirmation was needed — that the relationship between the Tower Cross and the Book is at best a rather distant one. But it does open up the possibility of a relationship of a rather different kind. If the Tower Cross was carved by the same workshop that produced the midland scripture crosses, as I believe it was, then it must have been carved about the same time as Muiredach's Cross at Monasterboice. If one accepts the conventional identification of Muiredach with the abbot who died in 924,[30] then the Tower Cross must presumably belong to the early years of the tenth century. Now the abbot of Kells at this time was of course none other than Máel Brigte mac Tornáin, who held the post jointly with that of Armagh. Is it an accident that the words of his obit in the annals, *comurba Patraic ocus Coluim Cille*,[31] echo the inscription on the Tower Cross,

worn by Christ in the Crucifixion scene at Kells finds one of its few parallels in stone on the West Cross at Monasterboice.

[28] The iconography of the three Hebrews in the fiery furnace is discussed by Harbison, I, 225-27. Seven examples are listed, those at Monasterboice and Kells being particularly alike.

[29] See for example angels' hems in the Book of Kells, folios 27v and 32v; also the hem of the seated figure drinking from a chalice, folio 201v.

[30] *AFM*, II (AD 922) 611; *AU²* (AD 924) 377. The inscription is discussed in Harbison, I, 364.

[31] *AU²* (AD 927) 378; see also Herbert, 74.

PATRICII ET COLUMBE CR[UX].[32] There is one further coincidence: Mael
Brigte's deputy as abbot of Armagh was Muiredach of Monasterboice.[33]

Mael Brigte and Muiredach were both powerful and influential men, who
towered over the ecclesiastical politics of southern Brega in the years
around 900. When the abbot of Monasterboice died in 924 he was described
as 'chief counsellor of all the men of Brega'.[34] His superior, Mael Brigte was
a diplomat of the highest order. His skilful diplomacy brought a halt to a
major battle in 892 and in 913 he charged off to Munster, where he had
sufficient authority to negotiate the release of a Welsh hostage.[35] He was the
first abbot of Kells to be styled comarb of Colum Cille and, as Máire Herbert
has shown, it was during his reign that Kells became the undisputed head
of the Columban federation.[36] It is not impossible that the commissioning of
high crosses played some part in the status these men acquired. The
prestige of Kells must have been in the ascendant in the 880s and 890s,
particularly when it became clear that the shrine and relics of Columba
would not be returning to Iona.[37] The carving of ornate crosses in the
decades around 900 could be seen as another symptom of this general
aggrandisement of the monastery.

Whatever the role of Muiredach and Mael Brigte, it is clear that the Tower
Cross was carved long after work on the Book of Kells had ceased. Does this
mean that the cross and the manuscript are entirely unrelated? The answer
is no. First, there are certainly parallels in the choice of decorative patterns,
though for the most part these belong to a common stock of insular motifs
and are not specific to the two works. More intriguing are glimpses of the
same visual subtleties and multi-levelled symbolism found in the Book. The
carving of Christ the Judge is one example. Another is the succinct witticism
of the two fishes on the east face: serving on the one hand as part of the
literal description of the feeding of the five thousand, but also as a reminder
of the letter Chi, ingeniously made up of fishes, which themselves serve as
an acrostic for Christ (**pl 82**). As Dr O'Reilly has pointed out,[38] the saltire
cross which we see on the cross is a constant refrain throughout the book.
There is one further connection which nobody seems to have noticed. In
carving their figures, the sculptors made some use of the so-called 'Kells

---

[32]The inscription is discussed by Harbison, I, 362.

[33]It is just conceivable that the link between the Tower Cross and the Monasterboice
crosses was even more direct. In 1934 Macalister claimed to have discovered a
second inscription on the Tower Cross which read: *DO RIGNE MUIREDACH* —
'which Muiredach made', R A S Macalister, 'The ancient inscriptions of Kells', *JRSAI*
64 (1934) 19. I have not been able to trace this inscription on the cross. Macalister
regarded Muiredach as a sculptor, rather than an abbot.

[34]*AU*[2] (AD 924) 377.

[35]*AFM*, I (AD 889 *recte* 892) 548; AU[2] (AD 913) 361.

[36]Herbert, 77.

[37]For the implication of the transfer of the shrine and relics of Colum Cille to Kells in
878 see Henderson, 190-95.

[38]Dr O'Reilly made this point in her lecture entitled 'Exegetical techniques and
liturgical themes in the iconography of the Passion', delivered at the Edinburgh
conference *Age of Migrating Ideas* on the 6th January 1992.

profile'. As we remember from the logo of the 1992 conference, throughout the Book one encounters human profiles with strong chins, large pointed noses and a prominent frontal eye.[39] These one-eyed individuals also turn up on the cross, as in the sculpture of Cain, for example (pl 90). While the masons in general followed the rounded style of the Muiredach workshop, they clearly knew something about those distinctive characters who inhabit the pages of the great gospel book of Columcille. The fact that the Tower Cross mixes the Muiredach style with the 'Kells profile' leads me to think that it was not one of the first scripture crosses, as many scholars have assumed in the past.

---

[39]The 'Kells profile' is discussed by S McNab, 'Styles used in twelfth-century Irish figure sculpture', *Peritia* 6-7 (1987-88) 271-74. Its origin remains a mystery, though Werckmeister has argued for a link with Visigothic art in Spain, O K Werckmeister, 'Three problems of tradition in pre-Carolingian figure style', *PRIA* 63 C, 167-89. From a different context, there is a striking parallel for Kells style heads on a bronze plaque of the fourth-third century BC in the Museo Nazionale Atestino at Este, J V S Megaw, *Art of the European Iron Age* (Bath 1970) 57 and pl 43 (I am grateful to Mary Ann Gelly, who gave me this reference). The pose of Abel on the Tower Cross at Kells echoes that used for the symbol of St Matthew on folio 187 of the Book of Kells, though the poses are reversed. There are also hints of the Kells profile at Clonmacnois (Cross of the Scriptures) and at Durrow (especially Resurrection panel).

High crosses and the Book of Kells

Peter Harbison

The question of when and where the Book of Kells was written has been exercising the minds of many scholars for a very long time without any agreement being reached on a date before or after 800, or on the respective claims for Iona, Kells, or indeed anywhere else, to be its place of origin. A comparison of the codex with the stone high crosses on either side of the North Channel may bring us no nearer to a solution of the problem, but it is nevertheless a worthwhile exercise, as it provides us with a fresh opportunity of looking at the book's illustrations and their analogues in other media, and of pointing to some similarities in ornament between codex and crosses.

Christ features in four of the full-page illustrations in the Book of Kells. Of the two narrative scenes, that on folio 202v has been generally accepted as 'Temptation of Christ on the pinnacle of the temple' (**pl 42**). It is the only one of the four which certainly has no possible comparanda on the high crosses. But, even in manuscripts surviving from the first millennium, the subject is an extremely rare one. The diagnostic feature of the devil with wings is found in three, presumably post-iconoclastic, ninth-century Byzantine manuscripts: the Chludoff Psalter in Moscow,[1] another psalter, MS 61 in the Pantokrator monastery on Mount Athos[2] and the Paris copy of the Homilies of Gregory Nazianzen.[3] A sooty winged devil is also illustrated in the Stuttgart Psalter[4] — a northern French manuscript of the 820s — but there it is the temptation of Christ upon the mountain and not on the temple that is represented. To find the devil in further temple Temptation scenes in western manuscripts we have to wait until the late tenth century, when we encounter him wingless in the northern French Psalter of St Bertin,[5] now in Boulogne, and winged in the so-called Gospels of Otto III[6] in Germany. We do know that a Temptation scene was present among the biblical subjects represented in the lost frescoes painted for the Emperor Louis the Pious in his imperial chapel at Ingelheim on the middle Rhine around 826, but its all-too-abbreviated description by Ermoldus Nigellus[7] does not identify which

[1] M V Shchepkina, *Miniatury Khludovskoi Psaltyri (no 129d)* (Moscow 1977) 92.
[2] Suzy Dufrenne, *L'illustration des psautiers grecs du moyen age, Pantocrator 61, Paris Grec 20, British Museum 40731*, Bibliothèque des Cahiers Archéologiques 1 (Paris 1966) pl 20.
[3] Sirarpie Der Nersessian, 'The illustrations of the Homilies of Gregory of Nazianzus Paris Gr. 510', *Dumbarton Oaks Papers* 16 (1962) 195-228, fig 6, middle.
[4] Henry, 189, fig 42.
[5] Peter Harbison, 'Three miniatures in the Book of Kells', *PRIA* 85 C (1985) pl IXa.
[6] ibid, pl IXb. Ernst Günther Grimme, *Das Evangeliar Kaiser Ottos III. im Domschatz zu Aachen* (Freiburg 1984) 30. Another late-tenth-century example in the Golden Evangeliar from Echternach is illustrated in Henry, 190, fig 43.
[7] Harbison (note 5 above) 187, note 42.

of the three Temptation scenes was illustrated, nor does it inform us whether or not the devil was painted with wings.

Because the Book of Kells,[8] the Stuttgart Psalter and the Ingelheim frescoes are probably the earliest known representations of the devil in medieval art, it is quite likely, as Gertrud Schiller[9] implies, that the Temptation was a newly invented composition of the Carolingian era, and it was perhaps its very novelty which led the Book of Kells illuminator to choose this rare subject for depiction, rather than to illustrate some other better-known, and visually longer-established, New Testament scene. Apart from the Book of Kells, more than half of the first-millennium manuscripts which illustrate a Temptation scene, and the majority of those showing the devil with wings, are psalters, so that there is quite a possibility that the Book of Kells illuminator may have derived some of the ideas for his Temptation scene from a psalter. We are obviously not in the position of being able to say where he may have seen his model, or where it was painted, but as the earliest surviving Carolingian psalters with narrative biblical illustrations — the Corbie, Utrecht and Stuttgart Psalters[10] — all emanated from northern France some time around the first third of the ninth century, there may well have been some link between a northern French psalter and the Book of Kells. In its decoration, the Corbie Psalter offers interesting comparisons with the Book of Kells as seen, for instance, in the similarity of the initial *M* of its *Magnificat*[11] to that on folio 191v of the Book of Kells, but while Henry[12] and others have already commented on the Kells-Corbie links, they are cautious about saying in which direction the borrowings may have gone in the absence of precise dates for the two manuscripts.

The second narrative scene, that on folio 114r (**pl 28**), is normally described as the Arrest of Christ, though doubts have been expressed recently about this identification.[13] Furthermore, the potential for ambivalent and multi-layered interpretation of the scene does not facilitate the task of comparing it with somewhat similar compositions in high cross panels, such as the possible Mocking scenes at Drumcliff, county Sligo (**pl 89**) and at Arboe, county Tyrone.[14] The other two full-page illustrations depicting Christ which remain to be discussed here are more static than narrative. The first of these, on folio 32v (**pl 20**), is difficult to define positively, but it is widely presumed *not* to be a *Majestas Domini*. Elsewhere,[15] I have tentatively identified its subject as being a variant of the Raised Christ motif, which is known to have decorated the apse of Roman churches as far back as the

---

[8]Teddy Brunius, 'Enter the Devil' in *Riforma Religiosa e Arti nell'Epoca Carolingia*, ed Alfred A Schmid, Atti del XXIV Congresso Internazionale di Storia dell'Arte, (Bologna 1983) 147-50.
[9]Gertrud Schiller, *Iconography of Christian art* (London 1971) I, 143-44.
[10]Wolfgang Braunfels, *Die Welt der Karolinger und ihre Kunst* (Munich 1968) 155-79.
[11]ibid, pl 77.
[12]Henry, 215.
[13]Harbison (note 5 above) 184-86. See also Jennifer O'Reilly in this volume.
[14]Harbison, III, fig 878.
[15]Harbison (note 5 above) 181-84.

fifth century,[16] and which may also have been present in the frescoes at Ingelheim. The arc around Christ's head may even be an echo of the Roman church apse. If my interpretation of folio 32v be anywhere near correct — and in the Kells adaptation from the original model(s) we must allow for manifold changes in both composition and meaning — then this scene may be compared to the Raised Christ panel on the high cross at Durrow in county Offaly (pl 91), which has Christ flanked by two angels above and SS Peter and Paul below.

The fourth of our full-page illustrations is that showing the Virgin and Child on folio 7v (pl 9). Closer in composition to most of the earlier representations of the pair[17] are the carvings on St Martin's and St Oran's crosses on Iona[18] and the cross at Kildalton on Islay.[19] It has, however, usually been overlooked that a simplified carving of the Virgin and Child is found on one Irish cross at Drumcliff, county Sligo, where it can be seen at the end of the south arm (pl 92). However, the lack of angels on the Drumcliff cross shows that it is further removed from the Book of Kells painting than are any of the three Scottish examples.

The echoes of the spiral decoration on some of the canon table columns on folio 5r of the Book of Kells as found on a panel on the south side of the shaft at Drumcliff (pl 93) also suggest that this county Sligo cross is closer to the Book of Kells than has been realised hitherto. Perhaps the comparison has been overlooked heretofore largely because the cross has usually been assigned to around the tenth/eleventh century,[20] but the spiral ornament and the Virgin and Child panel might make a ninth-century date more appropriate for the cross. One of the few other decorational details on Irish high crosses which suggest a link with the Book of Kells is the panel bearing beard-pulling men on the underside of the ring of the Market Cross at Kells (pl 94) which can be compared with a similar detail on folio 188r of the Book of Kells (pl 35). In contrast, the beard-pullers on the north side of the shaft of Muiredach's Cross at Monasterboice (pl 95) are closer in style to those in the Corbie Psalter,[21] though the playful nature of the animals in the

---

[16]Compare C Ihm, *Die Programme der christlichen Apsismalerei vom vierten Jahrhundert bis zur Mitte des achten Jahrhunderts*, Forschungen zur Kunstgeschichte und christlichen Archäologie 4 (Wiesbaden 1960).

[17]For a review of comparable early representations of the Virgin and Child, see Martin Werner, 'The *Madonna and Child* miniature in the Book of Kells', *Art Bulletin* 54 (1972) 1-23, 129-39. Compare also John L Osborne, 'Early medieval painting in San Clemente, Rome: the Madonna and Child in the Niche', *Gesta* 20/2 (1981) 299-310, and Douglas Mac Lean, 'Iona, Armenia and Italy in the early medieval period' in *Atti del Quinto Simposio Internazionale di Arte Armena*, ed B L Zekiyan (Venice 1992) 559-68.

[18]Royal Commission on the Ancient and Historical Monuments of Scotland; *Argyll: an inventory of the monuments*, IV, *Iona* (Edinburgh 1982) 193 (pl B) and 207 (pl B).

[19]W D Lamont, *Ancient & mediaeval sculptured stones of Islay* (Edinburgh 1968) pl VIII, a.

[20]Françoise Henry, *Irish art in the Romanesque period (1020-1170 AD)* (London 1970) 123-26.

[21]Harbison, III, figs 984-85. Compare also folio 253v of the Book of Kells and the contribution of Christian de Mérindol in this volume.

same position on the other three sides enters more into the spirit of the cats and mice on the Chi Rho page, folio 34r of the Book of Kells. It is, indeed, on such small decorational details, rather than the full-page iconographical subjects, that the parallels between Irish high crosses and the Book of Kells depend. It is certainly noticeable that the Irish high cross comparisons adduced here come largely from sites associated with the *paruchia Columbae* — Kells itself, Durrow, Drumcliff and possibly even Monasterboice.[22] They may be seen as being as close to the codex as the Virgin and Child parallels on the Scottish crosses mentioned above and, because of the possibility that the latter may have been copied not from the Book of Kells directly but from the presumably portable model on which the Book of Kells picture depended, we should perhaps conclude that the high cross evidence does not provide adequate proof of the place of origin of the Book of Kells.

Perhaps a more reliable way forward in attempting to solve the question of where the Book of Kells was written would be to try to establish an absolute, or at least a *post-quem*, date for the manuscript, if that should ever prove possible. A date before 804 — when the Columban monastery at Kells is first mentioned in the historical records[23] — would argue strongly in favour of Iona. But after the Vikings had raided the Hebridean island monastery for the second time in 806, when 68 of its monks were killed, conditions there would scarcely have been conducive to the peaceful production of a manuscript of such magnificence. Thus, if the codex could be shown to be later than 806, then its painters would be more likely to have been sitting in the safer surroundings of Kells, whither some of the Iona monks fled for refuge after the Viking depredations.

P.S. It may be of interest to mention that a show of hands taken at the concluding session of the Conference demonstrated that participants in favour of an eighth-century date for the manuscript marginally outnumbered those supporting a ninth-century date, whereas a much larger majority preferred Iona to Kells as the most likely place of origin for the Book.

---

[22]See A O'Kelleher and G Schoepperle, *Betha Colaim Chille: Life of Columcille* (Urbana, Ill. 1918) 96-97, §99, and Herbert, 189, 233 §41 and 258 §41.
[23]AU², 260-61.

The Book of Kells and metalwork

Michael Ryan

I

It would be perverse to deny that the entry in the *Annals of Ulster (AU)* for the year 1006 AD (correctly 1007) refers to a manuscript other than the Book of Kells. The entry notes the theft of the 'great gospel-book of Colum Cille', described as 'the chief relic of the western world' which was wickedly stolen from the *erdamh* of the stone church of Kells on account of its 'wrought shrine'. It was recovered after two months and twenty nights 'its gold having been taken off it and a sod over it'. Variants of the entry are to be found in *Chronicon Scotorum (CS)* s.a. 1005 and the Annals of the Four Masters *(AFM)* which recount essentially the same details but *CS* states that its recovery was 'before the end of a quarter after its gold and silver had been stolen off it'. In presenting the entries to you in this way, I am being a little mischievous because I have conflated the translations of a number of learned authorities who by no means agree about the significance of the detail contained in the laconic notices. The questions raised by these accounts are important and it is worthwhile examining them a little further here.

The subject of the annals has most recently, and in my view, most skilfully been surveyed by Meehan.[1] He has concluded that the *AU* entry is unlikely to refer to a treasure binding — a form of book cover not known to survive in Ireland. It should probably be taken to indicate a shrine of box form, a type of covering which is well-represented in the Irish tradition. (Of the eight surviving Irish book shrines, two are associated with the Columban tradition, the Misach and the Shrine of the Cathach, the latter probably made in Kells itself towards the end of the eleventh century[2]). It seems that

---

[1] Bernard Meehan, 'The history of the manuscript' in *Kells commentary*, 317-29. See also Ludwig Bieler, *Ireland: harbinger of the middle ages* (London 1963) 113; Henry, 150-52; Henderson, 179, 194-95. On the annals see *AU*, I, 518-19; *AU²* 438-39; W M Hennessy, *Chronicon Scotorum: a chronicle of Irish affairs from the earliest times to AD 1135* (Dublin 1866) 244-45; also *AFM*, II, 758 s.a. 1006. The relevant manuscripts of *AU* are TCD, MS 1282 (formerly H.1.8.) and Oxford, Bodleian Library, MS Rawlinson B 489. The significance of the entries relating to Kells are discussed in an unpublished manuscript catalogue of TCD manuscripts compiled in 1846 by J H Todd, A descriptive catalogue of some MSS in TCD Library (TCD, MS 1826a, p 15).
[2] The surviving Irish book shrines of early medieval date are as follows: in the National Museum of Ireland: the Lough Kinale shrine, the *Soiscél Molaise*, the Shrine of the Cathach, the Misach, the Shrine of the Stowe Missal, the *Domhnach Airgid*; in Trinity College Library, the Shrine of the Book of Dimma and in private possession, the Shrine of the Book of Moling. See E P Kelly in this volume.

Henderson[3] agrees with this view as he tentatively suggests that the Book of Kells first came to Ireland from Iona in 878 AD along with the other relics of Columba and that its cover may have been of ninth- or tenth-century Irish workmanship. He invokes instances of the enshrinement of other books at about this time: the cover made at the behest of Fland Sinna for the Book of Durrow and that recorded as having been made for the Book of Armagh c937 AD by Donnchad, son of Fland. He appears to suggest that the manufacture of a cover/reliquary for Kells would have been an appropriate benefaction for a prominent Uí Néill king prompted by contemporary fashion. He does however also hold out the possibility that the cover stolen in 1007 formed part of the original making of Kells and if so 'it seems certain that the cover would be pictorial, figurative, in view of the interest in illustration shown throughout the book'. He goes on to invoke the conservatism of the standing evangelist symbols on the front of the *Soiscél Molaise*, made in the early eleventh-century for an abbot of Devinish, as being perhaps dependent on a famous exemplar, the implication being that this might have been Kells itself. He seems not to allow for the possibility, if not probability, that the famous exemplar for the shrine was to be seen in the pages of the manuscript which it was made to protect.[4] The Athlone plaque and 'a number of other surviving openwork Irish book covers' suggest to Henderson another possible reconstruction of the lost Kells cover.[5]

To Henry the cover mentioned in the annals *must* have been a treasure binding because the disappearance of the folios from the beginning and end of the manuscript 'is as we have seen, readily explained by the theft in 1007 and the subsequent tearing of the jewelled binding and its adjacent pages'.[6] The argument that there might have been a metal-ornamented cover on Kells is, presumably, based on the frequent occurrence of treasure bindings on important continental manuscripts of the early medieval period. In an insular context it is also to an extent dependent on the late Old English colophon written into the Book of Lindisfarne by Aldred, provost of Chester-le-Street in 970 AD, which states that the book was written by Eadfrith, bishop of Lindisfarne church and that Ethelwald, also a bishop, 'impressed it on the outside and covered it' and that the anchorite, Bilfrith 'forged the ornaments which are on it on the outside and adorned it with gold and with gems and with gilded-over silver — pure metal'.[7] This seems

---

[3] Henderson, 194-95.

[4] R Ó Floinn (catalogue entry) in *Treasures of Ireland: Irish art 3000 BC to 1500 AD*, ed M Ryan (Dublin 1983) 161-63.

[5] There is no compelling evidence that the Athlone plaque and its analogues functioned as bookcovers — indeed the precedents are strongly against it. It is much more likely that the openwork plaques formed part of larger compositions such as crosses, altars, shrines and the like on which figured scenes were an important component of the ornament. See Ryan (note 4 above) 120 and Dorothy Kelly, 'Crucifixion plaques in stone at Clonmacnoise and Kells' in *Irish Arts Review* (Carrick-on-Suir 1990-91) 204-09, for an interesting suggestion about the relationship of crucifixion plaques to high cross iconography.

[6] Henry, 152; eadem, *Irish art during the Viking invasions: 800-1020 AD* (London 1967) 69.

[7] Conveniently discussed in Alexander, *Insular manuscripts*, 39-40 with refs.

to be a clear description of an elaborately decorated cover with applied metal ornaments but there may be an element of ambiguity here as the cover was already decorated by Ethelwald with embossed ornament in the manner, we might suggest, of the Stoneyhurst Gospels or those book covers frequently illustrated in manuscript illumination of the time.[8] Could Bilfrith's work have been on the front of a box? It is worth noting that the gospel book from which the readings were made at stational masses in Rome in the *Ordo Romanus primus* was invariably carried in a case (*capsa*) and on conclusion of the lections returned to the Lateran.[9]

The idea of a cased evangeliary was therefore known to the liturgists of the western church from the later seventh century onwards, certainly among those churches in southern Ireland, Northumbria and southern England which prided themselves on their communion with the See of Peter. It is difficult to believe that such a detail would have been missed by such devoted Romans as Wilfrid or Benedict Biscop or by the attentive students of John the Archcantor. Although such things cannot be proved, I would suggest that this Roman liturgical practice may have given rise to the Irish tradition of book enshrinement. The ritual of ceremonially returning the codex to a secure place emphasized not alone the solemn importance of the gospel book but also the need to safeguard so precious a testament to God's goodness. It is a small step from this show of reverence to enshrinement.

The precedents in the insular world, insofar as we know them, strongly favour the view that the cover referred to in the annals was in fact a box-reliquary. In instances where a manuscript remained accessible in a box which could be reopened the distinction is hard to make between a *capsa* in the Roman manner and a reliquary. If the internal evidence of Kells itself may be invoked, where books are illustrated, a simple panelled arrangement of the cover is depicted and nothing that approaches a jewel-encrusted binding. The illustrations have more in common with the comparatively simple covers shown in the bookcase in the Ezra portrait page of the *Codex Amiatinus*. This is especially true of the portrait of John in Kells (folio 291v) where the cover clearly bears the lozenge ornament which occurs on five of the nine bookcovers shown in *Amiatinus*.[10] I have been unable to find anywhere in the canon of early insular illumination a depiction of an elaborate jewelled bookcover.

Linguistic analysis is not of much help to us in deciding what sort of cover was stolen in 1007. Both the TCD and the Bodleian copies of the Annals of Ulster were written by Ruaidhrí Ó Luinín, the former as far as the year 1489 and the latter as far as 1510. The entry relating to Kells in TCD, MS 1282 at folio 54r is an addition in the original hand. Insufficient space was available

---

[8] For example in the bookcase depicted on the Ezra page of *Codex Amiatinus*, folio V. Alexander, *Insular manuscripts*, pl 27.

[9] ' ... et post hoc praeparato acolyto .. iuxta ambonem cum capsa in qua subdiaconus idem ponit evangelium ut sigilletur. Acolytus autem regionis eiusdem cuius et subdiaconus est revocat evangelium ad Lateranis', Andrieu (1948) II, 65.

[10] Alexander, *Insular manuscripts*, pl 27.

to the scribe to give the complete entry and he continued it at the head of the page. Unfortunately the descriptive phrase is trimmed off. Oxford, Bodleian, MS Rawlinson B 489 is a later recension of the work by Ó Luinín and the entry is completely incorporated in the text and is intact. I am deeply grateful to Dr Máire Herbert who kindly studied the entry (pl 96) in order to put the reading beyond question. The entry describes the Great Gospels (*Soiscelae mor*) as *Primhmind iarthair domain* (the chief relic of the western world) and makes it clear that the theft was *arai in comdaigh doendai* '... on account of its cumhdach/reliquary/cover *doendai*'. Dr Herbert states that the word *doendai* has no length-marks although these are shown elsewhere in the manuscript. The word has inspired a variety of translations. Todd in his 1846 manuscript catalogue rendered it as 'human' ornament but revised it twice to 'singular' and 'unique'. Hennessy in the Rolls Series edition of *AU* translated it as 'ornamental cover' while the latest editors of the text, MacAirt and MacNiocaill, preferred to revert to Todd's 'human ornamentation'.[11] Henry follows the translation proposed by Bieler who renders the words as 'wrought shrine' and which she regarded as more logical than the other translations.[12] O'Donovan in his edition of *AFM* calls it a 'singular cover'. Hennessy's edition of *AU* renders the qualifier as *dendai*, a slender 'd' while MacAirt and MacNiocaill give it as *doendai*.

The meaning of *doendai* is of more than passing interest because if we follow Hennessy, the word would carry the meanings 'made', 'accomplished' or Bieler's 'wrought'. If the latter, then 'human', perhaps in the sense of 'profane' or 'secular' rather than, say, 'figured' might be implied. The meaning 'made' is the choice of Byrne and Joynt in 1959 in the definition which they give to the word *dénta*.[13] Marstrander[14] quoting both *AU* and *AFM* derives the qualifier from the word *dáin*, delicate, fine. For what it is worth O'Donovan's *AFM* gives *daenda* which might be closer to a word signifying 'wrought' than *doendai*. The vagaries of orthography in the period when *AU* was compiled may render fine phonetic analysis difficult if not pointless. The best that can be said is that the word may imply meanings such as profane, secular, made, accomplished and even delicate or elaborate, all of which seem to carry an implication of manufacture. To render it as 'human ornament' creates an unwarranted ambiguity — is it man-made or figurative? The temptation to opt for the latter to some extent influenced Henderson's otherwise very even-handed approach to the question. The balance of probability is that 'wrought' or something like it is intended.

The word *cumdac* or *comdag* which appears here in the possessive case is not definitive. A variant of *cumtach*, it can mean either a cover, a case or shrine

---

[11]Meehan (note 1 above).

[12]Henry (1967, note 6 above) 69; Bieler (note 1 above).

[13]Mary E Byrne and Maud Joynt, *DIL* (1959) 24. They give the meanings 'skilfully fashioned, elaborate' and quote as their authority *comdaig dendai* from *AU*. As the reading on which they depended is not accurate, the relevance to the word discussed in their dictionary entry is moot.

[14]Carl Marstrander, *DIL* (1913) 27.

or more simply, ornament (eg *lebor chumdaigh* — a decorated book).[15]
However the stress laid by *AU* on the fact that the great gospel book was
'the chief relic of the western world' should be taken to favour the
interpretation that the object was a shrine.

To sum up, there is thus no firm evidence that the original manufacture of
the Book of Kells included the collaboration of a fine-art metalworker. All
that the evidence permits us to say is that at some point in its existence the
book was either provided with ornaments for its cover or, more likely, an
ornamental case or reliquary decorated in precious metal. We are not
entitled to claim with any certainty that the covering bore figured devices
not is it permissible for us to relate the loss of folios to the event in question:
there is for example no evidence that the book actually lost its binding in the
theft, the record testifies only to the removal of its gold and silver.[16] The
annals are likewise silent about what action was taken by the authorities of
Kells to repair the damage; the subsequent use of blank folios for the
copying of documents recording important transactions implies that the
book was safely kept and that the records added were considered unlikely
to be lost.

II

If we consider the nature of the ornament of Kells and its relationship to
that on approximately contemporary metalwork (enquiring parenthetically
what contemporary metalwork means when there is some uncertainty as to
the date of the manuscript) it becomes at once apparent that the range of
relevant motifs is broadly speaking the familiar one of interlace, animal and
human interlace, spiral and trumpet scrollwork, key and fret patterns, to
which we may also add, perhaps, some of the animals unencumbered by
tracery. The impression is further confirmed by features such as the
roundels with step- and cross-devices (eg canon tables folios 2v and 3) and
the cross-carpet page which are clearly translations into a painted medium
of the polychrome studs of so much of seventh- and eighth-century
jewellery in these islands. A similar effect like cloisonné enamels is to be
seen on the throne of the Virgin.

---

[15]*DIL* (1967) 627. However it is worth noting that the book shrines, the Shrine of the
Cathach and the Soiscél Molaise, are each called *cumtach* in their inscriptions. The
making of the shrine for St Patrick's Bell is denoted by the verb *rocumtaig* on the
inscription recording its manufacture. Neither the Cross of Cong nor the Lismore
Crosier is called *cumtach* in their inscriptions commemorating the patrons and
artisans: each is referred to by the word *gressa*. Françoise Henry, *Irish art in the
Romanesque period: 1020-1170 AD* (London 1970) 89, 94, 97, 107; Ó Floinn (note 4
above). There would appear to be strong contemporary evidence that in the
eleventh- and twelfth-century Irish church, the word *comdac/comdag* carried the
primary meaning of box-reliquary. The late fourteenth- or early fifteenth- re-
working of the Shrine of the Book of Dimma carries an inscription which refers to it
as a *mind*. Ó Floinn (note 4 above) 173.
[16]The subsequent vicissitudes of the manuscript could account for a greater loss than
actually happened. See Meehan (note 1 above).

The form of the Temple on the Temptation page (folio 202v) has been thought to reflect to some extent that of the house-shaped reliquaries of the insular tradition. The sources of this illustration have been shown to be very complex[17] which may account for the obvious differences between the Temple and the portable reliquaries — for example, the unsatisfactory 'props' at either end of the structure the pictorial origins of which O'Reilly has ingeniously explained — and the fact that there is a doorway in the long-side, a feature neither of the shrines nor of the surviving, if somewhat later, Irish stone churches. The figure in the doorway evokes the sources which have given us the Christ in Majesty on the scripture crosses and the pose of that on the Alfred Jewel. The flabella brandished by angels on a number of folios are another matter. No insular example survives — that said to have been Columba's own having been lost in the eleventh century.

We can conclude in broad terms that the aesthetic which informs the more ambitious insular metalwork of the eighth and ninth centuries has much in common with the ornament of Kells. This is especially true of two pieces, the Derrynaflan Paten and Ardagh Chalice (**pls 97 and 98**) which carry a repertoire of ornament which most closely approximates to that of Kells. That is to say that interlace, animal interlace, anthropomorphic motifs, fret, key, spiral and trumpet patterns occur mainly in alternating panels in a rhythm familiar from the border decoration of Kells pages. The paten, additionally carries small scenes of obvious symbolic importance. In qualifying them in that way, it is not implied that abstract motifs lacked a significance beyond the ornamental but it must be said that interpretations of them are little short of pure conjecture at this stage. Indeed it is highly likely that the arrangement of scrollwork on, say, the Chi Rho page (folio 34) was at least an aid to meditation if not much more, for those who had privileged access to the book.[18] It is more than likely that the actual work of illumination was in itself a devotional exercise. It has long been the contention of scholars such as Elbern and Stevenson[19] that animal ornament in metalwork may carry a symbolic significance which is in part recoverable as representations of the beasts of creation — those of Genesis, the creatures of earth, air and water — and this is taken a good deal further by Lewis.[20]

Arrangements of beasts have long been used to suggest homage to the Creator, the adaptation of the ancient device of symmetrically disposed beasts flanking a vine has numerous and obviously symbolic variants in christian art and is well represented in Kells itself. Many of these often repeated symbolic scenes have analogues in early medieval metalwork from

---

[17]See Jennifer O'Reilly's article in this volume.
[18]Alexander, 'Illumination', 274-75.
[19]V Elbern, 'Ein Frankisches Relquiar-Fragment in Oviedo, die Engerer Burse in Berlin und ihr Umkreis', *Madrider Mitteilungen* 2 (1961) 197-98; R Stevenson, 'The Hunterston Brooch and its significance', *Medieval Archaeology* 18 (1974) 38-40. See also in particular in relation to Kells, Isabel Henderson 'The Book of Kells and the snake-boss motif on Pictish cross-slabs and the Iona crosses' in Ryan, 64-65.
[20]Suzanne Lewis 'Sacred calligraphy: the Chi Rho page in the Book of Kells', *Traditio* 36 (1980) 139-59.

western Europe and it is wrong to ignore the importance of small metalwork objects as a medium for the transmission of iconography of a simple type but there are far too many precedents in manuscript painting and in christian sculpture to make any metalwork connection here particularly obvious. The eagle seizing the salmon in Kells, folio 250v, is a motif widely seen in medieval manuscript illumination; it is combined in the evangelist symbol twice in the Book of Armagh. It is represented on Migration Period helmets and other objects. It was a eucharistic symbol but also carried a freight of other meanings which varied with time. In insular hagiography there is a noteworthy episode in the *Life* of Cuthbert where the saint is sustained by a fish caught by an eagle.

I do not believe that we have in Kells any compelling evidence that the illuminators worked closely with, or were heavily influenced by, fine metalsmiths practising their arts in adjacent ateliers. There are very few parallels in the ornament of Kells to known motifs in metalwork that are so close as to suggest direct and immediate interaction. For example, there are no convincing metalwork comparanda for the snub-nosed feline beast which is so much a part of the Kells repertoire. The treatment of interlace shows an interesting divergence from the manner in which a metalworker would have treated it: the corners are sometimes broadened in a manner difficult to render in filigree wire and not represented to my knowledge in contemporary or earlier engraved and cast interlace. The treatment of the spirals is a case in point. As Henry has shown, these are now fully integrated into the repertoire and endings are not confined to the bird, trumpet and roll family. Instead the spiral may incorporate beasts and birds and men in a manner unprecedented in the metalworker's canon.

Additionally, the Kells ornamental repertoire incorporates plant-scroll ornament. This is wholly absent from metalwork found in Ireland and rare in metalwork in Scotland but it is known on Northumbrian pieces. It is of course widespread on sculpture in northern Britain and comparatively infrequent in Irish stone carvings.[21]

There are some interesting parallels between the decoration of the St Germain finials together with those from Gausel in Norway and the ornament of Kells.[22] These include the motif of the head in the jaws of a beast, the tightly-wound spiral boss with snakes which Isabel Henderson has so convincingly traced in Pictish sculpture and in the crosses of Iona. Much of the ornament of both shares a common ultimate inspiration in metalwork.[23] If any piece of metalwork has claims to be closely allied with

---

[21]Harbison, I, 323-24.

[22]Most recently discussed by L Webster in *The work of angels: masterpieces of Celtic metalwork, sixth to ninth centuries AD*, ed S Youngs (London 1989)145.

[23]Isabel Henderson, 'Pictish art and the Book of Kells' in *Ireland in early medieval Europe*, ed D Whitelock, R McKitterick and D Dumville (Cambridge 1982) 79-105; idem, 'The Book of Kells and the snake-boss motif on Pictish cross-slabs and the Iona crosses' in Ryan, 56-65 (pp 64-65). See also Royal Commission on Ancient

the ornament of Kells, it is that. However the lack of a provenance for the finials is to say the least unfortunate. Henderson has likewise stressed the relationship of the Kells feline, surely a lion, to the crouching beasts below Paul and Anthony on the Nigg slab, a sophisticated eucharistic composition which as Lewis has pointed out finds echoes in the iconography of Kells.[24]

The sculptural parallels, both with Pictish slabs and freestanding crosses of the Iona tradition, seem to me to be much closer than anything in metalwork and reflect perhaps partly the probable origin of the manuscript but also the fact that little is known of ambitious metalwork at the appropriate period from the hinterland either of Kells or Iona. The surviving major religious pieces of the later eighth and ninth century in Ireland belong in the main to the south midlands and north Munster although the Clonmore shrine, the Donore Hoard and various personal ornaments show that the highest quality metalwork was present in the midlands and Ulster in the seventh to the ninth centuries. Little survives from the Columba's home territory of the north-west. The north-east (including the lands of Dal Riada in Ireland) has produced a range of eighth/ninth-century pieces of distinction mainly personal ornaments. Some (the Loughan and Ballynagloch Brooches) show some familiarity with the Pictish tradition of highly decorated penannular cloak-fasteners. From co Antrim comes the fine enamelled wood and metal cross in the Hunt Museum, Limerick[25] — but none prompts especial comparison with Kells. Apart from the Monymusk shrine little metalwork of certain ecclesiastical character is know from Scotland at about the period of Kells and comparisons are therefore even more tenuous.

What can we say then about metalwork and Kells? Firstly, that the manuscript shares many generalised characteristics of taste with pieces of relatively late date — the Ardagh Chalice and Derrynaflan Paten — which may be of some chronological value. Secondly, that comparisons with metalwork are general in the main rather than particular which may suggest little contemporary interaction between the illuminators and metalworkers. Manuscript illumination in the tradition which gave rise to Kells had developed considerably — perhaps for as long as a century — from the stage at which interaction between the arts had been close. The best comparisons in another medium for the Kells decorative style are in sculpture as Henderson has shown beyond doubt.

We should expect that manuscript painting and goldsmithing should have diverged: they are two quite different arts and much of the former, of necessity derived from exotic models, was presumably constantly refreshed by the developing arts of the church overseas. The painter at his vellum enjoys a flexibility of design, speed of creation and use of colour not

Monuments of Scotland, *Argyll: an inventory of the monuments*, vol 4, Iona (Edinburgh 1982).

[24]Lewis (note 20 above) 155-56, n 69.

[25]P Harbison, 'The Antrim Cross in the Hunt Museum', *North Munster Antiquarian Journal* 20 (1978) 17-40.

available to the artist in metals. Things may be drawn in detail which simply cannot be matched by engraving or casting no matter how clever the metalworker. Ideas adopted by the graphic artist may be transformed and elaborated further and further away from their origins with great speed.

One cannot escape the impression that any cross-fertilisation with metalworking traditions had taken place long before Kells came to be illuminated and that metalworking influences had been already fully absorbed and transformed in monastic scriptoria.

There is nothing in Kells which shares so closely in workshop aesthetics as the Lindisfarne Gospels do. At the stage when Lindisfarne was produced we can see at least two works in metal, both from Ireland, which stand remarkably close to the decoration of that manuscript — the Tara Brooch and the Donore Hoard.[26] The comparisons with the Hunterston Brooch are less strong in my view, but are nonetheless also of importance. In the case of the Tara Brooch we have similar animal ornament but particularly close combination spiral-, trumpet- and stylised animal-head motifs. These are closely matched on the Donore discs where in some sense the technique of production mirrors that of painting. Kells has no such exact comparison.

Durrow, which in so many ways represents a stage in manuscript development from which Kells at least in part descends, has often been regarded as showing close connections with contemporary metalworking style. To some extent this is based on the spiral-decorated carpet page (folio 3v) which is thought to depend on the art of hanging-bowl escutcheons and this is likely to be in part true; of course it goes far beyond these in the number, layout and linking of elements in a manner not possible within the limitations of small metal discs in frames. More stress has been laid on the beast carpet page (folio 192v) and its links with Anglo-Saxon animal ornament as represented on the Sutton Hoo shoulder-clasps. It is not to deny the origin of the patterns to echo Haseloff's view that the beasts had diverged somewhat from their progenitors by the time they make their appearance in Durrow.[27] It is less compelling to compare the layout of the clasps themselves with that of the carpet page as a whole. The origins of the carpet page must be sought elsewhere in the wider traditions of christian book-design. If we reject this we become involved in pointless circular arguments about the inspiration for the layout of ornament on high-quality metalwork in early medieval, partly christianised contexts.

In short, even in Durrow we can see that there was divergence from the hypothetical origins in ornamental metalwork. Durrow has considerably less affinity in its generation with the artistic output of jewellers' workshops than Lindisfarne. Kells also stands somewhat apart from metalwork in its ornament but broadly reflects contemporary taste and broadly fits into the

---

[26]Ryan in Youngs (note 22 above) 66-70.
[27]G Haseloff, 'Insular animal styles' in Ryan, 46.

later part of eighth-century or earlier ninth-century ornamental style as we know it.

The Lough Kinale book shrine: the implications for the manuscripts

Eamonn P Kelly

In 1986 the remains of a metal-covered wooden box were found in Lough Kinale, county Longford, close to a small crannóg. The object was not intact when it was deposited in the lake, having been disassembled with considerable force. The close proximity of the components was such as to suggest that they had been bound together or placed in a bag at the time they were lost. Although a small number of components are missing, a full reconstruction is possible.[1] When intact, the book shrine measured 34.5cm in length, 28.0cm in width and 11.0cm in thickness. Once closed it would not have been possible to gain access to the contents without disassembling the box. For this reason and having regard for the iconographic nature of the decoration, the object has been identified as a reliquary, more precisely a *cumdach* or book shrine. Like many of the other surviving Irish book shrines it consists of a wooden box to which metal plates were nailed, the whole being bound with tubular strips along the sides and corners. The cover (**pl 99**) is dominated by a cross, with cusped sides, decorated with five cast bronze bosses which retain amber studs and four gilt bronze openwork panels of animal interlace. Each of the spaces between the cross arms bears a decorative roundel containing spiral openwork ornament and a central amber stud.

The border consists of four openwork gilt bronze strips laid over backing plates of tinned bronze. Along the top and bottom the decoration takes the form of interlocked peltae, terminating in spirals and lentoid openings, while the other two edges are decorated by a continuous pattern of spirals (**pl 100**). Four domed oval amber studs are placed diagonally at the corners.

Both sides of the shrine bear a central medallion flanked by two smaller medallions (**pl 101**). These are similar to those on the front but each have four projecting animal heads. The ends of the shrine bear fittings which formerly held a heavy leather strap (**pl 102**). Their arrangement is such that the shrine would have been carried on the flat. The base of the shrine is plain.

Discussion
The object is the earliest and largest of the Irish book shrines. Ultimate La Tène ornament is employed freely on the decorated components and many parallels can be drawn with major pieces of eighth-century metalwork. The point should be stressed that the object is not simply a box in which to store

---

[1] A full description of the shrine is given in E P Kelly, 'The Lough Kinale book shrine' in *The age of migrating ideas*, ed R M Spearman and J Higgitt (Edinburgh 1993) 168-74.

a valuable manuscript. It is a reliquary which contained a sacred relic which was not meant to be accessible for reading. The fact that the shrine would need to have been disassembled to extract the contents underlines this point. The carrying-strap implies that the shrine was carried on circuit on occasions and the fact that it was designed to be carried on the flat suggests concern to protect the contents from impact damage which would occur were the shrine to be transported on its side. Damage of this nature is evident, for example, on the Book of Durrow and *codex Usserianus primus*.

Overall, the decoration of the Lough Kinale shrine appears to be a compendium of both early and late eighth-century styles. Certain elements which compare closely with decoration on the Tara brooch, and which might be viewed as early, include the two smaller openwork zoomorphic panels on the interior of the cross arms and the Ultimate La Tène spirals on the side medallions. The border of the cover, particularly the peltae designs, are also stylistically early. Elements which are likely to be stylistically later in date include the projecting animal heads which relate to similar heads on objects such as the Cavan brooch[2] and the two larger zoomorphic panels which relate to animals represented on mounts from Oseberg[3] and on the Ahenny South Cross.[4] The extensive use of amber is also a late feature.[5]

The lay-out of the shrine cover is reminiscent of that found on the carpet pages of insular manuscripts. If the enshrined relic contained such a carpet page and were this to have inspired the decoration of the cover, then this fact could account for the occurrence of both early and late stylistic elements on the shrine — for it is certain that the manuscript would have been of some age when it was enshrined. In the case of the other surviving Irish book shrines or enshrined manuscripts, periods of between one hundred and six hundred and fifty years elapsed between the writing of the manuscripts and their enshrinement. The Lough Kinale book shrine appears to date to the late eighth century so it is likely that one is dealing with a manuscript which may date to the seventh or possibly early eighth century.

As is the case with the Lough Kinale shrine cover, many of the carpet pages found in insular gospel books are dominated by a prominent cross.[6] Cross forms, which are closely comparable to that which occurs on the Lough Kinale book shrine, are to be found on folio 16 of the *Codex Aureus*, a large mid-eighth century gospel generally thought to have been made in Canterbury.[7] The manner in which the border decoration on the Lough

---

[2]*Treasure of Ireland: Irish art 3000 BC to 1500 AD*, ed M Ryan (Dublin 1983) 135-37.

[3]*The work of angels: masterpieces of Celtic metalwork, sixth to ninth centuries AD*, ed S Youngs (London 1989) 118, 158.

[4]P Harbison, 'The Antrim Cross in the Hunt Collection', *North Munster Antiquarian Journal* 20 (1978) 17-40; N Edwards, 'An early group of crosses from the kingdom of Ossory', *JRSAI* 113 (1983) 5-46.

[5]M Ryan, 'The Roscrea Brooch', *Éile: Journal of the Roscrea Heritage Society* 1 (1982) 5-24.

[6]C Nordenfalk, *Celtic and Anglo-Saxon painting: book illumination in the British Isles, 600-800* (London 1977) pls 2, 14, 15, 19, 20, 26, 42.

[7]ibid, pl 33.

Kinale cover employs similar designs along the long sides, which differ
from those along the short sides, is also paralleled on the manuscripts: for
example folio 1v of the Book of Durrow, which depicts a double armed
cross[8] and folio 191v depicting the symbol of St John.[9] On the later book
shrines a cross, usually, is the major design element found on the cover and,
occasionally, the base. Although the form of the cross differs in these later
examples, there is a tradition of decorating the centre and extremities with
bosses, or large studs (which have the same effect).

Of this later group only the Soiscél Molaise[10] — which traditionally
contained the gospels of St Molaise — has its original cover[11] It dates to the
early eleventh century and consists of a cross and the symbols of the four
evangelists. Of the other shrines which contained gospel books, that is
Dimma,[12] the *Domnach Airgid*,[13] Stowe Missal[14] — which contained
fragments of a gospel of St John as well as a missal — and St Mulling,[15] all
except St Mulling employ a cross as the main decorative element on the
cover. In the case of the St Mulling book shrine, which probably dates to the
early fifteenth century, the main decorative element is a large crystal
flanked by smaller crystals and this decorative scheme relates it to the other
shrines discussed above. The Misach[16] and the Shrine of St Caillin[17] also
have crosses on their covers although the manuscripts associated with them
have not survived. No information exists as to the nature of the *Canoin
Phadraig*[18] which contained the Book of Armagh or the shrine (if such it was)
which housed the Book of Kells. It is clear however that the late-ninth- or
early-tenth-century shrine for the Book of Durrow, which disappeared
during the seventeenth century, had an inscribed silver cross on its cover.[19]

One shrine, known as the Cathach,[20] which contained a psalter, remains to
be discussed. It is perhaps significant that although there is a small
crucifixion scene placed to one side, the main decorative motif on the cover
is not a cross but an enthroned figure, perhaps representing Christ or St
Columcille, shown holding a book. The workmanship, which is fifteenth
century, may follow the original decorative scheme of the twelfth century.

---

[8]ibid, pl 2.
[9]ibid, pl 7.
[10]R Ó Floinn, 'The Soiscél Molaise', *Clogher Record* 13/2 (1989) 51-63.
[11]The cover of the Stowe Missal, although added to later, retains the origin eleventh-
century layout.
[12]R Ó Floinn, 'The shrine of the Book of Dimma', *Éile* 1 (1982) 25-37.
[13]R Ó Floinn in Ryan (note 2 above) 176-77, pls pp 71 and 179.
[14]ibid, 163-65, pl p 159.
[15]H S Crawford, 'A descriptive list of Irish shrines and reliquaries', *JRSAI* 53 (1923)
part I, 74-93; part II, 151-76.
[16]E C R Armstrong and H S Crawford, 'The reliquary known as the Misach', *JRSAI*
52/2, 105-12.
[17]Crawford (note 15 above) 154-55.
[18]ibid, 152.
[19]ibid, 154.
[20]ibid, 152-53.

Based on this analysis, which suggests that the covers of the shrines provide an indication of their contents, the fact that the Lough Kinale Shrine cover is dominated by a cross may suggest that it, too, contained a gospel book rather than any other form of manuscript.

The size of the shrine provides further clues to its original contents. When plotted against the dimensions of the other known or recorded book shrines (**fig 1**) it can be seen that the only one which would have come close to it was that which housed the Book of Kells. The other book shrines contained either pocket gospels or in the case of the Cathach, a small psalter, so it is unlikely that the Lough Kinale shrine was made to enshrine manuscripts of these types.

When all the illuminated insular gospel books are plotted (**fig 2**) they appear to fall into three groups:[21]

Group A consists of nineteen large gospel books which range in date from the mid-seventh to the early ninth centuries.
Durham Cathedral A. II. 10 (no 5) dates to the mid-seventh century while Utrecht 32 (no 8), Lindisfarne (no 9), Echternach (no 11) and Durham Cathedral A. II. 17 (no 10) date to the late seventh or early eighth centuries. Freiburg-im-Breisgau (no 25) is early eighth century while the Lichfield Gospels (no 21) and the Trier Gospels (no 26) are regarded as dating to the second quarter of the eighth century; Gotha (no 27) and the *Codex Aureus*, Stockholm (no 30), date to the mid-eight century while the *Codex Bigotianus* (no 34), Barberini (no 36), Leningrad (no 39), Rawlinson G. 167 (no 43) and the Vienna gospels (no 37) date to the second half of the eighth century. The remaining books — Kells (no 52), MacRegol (no 54) and the Book of Cerne (no 66) — may date to the early ninth century.

Group B consists of fourteen medium-sized gospel books which have the same date range as group A.
Two books, Durrow (no 6) and Garland of Howth (no 59) have Irish provenances and three — Cambridge 197B (no 12), BL, I. B. VII (no 20) and Hereford (no 38) — have English provenances. The remaining nine books have continental provenances. Three are associated with St Gall — St Gall 51 (no 44), St Gall 60 (no 60) and St Gall 1395 (no 57) — and two are in St Catherine's Church, Maaseik (nos 22-23). The remaining four books are in Turin (no 61), Leipzig (no 15), Augsburg (formerly Harburg) (no 24) and Würzburg (no 55).

Group C consists of eleven small pocket gospel books, four of which were enshrined, and all of which, with the possible exception of the Book of Deer, appear to be Irish.

---

[21]All dates and dimensions of manuscripts are after Alexander, *Insular manuscripts*. The dimensions given for the Book of Kells and the Book of Durrow are estimates of their original sizes. Although other manuscripts may also have been reduced in size over the centuries, it is considered that, for the purposes of this exercise, the approach remains a valid one. The numbers follow those in Alexander's catalogue.

— Shrines —

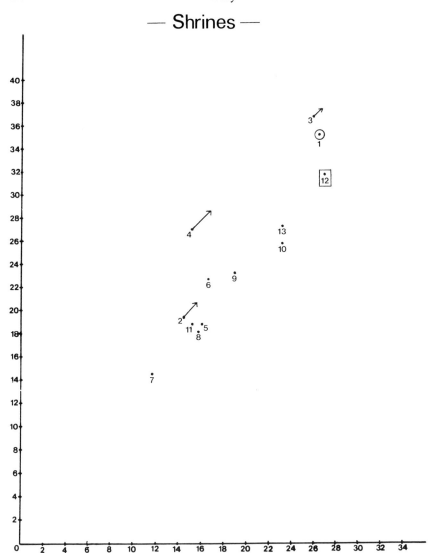

Fig 1 External dimensions are plotted in centimetres for each shrine. Where manuscripts which were formerly enshrined have survived, but not their shrines, the maximum dimensions of the manuscripts are plotted together with an arrow which indicates that the shrine's dimensions would have been greater than the values plotted.

(1) Lough Kinale shrine; (2) Canoin Phadraig; (3) Book of Kells; (4) Book of Durrow; (5) Dimma; (6) Domnach Airgid; (7) Soiscél Molaise; (8) Stowe Missal; (9) Cathach; (10) Misach; (11) St Mulling; (12) Satchel, Book of Armagh; (13) St Caillin

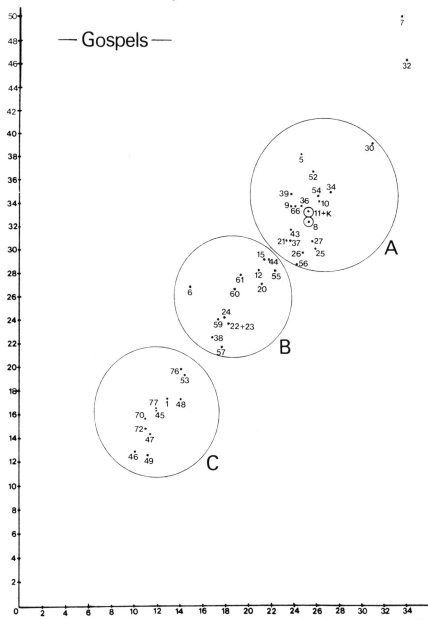

Fig 2 Dimensions of insular illuminated gospel books (plotted in centimetres). For explanation refer to text. The internal dimensions of the Lough Kinale book shrine are plotted. Its position is indicated by the letter K.

The earliest manuscript is the *codex Usserianus primus* (no 1) dating to the early seventh century. Five books — Mulling (no 45), BL, Add. MS 40618 (no 46), St John's gospel in the Stowe Missal (no 47), Dimma (no 48) and Fulda (no 49) —are believed to date to the second half of the eight century. Armagh (no 53) dates to early in the ninth century, *c*807, while Macdurnan (no 70) dates to the second half of the same century. The Book of Deer (no 72) is dated to the ninth or tenth centuries. The two remaining books, Harley 1023 (no 76) and Harley 1802 (no 77) date to early in the twelfth century.

The internal dimensions of the Lough Kinale shrine constituted the maximum size possible for the manuscript which it enshrined. When these dimensions (33.5cm x 22.5cm x 9.6cm) are plotted along with the gospel books then the shrine clearly appears to belong with the large illuminated gospels in Group A (**fig 2**).

The Lough Kinale shrine has also been plotted along with all the illuminated insular manuscripts, of all types, which appear to predate it (**fig 3**). This refinement suggests that the book shrine relates most closely to a group of large gospel books, all of which may have been produced in Northumbrian monasteries during the late seventh or early eighth centuries AD. The group includes the Utrecht Gospel (no 8), Lindisfarne (no 9), Durham A.II.17 (no 10), Echternach (no 11), Lichfield (no 21) and the Cologne *Collectio Canonum* (no 13). This may imply that the Lough Kinale book shrine also contained a Northumbrian illuminated gospel book of similar age.[22]

The loss, or deposition, of the shrine, in close proximity to a crannóg, is unlikely to have been fortuitous. Other major pieces of ecclesiastical metalwork have been found on or beside crannógs which, otherwise, are wholly secular in character.[23] The recent indications are that crannógs were aristocratic dwellings and may, therefore, have been the usual dwellings of aristocratic churchmen such as lay abbots. It is possible that objects, such as the Lough Kinale book shrine, were normally kept at such places.[24] That one important churchman, at least, had associations with Lough Kinale is demonstrated by a reference to the death, in 821, of 'Seachnasach of Lough Kinale'.[25] He is described as 'bishop and anchorite' but it is not stated with which ecclesiastical foundation he was associated. All the later book shrines are associated with powerful and important families such as O'Donnell/Magroarty (Cathach), O'Rourke (St Caillin), Kavanagh (St Mulling), O'Carroll Eli (Dimma), Maguire (*Domnach Airgid*), O'Kennedy (Stowe Missal), O'Morison (Misach) and O'Meehan (*Soiscél Molaise*). Two

---

[22]The comparison between the cross form on the cover of the book shrine and the cross forms in the *Codex Aureus* is viewed as relevant despite the fact that Canterbury was not part of the Northumbrian province.

[23]E P Kelly, 'Observations on Irish lake dwellings', *Studies in insular art and archaeology. American early medieval studies* 1 (1991) 81-98.

[24]ibid, 91.

[25]*AFM*, I, 433.

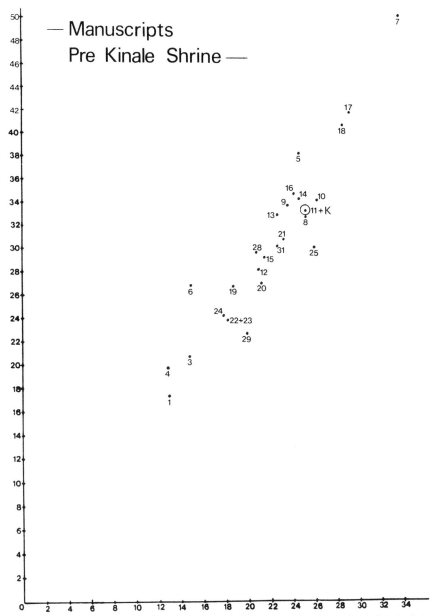

Fig 3 Illuminated insular manuscripts which pre-date the Lough Kinale book shrine (plotted in centimetres). For explanation refer to text.

manuscripts, Durrow and Armagh, were enshrined by monarchs styled king of Ireland: respectively Fland Sinna and Donnchadh, son of Flann. It seems likely that the Lough Kinale shrine was produced under the patronage of a local king and that the place where it came to be deposited, in Lough Kinale, is in proximity to where it was usually kept.

Another possibility is that important church valuables were removed to safe locations, such as crannógs, during the period of extensive Viking raids, around the middle of the ninth century. Wear on the bottom of the corner mouldings of the Lough Kinale shrine, which served as feet, and on the strap attachments shows that the shrine was in use for many years before its destruction. However the period involved is unlikely to have been very great as there are no repairs or additions such as are common on other shrines. Inscriptions are common features on shrines from the tenth century onwards and the fact that there is none on the Lough Kinale shrine may indicate that it was lost prior to then. The present condition of the Lough Kinale shrine, which resulted from an attempt to rob it of its decorative components, would not be inconsistent with the known practices of Viking raiders.

Material which is directly comparable to elements on the book shrine have been found in Viking graves in Norway. These include a decorated border from Vindal;[26] a medallion with projecting heads from Hofstad;[27] a strap end from Laland[28] and harness mounts from Oseberg.[29] The plundering of Lough Kinale by the Vikings, who attacked across the frozen surface of the lake, is recorded for the year 853 AD.[30] One hundred and twenty persons were slain and it is tempting to suggest that it was in the course of this raid that the book shrine was stolen and subsequently lost. A small silver chalice and a paten found on another crannóg in Lough Kinale, may have been concealed at that time.[31]

To summarise therefore: The indications are that the Lough Kinale book shrine was made to enshrine a large illuminated gospel book, of seventh or early eighth century date, which would have been about the same size as the Echternach Gospels. The book, which appears to have been associated with an unidentified saint[32], was enshrined during the late eighth century and was probably stolen and severely damaged in the course of a Viking raid around the middle of the ninth century.

---

[26]E Wamers, *Insular Metallschmuck in wikingerzeitlichen Gräbern Nordeuropas* (Neumünster 1985) pl 11.3.
[27]ibid, pl 19.1.
[28]ibid, pl 29.4.
[29]ibid, pl 27.5; Youngs (note 3 above) 118, 158.
[30]*AFM*, I, 487.
[31]Ryan, 'The formal relationships of insular early medieval eucharistic chalices', *PRIA* 90.C.10 (1990) 281-356.
[32]It was probably a saint of some importance. Saints associated with surviving Irish manuscripts are Patrick, Columcille, Cronan, MacCairtainn, Molaise, Maelruan, Cairneach, Mulling and Caillin.

If these conclusions are correct, then the presence of a large illuminated gospel book, possibly of Northumbrian origin, in the north midlands of Ireland during the seventh or early eighth centuries, must be taken into account in the debate concerning the place of manufacture of other illuminated manuscripts, most notably the Book of Durrow but also the Book of Kells.

Acknowledgements.
I wish to record, with thanks, the invaluable assistance of my colleague Paul Mullarkey, National Musuem of Ireland, who is conserving the book shrine. Thanks are also due to Bernard Meehan and Anthony Cains, Trinity College, Dublin, for information about the original dimensions of the Book of Durrow and the Book of Kells. I am grateful to Raghnall Ó Floinn for drawing my attention to the annalistic references.

Du Livre de Kells et du Psautier de Corbie à l'art roman: origine, diffusion et signification du thème des personnages se saisissant à la barbe

Christian de Mérindol

Le thème fameux des personnages se saisissant à la barbe est représenté dans le *Beatus* de Saint-Sever et sur le chapiteau dit 'de la dispute' de Poitiers, qui sont souvent rapprochés depuis Emile Mâle.[1] D'après les exemples connus, la diffusion de ce thème a paru orientée du sud vers le nord.[2] Depuis nos travaux sur le scriptorium de l'abbaye de Corbie en Picardie, au XIIème siècle,[3] qui ouvraient de nouvelles perspectives, nous avons réuni plus d'une douzaine d'exemples de ce thème. Certains sont inédits. L'étude approfondie de chaque exemple et une confrontation mutuelle, dans un cadre élargi, permettent de préciser la date d'apparition, l'origine, la diffusion et la signification de ce thème.

Pour un corpus

Les premiers exemples que nous avons repérés sont situés dans le nord de l'Europe occidentale vers 800. Ce point est totalement inédit. Deux personnages se prennent mutuellement la barbe dans deux miniatures de prestigieux manuscrits sensiblement contemporains, le Livre de Kells et le psautier carolingien de Corbie conservé à la bibliothèque d'Amiens, le manuscrit 18. Dans le premier manuscrit, au feuillet 253 verso (**pl 46**), le personnage de droite tient de l'autre main sa jambe pliée, celui de gauche les laisse pendre le long de son corps, permettant ainsi de former l'initiale synthétique N de l'évangile de saint Luc *Nemo servus potest duobus dominis servire* (Luc 16:13).[4] La tête du dragon qui achève l'initiale suivante lui mord le talon. Dans le psautier, au feuillet 73 (**pl 103**), les deux personnages se tiennent non seulement par la barbe mais par la main et animent le champ délimité par le cercle décoré de perles de l'initiale Q du verset du psaume 79 *Qui regis Israel, intende, qui deducis velut ovem Joseph*.[5] L'appendice de l'initiale est constituée du corps d'un monstre dont la tête a disparu. On retrouvera une initiale Q comparable dans un autre manuscrit du scriptorium de Corbie exécuté au début du XIIème siècle. Les points communs et les différences, nous le verrons, sont hautement significatives.

---

[1]E Mâle, *L'art religieux du XIIème siècle en France* (Paris 1922) 15-16.
[2]J Porcher, 'Enluminure angevine' dans *Anjou roman*, ed P d'Herbécourt et J Porcher, (La Pierre-Qui-Vire, coll. Zodiaque 1959) 219.
[3]C de Mérindol, *La production des livres peints à l'abbaye de Corbie au XIIème siècle. Étude historique et archéologique* (Lille 1976) (voir *infra* les notes 5 et 20).
[4]*Codex Cenannensis*, 41-42; F Henry, *L'art irlandais* (La Pierre-Qui-Vire, coll. Zodiaque 1964) II, fig 22.
[5]Mérindol (*supra* la note 3) 781-83, fig 38.

Les exemples suivants appartiennent à l'époque romane, les XIème et XIIème siècles. Le premier figure dans un manuscrit peint par Ingelard à Saint-Germain-des-Prés, entre 1030 et 1060 (Paris, BN, lat. 11685).[6] Dans le cadre d'une page du *De laudibus sancte Crucis* de Raban Maur, au feuillet 25 verso (**pls 105-06**), deux hommes s'empoignent par la barbe, l'autre main étant placée derrière la nuque de l'adversaire. Le personnage, à gauche, tire la langue. Cette image est associée à de petites scènes disposées dans un ruban en forme de grecque. On reconnaît des fables d'Esope et d'autres: dans le registre supérieur, une chasse en trois épisodes (un cavalier sonnant du cor, deux chiens courant et un cerf), dans le bord inférieur un berger et son troupeau (le berger et son chien, le troupeau de moutons et un loup), dans le cadre, à droite, successivement, dans le sens de la lecture, de bas en haut, le loup et la grue en deux tableaux (la grue face au loup, la grue plongeant son bec dans la gorge du quadrupède), et un singe lisant, enfin dans le cadre, à gauche, dans le sens de la lecture, ici de haut en bas, un personnage tenant un éventail, se protégeant la face de la main gauche devant l'attaque d'un insecte, une guêpe ou une abeille, puis l'âne et le lion, enfin notre scène. Selon May Vieillard-Troiekouroff, le modèle de ces sujets se trouvait dans les riches bordures des manuscrits de Saint-Denis de l'école du palais de Charles le Chauve; le modèle carolingien de ce manuscrit de Raban Maur provient de l'abbaye royale (Paris, BN, lat. 2421). Quoi qu'il en soit, ces trois exemples situés en Irlande, en Picardie et à Paris, ou ses abords, démontrent, pour la première fois et d'une manière valable, l'antériorité du nord sur le sud dans l'apparition figurée de ce thème. Il faudra l'expliquer.

Le premier exemple rencontré dans les régions méridionales est le fameux *Beatus* de Saint-Sever, écrit et décoré pour l'abbé Muntaner entre 1028 et 1060, ou avant 1072 (Paris, BN, lat. 8878).[7] À la page 184 (**pls 107-08**), deux hommes, comme dans l'exemple précédent, se tirent mutuellement la barbe, tandis que l'autre main est placée derrière la nuque de l'adversaire. La scène à présent se passe en présence d'une femme. Cette association se rencontrera fréquemment. La scène est accompagnée de deux inscriptions *Frontibus attristis barbas conscindere fas est* et *Calvi duo pro hac muliere (attriverunt) barbas*. Les deux hommes en effet sont chauves. Quant à l'antériorité du nord sur le sud, elle paraît trouver un écho à Saint-Sever même dans le domaine de l'architecture, de la sculpture et de la miniature.

---

[6] Y Deslandres, 'Les manuscrits décorés au XIème siècle à Saint-Germain-des-Prés par Ingelard', *Scriptorium* 9 (1955) 8 et suiv.; M Vieillard-Troiekouroff, 'Art carolingien et art roman parisiens. Les illustrations astrologiques jointes aux chroniques de Saint-Denis et de Saint-Germain-des-Prés (IX-XIème siècles)', *Cahiers archéologiques* 16 (1966) 85 et nn 47, 50.

[7] *Saint-Sever. Millénaire de l'abbaye*, Colloque international, 25-27 Mai 1985 (Mont-de-Marsan 1986). Ce recueil réunit plusieurs articles sur le *Beatus* de Saint-Sever, voir les notes suivantes. Sur ce manuscrit, voir aussi C O Nordström, 'Text and myth in some Beatus miniatures', *Cahiers archéologiques* 25 (1976) 7-37 et 26 (1977) 117-36, et F-M Besson, '"A armes égales". Une représentation de la violence en France et en Espagne au XIIème siècle', *Gesta* 36/2 (1987) 113-26 (p 119 et fig 20).

Ainsi sont respectivement citées la Normandie,[8] le Poitou[9] et plus
particulièrement, à propos du *Beatus*, des sources non hispaniques,
notamment dans les cycles de l'Apocalypse, et d'art français.[10] Charles
Higounet, en conclusion au colloque sur Saint-Sever, relevait la fusion des
différentes traditions et influences dans le manuscrit.[11] Réalisé avec
certitude pour l'abbaye, ce manuscrit exigeait, en son lieu d'exécution, qui
peut être Saint-Sever, le contexte indispensable d'une bibliothèque ou d'une
tradition intellectuelle. Sans vouloir trancher, il retenait les arguments des
deux camps de la controverse, une forme et une iconographie pour
l'essentiel hispanique et des sources non hispaniques. Quant à la relation
avec le portail de Moissac, il se posait la question de son sens, qui
amènerait, dans le cas d'une inversion, à un rajeunissement du *Beatus*.
Modestement le thème étudié ici souligne la dette du manuscrit envers une
iconographie apparue antérieurement dans le nord de l'Occident.

Vers 1100, les exemples, dans deux manuscrits, se situent l'un en Anjou,
l'autre dans la région d'Agen, et, sur deux chapiteaux, l'un en Bourgogne,
l'autre en Poitou. Dans une *Vie de saint Aubin*, exécutée à Saint-Aubin
d'Angers (Paris, BN, n. acq. lat. 1390), au feuillet 4 (**pl 111**), deux vieillards
luttent en se tirant la barbe et les cheveux dans un geste comparable à
l'image du *Beatus*. Jean Porcher a relevé des traces d'influences méridionales
dans l'art du peintre, notamment la dureté du dessin et les arcs à pans
coupés chargés de coupoles aplaties.[12] Les deux lutteurs sont accompagnés
de personnages disposés dans des rinceaux, qui sont parfois terminés par
une tête de monstre, et par un combat d'un homme armé et d'un monstre en
présence d'une femme. Dans un *Recueil des Pères de l'Église*, provenant peut-
être de Saint-Maurin, au diocèse d'Agen (Paris, BN, lat. 2819), au feuillet 87,
deux personnages se heurtent le front et se tirent violemment la barbe, leurs
mains saignent dans une coupe de vin, auquel se mêle le sang d'une
blessure qu'ils se sont faite à la tête. Jean Porcher proposait l'image d'un
serment de fidélité réciproque.[13]

Sur un chapiteau de l'église d'Anzy-le-Duc, les deux combattants se tirent
mutuellement la barbe et les cheveux.[14] Sur une autre face du chapiteau,

---

[8]À propos de l'isolement, relevé par P Héliot, de l'espace aménagé au-dessus d'une
chapelle latérale se terminant par une abside, par J Gardelles, *Saint Sever* (*supra* la
note 7) 236.
[9]Quelque analogie dans le répertoire ornemental et iconographique à cette époque,
par M T Camus, ibid, 245.
[10]P K Klein, ibid, 318, 320-22, 326-27, 329.
[11]ibid, 244, 245.
[12]Porcher (*supra* la note 2) 214, 219; J Vezin, *Les scriptoria d'Angers au XIème siècle*
(Paris 1974) 184. Les deux fagots (?) de part et d'autre des lutteurs se retrouvent à
Saint-Benoît-sur-Loire (Besson, *supra* la note 7, 118).
[13]J Porcher, 'Un manuscrit aquitain de la fin du XIème siècle', *Bulletin de la Société
Nationale des Antiquaires de France* (1950-51) 127-28; idem, *Manuscrits à peintures du
VIIème au XIIème siècle* (Paris 1954) no 315.
[14]A Kingsley Porter, *Romanesque sculpture of the pilgrimage roads*, 10 vols (Boston
1923) IV, fig 17; A Katzenellenbogen, *Allegories of the virtues and vices in medieval art*,
2ème éd (New York 1964) 59 n 3; P K Klein, 'Les sources non hispaniques et la
genèse iconographique du Beatus de Saint-Sever' dans *Saint-Sever* (*supra* la note 7,

voisine, deux hommes s'embrassent. Enfin sur le fameux chapiteau dit 'de la dispute', trouvé à proximité de l'église Saint-Hilaire de Poitiers (**pls 109-10**), deux hommes, armés d'une hache et d'une serpe, se battent en se tenant par la barbe, tandis que deux femmes, qui assistent à la scène, tentent de les séparer.[15] Sur les deux autres faces, à droite, un personnage taille un arbrisseau, et à gauche, deux estropiés, qui marchent avec des jambes de bois, s'embrassent. L'interprétation la plus fréquemment retenue est un groupement, comme dans le cas précédent, de la discorde et de la concorde, dont on connaît des figurations sous d'autres formes. L'inscription qui accompagne l'ensemble, malheureusement peu compréhensible, ne nous éclaire pas davantage. Meyer Schapiro a rapproché la facture de ce chapiteau, notamment pour les plis, avec celle du Christ de Rodez.[16]

Dans les premières décennies du XIIème siècle, le thème est principalement utilisé en sculpture sur des chapiteaux en Nivernais et dans le Bordelais. Un seul exemple manuscrit est connu. Il appartient à l'abbaye de Corbie et se trouve en relation étroite, nous l'avons dit, avec le prestigieux psautier carolingien que possédait le monastère. Sur une face d'un chapiteau de l'église de Saint-Pierre-le-Moutier, deux personnages se combattent en se tirant mutuellement la barbe et les cheveux; sur la face voisine, un homme combat un animal.[17] La proximité d'un monstre était déjà présente dans le Livre de Kells et le Psautier d'Amiens, vers 800, ainsi que, vers 1100, dans la Vie de saint Aubin (**pls 46, 103, 111**). Trois modillons du chevet de l'église de la Sauve-Majeure, du côté nord, le côté sinistre, l'un encore en place, méconnu, et que nous avons vu *in situ*, les deux autres à présent conservés à New York, au Cloisters, présentent ce thème avec des variations: trois personnages, celui du milieu à genoux tenant les cheveux des deux protagonistes qui lui tirent la barbe; deux autres lutteurs s'empoignant par la barbe; enfin, plus complexe, cinq personnages qui apparemment se tirent mutuellement la barbe et les cheveux.[18] Malgré la proximité des exemples antérieurs de Saint-Sever et d'Agen, sans négliger ceux du Poitou et de l'Anjou, l'origine corbéienne du fondateur de la Sauve-Majeure, saint Géraud, n'est peut-être pas totalement étrangère à la forte présence de ce thème en cette abbaye. Le fameux Psautier d'Amiens, qui était relevé, avec vraisemblance, dans le catalogue alphabétique de l'abbaye de Corbie dressé

325, n 22). La thèse de C S Pendergast, 'The Romanesque sculpture of Anzy le Duc' (Yale University) n'a pu être consultée.
[15]*Corpus des inscriptions de la France médiévale*, I, *Poitou-Charentes*, 1, *Poitiers* (1974) no 88 (bibliographie et inscription); Y J Riou, 'Réflexions sur la frise sculptée de la façade de Notre-Dame-la-Grande de Poitiers', *Bulletin. Société des Antiquaires de l'Ouest et des Musées de Poitiers* (1980) 512.
[16]Meyer Schapiro, *Romanesque art* (New York 1977) ('A relief in Rodez ...', 1963) 298 n 8.
[17]P Deschamps, *La sculpture française à l'époque romane. Onzième et douzième siècles* (Paris, Florence 1930) pl 36A; Katzenellenbogen (*supra* la note 14) 59, n 3; M Anfray, *L'architecture religieuse du Nivernais au moyen âge: les églises romanes* (Paris 1951) 276, pl XLIX, 3; Klein (*supra* la note 14) 325 et n 23.
[18]L Drouyn, *Album de la Grande-Sauve* (Bordeaux 1851) 20, pl VII, fig 3; *Sculpture médiévale de Bordeaux et du Bordelais* (Bordeaux, Musée d'Aquitaine 1976) 113, nos 107-08 (New York, Metropolitan Museum, The Cloisters, inv. no 34, 21. 1 et 2).

au XIème siècle, sous la forme de *psalterium depictum*,[19] ne pouvait pas être ignoré de ce moine qui joua un rôle important dans le monastère picard avant de fonder l'abbaye de la Sauve vers 1080. Cette liberté originale, par rapport aux autres exemples, montre une grande maîtrise du thème, qui paraît traduire une assimilation d'une tradition qui pouvait être d'origine locale.

L'exemple roman de l'abbaye de Corbie est particulièrement précieux puisqu'il permet de mesurer la relation avec un modèle carolingien qui était présent dans le monastère. Dans l'initiale Q de la huitième *homélie de saint Grégoire*, sur l'évangile de saint Luc (PL 76, 1103) **(pl 104)**, deux hommes au crâne plus ou moins dégarni, vus de profil, luttent face à face en se tenant par la barbe, qui s'encroise en longs rubans, et par la main.[20] Le modèle est incontestablement le manuscrit carolingien **(pl 103)**. Cette représentation est propre à ces deux seules oeuvres. Leur confrontation est remarquablement éclairante sur l'évolution de la sensibilité et de l'iconographie. Si cette scène est accompagnée d'un dragon comparable, qui forme l'appendice courbe de l'initiale, plusieurs traits nouveaux, qu'on pourrait appeler proto-héraldiques, apparaissent dans la seconde miniature: l'inversion de la position du dragon, qui accentue sa valeur péjorative puisqu'il est orienté à présent vers la gauche, le côté sinistre, le pointillé, signe particulièrement dévalorisant, qui recouvre l'animal ainsi que le champ délimité par l'initiale, enfin la position de la queue de l'animal qui, d'abord dressé comme celle d'un lion, se glisse ici honteusement sous le ventre, entre les pattes postérieures du monstre. Dès cette époque, les premières décennies du XIIème siècle, étaient ainsi assimilés plusieurs signes protohéraldiques ou de taxinomie. On ne peut malheureusement comparer les gueules, celle du monstre carolingien ayant disparu. La dette du monstre roman au précédent apparaît dans la forme de palmette qui, d'appendice de la queue, est devenu celui des oreilles. Le monstre roman laisse échapper de sa gueule la main et la jambe d'un personnage qu'il vient d'engouler **(pls 103-04)**.

À une date indéterminée du XIIème siècle appartiennent deux exemples apparemment peu connus, un chapiteau du portail de l'ancienne église d'Aubiac, en Gironde, où un homme paraît tenir sa barbe et celle d'un autre personnage,[21] et un manuscrit de l'abbaye de Marchiennes, dans le Nord, cité, sans autre précision, par Jean Porcher.[22]

À ces exemples s'ajoute celui d'une oeuvre qui, par son contexte étranger aux précédents, éclaire davantage la signification accordée à ce thème iconographique. Il s'agit de la galerie de la maison romane construite vers le

---

[19]Voir *supra* la note 5.
[20]Mérindol (*supra* la note 3) 971-73, fig 330.
[21]La lecture peu aisée dans L Drouyn, *Choix des types les plus remarquables de l'architecture au moyen âge dans le département de la Gironde* (Bordeaux 1846) (2. combat de deux personnages).
[22]Porcher (*supra* la note 2) 124, n 28.

milieu du siècle à Saint-Antonin, dans le Tarn et Garonne.[23] Deux personnages s'empoignent par la barbe et les cheveux. Des monstres, des sirènes-oiseaux, des sirènes-poissons, un combat d'un homme et d'un dragon sont figurés, comme dans des exemples précédents, sur plusieurs chapiteaux. On remarque aussi, à la suite de la précieuse lecture de Marcel Durliat, en complément de ce combat, un homme calme et serein tenant enchaînés deux lions domptés. La signification de cet ensemble s'éclaire et s'enrichit par la proximité de trois statues qui timbrent les piliers de la galerie, en façade, celle de Justinien, le législateur — le déchiffrement de l'inscription, qui subsiste partiellement sur la banderole qu'il tient, a été remarquablement résolu par Léon Pressouyre — et celles d'Adam et Eve, représentants de la faute originelle. Une double signification apparaît, comme fréquemment au moyen âge, une signification morale, la lutte contre le mal qui conditionne le salut éternel du chrétien, comme l'observe très justement Marcel Durliat, mais également sociale puisque située dans un lieu qui apparemment, d'après la référence à Justinien, devait avoir une fonction judiciaire. Ce lieu de justice d'époque romane vient heureusement compléter la série d'exemples cités dans un ouvrage récent.[24] Il déplace d'autant la date d'apparition d'une 'architecture judiciaire' et souligne, si besoin était, l'importance des textes de Justinien à l'époque médiévale.

Du sens moral à l'insertion dans la société, la justice.
L'évolution du thème est riche d'enseignement. Dans le Livre de Kells (**pl 46**), l'initiale est celle d'un texte soulignant le bon emploi de l'argent: 'nul ne servira deux maîtres, ou il haïra l'un et aimera l'autre, ou il s'attachera à l'un et méprisera l'autre. Vous ne pouvez servir Dieu et l'argent'. Le choix des deux personnages se tirant mutuellement la barbe est peut-être le signe du désordre, de la discorde créée par l'argent. Les exemples suivants semblent le confirmer. Dans le psautier carolingien (**pl 103**) la relation est également peu nette avec le texte. L'initiale Q est celle du psaume sur la prière pour la restauration d'Israël: 'Pasteur d'Israël écoute, toi qui mènes Joseph comme un troupeau, toi qui trônes sur les chérubins, resplendis devant Ephraïm, Benjamin et Manassi, réveille ta vaillance et viens à notre secours' (psaume 79).

Dans le manuscrit du XIème siècle de Saint-Germain-des-Prés (**pls 105-06**), la querelle est associée à des fables qui paraissent souligner des rapports conflictuels et la tromperie: le loup et la grue, l'homme se protégeant d'un insecte et le lion et l'âne. La chasse au cerf, dans le bandeau supérieur du cadre, place privilégiée, a peut-être une valeur christologique et annoncerait, comme dans des exemples postérieurs, la Rédemption.

La présence d'une femme apparaît dans le *Beatus* de Saint-Sever (**pls 107-08**). Les inscriptions commentent la scène. On peut les traduire par 'deux

---

[23]M Durliat, 'La maison romane de Saint-Antonin' dans *Le Haut-Languedoc roman* (La Pierre-Qui-Vire, coll. Zodiaque 1978) 320 fig; L Pressouyre, 'Lecture d'une inscription du XIIème siècle à Saint-Antonin-Noble-Val, Tarn et Garonne', *Bulletin de la Société Nationale des Antiquaires de France* (1986) 256-68.
[24]*La justice en ses temples* (Paris 1992) 29. Je remercie Madame Nadine Marchal-Jacob.

hommes chauves se tirent les barbes pour cette femme' et 'si les têtes sont chauves, on peut se tirer la barbe' ou 'si deux personnes se heurtent du front, elles peuvent se tirer la barbe'. Ainsi, apparemment avec une pointe de malice, est souligné le rôle de la barbe pour illustrer une querelle. Le caractère intime, personnel, de cet attribut masculin explique sans doute ce choix. Quant à sa relation avec le texte, retenons une des dernières propositions avancée par Peter K Klein, qui rejoint celle qui déjà se définit, l'illustration de la Discorde.[25] L'intervention de la femme ajoute cependant, semble-t-il, une valeur sociale à l'image. Dans le manuscrit angevin (**pl 111**), la scène de la querelle se situe parfaitement à la suite de la miniature du *Beatus*: deux hommes au front dégarni et une femme à proximité. Mais celle-ci n'assiste pas à cette lutte mais au combat d'un homme, armé d'une épée et d'un bouclier, qui lutte contre un griffon, un lion ailé à tête d'aigle. La femme est ainsi explicitement mêlée à l'illustration de la lutte de l'homme contre le démon. C'est la première association que nous rencontrons de notre thème avec celui de la lutte d'un homme et d'un monstre. Nous la retrouvons à Saint-Pierre-le-Moutier.

Selon Porcher, la peinture du manuscrit aquitain, nous l'avons dit, représente vraisemblablement un serment de fidélité réciproque, comportant effusion et mélange de sang. Le caractère intime, personnel, de la barbe justifiait sans doute le choix de cet attribut pour sceller l'engagement des deux personnages.

Les chapiteaux d'Anzy-le-Duc et de Poitiers associent la Discorde et la Concorde. La femme est à nouveau présente sur la seconde pièce (**pls 109-10**). Un indice, peu souligné, doit y être relevé. Les lutteurs sont barbus, les estropiés qui se tiennent enlacés ne le sont pas. La valeur négative de la barbe est ainsi bien marquée. Nous reviendrons sur ce point.

Les modillons du chevet de l'église de l'abbaye de la Sauve-Majeure sont tous placés au nord. On avait déjà remarqué qu'à l'intérieur de cette église, les tentations et les puissances du mal, le monde antérieur à la Rédemption, se trouvaient de ce côté.[26] Le chapiteau de la grosse colonne cylindrique, dans la baie qui sépare le choeur de l'absidiole nord, réunit les combats de deux centaures, de deux aspics, d'un homme armé et d'un lion, ainsi que deux griffons buvant dans un vase. Le chapiteau correspondant du côté sud est orné de pommes de pin, que l'on peut lire comme des grappes de raisin.[27] Dans la grande absidiole nord, ce sont des sirènes; dans la travée droite qui la précède, Adam et Eve, après la faute, de part et d'autre de la scène de la tentation. Du côté sud correspondant, ce sont les trois vainqueurs de la tentation: le Christ, Daniel et Samson. Une répartition

---

[25]Voir *supra* la note 11 (p 245).
[26]A Masson dans *Congrès archéologique* (1939) 224-27; P Dubourg-Noves, *Guyenne romane* (La Pierre-Qui-Vire, coll. Zodiaque 1969); Bonnet de la Borderie, 'Fenêtre ouverte sur la Gironde romane', *Archéologia* (1966) 84, 85; J Houlet et M Sarradet, *L'abbaye de la Sauve-Majeure* (Paris 1966) 76, 77 et 89; M Vieillard-Troiekouroff, 'Sirènes-poissons carolingiens', *Cahiers archéologiques* 19 (1969) 81 et n 52.
[27]Bonnet de la Borderie (*supra* la note 26) 85.

spatiale suivant les points cardinaux a été également observée dans la tour-porche de Saint-Benoît-sur-Loire. Les chapiteaux se référant aux vices et aux péchés paraissent également réservés au nord.[28] À la Sauve-Majeure, nos modillons sont accompagnés de monstres et d'autres scènes de combat, deux personnages dévorés par un dragon, un monstre qui avale un personnage qui s'efforce d'écarter les machoires qui le menacent. La lutte de l'homme contre le mal marque l'église du côté nord, à l'intérieur et à l'extérieur de l'espace oriental, qui est timbré par l'autel du sacrifice divin. La signification des lutteurs se tirant mutuellement la barbe et les cheveux est ainsi affirmée par l'ensemble de la décoration de l'église. Ces modillons ont échappé à l'attention des historiens et archéologues de l'abbaye.[29] Lorsqu'ils ont été exceptionnellement relevés, ces personnages ont été pris pour des acrobates.[30] Les formes imposées par la structure, suivant la priorité en usage à l'époque médiévale, ont ainsi pris le pas, dans la lecture, sur la signification de ces scènes.

Dans l'ancienne église d'Aubiac, c'est sur les quatre chapiteaux du portail que figure le monde antérieur à la Rédemption: en partant de la gauche, successivement, d'après les dessins de Drouyn, Adam et Eve, le combat qui nous occupe, un centaure et deux oiseaux superposés.[31]

La signification de l'initiale du manuscrit corbéien est également rendue plus claire par la décoration de l'ensemble du codex. Les deux lutteurs, qui occupent le champ délimité par l'initiale, et le monstre, qui forme l'appendice, illustrent la huitième homélie de saint Grégoire sur la naissance de Jésus et la visite des bergers (**pl 104**). La relation n'est pas évidente. Le manuscrit contient plusieurs illustrations: à la fin du codex, saint Grégoire, l'auteur, et saint Pierre, le patron de l'abbaye (folio 258 recto et verso), ainsi qu' en tête de trois extraits du texte sacré les personnages qui sont sans doute les évangélistes saint Luc (folio 26v), saint Matthieu auréolé (folio 33) et saint Jean écrivant (folio 51v), enfin, par deux fois, le Christ, le Christ triomphant dominant un combat d'un homme et d'un dragon, en tête de la onzième homélie, dont les premiers mots sont *Redemptor noster* (folio 43), et le Christ tenant le livre et l'hostie, devant la seizième (folio 47v).[32] Notre initiale représente le monde avant la Rédemption. Elle illustre parfaitement l'homélie sur la naissance de Jésus qui permit le triomphe sur le mal.

Le décor sculpté de la galerie de Saint-Antonin achève remarquablement l'évolution. La présence d'Adam et Eve, des monstres et de notre chapiteau illustrent le monde avant la Rédemption. Le Christ apparaît sous la forme

---

[28]P K Klein, 'Quelques remarques sur l'iconologie de la tour proche de Saint-Benoît-sur-Loire', *Cahiers de Cuxa* 14 (1983), 269-79 (p 269, fig 2). Voir cependant les réserves de E Vergnolle, *Saint-Benoît-sur-Loire et la sculpture du XIe siècle* (Paris 1985) 106.

[29]Ces modillons ne sont pas étudiés dans les travaux cités précédemment ni dans l'étude de H Couzy, 'Les chapiteaux de la Sauve-Majeure', *Bulletin monumental* (1968) 345-72. La première mention sérieuse est celle du catalogue cité à la note 18.

[30]Houlet et Sarradet (*supra* la note 26) 66-68.

[31]Voir *supra* la note 21.

[32]Voir *supra* la note 20.

d'un poisson que brandit une sirène-poisson, comme l'a judicieusement relevé Marcel Durliat.[33] L'homme calme et serein tenant enchaînés deux lions domptés prend alors toute sa signification. La statue de Justinien qui tient une banderole, sur laquelle on pouvait lire *l'incipit* des *Institutes* de Justinien,[34] insère l'ensemble dans un cadre nouveau, judiciaire, dans la société.

L'origine celtique du thème.

La source de ce thème reste inexpliquée. Une certitude se dégage de l'ensemble étudié. L'origine figurée et la transmission par les images paraissent limitées. Un seul cas d'une relation directe avec un modèle a été relevé, celui de Corbie. Il a montré une fidélité étonnante quant à la représentation de notre thème (**pls 103-04**). Tous les autres exemples se ressemblent plus ou moins avec des différences qui les séparent. Une source textuelle a été parfois proposée, une fable populaire, un fabliau, une poésie de troubadour ou un recueil d'apologues.[35] Le manuscrit de Saint-Germain-des-Prés associe le thème à des fables d'Esope. Mais jusqu'à présent aucun texte littéraire ou autre n'a été trouvé. Aucune scène comparable n'a été constatée dans les thèmes que transmettaient les fabliaux.[36] Nous suggérons une autre hypothèse.

A l'origine ce thème se place à la recontre du monde insulaire et du monde méditerranéen, telle que l'offre le Livre de Kells, et apparemment participe à l'apport des insulaires dans le nord de la France, sensible à Corbie avec le Psautier d'Amiens. Cette mise à l'honneur de la barbe paraît davantage appartenir au monde celtique. On connaît l'épisode fameux où des femmes demandent au jeune héros Cuchulainn de porter une barbe. Des guerriers refusent de le combattre parce qu'il est imberbe. Il décide alors de porter une fausse barbe qu'il fabrique avec de l'herbe.[37] Plusieurs passages du texte soulignent son absence de barbe. La pire injure 'honte à ta barbe' est prononcée dans un épisode concernant Owein, un des plus anciens compagnons d'Arthur.[38] Ritta Gawr arbitra la dispute entre les rois Nymiaw et Pebiaw en arrachant leur barbe. Puis y prenant goût, il arracha la barbe de tous les autres rois pour s'en faire un manteau.[39] Plus tard les preux porteront une barbe d'or (René II de Lorraine, au XVème siècle, en porta une pour pleurer la mort de Charles le Téméraire). En Occident, dans le sud, le port de la barbe était considérée comme une mode barbare. Saint Césaire d'Arles au concile d'Agde, en 506, prescrit à l'archidiacre de couper les cheveux et la barbe de force aux clercs qui se mettent à la mode barbare.[40] Charlemagne imposa à Grimoald, lorsqu'il lui conféra la

---

[33]Durliat (*supra* la note 23) 321.

[34]Pressouyre (*supra* la note 23) 260.

[35]Notamment Porcher, Crozet, Sandoz et Klein.

[36]Voir le *Corpus des inscriptions*, *supra* la note 15.

[37]E Windisch, *Irische Texte* (Leipzig 1905) V, 308-09.

[38]J-P Persigout, *Dictionnaire de la mythologie celtique*, 2ème éd (Paris 1990) 250.

[39]ibid, 269. Nous remercions pour son aide Michel Pastoureau. Ce thème apparaît en 1173 dans le *Tristan* de Thomas (vers 680 et suiv.).

[40]H Leclerq, l'article *Barbe* dans *DACL*, II, 1, col 486.

principauté de Bénévent, d'obliger les Lombards à se raser le menton afin de se conformer à l'usage des Romains.[41]

Ce ne serait pas le seul apport celtique de caractère littéraire au psautier d'Amiens. Nous en avons pour exemple l'initiale du psaume 108 *Deus, laudem meam ne tacueris, quia os peccatoris et os dolosi super me apertum est,* 'Dieu de ma louange, sors du silence. Bouche méchante et bouche d'imposture s'ouvrent contre moi'. La panse de l'initiale D (**pl 112**) est composée d'un monstre serpentiforme. Il s'enroule autour des jambes d'un personnage placé dans le champ que délimite la lettre capitale. Il lui enfonce la langue dans la bouche. L'illustration du texte est éloquente: bouche méchante et bouche d'imposture sont ainsi fécondées par le mal, le diable. On ne peut s'empêcher de rapprocher cette image de la fécondation par la bouche si fréquente dans les textes. Par exemple, en buvant l'eau du fleuve Conchobar, Ness avala un ver à chaque gorgée. Elle fut alors grosse et 'c'était de ces vers qu'elle était grosse'.[42] Dans un autre épisode du cycle d'Ulster, Dechtiré demanda à boire après la mort de son pupille. Elle sentit une petite bête venir avec la boisson. La bête fut 'entraînée par l'haleine de Dechtiré'. Elle fut alors enceinte. Une grande discussion à ce sujet s'empara des Ulates car elle n'était pas mariée. Son frère Conchobar la fiança à Sualdam, fils de Roeg. Avant de l'épouser, elle réussit à vomir 'et perdit le germe qu'elle portait dans son sein; et ainsi redevint vierge'.[43] Ceci souligne l'importance des zones frontières, marginales de la chrétienté médiévale: l'Irlande, l'Écosse, l'Islande notamment.[44]

Tirer la barbe d'un adversaire était ainsi l'injure suprême, une atteinte à sa virilité, à l'intimité de sa personne. Une dispute sous cette forme ne pouvait qu'y gagner en force. La naissance de cette image en Irlande n'est sans doute pas étrangère au succès des représentations de lutteurs, de combats d'hommes contre un animal ou d'animaux entre eux, notamment sur les croix à Kells, Durrow, Killamery, Kilrea ou Castledermot.[45] La valeur négative était sans doute une marque d'opprobre de la part de l'église. À Poitiers, la réconciliation entraîne la disparition de la barbe sur les protagonistes. Ne trouve-t-on pas, sur un chapiteau du choeur de Notre-Dame-du-Port, à Clermont-Ferrand, à l'époque romane, l'Ange qui chasse du Paradis terrestre Adam et Eve, en tirant le premier par la barbe et la seconde par les cheveux,[46] ou, dans une *Vie de saint Omer*, le bourreau qui entraîne le saint en le tirant par la barbe (Saint-Omer, BM, MS 698, folio

---

[41]ibid, col 487.

[42]H d'Arbois de Jubainville, *Cours de littérature* (Paris 1892) V, 16-17.

[43]ibid, 36-38.

[44]J Le Goff, dans *Pour un autre moyen âge* (Paris 1977) 386. Notre approche semble avoir échappé à l'attention des historiens, voir, par exemple, outre cette étude sur le rituel symbolique, l'article *Baiser* de F Cabrol dans le *DACL*, II, 117-30 et Y Carré, *Le baiser sur la bouche au Moyen Age: rites, symbles, mentalities, XIe-XVe siècles* (Paris 1992) 408-12 et passim.

[45]F Henry, *La sculpture irlandaise pendant les douze premiers siècles de l'ère chrétienne* (Paris 1932) 86, 132, 134, fig; eadem, *L'art irlandais*, La Pierre-Qui-Vire, coll. Zodiaque, I, 1963; II, 1964.

[46]*Congrès archéologique de Clermont Ferrand* (1924) fig p 49 et 50.

34).[47] Quant au caractère intime de cet attribut masculin, il subsistait dans les images de doute, de réflexion, de profonde interrogation comme dans la célèbre image des rois mages du Psautier de Winchester, de peu postérieur à 1150, où le plus ancien tire sa propre barbe devant l'Enfant Jésus.[48] Peu à peu cette image de dispute s'enrichit pour disparaître, au cours du XIIème siècle, sans doute sous l'influence de l'église et des ordres monastiques. Le poil, comme la fourrure, renvoyait davantage à la bête ou à l'homme en marge de la société, l'homme sauvage. La taxinomie se formait. À la même époque l'église imposa la suprématie du lion au détriment de l'ours celtique et germanique, un animal velu, jusque là considéré comme le roi des animaux.[49]

Le thème des deux personnages se tirant mutuellement la barbe, qui appartenait à l'héritage culturel venu du Nord, des Celtes, apparemment ne rencontra d'audience que dans la seule France et principalement dans les pays de l'Ouest.[50] Il céda le pas à d'autres représentations négatives de la dispute, de la discorde ou autre combat.[51]

---

[47]Porcher (*supra* la note 13, 1954) no 118 et couverture.

[48]M Rickert, 2ème éd (London 1965) fig 80.

[49]M Pastoureau, 'Quel est le roi des animaux' dans *Figures et couleurs. Étude sur la symbolique et la sensibilité médiévales* (Paris 1986) 159-75.

[50]Ces pays de l'Ouest méritent une attention particulière, voir C de Mérindol, 'La fourrure de vair dans les images à l'époque romane', *Histoire et généalogie* 40 (1992) 2-34, fig.

[51]À propos de notre thème sont citées d'autres oeuvres, mais il s'agit de luttes, parfois armées, ou d'accolades, ou de combats contre un monstre. Parfois l'un des deux personnages tire la barbe de l'autre comme à Saint-Benoît-sur-Loire. Une femme peut être témoin comme en cette abbaye, ainsi qu'à Nouaillé et à Saint-Lomer de Blois. Les oeuvres, qui ont pu être contrôlées, sont Notre-Dame-la-Grande, la Celle-Bruère, Lescure, une pièce du musée d'Agen, l'ancien évêché d'Angers, Carentan, Colombiers, Esclottes, Lauresque, Nouaillé, Saint-Benoît-sur-Loire, Saint-Lomer de Blois et Saint-Martin de Coux. N'ont pu l'être, Dorchet, Granville, Sainte-Honorine et Jou sous Monjou. Voir le *Corpus des inscriptions* et les articles de Riou, de Klein et de Besson, voir *supra* dans les notes 7, 14 et 15.

The Book of Kells and the Northumbrian type of classical drapery *

Douglas Mac Lean

Among those who favour a Carolingian dating framework for the Book of Kells, Dr Harbison has proposed placing the manuscript within the reign of Louis the Pious.[1] If he is correct, a number of figures in Kells would then depend upon a single figure in the Book of Armagh (Dublin, Trinity College Library, MS 52), the *imago hominis* on folio 32v, datable by the Ferdomnach inscription on folio 52v to 807-08 (**pl 73**).[2] The Armagh figure wears a cloak draped over both shoulders, with folds descending from both sides of each forearm; it clearly belongs to a family of Irish illuminations, found in St Gall, Stiftsbibliothek, MS 51, the Book of Mulling (TCD, MS 60), the excerpts from John's gospel bound with the Stowe Missal (Dublin, RIA, MS D.II.3), BL, Add MS 40618 and the Macdurnan Gospels (London, Lambeth Palace Library, MS 1370). I would propose, however, that this Irish group further developed the earlier experimentation of the Kells artists, who responded in turn to the previous emergence of the distinctive Northumbrian type of classical drapery, first detected by Ernst Kitzinger in his study of St Cuthbert's coffin.[3]

Whether worn over one or both shoulders, both ends of the classical *pallium* usually fall over the left arm, but the figures on Cuthbert's coffin, such as the standing Christ on the lid (**fig 1**), have one end draped over each arm, with an additional and improbable stretch of cloth between them. The only Mediterranean examples of this arrangement known to Kitzinger occur among the stucco figures in the Orthodox Baptistery in Ravenna,[4] making the availability of a Ravennate model more than likely at Lindisfarne, where the coffin was carved for the translation of the saint's relics in 698.

The 'double drapery' effect seen on Cuthbert's coffin first became established as an insular convention in Northumbria and is also found on

---

*This essay derives, in part, from my unpublished MA thesis, 'An analysis of the costumes worn by the human figures in the Book of Kells' (University of Texas at Austin 1979), which the late Julian Brown urged me to publish in its entirety when he read it in 1981. Until such time as I am able to do so, I offer this small bit of it in token of the affectionate memory of one who would still have had a great deal to teach us: *Mar chuimhneachan air ar maighstir*.
[1]P Harbison, 'The Carolingian contribution to Irish sculpture' in Ryan, 105-10.
[2]Alexander, *Insular manuscripts*, 76-77
[3]E Kitzinger, 'The coffin-reliquary' in *The relics of Saint Cuthbert*, ed C F Battiscombe (Oxford 1956) 292-97.
[4]ibid, 294, n 3.

Fig 1 St Cuthbert's coffin lid (*The Dean and Chapter of Durham Cathedral*)

the Ruthwell and Bewcastle crosses.[5] Fritz Saxl had argued that the mantle of the Bewcastle Christ derived from the *paenula*, the ancestor of the ecclesiastical chasuble.[6] For Kitzinger, however, the garment in question is 'basically ... a *pallium*', although he admits that it 'has been more thoroughly contaminated' than those of the Ruthwell figures, but he points out that the two edges of Christ's *pallium* in Ruthwell's Magdalene scene clearly overlap on his chest, something that would not happen with the semi-circular *paenula*.[7] Northumbrian artists did not rigidly adhere, however, to their adopted formula. Eadfrith most probably painted the Lindisfarne Gospels (London, British Library, MS Cotton Nero D.IV) while Lindisfarne woodcarvers were fashioning Cuthbert's coffin within shouting distance of the scriptorium. The ends of the *pallium* apparently drape over the left forearm of the Lindisfarne Luke (folio 137v) and both ends of the *pallium* are visible in the Lindisfarne John portrait (folio 209v), which Isabel Henderson relates to the large figure of David on the St Andrews Sarcophagus.[8] Insular artists were not congenitally incapable of rendering believable depictions of classical costume.

The two surviving evangelist portraits in the Lichfield Gospels (Lichfield, Cathedral Library) represent both the classical and Northumbrian versions of the *pallium*. However abstracted, Mark (p 142) wears his cloak over both shoulders, with the ends thrown over the left forearm, while the Luke portrait (p 218) employs the Northumbrian double drapery falling from both wrists.[9] Mediterranean models available in insular centres included conventional representations of classical costume as well as the Ravennate version seen on Cuthbert's coffin and the Ruthwell and Bewcastle crosses. Insular artists working in the same monastery or even a single artist preparing one manuscript could be equally enamoured of both.

Several figures in the Book of Kells are comparable to Kitzinger's examples of the Northumbrian type. Christ in the Ruthwell Magdalene scene and the possible evangelist figure in the upper left of the Kells *In Principio* page (folio 292r) each have their left hands draped while holding a book, with their *pallia* placed on both shoulders, drawn closed in front and a free end hanging from the right arm. A second free end falls from the covered left hand of the Ruthwell Christ, while a bent red line indicates the opposite end of the *pallium* on the Kells figure.[10]

---

[5]G Baldwin Brown and A B Webster, *The Ruthwell and Bewcastle crosses, the Gospels of Lindisfarne, and other Christian Monuments of Northumbria*, The arts in early England 5, (London 1921) pl XVII.

[6]F Saxl, 'The Ruthwell Cross', *Journal of the Warburg and Courtauld Institutes* 6 (1943) 1-19 (p 10).

[7]Kitzinger (note 3 above) 294, n1; Baldwin Brown (note 5 above) pl XIX.

[8]Alexander, *Insular manuscripts*, pls 30-1; I Henderson, 'Pictish art and the Book of Kells' in *Ireland in early mediaeval Europe: studies in memory of Kathleen Hughes*, ed D Whitelock, R McKitterick and D Dumville (Cambridge 1982) 79-105 (p 96, pl XIVa).

[9]Alexander, *Insular manuscripts*, pls 80, 82.

[10]In addition to the reproduction in the *Kells facsimile* a more accessible illustration may be seen in Henry, pl 95

The figure at the top of the Kells *Liber* page (folio 29r) closely follows the original Northumbrian type seen on Cuthbert's coffin, with the *pallium* draped over both shoulders and connected drapery falling from the arms (**pl 19**). The book-bearing figure in the lower left of the miniature introduces another line of development. Classical *clavi* decorate his tunic and he wears a mantle over both shoulders. A single, apparently right arm emerges from his *pallium*, terminating in a left hand, with a single drapery fold, bordered in yellow, descending from it. Analogous figures are found throughout the Book of Kells. The canon table on folio 3r provides two examples: the *imago hominis* under the arch and another in the central medallion.[11] The angel in the upper left on folio 285r correctly has a right hand on a right arm but the drapery again falls on one side, towards the viewer.[12] Another Kells variation shows the *pallium* falling on both sides of the single extended arm. Examples include the two upper angels attending Christ on folio 32v and the angel of the Crucifixion passage in Mark on folio 183r.[13]

All of the Kells variations of this type (and there are others) — figures in long costume thrusting one arm out from underneath the cloak — may belong to an insular pictorial lineage that began with the *Maiestas Domini* miniature in the *Codex Amiatinus* (Florence, Bibliotheca Medicea-Laurenziana, MS Amiatinus I, folio 796v).[14] Among the possible antecedents of the Northumbrian type of classical drapery, Kitzinger placed special emphasis on Mediterranean depictions of saints in procession, such as those in Sant'Apollinare Nuovo in Ravenna, carrying sacred objects in both hands, with the *pallium* slung over both arms, creating a 'curtain' in front of the body. The angel to Christ's right in the Amiatinus *Maiestas* and three of its four evangelists 'reproduce the type with a fair amount of accuracy'.[15] But Kitzinger thought that the bit of *pallium* enveloping the right hand of the angel to Christ's left suggested a second free end, in addition to the one draped over the angel's left hand, a potential link in the 'transition from the Mediterranean to the insular type'. The connection is well established between the *Codex Amiatinus* and the south Italian *Codex Grandior* made for Cassiodorus at Vivarium, but Hans Belting, Lawrence Nees and others have stressed Cassiodorus's long service in Ravenna to successive Ostrogothic rulers from Theodoric to Vitigis.[16] We may be looking at ripples of Ravennate sources for insular renditions of classical costume.

In some cases, the Kells artists advanced the type by adding a single protruding hand with drapery falling on one or both sides, as we have seen; they then took a further step by showing both hands. Three of the four angels in the Kells Virgin and Child miniature (folio 7v) have both hands

[11]ibid, pl 5.
[12]ibid, pl 89.
[13]ibid, pls 26, 55.
[14]Alexander, *Insular manuscripts*, pl 26.
[15]Kitzinger (note 3 above) 294-95.
[16]H Belting, 'Probleme der Kunstgeschichte Italiens im Frühmittelalter', *Frühmittel-alterliche Studien* 1 (1967) 94-143 (p 109); L Nees, *The Gundohinus Gospels*, Medieval Academy Books 95 (Cambridge, Mass 1987) 168-69.

visible.[17] Their mantles cover both shoulders and fall open over the chest, while separate folds dangle beneath each forearm; but the extra drapery, drooping between and connecting the arms, belies the logic of the arrangement and recalls the Northumbrian type incised on Cuthbert's coffin, prefiguring the Armagh *imago hominis*, although the Armagh figure lacks the stretch of cloth between the arms.

Insular ambiguity is less apparent in the garments of the figures attending Christ in the so-called Arrest miniature, folio 114r.[18] Their hands are visible, their mantles placed on both shoulders and no fabric connects the drapery falling on either side of their arms, although the figure on the right has two left hands and the left hand of the figure on the left is placed above the drapery that should itself be placed above the left hand. There is ambiguity here, too, but of a different kind.

Two sets of curving symmetrical lines, centrally placed on Christ's chest in the same miniature, seem to indicate a separation between the two edges of his open cloak. But that is rendered impossible by the continuity of the drapery between his arms, harking back, once again, to the Northumbrian archetype. In contrast, similar curving lines, set farther apart, on the *imago hominis* of the Four Symbols page, folio 129v, preceding Mark in Kells, do indeed indicate that the *pallium* of that figure falls open over his long tunic.[19] The colouring of Christ's tunic in the Arrest miniature, apparently intended to describe the location of his legs beneath it, recalls the coloristic ambiguity of the *Codex Amiatinus* Ezra (folio Vr).

The Kells St John portrait on folio 291v (**pl 51**) best represents the manuscript's re-interpretation of the Northumbrian variant of classical costume. The seated evangelist wears a long tunic and folds of his *pallium* fall on two sides of each arm. The open neck of the closed mantle forms a border which frames John's beard and descends, suggesting the meeting of the mantle's two edges in front of the figure. But the transverse lines of a fold of cloth, crossing over the vertical border between John's arms, render this conclusion doubtful, as does the linear continuity of the material of the mantle at the bottom of the drapery falling between the two arms. The expressive quality of John's costume in Kells becomes schematized in probably later Irish renditions of the formula. Vertical lines down the front of the figures of both Matthew and Luke in St Gall 51 (pp 2 and 128) seem to allude to the closure of the two ends of the *pallium*, but are contradicted by the continuous line defining the bottom sag of the drapery falling between their arms.[20] Luke is the more staid of the two and lacks the hollow scoops

---

[17]Henry, pl 10.
[18]ibid, pl 45.
[19]ibid, pl 50.
[20]Alexander, *Insular manuscripts*, 66-67, pls 204-05. Françoise Henry variously dated St Gall 51 to the middle or second half of the eighth century in *Irish art in the early christian period to 800 AD* (London 1965) 196; idem, *Irish art during the Viking invasions (800-1020 AD)* (London 1967) 58; and in Henry, 163. Alexander accepts the latter, broader framework, but Peter Harbison, 'The bronze crucifixion plaque said to be

of cloth proceeding outwards from Matthew' wrists, a feature already seen in the Armagh *imago hominis*, although the Armagh figure has no connecting drapery between the forearms. The combination of a vertical bisecting line at the front of Luke's cloak and its negation by the unbroken connection at the bottom of the drapery between the forearms, along with the double drapery effect on each arm, is peculiar to Kells, St Gall 51 and the later-ninth century Macdurnan Gospels, where it is seen in the Mark portrait (folio 70v).[21] The Northumbrian original is not as pointedly ambiguous. No line is employed to imply a bilateral separation of the mantle where it falls between the arms of the figure on Cuthbert's coffin or the Ruthwell and Bewcastle crosses, where the *pallium* sits on both shoulders and falls open over the front of the figure, yet an incongruously continuous piece of drapery also connects the arms. No further device is used to render impossible the logical arrangement of the garment in Northumbria, although the evangelists' manner of wearing their mantles depicted in Kells, St Gall 51 and Macdurnan would be as equally unattainable as it had been for their Northumbrian precursors with a large rectangular piece of cloth, such as the classical *pallium* or the Irish *brat*. But a fascination with ambiguity had long been characteristic of Celtic artists.

Other Irish versions of the Northumbrian type, with connected drapery between the arms but without the vertical line at the front of the cloak, also appear in St Gall 51. The John portrait (p 208) has a single starched scoop of cloth beneath the right wrist, while Mark (p 78), like Luke in the same manuscript, has none.[22] Stephaton and Longinus in the St Gall Crucifixion miniature (p 266) each have a single scoop, a feature also found among the apostles in the St Gall Last Judgement (p 267).[23] Pairs of scooped folds, reminiscent of the Book of Armagh, but with additional drapery linking the forearms, adorn both Matthew and John in the Macdurnan Gospels (folios 4v and 170v), as well as the Stowe St John (folio 11v) and the sole evangelist in BL, Add. MS 40618 (folio 21v).[24] The fully developed Irish variant of the Northumbrian type combines the connected drapery between the arms of the Kells John with the tubular folds of the Armagh *imago hominis*, but the Irish were no more congenitally incapable of reasonably accurate renditions of classical drapery than were their colleagues across the Irish Sea. Matthew's and Mark's cloaks in the Book of Mulling (folios 12v and 35v)

---

from St John's (Rinnagan), near Athlone', *Journal of Irish Archaeology* 2 (1984) 1-17 (pp 13, 15) argues for a ninth-century date. In view of the similarities between the drapery of the Matthew and John portraits in St Gall 51 and that of the John portrait in the Book of Mulling, Harbison's later dating is supported by the mid-ninth-century date for the Book of Mulling advocated by Lawrence Nees, 'The colophon drawing in the Book of Mulling: a supposed Irish monastery plan and the tradition of terminal illustrations in early medieval manuscripts', *Cambridge Medieval Celtic Studies* 5 (Summer 1983) 67-91.
[21] Alexander, *Insular manuscripts*, 86-87, pl 354.
[22] ibid, pl 208.
[23] ibid, pls 203, 206.
[24] ibid, 68-69, pls 209, 213, 326, 328.

drape conventionally over the left arm,[25] while John's mantle on folio 81v in the same manuscript (pl 114) follows the Irish double drapery formula.

It is perhaps to the common Gaelic culture of Ireland and Scottish Dalriada that we should look for the origins of the urge towards the distinctive insular treatment of classical costume, which first took root in Northumbria, and it is here that Professor Kitzinger and I cordially agreed to disagree when we discussed the matter in 1979. In his discussion of the figures on Cuthbert's coffin, Kitzinger repeatedly asserts that insular artists 'did not understand the nature of the garment they represented', that they 'misunderstood' a type which they themselves did not invent, that their 'desire for ornamental balance and symmetry ... for all the foreign influences that they evidently absorbed', was 'of insular origin' and shows that 'they were incapable to produce through lines a consistently pictorial effect'.[26] Whatever may have been true of the Lindisfarne woodcarvers who decorated Cuthbert's coffin, Eadfrith in the Lindisfarne Gospels, the Irish artist of the Book of Mulling and the Pictish sculptor of the St Andrews Sarcophagus were certainly capable of reasonably accurate versions of classical costume. Models descended from Ravennate exemplars, brought back to Northumbria from Rome in the baggage of Benedict Biscop and Ceolfrith, cannot alone account for the common insular predilection for closing the mantle in front, while drooping drapery from both wrists, which would seem to require an additional impetus.

I turn now to artistic observations drawn from contemporary life, rather than imported models, rejecting the long-accepted art-historical dictum that 'pictures came from pictures' in the middle ages. The closed mantles of three figures in the Book of Kells seem to fall realistically between their arms, but only one arm is visible of the *imago hominis* under the arch of the first Kells canon table on folio 1v as is also the case with the one in the upper left of the canon table on folio 5r.[27] Both figures appear to raise their single extended arms beneath a long side of the cloak and the part falling over the chest overlaps the other end of the mantle, where the two meet over the figures' torsos. The same may be said of the seated drinking figure in the margin of the genealogy of Christ on folio 201v in Luke, surely a figure drawn, to some extent, from the life.[28] These three minor figures in Kells may be the forerunners, in this regard, of the seated Matthew portrait in St Gall 1395 (p 418) whose mantle overlaps in front, while drapery falls on

[25]ibid, pls 210-11.
[26]Kitzinger (note 3 above) 293-96. In addition to Kitzinger's suggestion, discussed above, of Mediterranean models showing saints in procession, with drapery falling over both forearms while they hold sacred objects before them, he also proposes two other possibilities: insular artists might have relied upon depictions of figures wearing the *paenula*, which 'hangs evenly on all sides', or instead, upon figures with their *pallia* arranged with an end thrown over the shoulder, rather than a forearm, in which case the end hanging behind an arm could have been replaced on that arm. Each of Kitzinger's possibilities remains entirely dependent upon an imported model, whether it was clearly understood or not.
[27]Henry, pls 2, 9.
[28]ibid, pl 66.

either side of both wrists.[29] A related, if more mannered treatment, characterizes the Luke portrait (folio 115v) in the Macdurnan Gospels.[30]

It must be remembered that the traditional long costume of Christ, the apostles and evangelists consisted of both a large cloak or *pallium* and a long tunic. As such, it was not completely alien to the insular world. The same sort of garments were the prerogative of the Gaelic-speaking aristocracy, both male and female, the *brat* or mantle and the *léine* or long tunic, continually described, with numbing regularity, in Old-Irish secular literature, exactly contemporary with these illuminated manuscripts, only the elaborate descriptions of colours, stripes and fringes distinguishing one character from another.[31] The overlapping frontal closure of Matthew's *brat* in St Gall 1395 and its drapery over his arms may owe much more to contemporary Gaelic sartorial practice, in both Ireland and Dalriada, than to any Irish re-interpretation of a Northumbrian response to a Ravennate source.

Two adjacent panels on the west face of Muiredach's Cross at Monasterboice (pl 87) provide sculptural confirmation of such a possibility. The scene in the second panel from the bottom of the shaft has most often been identified as the Incredulity of Thomas,[32] although Harbison has recently argued that it is a representation of the Raised Christ.[33] If the former identification be accepted, the figure to the right of Christ may be John the Evangelist, who alone records the incident, while Harbison suggests instead that he is St Paul. In either case, the figure would represent one of the most important christian saints, but we are concerned here with his costume, whoever he may be. In addition to the two folds of drapery that fall along the outer edges of the figure on both sides, a third bit of cloth hangs between the right elbow and the left wrist. The curved line carved along the lower inside edge of this flap shows that it comprises two overlapping parts, reminiscent of the logical arrangement of Matthew's mantle in St Gall 1395. The figure's long hair and moustache are secular details, but it would not be unreasonable for an Irish sculptor to depict as an Irish aristocrat a saint attendant upon either the Raised Christ or the moment of Thomas's ultimate conversion. The arrangement of his *brat* includes both the double drapery effect on the arms and an additional connection of cloth between them.

The bottom shaft panel on the same face of the Muiredach Cross has generally been accepted as the Arrest of Christ, although Helen Roe offers

---

[29]Alexander, *Insular manuscripts*, pl 281.
[30]ibid, pl 327.
[31]See, for example, *Togail Bruidne Da Derga*, ed Eleanor Knott, Mediaeval and Modern Irish Series 8 (Dublin 1975) passim.
[32]Henry (1967, note 20 above) 157, 161; Helen M Roe, *Monasterboice and its monuments* (Dundalk 1981) 20, 31.
[33]Harbison, I, 144, 293-94. I thank Dr Harbison for bringing his views to my attention.

as an alternate possibility the *Ecce Homo*.[34] Harbison, however, points out that Pilate's use of that phrase is restricted to the account in John 19:5, which lacks the reed seen in Christ's right hand at Monasterboice, a detail found only in Matthew 27:27-31. He therefore proposes naming the scene the Second Mocking of Christ or *Ecce Rex Iudaeorum*.[35] In any event, the panel's central figure is Christ, whether his cloak is his own, or the purple or scarlet one insultingly provided by Pilate's minions. The garment in question has no additional connecting cloth between Christ's raised arms, other than the two edges pinned together with a brooch, although the two long folds that appear to fall on either side between his arms prompted McClintock, in his study of Old-Irish dress, to think that the *brat* was fitted with holes for the arms.[36] But the folds at the crook of the left arm suggest that this is not the case. It seems, rather, that the arms have been brought up under two opposite sides of the rectangular cloak, creating long folds of drapery on either side of both arms, in the manner of the St Gall, Stiftsbibliothek, MS 1395 Matthew.

The baffling drapery of the Cuthbert's coffin figures may have been suggested to Northumbrian artists by an acquaintance with Gaelic aristocrats and the garb of their class. The exile of King Oswald of Northumbria at Iona, the visits of Abbot Adomnán of Iona to Northumbria in the 680s, which now seem to have been more political than ecclesiastical in nature and could well have entailed secular gentleman in his entourage, and the creation of Mayo of the Saxons by Colmán of Lindisfarne after the Synod of Whitby are but a few of the historical events which support the high probability of an Anglo-Saxon awareness of Gaelic secular costume.[37] It is not enough to hunt down possible imported models; we must also account for the choices artists made when confronted with a multiplicity of pictorial sources. One would not expect the Gaelic gentry to bare the right shoulders of their tunics to the elements by wearing their mantles in the more customary manner of the classical *pallium*, but some Mediterranean models showed the *pallium* worn on both shoulders and contemporary Gaelic practice could have helped otherwise strange depictions of foreign and antiquated dress seem more familiar. The drapery of the figures on

---

[34]Henry (1967, note 20 above) 157, 181-82; Roe (note 32 above) 19, 31.

[35]Harbison, I, 143-44, 270-71. The John passage portrays Christ in the crown of thorns and a 'purple garment': *Exivit ergo Iesus portans coronam spineam, et purpureum vestimentum.* In Matthew's version, Pilate's soldiers dress Christ in the crown of thorns and a 'scarlet cloak' (*chlamydem coccineam*), put a reed in his hand, then mock him by saying *Ave rex Iudaeorum*. Although the Muiredach panel includes the reed found only in Matthew, Harbison notes that it lacks the crown of thorns mentioned in both gospels. For the First Mocking of Christ, see Harbison, I, 265-66.

[36]H F McClintock, *Old Irish and Highland dress and that of the Isle of Man* (Dundalk 1950) 2-3. The extended hand of the figure to Christ's right obscures the arrangement of the mantle along his right side.

[37]Primary sources for these events may be found in *HE*, 218-21, 346-47, 504-07, 550-51; *Adomnán's Life of Columba*, ed A O Anderson and M O Anderson, Oxford Medieval Texts, rev ed (Oxford 1991) xxvii, xl, 178-81; *Early sources of Scottish history AD 500 to 1286*, ed A O Anderson, 2 vols (Edinburgh 1922) I, 179, 196-99. For additional discussion, see H Mayr-Harting, *The coming of christianity to Anglo-Saxon England* (New York 1972) 94, 112-13; H Moisl, 'The Bernician royal dynasty and the Irish in the seventh century', *Peritia* 2 (1983) 102-26.

Cuthbert's coffin is intended to be classical but the classical model has been altered to accommodate the appearance of a secular costume which Northumbrian artists already knew, that of the Gaelic upper class. The Northumbrian system of depicting classical drapery then received characteristically experimental treatment in the Book of Kells, before becoming formulaic in Irish manuscripts in a process which may have begun in the Book of Armagh, only to be returned to its native source on the Muiredach Cross, in the secular costume of figures clad in the aristocratic *brat* and *léine*.

Acknowledgements: I am most grateful to the Samuel H Kress Foundation for the travel grant which enabled me to present this paper; to Dr Pádraig Ó Macháin for accommodation in Dublin: and to Dr Peter Harbison for kindly providing me with photocopies of the relevant portions of his new corpus of Irish high crosses.

Drolleries in the Book of Kells

Etienne Rynne

According to the *Concise Oxford Dictionary* the term 'drollery' means 'jesting; a facetious composition; quaint humour', any of which descriptions can readily be applied to the different types of humour leaping with amusement from the pages of the world-famous late-eighth-century Book of Kells. For three main types of drolleries are evident in the manuscript: firstly humorous details noticeable when one looks carefully in the illustrations, often perhaps private jokes for the artist and his colleagues, secondly initial letters which present funny positions and shapes or unnatural relationships between animals, birds, fish, worms and humans, and thirdly little figures, often contorted, of all the above animals, birds, etc used as space-fillers, in linking functions, or in run-over functions, not to mention many clearly haphazardly scattered drolleries in various odd places, merely for amusement.

Dr Françoise Henry has identified four major artists who worked illuminating the Book of Kells, artists whom she named the 'Goldsmith', the 'Portraitist', the 'Illustrator', and the 'Animal Painter'; in addition to these she allowed the work of some pupils/apprentices.[1] All these artists worked together, in harmony with one another and with one another's work. While not all of them may have had the same sense of amusement, it is clear that at least two of the major artists had an enormous sense of humour, namely the 'Portraitist' and, above all others, the 'Animal Painter', though the 'Illustrator' also could be humorous in his own quiet way; the 'Goldsmith' appears to have been a good deal more serious than the others but to nonetheless have appreciated (or merely tolerated?) their occasional escapes into humour — the little items in his work which raise a smile are more likely to be secondary additions by them. A few other humorous details, not always well drawn nor apparently always finished, are sneaked into the Book of Kells in such a way as to suggest the risqué efforts of the pupils/apprentices.

Various *raisons d'êtres* have been suggested for drolleries in illuminated manuscripts, perhaps best summed up by David M Robb.[2] He believes that they were primarily 'intended ... to entertain or amuse', that a 'drollery is independent of any restriction and appears where the whim of its creator pleases', and that 'it goes without saying that these figures have nothing to do with the text, either as illustration or interpretation. There is no explanation for them, in fact, save that they play the same role in the Gothic manuscript as the gargoyles and grotesques that their stone counterparts do

---

[1] Françoise Henry, *Irish art during the Viking invasions: 800-1020 AD* (London 1967) 73-77; Henry, 211-12.
[2] David M Robb, *The art of the illuminated manuscript* (Cranbury, NJ 1973) 225.

on the Gothic cathedral'. Though Robb is commenting on drolleries in Gothic manuscripts, what he states would appear to be equally valid for most, if perhaps not quite all, of those found in the Book of Kells. Indeed, J J G Alexander, commenting on the latter, makes much the same statement when he says that they 'are full of imaginative fantasy and humour which finds its nearest parallel in the marginal drolleries of Gothic manuscripts of five centuries later', and 'As with the Gothic marginalia there is a problem as to whether any meaning or connection with the text is intended ....'[3]

While accepting the viewpoint that drolleries were apparently incidental to the text as a general rule, it is clear that although they may not have had any particular *meaning* they usually had a *purpose*, maybe even a two-fold purpose: firstly to fill a space, to provide a link or to indicate a run-over, and secondly in decorating the page that they should also amuse the casual viewer. It is, therefore, with this in mind that one should approach any study or examination of the drolleries in the Book of Kells.

We should firstly try to put ourselves in the artist's place, and ask ourselves whether the artists were necessarily deeply involved in theology, philosophy, liturgy, exegesis, or religious symbolism, or were they perhaps not much more than highly qualified and dedicated artists with technique and flair in abundance who had been selected because of their ability to do the required job? Indeed, one might further point out that carefully and all as the Book of Kells was produced, it was apparently not meant to be read or treated as an ordinary book: it was quite obviously intended as a magnificent piece of art, which was to serve as an item to be proudly displayed on the high altar on special occasions for special ceremonies, an important status and symbolic object, and also perhaps, to paraphrase the well-known stock phrase, a masterpiece produced *do chum glóire Dé agus onóra Naoimh Colmchille*. It is a book, in fact, which was created perhaps not so much for the casual viewer as to be viewed casually (as opposed to being closely studied and interpreted in great detail).

One can over-interpret anything, and to interpret the work of the artists of the Book of Kells as anything more than a visual experience is dangerous. One must always keep in mind the fact that the artist may well have had quite a different idea/intention/interpretation when doing his work than that of the viewer, especially a viewer looking at it well over a thousand years later! Let us, therefore, try to look at this marvellous book with a fresh, not-too-questioning eye, just as would a rather ordinary Irishman of the period, whether he be a nominally literate and not-too-serious monk, a semi-literate king, or a member of the illiterate majority, all of whom would view the book with eyes full of wonder at its glory, ready to enjoy its beauty and not beyond being amused, even if in a rather unsophisticated way.

Let us start our enquiry into the humour and drolleries in the Book of Kells by having a quick, brief look at the first type mentioned above, namely the

[3] Alexander, *Insular manuscripts*, 73.

minor details found in the book's major pages which, whether done intentionally or not, raise a smile from today's viewer. There are several such pages, including the three illustrating scenes from the life of Christ, those showing the Madonna and Child, the Arrest of Christ, and the Temptation — a fourth illustration, the Crucifixion, was apparently intended to go on folio 123v, to face the *Tunc crucifixerant* text on folio 124r, but the page remains blank — did the artist die before the book was finished, perhaps being killed during the Viking raid on Iona in 806, or did he simply not travel to Kells with his colleagues where the Book was apparently finished?

To examine the Madonna and Child illustration (**pl 9**)[4] first: how many have noticed that the Virgin is depicted with two right feet and the Child with two left feet, as pointed out at least as long ago as 1914 by Edward Sullivan?[5] George Bain in 1951[6] added that one of the Child's feet had only four toes, that the angel in the upper left corner had an extra finger on the left hand, that the angel in the bottom right corner has two left hands, and that the one in the bottom left corner had a right hand on a left arm — he might also have added that Christ seems to have two left hands. Furthermore, neither of the two uppermost angels are either looking or pointing in the direction of the major figures, while the 'crowd scene' in a box-like cartouche interrupting the left side of the picture-frame is shown facing *away* from the child and his mother — the three 'crowd scenes' indented into the frame of the *Tunc crucifixerant* page (**pl 29**) might appear to be similarly out of sync with the page, but they would all have been looking at the Crucifixion scene on the opposing page (folio 123v) had it ever been painted. The scene generally identified as the Arrest of Christ (**pl 28**) is likewise mildly amusing: a very large Christ is being loosely gripped by two dwarf-like figures, both of whom have two left feet and one of whom has two left hands. Bain hints at an early Egyptian parallel for duplication of right or left hands and feet, but this seems unnecessary and it would seem more justifiable to regard its occurrence in the Book of Kells as being due to the inborn Celtic disinclination towards realism in art, or maybe as a private joke between the artists of the monastic atelier. The Temptation scene (**pl 42**) is different, the strangest thing about it, apart from the two angels hovering over Christ's head like love-birds, being the black stick-like devil, looking for all the world like a Javanese shadow-puppet giving a two-finger salute — but one does not joke about or laugh at the devil!

---

[4]As few possess either the 1950-51 Urs Graf Verlag edition, *Evangeliorum quattuor codex Cenannensis*, or the more recent *The Book of Kells*, Fine Art Facsimile edition (Luzern 1990), all the examples quoted in this paper will be confined to the coloured illustrations of the next best edition and one which is generally available in most good public and private libraries, namely *The Book of Kells: reproductions from the manuscript in Trinity College, Dublin* (London 1974) by Françoise Henry.

[5]Edward Sullivan, *The Book of Kells* (London 1914) 7.

[6]George Bain, *The methods of construction of Celtic art* (Glasgow 1951) 130, pl B.3.

Along with the three illustrative pages, there are some other very fine pages full of ornamental text which have similarly smile-provoking details, if not necessarily true drolleries. Facing the Virgin and Child on folio 7v is the *Natiuitas* on folio 8r (**pl 10**). Apart from the decorative but almost illegible lettering of *Natiuitas*, the page at first glance appears to be relatively straightforward yet beautiful. When one looks for the pictorial elements in it one notices firstly a seated cross-legged figure balancing on his knees an open book, one which appears as if it might be a book of waxed tablets such as the well-known late-sixth-century Springmount Tablets.[7] He might seem ordinary enough, but he does have two right feet. However, it is the second, not nearly so obvious figure who is really amusing: a small rotund man clad in checkered cloak and blue knee-breeches who is seated comfortably on a ball-like, tightly-wound spiral terminating a letter R at the end of the fifth line of ornamental lettering. He faces off the page, and is cock-a-snoot, thumbing his nose at us all and defying us to interpret him otherwise or to read a symbolic or liturgical meaning into his gesture — one wonders what the monastery's abbot or the book's patron made of this! This amusing, apparently purposeless character could, indeed, be regarded as a real drollery. The seated man fighting with a beast as if playing a harp, and together with the beast making up the *ci* of *In principio* at the beginning of St John's gospel (**pl 52**), is somewhat comparable though less of a true drollery.

The finest page of all in the Book of Kells is surely the Chi-Rho page (**pl 22**), also sometimes called the Monogram page or the *Christi autem* page (though the word *autem* is so abbreviated on it as to be well-nigh unrecognisable). Almost hidden in this page of extraordinary beauty, but successfully incorporated into its overall effect of wondrous whirling and flaring ornament, are several minor pictures of secondary importance, some of which have been recognised as near- or proto-drolleries. These include two moths tugging in opposite directions at a lozenge-shaped object, an otter catching a fish, and two comfortable catlike animals watching and holding on to the tails of two mice biting a disc between them, while two other mice stand on the cats' backs and nibble at their ears. It has often been suggested that these little cameos have each a religious symbolic meaning. Maybe so — the fish caught by the otter might well represent Christ being 'captured' by a convert to christianity,[8] but is it really likely that the casual, not so well-informed viewer would see the moths and the cats/mice as being 'emblems of the faithful partaking of the Eucharist'?[9] If the disc being held by the mice is to be interpreted as the host or eucharistic bread, are we then to interpret the little scene ending a line of script on folio 48r as a hound running off with the Eucharist in his mouth? Let us, rather, accept the more obvious

---

[7] R A S Macalister, 'Wooden Book with Leaves Indented and Waxed found near Springmount Bog, Co Antrim', *JRSAI* 50 (1920) 160-66.

[8] Since earliest times the fish has been regarded as a symbol representing Christ, the Greek word for a fish being *Ichthus*, an acrostic or anagram of Christ — the word can be spelled out by using the initials of *Iêsous Christos Theou Uios Sôter*, 'Jesus Christ [the Annointed One], God's Son, Saviour'.

[9] Henry, 199.

solution, namely that all the above little scenes are no more than amusing, or at least pleasing, drolleries.

Another somewhat humorous feature found on some of the major, more ornate pages is the piecemeal dissection or breaking up of human and animal figures in such a manner that only bits of them appear and then often in rather unexpected places. Excluding the many cases where disembodied heads appear as terminals of framelike borders (see folios 29r, 114r and v, 124r, 130r, 188r, 285r and 290v for animal heads so treated, and folio 34r for a human head used similarly — on the Rho), one is amused when the framelike border acts as a body, with the head at one end and legs at the other. This is particularly so on folio 8r, the *Natiuitas* page (**pl 10**), where a human head with a bent back arm, pulling its forelock at the centre top of the page, is attached to a frame which culminates after two right-angled bends in the bottom left-hand corner with two crossed and almost wildly swinging legs. A somewhat similar arrangement of a human head at one end of a long box-like border ending in crossed legs at its other end it to be found, though less easily, adjoining the elegant display initial *L* of *Lucas* on folio 16v. Intriguing but less amusing are the pair of interlaced animal legs terminating the border which starts with an animal's head on folio 292r (**pl 52**), the *In Principio* page. Somewhat different are the framing borders on either side of folio 187v (**pl 33**) where the borders are actual bodies complete with lion-like heads at the tops and well-shaped animal haunches and legs at the bottoms, and with extraordinarily long ribbon-like forelegs extending mantis-like from about midway between the heads and rear legs.

However, it is the completely dismembered animal and human bodies which protrude in places outside the edges of frames which amuse even more, though whether they were in every case intended to amuse or even to raise a smile is open to question. The best-known example is probably on folio 291v (**pl 51**), the portrait figure of St John (incidentally shown bearded). Emerging from behind the frame is a bearded head at the top, a right and left hand from the appropriate sides, and a pair of feet at the bottom. Unfortunately this page suffered from a too severe trimming by a binder in the early nineteenth century and the emerging figure is thus missing the top of his head while the left hand has been so closely cut that it is no longer certain if it ever held anything as, apparently, does the right hand. The figure behind the portrait has usually been identified as God, inspiring the evangelist in the writing of his work, though Françoise Henry is somewhat more specific when she identifies him as 'fairly obviously the Word',[10] ie as the text *In principio erat verbum* would warrant. Another example of such a dislocated figure is to be found behind a large panel at the end of genealogy of Christ in St Luke's gospel, on folio 202r (**pl 41**). In this case only the head and feet are shown, and which Henry identifies as 'surely "The Lord"'.[11] While one might reasonably accept the identifications suggested for the first figure, and perhaps even for the second, one is surely entitled to be far less certain of her identification of the human and lion

---

[10]Henry, 194.
[11]ibid.

similarly largely hidden on folio 188r (**pl 34**), the *Quoniam* page. This, Henry suggests, is 'the Christ of the Resurrection taking the place, on that page where he is nowhere represented, of the sacrificial calf one would have expected'.[12] Maybe, but those two disembodied beings, one an animal and the other a human, would hardly have been recognised as such a symbol by the overwhelming majority of those who saw the page at the time — or, indeed, at any time ever since! Surely it is preferable to believe that it would be more likely interpreted, whatever the artist intended, as a little joke showing a man performing the well-known circus act of bravely putting his head into the lion's jaws? Maybe it was intended to be the human-maneater equivalent of the playful cats-mice scene already noted in the Chi-Rho page.

However, the strangest and most amusing of all the disjointed bodies is to found on folio 183r (**pl 32**), the *Erat autem* page. Here there is no attempt at virtually any visual linking between the human head and shoulders resting like a sculptured bust on a pedestal-like panel in the upper right-hand corner of the page, and the lower limbs protruding below a similar panel in the lower left-hand corner. Surely this two-part figure must be regarded as a bit of a joke, and hardly as 'a representation of the Resurrection, with the partly hidden figure standing for Christ'?[13]

One of the large initials of display script type, the *M* of *Matheus* on folio 12r (**pl 12**), relates to the feature discussed above: centrally placed on the top of the letter are the head and shoulders of, presumably, the saint, while his legs flare out from the bottom of the middle line of the letter directly below. With the flared legs below and the wider shoulders above, the impression is given of the saint being squeezed into and pulled through the narrower straight-sided central vertical member of the letter *M*, much as a piece of two-by-four flannel is pulled through the barrel of a gun to clean it! Not only the display-script letter but also the more ordinary initial letters throughout the book are worthy of inspection in the present context. They are generally colourful, ornate and clever, many presenting interesting and amusing vignettes. To list, never mind describe, them all would be *de trop*, but a few selected examples ought to be examined to illustrate the general approach and treatment and also to savour the general flavour.

Strange, contorted, fighting, playing or otherwise, acrobatically cavorting men, animals, birds, fish, snakes or reptilian worms are undoubtedly the most common of themes encountered in these initial letters. For instance, dogs can be squabbling with other dogs as on folio 255r, with cats as on folio 243v, with humans as on folio 255v, with birds as on folio 91r, with fish as on folio 188v (**pl 13**; one of many cases shown of 'fish bites dog' rather than *vice versa*), or with reptillian worms/snakes as on folio 60r — all these examples could be multiplied several times, each example very different from the other — variety and imagination are paramount, but humour is seldom distant, witness such little scenarios as the *ménage-à-trois* on folio

---

[12]Henry, 198.
[13]Henry, 173.

283r (pl 49). But non-combative initials also abound and can be equally amusing. For instance, the cat and mouse pair on folio 83v (pl 24), where the cat looking to the left as he bites the nails of one paw while scratching his head with the other and has his hind paws in a twist, wondering all the while where the mouse has escaped to; the frightened mouse is immediately behind the cat and is also biting his nails as he puzzles out how he is going to get away. The scene antedates the modern animated cartoon films of Tom and Jerry fame by over one thousand one hundred years!

Individual figures, too, can be amusing. While the Q on folio 58v is merely odd rather than amusing, being made up from a human head attached to a single left foot and two vicious animal-heads, some of the others quickly raise a smile, for example, the contortionist forming the letter A on folio 53v. With the minimum of effort the artist seems able to indicate clearly a whole range of moods and expressions on the faces of his humans, animals and birds. This is exemplified, for instance, on the frightened face of the little animal curled up with his hind legs extended behind his head as if to stop himself rolling or falling down into an abyss — one can easily visualise a shriek for help emanating from that animal's mouth! Even as simple an initial as that on folio 24r (pl 16) consisting of a dog standing on his hind legs and reaching up will raise a nostalgic smile from viewers as they are reminded of a dog trying to peer through a window or reach up to food on a table. Likewise the little dog on folio 90v, with a satisfied look of relief on his face as he bends a leg backwards to scratch his own backside, will create nostalgia for all dog-lovers, while the monkey-like figure on folio 254r (pl 47), with his triangular headdress may raise a grin as it recalls the Tin Woodman of *Wizard of Oz* fame to modern viewers — the headdress might also be seen as antedating the funnels (as for pouring liquids) used as hats on many of the grotesque freaks in paintings by Hieronymus Bosch von Aachen some seven hundred years later.

Similar to the initials in many ways are the real drolleries, mostly appearing as space-fillers but sometimes gainfully employed in a linking function or a run-over function. Some are serious, or at least semi-serious, but most are of a humorous nature. Some, indeed, are almost realistic enough to be acceptable without question as drolleries were they in a Gothic manuscript, for example, the dog 'chasing' the hare on folio 48r (pl 23), or the three fowl, one a cock, on folio 67r.

It has often been said that the Celts in pre-christian times had a *horror vacui* and that in consequence whenever they saw a vacant space they yearned to fill it. This is equally applicable to the Celts of christian times, including the artists of the Book of Kells, with the result that empty spaces are few in the manuscript. Among the more pleasing, even amusing space-fillers, are the little horsemen, the best known being that on folio 89r, a really miniature composition — but whoever saw a rider, even a Cossack in a circus act, seated on a horse in quite that position, never mind the fact that the reins seem to be attached to the horse's eye! Somewhat more realistic is the cowering dog crouched at the end of a line of text on folio 241r — just one of many semi-realistic animals, birds and fish used as space-fillers. Humans appear much less frequently in such a role, but worthy of note is the strange, rather eerily staring head added as a space-filling extension to a letter *m* on folio 273r, and the realistic but tiny acrobatic, high-kicking one leg, on folio 45r.

But it is in the five folios listing the genealogy of Christ that little drawings appear almost as individuals rather than as space-fillers, thus giving the impression that they may even be associated with the text; this individuality may, in fact, be merely because the lines of the genealogy are short thereby leaving a lot of open space on the pages. However, some have attempted to equate these figures with specific people or as symbols tenuously associated with the adjacent text, but such attempts lack real foundation and seem to be little more than speculation. For instance, the little man on folio 201v (**pl 40**) gazing into a chalice-like vessel which he holds in front of him has been identified as Abraham because he is seated on the end of that name and Abraham had been, *inter alia*, instructed to be seated and to eat and drink with others. Françoise Henry, however, identifies him as being 'no doubt Melchisedek',[14] for whatever reason. But if he is to be identified as one or the other, then who is the nearly identical soul-mate seated in the upper right-hand corner of folio 292r (**pl 52**), St John's *In principio* page? It seems likely that the casual viewer would feel more inclined to regard both of these two figures as pictures of an alcoholic monk, unshaven and bleary-eyed on the morning after the night before, peering disconsolately into his now empty cup! Also in the genealogy, down the centre of folio 201r (**pl 39**), is a yellow hybrid figure, the upper half of which is human and the lower half with fish-fins and ending in two fish-tails — a mermaid or a merman. This has been identified as perhaps symbolizing Jonah on the grounds that he/she grasps the letter *t* in the line reading *Qui fuit Iona*.[15] Breasts seem to be indicated on this fish-human, thus suggesting that it is female — despite the fact that the presence of two fish-tails is more often associated with mermen than with mermaids. Besides, like the drunkard on the reverse folio, this creature has a near-parallel elsewhere in the Book of Kells, albeit without breasts and with only one tail: as a horizontal space-filler in folio 213r where no association with either Jonah or St Colmcille is justified. Whatever the artist may have intended, and we should not forget that a fairly close two-tailed parallel occurs on an eighth-century slab (no 22) at Meigle, in Pertshire, Scotland, though this has often been identified as the pagan Celtic god Cernunus,[16] it would seem more reasonable at this stage of our knowledge and at this distance from the artist to accept these fish-humans as drolleries, executed in the same spirit as the strange figures of medieval bestiaries. Even Françoise Henry points out that one can hardly go further and attempt to identify 'the six scraggy fowl above and below the

[14]Henry, 200.

[15]ibid.

[16]S Cruden, *The Early Christian & Pictish Monuments of Scotland*, 2nd edn (Edinburgh 1964) 21, pl 41.

fish-man',[17] or indeed the little warrior seated or squatting with his spear and buckler (it is far too small and insignificant to be a proper shield) in the lower right-hand corner of the first folio (200r; **pl 37**) in the genealogy; she did not include here or elsewhere the winged calf on folio 201v (**pl 40**), probably the only figure drawn in the genealogy which would have been immediately identifiable to every viewer — as the symbol of St Luke in whose gospel the genealogy appears.

Useful drolleries are also found in the Book of Kells, but not so frequently. Those with a linking function are rare enough, probably the best example being the rather cute little dog with a stick-like object behind his back on folio 293v (**pl 17**). He serves no obvious purpose other than to fill an otherwise awkward space and, in so doing, to add a bit of decoration to the page. Other less cute or exotic dogs also form a linking function in the text, for instance on folios 19v (**pl 15**), 145v, 212r, and twice on folio 309v, the first of them looking like a veritable flame-thrower! Birds, too, are sometimes utilised by the artist for the same purpose, either on their own (eg on folios 309r and 310v) or accompanied by other creatures (eg on folio 55r) or by flowers in flower-pots (eg on folio 276v), while a sprig of flowers on its own supplies a link on the fourth-last line in folio 309v; none of these latter, however, are drolleries nor even slightly amusing. The same might be said for the fish on folio 311v though it certainly serves more obviously as a link than do most of the others. Perhaps more interesting than most such drolleries is the fish biting a frightened dog on folio 254r (**pl 47**), a pair which combine to be both (or neither?) a linking drollery or an initial: the dog on its own would be a good example of the former while the fish forms the cross-bar of an initial *A* — but they are amusing and justifiably drolleries.

The other functional and drollery-related creatures are those serving as a run-over function, ie those used to indicate when a word or part of a word will not fit at the end of the line and has therefore to be fitted above, or, more commonly, below it. This feature, referred to as *cenn fo eite*, 'head under the wing', or *cor fo chasán*, 'turn in/under the path', may well be an idea developed in the Tiberius school of manuscript art in southern England during the mid-eighth century,[18] but it reached its zenith in the Book of Kells. Despite the reference to birds in the 'head under the wing' term, birds are not often used, though a small one can be found on folio 273r and a very feathery bird is on folio 274r. Dogs are much more frequent, many of them most attractive, eg at the end of folio 278r or the top of folio 165v and others definitely amusing, eg the thin green dog curled around the end of the last line of text on folio 283v, the little green dog at the bottom of folio 257r shielding his eyes from the word *uxores* above (an extra little joke?), or the blue and green dog on folio 327r (**pl 53**) who looks like a most miserable footballer who has inadvertently scored an own goal! Reptilian worms, too, though not used that often as run-over drolleries, would appear to be

---

[17]Henry, 200.
[18]I am grateful to Michelle Brown for this information.

eminently suitable for such a purpose, witness the yellow one on folio 52v
or the bluish-grey one on folio 337v.

Work which appears to be that of pupils or apprentices can belong to the
drollery class, not because it is less competent, but because it can be
amusing and irrelevant. It can, too, be recognised by having an unfinished
look or the appearance of not really belonging where it appears. A good
example is the faintly outlined fish catching a writhing worm on folio 188v
(pl 13) — the student seems to have drawn this perhaps as a lesson or
because he felt like copying the fish in the nearby initial painted by his
master, but still not being experienced enough to copy the dog he therefore
replaced it by a worm, a more natural victim for a fish to bite; a drollery
resulted though only accidentally funny. A similar outline/unfinished
figure is on folio 329v. It is of a cross-legged seated man pulling his beard
and may also be apprentice work, but by one who had virtually completed
his training. This, too, is a true drollery, but can one say the same for the
lounging purple-clad man on folio 99v (pl 25)? He is very amateurishly
drawn and looks like an afterthought where the pupil noticed a gap the
master-artist had inadvertently forgotten to fill and decided to attempt
something suitable himself — it is far more amusing than the pupil may
have intended, but it is a drollery nonetheless, one of the more amusing
even if the humour is largely accidental — and, like almost everywhere, in
the eye of the beholder, not necessarily in that of the artist.

One could continue listing and enumerating interesting little detailed
illuminations in the Book of Kells for a long time, nearly all pleasing to the
eye and often amusing to the mind, but the above selection should suffice to
reveal the possibilities. Undoubtedly the Book of Kells is the most profusely
and humorously decorated early manuscript, and raises the question as to
the origin of the idea of drolleries found in it. If one were to be very
pedantic one could perhaps agree with Robb when he states that 'it can
hardly be doubted that the Gothic drollery was invented in England early in
the 13th century and spread to the Continent' and that 'it is not difficult to
recognise the humour of the Gothic drollery as a 13th-century realisation of
this characteristically English trait' — although he almost covers himself
when he comments that 'the Gothic drollery is not without ancestry. In the
Christi autem monogram on folio 34 of the Book of Kells, cats are watching
mice at play in the lower part of the miniature'.[19] However, as has been
demonstrated above, hopefully, the Book of Kells presents many true
drolleries and countless other near-drolleries and humorous details thus
bringing the idea back almost half a millennium, and to an Irish origin.

But there were near-drolleries in some illuminated manuscripts even before
the Book of Kells. The little animal-head, thought perhaps to be that of a
dolphin (ichthus, the christian symbol) by some authorities, on the leg of a
letter Q on folio 48 in the Cathach, can perhaps be considered a proto-
drollery which brings the idea back perhaps to 561 and even more securely

[19]Robb (note 2 above) 225.

to Ireland. The next earliest drollery-related illustrations can be found in the Gelasian Sacramentary (notably on folios 3v and 4), a manuscript painted somewhere near Paris, *c*750. Robb opts for 'some monastery in north-eastern France affiliated with the very important foundation established by monks from Luxeuil at Corbie about 660'[20] — and it should be noted that the Irish connection is still present: Luxeuil was founded *c*590 by St Columbanus, from Bangor, county Down. Another northern French manuscript, the Gellone Sacramentary, also antedates the Book of Kells which, among several other drollery-like initials,[21] on folio 99v has an initial *D* with a protruding hand spearing a large fish, described by Robb as 'an idea that anticipates the drolleries that enliven the pages of later Gothic manuscripts':[22] it dates from *c*750-800 but has no obvious Irish associations though Henry sees 'traces of Insular influence in the use of some patterns'.[23] Features in the St Gall gospel book (Stiftsbibliothek 51), the Book of Dimma, and the Codex Bonifatianus 3, all mid-eighth century Irish manuscripts, occasionally have humorous details such as one later encounters in the Book of Kells, as indeed do later manuscripts with Irish associations such as the Book of Deer of *c*900 (Deer was a Columban foundation in Scotland), the Corpus Christi Missal of *c*1130, and perhaps the most humorous (albeit probably unintentionally so) after the Book of Kells itself, the Southampton Psalter of early-eleventh-century date. Later than that one encounters the Gothic drolleries, which in their realistic naturalism owe more to a Germanic, be it Saxon, Frankish or Teutonic, than to an Irish background.

With our modern-day approach to everyday things of the past which we might not fully understand, we often tend to vest the emperor with new clothes which he may never have worn. In the present case this can mean allocating symbolism to probably straightforward features, or, as G K Chesterton pointed out a long time ago, thinking that what is obvious and intelligible to the common sense of the masses must be wrapped in layers of waffling mystagoggery by academic middlemen.

We should, therefore, look at the Book of Kells for what it most obviously is: a beautifully illuminated evangeliar, one created by real people, not angels (*pace* Giraldus Cambrensis), but Irish people with a strong Celtic background who had therefore a different approach to art from the rest of their European contemporaries, artists who eschewed realism as unnecessary or undesirable, and who, most importantly, had a strong sense of humour which they were not afraid to allow stray into their marvellous work.

---

[20]Robb (note 2 above) 77.
[21]Henry, 216, fig 69.
[22]Robb (note 2 above) 78.
[23]Henry, 216.

The origin of the beast canon tables reconsidered

Nancy Netzer

'We are still unable to state with any certainty either the probable date or the probable origin of the Book of Kells.' So begins J J G Alexander's conclusion in the manuscript's recent facsimile.[1] To be sure, the date of the Book of Kells has been much debated over the last century. In his comprehensive volume on pre-Carolingian miniatures that appeared during the first World War, E H Zimmermann somewhat arbitrarily dated the Book of Kells, along with the Book of Durrow and the Lindisfarne Gospels, to the early eighth century.[2] In the first edition of the second volume of *Codices latini antiquiores*, the palaeographer E A Lowe proposed a date in the late eighth to early ninth century.[3] Later, Lowe had doubts and turned for guidance in dating the manuscript to the palaeographer, T J Brown, who argued that, as the script and layout of the Book of Kells resemble those of the Lindisfarne Gospels datable to about 700, there could not be as much as a century between the two.[4] For Lowe's second edition he changed the date of the Book of Kells to the second half of the eighth century.[5] In the meantime, between Lowe's two editions, the art historian A M Friend published what remains the strongest argument for dating the Book of Kells after 800.[6] The presence of beasts in the tympana of several of the Kells canon tables (folios 1v-3r, **pl 1**) led Friend to propose that much of the unusual iconography in the illustrations of the Book of Kells was based on a gospel book produced in Charlemagne's court scriptorium in the late eighth century. This Carolingian book was thought to have been sent to Iona, where, Friend believed, the Book of Kells was produced. His arguments were based primarily on a careful examination of the beast canon tables in the Book of Kells and in the Harley Gospels[7] (**pl 115**), one of the earlier of a series of gospel books produced in Charlemagne's scriptorium and considered to date from about 800. Friend noted that both the Harley and Kells tables employ, under the main arch, full-length symbols of the evangelists whose works are compared in the tables below and that both have triangular corner pieces above their main arches, providing a rectangular shape to the overall design. What Friend neglected to underscore, however, is that the symbols in the two manuscripts belong to different traditions. Rendered in the illusionistic style, those in the Harley Gospels have wings and halos and carry books. The Kells beasts are winged

[1] Alexander, 'Illumination', 288.
[2] E H Zimmermann, *Vorkarolingische Miniaturen* (Berlin 1916).
[3] *CLA* (1935) II, no 274.
[4] Brown, 219-46 (pp 234, 243).
[5] *CLA* (1972) II, no 274.
[6] A M Friend, 'The canon tables of the Book of Kells' in *Medieval studies in memory of Arthur Kingsley Porter*, ed W Koehler (Cambridge 1939) 611-40.
[7] BL, MS Harley 2788; for illustrations and description see W Koehler, *Die Karolingischen Miniaturen II: die Hofschule Karls des Grossen* (Berlin 1958).

and lack halos; only some of the men (folios 1v, 2v, 3r, 3v, 4r, **pls 1-5**) and one eagle (folio 5r) hold books. Depicted in a manner similar to others in the same manuscript, the beasts on the Kells canon tables conform to insular types, many of which were found earlier in the Book of Durrow.[8]

Friend also does not take into account another difference between the two series. In the Book of Kells the beasts are not always in the tympana, but on the fifth and sixth tables (folios 3v-4r, **pls 4-5**) the symbols are placed within the arches of the arcade. Neglecting this change of format, Friend goes on to stress the importance of a break in format in both the Harley and Kells series after Canon IV, ie on the seventh table. In Kells, Canon IV (folio 4r, **pl 5**) shows beasts, albeit confused, heading each column. On the verso, containing Canon V (folio 4v, **pl 6**) the beasts have disappeared.[9]

In the Harley tables, the design changes from one with flat pillars and decorative stepped bases (folios 6v-9r, **pl 115**) to one with marble columns, three-dimensional bases and beasts supporting a *tabula ansata* (folios 9v-10v). Friend believed the changes in the Harley tables to be the result of the artist's having used two different models, one of which was defective after Canon IV. On the basis of the placement of the symbols and the supposed similar break in the formats of the Kells and Harley tables, he argued that this defective model was transported from Charlemagne's court scriptorium to Iona and later used by the artist of the Book of Kells for his tables I through IV. This supposed sharing of models indicated that the Book of Kells must be later than the Harley Gospels, ie, after 800.[10]

The question is whether, in fact, these similarities, as Friend would tell us, are the result of the Kells artist's dependence on a Carolingian court school model, or if, perhaps, another explanation is more likely. Indeed, an alternative solution involving a more indirect series of connections may be proposed.

For this argument two additional insular manuscripts datable to the first part of the eighth century must be introduced. The first is a gospel book in Augsburg (**pls 117-18**).[11] By virtue of an acrostic at the end, this codex may be attributed to a scribe working at the beginning of the eighth century at the continental centre of Echternach.[12] This centre was founded in about 697

---

[8]TCD, MS 57; for illustrations see Alexander, *Insular manuscripts*, no 6.
[9]See also Henderson, 131-41 for discussion of breaks in format in the Kells tables and problems with Friend's argument.
[10]The court scriptorium is thought to have been active from about 780 until Charlemagne's death in 814. Within this period, the Harley Gospels is usually dated to about 800. See Koehler (note 7 above).
[11]Augsburg, Universitätsbibliothek Cod. I.2.4°2 (formerly Maihingen and Harburg, Öttingen-Wallersteinsche Bibliothek). For description and illustrations see Alexander, *Insular manuscripts*, no 24.
[12]For discussion see C Nordenfalk, 'On the age of the earliest Echternach manuscripts', *Acta Archaeologica* 3 (1932) 57-62; and more recently N Netzer, 'The early scriptorium at Echternach: the state of the question' in *Willibrord: Apostel der Niederlande Gründer der Abtei Echternach*, ed G Kiesel, J Schroeder (Luxembourg 1989) 128-30.

by St Willibrord, who was born and educated in Northumbria and, who, at the age of twenty, joined Egbert's English community at the monastery of Rath Melsigi in Ireland, from whence he set off in 690 to the Continent to convert the Frisians.[13]

The other manuscript, which Friend mentioned, but dismissed summarily as thoroughly confused and unimportant,[14] is a gospel book now in the Church Treasury at Maaseik.[15] It contains two sets of canon tables, of which one (**pl 116**) is incomplete. Both Maaseik sets, however, contain mistakes in their numerals that reveal they were copied from the same model and made in the same scriptorium.[16] As has been shown elsewhere, the Maaseik and Augsburg Gospel Books, of nearly identical dimensions and quire structure, copy the same exemplar for their texts and were both produced in the scriptorium at Echternach. The Maaseik Gospel Book was probably given to the Abbey at Aldeneik, where it was preserved, by Willibrord himself, who consecrated its first abbess Harlindis.[17]

The incomplete series of Maaseik canon tables shows that the inclusion of beasts at the head of each column (the *Autorenbild* type) is incompatible with the standard four intercolumniations found not only throughout this series of tables but in several other insular canon series as well.[18] As the first two tables comparing all four gospels are missing, the next five extant tables (folios 3r, 3v, 5v, 5r, 2r, **pl 116**) compare different combinations of only three gospels. Where the fourth intercolumniation is not needed, the artist filled the arch above the unused space with an animal in order to balance the design. Frequently, he employs the extra evangelist symbol (folios 3r, 5r, 2r). Twice (folios 3v, 5v, **pl 116**), however, the artist uses what appears to be a long-necked dog in profile. This series of Maaseik tables is not very well worked out and, in fact, because the artist has made another more serious mistake,[19] the artist abandons it before completing the numerical text on the last four extant tables. It, therefore, appears to be an artist's bold and unsuccessful attempt to incorporate beasts from a model different from that which supplied its frames with four intercolumniations and its numerical

---

[13]On the scriptorium at Echternach see, most recently, Netzer (note 12 above) 127-34; R McKitterick, 'The diffusion of insular culture in Neustria between 650 and 850: the implications of the manuscript evidence' in *La Neustrie. Les pays au nord de la Loire de 650 à 850*, ed H Atsma (Sigmaringen 1989) 422-29; and N Netzer, *Cultural interplay in the eighth century: the Trier Gospels and the making of a scriptorium at Echternach* (forthcoming, Cambridge University Press).

[14]Friend (note 6 above) 620.

[15]Maaseik, Church of Saint Catherine, Trésor, s.n.; for description and illustrations see Alexander, *Insular manuscripts*, nos 22-23.

[16]For example, both tables for Canon II (folios 3r, 7r) are missing the thirty-fourth and thirty-fifth numerals (CLXV and CLXXVI) in Luke's list.

[17]For discussion see Netzer (note 12 above) 130; and Netzer forthcoming (note 13 above) chs 2, 6, 11.

[18]See, for example, the canon tables in the Barberini Gospels (Vatican, Biblioteca Apostolica, MS Barb. lat. 570) and the Royal Gospels (London, BL, MS Royal I.B.VII). For descriptions and illustrations see Alexander, *Insular manuscripts*, nos 20, 36.

[19]The artist reversed the tables on the recto and verso of folio 5. For discussion see Netzer, forthcoming (note 13 above) ch 6.

text. This second model, providing frames and text, probably was produced in Italy in the sixth century and, with the notable exception of including apostle medallions, resembled in design the tables from a fragment now in the Vatican Library.[20] The model was copied more faithfully in another gospel book produced at Echternach, the Trier Gospels.[21] In this regard, it should be mentioned that two later insular manuscripts with canon tables with four intercolumniations throughout, the Barberini[22] and Cutbercht Gospels,[23] avoid the problem of matching the number of figures and intercolumniations by placing their respective anthropomorphic beasts and portraits of the evangelists only on the first table of the series, where all four gospels are compared.

The source of the beasts on the incomplete series of Maaseik tables appears to have been the model for the canon tables of the other gospel book produced at Echternach mentioned above, the Augsburg Gospels. Unlike the Maaseik tables, the width of the Augsburg tables varies according to the number of intercolumniations required for each canon. Most significant here, however, is the provision of additional arches for the beginning of each canon, resulting in some pages having more than one arcade (**pls 117-18**). A similar feature occurs in several later manuscripts, including the Montpellier Gospels[24] and a Bible of Theodulf,[25] both written in northern France in the late eighth century; a gospel book written at Salzburg in about 830;[26] and two Spanish Bibles of the tenth century in León.[27] Neither the design nor the distribution of any of these later examples is close enough to the Augsburg tables to reveal a direct connection. Rather, they indicate widespread use of additional arcades in later manuscripts, and suggest that the device was not invented in Willibrord's scriptorium at Echternach. The design probably existed in the model of the Augsburg Gospels.

---

[20]Vatican, Biblioteca Apostolica, MS lat. 3806, folios 1-2. For description and illustrations see C Nordenfalk, *Die spätantiken Kanontafeln* (Goteborg 1938) 174, pls 48-51; and D Wright, 'The canon tables of the Codex Beneventanus and related decoration', *Dumbarton Oaks Papers* 33 (1979) 137-55.

[21]Trier, Cathedral Treasury, MS 61. For description and illustration see Alexander *Insular manuscripts*, no 26; for detailed discussion of the hypothetical Italian model employed in the scriptorium at Echternach see Netzer, forthcoming (note 13 above) ch 6.

[22]Here, however, the symbols for Mark and Luke are reversed.

[23]Vienna, Nationalbibliothek, MS lat. 1224; for description and illustration see Alexander *Insular manuscripts*, no 37.

[24]Montpellier, Bibliothèque de Ville, MS 3. The manuscript was written in northeastern France. See *CLA* (1953) VI, no 791

[25]London, BL, Add. 24142. For these tables see, most recently, L Nees, *The Gundohinus Gospels* (Cambridge 1987) 33-81, where it is argued that they depend on a Ravennate model of the sixth century.

[26]Augsburg, Universitätsbibliothek, Cod. I.2.2° 2. (formerly in Harburg, Öttingen-Wallerstein'sche Bibliothek). See K Holter, 'Drei Evangelienhandschriften der Salzburger Schreibschule des 9. Jahrhunderts', *Österreichische Zeitschrift für Kunst und Denkmalpflege* 11 (1957) 85-91.

[27]León, Cathedral Cod. 6, folio 153r; León, Colegiata de San Isidoro, Cod. 2, folio 402v. For description and illustrations see Friend (note 6 above) 619-20, pl 655; and J Williams, 'The illustrations of the León Bible of the year 960 — an iconographic analysis', PhD dissertation, University of Michigan (1962) 137-44.

Most importantly, the use of beasts to label the numerical lists in the León Bibles suggests that an original function of additional arcades to mark the beginning of a new canon may have been either to support or to enclose such symbols. In fact, the poem on the evangelical canons by the seventh century Irish poet Aileran (died 655) on folio 1v of the Augsburg Gospels strongly suggests that the model of the Augsburg tables contained beasts. As can be seen in the transcription (Appendix A),[28] the poem describes in ten separate sections (one for each canon) a discourse among (or between) the appropriate beasts for the gospel compared in each of the ten canons. It also mentions, both in the text and in red numerals in the margin, the number of comparative passages belonging to most canons. For example, the first section refers to a man, lion, calf and eagle (*homo, leo, vitulus et aquila*) speaking together as one about the Lord through seventy-one (*LXX*[29] *unum*) chapters. Similarly, section seven describes the man and the bird (*homo auis*) speaking words in agreement about the Lord seven (*septies*) times. Most significant is that the number of passages cited in the poem matches the number of numerals in Augsburg's tables,[30] especially where Augsburg's numbers differ from those that are standard in early canon tables.[31] One example is found in the last two lines of the poem in section ten. It mentions ninety-seven (*nonagies ... atque septies*, literally nine plus seven) passages in which the one flying to the stars (*subvolantem ad astra*), ie, the eagle for John, speaks alone. The standard number of passages for John in Canon X is either ninety-six or ninety-eight. The latter is found in the canon tables of the two other gospel books produced at Echternach, the Maaseik and Trier Gospels. Ninety-seven, on the other hand, is a rare number, matched among early medieval canon series only in a few other insular gospel books including the Books of Durrow,[32] Armagh,[33] and Kells and the Echternach Gospels.[34] Thus, there can be little doubt that the Irish

---

[28]On the poem and its witnesses see the critical edition of D DeBruyne, *Préfaces de la bible latine* (Namur 1920) 185. See also D DeBruyne, 'Une poesie inconnue d'Aileran le Sage', *Revue bénédictine* 29 (1912) 339-40; M Esposito, 'Hiberno-Latin manuscripts in the libraries of Switzerland', *PRIA* 30 (1912) 36-40; and B Bischoff, 'Wendepunkte in der Geschichte der lateinischen Exegese im Frühmittelalter', *Sacris Erudiri*, 6, 2 (1954) 237-38. 'Aileranus dixit' precedes the poem in a gospel book of the ninth century (Paris, BN, MS lat. 258) and a bible of the eleventh century (Vatican, Biblioteca Apostolica, MS Barb. lat. 587).

[29]The standard text (see DeBruyne, note 28 above, p 185) contains *septuaginta*. The substitution of numerals here and elsewhere in the text may be attributed to the scribe of the Augsburg Gospels.

[30]The one exception is Canon X for Mark where the poem mentions nineteen passages, an unusual number found also in the Book of Kells. Although, the Augsburg canon table (folio 12r) now contains twenty numerals, the traditional number. The final passage (*CCXXXIIII*) is a later correction written in a different hand between two lines.

[31]For the list of standard numerals see *Biblia Sacra Iuxta Vulgatam Versionem*, ed R Weber (Stuttgart 1969) 1516-26.

[32]See note 8 above. The gospel book is usually dated to the second half of the seventh century and has been assigned variously to Ireland, Iona, and Northumbria.

[33]TCD, MS 52. According to an inscription (folio 52v) the manuscript was written at Armagh in about 807. See Alexander, *Insular manuscripts*, no 53.

[34]Paris, BN, MS lat. 9389. See Alexander, *Insular manuscripts*, no 11. This gospel book is generally thought to have been written at Lindisfarne in about 700. For discussion of other possible places of origin see D Ó Cróinín, 'Pride and Prejudice', *Peritia* 1

poem describing the beasts in discourse belongs with the Augsburg canon tables, and that the poem must have been present in Augsburg's model. In fact, the poem may have been conceived as a series of *tituli* for individual tables.[35] Most important, however, is the fact that Aileran's poem suggests that beast canon tables were probably known in the poet's native Ireland in the seventh century. If so, the Kells and Augsburg tables could derive from the same archetype with beasts.

Support for this latter hypothesis comes from examination of unusual features in the Kells and Augsburg tables that points to a common archetype. The first is the layout of Canon II in the Kells tables, which Friend incorrectly viewed as an idiosyncratic feature.[36] Folio 3v (**pl 4**) shows the last nine lines of Canon II at the top and all of Canon III below. This arrangement is matched only in the Augsburg tables (folio 9v, **pl 117**), where a second arcade is placed after the last nine lines of Canon II to mark the beginning of Canon III. A related arrangement appears in one other insular manuscript, the Codex Aureus in Stockholm produced in Kent (probably at Canterbury) in the mid-eighth century.[37] Stockholm's fifth table (folio 7r) with numerals for the end of Canon II contains two incipits for the beginning of Canon III. One is in its proper position at the end of Canon II; the other is nine numerals above. The first incipit is misplaced, and best explained by the use of an exemplar similar to the Augsburg and Kells tables where the final nine lines of Canon II began a new table. Presumably, when the Stockholm scribe reached the end of the third page of Canon II in his exemplar, he assumed, as is traditional, that Canon II was complete. He may even have had a second model which he used for the frames of some of the more classically inspired tables (folios 5r, 5v, 8r, 8v)[38] in front of him in which Canon II comprised three tables and from which he copied the incipit for Canon III). It was only after turning the page in the exemplar from which he was copying the numerals that he realised his error in eliminating nine lines. The fact that the Stockholm tables also have circular capitals and a 'vestigial' medallion (without an apostle portrait) on one encompassing arch (folio 6v) — both devices that appear on the Maaseik tables (folios 5v, 5r) — suggests dependence on a model from Echternach, which possessed features of the frames in the Maaseik Gospels and the numerical layout of

---

(1982) 352-62; and N Netzer, 'Willibrord's scriptorium at Echternach and its relationship to Ireland and Lindisfarne', *St Cuthbert, his cult and his community to AD 1200*, ed G Bonner, D Rollason, C Stancliffe (Woodbridge 1989) 203-12.

[35]Fragmentary *tituli* from an unidentified poem are found at the top of several canon tables in a gospel book of about 800 written in the area of Saint Amand and now in the church of Saint Bavo in Ghent (MS 17). These tables closely reflect a late antique Mediterranean model. For illustrations see Nordenfalk (note 10 above) pls 104-12.

[36]Friend (note 6 above) 615-16.

[37]Stockholm, Royal Library, MS A. 135. See Alexander, *Insular manuscripts*, no 30.

[38]C Nordenfalk, *Celtic and Anglo-Saxon painting* (New York 1977) 38, believes that the more classical tables on the outer bifolium (folios 5r, 5v, 8r, 8v) are by a different artist than the more insular tables with circular capitals and bases on the central bifolium (folios 6r, 6v, 7r, 7v). Similarity between the rendering of the insular ornament on the two different types of frames suggests, rather, that a single artist is using two different models.

the Augsburg Gospels.[39] The appearance of circular bases and/or capitals in the Kells (folios 4v, 5r, **pl 6**), Stockholm, and Maaseik tables could then be seen as derivations from a common archetype known in Ireland in the seventh century. At least some of the features of this archetype would have made their way to Echternach (probably in the model of the Augsburg tables), whence they were transferred to Kent.

Given the illusionistic design of the frames with columns, capitals and bases in the Augsburg Gospels, the frames of the archetype common to the Kells and Augsburg tables would, at least, have had their roots in the Mediterranean world. In fact, some of the odd-shaped capitals in the Book of Kells, like those with curved indentations in their sides (folios 3v, 4r, **pls 4-5**), become more understandable if one views them as further abstractions of some in the Augsburg tables (folios 10v, 11r, **pl 118**) which, in turn, are probably debased forms of Corinthian capitals in the Mediterranean archetype. Whether the beasts were incorporated into the frames in the Mediterranean world or later in Ireland is impossible to know. In any case, the correspondence between numerical text and that mentioned in the Irishman Aileran's poem leaves little doubt that the model for the Augsburg Gospels, either a Mediterranean original or a relatively faithful Irish copy thereof, came to the Continent, and specifically to Echternach, via Ireland. It may well have been brought by Willibrord himself, as Bede tells us that it was from Ireland that Willibrord set off for the Continent. Echternach, then, may have been the way station through which beast canons were transmitted from Ireland to Charlemagne's court scriptorium. This scenario would also explain the insular influence on the first tables of the Harley Gospels (folios 6v-9r), ie, the flat embracing arches, columns with inset panels of interlace, and flat stepped bases filled with animal ornament.

As Beornrad, abbot of Echternach (774-797), commissioned Alcuin to write both a prose and metrical *Life of Saint Willibrord*,[40] the connection between Echternach and the court scriptorium might be attributed to Alcuin. Although no evidence exists to prove that Alcuin came to Echternach, he must have been in contact with the monastery in order to write these works, and may even have worked there on the texts before serving as one of the chief scholars at Charlemagne's court in Aachen.

Whether or not Alcuin was the link, another Court School manuscript clearly reveals that influence from Echternach existed in Charlemagne's scriptorium. The three pillar canon frame, with an embracing arch and two smaller arches of the other Maaseik canon series, finds its only close parallel in the canon tables from the Arsenal Gospels, the earliest gospel book from the court scriptorium.[41]

---

[39]For discussion see Netzer, forthcoming (note 13 above) chs 6, 11.

[40]Alcuin, *Vita Willibrordi*, Monumenta Germaniae Historica, Scriptores rerum Merovingicarum 3, ed W Levison, pt 1 [1920], 81-141).

[41]Paris, Bibliothèque de l'Arsenal, MS 599 (folios 8r-15v). For illustrations see W Koehler (note 7 above).

Most importantly, the triangular corner pieces, which Friend saw as an invention in the Harley Gospels and therefore a significant feature linking the Kells tables to Harley's,[42] appear already in the Maaseik tables as dotted outlines, which are now very faded. This design with an embracing arch and squared spandrels may well have been found in the model of the Augsburg tables (and the proposed common archetype) and may have been eliminated by the Echternach artist along with the beasts, possibly because he was producing a manuscript of more modest size than that of his model. In any case, the squared spandrel design existed at Echternach before the Court School manuscripts, and it may have been brought from Ireland to Echternach from whence it was disseminated on the Continent.

What all this means, then, is that the scenario for artistic connections proposed by analysis of the beast canon tables may not be as Friend and others saw it. The iconography may not have originated either in Spain or the Mediterranean world, moved to Charlemagne's court and then travelled westward to Iona. Instead, the iconography may have its roots either in the Mediterranean world or Ireland and, in either case, would have travelled from Ireland to Charlemagne's court scriptorium via Echternach.

The other two insular manuscripts with pictorially labelled columns, the Barberini and Cutbercht Gospels, would not contradict this theory. Links to Echternach may be demonstrated for them as well. As I have shown elsewhere, the gospel text of the Barberini Gospels is closely related to that in the Augsburg and Maaseik Gospels,[43] and its anthropomorphic winged symbols with books (folio 1r) are of the same type as those in the medallions on the arches of the second series of canon tables in the Maaseik Gospels (folios 10r, 10v, 11r, 11v). In the Cutbercht Gospels the distribution and some unusual features of the numerals of the canon tables, as well as the rare series of chapter summaries bound together at the beginning of the codex, reveal dependence on a model from Echternach.[44]

The theory of an indigenous Irish model for the Kells tables also receives indirect support from the observation that the change to grid frames in the Book of Kells occurs at the same point, ie, before Canon IX, where the arches cease in the fragmentary tables of another insular gospel book, from the Royal collection in the British Library.[45] The Royal tables are datable, at the latest, to the middle of the eighth century. It has correctly been concluded that, given the concurrence in the two manuscripts and the similarity of the design of their canon frames (revealed by an offset on one of the extant Royal tables), the break probably derives from an earlier, 'venerable and

---

[42]Friend (note 6 above) 621, 634-35.
[43]Netzer, forthcoming (note 13 above) ch 2.
[44]For discussion see, Netzer, forthcoming (note 13 above) chs 2, 6, 11.
[45]London, BL, MS Royal 7.C.xii, folios 2-3. An offset of arcades similar to the Book of Kells is visible on folio 3r. For discussion see P McGurk, 'Two notes on the Book of Kells and its relation to other insular gospel books', *Scriptorium* 9 (1955) 105-07; McGurk, 'Texts', 53, 57; Alexander, 'Illumination', 270-71.

sanctified' pre-Carolingian and probably insular model, that was copied independently by the artists of the Kells and Royal tables.[46]

In addition, the numerical text of the Kells tables recently has been shown probably to depend not on a Carolingian exemplar but on another insular manuscript, the Book of Durrow, where the tables are written throughout in grids.[47] Thus, careful study of several aspects of the Kells tables provides little support for the origin of either their beasts or other aspects of the tables in a Carolingian model.

What then does this mean for the dating the Book of Kells? Simply stated, it overcomes the chief obstacle to previous attempts to relate the production of the codex at Iona to the translation of Columba's relics there in the mid-eighth century,[48] and to place the Book of Kells within the development of insular half-uncial script in the middle of the eighth century.[49]

Instead of a Carolingian model, one might now begin to develop the theory of a lost generation of insular illuminations datable between the beginning and middle of the eighth century. These might stand behind what have been perceived as innovations in the Book of Kells, like the introduction of miniatures in the text and human ornamental initials.

Indeed, concerning the latter, investigation of the origin of the Merovingian initials in the Trier Gospels points independently to such a lost intermediary development.[50] An initial in the Trier Gospels (folio 112v) showing a human figure contorted to form the letter E with a feeble attempt to copy an interlaced knot in the central body, is — like others in the same manuscript — probably based on an earlier insular example, that predates the more complex, advanced forms in the Book of Kells (eg H, folio 68v). Similarly, the mysterious crouching figure grasping his beard in the central column of the first canon table in the Barberini Gospels (folio 1r) might reflect an earlier insular tradition that stands behind the profile crouching figures grasping their beards that fill the columns of several of the beast canon tables in the Book of Kells (folios 1v, 2r, 3v; **pls 1** and **4**).[51]

Alas, however, the discussion must end where it began, stressing that there is still insufficient evidence to firmly date the Book of Kells. Having eliminated the chief impediment to a date earlier than about 800 — the dependence of the Kells beast canon tables on a Carolingian invention — one is at least a step closer to solving the problem. The answer may well come from investigation of the still relatively unexplored relationship of the

---

[46]See McGurk, 'Texts', 57.

[47]ibid, 52-57.

[48]For discussion see I Fisher in RCAMS, *Argyll: an inventory of the monuments*, vol 4, *Iona*, (Edinburgh 1982) 47; and P Meyvaert, 'The Book of Kells and Iona', *Art Bulletin* 71 (1989) 6-19.

[49]See Brown.

[50]On the initials in the Trier Gospels see, Netzer, forthcoming (note 13 above) ch 5.

[51]This comparison was suggested by a student Sean Connolly.

Kells decoration to that manifest in other media, especially contemporary metalwork.

APPENDIX A

Poem on the Evangelical Canons

(Augsburg Gospels, folio 1v)*

I.   Quam in primo speciosa quadriga
             homo leo uitulus et acquila
LXXI   LXX unum per capitula
             de domino conloquntur paria.

II.   In secundo subsequente protinus
             homo leo loquitur et uitulus;
CVIIII   quibus inest ordinate positus
             centum in se atque VIIII numerus.

III.   Tum diende tertio in ordine
             homo et bos loquitur cum uolucre
XXII   numero quo consistunt antiquae
             albabeti ebreorum litterae.

IV.   Quarto loco fatentur aequalia
             una leo homo atque aquila
XXVI   uno ore loquentes kapitula
             uerbi summi sena atque uicena.

V.   Quinta uice concordant in loquella
             homo prudens atque mitis hostia
LXXXIII   ihesu christi emitantes agmina
             iuda sine saluatori credula.

VI.   Ecce sexto pari sonant clamore
             natus adam cum clamoso leone
             conputata traditis pro munere
XLVIII   sacerdotum oppidis in honore.

VII.   En loquntur septies in septimo
VII   homo auis consona de domino.

VIII.   In octauo nunc leonis catulus
                 dei uerba profert atque uitulus
XIII   quorum simul conputatur numerus
                 adiecto paulo apostolicus.

VIIII.   Nonus ordo in quo duo pariter
                 conloquntur, uitulus et uolucer
XXI   inspirati sensu spiritaliter
                 proloquntur ternum septipliciter.

X.   Homo nimpe uerbum profert proprium
LXII   sexaginta et per duo numerum.
                 Rugientemque leonem audies
XVIIII   solum sane decies et noies.
                 Bouem solum fatentem inuenies
LXXII   uerba dei bis et septuagies.
                 Subuolantem ad astra repperies
XCVII   nonagies loqui atque septies.

*numerals written in red are underlined

Echoes: the Book of Kells and southern English manuscript production

Michelle P Brown

The Book of Kells is indeed all things to all men and women. The wide ranging debate as to its date and origins bears witness to its encyclopaedic quality. For all the cultural elements present in the insular world and its neighbours are held up to the mirror of Kells and converted by its own distinctive matrix into tantalisingly elusive reflections, only fleetingly reminiscent of well-known forms. The recognition of echoes and shades within this enchanted mirror has led many scholars to seize upon specific links and to elevate them to the status of tangible affiliations. Thus Irish, Pictish, Hiberno-Saxon and Carolingian echoes have jostled one another in the academic, and popular, imagination and have been used as the basis for specific claims of date and origin.

I make no such claims on the grounds of echoes which I may discern of the southern English *Tiberius* group manuscripts, but I do think that, with the exception of some tentative but useful suggestions by Françoise Henry, the 'Southumbrian' connection has been detrimentally excluded from the equation.[1] The recent exhibition 'The making of England, Anglo-Saxon art and culture AD 600-900' avoided direct confrontation of this issue, but it did assemble a wealth of material in which a great complexity of relationships was revealed.[2] Several scholars who are currently working with material of a more specifically 'Celtic' character encountered surprising connections and overlaps, and this should act as a warning against the dangers of rigidly excluding overtly 'English' material from that useful but ill-defined term of cultural collaboration, 'insular'.

In this paper I wish to explore the nature of the Kells/*Tiberius* group echoes. Which stem from a common ultimate debt to Irish and Hiberno-Saxon roots? Which reflect continental trends, or shared responses to the early christian legacy? Which may be indicative of more direct, up-to-date contacts between the insular world and southern England, and do these carry implications, especially concerning date?

The areas of discussion will be: connections of exegesis and image; minor decoration; zoomorphic decoration; display script; aspects of cursive minuscule; patterns of transmission, and some implications of exemplars

---

[1] Henry, 163, 215, 220. On the Tiberius group, see M P Brown in *The making of England, Anglo-Saxon art and culture AD 600-900*, ed J M Backhouse, L Webster (exhibition catalogue, London 1991) 195-96, and eadem, 'Cambridge, University Library, MS Ll.1.10, The Book of Cerne' (PhD thesis, University of London, forthcoming 1993).

[2] Backhouse and Webster (note 1 above).

and historical evidence. Let us begin with matters concerning the iconography of the Kells miniatures. This is an area which is yielding some of the most interesting recent thought on this complex book. The work of Jennifer O'Reilly and Carol Farr, in particular, has revealed something of the labyrinthine relationships between image, text and exegetical thought.[3] Carole Farr has argued convincingly for a multivalent interpretation of the Temptation miniature (Kells, folio 202v, **pl 42**), which simultaneously represents a visual summary of the concept of the *Communio Sanctorum*.[4] I shall suggest elsewhere that the selection and arrangement of texts in the Book of Cerne (Cambridge, University Library, MS Ll.1.10), one of a group of Mercian prayerbooks which developed thematic devotional compilations, also reflects the *Communio Sanctorum*, embodying Christ, the 'Church Triumphant', the 'Church Militant' and the 'Church Expectant'.[5] Although of interest, this shared preoccupation with a theme alone indicates nothing more than participation in a common climate of doctrine and exegesis, of the sort which would have prevailed throughout Britain and Ireland.

An area of more significant overlap is that of the depiction of the evangelists. The Book of Cerne is notable for its departure from any of the conventional formulae for depicting the evangelists with their symbols.[6] The symbols are not used to identify the evangelist portraits, but revert to full-length types, with attributes, set beneath arches, with roundels above containing busts of the evangelists in human guise (**pl 126**). These are accompanied by inscriptions, each worded differently and distinctively, which highlight the nature of the human and symbolic guises. I shall suggest elsewhere that these images not only depict the dual natures of the evangelists, but of Christ.[7] Thus Christ appears in his *humanitas* and in the symbolic forms of the man, personifying his Incarnation (**pl 126**), the lion, symbolising the Resurrection, the bull, the immolatory victim of the Passion, and the eagle, the symbol of the ascended Christ. This interpretation, derived from the visions of Ezekiel and the Apocalypse, was explored in a number of patristic exegetical sources, of which the most explicit, and probably most widely read, was that of Gregory the Great in his Homily on Ezekiel (Book I, Homily VIII, chs 20-21).[8] For the purposes of this paper it will suffice to concentrate upon the miniature of Matthew in the Book of Cerne (**pl 126**). Here the human bust, which is of the early christian 'youthful Christ' type, is accompanied by a cross and an inscription emphasizing the human guise. Matthew's symbol, the man, departs, however, from its usual form and is explicitly depicted and

---

[3]See, for example, their contributions to the present volume.

[4]Farr, 'Lection'.

[5]Brown forthcoming (note 1 above) and in Backhouse and Webster (note 1 above) 211.

[6]ibid, and on the Book of Cerne generally see also Alexander, *Insular manuscripts*, 84-85, pls 312-15 (henceforward cited as Alexander); A B Kuypers, *The Prayer Book of Aedeluald the Bishop, commonly called the Book of Cerne* (Cambridge 1902); H Wheeler, 'Aspects of Mercian art: the Book of Cerne' in *Mercian studies*, ed A Dornier (Leicester 1977) 235-44.

[7]Brown, forthcoming (note 1 above).

[8]PL 76, col 815.

labelled as an angel, with the words *hic matheus in angelica asspectu videtur*. This is unusual, for when this symbol is labelled elsewhere it is termed *homo*. The key to the reading of this image may be found in Gregory's Commentary where, in his discussions of the role of the symbol in depicting Christ's humanity, he deals with a tricky point of theology. For mankind was created as a lower order to that of the angelic hosts, and yet Christ, in his humanity and by virtue of his resurrection, ascended the throne and thereby transcended the orders of angels (including the order of thrones, which are picked out in a characteristic piece of theologian's word-play). The Cerne miniature might, therefore, be interpreted on one level as a depiction of Christ Incarnate set above the angels.

This theme is rendered more explicit in the portrait of Christ enthroned which precedes Matthew's gospel on folio 32v of the Book of Kells (pl 20). The placing of the miniature in relation to Matthew's gospel emphasizes Christ's humanity, and his triumphant ascension of the throne is emphasized by the presence of the two peacocks which flank his person and which symbolise the Resurrection. Flanking the lower half of Christ's body are four angels who are distinguished by different attributes. One is clearly a seraph, as indicated by its wings, another holds a sceptre, perhaps symbolising principalities, dominations or powers, and the other two, although harder to interpret, are differentiated by their wings and garb. Thus, in one reading of what is probably a multivalent image, Christ Incarnate is enthroned above the orders of angels.

Once again, this merely indicates common reference to a popular exegetical source, but there are no other readily discernible workings of this particular theme in a British or Irish visual context, nor did insular writers, such as Bede, choose to focus upon this specific point, although he did enlarge upon the theme of the symbols as images of Christ's being.[9] These themes were, however, taken up in Carolingian circles during the ninth century, but whether this was an independent development, or one which inspired or was inspired by the insular world, it is not possible to tell. What it is possible to say is that the Book of Kells, the Book of Cerne and the Book of Armagh seem to share a mutual preoccupation with the nature of the evangelists and the ways in which they symbolise Christ's manifestations, and with the harmony of the gospels. Experimentation in depicting the evangelists was an established tradition in Anglo-Saxon and Celtic art of the seventh and eighth centuries, but the concerns which I have just outlined do seem to represent a further stage of development within this tradition and one which built and expanded upon earlier depictions.[10] We have discussed some of the ways in which this preoccupation is developed in Kells and Cerne. Other of the Kells miniatures presumably carry similar implications,

---

[9]For the relevant Bedan commentaries on the evangelists and their symbols, see his *Explanatio Apocalypsis*, Book I, ch 4, PL 91, col 403.

[10]On insular depictions of the evangelists and their symbols in general, see Brown forthcoming (note 1 above); Henderson, 115-22 et passim; C Nordenfalk and A Grabar, *Early medieval painting from the fourth to the eleventh century* (Skira 1957) 62, 109, 113, 118, 126 et passim; Alexander, passim.

and the plethora of evangelist symbols which together occupy their own pages and which desport themselves throughout the canon tables (often accompanied by images of Christ) are almost obsessive (**pl 1**). In Armagh the theme of harmony is expressed in a visual fashion which is dependent upon Ezekiel (1:6 and 1:10-11), in which symbols are depicted with double wings, some of which carry roundels containing heads of the other evangelist symbols.[11] In the four symbols page of Armagh (folio 32v) the relationship between the symbol of the eagle and the Christ of the Ascension is rendered explicit by the way in which the flying eagle carries the fish, another symbol of Christ, heavenwards.[12] The Book of Cerne may be dated stylistically to c820 to 840 and the Book of Armagh to c807, and this begs the question of whether this shared climate of renewed exploration of the nature of the evangelists might carry dating implications for Kells.[13]

Moving on to minor decoration, one of the most distinctive and enlivening elements of the mise-en-page of the Book of Kells is its use of a parade of animals, human figures and mythical creatures which serve as line-fillers and run-over symbols (**pl 15**). The latter device has often been called the *ceann fa eite* or 'head-under-wing', a term used by Irish scribes during the later middle ages, and the frequent use of the zoomorphic run-over symbol in Irish manuscripts from the ninth century onwards has led to the assumption of an Irish origin for the device.[14] However, a detailed examination of the surviving evidence gives quite a different picture. Linear and dumb-bell-shaped run-overs are found in insular manuscripts from an early date, but the earliest occurrences of zoomorphic symbols are in manuscripts of the *Tiberius* group, dating from the second half of the eighth century and the first half of the ninth, and in the Book of Kells.

Possibly the earliest occurrence of a zoomorphic run-over symbol is to be found in the *Codex Bigotianus* (Paris, BN, lat. 281 and 298), a book generally accepted as the work of a Southumbrian scribe working in Mercia or Kent during the second half of the eighth century, although the possibility that it was produced by an English scribe working on the Continent cannot be completely excluded.[15] On folio 50v of this work the scribe has lightly drawn a bird, perhaps a dove, to mark a word which has run-over from the line above and which nestles into the gutter of the book. Elsewhere the scribe has avoided running over, and this, coupled with the discreet nature of the drawing, would suggest that this might represent a new solution to a problem encountered during the act of writing. *Bigotianus* is a member of the *Tiberius* group, as are two of the other major exponents of this device,

---

[11]On the Book of Armagh, see Alexander, 76-77, pls 221, 226-27, 229-30 and *CLA* (1972) II, no 270.
[12]See Alexander, pl 230.
[13]See notes 11 and 5, above.
[14]On the *ceann fa eite* see D N Dumville, 'Liturgical drama and panegyric responsory from the eighth century? A re-examination of the origin and contents of the ninth-century section of the Book of Cerne', *Journal of Theological Studies*, ns 23, part 2 (1972) 374-406 (p 396).
[15]On the *Codex Bigotianus*, see *CLA* (1950) V, no 526; Alexander, 60, pls 166-68; Backhouse and Webster (note 1 above) 201-02.

namely the Barberini Gospels (Vatican, Bibl. Apost., lat. 570) and the Book of Cerne.[16] A number of grotesque and zoomorphic run-overs and line-fillers enliven the work of one of the four scribes of the Barberini Gospels (pl 123). This scribe seems to be fulfilling a subsidiary role in the work and may have been learning from the other scribes, two of whom employ a Phase II half-uncial of Northumbrian character. His script is rather different and features some of the hybrid and cursive features encountered in Merican charters and books of the late eighth century, suggesting that he, and the book, may have had something of a Mercian background. The next work to take up and develop the device, the Book of Cerne, was of Mercian origin and the breviate psalter which forms part of this devotional compilation provides a habitat for a menagerie of what has been termed 'pretentious worms' which serve to preserve the verse-form whilst saving space (pl 122).[17] The *Tiberius* group may therefore be seen to provide a context for the development of the device, from one tentative, isolated example in *Bigotianus*, through the work of one innovative scribe working in a more conventional team in the Barberini Gospels, to a more standardised depiction and application of the motif in Cerne. I have, furthermore, been unable to locate any earlier use of the zoomorphic run-over symbol in works produced on the Continent and one is left, as in the case of the development of the historiated initial, with the likelihood of an English invention.

Where does the Book of Kells fit into this picture? It has certainly mastered the art of the device and elevated it to new heights, but should it be seen as an isolated and precocious earlier exponent of the genre, or should it be viewed as a contemporary response to the feature as encountered and developed in the *Tiberius* group. The absence of the feature from extant Irish, Northumbrian and continental manuscripts and its presence in Southumbrian works of the late eighth century onwards would argue for a southern origin for the device and perhaps, by implication, for a later date for the Book of Kells. The subsequent popularity of the motif in Ireland may have stemmed from its introduction via the monastery of Kells, the later medieval home of the manuscript. Similarly, the use of zoomorphic abbreviation bars is a shared feature of Kells, the Book of Armagh and of several *Tiberius* group manuscripts, notably the Book of Cerne. In this case, however, the motif also occurs in a number of pre-Carolingian manuscripts of the second half of the eighth century, such as the Sacramentary of Gellone.[18] Continental manuscripts of this period, such as the Gelasian Sacramentary, also furnish a link with the *Tiberius* group in their use of zoomorphic and anthropomorphic motifs as spacers between letters and

---

[16]On the Barberini Gospels, see *CLA* (1934) I, 63; Alexander, 61-62, pls 169-78; Backhouse and Webster (note 1 above) 205; Brown forthcoming (note 1 above).

[17]See note 6 above.

[18]On the Sacramentary of Gellone and other relevant Frankish manuscripts see Nordenfalk and Grabar (note 10 above) 126-35 and *La Neustrie*, ed P Périn, L-C Feffer (exhibition catalogue, Paris 1985). For zoomorphic abbreviation bars, see Alexander, pl 227 (Book of Armagh), Henry, 116 (Kells, folio 179v) and Dornier (note 6 above) fig 66a (Book of Cerne).

words in display script. The Vespasian Psalter (BL, Cotton MS Vespasian A. 1), the earliest extant representative of the *Tiberius* group, thought to date to the second quarter of the eighth century, is the earliest book to exhibit this feature (**pl 121**), and its use continues in other eighth-century members of the group, appearing in the Stockholm *Codex Aureus* and the Blickling Psalter.[19] This device may, in turn, have stimulated the development of the zoomorphic line-filler, a device to which I have already referred. By the late eighth century, however, the figural spacers in *Tiberius* group display script had been absorbed into the script itself, with human and animal heads serving as terminals to letters and, by battening upon adjacent letters, serving to link them into what I would term 'lacertine display script'. This development may be seen in the Barberini Gospels (**pl 124**) and in ninth-century members of the *Tiberius* group, such as the Tiberius Bede (BL, Cotton MS Tiberius C. II), the Book of Cerne (**pls 119-20**) and the Royal Bible (BL, Royal MS I.E.VI), and also in the Cutbercht Gospels (Vienna, Nationalbibliothek, Cod. 1224), thought to have been made at Salzburg during the late eighth century with the assistance of an Anglo-Saxon scribe and exemplars, which may have included *Tiberius* group material.[20]

The use of such embellished terminals as part of initials is a regular feature of earlier insular calligraphy, but the incorporation of the device within display script finds only limited precedent, in the Lindisfarne Gospels (BL, Cotton MS Nero D.IV), where such terminals do not generally fulfil an actual linking function.[21] Presumably the fusion of the two types of 'inhabited' display script, Southumbrian and Hiberno-Saxon, gave rise to the lacertine display script of the later members of the *Tiberius* group, and perhaps also to that found as part of the repertoire of display scripts in the Book of Kells. Here animal and human heads and figures entwine themselves in a game of 'follow-my-leader', producing a more opulent and

---

[19]See, for example, Périn and Feffer (note 18 above) pl 96. On the Vespasian Psalter, see *CLA* (1972) II, no 193; Alexander, 55-56, pls 143-46 and fig 7; Backhouse and Webster (note 1 above) 197-99; D H Wright, *The Vespasian Psalter*, Early English Manuscripts in Facsimile 14 (Copenhagen 1967). On the Stockholm *Codex Aureus*, see *CLA* (1966) XI, no 1642; Alexander, 56-57, pls 147, 152-59; Backhouse and Webster (note 1 above) 198-200. On the Blickling Psalter, see *CLA* (1966) XI, no 1661; Alexander, 57-58, pls 148-51. For their use of zoomorphic and anthropomorphic spacers, see Alexander, pls 145, 148-49, 152 and fig 7. On their use in Kells, see Henry, 95 (Kells, folio 292) and 11 and 103 (Kells, folio 8).

[20]On the Barberini Gospels, see note 16 above. On the Book of Cerne, see note 6 above. On the Tiberius Bede, see *CLA* (1972) II, no 191; Alexander, 59-60, pls 134, 165; Backhouse and Webster (note 1 above) 215-17. On BL, Royal I.E.VI, see *CLA* (1972) II, nos 214, 245, 262 and Suppl. p .5; Alexander, 58-59, pls 160-64; Backhouse and Webster (note 1 above) 217; M O Budny, 'London, British Library MS Royal I.E.VI: the anatomy of an Anglo-Saxon Bible fragment' (unpub. PhD thesis, University of London 1985). On the Cutbercht Gospels, see *CLA* (1963) X, no 1500; Alexander, 62-63, 180-87. To compare the 'lacertine display scripts' used in these volumes, see Alexander, pls 134, 161, 165, 171-72, 183, 310-11. For its use in Kells, see Henry, 103 (Kells, folios 8 and 19v, details).

[21]On the Lindisfarne Gospels, see *CLA* (1972) II, no 187; Alexander, 35-40, pls 28-46 and fig 2; Backhouse and Webster (note 1 above) 111-14; *Evangeliorum quattuor codex Lindisfarnensis*, ed T D Kendrick and others, 2 vols (Olten, Lausanne 1956 and 1960); J M Backhouse, *The Lindisfarne Gospels* (London 1981). For its limited use of display script linked by zoomorphic terminals, see Alexander, pl 40.

complex effect than that of the *Tiberius* group manuscripts, but nonetheless resembling them most closely in mechanics and application (**pls 15, 119-20, 124**).

Alongside this development, display letter-forms tended to become more fluid and ribbon-like, with greater mixing of capital, uncial and half-uncial forms. Perhaps in an attempt to impose a measure of discipline and order upon these exuberant strings of lettering, frames became a feature of later *Tiberius* group display script. One has only to consider the ill-disciplined effect of the display script of the Leningrad Gospels (St Petersburg, Public Library, Cod. F.v.I.8) to be aware of the dangers of dispensing with a framing device for lines of script.[22] A feature shared by the Book of Kells and by later members of the *Tiberius* group, such as the Tiberius Bede and the Book of Cerne, is their use of framed panels of lacertine display script for major text breaks in the case of the *Tiberius* manuscripts, and for minor textual divisions in the case of Kells (**pls 14, 119-20**).[23] The use of rectilinear frames for panels of display script which do not occupy a full incipit page finds precedents in early Northumbrian books, such as BL, Royal MS 1.B.VII, in eighth-century works from continental scriptoria with an insular background, such as a psalter from Echternach (Stuttgart, Württembergische Landesbibl., Cod. Bibl. 2° 12) and the Cutbercht Gospels, and in southern English books, such as the Vespasian Psalter, the Blickling Psalter and the Stockholm *Codex Aureus*.[24] In Kells and the later *Tiberius* manuscripts these frames often sprout zoomorphic extensions at their corners (**pls 14, 119-20**) and may be traced back to Hiberno-Saxon sources, notably the Lindisfarne Gospels and the Lichfield Gospels (Lichfield, Cathedral Library, s.n.).[25] This might merely represent a parallel descent from a common insular genre, but, taken along with the other similarities of display script and zoomorphic features, the parallel might be suggestive once again of participation in a shared current climate of ideas and motifs.

There are certain other intriguing parallels between Kells, Armagh and the *Tiberius* manuscripts. Initials are often composed in a very similar manner. Compare, for example, the initials A on folio 160 of the Book of Armagh and folio 4v of the Book of Nunnaminster (BL, Harley MS 2965), a Mercian

---

[22]On the Leningrad Gospels, see *CLA* (1966) XI, no 1605; Alexander, 64, pls 188-195. For its undisciplined display script, see Alexander, pl 192.

[23]For a comparison of framed display panels in Kells and in later members of the *Tiberius* group, see Alexander, pls 165, 310-11 and Henry, 12-14 (Kells, folios 12, 13, 15v, 16v, 18, 19v) and 46-48 (Kells, folios 114v, 124, 127v).

[24]On BL, MS Royal 1.B.VII, see *CLA* (1972) II, no 213; Alexander, 48, pls 70-73; Backhouse and Webster (note 1 above) 119. On the psalter from Echternach (now in Stuttgart), see *CLA* (1959) IX, no 1353; Alexander, 54-55, pls 140-42; Backhouse and Webster (note 1 above) 162-66. For the use of framed display panels in these and other insular volumes, see Alexander, pls 70, 73, 140-44, 148-49, 152, 156, 183.

[25]On the Lichfield Gospels, see *CLA* (1972) II, no 159; Alexander, 48-50, pls 50, 76-82; Backhouse And Webster (note 1 above) 127. On the use of framed display panels with zoomorphic corner extensions, see Alexander, pls 39 and 45-46 (Lindisfarne Gospels, folios 27, 95 and 211), pl 165 (Tiberius Bede, folio 5v), pls 310-11 (Book of Cerne, folios 32 and 43) and Henry, 12-13, 122 (Kells, folios 13, 15v, 124).

prayerbook of the first quarter of the ninth century (**pls 74** and **125**).[26] Is this resemblance an echo of common ultimate source material, or is it the result of more recent contacts? The way in which zoomorphic terminals serve to link letter-strokes in initials and their continuation lettering is again comparable in Kells, Armagh and *Tiberius* manuscripts such as Cerne and Paris, BN, lat. 10861, a collection of saints' lives made by a Canterbury-trained scribe whose script may be dated to *c*805-25.[27] In each of these books amorphous beast-heads bite hungrily onto adjacent letter-strokes to form chains of letters, in a similar fashion to that encountered in lacertine display script. In all of them human heads, and sometimes grotesques, also act as terminals to minor initials and are drawn in a calligraphic, comic fashion. The character of these heads and of the menagerie of simplified, eager and whimsical little beasts whose heads play such an essential decorative role are extremely similar in all of the manuscripts in question. The simplified beast-heads, denuded of any distinctive canine, feline or leoine characteristics, also feature in other Irish manuscripts, such as the Stowe Missal (Dublin, RIA, MS D.II.3) and the Book of Mulling (Dublin, TCD, MS 60).[28]

Turning now to the question of text script, there are again similarities in approach. The hybrid and cursive minuscule scripts which are a feature of southern English manuscript production during the late eighth and ninth centuries are characterised by a love of calligraphic embellishment, a mixing of letter-forms, a move towards an increasingly pointed aspect and the use of minuscule script for a wider range of texts, including those of a liturgical nature. Charters provide a useful context for the dating and to some extent the localisation of these developments (and the books which reflect them) which commence during the later years of the reign of Offa in the 780s and 790s and which reach a peak in what I have termed the 'mannered minuscule' produced at Christ Church, Canterbury, under Archbishop Wulfred (805-32).[29] The 'mannered' features of this script include a heightened linking of letters, with monograms, ligatures, loops, reversed ductus with open bows and calligraphic distortion and embellishment of letters. Many of these characteristics find an ultimate source, although

---

[26]On the Book of Nunnaminster, see *CLA* (1972) II, no 199; Alexander, 65, pls 135, 137-39; Backhouse and Webster (note 1 above) 210-11; W de Gray Birch, *An ancient manuscript belonging to St Mary's Abbey, or Nunnaminster, Winchester* (London 1889).

[27]On BN, MS lat. 10861, see Alexander, 85, pl 319; Backhouse and Webster (note 1 above) 214; M P Brown, 'Paris, Bibliothèque Nationale, MS lat. 10861 and the scriptorium of Christ Church, Canterbury', *Anglo-Saxon England* 15 (1987) 119-37. For the use of beasts and beast-heads to link chains of continuation lettering and initials in this and related volumes, see Alexander, pls 227 (Book of Armagh), 319; Dornier (note 6 above) fig 65a (Book of Cerne), and Henry, 75, 116, 123-24 (Kells, folio 254, lines 16-17, folios 179v, 250v, 60).

[28]On the Stowe Missal and gospel of St John, see *CLA* (1972) II, nos 267-68; Alexander, 68, 70-71, pls 209, 217, 220. On the Book of Mulling, see *CLA* (1972) II, nos 276-77; Alexander, 67-68, pls 210-12, 214-16, 218. For human-headed terminals, see Henry, 116 (Kells, folios 170v, 179v), Dornier (note 6 above) fig 64a (Book of Cerne) and M P Brown, *A guide to western historical scripts, from antiquity to 1600* (London 1990) pl 19 (Book of Armagh).

[29]See Brown (note 27 above); Backhouse and Webster (note 1 above) 214.

different in interpretation, within Phase I minuscule.[30] These influences may have been derived from earlier Northumbrian works, but closer similarities of treatment and detail are once more to be found in the Book of Armagh. The Book of Kells does not contain minuscule script *per se*, but its baroque treatment of display half-uncial is akin to Armagh's treatment of cursive minuscule, which it elevates to a similar display status. The *Tiberius* manuscripts and the southern English charters do not indulge in such exuberant excess, but striking comparisons of detail do occur, as does a general similarity of aspect with the more restrained passages of Armagh's script. This could be a case of simultaneous echoes from a common Phase I source, which, although supplanted in England by Phase II forms, was perpetuated in Ireland alongside more recent developments.[31]

However, there is a piece of evidence which suggests that the evolution of cursive minuscule in southern England may have received a more direct stimulus from Irish sources. The Book of Nunnaminster, a Mercian prayerbook of the first quarter of the ninth century which may have been owned by a woman, has a stylistic break towards its end, at folio 37.[32] The ink, weight of script and general aspect are similar enough in the two sections to suggest that the same scribe may be at work, and the rubric which heads the new section is certainly in his or her hand, but the set minuscule script of the first section begins to assume a more cursive ductus and calligraphic details are added, such as extended letter-strokes, pen-held terminals and open bows. The character of the text also changes at this point, for although the devotional materials contained in the volume are of mixed 'Roman' and 'Celtic' character the prayers from this point onwards come from a purely Celtic, and more specifically, Irish background. The style of initial also alters at this point, with blue replacing the green used earlier in the book, and a more amphorous beast-head is used as a terminal for initials, of the sort which becomes standardised in the 'pretentious worms' of the Book of Cerne (**pls 120** and **122**) and which has already been discussed in the context of Irish manuscripts and parts of the zoomorphic repertoire of the Book of Kells. This shift in the character of text, script and decoration would suggest that the scribe (or scribes, if the identity of hand is not accepted) was responding to a new exemplar of Irish origin.

The Celtic components of the Mercian prayerbooks of the *Tiberius* group have long been acknowledged, but it has been assumed that any such influences must have been pre-digested and transmitted via an Hiberno-

---

[30]On Phase I minuscule, see T J Brown, 'The Irish element in the insular system of scripts to c AD 850' in *Die Iren und Europa im früheren Mittelalter*, ed H Löwe (Stuttgart 1982) 101-19; Brown (note 28 above) 48-49.

[31]On Phases I and II of the insular system of scripts, see ibid. For the script of the Book of Armagh, see Brown (note 28 above) pl 19.

[32]On female ownership of the Book of Nunnaminster and on the use of an Irish exemplar, see M P Brown, 'Female book-ownership in England during the ninth century: the evidence of the prayerbooks' in *Reformed Englishwomen*, ed L Abrams, D N Dumville (forthcoming 1993) and in Backhouse and Webster (note 1 above) 210-11 (with accompanying plate illustrating the point of transition between exemplars); Birch (note 26 above).

Saxon milieu. Stylistic considerations, some details of text and the case of
the Irish exemplar for part of the Book of Nunnaminster would imply,
however, that there may have been an element of more up-to-date contact
with the Celtic world. This is not a popular argument historically, but bit by
bit evidence emerges which points in this direction and confirms the
stylistic links which are seen, but seldom believed. Kathleen Hughes
attempted to draw attention to the possibility of continued Anglo-Irish
relations in the post-Whitby period, but her work in this area has received
inadequate attention and supplementation.[33]

The Irish and Hiberno-Saxon background of the Mercian church has often
been overshadowed by a concentration upon Wilfrid's intervention. The
first bishop of the Mercians and Middle Angles was Diuma (656-58), an
Irishman, consecrated by Finan of Lindisfarne; his compatriot and
successor, Cellach (658-59) returned to Iona, but the two subsequent Anglo-
Saxon bishops were both consecrated by Irish bishops. Then came Chad of
Lindisfarne (664-72), whose original consecration was opposed by Wilfrid,
ostensibly on the grounds of British participation. The Mercian church
henceforward adopted a more romanophile stance, but its roots were
embedded in the Celtic world.[34] Another source of direct contact between
the English and Irish churches during the eighth and ninth centuries was
that the bishop of Mayo continued to attend English synods as a
suffragan.[35] Hughes drew attention to the references in the correspondence
of Offa, Alcuin and Charlemagne to the reception of Irish scholars and
prelates at the court of King Offa (757-96) and Isabel Henderson has
recently pointed to links between Mercia and Pictland at this time.[36] The
Southumbrian Synod of Chelsea of 816 contains a condemnation and
negation of the validity of ministrations by Irish priests and this has been
cited as evidence of an anti-Irish movement which would preclude cultural
exchange.[37] This is not necessarily a correct premiss, and, furthermore, this
text may show that the presence of Irish clerics was a significant factor in
the southern English church at this period and that it posed something of a
threat to attempts by the episcopate to consolidate control of the
Southumbrian church under its rule, from which such itinerant clergy
would be largely exempt. This reflects similar trends in the Carolingian
orbit.[38] Other random pieces of evidence might also have some bearing

---

[33]K Hughes, 'Evidence for contacts between the churches of the Irish and the English
from the Synod of Whitby to the Viking Age' in *England before the Conquest: studies in
primary sources presented to Dorothy Whitelock*, ed P Clemoes, K Hughes (Cambridge
1971) 49-67.

[34]See Dornier (note 6 above) passim, and H Mayr-Harting, *The coming of christianity
to Anglo-Saxon England* (London 1972) passim.

[35]On the attendance of the bishop of Mayo at Northumbrian synods, see C Cubitt,
'Anglo-Saxon church councils c650-c850' (unpubl. PhD thesis, University of
Cambridge 1990) 40, 260.

[36]See note 33 above; I Henderson, unpubl. paper delivered to a conference of the
Association of Art Historians, Dublin, 1990.

[37]See note 33 and Cubitt (note 35 above) 246, 340, 345.

[38]See Cubitt (note 35 above) 340, 345, and 422 and Brown forthcoming (note 1
above).

upon the matter. For example, Françoise Henry noted that the Annals of Ulster reveal that there was an English quarter at Armagh, certainly by the late eleventh century.[39] We do not know when this was established, but it might reflect the continuation of contacts established earlier, and is suggestive given the parallels noted between the Book of Armagh and the southern English *Tiberius* manuscripts.

These shreds of historical evidence would at least provide some context for continued cultural exchange between southern England, Ireland and the area where the Book of Kells was probably written which may have led to some of their shared features. Some of these features may simply represent echoes from a common wellspring of influences, but others would tend to suggest that the books in question emerged from a related climate of stylistic and eschatological development. If the Book of Kells did participate in this climate, a date in the late eighth or early ninth century would be suggested for its production. If it did not, then it must be viewed as a bizarre and precocious innovator in the areas concerned, which stands alone, but which exerted an influence upon subsequent Irish, southern English and continental book production. Given the extraordinary nature of Kells this is not impossible, but the evidence set forth in this paper would, I suggest, imply that it bears a chronological relationship to ninth century books such as the Book of Armagh, which is datable from its colophon, and the later members of the *Tiberius* group, which are datable from the place of their scripts in the evolutionary scale determined by charter evidence. Like them, it drew to some extent upon a common fount of ultimate Irish and Hiberno-Saxon experience, producing echoes of varying intensity, but these combined with the voices of the present.

---

[39]F Henry, *L'Art Irlandais* (St Léger-Vauban 1964) 49.

Exegesis and the Book of Kells: the Lucan genealogy

Jennifer O'Reilly

The Book of Kells was produced in a culture where the use and production of exegesis was well-established and sophisticated. The early reception date of a wide patristic inheritance and the impact of biblical and patristic concepts and techniques on a large vernacular as well as Hiberno-Latin literature have all been radically reappraised in recent years. The identification of various early works of biblical commentary as Irish, or as belonging to the Hiberno-Latin tradition, has been fundamental.[1] Since the pioneering work of Patrick McGurk in the different medium of insular gospel books, there has been growing awareness both of the antiquity of some features of their preliminary texts, and of their layout and decorative highlighting of the gospel text, and of the variety of functions carried out by such visual structuring of the page, particularly in the Book of Kells. The work of Suzanne Lewis and others has also shown an expository and symbolic element, not only in some of the full-page illustrations, but in its sacred calligraphy.[2] There remains some caution, however, about reading meanings in (or into) the Book of Kells. This caution is justifiable in view of the manuscript's uniqueness, the still unanswered questions about its precise date, place of origin and function and the fragmentary nature of surviving evidence about earlier insular gospel books and the tradition of early christian book production and illustration on which they drew. The present paper is a contribution to the task of trying to understand the layout and decoration of the gospel text in Kells by viewing it in the context of how scripture itself was read. The insular inheritance was not only of particular patristic commentaries but of a whole way of reading the sacred text. Some of the decoration in the Book of Kells may represent an adaptation into visual form of exegetical techniques and figures. The approach is here applied to the Lucan genealogy.

In surviving insular gospel books the tradition for the layout and decoration of Christ's genealogy in Luke 3:23-38 is far less developed than

---

[1]B Bischoff, 'Turning-points in the history of Latin exegesis in the early Irish church: AD 650-800' in *Biblical studies: the medieval Irish contribution*, ed M McNamara (Dublin 1976) 74-160; J F Kelly, 'A catalogue of early medieval Hiberno-Latin biblical commentaries' (I) *Traditio* 44 (1988) 537-71; (II) *Traditio* 45 (1989-90) 393-434. C D Wright, 'Hiberno-Latin and Irish-influenced biblical commentaries, florilegia and homily collections' in *The sources of Anglo-Saxon literary culture: a trial version*, ed F M Biggs, T D Hill, P E Szarmach (Binghampton, NY 1990) 87-123: I am grateful to Damian Bracken for this reference and for helpful discussion of the material.
[2]McGurk, *Gospel books*; idem, 'Two notes on the Book of Kells and its relation to other insular gospel books', *Scriptorium* 9 (1955) 105-07; S Lewis, 'Sacred calligraphy: the Chi Rho page in the Book of Kells', *Traditio* 26 (1980) 139-59.

for the version in Matt 1:1-17. There is nothing comparable to the title-page opening of Matthew's *Liber generationis* which also forms the opening of his gospel and of the gospel text of the whole codex, nor is there any significant parallel to the decorative climax of the Chi Rho in Matt 1:18. As early as the Book of Durrow, however, the genealogy had been treated as a unit within Luke's text. The Hebrew names of Christ's ancestors were listed one beneath the other, each preceded by the formula *qui fuit*, meaning 'who was (the son) of X'. The three words of each entry were well spaced forming three vertical columns down the page and the listing could be continued in parallel on the same page to form six columns in all, as in the Book of Durrow and BL, Royal MS I. B. VII, or even nine columns, as in the Book of Armagh.

As with its treatment of the Matthean genealogy, the Book of Kells both expands established features of the insular tradition and goes beyond it. The columnar listing is retained but there is only one Hebrew name with its accompanying *qui fuit* on each line so that the list is lavishly spaced over five pages, folios 200r-202r. The repeated initial *Q*s, slightly enlarged or coloured in earlier examples, are in Kells decorated with prodigal variety and richness. On the first two folios they are composed of entwined birds and beasts, on the third page they are made up of quadrupeds, on the fourth page several interlaced human figures appear and then entirely geometric patterns are used, the shape of the *Q* undergoing frequent metamorphosis in the process (**pls 37-41**). The vertical linking of the *Q*s serves to unify without monotony the seventy-seven names so that the Lucan genealogy, though not formally framed like the Matthean one in Kells, folios 29v-31r, nevertheless presents a magnificent counterpart to its layout. Not only are the columns of words enlivened by touches of colour, ornament or calligraphic flourishes, but inter-columnar figures are introduced which have no precedent in surviving insular gospel books.

Iona

On the third folio of the Lucan genealogy is a curious hybrid figure which has a counterpart later in Luke's text. Both figures are youthful beardless men with arms crossed and contorted and with the lower body made up of interlace and two sets of fin-like projections: one has a single fish tail, the more elaborately interlaced variant in the genealogy has two fishtails in place of feet. On folio 213 the figure has been placed horizontally at the end of a line of text (Luke 6:31), parallel with the lines of text above and below. Because no 'meaningful' connection has been detected between the figure and the text at this point, it has generally been regarded as a decorative space-filler. The similar figure placed vertically between columns of words on folio 201 in the listing of Christ's ancestors, however, has attracted considerable interest from modern scholars.

Because the figure grasps the final letter of the phrase *qui fuit* which precedes the Hebrew name Iona (= Jonah), Carl Nordenfalk read it as a *nota bene* symbol singling out the name of 'Iona the prophet' and he speculated that 'it is quite likely that the artist wanted to draw attention to the place where the manuscript was written'.[3] The name Iona is not the only one to be so singled out on this folio, however: the six birds also grasp the terminal *t* of the phrase preceding the names of six other ancestors in the list and the ambiguous crossed-arms gesture of the fish-man pointing both up and down could be read as indicating those birds who are grouped above and below him. Furthermore, as Nordenfalk himself later noted, the name of the island of Iona was not spelled thus in Hiberno-Saxon texts so the fish-man could not have been intended as a visual pun on the name of Columba's island monastery. Nevertheless, Nordenfalk ingeniously suggested that 'the Irish scribe, knowing that *Ionas interpretatur columba* from Isidore, *Etymologiae* 7.8.18, was pointing to Jonah's name because it called to mind Columba in whose honour the Book of Kells may have been produced'.[4]

Paul Meyvaert also believes that the raised right hand of the fish-man 'undoubtedly has the purpose of directing our attention to the name Iona: it is a *nota bene* symbol containing a clue to the manuscript's place of origin'.[5] He too cites the patristic exegetical device of translating Hebrew biblical names, a practice popularised by Jerome's *Liber interpretationis hebraicorum nominum* which interprets the name Iona as Columba. An abbreviated list of Jerome's Hebrew names survives in a number of insular gospel books. Dr Meyvaert makes the important observation, however, that the list of names appearing in Luke's gospel in a small sub-group of insular manuscripts including the Book of Durrow and the Book of Kells, is strangely defective and does not have Iona but *Iori (sic) columba mea* which does not suggest that it was the Hebrew name list of Luke being copied out that inspired the scribe-illuminator to draw attention to Iona-Columba. Instead, Dr Meyvaert turns to two famous non-biblical Irish applications of the Iona-Columba interpretation.

In 615 Columbanus wrote, 'I am called Jonah in Hebrew, Peristera in Greek and Columba in Latin'; in correspondence he several times used the Hebrew name Iona of himself. Similarly, in the second preface to the *Vita Columba* written before 700, Adomnán, ninth abbot of the island monastery of Iona noted 'what is pronounced *iona* in Hebrew and what Greek calls *peristera* and what in Latin is named *columba*, means one and the same thing'. Adomnán comments at length on the appropriateness of this name given to St Columba. Dr Meyvaert observes:

> From this evidence one can safely conclude that the scribe-illuminator is subtly indicating that the great name of Columba lies concealed on folio 201r of the Book of Kells. There seems little reason to doubt that the Columba in question here is the northern Columba, the founder of

---

[3]C Nordenfalk, 'Another look at the Book of Kells' in *Festschrift Wolfgang Braunfels*, ed F Piel and J Traer (Tübingen 1977) 275-79 (p 278).
[4]Noted by Lewis (note 2 above) 139 n 1.
[5]P Meyvaert, 'The Book of Kells and Iona', *Art Bulletin* 71 (1989) 6-19, 6 n 4.

Hy (ie the island monastery of Iona), praised by Adamnán. But if this is so, it provides an important clue regarding the place of origin of the Book of Kells. The manuscript can only have been produced in Columban territory — in other words, where the veneration of St Columba was dominant and probably also where Adamnán's Life of Columba was known.[6]

Northumbria is excluded by this definition because the cult of Columba had been superseded there by the end of the seventh century following the controversy over the dating of Easter.[7] Both Bede's *Historia ecclesiastica* and the *Life* of Wilfrid show the Columban monks of Lindisfarne (which had been founded from Iona in the 630s) losing the debate at the Synod of Whitby in 664 about the relative authority of St Columba and St Peter.

Columba

One difficulty with this interpretation of the significance of the fish-man figure in the Book of Kells is that the play on the Hebrew name Iona/Jonah and its Latin version Columba was by no means confined to Adomnán's account of St Columba but was widely used in exegesis to describe St Peter, whose original name was Simon bar-Jonah. Moreover the context for such discussion was exegesis of Matt 6:15-19, the Petrine text, which also figured largely in the insular literature of the Paschal controversy. The Hiberno-Latin pseudo-Jerome says of Peter's name Bar-Jonah, 'id est, filius Iona, id est columba'; a commentary on Matthew from the eighth-century circle of Virgil of Salzburg has, 'Petrus vocatur filius columbae quia iona columba interpretatur acsi dixisset filius sancti Spiritus es, quasi in columba spiritus venit'.[8] Isidore's *Etymologiae*, well-known to Irish commentators, says 'Simon Bar-iona in lingua nostra sonat filius columbae, et est nomen Syrum pariter et Hebraeum. Bar quippe Syra lingua filius, Iona Hebraice columba; utroque sermone dicitur Bar-iona'.[9] In his *Liber interpretationis hebraicorum nominum* Jerome briefly notes the meaning of the name Iona when it appears in Luke's gospel, the Acts of the Apostles and the Book of Jonah : 'Iona columba' or 'Iona columba vel dolens'. In the section on St Matthew's gospel however, Jerome comments more fully on Peter's original name: 'Bariona filius columbae. Syrum est pariter hebraeum. Bar quippe lingua syra filius, et iona columba utroque sermone dicitur'. Furthermore, in his gospel commentary on Matthew, which was extremely influential with Irish exegetes, Jerome applies this interpretation of names to the Petrine text in which Christ says, 'Blessed are you Simon Bar-iona' (Matt 16:17). Jerome explains that Simon's

---

[6]ibid, 9, nn 10-12, quoting *Sancti Columbani opera*, ed G S M Walker, Scriptores Latini Hiberniae 2 (Dublin 1970) 2, 54 and *Adomnan's Life of Columba*, ed A Anderson and M O Anderson (Edinburgh 1961), revised M O Anderson (Oxford 1991) 2-4.

[7]Meyvaert (note 5 above) 9-10 nn 14-16.

[8]*Expositio in IV evangelia*, PL 30, 554; F J Kelly, 'Irish monks and the see of St Peter', *Monastic Studies* 14 (1983) 207-23 (p 217).

[9]*Etymologiae*, ed W M Lindsay, 2 vols (Oxford 1985, facs. repr of 1911 edn) I, book 7, 9:4.

acclamation of Christ in the preceding verse was inspired by the Holy Spirit, whose son he was, as is shown in his name: the Holy Spirit is signified by a dove and 'siquidem Bar Iona in lingua nostra sonat filius columbae'.[10]

If this exegetical tradition suggests that the fish-man figure on folio 201r of the Book of Kells cannot, by itself, be read exclusively as a coded allusion to St Columba, does it have any significance or offer any comment on the text it decorates?

In an early commentary on the Acts of the Apostles, c709-16, Bede specifically refers to Jerome's list of Hebrew names and says, 'Wherever the sacred scriptures give the names of things or persons with an interpretation, it certainly indicates that a more sacred sense is contained in them ... Thus blessed Peter, on account of the grace of the same Spirit, was called Bar-iona, that is son of the dove'.[11] Bede's homily on the Chair of St Peter which focuses on the Petrine commission in Matt 16, is of particular interest here in that it offers a number of parallels with Adomnán's account of St Columba. Bede says that the name Simon Bar-iona, meaning *filius columbae* in latin, properly glorifies this perfect confessor of Christ's name because he was divinely inspired to recognise Christ's true identity with the acclamation, 'Thou art Christ, the son of the living God' (Matt 16:16). He was rightly called the son of a dove because the dove is a simple creature and Simon Bar-iona followed the Lord with pious simplicity mindful of the command that the Lord's followers be prudent as serpents and simple as doves (Matt 10:6). Furthermore, adds Bede, because the Holy Spirit descended on the Lord at his baptism in the form of a dove, one who is full of spiritual grace may properly be given the name 'son of a dove' or 'son of the Holy Spirit'.[12]

Similarly, Adomnán had drawn upon the patristic tradition of translating the Hebrew name Iona as Columba and also sought the significance of that divinely-given name, meaning dove, in the authority of the gospel. Like Bede, he refers both to the descent of the Holy Spirit in the form of a dove at Christ's baptism and to the exhortation in Matt 10:6 that the simplicity of the dove be taken as a model for discipleship:

> So good and great a name is believed not to have been put upon the man of God without divine dispensation. According to the truth of the gospels, moreover, the Holy Spirit is shown to have descended upon the only-begotten Son of the eternal Father in the form of the little bird that is called a dove. Hence often in sacred books a dove is understood to signify mystically the Holy Spirit. Similarly, in the

[10]*Liber interpretationis hebraicorum nominum*, CCSL 72, 140, 146, 124, 135. *Commentariorum in Matheum*, CCSL 77, 141.
[11]*Expositio Actuum Apostolorum*, CCSL 121, 28; *The Venerable Bede. Commentary on the Acts of the Apostles*, trans L T Martin (Kalamazoo 1989) 52-53.
[12]*Opera homiletica*, CCSL 122, 143-44.

gospel, the Saviour himself bade his disciples to have implanted in a pure heart the simplicity of doves. For indeed the dove is a simple and innocent bird. Therefore a simple and innocent person (Columba) also was rightly called by this name, since he with dove-like disposition offered to the Holy Spirit a dwelling in himself.[13]

The play on the forms of Columba's name does not simply allow Adomnán to display his erudition and *urbanitas*.[14] The power of Adomnán's claims here lies in his use of language traditionally used to exalt the discipleship of the Prince of the Apostles, not in order to lessen Peter's glory (the Columban monks at Whitby did not deny Christ's commission to St Peter), but to reveal Columba too as 'a man very dear to God and of high merit in his sight' on whom the grace of the Holy Spirit was poured out abundantly and in an incomparable manner.[15] In Bede's homily, Simon Bar-iona was through his divinely-inspired prophetic recognition of Christ's identity granted a share in Christ's name, the rock: 'Thou art Peter and on this rock I will build my church' (Matt 16:8; cf I Cor 10:4); Adomnán presents Columba, 'the father and founder of many monasteries' as, by divine dispensation, an exemplary dove or dwelling-place of the Holy Spirit in the latter-day western world: although Columba 'lived in this small and remote island of the Britannic ocean, he merited that his name should not only be illustriously renowned throughout our Ireland, and throughout Britain', but that it should reach Spain, Gaul and Italy and 'the Roman city itself, which is the chief of all cities'.[16]

In a very different rhetorical register and nearly a century earlier, Columbanus had also assumed contemporary familiarity with the traditional exegetical interpretation of Iona-Columba when he frequently used it of his own name, even calling himself Bar-iona in a letter to Gregory I. This has recently been described as 'self-righteous' and 'intentionally offensive': 'the Irishman could hardly have expected a Pope to find his claim to be Bar-iona either clever or amusing'.[17] It does, however, point to a wider application of the Iona-Columba exegesis than that encountered so far and one which may well have some relevance in the attempt to read the fish-man symbol in the Book of Kells.

Columba and its various forms and diminutives — Colum, Colman and Columban — was 'very common among the Irish saints'[18] and exegesis of the Petrine and related texts makes it clear that *all* the faithful are called to be *columbae* or doves, because at their baptism they are filled with the Holy Spirit (albeit each according to his capacity). Whereas Bede and Adomnán show St Peter and St Columba respectively to have

[13] Anderson (note 6 above) 4-5.
[14] J-M Picard, 'The purpose of Adomnán's *Vita Columbae*', *Peritia* 1 (1982) 176-77.
[15] Anderson (note 6 above) 209.
[16] ibid, 233.
[17] J F Kelly, 'The letter of Columbanus to Gregory the Great', *Gregorio Magno e il suo tempo*, Studia Ephemeridis Augustinianum 33 (Rome 1991) 216, 218.
[18] Walker (note 6 above) xii n 3.

been very full vessels of the Holy Spirit, Columbanus, in describing himself, immediately follows the phrase *ego Bar-iona* with the self-deprecatory words *vilis Columba*, and elsewhere in his correspondence repeatedly refers to himself as *Columba peccator*. Particularly when understood in the context of his idiosyncratic use of the authorial humility topos,[19] Columbanus seems to be saying that as a member of the church he is a dove, his very name proclaims it, though he is a small and wretched one; far from abrogating the authority of Simon Bar-iona he presumes to offer advice, and even admonition, to Popes Gregory I and Boniface IV only in the interests of the church's unity which St Peter represents. In exegetical parlance — and his letter of 600 is addressed to a great exegete whom he revered — unity was a very dovelike preoccupation.

As early as Cyprian's *De ecclesiae catholicae unitate*, which was well-known to insular commentators, the nature of the dove is allegorically expounded. The reason why the Holy Spirit came in the form of a dove is because doves are without rancour or bitterness, they fly in formation, assemble and eat in one house and are, in short, an image of unity and concord whose example the church must follow, 'that we may imitate the doves in our love for the brethren'. In the second version of the text, Cyprian quotes the Petrine commission in Matt 16 to demonstrate that although after the Resurrection, the other Apostles also received the Spirit and shared in Peter's power, nevertheless 'It is on one man Christ builds his church ... in order to show that the church of Christ is unique. Indeed this oneness is figured in the Canticle of Canticles when the Holy Spirit, speaking in the Lord's name, says, "One is my dove, my perfect one" (Cant 6:8)'.[20] This classic text (Cant 6:8) is echoed in the very interpretation of the Hebrew name Iona, not simply as *Columba*, but as *Columba mea* in Jerome's list of the Hebrew names used in Luke.

Bede, who draws on Cyprian and the Song of Songs in his homily on the Chair of Peter, explains that although the same office is committed to the whole church in her bishops and priests, the special way in which Peter was blessed and given the keys in Matt 16:17-19 represented the unity of faith and fellowship of all believers. Playing on the interpretation of the name Bar-iona as *filius columbae*, Bede urges: 'if we imitate Peter's example ... we also will be capable of being called blessed ... on account of the gift of virtues we have received from the Lord, we will be called "sons of a dove" and Christ himself, rejoicing with us in the spiritual progress of our souls will say, "How beautiful you are ... your eyes are those of doves" (Cant 4:1)'.[21]

---

[19] M Lapidge, 'Columbanus and the Antiphonary of Bangor', *Peritia* 4 (1985) 107-08.

[20] Cyprian, *De ecclesiae catholicae unitate*, CCSL 3, 255-56, 252. Note on authenticity of Primacy Text, ibid, 244-45. This work was used in the insular paschal controversy, eg *Cummian's letter* De Controversia Paschali *and the* De Ratione Conputandi, ed M Walsh and D Ó Cróinín (Toronto 1988) 78-79 n 151.

[21] *Opera homiletica*, CCSL 122, 146-47; *Bede the Venerable. Homilies on the Gospels*, trans L T Martin and D Hurst (Kalamazoo 1991) I, 204.

Baptism

The dove, a vessel or dwelling-place of the Holy Spirit, was a familiar image of the church or the soul and could thus be applied to the particular examples of St Peter, Columba or Columbanus. Exegesis on the dove was not peculiar to exegesis of the Petrine text in Matt 16 or to the traditional interpretation of Iona as Columba, however, but was found in two other important contexts: commentaries on the gospel accounts of Christ's baptism and catechetical and mystagogical works on the sacrament of baptism. Ambrose's *De Mysteriis*, for example, links together the account of the descent of the Holy Spirit in the form of a dove at Christ's baptism, the injunction of Matt 10:6 'be simple as doves' (which is directly applied to those who are baptised) and the words of Cant 4:1, addressed by Christ to the pure soul of those regenerated in baptism: 'How beautiful you are ... your eyes are those of doves'.[22] This is one of a number of quotations about doves in the *Song of Songs* cited by Bede in a homily expounding Christ's baptism and the sacrament it prefigured. Elsewhere he notes that the Holy Spirit by descending at Christ's baptism as a dove 'does not represent merely its own innocence and simplicity, or that of him on whom it descended, but likewise that of those who think of him in goodness and seek him in simplicity of heart (Wisdom of Solomon 1:1). The Lord himself says in praise of the piety that they share with one accord ... granted by a spiritual grace: 'One is my dove' (Cant 6:8)... The church is appropriately given the name 'the one dove of Christ' ... for undoubtedly it is not because of her own merits, but because of a gift of spiritual grace she has received, that she is gathered into the unity of the Christian faith from many nations'.[23]

Any discussion of whether this exegetical chain of texts concerning the dove has any relevance to an interpretation of the hybrid figure, apparently drawing attention to the name Iona on folio 201 in the Book of Kells, needs now to view both this exegesis and the figure of the fish-man in the context of the whole folio and in the larger decorated unit of text of which folio 201 forms a part. Two practical questions also need to be addressed: why is the fish-man accompanied by six birds to which he appears to be pointing? And why are these figures placed within the Lucan text of Christ's genealogy?

It is clear from the traditions briefly sketched here that the dove was universally regarded as an image of the baptised christian soul or of the church collectively, filled with the Holy Spirit. The key text in the exegetical chain and the unambiguous reason why the dove was so widely used as the image of the Holy Spirit filling the soul or the church is that at Christ's own baptism the Holy Spirit descended *in specie columbae*. This reason is quoted by Adomnán in the very next sentence after his play on Iona-Columba and forms the basis of his explanation of the suitability

---

[22]*Ambroise de Milan. Des sacrements. Des mystères*, ed B Botte, Sources Chrétiennes 25, 168-76.
[23]*Opera homelitica*, CCSL 122, 107-08; Martin and Hurst (note 21 above) 151-52.

of the name Columba for one who 'with dove-like disposition offered to the Holy Spirit a dwelling in himself'. If the Book of Kells was produced in a Columban monastery, the detail of the hybrid figure alongside the name of Iona would doubtless have had a particular significance but it could not have been an exclusive allusion to St Columba since all the baptised are called to be doves, to become the dwelling-place or temple of the Holy Spirit. At their baptism and post-baptismal confirmation the faithful are anointed with oil and chrism to signify their participation in Christ's spiritual anointing with the Holy Spirit at his incarnation, which was proclaimed at his baptism by the descent of the dove and in the words of the Father, 'This is my beloved son'. In St Luke's gospel alone the account of Christ's baptism is immediately followed by his genealogy. In the Book of Kells the two lines of text concluding the Lucan baptism narrative are inscribed at the top of folio 200r above the opening of the genealogy (pl 37). The top line bears the words of the Father, *tu es filius meus dilectus*. The list of Christ's human ancestors thus immediately follows the revelation of his divine sonship at his baptism, a point also stressed at the end of the genealogy where Christ's earthly ancestors are traced back to Adam 'who was the son of God'. The Durham Gospels sets out the Lucan baptism and genealogy in one large double opening.[24] Patristic and insular commentators were responsive to the theological implications of Luke's genealogy and its context. Following St Ambrose, an eighth-century Hiberno-Latin commentary on Luke's gospel notes that the account of Christ's genealogy is placed after the account of the baptism in order to demonstrate that God is Father not only of Christ but of all Christians through baptism.[25] Bede's commentary on Luke's gospel shows that the real significance of the coming of the dove at Christ's baptism was its descent into his body, the church; thus those who are baptised receive the Holy Spirit and become the sons of God.[26]

In that same gospel commentary and in the context of discussing the importance of the number seven in Luke's listing of the seventy-seven generations of Christ's ancestors, Bede refers to the seven gifts of the Holy Spirit which Isaiah prophesied would descend on the Messiah (Isaiah 11:2-3). Allusion to Isaiah's prophecy in the context of baptism was a patristic commonplace. It is used by Ambrose, for example, to explain that

---

[24]Durham, Cathedral Library, MS A.II.17, folios 74v-75r, *The Durham Gospels*, ed C D Verey, T J Brown, E Coatsworth, Early English manuscripts in facsimile 20 (Copenhagen 1980).

[25]J F Kelly, editor of the Hiberno-Latin commentary on Luke, Cod. Vind. lat. 997, *c* 780-85 (CCSL 108C), notes its dependence on Bede's Lucan commentary, *c* 709-716, and other evidence of the early familiarity of Irish commentators with some of Bede's works: 'To study Hiberno-Latin exegesis without reference to Bede is to ignore not only an important source for the Irish exegetes, but also a part of the tradition in which they stood'; Bede's own use of earlier Hiberno-Latin works is also noted: 'Bede and Hiberno-Latin exegesis' in *Sources of Anglo-Saxon culture*, ed P Szarmach (Kalamazoo 1986); J Kelly, 'The Hiberno-Latin study of the gospel of Luke' in McNamara (note 1 above) 10-29.

[26]Bede, *In Lucae evangelium expositio*, CCSL 120, 84; cf Ambrose, *Expositio evangelii secundum Lucam*, CCSL 14, 81-82.

the faithful also receive the spiritual seal of these seven gifts of the Holy Spirit at their own post-baptismal anointing with chrism at which they participate in Christ's anointing. The seven gifts, 'spiritum sapientiae et intellectus, spiritum consilii atque virtutis, spiritum cogitationis atque pietatis, spiritum sancti timoris', dispose the faithful to virtue.[27] In his homily expounding Christ's baptism Bede shows how the seven-fold nature of the dove, allegorically revealed in the Song of Songs, exemplifies the seven types of virtue necessary to the life of the baptised: 'And this is rightly done because the grace of the Holy Spirit, who descended as a dove, is sevenfold'.[28] The eighth-century Hiberno-Latin commentary on Luke's gospel (which was influenced by Ambrose's Lucan commentary) interprets the evangelist's description of Jesus after his baptism 'full of the Holy Spirit' as meaning the seven gifts of the Holy Spirit 'and of this fullness have we all received'.[29]

It has been seen that St Luke's gospel uniquely connects Christ's baptism and his genealogy and that the exegetical tradition emphasized both Christ's divine Sonship, made known in the words of the Father and the descent of the dove at his baptism, and his human ancestry revealed in the genealogy. Commentators further noted the allusion of the dove to the descent of the Holy Spirit on the church whose earthly members, re-born in baptism, become sons of God. Related themes, which also exist in other contexts, were drawn into Ambrose's magisterial treatment of the Lucan baptism and genealogy: the exposition of the nature of the dove as an image of the church or the individual soul filled with the Holy Spirit and the application of this image of the dove to all the faithful who in their baptism and post-baptismal confirmatory anointing with chrism share in Christ's anointing with the seven-fold gifts of the Holy Spirit. Finally, the patristic interpretation of the Hebrew name Iona as *columba* meaning dove had long been familiar in insular monastic culture and, in the *Life of Columba*, had found early expression in connection with a number of the exegetical themes itemised here. Seen from the perspective of exegesis on Luke's text and its themes, therefore, the possibility that the hybrid figure on folio 201r in the Book of Kells may be a witty visual play on the Hebrew name Iona and its latin meaning *columba* or dove, seems strengthened rather than diminished by his gnomic gestures. He is pointing both upwards and downwards, linking him to the six birds grouped directly above and below, so that the whole column of figures may be read as seven 'doves' in all. A number of puzzles remain. Why, for example, is the central 'dove' depicted as half-man, half-fish? Is this just incidental, an idiosyncratic drollery, or is it integral to the meaning of the page suggested here?

---

[27]Botte (note 22 above) 74-75.
[28]*Opera homiletica*, CCSL 122, 86.
[29]*Scriptores Hiberniae minores*, ed R E McNally, CCSL 108C, 29.

The Sign of Jonah

Françoise Henry's observation that the Hebrew name Iona in Luke's genealogy had itself 'probably suggested the fish-human figure' on folio 201[30] and Paul Meyvaert's comment that 'there may be a playful allusion here to Jonah and his whale'[31] tacitly depend on conflating Christ's ancestor Iona (about whom nothing is known) with the prophet Iona who was often depicted as a half-length figure emerging from the jaws of the whale or sea monster in early christian art. In early Irish monastic circles the Hebrew name Iona certainly evoked the prophet of that name. Using word-play on his own name, Columbanus frequently and unambiguously likened himself to the prophet Jonah and his shipwreck and Adomnán in interpreting St Columba's name says he 'received the same name as the prophet Jonah'.[32] The scriptural and exegetical associations of the prophet Jonah may, therefore, have some significance in interpreting the fish-man figure in the Book of Kells.

Jonah was cited by Christ in Matt 12:39-40; 16:4 and Luke 11:29-30 as the sign of the Son of Man, expanded in Matthew's version to a specific image of Christ's own death and resurrection. Because the faithful sacramentally participate in Christ's death and resurrection at their descent into the waters of baptism, from which ritual death they emerge to a new life, they too were in early exegesis likened to Jonah and his deliverance from the whale. In his commentary on the Book of Jonah, Jerome refers to Christ's baptism to explain that the prophet's name means *columba* because *Spiritus Sanctus in specie columbae descendit*. He directly links Jonah's mission to the Ninevites with the risen Christ's injunction to his disciples to baptise all in the name of the Father, the Son and the Holy Spirit (Matt 28:19).[33]

Royal priesthood

Genealogy has an extremely important function in both the Old and New Testaments:

> The very interest in ancestry reflects Israel's tribal origins ... Besides establishing identity, biblical genealogies are sometimes used to undergird status, especially for the offices of king and priest where lineage is important ... to structure history into epochs and to authenticate a line of (cultic) office holders.[34]

The two versions of Christ's genealogy in the gospels of Matthew and Luke received extensive exposition in patristic commentaries but were of particular interest for a clerical caste within barbarian society who shared many of the assumptions and techniques of the authors of biblical

---

[30]Henry, 200 and n 95.
[31]Meyvaert (note 5 above) 6.
[32]Walker (note 6 above) 19, 35, 55; Anderson (note 6 above) 3.
[33]*Commentariorum in Ionam prophetam*, CCSL 76, 380, 404.
[34]R E Brown, *The birth of the Messiah* (London 1977) 65.

genealogies. Donnchadh Ó Corráin has shown that early Irish churchmen themselves produced a vast corpus of genealogical material, shaped for ecclesiastical and political purposes.[35]

On the same page as the Iona figure in the Book of Kells is the name of Christ's ancestor David. Ambrose's Lucan commentary, followed by insular exegetes, explains that in Matthew's genealogy the descent is through David's son and royal heir, Solomon, but in Luke's version the sacerdotal line is traced through another of David's sons, Nathan.[36] Christ as a member of the royal house of Judah was not in the direct descent of the priestly tribe of Aaron (Num 3:3,10; Heb 7:14), but St Luke is at pains to explain that the Virgin Mary was the cousin of John the Baptist's mother, Elizabeth, who was 'of the daughters of Aaron' (Luke 1:5) and that Elizabeth's husband, the priest Zachariah, was descended through Abia from Aaron, the first anointed priest under the law. Insular commentators document other examples of such links by inter-marriage between the royal and priestly lines in order to show that Christ belongs in the flesh to both tribes and that in his assumed humanity he has the person of priest and king.

Furthermore, all the baptised when anointed with chrism through which they sacramentally share in Christ's anointing are called to be prophets, priests and kings, as the liturgy also makes evident.[37]

There were other important factors in the particular association of Luke's gospel with Christ's (and therefore with the church's) royal priesthood. Luke's account of the incarnation is symbolically prefaced by the scene of Zachariah, a priest of the Old Covenant, making an offering at the altar in the temple at Jerusalem. This was important in late antique and early medieval manuscript art. In the sixth-century Rabbula Gospels Zachariah

---

[35]D Ó Corráin, 'Irish origin legends and genealogy: recurrent aetiologies' in *History and heroic tale*, ed T Nybey, I Pio, P Sorensen, A Trommer (Odense 1985) 51-96; K McCone, *Pagan past and christian present in early Irish literature* (Maynooth 1991) 233-44.

[36]Ambrose, *Expositio evangelii secundum Lucam*, I, CCSL 14, 82-83; cf Bede, *In Lucae evangelium expositio*, CCSL 120, 89-90. Also in the Hiberno-Latin tradition, eg in the commentary on the Matthean genealogy in Munich, Clm. 6233, folio 22v, lines 692-98, c770-80, and the commentary on the Lucan genealogy in the eighth-century Irish 'Reference Bible', Paris, BN, MS lat. 11561, folio 164v and Munich, Clm. 14277, folio 253r. I am most grateful to Dr Seán Connolly, who is editing the 'Reference Bible' New Testament, for making his transcripts of the genealogical material in these unpublished manuscripts available to me. Ambrose is the most important patristic source for the commentary on Luke in the Reference Bible but 'Ambrose's own source, Origen's Homilies on Luke, is known to the Irish exegete, in latin translation, and the Alexandrian is cited by name', J F Kelly, 'Das Bibelwerk, organisation and Quellenanalyse of the New Testament section' in *Irland und die Christenheit*, ed P Ní Cháthain and M Richter (Stuttgart 1987) 113-123 (p 116). The contrast in Christ's descent traced through Solomon and Nathan was also perpetuated through the 'Monarchian' prologues prefacing insular gospel books, including the Book of Kells: J Chapman, *Early history of the Vulgate gospels* (Oxford 1908) 230.

[37]*Ex dictis sancti Hieronimi* (Munich, Clm. 14426), CCSL 108B, 229-30 and Bede, *Opera homiletica*, CCSL 122, 19-20 for royal and priestly intermarriage; see below and n 90 for anointing.

is paired with Aaron but in Carolingian and later Anglo-Saxon examples the scene is depicted as a literal illustration of Luke's text (1:9-11) and usually shown in the spandrels or historiated initial of the gospel incipit.[38] In exegesis however, the underlying meaning of the scene was expounded in great detail. Following Ambrose, Bede notes that the appearance of an angel beside the altar of Zachariah's offering was to proclaim 'the coming of the true and eternal high priest who would be the true sacrificial offering for the salvation of the whole world'.[39]

Ambrose in turn, like Origen before him, was drawing on the exegesis already well-developed in the Epistle to the Hebrews which shows how Christ was called by God to be the new High Priest of the heavenly sanctuary superseding the Aaronic priesthood and the sacrifices of the Old Covenant and of the earthly tabernacle. The Epistle repeatedly cites Christ's fulfilment of the Messianic prophecy from Ps 109:4, 'Thou art a priest for ever, after the order of Melchisedech' (Heb 5:6,10; 6:20; 7:2,17). Melchisedech does not feature in Luke's list of Christ's ancestors because this mysterious priest-king was 'without father, without mother, without genealogy' (Heb 7:3). In Hebrews, however, the first of the repeated acclamations of Christ as 'Thou art a priest forever after the order of Melchisedech' is directly coupled with another prophetic text: 'Thou art my son: this day have I begotten thee' (Ps 2:7; Heb 5:5-6). Commentators, including Ambrose's work on Luke's gospel, regularly noted the fulfilment of this prophecy in the gospel accounts of Christ's baptism when the psalm words are alluded to in the proclamation of his divine sonship. Exegesis on St Luke's combined account of Christ's baptism and his priestly genealogy therefore regularly makes substantial use of the Epistle to the Hebrews' revelation of Christ as the divinely appointed great high priest 'after the order of Melchisedech'. The image carried a further and widely known allusion to Christ's priesthood and sacrifice because the priest-king Melchisedech had offered bread and wine to Abraham (Gen 14:18), a standard type or prefiguring of the Eucharist which was frequently cited in commentaries on the Last Supper and on the Eucharist and recalled in the Roman canon of the mass.

The twelfth-century Mosan Floreffe Bible (London, BL, Add. MS 17738) sets out the major themes of this exegesis in pictorial form at the beginning of St Luke's gospel at the place reserved in earlier gospel books for a literal illustration of Luke's account of Zachariah at the altar in the

---

[38]Florence, Bibl. Medicea-Laurentiana (Plut. I, 56). *The Rabbula Gospels*, ed C Ceccheli, G Furlani, M Salmi (Oltun and Lausanne 1959), Canon I, folio 3v, pl 9.2. The Annunciation follows, accompanied by the O.T. priest Samuel with the oil for royal anointing, then Christ's baptism, with the enthroned figures of David and Solomon. Early western representations of Zachariah at the altar reviewed by R Walker, 'Illustrations of the Priscillian prologues in gospel manuscripts of the Carolingian Ada school', *Art Bulletin* 30 (1948) 1-10; W Koehler, 'An illustrated evangelistary of the Ada school and its model', *Journal of the Warburg and Courtauld Institutes* 15 (1952) 48-66.

[39]*In Lucae evangelium expositio*, CCSL 120, 24; cf Bede, *Homelia* II, no 19, *Opera homiletica*, CCSL 122, 318-27 (p 323).

Temple (**pl 127**). On the double-columned page on folio 187 the picture is positioned alongside the literal text of Luke's account of Zachariah but, with the aid of inscriptions, provides a detailed comment on its underlying spiritual meaning. St Luke stands holding an emblem of his evangelist symbol, the winged calf, immediately beside a scene of the sacrifice of a calf on an altar by a priest of the Old Covenant. This blood sacrifice is superseded by the Crucifixion shown in the upper register of the picture and on the same central axis as the sacrificial altar below. The lance thrust which pierces Christ's side on the Cross parallels the knife thrust into the sacrificial calf on the altar below which, under the Old Covenant, had to be made to repeated victims in expiation for sin. That Christ's Passion is to be seen as the priestly sacrifice of the New Covenant is made unambiguously clear by the addition of portrait busts with banderoles. King David quotes from his own Ps 109: 'Thou art a priest for ever after the order of Melchisedech' and St Paul, the presumed author of the Epistle to the Hebrews, quotes from 9:12: 'But by his own blood he entered once into the holy place'. The inscription over the Sanctuary arch, which encloses the entire picture, directly relates Christ and the sacrificial calf.

The Book of Kells has no such didactic intent: its illustration will not teach what is not already known. Instead of attaching a coherent centralised design to the narrative of Zachariah in Luke 1, providing a clear commentary on it, the Kells artist has added enigmatic and apparently unconnected figures to the margins of a genealogy where they may be read by the casual eye as simply decorating or animating the page. But viewed in the context of the exegetical tradition just outlined, they may also be seen as a series of pictorial cues both recalling and prompting a meditative reading of a mysterious text, namely the list of Hebrew names. Similarly, the author of the Hiberno-Latin commentary on Matthew's gospel in Munich, Clm 6233 uses the bare list of Hebrew names and their etymologies as a series of hooks on which to hang exegetical chains of texts. Their precise relevance to the particular names against which they are positioned varies considerably — sometimes it is very close, sometimes it seems slight, forced or non-existent — but they are united in providing a series of insights into the nature of Christ within the framework of a genealogy whose very function is to elucidate that identity.[40]

On folio 201v in Kells a figure with a chalice is placed over the name of Abraham (**pl 40**). At the foot of the page is a small winged calf placed vertically, as in the evangelist symbol of Luke on folio 27v, where a cross appears in its halo. The patristic tradition of associating St Luke and his symbolic calf with the Passion and priesthood of Christ was very

---

[40]The Hebrew names in Matt 1:4-5, for example, prompt succinct allusion to biblical texts on the Crucifixion as exaltation (linking John 12:32 and Phil 2:8-11), on the body of Christ as the prophesied new sacrifice for remission of sin, on the church drawn from the Gentiles and on Christ's royal and priestly lineage 'after the order of Melchisedech'.

familiar in Hiberno-Latin exegesis on the four evangelists.[41] Ambrose refers to the suitability of the calf as the symbol of St Luke precisely in his discussion of the Lucan genealogy which reveals Christ as a priest for ever 'according to the order of Melchisedech': Ambrose observes that the calf always points to this sacerdotal mystery.[42] In Kells the calf is depicted with its back to the names of three of Christ's ancestors (Eber, Sala and Cainan) who merit no particular comment in exegesis. More important, perhaps, in explaining the calf's position on the page is the fact that it is directly facing the ornament at the end of the genealogy on the facing page and that the calf's legs are outstretched so that its whole body forms a kind of bracket exactly spanning the depth of that decorative panel and visually relating the two.

The panel on folio 202r (**pl 41**) is formed by entwined peacocks and a vinescroll stemming from a chalice and partly conceals a bearded figure standing behind it. The idea that this is not simply a decorative endpiece but also carries the standard early christian allusions to the motif of the Eucharist is strengthened by comparison with the decorative panel marking the *Breves causae* of Luke which begins on folio 19v with the words *Zachariae sacerdoti*. The opening letters, *Zacha*, clouded by ornament and enlarged on a panel to fill the width of the page, are ingeniously formed from an inhabited vinescroll stemming horizontally along the panel from a chalice, so that an allusion to the eucharistic sacrifice of the new high priest may be discerned, concealed in Zachariah's name.

The Temple
Ambrose's commentary on St Luke's gospel contrasts the Aaronic priesthood represented by Zachariah with the eternal priest of whom it is said: 'Thou art a priest for ever'. Ambrose expounds this text as referring to 'the priest who is to come, whose sacrifice would not be like others, for he would not offer sacrifice for us in a temple made with human hands but he would offer propitiation for our sins in the temple of his body'.[43] This draws heavily on the Epistle to the Hebrews 9 which contrasts the blood sacrifices of the Levitical priesthood with Christ's redemptive single sacrifice of his own blood. The 'former tabernacle' is to be superseded by 'a greater and more perfect tabernacle, not made with hands, that is, not of this creation'; as the new high priest, 'Jesus is not entered into the (Holy of) Holies made with hands, the pattern of the true, but into Heaven itself, that he may appear now in the presence of God for us' (Heb 9:11, 24). But Ambrose links the Hebrews text to another important scriptural chain.

---

[41]R McNally, 'The evangelists in the Hiberno-Latin tradition' in *Festschrift Bernhard Bischoff*, ed A Hiergemann (Stuttgart 1971) 111-22.
[42]Ambrose, *Expositio evangelii secundum Lucam*, CCSL 14, 83; cf 5: in the prologue dealing with the priest Zachariah Ambrose also speaks of the calf as the symbol of Luke's gospel which begins with a priest and ends with a victim.
[43]ibid, 17.

The earliest christian preachers declared that the Lord who created heaven and earth 'dwells not in temples made with hands' (Acts 17:24, 7:48). To the Jews who demanded Jesus give them some sign of the divine authority by which he had cleansed the Temple in Jerusalem, he replied: 'Destroy this temple and in three days I will raise it up'. They understood this literally. 'But he spoke of the temple of his body' (John 2:19-22). During his trial before the chief priests his accusers said, 'We heard him say, I will destroy this temple made with hands and within three days I will build another not made with hands' (Mark 14:58; Matthew 26:61). The Jews failed to discern the spiritual fulfilment of his prophecy in the Crucifixion and Resurrection: 'Thou that destroyest the temple of God and in three days will rebuild it, save they own self. If thou be the Son of God, come down from the cross' (Matt 27:40; Mark 15:29).

Ambrose's contrast of the Old Covenant priesthood represented by Zachariah with 'the priest who is to come' depends on the Epistle to the Hebrews, some of whose themes have been traced here in the decoration of the last double-opening of Jesus's priestly genealogy in the Book of Kells, folios 201v-202r. But Ambrose's contrast of the Old Covenant sacrifice in the 'temple made with human hands' with the new priest's offering of 'propitiation for our sins in the temple of his body' also draws on the chain of gospel texts, centred on John 2:19-22, which identify the new temple, the place of the divine presence, as the human body of Jesus.

Furthermore, Ambrose applies the image of the Temple not only to the incarnate body of Jesus but to the church. Commenting on Luke's account of the baptism, which points to the descent of the Holy Spirit on the church at Pentecost, Ambrose pictures the birth, growth, composition and calling of the church through the image of the Temple building, drawing on a chain of scriptural texts.

He describes the Temple built by Solomon in Jerusalem as the type of the church built by God and quotes Ps 126:1: 'Except the Lord build the house, they labour in vain who build it'. In particular he comments on the constituent phrases of two key texts in the chain. He calls on the faithful to be 'as living stones built up, a spiritual house, a holy priesthood, to offer up spiritual sacrifices' (I Peter 2:5) and pictures this spiritual house as 'built upon the foundation of the apostles and prophets, Jesus Christ himself being the chief cornerstone in whom all the building framed together grows into a temple' (Eph 2:20-21).

Ambrose's interpretation of the Lucan baptism and genealogy in terms of the new priesthood and Temple illumines the extraordinary picture in Kells which immediately follows the genealogy and precedes Luke's description of Jesus returning from his baptism 'full of the Holy Spirit'. On folio 202v a bust-length portrait of Christ is set on a smaller-scale church building (pl 42). With metaphysical wit the picture gives a literal rendering of the gospel image of 'the temple of his body', prompting the search for a spiritual interpretation. The image faces, and is complemented by, an elaborate framed display text of the opening words of Luke 4:1: 'Jesus full of the Holy Spirit' (pl 43): this text and image positioned at the end of Luke's account of the baptism and genealogy, which together show Jesus to be Son of God and of human descent, thus reveal the Temple as the body or humanity of Jesus filled with the Holy Spirit. The rows of little figures beneath the building enable it to be read not only as the incarnate body of Jesus but also as his body the church, made up of 'living stones' with Jesus as 'the chief corner stone'.

The visual ambiguities of the Temple picture in Kells mirror some of the multiple allusions of the exegetical chain of scriptural texts on the image of the Temple used by Ambrose in his Lucan commentary. The idea, central to Ambrose's use of the Temple image, that it can allude simultaneously to Christ and his church is clearly stated in Bede's homily on the chief gospel link in the chain, John 2:12-22. Referring to the Temple in Jerusalem Bede says 'the temple made by hands prefigured our Lord's most sacred body' but adds that it also 'pointed to his body the Church and to the body and soul of each one of the faithful (as we find in quite a few places in the scriptures)'.[44] This mode of interpretation is set out more fully at the beginning of his allegorical exposition on the description of the Temple in III Kings 5:1-7:51:

> The house of God which king Solomon built in Jerusalem was made as a figure of the holy universal Church which, from the first of the elect to the last to be born at the end of the world, is daily being built through the grace ... of its redeemer. It is still partly in pilgrimage from him on earth and partly, having escaped from the hardships of its sojourn, already reigns with him in heaven where, when the last judgement is over, it is to reign completely with him ... to it belongs the very mediator between God and men, himself a human being, Christ Jesus (I Tm 2:5), as he himself attests when he says, 'Destroy this temple and in three days I shall raise it up'. To which the evangelist by way of explanation added, 'But he was speaking of the temple of his own body' (John 2:29, 21). Furthermore, the Apostle says of us, 'Do you not realise that you are a temple of God with the Spirit of God living in you?' (I Cor 3:16). If, therefore, he became the temple of God by assuming human nature and we became the temple of God through his Spirit dwelling in us (Rm 8:11), it is quite clear that the material temple was a figure of us all, that is, both of the Lord himself and his members which we are. But (it was a figure) of him as the uniquely chosen and precious cornerstone laid in the foundation (cf Is 28:16, I Peter 2:6) and of us as the living stones built upon the foundation of the apostles and prophets, i.e. on the Lord himself (Eph 2:20, I Peter 2:5-7, I Cor 3:11) ... the figure (of the temple) will apply to our Lord himself in some respects, in others to all the elect.[45]

---

[44]*Opera homiletica*, CCSL 122, 189; Martin and Hurst (note 21 above) II, 8-9.
[45]Bede, *De tabernaculo, de templo, in Esdram et Nehemiam*, ed D Hurst, CCSL 119A, 148. Translation used here is by Seán Connolly: I wish to thank Dr Connolly for

Bede's treatise shows the familiarity within an early eighth-century insular monastic context of the patristic tradition and, like the Kells picture, illustrates its highly creative re-working. It demonstrates that the Temple in Jerusalem prefigured both 'the temple of his body' (John 2:19, 21) and the temple made of 'living stones' (I Peter 2:5-7; Eph 2:20) and shows that the use of the Temple as an image of the church as the body of Christ does not simply refer to the church on earth but to his mystical body, beyond temporal and spatial limitation: it includes the dead and those yet to be born. The faithful who died before the Incarnation are not regarded simply as part of the fabric of the Temple in Jerusalem which was superseded by the christian church: they are shown to be part of the single body of Christ which will be completed only in the kingdom of heaven. Though Bede's treatise cannot be seen as the 'source' of the picture of the Temple in the Book of Kells, it can assist a clearer understanding of the conceptual connection between the image of the Temple on folio 202v and the iconography of the genealogy in the pages leading up to it, a connection which, it has been suggested here, reflects patristic exegesis of Luke's text. Seen within this exegetical tradition, the Temple image and its facing text in Kells transforms a literal reading of the foregoing list of Hebrew names and reveals it as chronicling both the earthly ancestors from whom Christ took 'the temple of his body' in historical time *and* the spiritual ancestors of his body the church, still awaiting its completion at the end of time. From the moment of the Incarnation the 'temple of his body' is shown to be 'full of the Holy Spirit'; the revelation of this at his baptism signifies that his body, the church, is also the habitation of the Holy Spirit.

Abraham
Folios 201v-202r in the Book of Kells have already received some comment in the light of Ambrose's exegesis on the priestly genealogy and related themes in Luke contrasting the Old Covenant priesthood and repeated blood sacrifice in 'the former tabernacle' with the single sacrifice of Christ, the new high priest, in 'the temple of his body'. The suggested connection between this exegesis and iconography and the picture of the Temple on the page immediately following the genealogy may now be considered further.

Directly above the calf in the inner margin of folio 201v, and facing the final page of the genealogy, is a bearded figure reclining over the name of Abraham and alongside the names of Isaac and Jacob. In the New

---

generously making his work available to me before its publication. In *De schematibus et tropis* Bede explains that a single word or event may figuratively designate a mystical, tropological and anagogical sense at the same time. He cites the Temple as an example. Historically, it is the house built by Solomon; allegorically, it is the body of the Lord (John 2:19) or his church (I Cor 3:17); tropologically it can refer to the individual faithful (I Cor 3. 16), and anagogically it signifies the joys of the heavenly dwelling (Ps 84:4): 'The Venerable Bede. Concerning figures and tropes', trans G H Tannenhaus in *Readings in medieval rhetoric*, ed J M Miller, M H Frosser, T W Benson (Bloomington, Ind. and London 1973) 120-21.

Testament, in early exegesis, liturgy and iconography, Abraham is an immensely important figure of faith whose sacrifice of Isaac and reception of bread and wine from Melchisedech were seen as major prefigurings of the eucharistic sacrifice. Although Melchisedech was often represented with bread and wine in early christian art there is no iconographic parallel showing him as a seated figure with only the chalice. Exegesis on Abraham however is of direct interest in deciphering the possible meaning of the figure in the context of Christ's genealogy.

In a solemn covenant the patriarch had received from God his new name Abraham, meaning the father of many nations (Gen 17:5), and was promised 'in thy seed shall all the nations of the earth be blessed' (Gen 22:18). Already in the New Testament this is very fully interpreted and in his commentary on the Lucan genealogy Ambrose quotes from Galatians 3 to show that all the faithful, including Gentiles, are the children of Abraham: the seed of Abraham was his son Isaac, according to the flesh, but, according to the Spirit, it is Christ. All the faithful who have been baptised in Christ have put on Christ and therefore receive through him the promise of the Spirit made to Abraham: 'There is neither Jew nor Greek ... For you are all one in Christ Jesus. If you be Christ's then are you the seed of Abraham, heirs according to the promise' (Gal 3:29). Ambrose stresses that the patriarchs, including Abraham, Isaac and Jacob, lived before the age of the Law and lived in faith: grace precedes the Law and faith precedes the letter. The status accorded in the New Testament and patristic exegesis to Abraham and other patriarchs, who lived before the Incarnation and even before the Mosaic Law, would have been of particular interest to a barbarian culture concerned with the fate of its own ancestors who had lived according to 'the law of nature' before the conversion to christianity.[46] Ambrose shows the working of grace through the patriarchs quoting: 'Abraham believed in the Lord and it was counted to him for righteousness' (Gen 15:6; Gal 3:6) and 'Your father Abraham rejoiced to see my day' (John 8:56).

In a considerable variety of contexts insular exegetes elaborated this interpretation. In the Hiberno-Latin commentaries on the Catholic Epistles Abraham is 'pater noster, id est apostolus non tantum carne sed et fide' or 'pater nostrae fidei'; 'filii Abrahae omnes fideles sunt'.[47] In the Irish glosses on Romans in the Würzburg copy of the Pauline Epistles Abraham is also seen as the father of all the faithful who spiritually inherit the promised blessing made to him.[48] Bede repeatedly returns to the theme:

---

[46]D Ó Corráin, L Breatnach, A Breen, 'The laws of the Irish', *Peritia* 3 (1984) 382-438 (pp 390-96); McCone (note 35 above) 71-72, 92-100.

[47]*Scriptores Hiberniae minores*, CCSL 108B, 14, 65.

[48]Rm 4:1, 12, 13, 16, 17. University of Würzburg, M.p.th.f.12. L C Stern, *Epistolae Beati Pauli glosate glosa interlineáli* (Halle 1910); P Ní Chátháin, 'Notes on the Würzburg glosses' in Ní Chátháin and Richter (note 36 above) 190-99.

The house of Jacob (Abraham's descendants) refers to the universal Church; even though many of the faithful do not take their physical origins from the stock of the patriarchs they are by baptism reborn in Christ and so receive the heritage of the patriarchs.[49]

In the opening chapter of Luke's gospel both Mary and the priest Zachariah recognise the coming of Christ as the fulfilment of God's promises made 'to Abraham and his seed for ever', 'to Abraham our father' (Luke 1:55, 73) and their testimony, enshrined in the *Magnificat* and *Benedictus* respectively, formed daily canticles in the monastic office. In a homily on Luke's text Bede shows that Mary properly names Abraham in particular in the *Magnificat* because

> although many of the fathers and holy ones mystically brought forward testimony of the Lord's incarnation, nevertheless it was to Abraham that the hidden mysteries of the Lord's incarnation were first clearly predicted and to him it was specifically said: 'And in your seed all the tribes of the world earth will be blessed' (Gen 12:3) ... However, 'the seed of Abraham' does not refer only to those chosen ones who were brought forth physically from Abraham's lineage but also to us who, having been gathered together to Christ from the nations, are connected by the fellowship of faith ... We too are the seed and children of Abraham since we are born by the sacraments of our Redeemer, who assumed his flesh from the race of Abraham.[50]

Moreover, Bede shows that the divine promise made to Abraham does not end with the coming of Christ at his incarnation but that 'to Abraham and his seed for ever' there will remain, until the end of the world, 'the everlasting glory of future blessedness'. Viewed in the light of this exegetical tradition, the genealogy of Christ is not only the record of a heritage but the sign of a continuing expectation; it is also the genealogy of the church whose members, whether Gentile or Jew, are reborn in baptism and foretaste future blessedness in the sacrament of the Eucharist.

The heavenly banquet
On folio 201v (**pl 40**) in the Book of Kells the figure seated above the name of Abraham, with his back alongside the names of Isaac and Jacob, is raising a chalice, as though about to drink from it. The chalice is similar in shape and colour to the chalice from which the vinescroll stems in the genealogy's endpiece on the facing page. The eucharistic motif of the chalice, vine and peacocks was often used in early christian funerary art to allude to the eschatological banquet which the Eucharist anticipates and it is used in the scene of Christ in the heavenly liturgy on folio 32v at the end of the Matthean genealogy in the Book of Kells. At the end of the institution of the Eucharist during the Last Supper, Christ promised the faithful he would celebrate that heavenly banquet with them:

---

[49]*Opera homiletica*, CCSL 122, 17; Martin and Hurst (note 21 above) I, 23.
[50]Op. cit. CCSL 122, 29-39; Martin and Hurst above, I, 41.

I will not drink from henceforth of this fruit of the vine until that day
when I shall drink it with you new in my Father's kingdom' (Matt
26:29).

In the Book of Kells these words in Matthew's gospel are immediately
followed on the facing page, folio 114r, by an inscribed full-page picture of
Christ with priestly orant gesture, flanked by two figures and by chalices
and vines. Like the Temple picture on folio 202v, the image of the high
priest within the sanctuary offers an allusive visual metaphor of the
incarnate and mystical body of Christ and the incorporation of the
faithful in him.[51] In liturgy and exegesis the three patriarchs, whose
names seem to be highlighted by the reclining figure with raised chalice
on folio 201v in the Lucan genealogy of Christ and his church, are
specifically associated with the promised heavenly banquet of Matt 26:29
because they are named in Christ's prophecy:

Many shall come from the east and the west and shall sit down
(recumbent) with Abraham and Isaac and Jacob in the kingdom of
heaven (Matt 8:11).

The names of the three patriarchs, in allusion to this text and the
heavenly banquet, are cited in a mass for the dead in the Stowe Missal.[52]

The exegetical connection between the texts of Matt 8:11 and Matt 25:29
had been fully developed in Origen's allegorical interpretation of the Old
Covenant priesthood and sacrifice in his important homilies on Leviticus.
He describes Christ at the Last Supper on the eve of his Passion as the
high priest entering the sanctuary who will not drink the fruit of the vine
until his priestly task is accomplished, that is, until he has brought his
whole creation to perfection. Origen explains that, therefore, even the
apostles and saints have not yet received their joy and that the faithful
patriarchs of the Old Testament have still not received the completion of
the promise made to them since they will 'not be perfected without us'.
(Heb 11:40). When the perfection is accomplished, the high priest will
drink the new wine 'in a new heaven and a new earth' and will 'gather up
all the faithful together to build up that holy body which is the Church'.
He who is the head of the whole body 'does not want to receive his
complete glory without us, that is, without his people who are his body
and members. For he wants to dwell in this body of his Church'. This
interpretation of Matt 26:29, Origen says, glosses the text 'many shall
come from the east and west and shall sit down with Abraham and Isaac
and Jacob in the kingdom of heaven' (Matt 8:11):

---

[51] J O'Reilly, 'The Book of Kells, folio 114r: a mystery revealed yet concealed' in The
age of migrating ideas, ed R M Spearman and J Higgitt ((Edinburgh 1993) 112-13, fig
12.1
[52] F E Warren, The liturgy and ritual of the Celtic church (Oxford 1881) 248.

> Abraham is still waiting to receive his perfection. Isaac is waiting, Jacob and all the prophets are waiting for us, that with us they may receive their perfect happiness. Here is the reason why this mystery is kept till the Last Day ... For it is one single body that awaits its perfection, one body that is promised a future resurrection: 'There are many members, yet one body' (I Cor 12:20).[53]

The quotation is from the classic description in I Cor 12:4-27 of Christ and his church in terms of a single body with many members:

> For in one Spirit were we all baptised into one body, whether Jews or Gentiles, whether bond or free: and in one Spirit we have all been made to drink (I Cor 12:13).

In the context of the interpretation already suggested here for folios 201v-202v in the Book of Kells, the figure with raised chalice may allude to the expectation of the heavenly banquet when the new high priest, his priestly task accomplished, enters the second sanctuary and gathers Abraham, Isaac, Jacob, the prophets, saints and all the faithful into a single body. That drawing together of the faithful into the body of Christ is visualised in the picture of the Temple immediately following Christ's genealogy.

Christ's priestly descent, spiritually interpreted, reveals him as the successor of the Aaronic priesthood, the eternal priest 'after the order of Melchisedech'. The figure, partly concealed by the decorative endpiece of this Old Testament lineage on folio 202r, waiting behind the eucharistic vinescroll and chalice, occupies exactly the same position on the page as the haloed priestly figure placed at the door of the sanctuary in the Temple picture on the verso.

The Old Irish treatise on the mass appended to the Stowe Missal relates stages of the eucharistic liturgy to the successive uncovering of the mystery of Christ through history. From the Introit to the Epistle and Gradual is regarded as 'a figure of the law of nature, wherein Christ has been renewed through all his members and deeds'; from the Gradual to the uncovering of the chalice 'is a commemoration of the law of the Letter wherein Christ has been figured, only that what has been figured therein was not yet known'; from the uncovering of the host and chalice to the oblation 'is a commemoration of the law of the Prophets, wherein Christ was manifestly foretold, save that it was not seen until He was born'. The full uncovering and elevation of the chalice then commemorates the incarnation of Christ and his glory.[54]

---

[53]Homily 7:2, as quoted by H de Lubac, *Catholicism* (London 1950) 256; cf *Origen. Homilies on Leviticus*, trans G W Barkley (Washington DC 1990) 137.
[54]*The Stowe Missal*, ed G F Warner, 2 vols (London 1915) II, 40.

The new chosen people

The 'living stones' arranged in regular courses on either side of the priestly figure on folio 202v (**pl 42**), are shown to be beneath the Temple which may be seen as 'built upon the foundation of the apostles and prophets' (Eph 2:20). The body of this priestly figure descends right to the foundation of the building and joins the two groups of people who face inwards to him and hence to each other. In his commentary on the Lucan genealogy, Ambrose twice quotes from the Ephesians text to show that Gentiles and Jews are reconciled by the incarnate crucified body of Christ:

> For he is our peace, who has made both one, and breaking down the middle wall of partition, the enmities in his flesh ... that he might make the two in himself into one new man (Eph 2:14-18).

Gentiles and Jews then form part of his body, the church, pictured as 'a holy temple', 'a habitation of God in the Spirit', with Jesus Christ himself being the 'chief cornerstone' (Eph 2:20-22, cf 1 Peter 2:5-8).

The themes of priesthood, sacrifice and the Temple which are featured in patristic and insular exegesis on Luke's account of the baptism and genealogy of Christ, and which seem reflected in the iconography of the genealogy in the Book of Kells, thus reach a climax in the picture of the Temple. The royal and priestly lineage of Christ, inherited when he took on human flesh ('the temple of his body') is revealed to be that of his church also. His Old Testament earthly ancestors are the spiritual ancestors of all those who, in baptism, share in Christ's anointing as prophet, priest and king and, whether Jew or Gentile, are reborn as sons of God to form the new chosen people. These themes are also gathered up in the chain of scriptural texts on the Temple image used in Ambrose's commentary on Luke's account of the baptism. Most notably, I Peter 2:5, 9-10 addresses the faithful both as 'living stones built up, a spiritual house' *and* as 'a chosen people, a royal priesthood ... who in time past were not a people but are now the people of God'.

Seventh-century Hiberno-Latin exegesis on the Catholic Epistles highlights a number of ways in which the text of I Peter 2:5-10 was related to themes already noted here in connection with patristic and insular exegesis on the baptism and genealogy of Christ. In the *Commentarius in Epistolas Catholicas Scotti Anonymi* the 'living stone rejected by men', but now chosen by God to be the chief cornerstone of the spiritual building (verses 4-8), is identified with Christ whose divinity was proclaimed in the words of the Father: 'This is my beloved Son'. The faithful are admonished to be 'as living stones built up, a spiritual house, a holy priesthood, to offer up spiritual sacrifices acceptable to God' (verse 5); the commentary notes that each of the faithful is a member of the eternal priest of whom it was said: 'Thou art a priest for ever (after the order of Melchisedech)'.[55] The *Tractatus Hilarii in Septem Epistolas Canonicas* glosses the acceptable 'spiritual sacrifices' of the holy priesthood of the faithful as the offering of hymns, psalms and prayers (Col 3:16) and directly contrasts them with the unacceptable blood sacrifice of a calf. In this commentary's gloss on the individual phrases in I Peter 2:9: 'You are a chosen people, a royal priesthood, a holy nation', themes from exegesis on the baptism and Lucan genealogy again appear: *genus electum: in Abraham; regale sacerdotium: in Aaron; gens sancta: id est in baptismo*.[56] The importance of baptism in the formation of this new people of God, pictured both as a single body and as a holy temple or habitation of God, is again stressed in the early Irish glosses on Ephesians 2. The phrase in verse 16, 'he might reconcile both (Jews and Gentiles) unto God in one body', is glossed: 'by bestowing the gifts of the Spirit on all'.[57]

These biblical images of the formation of the new chosen people of God through baptism were applied by insular writers to their own society. The text from Matt 8:11, for example, 'Venient ab oriente et occidente et recumbent cum Abraham et Isaac et Iacob in regno caelorum', is quoted by St Patrick in each of his pastoral letters where those coming from east and west to join the patriarchs and 'banquet with Christ' in the heavenly kingdom are clearly identified by Patrick with recent converts, anointed with chrism, 'a people newly coming to belief whom the Lord took from the uttermost parts of the earth as long ago he promised through his prophets'. Patrick shows the prophecy of Hosea 1:10 has been fulfilled through baptism and the outpouring of the Holy Spirit on them:

> Those who were not my people I will call 'my people'. And in the very place where it was said: 'You are not my people', they will be called 'sons of the living God'. Consequently, then, in Ireland, they who never had knowledge of God ... have lately been made a people of the Lord and called the children of God.[58]

The same Hosea text is cited in I Peter 1:9-10 where the 'living stones' of the spiritual house, who are also a 'royal priesthood', are further identified as 'a holy nation, a chosen people ... Who in time past were not a people, but are now the people of God'.

Abraham, Isaac and Jacob, together with other patriarchs and the Old Testament prophets are related not only to the image of the church as the body of Christ but to the other great New Testament image of the church as a building or temple made up of the living stones of the faithful. The

---

[55] *Scriptores Hiberniae minores*, CCSL 108B, 31-33, dated c650-90, the *Tractatus Hilarii* to c690-708, Bede's commentary on the Catholic Epistles to c708-709.

[56] ibid, 82, 32.

[57] See note 48 above. The middle wall of partition (verse 14) is glossed as sin, which was between God and man, between body and soul. The word 'temple' in Eph 1:21 is glossed as 'the assembly of the saints; they are called a temple because Christ dwells in them, that is, it is a habitation for God'.

[58] D Conneely, *The letters of Saint Patrick* (Maynooth 1993) 71, 80.

temple building image can refer variously to the Jewish Temple built in the city of Jerusalem in the Promised Land, which is a type or pre-figuring of the christian church, and also to the Temple in the heavenly Jerusalem described in Revelation. It could be used interchangeably in some contexts with the image of the heavenly city or paradisal promised land towards which the church on earth is journeying in pilgrimage. The Epistle to the Hebrews describes Abraham, together with Isaac and Jacob 'the co-heirs of the same promise', looking beyond their earthly inheritance 'for a city that has foundations whose builder and maker is God'; like other patriarchs and prophets they died 'according to the faith, not having received the promises but beholding them afar off' as pilgrims and strangers seeking a heavenly country: 'Therefore God ... has prepared for them a city' (Heb 11, 10, 13-16). Bede, in his allegorical commentary on the Temple shows that 'many of the patriarchs of the Old Testament attained such a peak of perfection ... that they are not to be considered inferior to the apostles'; 'although still separated from the mysteries of the Lord's incarnation, nevertheless by their faith and preaching they were very near'. The patriarchs and prophets are, accordingly, visualised as part of the fabric of Solomon's Temple which is 'a figure of the holy universal church'.[59]

The Epistle to the Ephesians shows that the Gentiles are reconciled in Christ to these chosen people of the Old Covenant, no more strangers and foreigners but 'fellow citizens and members of the household of God' (Eph 2:19). They are also visualised as forming part of the building fabric of the house or temple which represents the single community of the new people of God and is built upon the apostles *and* prophets. This image is animated by allusion to the Pauline image of the body as the temple or habitation of God so that the church is seen as both building and body (Ephesians 2:20-22), as in the picture in the Book of Kells on folio 202v.

The second Adam
In Luke's gospel alone the line of earthly ancestors from whom Christ took his humanity is traced right back, beyond Abraham and the patriarchs, to Adam 'who was the son of God' (Luke 3:38). The genealogy ends with these words in the Book of Kells on folio 202r and the image of the Temple appears on the following page. Augustine's commentary on the image of 'the temple of his body' throws additional light on the appropriateness of the Temple image at this juncture of Luke's text. Augustine describes how Adam, who was both one man and the whole human race, was broken and scattered by sin but gathered together and renewed in Christ:

> because an Adam has come without sin that he might destroy Adam's sin in his flesh and that Adam might restore the image of God to himself. From Adam, therefore, is Christ's flesh; from Adam, therefore, is the temple which the Jews destroyed and the Lord raised up again in three days. For he raised up again his flesh ... Our Lord

---

[59]*De templo*, CCSL 119A, 161-62.

Jesus Christ received his body from Adam, but did not take the sin of Adam — he took his bodily temple from him, not the iniquity which must be driven from the temple — but this flesh which he took from Adam — the Jews crucified. They destroyed the temple built in forty-six years and he raised it up in three days.[60]

The association of Adam and Christ with the image of the Temple had already been expressed in insular art. In an exegesis well-known to Bede and to Hiberno-Latin commentators, Augustine noted that all peoples originate in Adam and that in the four letters of his name the four quarters of the earth are signified: the initial letters of the Greek words for east, west, north and south spell out the name of Adam.[61] The numerical values of the four letters of Adam's name add up to forty-six, the number of years it took to build the Temple in Jerusalem which Christ said he would raise up in three days (John 2:19-21). Cassiodorus had a picture of the Temple of Solomon in his *Codex Grandior* which Bede knew of and referred to in his own treatises on the Tabernacle and the Temple. In the *Codex Amiatinus*, produced at Wearmouth-Jarrow, a large diagram of the 'former Tabernacle' is inscribed with the names of the twelve tribes of Israel descended from the sons of Jacob and the four cardinal directions which conceal the name of Adam and the number forty-six, thus alluding to the Second Adam and the temple of his body which superseded the temple made with hands.[62]

In Ambrose's commentary on the Lucan baptism, it is precisely in the context of discussing Christ as the Second Adam from whose body on the Cross the church was born, that he describes the church by quoting from Eph 2, I Peter 2 and other texts in the biblical chain which pictures the church as the body of Christ through the image of the Temple building. Ambrose notes that the name of Adam comes at the end of the Lucan genealogy, thus one made *in* the image of God (Gen 1:27) comes before his descendant who *was* the image of God. Adam, the created son of God, is 'a figure of him to come' (Rm 5:14), that is the Son of God.[63]

The Pauline image of the individual member of the church as the temple of God (1 Cor 3:17, 6:9; 2 Cor 6:16) is part of the very language of baptismal rites where the sin of Adam is renounced and the devil expelled.[64] A long exegetical and catechetical tradition stressed the need for the baptised,

---

[60]*In Iohannis evangelium tractatus 124*, CCSL 36, 108; *St Augustine. Tractates on the gospel of John 1-10*, trans J W Rettig (Washington DC 1988) 222-24.

[61]For Adam's name as a cosmic tetragrammaton in the Fathers, the Book of Enoch, Isidore's *Etymologiae* and in Hiberno-Latin exegesis, see McNally (note 41 above) 115-16.

[62]Alexander, *Insular manuscripts* no 7, pl 23. For the uses of the Temple symbolism of 46 in Augustine and Bede, see W Berschin 'Opus deliberatum perfectum: Why did the Venerable Bede write a second prose Life of St Cuthbert?' in *St Cuthbert, his cult and community to AD 1200*, ed G Bonner, D Rollason, C Stancliffe (Woodbridge 1989) 95-102.

[63]Ambrose, *Expositio evangelii secundum Lucam*, CCSL 14, 103-04.

[64]See below and note 99.

who have renounced the Old Adam and become sons of God, to remain
vigilant, under Christ, against the continuing assaults of the devil. This is
prefigured in the Second Adam's own temptation by the devil in the desert
and recalled in the church's liturgy at the beginning of Lent. The tradition
helps illumine the Kells picture of the Temple and its facing text, which
are followed by the account of Christ's Temptation. The double opening
may be read as showing the baptised christian or the whole church 'full of
the Holy Spirit' and defended by Christ from the devil. George Henderson
has stressed the importance of the expulsion of the devil by baptism for an
understanding of the picture and has captured the sense of the pivotal
positioning of the picture of the second Adam in Luke's text:

> The Book of Kells picture, dominated by Christ in his church,
> surrounded by his redeemed people, glorified by angels, easily
> confuting the black tempter, tackles the contents of the Gospel
> chapters before and after and gives full weight to the words
> displayed on the facing recto.[65]

The Temptation
Most modern scholars, however, have seen the picture on folio 202v **(pl 42)**
in the Book of Kells in isolation from the texts which precede it and have
identified it as the Temptation of Christ. Carol Farr believes that the
Kells picture 'almost undoubtedly depicts the Temptation on the Temple
roof' but quite transforms the traditional reading of the picture as a
narrative illustration by viewing it in the context of lenten liturgical
themes and through exegesis on the gospel account of the Temptation and
on the Old Testament texts it cites, particularly Ps 90.[66] Dr Farr shows
how, in the Tyconian tradition of reading Ps 90 in terms of the figure of
'Christ the Head and his Body the church', Augustine's commentary on
the psalm relates it not only to the Temptation of Christ but to the
continuing temptation and ultimate triumph of his church which, it is
argued, is the theme of the picture in Kells. In this argument's detailed
review of the familiarity in insular monastic culture of patristic exegesis
on the image of the church as the Body of Christ and on the related New
Testament image of the church as a spiritual building prefigured in the
Tabernacle and the Temple of Jerusalem, there is much that is
complementary to the interpretation of the picture suggested in the
present discussion. Dr Farr herself points to several remaining enigmas,
however, if the picture is seen primarily as a symbolic exposition of the
Temptation narrative.

First, there is the question of why the Temptation should have received
the extraordinarily elevated decorative status of a full-page picture

---

[65]G D S Henderson, *Bede and the visual arts* (Jarrow Lecture 1980) 17-18; Henderson,
168-74: 'The emphasis in the Stowe Missal on the expulsion of the devil by baptism is
sufficient in itself to explain the iconography of the Kells picture. It subsumes Christ's
"Temptation" in the general victory offered by Christ to mankind', 174.
[66]Farr, 'Lection', 20, 74-112.

facing a framed display text. The placing of pictures within the gospel text (rather than at its opening or in the prefatory pages of the codex) is exceedingly rare in surviving early medieval gospel books. Kells has two such pictures and, arguably, folio 123v was reserved for a third which was not executed. Folio 123v faces an elaborate framed display text of Matt 27:38 from the account of the Crucifixion and the picture on folio 114r, which has a framed display text on its verso, is also placed in a position of great theological importance at Matt 26:30, after Christ's institution of the Eucharist at the Last Supper and before the account of the Passion.

Secondly, not only does Kells lavish apparently disproportionate decorative attention on the Temptation but chooses to do so in the context of Luke's gospel rather than Matthew's, which was the version of the story read on the first Sunday in Lent in most known early lection systems. Nor is Kells entirely idiosyncratic in this respect, as a number of other insular gospel books also highlight the opening of Luke 4:1, though on a much more modest scale than Kells, folio 203r (pl 43). Dr Farr concludes that the Lucan version of the Temptation narrative was probably used as a lection for Quadragesima in some lost non-Roman liturgy.[67] While this may well be so and would have important implications for understanding the function of the image in the book and in the life of the community in which it was used, it is obviously difficult to demonstrate as so little insular liturgical material remains and because the decorative structuring of texts in insular gospel books seems to have served a variety of functions, not only liturgical.

Thirdly, the three Temptations of Christ are recounted in Matt 4:1-11 and Luke 4:1-13, but in Luke's version the Temple incident is the last of the three Temptations: it does not appear in the text of the Book of Kells, therefore, until folio 204r, which is three folios after the Temple picture. Nor is the particular importance of the third Temptation (Luke 4:9-12) signified in the layout and decoration of its text on folio 204r, in marked contrast to the embellishment of the opening of Luke 4:1 which actually faces the picture.

Finally, if the Temple picture on folio 202v is seen as only referring forwards, to the text of the Temptation, and if the decoration of Luke 4:1 on folio 203r is explained as a structural break from the preceding text of the genealogy, it is difficult to explain why the picture is positioned *between* the end of the genealogy and the beginning of Luke 4:1.

In the present discussion it has been suggested that the layout and decoration of the Lucan genealogy and the Temple picture in the Book of Kells are related and that they are responsive to the theological significance of the gospel text as perceived in patristic and insular exegesis. Ambrose devoted the whole of Book III of his commentary on Luke to the text of the genealogy alone: the exegetical tradition of reading

---

[67]eadem, 141-61.

scripture did not regard the list of Christ's ancestors as an awkward editorial intrusion into Luke's narrative of the baptism and Temptation but as an integral part of an important statement about the identity of Christ and the collective personality of his church. It is worth recalling at this point that commentators stress that Luke's juxtaposition of baptism and genealogy sets out Christ's divine Sonship as well as his earthly ancestry and that the indwelling or invisible anointing of the Holy Spirit begun at the incarnation was manifested on the eve of his public ministry when, at his baptism in the Jordan, the Holy Spirit descended as a dove and the Father proclaimed 'You are my beloved Son' (Luke 3:22). The last verse of the Lucan genealogy again reveals him to be 'the son of Adam, who was the son of God' (Luke 3:38) and the very next words of Luke's text specifically recall the baptism before setting the scene for the Temptation: 'And Jesus full of the Holy Spirit returned from Jordan and was led by the Spirit into the desert' (Luke 4:1). Matthew's version, which continues directly from his account of the baptism with no intervening genealogy, simply says, 'Then Jesus was led by the Spirit into the desert to be tempted by the devil' (Matt 4:1). Bede notes the difference in his Lucan commentary.

In the Temptation which immediately follows, the devil finally taunts Jesus to prove his divine Sonship ('If thou be the son of God ...') by casting himself from the top of the Temple and literally fulfilling the Messianic prophecy of Ps 90:11-12. After the Temptation (Luke 4:2-13) Jesus returns to Galilee 'in the power of the Spirit' (4.14) and in the synagogue at Nazareth publicly reads from the Messianic prophecy of Isaiah 61:1-2: 'The Spirit of the Lord is upon me. Wherefore he has anointed me ... to preach deliverance to the captives ...', a prophecy Jesus claims has been fulfilled in himself (4:18-21). Those present fail, like the devil, to 'see' who he is and demand 'Is this not the son of Joseph?' (4:22) which vividly recalls Luke's introduction to the genealogy 'Jesus ... being, as was supposed, the son of Joseph' (3:12). The irony continues as only the devil or unclean spirit of one possessed recognises who he is and acclaims him: 'I know thee who thou art, the holy one of God' (4:34); other devils finally acknowledge his divine identity: '"Thou art the Son of God" ... they knew he was the Christ' (4:41). An eighth-century Hiberno-Latin commentary on Luke illustrates contemporary interest in connections within the passage. It shows the fulfillment of the prophecy 'The Spirit of the Lord is upon me' in the descent of the Spirit at the Incarnation and baptism in the Jordan and notes that the prophecy of 'deliverance to the captives' refers to the redemption of all people captive in Adam to the devil. The question, 'Is this not Joseph's son?' is directly linked with the taunt of the devil at the Temptation, 'If you are the Son (of God) ...'.[68] The sequence in Luke demonstrates the fulfillment of the prophecies of Ps 90 and Isaiah 61:1-2, but the largest prophecy is the genealogy itself which shows Jesus

---

[68]*Scriptores Hiberniae minores*, CCSL 108C, 36, also 29 for the relation of Luke 4:1 to the theme of baptism: the phrase 'regressus est a Iordane' is associated with the four rivers of Eden rising from a single font.

prefigured throughout the history of his people going back to the patriarchs before the Law, and indeed the whole of human history back to Adam.

The sacred monogram
The isolation of just the opening words of Luke 4:1 'Jesus full of the Holy Spirit' on folio 203r (**pl 43**) in Kells would seem, therefore, not simply to be marking the re-opening of the narrative after the genealogy but to be identifying the great theme of this whole sequence of Luke's text which reveals that Jesus of Nazareth is also Son of God, hence the picture of his human body 'full of the Holy Spirit'. Several insular gospel books highlight this verse by the enlargement or other embellishment of the opening initial, word or line but in Kells alone the opening words, *Ie(su)s autem plenus Sp(iritu)s S(an)c(t)o*, though written in abbreviated form, are enlarged to fill the whole page and are elaborately framed and veiled with ornament which elevates the text to the level of a gospel incipit. The first two letters of Jesus's abbreviated name dominate the upper half of the page. The decoration of the *nomen sacrum Ihs* meaning Saviour, and the epithet 'full of the Holy Spirit' at the end of the Lucan genealogy, may be seen as a counterpart to the treatment of his Greek title Christ (meaning the Anointed One) in the Chi Rho monogram at the culmination of the genealogy in Matthew. The two names and genealogies together reveal him as Jesus and as Christ, as human and divine, the Davidic Messiah and the Son of God, as king and priest. The very differences in the ancestral names, the number of generations and the direction of tracing descent in the two gospel versions of Christ's genealogy help explain why they received such a burden of exposition to show that, properly read, they were in fact complementary revelations of the same truth. The mysterious latent power of names, genealogies and epithets to reveal identity was an important feature of patristic exegesis which touched a vital chord for insular, and especially Hiberno-Latin, commentators and received eloquent expression in the Book of Kells. The convention of writing the Greek title Christ and the Greek version of the name Jesus in romanised versions of their initial letters, with latin endings, offers some kind of cryptic calligraphic parallel to the exegetical practice of expounding the significance of a name or title through its etymology and its Greek, or even Hebrew, equivalent. The primary function of the *Xpi* monogram on folio 34r and of the *Ihs* monogram on folio 203r in Kells was patently not as an aid to reading aloud. The splendour of the page and the difficulty of deciphering the veiled letter forms of its literal text compel the reader to pause and ponder the significance of the sacred names.

Remarkable though folio 203r is, the modern reader may feel it is less magnificent in conception than the Chi Rho design and lacking in the kind of exegesis hidden on folio 34r in the embellishment of the name of Christ.[69] Among the display pages in the Book of Kells, folio 203r is unique in preserving the panelled vertical shafts of the first two combined

---

[69]Lewis (note 2 above).

letters, the *I* and *h* of the name of Jesus, as discreet elements, rather in the manner of earlier insular gospel book incipts. A further unique feature is the curiously exotic six-lobed pierced ornament within the bowl of the *h*, the number six emphasized a second and a third time by concentric rings of dotting within the lobes, which in turn are encircled by three concentric circles of colour interspersed by decorative bands and with rectangular mounts marking off the outer band at three of its cardinal points. This abstract circular shape within the sacred name is, like the golden rhombus at the centre of the letter chi on folio 34r, the focal point of the design.

On the folio facing the *Ihs* monogram, the side panels of the Temple picture's frame have been rendered as stylised columns filled with golden ornament and with crosses in the place of bases and capitals, a device used for the capitals of the two columns supporting the arch over Christ in folio 114r. In the exegetical context in which the Temple picture has been located, the columnar frame may also be read as alluding to the two bronze pillars erected either side of the Temple entrance by Solomon (2 Chron 3:15). Bede has a detailed interpretation of this verse and of the multiple underlying meanings of the columns which can refer to the apostles and spiritual teachers who are pillars of the church (cf Gal 2:9) and bulwarks of truth (cf I Tm 3:15) and particularly to their drawing together both Jews and Gentiles, through baptism, into the church. The 'mystery of the material pillars' at the entrance to the Temple is also a reminder that 'both in prosperity and adversity we must keep the entrance to our heavenly homeland firmly before the eyes of our mind'. The great height of the pillars fittingly alludes to the spiritual ascent of the elect 'that they may merit to see their creator face to face, for they will have nothing further to seek when they reach him who is above all things'. The capitals of the pillars in the Kells picture are on a level with the head of Christ and with the upper row of little figures ascending towards him. Finally Bede reveals 'the more profound sense' of the two pillars when he discerns in the scriptural account of their dimensions an established sacred numerology, for, concealed in the eighteen cubits of their height is the name of Jesus. Not only is eighteen the multiple of three and six, which carry their usual associations with the Trinity and the six days of creation, but 'the name of Jesus begins from this number among the Greeks. With them the first letter of this name means ten and the second eight'.[70] The column-like shafts of the first two letters of Jesus's name on folio 203r and the incorporation of the repeated motifs of three and six in the decoration of the letter *h* may, therefore, conceal an arcane exegesis on the sacred name, identifying Jesus with the Temple and further linking word and image.

The language of paradox
Similarly, the striking ambiguities of the mixed visual metaphor on folio 202v facing the name of Jesus in the Book of Kells can yield a spiritual

---

[70]*De templo*, CCSL 119A, 199. This interpretation of 18 is common in exegesis on Gen 14:14.

insight. The picture adopts a familiar exegetical technique in telescoping the New Testament image of the Temple with that of the body (1 Cor 12:12-27; Eph 4:15-16; Col 1:18) so that the Temple, which can denote the incarnate body of Christ, is also revealed as representing the mystical body of Christ, with Christ as its head, its members forming the 'living stones' of a curiously organic building which grows up into a Temple of the Lord (cf I Peter 2:5-6; Eph 2:21).

Some of the features that may still puzzle us in the Kells picture also exercised the Fathers commenting on the texts which ultimately underlie this extraordinary image because the scriptural chains themselves, read at a literal level, are often self-contradictory, irrational or bizarre. Augustine, for example, in his commentary on Ps 86, raises the question of how can the Temple of God be 'built upon the foundation of the apostles and the prophets' (Eph 2:20) when it was also written that 'other foundation no man can lay, but that which is laid: which is Jesus Christ' (I Cor 3:11)? Augustine replies with another paradox: the apostles and prophets are foundations in the sense that they sustain our weakness (lesser 'living stones' in the fabric of the building) but Christ is the foundation of all foundations, the pillar of pillars in this building. Both scriptural statements are spiritually true, though literally incompatible. The small priestly haloed figure in the Kells picture, whose head is in the sanctuary but whose pillar-like body penetrates to the very foundation of the building which may also be read as being built upon the apostles and prophets, may be a pictorial equivalent of the exegetical attempt to resolve this paradox. Augustine also asks how can Christ be both the foundation and the keystone of this building, both at the base and the top? He explains that, unlike earthly bodies which have spatial limitations, 'the divinity is present in all places and the likeness of all things can be applied to it, though in reality it is none of these things'. On the contrary, all things have their reality in Christ. Augustine finds no incongruity, therefore, in the idea that 'Just as the foundation of an earthly building is at the base, so the foundation of the heavenly building is at the top, in heaven'.[71] Rightly understood in *lectio divina* this building is complemented, not contradicted, by the corporeal image of the church as the pilgrim body still on earth, its Head in heaven. Similarly, the large portrait bust of Christ in the Kells picture may be read as both the head of the body and as the cornerstone or keystone of the building.[72]

---

[71]Augustine, *Enarrationes in psalmos, 51-100*, CCSL 39, 1198-1203.

[72]G Ladner, 'The symbolism of the biblical cornerstone in the medieval West' in *Images and ideas in the middle ages. Selected studies in history and art* (Rome 1983) I, 171-96, notes that the *lapis angularis* of Ps 117:96 (cited in the synoptic gospels, Acts 4:11 and I Peter 2:7) is usually combined with Isaiah 28:16 and interpreted not exclusively as a coping stone but as a cornerstone or foundation stone (173). The *caput anguli* image was identified with Christ as head of the church in the body metaphor used in Ephesians 4:15 (194). Nordenfalk (note 3 above) 277, suggests the possible influence on the Kells picture of an illustrated copy of Prudentius's *Dittochaeum* where 'the stone which the builders rejected' is raised to the top of the Temple in Jerusalem: 'Now it is the head of the Temple and holds the new stones

Such apparent contradictions and obscurities in scripture were regarded as pointing to a hidden significance and attracted the particular interest of exegetes. Augustine provides a second example of relevance in considering the Kells Temple picture and its role in the larger decorative unit formed by folios 200r-203r. In the synoptic gospels the disbelieving Jews ask for a sign of Jesus's identity. He replies, 'A sign shall not be given (this generation) but the sign of Jonah the prophet' (Matt 12:39, Luke 11:29). However, in St John's gospel he does give another sign 'Destroy this temple and in three days I will raise it up' (John 2:19). Augustine was drawn to reconcile the two apparently contradictory signs given by Jesus, Jonah and the Temple, in the significant context of explaining the spiritual blindness of those who failed to see the hidden God, the Lord of glory, in the crucified and resurrected body of Jesus. He quotes Matthew's story of the sign of Jonah and then says, Jesus also spoke 'through another similitude of this same sign' and quotes John's story of the Temple of Jesus's body: 'His flesh was the Temple of the divinity hidden within. Whence the Jews outwardly saw the Temple, the Deity dwelling within they saw not'.[73]

Reasons have already been considered here for supposing that the fish-man figure in the Lucan genealogy in the Book of Kells, folio 201r, may well be an allusion to the prophet Jonah and to the latin meaning of his name, *columba*, and that Jonah's established association with the sacramental sharing of Christ's death and resurrection in baptism is particularly fitting in the context. It has been noted that the descent of the Holy Spirit as a dove at Christ's baptism, immediately preceding the genealogy, signifies the descent of the seven-fold gifts of the Spirit into his body the church. The individual soul thus becomes a dove (a *columba* or a Jonah) at baptism, that is, a vessel or habitation of the Holy Spirit, like Christ. Both Jonah and the Temple are signs given by Christ himself in response to demands for proof of his divine power, yet in the gospels both are explicitly interpreted as referring to his incarnate, crucified and resurrected body. In exegesis, both the dove and the Temple are habitations of the Holy Spirit, both can be used as images of the individual Christian, both can also represent the unity of the whole church, both are particularly associated with baptism and with the spiritual life of the baptised.

The underlying spiritual similarity of dove and temple is obscured by their manifest material differences. But it was precisely the puzzling decision of the Holy Spirit to descend in so small and simple a creature as a dove which prompted exegetical ingenuity in penetrating beneath the literal letter of scriptural passages about doves and finding that, spiritually interpreted, they revealed the dove to be a particularly appropriate vessel or habitation of the Holy Spirit. Ambrose raises this

---

together'. This may also explain the two Ottonian representations of the Temptation which, like Kells, show Christ as a half-length figure at the top of the Temple.
[73]*Enarrationes in psalmos, 51-100*, CCSL 39, 843-845

very question in his commentary on Christ's baptism in Luke's gospel, the same context in which he also explores the multiple allusions of the image of the Temple. Moreover, he directly compares the corporeal appearance of the Holy Spirit as a dove at Christ's baptism with the invisible presence of God in the Temple.[74] In the Book of Kells the evident differences between the diverting 'Jonah' figure with six birds enlivening the column of Hebrew names on folio 201r and the solemn full-page picture of the Temple on folio 202v obscure the fact that they distinctively point to the same truth. They function as metaphysical conceits and, placed within the same decorative sequence in the gospel text, can illuminate each other, like scriptural texts in an exegetical chain.

If the illustrations in the Book of Kells were partly inspired by exegesis of the gospel text and incorporate pictorial adaptations of rhetorical techniques, then the objectives of exegesis may offer some guide to the composition and function of the images. By this criterion, it seems unlikely that the picture of the Temple on folio 202v was intended as a static and didactic representation of theological or ecclesiological truths or that it was intended to be read, in a manner more suited to some later medieval works, as an onion-layered series of fixed meanings denoting successively the body of Christ, of the individual faithful and of the church. Patristic exegesis, in contrast, is concerned to show the *simultaneity* of such truths as aspects of a single truth and to show the continuing significance of the spiritual interpretation of the literal text for the present reader who is provided with images for *meditatio* and *imitatio*. The objective, using the image of the Temple, is nowhere more fully and clearly demonstrated than in the commentaries and homilies of Bede and especially in *De tabernaculo* and *De templo*, which are detailed allegorical commentaries on Exodus 24:12-30, 21 and on 3 Kings 5:1-7:51 respectively.

Images of tabernacle, temple and the heavenly Jerusalem
Bede distinguishes between the temporary Tabernacle built by Moses in the desert 'on the route by which one reaches the land of promise' and the Temple, built by Solomon in the land of promise itself in the royal city of Jerusalem 'on an ever inviolable foundation until it fulfilled the task of the heavenly figures imposed upon it. For these reasons the former can be taken to represent the toil and exile of the present Church, the latter the rest and happiness of the future Church'.[75] Tabernacle and Temple cannot simply be equated with the church on earth and in heaven respectively, however. Because the Tabernacle was made by the people of Israel alone, it 'can be chiefly taken as a symbolic expression for the Fathers of the Old Testament and the ancient people of God'. The Temple of Solomon was also built long before the incarnation but, because Solomon used the servants of Hiram, king of Tyre, in its construction, it may be seen as representing 'the

---

[74]Ambrose, *Expositio evangelii secundum Lucam*, CCSL 14, 72-74. Lapidge (note 19 above) 108, n 18.
[75]*De templo*, CCSL 119A, 147-48.

Church assembled from the gentiles', that is, the new chosen people. *Both* these Old Testament sanctuaries, however, when spiritually interpreted,

> can be shown in many ways to suggest symbolically both the daily labours of the present Church and the everlasting rewards and joys in the future and the salvation of all nations in Christ.[76]

The literal text of the Old Testament's detailed description of the construction, layout, dimensions, ornaments and furnishings of Tabernacle and Temple therefore provides a rhetorical figure in which the nature of Christ and of his church, past, present and to come, are delineated and the reader finds a model of the spiritual life. The process of reading the figure to reveal this underlying significance is conducted and validated through reference to other scriptural texts.

The key links in the chains are set out in the opening section of Book One of *De templo*. The house of God built by Solomon 'as a figure of the holy universal Church' refers both to Christ who said of the temple of his body, 'Destroy this temple and in three days I will raise it up' (John 2:19-21) and to the faithful who are 'the temple of God' (I Cor 3:16):

> If, therefore, he became the temple of God by assuming human nature and we became the temple of God through his Spirit dwelling in us (Rm 8:11), it is quite clear that the material Temple (of Solomon) was a figure of us all, that is both of the Lord himself and his members which we are ... of him as the uniquely chosen and precious cornerstone laid in the foundation (Is 28:16) and of us as the living stones built upon the foundations of the apostles and prophets, that is, on the Lord himself (Eph 2:20; I Peter 2:5-6).[77]

The texts Bede uses here to expound the Old Testament description of the Temple as a figure referring simultaneously to Christ's incarnate body, to the individual faithful and to the community of the new chosen people, the church, on earth and in heaven, are paralleled in Ambrose's much earlier use of the same array of texts to expound the figure of the Old Testament Temple used by Luke in the opening chapters of his gospel. While the physical appearance of the single house-shaped structure on folio 202v in the Book of Kells does not seem to have been significantly influenced by the Old Testament descriptions of the fabric of Tabernacle and Temple, nevertheless, it may reflect their treatment in the New Testament which strongly suggests their interrelatedness, their combined role in the whole history of salvation and the sense that they are both but the copies or shadows of a heavenly reality (Heb 8:5, 10:1).

---

[76]ibid, 148.
[77]ibid, 147.

Descriptions of the heavenly Jerusalem in the Book of Revelation consciously evoke both Tabernacle and Temple.[78] The vision of the power of God filling the heavenly Temple (Rev 15:5, 8) recalls scenes of God taking possession of his Tabernacle in the desert (Ex 40:34-35) and of his Temple in Jerusalem (3 Kg 8:10-11; Is 6:4). The eschatological vision of the new Jerusalem in 'a new heaven and a new earth' is announced: 'Behold the tabernacle of God with men: and he will dwell with them. And they shall be his people' (Rev 21:3). Thus all three sanctuaries — the Tabernacle, the Temple and the heavenly Jerusalem (variously described as Temple or city) — represent the place where God dwells with his people.

At the Incarnation the human body of Jesus became the new place of the divine presence. This is expressed in St John's gospel by the image of 'the temple of his body' which compares Jesus with the Temple building in Jerusalem and implicitly presents him as the new Temple. In St Luke's gospel the concept is expressed through his long introduction to the account of the Incarnation by the theme of the Old Covenant priesthood and Temple which Jesus came both to fulfil and replace. Ambrose's development of Luke's own image and his use of the techniques of the Epistle to the Hebrews in comparing Christ with 'the tabernacle made with hands' explicitly incorporates John's image of 'the temple of his body'. Ambrose's continued use of the Temple theme in his exegesis on Luke's account of Christ's baptism and priestly genealogy reveals the significance of the Incarnation by showing Jesus of Nazareth to be Son of God and 'full of the Holy Spirit', a concept which, it has been suggested here, is expressed by the Temple picture in the Book of Kells showing the human body of Jesus as the Temple, 'full of the Holy Spirit'. The other readings of the Temple image which its context in Kells suggest — its allusion to the individual baptised and to the new chosen people — explore the implications of the central theme and so lead to a renewed and more profound understanding of 'the body of Christ' as the *mystical* body of Christ which transcends time and encompasses the Tabernacle, the Temple, the church on earth and the heavenly sanctuary.

There was a Jewish and early christian tradition of architecturally ambiguous images which allowed a stylised representation of a single building to be read as referring to both Tabernacle and Temple and even to the heavenly Jerusalem as well. Bianca Kühnel has shown that the diagram of the Tabernacle in the *Codex Amiatinus*, for example, derived from the description in Exodus 25 and 26, is transformed by the addition of a cross over its entrance from the historical, perishable desert tent of the Old Covenant into the Tabernacle of God, the eternal Temple and city of the New Covenant.[79] It might be added that, like the building in the

---

[78]B Kühnel, 'Jewish symbolism of the Temple and the Tabernacle and christian symbolism of the Holy Sepulchre and the heavenly Tabernacle', *Jewish Art* 12/13 (1986-87) 147-68 (p 152).
[79]ibid, 166.

Kells picture, the *Codex Amiatinus* Tabernacle can also be read as the temple of the body of Christ because of its concealed allusion to that image in John 2:19-21.[80] Insular awareness of the early christian pictorial tradition was not confined to Jarrow. At the end of the Apocalypse in the Book of Armagh, *c* 807, the ground plan of the heavenly Jerusalem, almost foursquare, like the Holy of Holies in the Temple of Solomon (Rev 21:16; I Kg 6:20), its inscriptions including the names of the twelve tribes of Israel (Rev 21:12, 14) also shown on representations of the Tabernacle, bears in addition the simple caption *dns noster ihs xps*.[81]

This tradition of sacred diagrams and rectangular plans did not provide the 'source' for the physical features of the building in the Kells picture but indicates it was not conceived in a vacuum. The importance accorded the image of the Tabernacle-Temple as frontispiece to the entire Bible, both in Cassiodorus's *Codex Grandior* and in Ceolfrith's *Codex Amiatinus*, gives some perspective to the initially puzzling degree of decorative crescendo accompanying the image of the Temple in the Book of Kells. The early christian pictorial tradition reflects the immense importance of Tabernacle and Temple in scripture, and hence in exegesis, as representing the whole complex relationship of the Old Covenant and the New, historically distinct, antithetical and yet mystically united.

The ambiguity of the design on folio 202v in the Book of Kells provided another way of dealing with the problem of attempting to represent both the unity of the Temple image and the physical diversity of its various aspects in time. It is possible to read the central structure as the Ark of the Covenant, with the Old Testament 'reliquary' pictured like an insular house-shaped shrine with two carrying poles and two over-arching cherubim. The Ark was placed in the Holy of Holies in the Tabernacle at the time of Aaron, accompanied the chosen people through the desert to the Promised Land and was eventually transferred to the Holy of Holies in the Temple of Solomon. The Ark is also revealed in the apocalyptic theophany of the temple of God in the New Jerusalem (Rev 11:19). It is therefore a constant feature and a connecting link between Tabernacle, Temple and heavenly sanctuary and may well function as a synecdochal representation in the Kells picture.

In both Tabernacle and Temple the Ark was set beneath two cherubim (Ex 25:18-22; I Kg 6:23-28; 2 Chron 3:10). God promised 'And there I will meet thee and commune with thee, from between the two cherubim'. In exegesis the cherubim are interpreted as a fulfilment of the prophecy that the Lord would be made known or recognised between two animals (Hab 3:2) and as representing the Old and New Testaments which respectively

---

[80]See above and note 62.

[81]TCD, MS 52. J Gwynn, *Liber Ardmachanus: the Book of Armagh* (Dublin 1913) folio 171r.

prophesy and announce the Incarnation.[82] The paired cherubim appropriately flank the head of Christ, suggesting he is the new Temple, in the Kells picture which represents his incarnate body and hidden divinity.

The association of the incarnate body of Christ with the Temple in John 2:19-22 forms a key link in another chain which identifies the piercing of Christ's crucified body, the source of the sacraments (John 19: 34, 37), with the issue of the water of life from the Temple in the heavenly Jerusalem (Ezek 47:1; Rev 22:1). This heavenly Temple is identified with the glorified Christ in Rev 21:22; in an early christian apocalypse cycle preserved in Carolingian copies he is literally depicted as the Temple building with the river of life flowing from its side but without any anthropomorphic features, which obviously limits the range of its allusion.[83] Among the early tenth-century Anglo-Saxon miniatures inserted in the Athelstan Psalter, and almost certainly reflecting earlier pictorial influences, folio 21r presents much closer similarities with the Temple image in Kells in the pictorial conventions used to depict Christ and his church.[84] Both employ elements of the New Testament images of the Temple and the body, both combine the themes of the living stones, the cornerstone and the holy priesthood found in I Peter 2:5-9. In both, a large-scale figure of Christ is placed immediately over a small basilica- or house-shaped church with tiled and gabled roof and a door in its long side. In both, Christ is long-haired and beardless and is attended by angels and by seried ranks of small, bust-length figures looking inwards. The features peculiar to the Athelstan Psalter help define the Book of Kells' distinctive treatment of the exegetical chain on which they both draw. In the Psalter, Christ is a full-length figure bearing the Cross, marked with the side wound and flanked by the letters alpha and omega in clear reference to the vision of his Second Coming in Rev 1:7-8, recalling John 19:37 and Zach 12:10. This image, like the apocalyptic text, identifies his incarnate crucified body with his triumphant glorified body. The crucifixion is further evoked by his enthronement on a sacrificial stone altar which Robert Deshman identified as the cornerstone.[85] I Peter 2:6-7, a key text in the chain concerning the Temple image, cites three Old Testament texts, Ps 117:22, Is 8:14 and 28:16, to evoke the nature of the living stone around whom the members of the church are to form themselves as living stones: it is the stone rejected by men but chosen by God to be the chief cornerstone, the precious stone laid in the foundation of Sion yet placed *in caput anguli*. In the Athelstan Psalter

---

[82]Jerome, *Commentariorum in Abacuc*, CCSL 76A, 621; Bede, *De tabernaculo, De templo*, CCSL 119A, 19-20; 178-81. See note 114 below for exegesis on the Ark which can represent Christ, the church and the soul. See Eamonn Ó Carragáin's paper in this volume, n 69.

[83]Trier, Stadbibl. Cod. 31, folio 73. R Laufner and P Klein, *Trierer Apokalypse* (Graz 1975) pl 26.

[84]London, BL, Cotton MS Galba A.XVIII, folios 2v, 21. E Temple, *Anglo-Saxon manuscripts, 900-1066* (London 1976) pls 32, 33.

[85]'The imagery of the living Ecclesia and the English monastic reform' in Szarmach (note 25 above) 267-72.

picture the stone is clearly located in Sion and placed above the church building, like the anthropomorphic representation of Christ which overlays it. The 'living stones' of the new Jerusalem are arranged in groups, identified by inscription as all the choirs of the martyrs, confessors and virgins: a companion picture at folio 2v depicts the ranks of the angels, prophets and, by implication, the apostles, so the two expand into an eschatological image of the heavenly choirs, the citizens of the heavenly Jerusalem. In contrast, there is a greater integration of the images of the body and the Temple in the Kells picture, a more allusive and ambiguous range of temporal reference to Tabernacle, Temple and the heavenly sanctuary. Its role as part of a larger decorative unit and its positioning within the Lucan text as already described, also allow a wider and more flexible range of readings. Three further features distinguish it from the Athelstan Psalter picture, namely, the small priestly figure within the sanctuary, the black devil, and the all-male composition of the groups outside and beneath the Temple. They may offer some further insight into how contemporaries viewed the Kells image.

The priests of Aaron and baptism

In the Kells picture the horizontal line separating the main structure from the rows of bust-length figures below, also cuts across the body of the small but full-length figure standing in the lower part of the Temple so that the head, torso and hands are heavily framed and outlined in the doorway of the Temple, while the lower body reaches to the bottom edge of the picture through the middle of the 'living stones'. It is a hieratic and archaic-looking figure clad in a purple tunic with a gold inset at the neck and covered with groups of three dots, like the long-sleeved tunic of Christ at the top of the Temple. The closest analogy is with the magisterial evangelist portrait on p 218 in the Lichfield Gospels. Like the Kells figure, the evangelist is not in the so-called Osiris pose but holds up two staffs whose shafts are crossed so that they form a chi. In both cases they are ceremonially displayed as sceptres and extend beyond shoulder height. In the Lichfield Gospels example, one rod is green and budding, though with a chamfered base, and the other is a long shafted golden cross with an encircled eight-petalled rosette at its centre. In the Kells example, both golden rods terminate in eight-petalled rosettes. Significantly for this comparison, the Lichfield portrait is of St Luke who is accompanied by his winged calf. The standard association of this evangelist's gospel and symbol with the priesthood and sacrifice of Christ, replacing the blood sacrifice of the Aaronic priesthood of the Old Covenant, and the common exegetical interpretation of Aaron's budding rod as a prefiguring of the Cross, the tree of life, suggest this iconic evangelist portrait is a Christ-bearing image.[86]

---

[86]Lichfield Cathedral Library. Henderson, 122-124, pl 180 also interprets the portrait with reference to exegesis on Luke, CCSL 120, 424-25. The portrait of Aaron accompanying Zachariah in the Rabbula Gospels shows the influence of Ex 20 and Lev 8 in the depiction of his priestly garments, including the sacerdotal diadem and the ephod, but the cross on his breastplate shows Aaron to be 'a prophet of Christ', *Rabbula Gospels* (note 38 above) 53, pl 92.2.

Exegesis on Luke's account of Christ's baptism and genealogy, to which the Kells Temple picture has here been related, follows the Epistle to the Hebrews in revealing the blood sacrifices of the Aaronic priesthood under the Mosaic Law to have been 'a shadow of good things to come', namely the high priesthood of Christ (10:1). The rod or staff of the tribe of Levi, inscribed with the name of Aaron, had budded and blossomed in the tabernacle (Num 17:8), signifying that Aaron and his sons had been divinely chosen for the priesthood. Exodus 28-29:30 and Leviticus 8:1-13 describe the consecration of Aaron and his sons by the anointing of the head with unction, the consecration of the hands, the ritual purification and solemn vesting with the priestly garments — the linen ephod, the rational or breastplate, the purple tunic and girdle, the headdress with a gold plate inscribed 'Holy to the Lord' placed over the brow. The figure in the Kells picture cannot be crudely identified as Aaron for, like the figure of Christ above, he is beardless (cf Lev 21:5) and haloed, but within the red rim of the halo may be discerned a strange headdress with a tiny lozenge at the centre of the prominent golden ornament placed over the brow.

Donnchadh Ó Corráin has shown that early Irish churchmen's conception of themselves as 'the tribe of the church' was in some respects influenced rather literally by the Pentateuch model of the tribe of Levi and the hereditary priesthood of Aaron.[87] While this helps explain their interest in Old Testament accounts of the priesthood, the depiction of the archaic priestly figure surrounded by an entirely male community in the Book of Kells' picture of the church through the image of the Tabernacle/Temple cannot be read as a simple reflection or promotion of clerical exclusiveness. The very reverse is suggested by the exegetical tradition in which the image has been interpreted here. The picture may, however, offer a pictorial equivalent of a topos in monastic hagiography by suggesting that the monastic community grouped around its abbot, who has the place of Christ in its midst, represents the whole people of God, the universal church.

The christian interpretation of the Aaronic priesthood, already established in the Epistle to the Hebrews, was greatly extended by Origen, particularly in the sixteen homilies he devoted to the interpretation of Leviticus, which were known through the elaborated

[87] 'A large party in the Irish church in the seventh and eighth centuries consciously conceived of the mandarin caste of churchmen, scholars, jurists, canon lawyers, historians and poets, to which they belonged, as priests and levites in the strict Old Testament sense of these terms', Ó Corráin et al (note 46 above) 394, examples 394-400. 'That is not to say that they thought of themselves always as priests and levites: rather, the function of that class in the Old Testament was a model useful in teaching, in forming legal concepts within which to adapt and develop rules about the churches, their rights and relationships with secular society', D Ó Corráin, 'Irish vernacular law and the Old Testament' in Ní Cháthain and Richter (note 36 above) 284-307 (p 284).

translation of Rufinus and through intermediaries.[88] Origen's homilies on Luke have not survived intact but influenced Ambrose's commentary, particularly on Luke's opening chapters, so it may be presumed this was another context in which Origen had taken up the theme of the priesthood of Aaron and of Christ. Angers, MS 55 gives a tantalising glimpse of the lesser-known early writers who also fed the eighth-century Hiberno-Latin exegetical tradition. Its citation from the lost commentary by Fortunatian gives a christian allegorical interpretation of Aaron's priestly garments — which are related to baptism — and of his rod, whose budding in the Holy of Holies represents the incarnation, its fruit the evangelists, its taste the Old and New Testaments which together bear witness to Christ, its wood is the Cross and so on.[89]

The eighth-century Irish Reference Bible describes how Aaron, under the Law, was anointed to his office and thus became the first *Messias* or *Christus*. He is compared with Christ, the Anointed One, who was anointed at his incarnation, however, not physically with oil or chrism like Aaron, but invisibly by the Holy Spirit as 'a priest for ever, according to the order of Melchisedech' and also as a prophet and a king.[90] It is this spiritual anointing which was made manifest at Christ's baptism when the Holy Spirit descended in the form of a dove to the body of Christ, his church. In this sense, all the baptised when anointed with chrism, through which they sacramentally share in Christ's anointing, are called to be prophets, priests and kings, as the liturgy makes evident.

Basic baptismal catechesis further reveals the relevance of the evocation of Aaron's priesthood in the Kells picture placed at the culmination of the royal and priestly genealogy of Christ, which is also, through baptism, the spiritual genealogy of his church:

> Just as Aaron's rod was dry and then blossomed, signifying he was a priest chosen by God, so catechumens, dry because of their sins, begin to flower when they come into the baptistery and are watered by the

---

[88]M Bonnet, *Origène, Homilies sur le Levitique SC* (Paris 1981). C Bammel, 'Insular manuscripts of Origen in the Carolingian empire' in *France and the British Isles in the Middle Ages and Renaissance*, ed G Jondorf and D N Dumville (Woodbridge 1991) 5-16 notes the survival of two seventh-century manuscripts (from Gaul) of Rufinus's translation of the homilies on Leviticus. To the examples of insular uses of Origen may be added the citation from Homily 9 on Leviticus in Walsh and Ó Cróinín (note 20 above) 63 and frequent uses of 'Origenes dicit' in the Lucan commentary of the Irish Reference Bible.

[89]*Ex dictis sancti Hieronimi*, CCSL 108B, 145.

[90]*Christus unctus chrismate utique Spiritus Sancti ut 'unxit te Deus, Deus tuus, oleo'* (Ps 44:8) *Oleo enim laetitiae in lege sacerdotes et reges et prophetae unguebantur, Christus vero prae consortibus non oleo corporali sed oleo Spiritus Sancti in sacerdotem et regem et propheten unctus est ut dicitur, 'tu es sacerdos in aeternum secundum Melchisedech'* (Ps 109:4), from commentary on Matthean genealogy, Paris, BN, lat. 11561, folio 138r, Munich, Clm. 14277, folio 219v. Angers 55 also gives other scriptural references for Christ's three-fold anointing which is related to his baptism and his title in the *tres linguae sacrae*: *Christus, Unctus, Messias*, CCSL 108B, 147-48. All three features are related in a commentary on the incarnation in Verona, Bibl. Capit. LXVII (64), folio 42r quoted by Kelly (note 25 above) 21-22.

font. Perhaps you may be saying: 'What had this to do with the people if the rod of the priest was dry and blossomed again?' But what is the people if not priestly? To them was said, 'You are a chosen race, a royal priesthood' (I Peter 2:9). Each catechumen is anointed to a spiritual priesthood and a spiritual kingdom.[91]

The text cited by Ambrose, from Peter's description of the spiritual house formed by the 'holy priesthood' who are also 'living stones' in the building, is used by Bede in his commentary on the Temple in order to demonstrate the universality of this priesthood:

> It was not to bishops and priests alone but to all God's Church that the apostle Peter was speaking when he said: 'But you are a chosen generation, a royal priesthood, a holy nation'.

Giving a spiritual interpretation to the great laver which stood within the court of the priests in the Temple of Solomon for the purposes of their ritual cleansing, Bede says that although the priests washed in it, 'all the elect are called priests in a typological sense in the scriptures since they are members of the high priest Jesus Christ'; the priests of Aaron's line who were washed in the Temple laver 'represent those who through Baptism are made sharers in the high priesthood which is in the Lord Jesus Christ'.[92]

The same text from Peter's epistle had been used by Origen to expound the same image of the anointed Aaronic priesthood as prefiguring the new chosen people who, through their baptismal anointing, share in Christ's priesthood which supersedes that of Aaron. Origen links this image to the great architectural metaphor of the Tabernacle and the Temple. He explains that 'the first and visible sanctuary' described in the Old Testament was open to the priest but that only the high priest passed beyond the veil to offer sacrifice on the Day of Atonement. This first sanctuary, therefore,

> can be understood as this church in which we are now placed in the flesh ... (but) I do not want you to marvel that this sanctuary is open only to priests. For all who have been anointed with the chrism of the sacred anointing (i.e. Baptism) have become priests, just as Peter also says to all the Church: 'You are a chosen race, a royal priesthood, a holy people. Therefore you are 'a priestly race' and because of this you approach the sanctuary.[93]

---

[91] Ambrose, *De sacramentis*, CCSL 73, 74-75. Isidore of Seville relates Aaron's priestly anointing with the anointing of Christ and of all the members of the church as priests and kings, *De ecclesiasticis officiis*, CCSL 113, 106.

[92] *De templo*, CCSL 119A, 207, 214.

[93] Barkley (note 53 above) 196.

The image is applied not only to the church but to the individual faithful. Aaron's priestly headdress and garments, itemised in Leviticus, are all allegorically expounded as facets of the spiritual life with which the baptised should clothe themselves in order to make a sacrificial offering of their own lives. Whoever adorns his head with priestly ornaments, that is, by acts which bring glory to Christ, has adorned 'his head who is Christ' (Eph 4:15).

> You too can function as a high priest before God within the temple of your spirit if you would prepare your garments with zeal and vigilance, if ... the anointing and grace of your baptism remains uncontaminated ... 'For you are the temple of the living God' if 'the Spirit of God lives in you' (2 Cor 6:16; 1 Cor 3:16).[94]

In this the faithful follow Christ the true high priest who was clothed with 'a sanctified linen tunic' — that is his human flesh, begotten of the Holy Spirit — when he made his offering. The homily twice cites the prophecy of Zech 3:1-3 and its image of the purification of priestly garments: 'And I saw Jesus, the great priest, dressed in filthy garments, and the devil standing at his right hand to speak against him (be his adversary)': the garment of Jesus's human flesh is sanctified by the blood of his Passion.[95]

But although the baptised can enter 'the first and visible sanctuary' which is the church and share in the priesthood of Christ, who once entered the Holy of Holies to offer his own blood for atonement (Heb 9:11-12), he alone enters beyond the veil into a 'second and invisible sanctuary',

> not into a sanctuary made by hands, but into Heaven itself, and he appears for us before the face of God' (Heb 9:24). Therefore the place of heaven and the throne itself of God are designated by the figure and image of the interior sanctuary.[96]

This is precisely the same passage from Hebrews cited by Ambrose in his Lucan commentary when he distinguishes 'the former tabernacle' of the Aaronic priesthood, both from the 'temple of his body' (John 2:21) in which Christ's propitiatory sacrifice was made, and from the heavenly sanctuary (Heb 9:24). This does not mean that Christ makes a second sacrifice in the heavenly sanctuary but that 'the destruction of sin by the sacrifice of himself' (Heb 9:26), the 'day of Atonement', is made eternally present. Origen explains that human beings cannot yet follow him into the heavenly sanctuary because of their mortality, but cites St Paul:

---

[94]ibid, 125.

[95]ibid, 184. The same text from Zachariah's vision of the Temple is quoted by Bede (*Opera homiletica*, CCSL 122, 121) as a prophecy of Jesus's victory over the devil and may help explain the curious posture of the two in the Kells picture: Christ's body is placed frontally but his arms reach out so that the devil is 'at his right hand'. The devil's own left hand is raised in a gesture of speech or debate ('his adversary').
[96]ibid, 197, cf 178.

Death, the last enemy, will be destroyed' (I Cor 15:26). This 'enemy' is the Devil.[97]

Meanwhile, until its consummation at the end of the world, the church on earth must wait, like the people standing outside and below the sanctuary doorway. For Origen and many other commentators, including Bede, this waiting itself becomes a metaphor of the spiritual life as the church is urged to

> Stand before the gates (Jas 5:9) waiting for our high priest who remains within the Holy of Holies, that is, before the Father, and intercedes ... 'for the sins' of 'those who wait for him' (Heb 9:28) ... who 'do not depart from the Temple, who are not absent from fasting and prayers' (Luke 2:37) ... 'To meditate on the Law of the Lord day and night' (Ps 1:2) ... is truly 'to wait before the gates for the high priest who waits within the Holy of Holies.'[98]

Origen observes that anyone who examines the epistle to the Hebrews, especially where the apostle compares the high priest of the Law (the priesthood of Aaron) to the high priest of promise, Christ, about whom it is written, 'You are a priest forever after the order of Melchisedech' (Heb 5:6), will find 'that those things which were written in the Law are copies and forms of true things' (cf Heb 8:5; 9:8-11; Acts 7:44).

Ambrose also adopts this method of spiritual interpretation when commenting on the image of the Old Covenant priesthood which prefaces and permeates Luke's account of the incarnation and when showing, through Luke's account of the baptism and genealogy, the spiritual anointing and royal priesthood of Christ and his church. It is in this context that Ambrose uses the chain of scriptural texts referring to the temple of Christ's body, the temple of the Holy Spirit which is every baptised christian, the temple of the church and the heavenly sanctuary, the temple or city of the new Jerusalem. The picture on folio 202v placed at this point in Luke's text demonstrates the essential exegetical characteristic of revealing the simultaneity of truths which cohere and find their reality in Christ. Viewed in this context, the priestly figure standing in the doorway of the Temple in the Kells picture may help articulate a reading of the image which depicts a single building but alludes simultaneously to others: like the Temple, the priestly figure transcends temporal limitations. His archaic appearance and distinctive headdress may recall the priesthood of Aaron in the Tabernacle and of Aaron's descendants in the Temple in Jerusalem, yet his hieratic stance, halo and twin budding rods, also suggest the new high priesthood of Christ 'after the order of Melchisedech' who was priest and king. The members of the new chosen people drawn together around the priestly figure share in this royal priesthood through baptism and are able to

---

[97]ibid, 200.
[98]ibid, 187.

enter the sanctuary because they are 'sanctified by the oblation of the body of Jesus Christ' (Heb 10:10, cf 12,14); they enter into the Holy of Holies 'through the veil, that is to say, his flesh' (10:19-20). This helps illumine the picture's major image of Jesus, 'full of the Holy Spirit', as the place where this propitiation was offered, the temple of his body.

The iconography of the previous double opening in Kells has already contrasted the blood sacrifice of the Aaronic priesthood and the sacrifice of the new high priest in its juxtaposition of the calf and the eucharistic chalice and vine. The horizontal endpiece of the genealogy on folio 202r showing the vine is complemented by the horizontal courses of 'living stones' in the corresponding position overleaf on folio 202v, which are built up to form a single spiritual house. Like the vine, the spiritual house or temple is an image of the incorporation of the faithful into the body of Christ. The thematic connection between the iconography of the genealogy and the Temple picture in Kells is further emphasized, assisting a reading of the Temple picture, by the way in which the half-concealed figure waiting behind the vinescroll at the end of the list of the church's spiritual ancestors on folio 202r exactly foreshadows the high priestly figure standing among the new chosen people in the corresponding position on folio 202v. The connection shows the importance of the sacraments as the means of incorporation into the body of Christ. Meditation on the Temple image in its exegetical context gradually expands and deepens an understanding of the temple of Jesus's human body, 'full of the Holy Spirit', leading in to the image of his sacramental body, the church, and finally to an image of his mystical body, transcending time and space, including the church's spiritual ancestors and the future elect. The importance of the sacraments in understanding this is that they take their origin from the crucified body of Christ, as Ambrose explains during his meditation on the chain of Temple texts in his commentary on the Lucan baptism, but they also participate in the 'heavenly realities' of which earthly institutions are the shadows or copies. The sacraments therefore link the present age and the age to come, the visible and invisible, earth and heaven.

It is possible to view the side frames of the Temple picture as two pillars supporting a roofline and therefore to see the 'living stones', who are also 'a chosen people, a royal priesthood' (I Peter 2:5,9), as within the sanctuary that is the church on earth. Their sharing in the priesthood of Christ is foreshadowed in the priesthood of Aaron at the sanctuary doorway of the Tabernacle. But the house-shaped, Ark-like structure can also be regarded as separated from the little figures below, the outlining of the haloed high-priestly head alone in its doorway suggesting the heavenly sanctuary. The group of figures around his feet then appear as the earthbound church waiting its own completion outside the heavenly sanctuary as the high priest reappears at the end of time. By being partly on earth, partly in heaven, alluding both to Christ's priestly sacrifice in 'the temple of his body' and to his entry to the heavenly tabernacle 'not made with hands', the sceptre-bearing high-priestly figure in the Temple picture acts as a key to exploring, through scriptural chains, the multiple significance of the Temple as an image of the body of Christ.

Recapitulation

The foregoing argument has tried to show how the meaning of the Temple picture is *articulated*; the meaning itself has here been discerned within the context of the decorative unit, of which the picture and its display text form the culmination, and of the gospel text in which the decorative unit is placed. In particular, the picture has been related to the combined account of the baptism and genealogy which immediately precedes it and is recalled in Luke 4:1 whose opening words immediately follow the picture on the facing recto. The broad features of commentators' expositions of Luke's extensive use of the image of priesthood and Temple in his opening chapters and its relevance to the picture may be briefly recalled. As exegesis emphazises that the baptism and priestly genealogy in Luke reveal Christ's identity as both human and yet Son of God, so the double opening of folios 202v-203r shows the temple of his human body 'full of the Holy Spirit'. Secondly, it has been seen that commentators stress that Christ's baptism signifies the sacramental baptism of all the faithful who are reborn as sons of God and participators in Christ's priesthood: the picture similarly may be seen as referring to each of the baptised as being a temple of the Holy Spirit. Thirdly, through baptism, the faithful become the spiritual heirs of Christ's ancestors and are drawn together into one single community of the new chosen people of God, destined for the heavenly Jerusalem. In this sense, the picture may also be read as referring to the church, the body of Christ, a living building existing partly on earth and partly in heaven where it will eventually receive its completion.

Baptism

It may reasonably be asked why so much attention should have been lavished on themes of baptism in the Book of Kells: produced in an established monastic culture whose members were already baptised, it can hardly be regarded as a didactic aid to evangelisation. The rite of baptism in the Stowe Missal has an unusually detailed enumeration of the parts of the body from which the devil is exorcised but the idea that the body of the newly baptised, anointed with oil and chrism, becomes 'the temple of the living God' (cf 1 Cor 3:16-17, 6:19) is quite conventional.[99] In the language of catechesis, however, the baptised still have to ward off recurrent attacks of the devil or, to use another metaphor, they have constantly to cleanse the temple their bodies became at baptism to make a fitting dwelling place for the Holy Spirit:

---

[99]Stowe Missal, Warren (note 52 above) 207, 210, 213; cf Gallican sacramentary ordo for Easter Saturday baptism with provision for exorcism *omnes exercitus diaboli ... ut fiat templum Dei sanctam* in *The ancient liturgies of the Gallican church*, ed J M Neale and G H Forbes (Burntisland 1855) 269.

You are associated with the divine nature, do not turn back to your base condition by a degenerate way of life. Remember that you have been rescued from the power of darkness ... By the sacrament of baptism, you have been made the temple of the Holy Spirit. Do not make such a guest take flight by perverse actions nor submit yourselves again to the devil's slavery.[100]

The Ninevites saved by Jonah's mission are often identified with the Jews to whom Christ brought the means of deliverance from sin, enabling them to enter the church through repentance and baptism. Christ's reference to Jonah occurs in both Matthew 12:39-45 and Luke 11:24-32 in the context of an exorcism and of Christ's teaching about an exorcised man who is re-possessed by seven unclean spirits or devils and becomes their dwelling-place. Ambrose, in his commentary on Luke's gospel, sees the seven devils as signifying the spiritually arid life of the unrepentant Jews, still living under the Law, contrasted with the seven-fold grace of the Holy Spirit which fills the baptised. In Bede's homily 1:12 already referred to, this gospel passage is integrated into the time-honoured chain of texts linking Christ's baptism and the sacrament of baptism, the importance of the dove and the seven gifts of the Holy Spirit. By fasting in the desert after the descent of the dove at his baptism, Christ showed by example 'that after we have received the forgiveness of sins in baptism, we should devote ourselves to vigils, fasts, prayers and other spiritually fruitful things, lest ... the unclean spirit which had been expelled from our heart by baptism may return and finding us fruitless in spiritual riches, may weigh us down with a seven-fold pestilence and our last state be worse than our first.' Accordingly, Bede admonishes his readers to study and follow the example of the dove whose seven-fold nature described in the Song of Songs presents seven examples of virtue as 'the grace of the Holy Spirit, who descended as a dove, is seven-fold'.[101] The story of the seven devils attached to the gospel citations of Jonah is thus applied in some detail to the spiritual life of the baptised, who are continually threatened by the devil and continue to need the operation of the seven gifts of the Holy Spirit received in their post-baptismal anointing. How to remain a fitting habitation of the Holy Spirit is, therefore, the purpose of the post-baptismal life; its achievement, only with the help of the seven gifts of the same Holy Spirit, is the distinction of saints. Approached from this premiss, the reading of the Temple picture in the Book of Kells established so far may be refined a little. Its depiction of the bodily temple of Jesus's humanity 'full of the Holy Spirit' simultaneously reveals his identity and the vocation of the baptised who are called to a life-long process of 'conversion' to become like him.

---

[100] *Sancti Leonis Magni, Tractatus septem et nonaginta,* CCSL 138, Tractatus 21, 88, quoted by L Bouyer, *The spirituality of the New Testament and the Fathers* (London 1968) 530.
[101] *Opera homelitica,* CCSL 122, 83-86.

The monastic life

The call for vigilance, under Christ, against the continuing attacks of the devil, prefigured by Christ's own triumph over the devil in the desert and recalled in the church's lenten liturgy, is a recurring theme of catechetical literature and applies to the spiritual life of all the baptised. It has a particular importance for the monastic life, however, which simply seeks more fully the perfecting of the seven gifts of the Holy Spirit granted to all the baptised. The eighth-century Hiberno-Latin commentary on Luke's gospel which glosses the phrase in Luke 4:1, *Iesus autem ... plenus spiritu sancto* as *id est, septem dona Spiritu(s) sancti habens, et de hac plenitudine ... eius nos omnes accipimus*, sees the same verse's reference to Christ returning from the Jordan and going into the desert as a model for the monastic life: *Et hanc deserti regulam sancti monachi sequebantur*. The devil in this desert, who once tempted and overcame Adam, will overcome the man who is earthly but will be overcome by the heavenly man; it is good, therefore, to flee the crowds of vices and seek the secrets of perfection.[102]

The image of the monastic community and individual monks under spiritual attack from black silhouetted figures of devils accompanied many manuscript copies of a treatise by John Climacus, sixth-century abbot of Sinai. In common with other monastic writings, including the Rule of St Benedict, his treatise, known as the *Scala paradisi*, uses the ladder (recalling Jacob's Ladder in Gen 28:11-18) as an image of the spiritual life. Its thirty rungs signify the age of Christ at his baptism (Luke 3:23), and the ascent of its rungs marks the monk's ascent of the spiritual precepts or virtues so that 'he may come unto a perfect man, unto the measure and fullness of Christ'. The manuscript tradition shows the monks assisted by angels and the prayers of the elders but tempted by devils or vices who fire darts and try to deflect monks from the straight and narrow way.[103] Like the *scala paradisi* scene, the picture on folio 202v in the Book of Kells shows Christ as a half-length figure with a scroll and attended by angels and has some of its figures arranged in an upward diagonal. It has often been noted that its black silhouette type of devil seems ultimately derived from Byzantine art. Further, in the late descendant of the Climacus manuscript tradition shown as (pl 128), the lassooing devils towards the bottom of the ladder provide a striking parallel for the strange extension to the devil's right hand in the Kells scene. It is the kind of inconsequential detail which can be carried over into a new context, perhaps not entirely understood, leaving a hint of its origins.

That the monastic life was imaged in such terms of contests with the devil or devils in insular monastic culture is clear from hagiographic evidence of familiarity with materials such as Athanasius's *Life of Anthony* and

---

[102]*Scriptores Hiberniae minores*, CCSL 108C, 28-30.
[103]J R Martin, *The illustrations of the Heavenly Ladder of John Climacus* (Princeton 1954).

with Gregory's *Dialogues*.[104] Again, the New Testament provides authority for the metaphor. St Paul counsels the Ephesians to 'put on the whole armour of God' — the invisible girdle of truth, shield of faith, helmet of salvation and sword of the Spirit (which is the word of God) — in order to withstand 'the deceits of the devil' and 'to extinguish all the fiery darts of the most wicked one', 'praying at all times in the spirit' (Ephesians 6:10-18). Cuthbert fought in solitude for some time against the devil by prayer and fasting in the outer precincts of the monastery at Lindisfarne, then retreated to the remoteness of Farne and, aided by the Pauline spiritual armour, quenched 'all the fiery darts of the wicked one' (Eph 6:16,17), routed the devil and his hosts and built there a city (meaning his monastic cell). It is described as a place of combat where the hosts of the devil continued to seek his overthrow and where he counselled those beset with temptation about the wiles of the devil.[105]

Similarly, St Columba had been described by Adomnán as praying in a remote spot on Iona when,

> as he afterwards informed a few brothers, he saw a foul and very black array of demons making war against him with iron spits. They, as was revealed by the Spirit to the holy man, wished to assail his monastery and with these same spikes to slaughter many of the brothers. But he, one man against these innumerable enemies, fought a strong fight, taking to himself the armour of the apostle Paul.

The battle continued for the greater part of a day until the angels of God came to Columba's support and the demons were repelled from the island and sought out neighbouring monasteries, one of which at least Columba prophesied would not be stricken as the community was defended under a good abbot by fasts and prayers from the assault of demons.[106] It is possible that the idea of the contemporary monastic community defended under Christ by the merits and intercession of its heavenly patron may have had some influence in the visualisation of the great universal biblical metaphor of the Temple on folio 202v in the Book of Kells.

The depiction of Winchester's heavenly patron St Swithun as literally 'a pillar in the house of God' in the Benedictional of St Aethelwold, *c*973, shows his column-like body supporting an architectural arch and outlined against an open arch or doorway.[107] His vestments and Petrine tonsure identify his priestly status, his halo shows he is a part not simply of the church on earth, but of the Temple of the heavenly Jerusalem: he has

---

[104]C Stancliffe, 'Irish saints' Lives' in *The seventh century: change and continuity*, ed J Fontaine and J N Hillgarth (Warburg Inst, London Colloquium 1988) 87-115; 105-10 on appearance of devils in Irish hagiography. I am grateful to Máire Herbert for this reference.

[105]B Colgrave, *Two Lives of St Cuthbert* (Cambridge 1940) 215-17 (p 220).

[106]Anderson (note 6 above) 193-95.

[107]London, BL, Add. MS 49598, folio 97v. Facsimile, *The Benedictional of St Aethelwold*, ed G F Warner and H M Wilson (Oxford 1910).

received the apocalyptic promise, 'He that shall overcome, I will make him a pillar in the temple of my God' (Rev 3:12). There is some broad similarity with the timeless, more hieratic, priestly haloed figure in the Kells picture whose lower body is set like a pillar among the 'living stones' in the foundations of the Temple building on earth and whose head and symbols of priestly authority are outlined against the doorway of the heavenly sanctuary above. The assimilation of the 'living Ecclesia' metaphor used in I Peter 2:4-10 into the liturgy, hagiography and art of the later Anglo-Saxon monastic reform and the application of epithets such as stones, columns, pillars and even cornerstone both to individual leaders, such as Dunstan and Oswald, and to features of the monastic life whose practice characterised them as exemplary spiritual houses, has been demonstrated by Robert Deshman. In particular, he has shown that the mass for the Translation of St Swithun, which describes Swithun as an apostle and a 'column of shining glory', and the picture for this feast in the Benedictional of St Aethelwold 'commemorated the saint's literal incorporation into the cathedral'; in 971 his relics were moved in from outside and appear to have occasioned rebuilding to provide a suitable architectural setting.[108]

Already by 731, however, Bede had recounted a miracle of Aidan, who is also cast in the apostolic mould, which reveals him as a pillar of the church and a bulwark of truth. The plank buttressing the west wall of a church, against which he leaned as he breathed his last, proved miraculous and when the church was rebuilt 'they put the buttress not outside as before to support the structure, but inside the church itself as a memorial of the miracle'.[109] The death of some of the community of the Irish-trained monastic bishop Chad is described as the translation of 'the living stones of the church from their earthly sites to the heavenly building', and in homilies for the dedication of the monastic church at Jarrow, the themes of the physical and spiritual building of the house of God are linked, with the monastic perfection of the lives of the monks forming 'living stones'.[110] Moreover, Bede's commentary on the Temple systematically interprets the physical features of Solomon's Temple as referring both to aspects of the individual and collective spiritual life and to various members of the church, past, present and future, not as named individuals but as categories within the christian body — patriarchs and prophets, apostles and evangelists, preachers, teachers and the whole 'multitude of believers' drawn from the nations.

Repeatedly it shows the interpenetration of the image of the Temple as the universal church stretching throughout time and space and as the immediate individual experience of the church. In reconciling apparently conflicting scriptural texts within the exegetical chain, Bede explores the

[108]Deshman (note 85 above) 261-62, 273-77.
[109]HE, 265. Farr, 'Lection', 56-57, n 109 suggests this passage may have been influenced by De tabernaculo 2, CCSL 119A, 59-60.
[110]HE, 339.

paradox of how words and images used of Christ or of his saints may also be applied to the faithful. While it is true that 'there is no other foundation that can be laid but that which has been laid, namely Jesus Christ' (I Cor 3:11), nevertheless

> into this foundation, great and costly stones are carried when men eminent in deeds and sanctity adhere by their habitual sanctity of spirit to their Creator, so that the more firmly they place their hope in him, the greater is their capacity to direct the life of others, which is to act as a broad foundation supporting a massive building.

Similarly the biblical image of the apostles as pillars (Gal 2:9) is extended to include 'all spiritual teachers' who are strong in faith and works and 'elevated to heavenly things by contemplation'; whoever teaches everything the Lord commanded the apostles 'is indeed a pillar in God's house ... a bulwark of truth'.[111]

A final illustration of the kind of resonances the image of the Tabernacle or Temple may have had for a monastic readership concerns *lectio divina*. The major works on the image referred to here, such as the Epistle to the Hebrews, Origen's homilies on Leviticus, Ambrose's commentary on Luke's gospel and Bede's treatises on the Tabernacle and Temple, are all works of spiritual interpretation of the literal text of scripture which found in the image of the house of God, as the place of the divine presence with his chosen people, a key to the mystery of Christ and the whole history of salvation. The sanctuary of the Tabernacle or Temple or the Ark itself became an image of the discernment of scripture in which the truth is revealed. Cummian describes cloistering himself for a year and 'entering the sanctuary of God (that is sacred Scripture)' before writing the *De controversia paschali* which, in an important sense, is about the spiritual interpretation of Scripture.[112] In a more affective, contemplative vein, Columbanus used the image of the Tabernacle, in which the priestly sons of Aaron kept a lamp burning perpetually (Ex 27:20-21), in his prayer for enlightenment

> my lamp might ever burn by night in the temple of my Lord that to all entering the house of God it might give light ... Do thou enrich my lantern with thy light ... so that by its light there may be disclosed to me those holy places of the holy, which hold thee the eternal priest ... entering there in the pillars of that great temple of thine, that constantly I may see, observe, desire thee only ...[113]

---

[111]*De templo*, CCSL 119A, 154, 200.

[112]Walsh and Ó Crónín (note 20 above) 58-59.

[113]Walker (note 6 above) Sermon 12, 115. The Tabernacle lamp is given a detailed spiritual interpretation in Origen's thirteenth homily on Leviticus 233-36 and in Bede's *De templo*, CCSL 119A, 93-95.

The image of the sanctuary Ark, the core of Tabernacle and Temple, as both the revelation or discernment of truth and the prompting of an inner conversion, had been given a masterly exposition by John Cassian, a favourite author for Irish exegetes and an important mediator of the traditions of desert monasticism to the West. In the fourteenth Conference he counsels the monk to apply himself so constantly to meditation on Scripture that it impregnate his soul, forming it to its own image. Drawing on the description in Heb 9:4-5 of the Ark of the Covenant and its sacred contents housed within the Tabernacle, Cassian shows how, through meditation on Scripture, the soul becomes like the Ark, enclosing the two tablets of stone that are the two testaments, the golden urn of manna which figures spiritual thoughts and the bread of angels, 'and the rod of Aaron, that is to say the standard, the saving sign of our sovereign and true pontiff, Jesus Christ, always flowering anew in an undying memory'. All these are covered by the two cherubim who signify fullness of knowledge; they are placed over the propitiatory of God, 'that is, the tranquillity of your heart', and protect it from evil spirits. The soul, by its love of purity, thus becomes the Ark of the priestly kingdom, absorbed in spiritual understanding and so

> carries out the commandment given to the pontiff (Aaron) by the law-giver (Moses): 'He is not to go out of the sanctuary, lest he profane the sanctuary of God' (Leviticus 21:12), that is, his heart, where the Lord promises to make his abiding dwelling-place.[114]

Similarly, the pictorial image of the divine dwelling-place in Kells is not simply typological but provides an aid to meditation on the indwelling of the divine. The process of reading an exegetical chain of scriptural texts involves constant recapitulation which is not merely repetition but returns the reader to continuous reconsideration of the apparently familiar primary image to extend and deepen understanding of its significance.

The chief relic of the western world?
Set at the end of the Lucan account of Christ's baptism and human ancestry, in which his divine Sonship is revealed, the picture and facing text on folios 202v-203r in the Book of Kells present the incarnate body of Jesus, full of the Holy Spirit. The Temple is also an image of his sacramental and mystical body, the church on earth and in heaven, spiritually descended from Christ's ancestors and sharing in his royal priesthood. The spiritual building with Christ as its foundation and cornerstone, the faithful as living stones and pillars, shows the incorporation of the faithful in the body of Christ. In exegesis, the images of Tabernacle, Temple and the Ark are used with great flexibility to describe aspects of that whole process of incorporation. It is begun at baptism when the devil is exorcised and each of the faithful becomes the

---

[114]Cited by Bouyer (note 100 above) 506. There is a detailed spiritual interpretation of the Ark and its contents in Munich, Clm. 6233, 11.92-120 and in Bede's *De tabernaculo*, CCSL 119A, 13-17.

habitation of the Holy Spirit; with constant vigilance under Christ against the continuing temptations of the devil, it continues in the whole development of the spiritual life which aspires to be like Christ and to journey towards the heavenly sanctuary of the New Jerusalem. It has been seen that some of these themes would have had particular interest for the monastic life and that images of the monastic community and its heavenly patron may have helped form the visualisation of the image which is derived from scriptural chains applying to the universal church. This is very different from saying that the iconography alone may be used to associate the manuscript conclusively with any particular cult or community. Surveying a wide range of other types of evidence for assigning a date and place of origin to the Book of Kells, George Henderson added the supporting testimony of the cumulative effect of the illustrations to the argument that it is a Columban book and judiciously observed:

> In its general ecstatic visionary quality and in the specific slant of its iconography, the Book of Kells is at least consistent with the interpretation of St Columba offered in his official biography.[115]

The present discussion of the Temple picture set in the larger unit of folios 200r-203r would support this judgement. Columba was a priest of royal descent and prophetic power. In the conventions of hagiography, Adomnán shows him to be of apostolic stature, with power to bind and loose, one in whom Christ himself was manifested through his signs and miracles (69,95).[116] His vigilance in heroic feats of prayer defends his monastery from the assaults of devils (193-95) and after death he remains a powerful patron and intercessor. He is specifically described as 'the pillar of many churches' (227) and at death his soul leaves 'the tabernacle of his body' (227, 233). He joins the company of the saints in the New Jerusalem and 'has a glorious eternal place in the heavenly land among both companies, namely of prophets and apostles, as a man prophetic and apostolic' (141, 233). By divine favour his name is illustriously renowned in the city of Rome and throughout the universal church (233).

Columba is shown to be a point of contact between earth and heaven, who slept on a stone pillow, like Jacob (225), frequently conversed with angels and witnessed them aiding the souls of the departed to heaven. Angels continue to visit his burial place 'down to the present day' (233). In a vision Columba appears 'radiant in angelic form, whose lofty height seemed with its head to touch the clouds' (15). At his death, a pillar of fire illumined the whole world and pierced the sky (229). Above all, there are striking images of how he was filled with the Holy Spirit. The biography is an extraordinary portrait of the divine indwelling. It has been seen that the very name, Columba, the same name as the prophet Jonah, was divinely given and absolutely appropriate because 'he with dove-like disposition offered to the Holy Spirit a dwelling in himself'

---

[115]Henderson, 194, cf 180.

[116]Anderson (note 6 above) page numbers in parentheses in text.

(5). As he entered the church to pray, he was accompanied by a dazzling golden light 'descending from highest heaven and wholly filling the inside of the church' (211); a fiery radiance rose from his head like a column as he consecrated the eucharist' until those holiest ministries were completed' (207). Adomnán records Columba's preoccupation with reading and copying scripture, the miraculous powers of books he wrote or possessed. Most significantly, he is shown to be the divinely inspired interpreter of the sacred text. Once, for example, 'the grace of the Holy Spirit was poured out upon him abundantly and in an incomparable manner and continued marvellously for the space of three days'. Caught up in ecstatic prayer, alone, without food or drink, 'he saw, openly revealed, many of the secret things that have been hidden since the world began. Also everything that in the sacred scriptures is dark and most difficult became plain, and was shown more clearly than the day to the eyes of his purest heart' (209).

There is a strong sense here of the apostolic spiritual interpretation of scripture: 'We speak the wisdom of God in a mystery a wisdom which is hidden, which God ordained before the world ... But to us God has revealed (it) by his Spirit' (I Cor 2:7, 10). It is the mystery of Christ, 'the mystery which was kept secret from eternity which is now made manifest' (Rom 16:25-6); 'the mystery of Christ which in other generations was not known to the sons of men as it is now revealed to his holy apostles and prophets in the Spirit' (Eph 3:4-5). In this sense, the spiritual interpretation of scripture revealed in the visual exegesis of folios 202v-203r in the Book of Kells would have offered an eloquent tribute to a monastic founder and heavenly patron who was so pre-eminently 'full of the Holy Spirit'.

'Traditio evangeliorum' and 'sustentatio': the relevance of liturgical ceremonies to the Book of Kells

Éamonn Ó Carragáin

Most interpretative scholarship on the Book of Kells has, quite correctly, focused on how the book could have been used for private meditation. But the rich decoration of the manuscript suggests that it had public roles to play as well as private ones. This paper propounds some ways in which such a lavish gospel book might have been put to communal liturgical use in the context of monastic liturgy.[1]

The Book of Kells does not seem to have been intended as a working manuscript. Concluding that the book was intended for display during liturgical ceremonies, Françoise Henry remarked on 'the extraordinary carelessness with which the text has been handled', and judged that 'the treatment of the canon-tables ... is unbelievably irresponsible'. Patrick McGurk also pointed out that the Eusebian numbers in the canon tables are arranged so as to be 'almost unusable'; in any case the relevant Eusebian reference numbers are copied only sporadically into the gospel text itself. Therefore, Françoise Henry reasonably argued that 'it looks as if the Kells scribe did not care very much, knowing that nobody was going to use the volume for reference, and that it had, first of all, to be a beautiful object'.[2] The makers of the book may have thought of their audience in terms of the unseen as well as the seen: God, the angels and saints, the church already

---

[1] Françoise Henry concluded that 'the fantastic lavishness of the decoration and the unusually large size of the Book show clearly that it was an altar-book, made to be used for liturgical reading, and probably intended to be displayed open as a sumptuous ornament during ceremonies when pomp was especially required': Henry, 153. George Henderson (pp 15-16) also placed the insular gospel books in a liturgical context. The most scholarly and far-reaching study to date of the relationship between the Book of Kells and the liturgy is Carol Ann Farr, 'Lection'. Some of its most important conclusions are summarised in Farr, 'Liturgical influences', 127-41. See also Dr Farr's contribution to the present volume. I am grateful to Michelle Brown, of the British Library, who allowed me to read portions of her forthcoming thesis on the Book of Cerne dealing with evangelist symbols and with the *Apertio aurium* ceremony. I wish to thank Tomás Ó Carragáin and Eoghan Ó Carragáin for their close and instructive examination (in facsimile) of folios 2v-3r, and for their most helpful discussions of details of the design of this opening and other details in the book. The Humanities Research floor of the Boole Library, University College, Cork, and in particular Helen Moloney Davis, were generous in their help with bibliographical questions. For shared knowledge, insights and encouragement I owe to my colleague Dr Jennifer O'Reilly a debt incurred over many years of shared teaching and discussion of early monastic culture and its iconography.
[2] Henry, 153; McGurk, 'Texts', 56.

reigning in heaven and already helping men and women on earth.[3] Such a heavenly audience would appreciate the labour and skill devoted to the presentation and adornment of a precious liturgical object, and such a heavenly audience would not have been confused by the absence of Eusebian canon numbers. But such an idea already puts us in a context of performed liturgical acts. The liturgy was seen as inspired by the Holy Spirit, who enabled the members of Christ's body on earth and in heaven together to participate with the angels in Christ's own prayer to the Father.[4] The idea that visible and invisible creatures, drawn together from all nations and all periods of history down to the end of time, could form one body and participate in the same life, that of the Trinity, enables us to realise why so much attention and skill might be lavished on a book which may have been used liturgically but seldom actually read, privately or aloud. But a great book can be a presence to a community which has seldom read it. This can be true even today: the Book of Kells is a great presence in Trinity College, though I suspect that a rather small percentage of the TCD community has read the book, even in facsimile. I expect that the same was true (though for different reasons) at Iona, or Kells, or whichever monastic community produced or possessed the book in the early medieval period.

I wish briefly to consider the different ways in which gospel books could become present to communities which were mostly illiterate.[5] The liturgy

---

[3]See especially the Rule of St Benedict 19:6-7: 'Let us consider, then, how we ought to behave in the presence of God and his angels, and let us stand to sing the psalms in such a way that our minds are in harmony with our voices': ed and trans Timothy Fry and others, *RB 1980: the rule of St Benedict in Latin and English with notes* (Collegeville, Minnesota 1981) 216-17. On the unity of the invisible and visible participants in the liturgy, see Eric Peterson, *The angels and the liturgy: the status and significance of the holy angels in worship* (London and New York 1964); and R A Markus, *The end of ancient christianity* (Cambridge 1990) 21-25.

[4]The classic liturgical expression of this theme is to be found in the various Prefaces to the Roman canon of the mass: eg *The Stowe Missal*, ed George F Warner, HBS 31-32, 2 vols (London 1906-15) II, 9-10: '*Uere dignum et justum est equm et salutare est nos tibi hic semper et ubique gratias agere domine sancte omnipotens aeterne deus per christum dominum nostrum qui cum unigenito tuo et spiritu sancto deus es unus et inmortalis ... Per quem maestatem tuam laudant angeli adorant dominationes ... ac beata seraphim socia exultatione concelebrant cum quibus et nóstras uoces ut admitti iubeas deprecamur suplici confessione dicentes sanctus ... Sanctus sanctus dominus deus sabaoth ...*'. The most important modern studies of the theme are Henri de Lubac, *Corpus mysticum. L'Eucharistie et l'Église au Moyen Age: étude historique*, 2nd edn (Paris 1949) 9-137; Yves Congar, *L'Ecclésiologie du haut moyen âge de Saint Grégoire le Grand à la désunion entre Byzance et Rome* (Paris 1968) 61-248; J A Jungmann, *The mass of the Roman rite: its origins and development*, trans Francis A Brunner, 2 vols (New York 1951-55; repr. Westminster, MD, 1986) II, 101-38; and *Corpus praefationum*, ed Edmond Moeller, CCSL 161-161D, 5 vols (Turnhout 1980-81) I, 'Étude préliminaire', xix-xxxii and (on the Stowe Missal and other Celtic prefaces) xxxvi-xxxvii.

[5]On the importance of ritual in early medieval Europe, see Arnold Angenendt, *Kaiserherrschaft und Königstaufe: Kaiser, Könige und Päpste als geistliche Patrone in der abendländischen Missionsgeschichte*, Arbeiten zur Frühmittelalterforschung 15 (Berlin and New York 1984) 45-48; Arnold Angenendt, *Das Frühmittelalter. Geschichte des abendländischen Christentums von der Völkerwanderung bis zum Reich Karls des Grossen*, Christentum und Gesellschaft 4 (Stuttgart 1989) 49-50, 56-60, 151-58, 245-50, 327-48; *Pastoral care before the parish*, ed John Blair and Richard Sharpe (Leicester 1992) especially chapters 6 (by Alan Thacker), 7 (by Sarah Foot) and 8 (by Catherine Cubitt).

expressed itself primarily through communal actions, gestures, singing and hearing. Books were indeed used in liturgical ceremonies: but in these, ideally, books were used to help the memory to recall already-familiar texts. One of the aims of monastic education, in fact, seems to have been to prepare people to do without the aid of books if necessary: monks were encouraged to get by heart not only the psalter, but even the scriptural lections which they might have to sing aloud in the night office. When a book was used in a solemn ceremony, its use is likely to have been to a large degree mnemonic: a memory aid for texts that had, ideally, been already committed to memory by the liturgical actors. In short, the liturgy made sacred texts part of communal life. In its reliance on gesture, song and memory, early medieval monastic culture was at one with its contemporary secular world, which, as Marc Bloch has shown, saw ceremonies and gestures (such as the ceremony of allegiance) as the primary records of social agreements, and the actual manuscript charters recording such acts as secondary aids to memory.[6]

The monastic communities which used the Book of Kells are likely to have been familiar, at least by hearsay and perhaps even by practice, with a striking set of lenten ceremonies in which the gospels were 'presented' symbolically to a largely illiterate audience.[7] From its opening words, the ceremony of the handing on of the gospels was known as the 'opening of the ears' (*Apertio aurium*). The ceremony took place during the fourth week of Lent, just two weeks before Holy Week in which the Passion was commemorated. This was the third and most important of seven scrutinies. Scrutinies were ceremonies in which the catechumens, preparing for baptism on the Easter vigil, were exorcised of evil spirits and instructed in the rudiments of their faith. In the *Apertio aurium* ceremony, the catechumens were asked to come forward (if those to be baptised were babies they were carried in the arms of their sponsors). Two lections were read first. The first emphasized the importance of conversion (Isaiah 55:2-7: 'All you that thirst, come to the waters'). The second, an assemblage of short texts from St Paul, drove home that it was necessary to put off the old man and put on the new (Colossians 3:9-10), and that the gospel has been preached to the ends of the earth (Romans 10:18).[8]

---

[6]See the Rule of St Benedict, 10:2 '*memoriter dicatur*', Fry (note 3 above) 204-05; 13:11 '*lectio una … memoriter recitanda*', Fry (note 3 above) 208-09; Marc Bloch, *Feudal Society*, 2 vols (London 1971) I, 72-87, 145-47. On the importance of memory in medieval culture, see now Mary J Carruthers, *The book of memory: a study of memory in medieval culture* (Cambridge 1990).

[7]The classic introduction to the *Apertio aurium* ceremony is still Pierre de Puniet, 'Apertio aurium', DACL, I, part 2 (1924) cols 2523-37. On the lenten catechumenate in general, see Thierry Maertens, *Histoire et pastorale du rituel du catéchuménat et du baptême*, Paroisse et liturgie 56 (Bruges 1962).

[8]Andrieu, *Ordo XI*, nos 42-3, II, 427-8. The ceremony is translated in E C Whitaker, *Documents of the baptismal liturgy*, 2nd edn (London 1970) 172-74 (Gelasian sacramentary), 199-201 (*Ordo XI*), 204-06 (Bobbio Missal). In a paper on the Roman Liturgy and the Ruthwell Cross, delivered at the Conference of the International Society of Anglo-Saxonists at Cambridge, in August 1985, I argued for the relevance of the *Apertio aurium* ceremony to insular gospel books as well as to Ruthwell. Dr Patrick Sims-Williams told me afterwards, in private conversation, that he had

Then four deacons came forth from the sacristy, each carrying a gospel book (*cum quattuor libris evangeliorum*). At this early period, the sacristy or private vesting-hall (*sacrarium, secretarium*) usually stood near the entrance door (either inside the church or outside it, in the atrium); in such churches, the deacons would have had to proceed the length of the nave.[9] They came in a solemn procession, headed by clerics carrying two candles, thuribles and incense. They placed the four gospel books on the four corners of the altar. The celebrant first briefly instructed the catechumens on what a gospel is: it is defined as 'the divine actions' (*id est gesta divina*) and as good tidings, which always is an annunciation of our Lord Jesus Christ: *bona adnuntiatio quae utique adnuntiatio est Jesu Christi domini nostri*. Then the four beasts of Ezechiel's vision (Ezechiel 1:10) were described, and their relation to the four evangelists explained. The first emphasis of the ceremony was therefore on the unity of the gospels, and on the centrality of Christ and his actions to their meaning.[10]

independently made the same suggestion in a review of Kathleen Hughes, *Celtic Britain in the early middle ages*, in *Journal of Ecclesiastical History* 36 (1985) 306-09 (p 308). As far as I am aware, Dr Sims-Williams was the first to suggest in print the relevance of the *Apertio aurium* ceremony to insular art; see now his *Religion and literature in western England, 600-800* (Cambridge 1990) 293-95. I have examined the relevance of the ceremony to some Northumbrian monuments: 'A liturgical interpretation of the Bewcastle Cross' in *Medieval literature and antiquities: studies in honour of Basil Cottle*, ed Myra Stokes, Tom Burton (Woodbridge, Suffolk and Wolfeboro, NH 1987) 15-42 and pls I-IV (pp 20-24); and 'The Ruthwell crucifixion poem in its iconographic and liturgical contexts', *Peritia* 6-7 (1987-88) 1-71, pls 1-3 (pp 46-8).

[9]Jungmann, I, 320 and, for the later positioning of the sacristy close to the choir and altar (from the Romanesque period), I, 268-71; see also Pierre Batiffol, *Leçons sur la Messe* (Paris 1927) 71; E G Cuthbert F Atchley, *Ordo Romanus Primus*, Library of liturgiology and ecclesiology for English readers 6 (London 1905) 23. The *secretarium* or *sacrarium* was, as well as a hall for vesting, often a reception hall (thus sometimes called also *salutatorium*). It was capable of being closed off, and was sometimes of considerable size. The regular positioning of the sacristy or vesting hall at the entrance of a basilica, ie at the western end of an oriented church, provides an interesting context for the statement in the Annals of Ulster at AD 1007 that 'The Great Gospel of Colum Cille was wickedly stolen by night from the western sacristy [*asind airdom iartharach*] in the great stone church at Cenannas' (see Bernard Meehan, 'The history of the manuscript' in *Kells commentary*, 317-19). The word *airdam, airdom* was 'variously applied to any extraneous building attached to a larger one, *vestibule, porch*, etc' (*DIL*, sv. *airdam*). *Airdam* or *airdom* is made up of two elements, the prepositional prefix *air* 'before, in front of', and the noun *dom* (Lat. *domus*?) 'house, hall, church' (cf *DIL* svv. *air, dom*). It would be a suitable term for a vesting hall at the entrance to a church, ie for an insular analogue of the Roman *sacrarium, secretarium* or *salutatorium*. It is clear that *airdom* refers to a room-like structure 'attached to the main structure of the church'; and it is therefore possible that the *airdom* of the Annals of Ulster might refer to 'a chapel attached to the main structure of the church in which the relics, including the Gospel Book of Columba, were kept' (Paul Meyvaert, 'The Book of Kells and Iona,' *Art Bulletin* 71 (1989) 6-19 (p 11 n 22)). But as the western position of the *airdom* is specified in the annals, and as liturgical manuscripts (in their book shrines) were regularly stored with liturgical vestments and liturgical vessels, as in the *vestiarium* of the Lateran (see below, p 414), it is also possible that 'sacristy-cum-treasury' gives a better idea than 'chapel' of the use of the *airdom iartharach* at Kells. I am grateful to my colleagues Jennifer O'Reilly, who reminded me of the Annals of Ulster account, and Seán Ó Coileáin who helped me with the etymology and meaning of *airdam*.

[10]Andrieu, *Ordo XI*, nos 44-45, II, 428-29. The fact that the processions in which gospel books were borne, here and in *Ordo I* (discussed below) were headed by two clerics bearing candles is symbolically significant. In Roman secular ceremonial, it

Next, the individuality of each gospel was emphasized. A deacon took the gospel book from the front left hand corner of the altar and went in solemn procession (again preceded by the candles and thuribles) to the ambo or pulpit, which he ascended. He began *Initium sancti evangelii secundum Matheum*, and recited the first twenty-two verses of Matthew's gospel. Then a subdeacon solemnly received the book from the deacon and, carrying it reverently on a linen cloth (*super linteum*), brought it back to the sacristy. If the sacristy was situated near the entrance door, the subdeacon would have had to bring the gospel book back down the length of the nave: the congregation would have had plenty of opportunity to look at the book at this point. When the book had been carried out of sight, the celebrant recited a brief homily explaining why Matthew's symbol should be the figure of a man. Then the deacon took the gospel book, open at the beginning of Mark's gospel, from the rear left hand corner of the altar, brought it in procession to the ambo, and again recited *Initium sancti evangelii secundum Marcum* (Mark 1:1-8). When the gospel book had been brought back down the nave to the sacristy, the priest recited a brief homily explaining Mark's symbol, the lion. The same procedure was followed for Luke and John.[11] By the end of the ceremony, when all four gospel symbols had been explained, the four gospel books had been removed from the altar and brought down the nave to the sacristy; the congregation were left with the image of the altar itself. The overwhelming visual effect of the ceremony must have been to associate the four gospel books with the altar, and so to drive home the words of the opening homily, that all four gospels announce the same truth: Christ, known through his incarnation and actions. The ceremony concentrated the attention of the onlookers first on the gospel books and then gradually on the altar itself. This visual progression is analogous to the structure of the mass, which began with readings from scripture and the gospels, and ended with the eucharistic sacrifice, celebrated on the altar. After the symbolic 'handing on' of the gospels, the *Apertio aurium* ceremony then proceeded with the symbolic handing on of the creed and the 'Our Father' (ie they were explained to the catechumens by the celebrant, who again recited prescribed homilies). The catechumens were then commanded to retire from the church. *Ordo* XI, which envisages a ceremony of infant baptism, specifies that the parents were to go outside with their children, give the children into the care of others (*in custodia*), and then re-enter the church with the sponsors (who were to receive the children from the font) to offer their gifts at the offertory of the mass. The children remained under care outside until mass, '*missarum sollemnia*', was finished.[12] It is particularly interesting that the *Apertio aurium* ceremony, which in its *Traditio evangeliorum* used a dramatic structure analogous to the mass, culminated in a celebration of the mass itself. The relationship which

---

was customary to honour the official portraits (icons) of emperors by flanking the portraits with candles; see Jungmann, I, 68-69 and note 7 above; and Pierre Batiffol, *Études de liturgie et d'archéologie chrétienne* (Paris 1919) 210-13. The gospels, which provided the directly inspired image of Christ, were given the same symbolic honour as the icons.

[11]Andrieu, *Ordo* XI, nos 46-50, II, 429-33.

[12]For '*missarum sollemnia*', Andrieu, *Ordo* XI, no 74, II, 441.

the *Traditio evangeliorum* ceremony established between the gospel books and the altar must have been easy for the adult congregation to appreciate. The *Traditio evangeliorum* and the mass both focused the attention of the congregation on the same altar; and the altar was seen as a multivalent symbol: of Christ, of his sufferings and sacrifice and that of the martyrs, and of the hearts of the congregation who offered the mass.[13]

When new, the Book of Kells itself may, like many insular gospel books, have had in its prefatory material the extract from Jerome's commentary on Matthew, *Plures fuisse*, which briefly explains the evangelist symbols.[14] But such prefatory material was for learned readers. The importance of the *Apertio aurium* ceremony is that it provided even the illiterate with a public dramatisation of such learned traditions. The existence of the *Apertio aurium* ceremony makes it clear that an interest in the symbolism of the evangelists and their beasts was by no means confined to the learned. On the contrary, it is evident that the evangelist symbols were used to instruct the illiterate in the basic facts (a) that each gospel had its own individuality and (b) that all four together made Christ present, in a way analogous to the way he was present in the mass itself. It is clear that such ceremonies were enacted not just for the catechumens but for their parents, sponsors, relations and the whole congregation (this was particularly true in the case of infant baptism). If the gospel books (each open at the beginning of the appropriate gospel) which were carried to the altar for the *Apertio aurium* ceremony happened to be equipped with full-page miniatures of the evangelist symbols (each at the beginning of the appropriate gospel), this would have been a most practical way to prepare the congregation in advance for the actions and spoken words of the ceremony. The congregation would have had ample time to gaze on such brightly coloured symbols: as they were carried in procession with candles and incense at the beginning of the ceremony, perhaps as they lay on the altar, and particularly as the books were carried back to the sacristy (if the *sacrarium* was at or near the back of the church). Only after the congregation had several opportunities of contemplating each symbol, and of appreciating the honour with which the relevant gospel book was carried and chanted by the clerics, did the celebrant explain the significance of the relationship between the symbol and its book. The ceremony, like most liturgical ceremonies, operated first of all at the level of dramatic sense-experience (solemn processions and actions, visual images and chant); only secondarily were the actions, images and chants supplemented by verbal explanation.[15] The existence of the *Apertio aurium*

---

[13]*Lexikon der christlichen Ikonographie*, ed Engelbert Kirschbaum, Wolfgang Braunfels, 8 vols (Freiburg-im-Breisgau 1968-74) I, 106-7, under 'Altar'; Olivier Rousseau, 'Le Christ et l'autel: note sur la tradition patristique', *La Maison-Dieu* 29 (1952) 32-39; Joseph Schmitt, '*Petra autem erat Christus*', *La Maison-Dieu* 29 (1952) 18-31.
[14]McGurk, 'Texts', 37; Henry, 153.
[15]It is relevant to ask, and difficult to answer, the question: when and where were the Latin homilies prescribed for the ceremony (the explanation of the evangelist symbols, Creed and Pater Noster, which de Puniet sees as possibly the work of Pope Leo I), paraphrased for insular congregations in their vernaculars? The Latin homilies are critically edited by Pierre de Puniet, 'Les trois homélies catéchètiques du sacramentaire gélasien pour la tradition des évangiles, du symbole, et de

ceremony is important evidence that the custom of equipping gospel books with evangelist symbols is unlikely to have been simply a learned custom familiar to monks who meditated on books. At times, a gospel book may have been intended for use in the catechumenal scrutinies themselves. Even when there was no such practical intention, provision of gospel symbols may have been intended as a reminder of the heroic ages of christian evangelisation, a reminiscence or citation of the beautiful ceremony (*pulcher ac salubris*) in which gospels were symbolically handed on even to the illiterate, who for the rest of their lives, as christians, would hear them read or chanted at mass.[16]

Such books as the Lindisfarne Gospels or the Echternach Gospels, with their full-page evangelist symbols, would have been suitable for use in an *Apertio aurium* ceremony. The *ordines* quoted above describe an ideal ceremony, based on the ceremonies of a large episcopal city like Rome itself, in which four gospel books were available. But early medieval *ordines* were primarily descriptive, not prescriptive. They described a real ceremony, usually at Rome, or an ideal ceremony, usually based on or adapted from ceremonies at Rome. But it was presumed that these ceremonies could be adapted, radically at times, to suit local circumstances and the means available.[17] It would have been easy to perform the ceremony with only one book like the Lindisfarne or Echternach Gospels (bound or unbound). An unbound gospel book could have been carried out in procession as four separate booklets, each containing a gospel. Even if the book was bound, the celebrant or an assistant could have opened the gospel book, in turn, at each of the four evangelist symbols at the *incipits* of the individual gospels. The Book of Durrow (folio 2r) also contains a single page in which all four evangelist symbols appear: they fill the four quarters of the page, and the

l'oraison dominicale', *Revue d'histoire ecclésiastique* 5 (1904) 505-21 and 755-86; 6 (1905) 15-32 and 304-18.

[16]Bede, who twice describes the ceremony, each time refers to it as beautiful: '*pulcher*' in *Bedae Venerabilis opera*, Part II, *Opera exegetica*, 24, *De Tabernaculo* II, lines 1849-55, CCSL 119A, ed D Hurst (Turhout 1969) 89; '*pulcherque ac salubris*', *In Ezram et Neemiam* II, lines 924-27, CCSL 119A, 310-11. The ceremony of the *Apertio aurium* poses the problem of the Latin liturgy in general. How was it experienced by an illiterate audience whose speech was not based on or descended from Latin? Were its homilies paraphrased in the vernacular in insular ceremonies? How did illiterate audiences respond to the Latin mass? For discussions of the long-term effects of holding to Latin as a liturgical language in early medieval Europe, see Jungmann, I, 81-92; Angelus Albert Häussling, *Mönchskonvent und Eucharistiefeier: eine Studie über die Messe in der Abendländischen Klosterliturgie des frühen Mittelalters und zur Geschichte der Messhäufigkeit*, Liturgiewissenschaftliche Quellen und Forschungen 58 (Münster, Westfalen 1973) 251-55, 268-71.

[17]The classic account of the descriptive (rather than prescriptive) nature of early medieval *ordines* is Andrieu's introduction to the genre, II, pp xvii-xlix: see especially pp xxvi-xxix, xxxi-xxxiii, on the primary importance of oral tradition, of the personal experience of the cleric who had 'been there' (at Rome, some other cathedral city, or some great monastery) and could report the order of their ceremonies. The individual community then had to make their own of this reported tradition. Written *ordines* were often makeshift documents, secondary records of the living liturgical tradition which was the primary authority. See also the important discussion of how early medieval notions of 'copying' left an individual community free to 'cite' a model while adapting it to their own requirements, in Häussling (note 16 above) 102-07.

page is divided into four by an elaborate cross.[18] While presenting all four evangelist symbols, the page subordinates them to the cross, a symbol of Christ's sacrifice (re-enacted at the altar at mass). The Four Symbols pages are visual equivalents of the statement at the beginning of the *Traditio evangeliorum* ceremony that the gospels are a *bona adnuntiatio, quae utique adnuntiatio est Jesu Christi domini nostri*.

It is not impossible that the Lindisfarne or Echternach Gospels were intended for use in an actual *Apertio aurium* ceremony; there were plenty of adult pagans to be converted, in Frisia and Saxony and perhaps even in Northumbria, in the early eighth century; and when infant baptism was the rule, the sponsors, parents and congregation needed yearly reminders, in Lent, of what the gospels were about. The *ordines* make it quite clear that the ceremony continued to be performed in an established christian society where infant baptism was the rule. But it is also possible that in monastic *scriptoria* gospel books may have been provided with evangelist symbols, not for practical use, but rather to emphasize the 'great ancestry' of such a work by citing or referring throughout the book to what was thought to be ancient liturgical tradition.[19] This may account for the way in which, in the Book of Durrow, Mark's gospel is preceded by an eagle (folio 84v), and John's gospel by a lion (folio 191v). Such anomalies may have been preserved or tolerated if the intention was simply to cite or refer to the *Apertio aurium* ceremony in a gospel book, not to perform the ceremony using that book.[20] The 'ancient custom' of the *Apertio aurium* was described, not merely in collections of *ordines*, but in manuscripts of the celebrant's

---

[18]On the origins of the four symbols tradition, see Martin Werner, 'The four evangelist symbols page in the Book of Durrow', *Gesta* 8 (1969) 3-17; Laurence Nees, 'A fifth-century book cover and the origin of the four evangelist symbols pages in the Book of Durrow', *Gesta* 17 (1978) 3-8; Martin Werner, 'The Durrow four evangelist symbols page once again', *Gesta* 20 (1981) 23-33.

[19]Bede stresses the antiquity of the ceremony, *mos antiquitus: De Tabernaculo* (note 16 above). But De Puniet (*Apertio aurium*, cols 2528-29) argues convincingly that it replaced a different rite in the course of the sixth century. The earliest written reference to the rite (and this reference is brief and inconclusive) is by Gregory the Great, in a letter written in 601 (PL 77, col 1146). Bede, in the passages already referred to, provides the earliest unambiguous evidence of knowledge of the ceremony.

[20]Alexander, *Insular manuscripts*, favours the theory that the Durrow artist followed the order of equivalence proposed by St Irenaeus of Lyons (c130-200) (p 31). Henderson (p 24) adds that Irenaeus's identifications were copied by the fourth-century Spanish writer Juvencus, whose poetry was known in Ireland (it is quoted in the Macregol Gospels, Oxford, Bodleian Library, MS Auct. D.2.19). Such an equivalence would have been highly unusual in seventh-century Northumbria. Bede was sharply criticized, and replied sharply to the criticism, when in his commentary on the Apocalypse (PL 93:144), he followed Augustine in identifying the lion with Matthew and the man with Mark. A Northumbrian bishop, like Acca of Hexham, might be expected to be uneasy at divergence from the Roman tradition (even when the authority for the divergence was Augustine) if it was not merely a learned tradition but had been enshrined, through the *Apertio aurium* ceremony, in the Roman liturgy of the catechumenate. See Acca's letter to Bede, prefaced to Bede's *In Lucae evangelium expositio, Bedae Venerabilis opera*, Part II, *Opera exegetica*, 3, CCSL 120, ed D Hurst (Turnhout 1960) 6, and Bede's lengthy and irritated defence of his suggestion (pp 7-10). Perhaps Durrow was produced at an Irish monastery which may have heard of, but did not practice, the *Apertio aurium*.

own liturgical book, the sacramentary.[21] The purpose of a sacramentary was to record the prayers that a celebrant should recite at mass; the frequent occurrence of detailed directions for this ceremony in sacramentaries is a striking example of the importance which the ceremony, and the catechumenate in general, was still felt to have in the eighth and ninth centuries. It seems inconceivable that great Columban monasteries like Kells or Iona would not know of such a ceremony (whether or not they actually administered catechumenal ceremonies) as it is described not only in Roman sacramentaries and *ordines* but in the *Gallicanum Vetus* and in the Sacramentary of Bobbio.[22]

The Book of Kells is not designed for practical liturgical use in the *Apertio aurium* ceremony. Kells completely avoids the full page representations of evangelist symbols found in Durrow, Echternach and other gospel books. In the two evangelist portraits in Kells (St Matthew, folio 28v, and St John, folio 291v) these evangelists are represented as human figures, not as evangelist symbols, nor with their own symbolic 'beasts'. On the other hand, Kells has no fewer than three elaborate Four Symbols pages (preceding the gospel of Matthew, folio 27v, of Mark, folio 129v, and of John, folio 290v). In the Four Symbols pages preceding Matthew and Mark the symbols are unified around elaborate crosses; in the Four Symbols page preceding John the symbols are unified by an elaborate Chi-symbol (or St Andrew's Cross). The letter Chi was, like the Cross itself, an important symbol of Christ, separately elaborated on folio 34r of the Book of Kells.[23] As well as these elaborate Four Symbols pages, some or all of the evangelist symbols are combined in various ways in several of the canon-tables pages (folios 1r-5r), and on the final text page of St Mark's gospel (folio 187v). It is as if the designers of Kells wished throughout their book to refer to the ancient liturgical tradition of the *Apertio aurium*, with its emphasis on the individuality and unity of the gospels as symbols of Christ, but that they never intended their book to be actually used in such a ceremony. Such an indirect and symbolic, rather than a practical, use of the tradition may be a sign that Kells comes from a more developed monastic culture than, say, Lindisfarne or Echternach. It is after all not in a monastic setting *per se*, but in the early stages of the christianisation of a culture, that evangelisation is an urgent priority. To take the analogy of Anglo-Saxon sculpture: it is not at Monkwearmouth-Jarrow, Lindisfarne, nor even Hexham that the most extended surviving programme of early Northumbrian iconography is found, but at Ruthwell (730-750?), possibly a small monastery in territory that had only recently come into Anglo-Saxon hands. The programme of the

---

[21]In Roman Gelasian sacramentaries, the ceremony is found both in the Old Gelasian and in the Gelasians of the eighth century (eg the sacramentaries of Gellone and Angoulême. The ceremony appears also in the so-called Pontifical of Poitiers, from the Paris region, *c*900). Among Gallican sacramentaries, it is found in the *Missale Gallicanum Vetus* and the Sacramentary of Bobbio. De Puniet (note 7 above) col 2523, gives a comprehensive list.

[22]See De Puniet (note 7 above).

[23]See Suzanne Lewis, 'Sacred calligraphy: the Chi Rho page in the Book of Kells', *Traditio* 36 (1980) 139-59.

Ruthwell Cross makes unmistakable references to the Roman ceremonies of catechumenate and public penance found in the early eighth-century Roman books. The Ruthwell programme culminated precisely in four separate but related images of the evangelists, each evangelist duly presented in a separate small panel, matched with his appropriate beast, probably surrounding a head-and-shoulders bust of Christ, or a roundel representing the Agnus Dei.[24]

Other ways in which a precious gospel book could form part of liturgical action are to be seen in the *Ordo Romanus Primus*.[25] This account of the solemn stational mass describes how the Eucharist was celebrated (cAD 700) by the pope in Rome. But from the seventh to the ninth centuries there was great interest throughout Europe, in Ireland as well as in Northumbria, in the lavish ceremonies of the city of Rome.[26] The earliest documented and precisely dated pilgrimage to Rome by Irish clerics, the delegates from the Synod of Mágh Léine (from the southern half of Ireland) who were at Rome in Easter 631, provides first-hand evidence of the impression made on these Irishmen by the city, by its pilgrims from East and West, and by its basilicas and relics. The delegates were appealing to 'the chief of cities' (*ad capud urbium*), 'as children to their mother' (*uelud natos ad matrem*) for a ruling on the Easter controversy. They stayed in a hospice in the precincts of St Peter's on the Vatican.[27] The hospice housed pilgrims from several nations, and the unanimity of these pilgrims on the question of the date of Easter impressed the Irish delegates with the catholicity of the Roman method of reckoning Easter. It is clear that their visit to Rome confirmed, by actual experience,

---

[24]See Rosemary Cramp, 'The evangelist symbols and their parallels in Anglo-Saxon sculpture' in Robert T Farrell, *Bede and Anglo-Saxon England*, British Archaeological Reports, British series 46 (Oxford 1978) 118-30; and Ó Carragáin, 'Ruthwell crucifixion poem' (note 8 above) 42-50.

[25]Andrieu, II, 65-108; English translation and commentary in Atchley (note 9 above). There are good summaries of the ceremonies of *Ordo Romanus primus* in Jungmann (note 4 above) I, 67-74, 'The Roman stational services in the seventh century', and in Batiffol (note 9 above) 65-99, 'Le cérémonial de l'Ordo Romanus I'.

[26]It is important once more to stress that an interest in 'imitating Rome' did not by any means imply, in this early period, an ultramontane attitude to the liturgy. Such an interest could coexist happily with a desire to adapt Roman customs radically to suit local circumstances, and a care to preserve and develop local traditions within the same liturgy. See the remarks of Jungman, I, 67: 'The effect of this example (*Ordo Romanus primus*) would be felt in the divine service of every village church and would even touch the ceremonial of low Mass'; Batiffol (note 9 above) 98-99; the references on liturgical imitation, (above, p 404), and the references in note 17.

[27]Cummian's letter 'De Controversia paschali', ed Maura Walsh, Dáibhí Ó Cróinín, *Together with a related Irish computistical tract 'De Ratione conputandi'*, ed Dáibhí Ó Cróinín, Studies and Texts 86 (Toronto 1988) 92-95. On early pilgrim hospices in the precincts of St Peter's, see Louis Reekmans, 'Le développement topographique de la région du Vatican à la fin de l'antiquité et au début du moyen âge (300-850)' in *Mélanges d'archéologie et d'histoire de l'art offerts au professeur Jacques Lavalleye*, Université de Louvain, Recueil de travaux d'histoire et de philologie, 4e série, fascicule 45 (Louvain 1970) 197-235. Cummian's impression, that the hospice was situated 'in aecclesia sancti Petri', was probably not very misleading: we know that dwellings for clerics were built even in the shadow of St Peter's. Pope Sergius I, cAD 700, repaired the lodgings (*cubicula*) which had been damaged by rain and by fragments falling from the roof of the basilica (Reekmans, 217).

oral accounts of the city and its traditions with which these clerics were already familiar:

> And they saw all things just as they had heard about them, but they found them more certain in as much as they were seen rather than heard. And they were in one lodging in the church of St. Peter [*in uno hospicio … in aecclesia sancti Petri*] with a Greek, a Hebrew, a Scythian and an Egyptian at the same time at Easter, in which we differed by a whole month. And so they testified to us before the holy relics [*et ante sancta sic testati sunt nostris*],[28] saying 'As far as we know, this Easter is celebrated throughout the whole world.' And we have tested that the power of God is in the relics of the holy martyrs and in the writings which they brought back. We saw with our own eyes a totally blind girl opening her eyes at these relics, and a paralytic walking and many demons cast out [*Et nos in reliquiis sanctorum martyrum et scripturis quas attulerunt probauimus inesse uirtutem Dei. Uidimus oculis nostris puellam caecam omnino ad has reliquias oculos aperientem, et paraliticum ambulantem, et multa demonia eiecta*].[29]

The Irish delegates were as careful to bring back relics as they were to bring back written books. Cummian establishes a close association between the relics and the written books (*scripturis*: the word could refer to books of Holy Scripture, as well as to other books such as computistical writings). Cummian specifies that miracles took place in the presence of the relics (*ad has reliquias*), in order to demonstrate that both forms of evidence brought from Rome, writings and relics, embody the power of God (*inesse uirtutem Dei*). In order to heighten the sense that everything to do with the Roman experience of the delegates embodied the power of God, Cummian describes the miracles in a cumulative series (the blind see, the lame walk, and demons are cast out). The series is clearly intended to recall the Lucan account of how Jesus himself directed the followers of John the Baptist to list for John the signs that the Kingdom of God was now present:

> And when the men had come to him, they said, 'John the Baptist has sent us to you, saying, "Are you he who is to come, or shall we look for another?"' In that hour he cured many of diseases and plagues and evil spirits, and on many that were blind he bestowed sight. And he answered them, 'Go and tell John what you have seen and heard: the

---

[28]I would translate *nostris* as 'our people', 'our delegates' (certainly not 'us'). The phrase *ante sancta* may mean that the delegates, anxious to have the most weighty testimony, persuaded their fellow-pilgrims to attest solemnly to their Easter traditions at the *martyrium*, the burial place of St Peter, in the basilica itself. Alternatively, it may mean that they got the pilgrims to attest on eucharistic species preserved outside mass. The term *sancta* was sometimes applied to eucharistic species, seen as the relic *par excellence* of Christ's presence with the Church: see Jungmann, I, 70, n11, II, 307-21; Batiffol (note 9 above) 90-93; Atchley (note 9 above) 106-09; De Lubac (note 4 above) 26, 66; Nathan Mitchell, *Cult and controversy: the worship of the Eucharist outside mass* (New York 1982) 56-61. On the Eucharist as relic, see also Häussling (note 16 above) 251-55; Mitchell, 108-09.

[29]Ó Cróinín and Walsh (note 27 above) 92-95.

blind receive their sight, the lame walk, lepers are cleansed, and the deaf hear, the dead are raised up, the poor have the good news preached to them. And blessed is he who takes no offence at me'.[30]

Cummian's implication is clear. Those who reject the Roman writings reject the Roman relics; but the miracles, performed at the Roman relics back in Ireland, demonstrate that to reject either Roman tradition would be to reject manifest signs of the presence in both traditions of the power of the Kingdom of God.

Granted such attitudes to Rome, it was natural that the liturgy performed in *caput urbium* should become an inspiration for a whole variety of liturgies throughout Europe. Roman ceremonies were carefully recorded, not that they should be copied to the letter, but so that they could be used as models on which local ceremonies could be freely developed. For example, the Irish Stowe Missal proclaims that its prayers for mass are *Orationes et preces misae aeclesiae romane*, and that its canon of the mass is *Canón dominicus papae Gilasi*.[31] The so-called *Vita prima* of St Brigit provides further striking evidence of such interest in eighth-century Ireland:

Another day also a holy man came to the house where Brigit was praying alone and found her standing with her hands outstretched to heaven in prayer and she did not see or hear anything else. At the same time the residents of the place could be heard making a great din, for the calves had just then rushed to the cows, but the saint, intent on God in an ecstasy of spirit, heard nothing. Then the man left her for the time being. But he came back to her at a different time and said to her, 'Holy one of God, why didn't you run when the people were shouting?' And she said, 'But I didn't hear the shouting'.
The man said to her, 'What did you hear instead?' Brigit replied, 'I heard masses in Rome at the tombs of Sts Peter and Paul and it is my earnest wish that the order of this mass and of the universal rule be brought to me'.
Then saint Brigit sent experts to Rome and from there they brought the masses and the rule. Again after some time she said to the men, 'I discern that certain things have been changed in the mass in Rome since you returned from there. Go back again'. And they went and brought it back as they had found it.[32]

---

[30]Luke 7:20-23; Cummian seems to have been thinking of the Lucan text, which includes all the elements of Cummian's passage (including the casting out of demons, 'he cured ... evil spirits', Luke 7:21), rather than the shorter parallel passage in Matthew 11:1-6, which has no reference to demons. Both Luke and Matthew are referring to such messianic images as Isaiah 35:5-6, 29:18-19 and 61:1.

[31]Warner (note 4 above) II, 5, 10. For some early Roman influences on the Stowe Missal, see Klaus Gamber, 'Die irischen Messlibelli als Zeugnis für die frühe römische Liturgie', *Römische Quartalschrift* 62 (1967) 214-21.

[32]*Vita prima*, ch 90: trans Seán Connolly, 'Vita prima Sanctae Brigitae: background and historical value', *JRSAI* 119 (1989) 5-49 (p 41).

I quote the last two sections of the chapter in the original Latin from Dr Seán Connolly's forthcoming edition of the *Vita prima*:

4 *Dixit ei uir ille: 'Quid aliud audisti?' Respondit Brigita: 'In urbe Roma iuxta reliquias sancti Petri et Pauli audiui missas et nimis desidero ut ad me ordo missae istius et uniuerse regule deferatur'.*
5 *Tunc misit Brigita uiros sapientes ad Romam et detulerunt inde missas et regulam. Item post aliquantum tempus dixit Brigita ad illos uiros: 'Ego sentio quod quaedam commutata sunt in Roma in missa postquam uenistis ab ea. Exite iterum'. At illi exierunt et detulerunt ut inuenerunt.*[33]

There are a number of striking features in this passage. The saint, rapt in prayer, experiences a divinely inspired vision of the mass at St Peter's on the Vatican, and possibly of St Paul's outside the walls.[34] Her first reaction is to want to have a copy of the order of celebrating this mass; it is associated by the hagiographer with the 'order of the universal rule'.[35] Wise men go to Rome, presumably to record (perhaps in writing: *detulerunt inde*) the words and actions of the Roman ceremonies (*ordo missae istius ... [ordo] uniuerse regule: ordo, ordines* were accounts, which could be oral or written, of the 'order', or directions for the production, of liturgical actions; the words of the ceremonies would be recorded in a variety of other books, such as antiphonaries, lectionaries, sacramentaries). The wise men of Kildare have themselves to go to Rome, because at this stage neumed musical notation had not been invented in the monasteries of the West, and liturgical music had to be learned by the direct method, from imitation of a trained singer.[36]

---

[33]I am very grateful to Dr Connolly for allowing me to publish this extract from his forthcoming edition of the *Vita prima*. Dr Connolly dates the *Vita prima* to about 750, and assigns its provenance to the territory of the Southern Uí Néill in the Clonard-Ardbraccan areas (note 32 above, pp 6-7). An uncritical text of the Latin life may be found in *Acta Sanctorum*, Februarii, I, 118-36 (the Rome-vision episode is in Caput XV, p 131).

[34]In the canon of the Roman mass, the names Peter and Paul were linked in the *Communicantes* prayer, the memento of the living; the liturgical commemoration of one of the pair regularly involved the commemoration of the other (eg the feast of St Peter on 29 June; of St Paul on 30 June): see V L Kennedy, *The saints of the canon of the mass*, Studi di Antichità cristiana 14, 2nd edn (Rome 1963) 30, 69, 101-11. In his phrase *iuxta reliquias sancti Petri et Pauli* the hagiographer may have had no more specific topographical details in mind than 'at the shrines of the two chief saints of Rome'.

[35]The phrase *ordo ... uniuerse regule* is reminiscent of a phrase used in the earliest *Vita* of St Wilfrid when it describes his first visit to Rome in 654: his Roman friend Boniface, archdeacon of the city, taught him a perfect knowledge of the four gospels, of the Easter computus (*paschalem rationem*) which the British and Irish schismatics did not know, and 'many other rules of ecclesiastical discipline' (*et alias multas ecclesiasticae disciplinae regulas*). In both *Vitae* the contexts suggest that the *regulas* included liturgical traditions; but both *Vitae* may also have wider ecclesiastical regulations in mind.

[36]The date of the invention of neums, and their spread from Francia to the rest of Europe, is much debated among musicologists. At present the issue seems to lie between two theories: (a) the early dating (770-850): that neums were invented in the latter half of the eighth century in Francia, and spread slowly in the great Carolingian monasteries as a means for ensuring the standardization of chant required by the emperor; or (b) the late dating (850-950): oral tradition reigned supreme until a century later; the use of neums spread very slowly from the latter half of ninth century, spreading widely only in the tenth. For a good defense of the

But soon after they return they have to set out a second time: the saint is aware that the Roman mass is developing fast, and wants her monastery to be kept up to date with it. She therefore commands them to prepare a new edition incorporating the latest developments (they have to travel to Rome again, because while words could be copied and brought by junior messengers, complex music and production techniques had to be learned orally at first hand).[37]

This passage corresponds closely with a widespread attitude to Rome, in Francia and Northumbria as well as in the Irish centre that produced this *Vita*, between the years 650 and 750.[38] There was in all these countries a growing awareness that the Roman liturgy was changing fast and becoming more and more splendid, and that new chants were continually being introduced. Therefore repeated visits to Rome were necessary to keep up to date. There was a great curiosity about old and new Roman ceremonies, so that the splendid liturgy performed at the bodies of St Peter and St Paul could be imitated, emulated or adapted to local use (for in this period a lively interest in using features of the Roman liturgy could coexist happily with a confident attachment to local traditions). Where an actual pilgrimage to Rome was impossible, visions could in this period be granted to satisfy the frustrated pilgrim. The Irish vernacular life of St Berach, though later than the *Vita prima* of St Brigit, provides a remarkable parallel to St Brigit's visions of the Roman liturgy. The life of Berach also shows how it was possible to supplement and commemorate a vision of the Roman liturgy by the erection of a high cross dedicated to Saints Peter and Paul. It provides a fascinating example of an Irish monastery using art to effect a symbolic

---

early dating (*c*770-850), with a fine bibliography of the controversy, see Kenneth Levy, 'On gregorian orality', *Journal of the American musicological society* 43 (1990) 185-227. A good defense of the late dating theory can be found in Leo Treitler, 'Reading and singing: on the genesis of occidental musical writing', *Early music history* 4 (1984) 135-208. See also Michel Huglo, *Les livres de chant liturgique*, Typologie des sources du moyen âge occidental, fasc. 52 (Turnhout 1988) 48-51, 53-57, 60-82.

[37]Stephen J P van Dijk, 'The urban and papal rites in seventh and eighth-century Rome', *Sacris Erudiri* 12 (1961) 411-87 (pp 469-70), associates this awareness of swift liturgical change at Rome with the pontificate of Pope Vitalian (657-72); but the pace of liturgical change hardly lessened in the reign of Pope Sergius I (686-701), and still continued under Gregory II (715-31). The story could reflect the early eighth as well as the late seventh century.

[38]For relations between Northumbria and Rome in this period, see the bibliographical references in Ó Carragáin, 'Ruthwell crucifixion poem' (note 8 above) 18-22, 42-50. On contacts between Rome and Francia, see André Borias, 'Saint Wandrille et la crise monothélite', *Revue bénédictine* 97 (1987) 42-67; Theodor Klauser, 'Die liturgischen Austauschbeziehungen zwischen der römischen und der frankisch-deutschen Kirche, vom 8. bis 11. Jahrhundert', *Historiches Jahrbuch der Görresgesellschaft* 53 (1933) 169-89; Cyrille Vogel, 'Les échanges liturgiques entre Rome et les pays francs jusqu'à l'époque de Charlemagne' in *Le Chiese nei regni dell'Europa occidentale e i loro rapporti con Roma sino all'800. 7-13 Aprile, 1959*, Settimane di studio sull'alto medioevo 7, 2 vols (Spoleto 1960) I, 185-295, with discussion, I, 326-30; Cyrille Vogel, 'Saint Chrodegang et les débuts de la romanisation du culte en pays franc' in *Saint Chrodegang. Communications présentées au colloque tenu à Metz à l'occasion du douzième centenaire de sa mort* (Metz 1967) 91-110; Kassius Hallinger, 'Römische Voraussetzungen der bonifatianischen Wirksamkeit im Frankenreich' in *Sankt Bonifatius. Gedenkgabe zum zwölfhundertsten Todestag*, 2nd edn (Fulda 1954) 320-61.

imitatio Romae (were the two crosses wooden or stone? if stone, were they plain or with sculptural panels?). The whole episode is therefore relevant to the question, whether Roman ceremonies can be used as background material for the Book of Kells. It is particularly interesting to find Rome being symbolically 'imitated' in a monastery where actual pilgrimage to Rome was discouraged. Berach's attitude to Roman pilgrimage may even have resembled that of the poet who composed the famous quatrains, *Téicht doróim*:

> To go to Rome, much labour, little profit: the King whom thou seekest here, unless thou bring him with thee, thou findest him not. Much folly, much frenzy, much loss of sense, much madness (is it), since going to death is certain, to be under the displeasure of Mary's Son.[39]

As the life of Berach makes clear, an Irish monastic community could, by means of a monument, artistically 'imitate' Rome precisely in order to free the imaginations of members of the community from the seductions of Rome-pilgrimage. For a monastic community, only one pilgrimage really mattered, preparation for the journey forth from the body ('since going to death is certain'). Pilgrimage to Rome could be a distraction from this necessary concentration on the last things; and one way of combatting this distraction may well have been to provide symbolic substitutes for Rome -pilgrimage as in Berach's monastery; possibly combined with local adaptations of the Roman liturgy such as we find in the Stowe Missal. If this were done, then in all senses that really mattered, a monastery could claim to have Rome at home:

> On another occasion Colman Cáel (the lean) of Cluain Ingrech determined to go to Rome; he was a pupil of Berach, and it was Berach who appointed him to Cluain Ingrech. He went therefore to his tutor and master Berach. Berach tried to stop him from going, and could not. Colman Cáel set out, and Berach went a little way with him on the road [*sealat 'san slighidh*]. They met with Ciaran Máel (the Bald) at the end of the lawn [*i cind na faitce*]. And he and Berach tried once more to stop Colman Cáel from going. And Colman Cáel said that he would not rest till he should see Rome with his eyes [*na hanfadh no co ffaicedh dia suilibh in Roimh*]. Berach sained the air, and made the sign of the cross over Colmán's eyes; and they three, Berach and Colman Cáel, and Ciarán Máel, saw Rome, and praised the Lord in that place [*atconnncatar a ttriur ... inni Roimh, 7 ro molsatar an Coimde annsin*], and erected a cross and a mother church there to Berach, and to Ciaran Máel, and to Colman Cáel. And another cross was erected there to Paul and to Peter. And the visiting of those crosses is the same to any one as if he should go an equal distance of the road to Rome [*as ionann do neoch ionnsaigidh na*

---

[39]*Thesaurus palaeohibernicus: a collection of Old-Irish glosses, scholia, prose and verse*, ed Whitley Stokes, John Strachan, 2 vols (repr Dublin 1975) II, 296 (*Codex Boernerianus, Misc. Dresd. A. 145b*).

ccros sin 7 do imeochadh a coimhmeit do shligidh na Romha]. And (Berach) stopped Colman Cáel there.[40]

The interest of northern pilgrims in seeing and imitating the shrines of Rome became reflected in papal policy only from the early eighth century; imitation of the Roman liturgy only began to be actively encouraged by Pope Gregory II (715-31) and his successors. What was done in Rome had long been revered as the authentic tradition stemming from St Peter himself. But by the middle of the eighth century it was gradually coming to be seen as normative, a 'universal rule', not only in Bede's Northumbria or Boniface's Francia, but also (*c*750) apparently in the *Vita prima* of St Brigit. In his idea that the *ordo ... universe regule* is to be found in Rome, the author of the *Vita prima* was thinking in the ways his contemporaries throughout mid-eighth-century Europe were also beginning to think.[41]

Angelus Albert Häussling has demonstrated that the feature of the Roman liturgy which most impressed northern observers was the centrality to it of processional movement, between the different basilicas, *tituli* and *martyria* of the city. The papal liturgy involved a planned programme (which spanned the liturgical year but was particularly intensive in Lent and Holy Week) of processions to celebrate solemn mass at the various stational churches of the city. *Ordo Romanus Primus* provides striking evidence of how elaborate these processions were, and how important a feature of them were gospel books.[42] *Ordo I* describes in detail the papal procession to the

---

[40]Life of Berach, xxx, ed Charles Plummer, *Bethada náem nÉrenn; lives of Irish saints*, 2 vols (Oxford 1922) II, 41-42; extracts from the Irish text (recorded in the seventeenth century by O'Clery) supplied (in square brackets and italics) from I, 42. I am grateful to Dr Michael Ryan for this reference. Professor Pádraig Ó Riain has kindly informed me that this life is likely to have been redacted in the twelfth century, but that individual episodes may reflect earlier traditions. In the Latin life of Berach, the saint invites the unnamed monk who wishes to go on pilgrimage to Rome to fast and pray with him. After three days and nights, the monk tells Berach of a dream in which an angel, in appearance like a young man, conducted him to Rome, and so enabled him to fulfil his vow of pilgrimage: *Vitae Sanctorum Hiberniae*, ed Charles Plummer, 2 vols (Oxford 1910) I, 85-86, ch xxv. There is no mention of high crosses in this episode of the Latin life. Plummer calls this Latin life 'a late recension', and says that the Irish life 'is much fuller and more original than this degenerate Latin text' (I, p xxxiii; for useful comparative material on Irish attitudes to pilgrimage and on Irish interest in Rome, see I, pp cxxii-cxxiii).

[41]For early Irish attitudes to Rome, see John Ryan, 'The early Irish Church and the See of Peter' in *Le Chiese nei regni dell'Europa occidentale e i loro rapporti con Roma sino all'800. 7-13 Aprile, 1959*, Settimane di studio sull'alto medioevo 7, 2 vols (Spoleto 1960) II, 549-74, discussion, II, 583-91; Richard Sharpe, 'Armagh and Rome in the seventh century', and Charles Doherty, 'The use of relics in early Ireland', both in *Irland und Europa: Die Kirche im Frühmittelalter*, ed Próinséas Ní Chatháin, Michael Richter (Stuttgart 1984) respectively 58-72, 89-101.

[42]The best introduction to the importance of processions in the Roman liturgy is John Baldovin, *The urban character of christian worship. The origins, development, and meaning of stational liturgy*, Orientalia christiana analecta 228 (Rome 1987) 105-67. See also G G Willis, 'Roman stational liturgy' in his *Further essays in early Roman liturgy*, Alcuin Club collections 50 (London 1968). On liturgical processions in general, see Terence Bailey, *The processions of Sarum and the Western Church*, Pontifical Institute of Medieval Studies, Studies and texts 21 (Toronto 1971) 79-119. Häussling provides conclusive evidence that the Roman stational system was imitated in Frankish monasteries from the 780s onwards: (note 16 above) 55-72 and *passim*. There are

stational church, and the pope's solemn entry from the *secretarium* to the church at the beginning of mass.[43] The precious vessels to be used in the mass were carried on the stational procession. Among these was the book of gospel readings, brought to be used in the stational mass. When the papal stational mass was celebrated on ordinary feast-days, the gospel book was carried in procession by the archdeacon, the senior deacon of the Roman Church. On special feasts, however, particularly valuable liturgical vessels were used (*calicem et patenam maiores*). On these days, the 'great gospels' (*evangelia maiora*) were solemnly carried on the procession from the Lateran to the church at which the stational mass was to be held (eg on Easter Sunday morning, Santa Maria Maggiore).[44] The 'great chalice and paten' and the 'great gospels' seem both to have been kept in the *vestiarium*, the department of the Lateran where the papal collection of liturgical garments and vessels were stored (*de vestiario dominico*). For fear lest the precious jewels of its binding might be lost, the book was carried in a sealed book shrine, under the personal seal of the *vesterarius*, the official at the Lateran palace who had care of the *vestiarium* (*exeunt sub sigillo vesterarii per numerum gemmarum, ut non perdantur*).[45] The stational procession made it clear that the gospel book was seen, like chalices and patens, as a precious liturgical object. A great Columban monastery which wished to cite or emulate (if not to imitate) the Roman liturgy might well have felt that it was necessary to provide its abbot, for processions on major feasts, with jewelled *evangelia maiora* in a sealed book shrine.

On arrival at the church, the deacon who was to read the gospel prepared the gospel book. At the command of the archdeacon, the book was unsealed (removed from its shrine), and placed in the hands of the acolyte. Following byzantine court ritual, the acolyte bore the book, not on his bare hands, but with hands covered by his outer garment (*super planetam*). The great gospels or evangeliaries (sets of gospel readings arranged in the order of the liturgical year) used on major feasts needed two acolytes to carry them.[46]

---

clear references to the Roman stational procession to the Holy Cross in Jerusalem on Good Friday on the Ruthwell Cross, both in its iconography and in its vernacular English poem (the monument is dated 730-50): see Ó Carragáin, 'Ruthwell crucifixion poem' (note 8 above) 42-50.

[43]The entrance of the celebrant was an important feature, not only of the Roman rite, but also of the Milanese rite (and thus familiar to Irish foundations like Bobbio): see Pietro Borella, 'L'ingressa della messa ambrosiana', *Ambrosius* 24 (1948) 83-90; Pietro Borella, *Il rito ambrosiano*, Biblioteca di scienze religiose (Brescia 1964) 141-54.

[44]Andrieu, *Ordo* I, nos 20-22, II, 73.

[45]Andrieu, *Ordo* I, no 22, II, 73: the great paten and chalice were likewise carried *sub sigillo*. That carrying the gospels *sub sigillo* meant carrying them in a sealed book shrine (*capsa*) is made clear later, when, after the gospel has been read, *ponitur in capsa, ut sigilletur*: *Ordo* I, no 65, Andrieu, II, 89. There is a fine discussion of the social background of *Ordo Romanus Primus* (ie the papal administration in the Lateran, and its relations with the other ancient titular churches of Rome) in Thomas F X Noble, *The republic of St Peter. The birth of the papal state, 680-825* (Philadelphia 1984) 212-30; on the *vesterarius*, see Noble, 226.

[46]Andrieu, *Ordo* I, no 30, II, 77. Acolytes were adult clerics: the office of acolyte was a career office in the Roman church, and acolytes could replace deacons who had died: see Noble (note 45 above) 217. Their status in the Roman ecclesiastical career structure might perhaps be described as 'deacons in waiting'.

The acolyte(s) brought the gospels up the nave to the sanctuary area in procession, preceded by a subdeacon who, taking the book from the covered hands of the acolyte(s), placed it with ceremony on the altar (*manibus suis honorifice super altare ponat*).[47] During this enthronement of the gospels on the altar, the pope had already gone to be vested in his liturgical garments in the *sacrarium* or *secretarium*, which as we have seen was near the main entrance, adjoining the *atrium* of the basilica. While the choir sang the *Introit* chant, the pope proceeded solemnly up the nave, supported (*sustentatus*) by his archdeacon and another deacon, and preceded by seven acolytes from the local ecclesiastical region of the city carrying seven lighted candles, as well as by a subdeacon with a thurible. The pope prostrated himself in prayer, on a special carpet (*oratorium*) spread for this purpose before the altar, until the choir finished the *Introit*. Before giving the signal for the choir to begin the *Gloria*, the pope rose and kissed both the gospels and the altar.[48] The ceremonial of enthroning the gospels on the altar, and solemnly kissing both book and altar, established once more (as in the *Apertio aurium*) a close connection between book and altar, ie, between the symbol of Christ's word and the symbol of Christ's sacrifice.

When in the solemn papal mass the gospel came to be read, the ceremonial honour given to the gospel book was even more elaborate than that described in the *Apertio aurium* ceremony. After the epistle had been read and the responsory chants sung, the deacon, again following ancient court ceremonial (in this case the gesture of *proskynesis*), kissed the feet of the pope, who in an undertone blessed him for the office he was to perform (*et tacite dicit ei pontifex: 'Dominus sit in corde tuo et in labiis tuis'*).[49] Then the deacon approached the altar, kissed the gospels, and, taking the codex in his hands, brought it in solemn procession to the ambo. The procession was headed by two acolytes with candles; they were followed by two subdeacons from the local region of the city, one carrying a thurible with incense; then came the deacon carrying the gospels. The deacon, as he passed in procession bearing the gospels, was blessed by the bishops assisting at the mass (with the words *Dominus tecum*) and by the attendant priests (with the words *Spiritus domini super te*). Even the act of opening the gospel book had its appropriate ceremony: the subdeacon who was not carrying the incense offered the deacon his left arm on which to rest the book, so that the deacon could open it with his right hand at the place where a bookmarker had already been placed. The deacon ascended the ambo with his finger on the place where he was to begin. During the reading, the five clerics formed a symmetrical tableau centred on the book.

---

[47]Andrieu, *Ordo* I, no 31, II, 77.

[48]Andrieu, *Ordo* I, no 51, II, 83. Batiffol (note 9 above) 75-77. Batiffol sees in the seven candlesticks a tableau based on the Apocalypse of St John (Apocalypse 1:12-13; 2:1): 'L'evêque, qui figure le Christ, marchera lui aussi au millieu de sept chandeliers' (p 76). On the *oratorium*, see Jungmann (note 4 above) I, 70 and n 12.

[49]On *proskynesis*, see Jungmann, I, n 71 and note 15; also Ute Schwab, 'Proskynesis und Philoxenie in der altsächsischen Genesisdichtung', with an appendix by Walter Berschin, 'Die Tituli des Halberstädter Abrahamsteppichs' in *Text und Bild. Aspekte des Zusammenwirkens zweier Künste in Mittelalter und früher Neuzeit*, ed Christel Meier, Uwe Ruberg (Wiesbaden 1980) 209-77.

In the centre of the tableau was the deacon, standing on the raised ambo to read aloud from the gospel book. The two acolytes with their candles flanked the steps by which the deacon had gone up into the ambo. At the other side of the ambo, the two subdeacons (one holding the incense) flanked the steps by which the deacon would descend from the ambo after he had read the gospel.[50] At the end of the gospel reading, the pope again blessed the deacon (with the words *Pax tibi*); he replied courteously (*Et cum spiritu tuo*). Then the deacon, descending from the ambo by the steps flanked by the subdeacons, solemnly handed the gospels to the subdeacon who had helped him to open it. He in turn handed the book to a third subdeacon, who, holding it before his breast with his hands covered by his outer garment, brought the gospels to be kissed by all the clerics standing in the sanctuary, in order of rank. Finally, the book was replaced in its book shrine: the shrine was sealed, and the gospel book brought back by an acolyte to the Lateran. As in the *Apertio aurium*, the gospel book was treated with the greatest honour, and, when it had been read, disappeared from view; from that moment of the solemn mass, ie during the offertory and canon of the mass, the attention of the onlookers was focused on the eucharistic action which took place on and around the altar.[51] The early medieval church was consistent in its attitude to the relations between the mystical eucharistic action and the mystical word of the gospels. They saw both together as manifesting the natures, person and actions of Christ the Word. They saw both as prophetic: not only as commemorating past actions and events, but as adumbrating the present and future history of mankind until the full revelation of Christ and of the church. Thus they presented the gospel as far as possible in the context of, and subordinated only to, the enactment of the eucharistic mystery. The mass progresses from rumination on Christ's word to performance of the eucharistic action prescribed in the gospels. Through the eucharistic mystery, they believed, Christ effected what the gospels prophesied: he continually unified the church in its members, and the members to himself until, 'when the perfect comes' and human history had been brought to completion, the church would be revealed in its perfection as his glorified body.[52]

---

[50]This would seem to be the visual result of *Ordo* I, no 59 (Andrieu, II, 88), which specifies that at the ambo the acolytes divide so that the senior clerics can pass between them: *venientes ad ambonem dividuntur ipsi acolyti ut per medium eorum subdiaconi et diaconi cum evangelio transeant.* Before the reading, the subdeacons go back and stand before the steps, at the opposite side of the ambo, by which the deacon comes down from the ambo: *et illi duo subdiaconi redeunt stare ante gradum discensionis ambonis*: Andrieu, *Ordo* I, no 62, II, 89. Atchley (note 9 above) illustrates three examples of ambos with two sets of steps: from Ravello (frontispiece), from San Clemente, Rome (pl XIV, p 150 and pl XII, p 77) and S Apollinare Nuovo, Ravenna (pl XV, p 178).

[51]Andrieu, *Ordo* I, nos 59-65, II, 87-90. The text specifies, in the present tense, that the gospels are brought back to the Lateran: *Acolytus autem regionis eiusdem cuius et subdiaconus est revocat evangelium ad Lateranum*: Andrieu, *Ordo* I, no 65, II, 90. This seems to mean that the gospels were immediately carried back down the nave out of the stational basilica before the offertory of the mass began, and this is how Jungmann, I, 71, interprets the passage: '... the papal subdeacon ... hands it to an acolyte who immediately carries it back to the Lateran'.

[52]Cf I Corinthians 13:10. A good example of how closely, in patristic and early medieval thought, the act of understanding the multivalent texts of scripture was

The papal mass described in *Ordo Romanus Primus* makes consistent use of symbolically significant tableaux. When the deacon read the gospels from the ambo flanked by two pairs of less senior clerics bearing incense and candles, the flanking pairs expressed the dignity of the book he read. One such recurring tableau is particularly relevant to the Book of Kells. On his arrival at the church, the pope was assisted from his saddle by two deacons who flanked and supported him while he walked to the *secretarium* to vest for mass. In the words of the Ordo, the pope proceeded *sustentatus a diaconibus*.[53] Ernst Jerg has shown that we have here a reference to an ancient royal ceremonial, found in Roman imperial state ceremonial both in the West and in the East, but also found in the Old Testament, in Persia, and as far afield in space and time as Tibet in the lifetime of the present Dalai Lama.[54] The essence of the ceremonial was that the dignity of a king or priest or great personage was to be expressed by having two officials of lesser importance flank him and support him with their hands while he advanced in solemn state. In a clearly related tableau, the dignity of a great personage could also be expressed by having two supporters flank the throne on which he sat in state.[55] In the *Ordo Romanus Primus*, when the pope had vested in the *secretarium* and the choir in the sanctuary had begun the *Introit* chant, the pope began his solemn procession up the nave as follows: he first gave his right hand to the archdeacon, and his left hand to the deacon second in rank. They kissed his hands, and then proceeded up the nave supporting him: *et illi, osculatis manibus ipsius, procedunt cum ipso sustentantes eum*.[56] Similarly, at the beginning of the offertory, the pope advanced to receive the gifts supported by two high officials of the city of Rome: the *primicerius notariorum* (the senior notary) held his right hand, and the *primicerius defensorum* (the senior legal advocate) held his left: *tenente manum eius dexteram primicerio notariorum et primicerio defensorum sinistram*; they again supported him when he had received the gifts and returned to his seat.[57] Finally, at the communion, the pope proceeded from his seat to

---

associated with the reception of Christ's *corpus mysticum* in the Eucharist, is the widespread idea that Christ's breaking of bread (in the feedings in the desert, the Last Supper, and the supper at Emmaus) involved his fulfillment and opening (= explanation) of scripture: De Lubac (note 4 above) especially pp 80-82 and also 102, 266-67, 340-42; on this and related metaphors, see Hans-Jörg Spitz, *Die Metaphorik des geistigen Schriftsinns*, Münstersche Mittelalterschriften 12 (Munich 1972) 41-104. On the way in which the Eucharist was seen in this period as unifying and vivifying the Church and uniting it (his body: *corpus Christi*, I Cor. 12:27) to Christ (its head), see De Lubac, 19-137; Congar (note 4 above) 81-98.

[53] Andrieu, *Ordo* I, no 29, II, 76.

[54] Ernst Jerg, 'Die *sustentatio* in der römische Liturgie vor dem Hintergrund des kaiserlichen Hofzeremoniells', *Zeitschrift für katholische Theologie* 80 (1958) 316-24; see also the extended note on the history of the tableau by Jungmann, I, 69, n 10. For the use of *sustentatio* in twentieth-century Tibet (mentioned by Jerg, 323), see Heinrich Harrer, *Seven years in Tibet*, Reprint Society edn (London 1955) 169, 230, 254, and the photograph between pp 176-77 showing the young Dalai Lama proceeding, flanked by advisers.

[55] As in the Agilulf bronze helmet-frontal, now in the Bargello Museum, Florence, reproduced in *L'Europa delle invasioni barbariche*, ed Jean Hubert, Jean Porcher and Wolfgang Fritz Volbach (Milan 1968) 247, fig 271.

[56] Andrieu, *Ordo* I, no 45, II, 81.

[57] Andrieu, *Ordo* I, nos 69 and 76, II, 91, 92. The *primicerius notariorum* was in charge of the papal chancery; the office has been termed 'the pope's prime minister' (Noble,

give communion to the noble laymen, with the same senior officials again holding his hands: *tenentibus ei manus*.[58]

This symbolic tableau is clearly relevant to the figural page in the Book of Kells labelled in modern scholarship the 'Arrest of Christ' (folio 114r, pl **28**). Here, at the beginning of Christ's Passion, after the Last Supper, the gospel text briefly describes how Christ and his disciples went to the Mount of Olivet: *Et ymno dicto exierunt in montem oliveti*. The Kells artist has incorporated this text, a text which clearly describes movement by Christ and his disciples from place to place, into a scene in which two figures grasp Christ's arms (and yet Jonathan Alexander has rightly stressed that there is a sense that the figures are immobile, 'as if they were frozen at a particular moment').[59] In various ways, including this combination of movement and immobility, the Kells artist has deliberately exploited the multivalence of the *sustentatio* image. The *sustentatio* tableau formed part both of religious and of secular ceremonies. As we have seen, even in the solemn Roman mass the celebrant could be supported by subdeacons or by senior administrative officers (who at this period, in Rome, would have been clerics: either deacons, or clerics in minor orders, who could marry). To hold the hands of an honoured figure as he advanced in procession was a sign of recognition and honour, but obviously to grasp someone's arms could also become an act of arrest or capture. The essence of the principle of multivalence is that of a particular image, through its design and through its context, is intended to suggest at once a variety of meanings.[60] No element of the meanings should be excluded, either by tying the image down too firmly in time or place, or by restricting its symbolic import by identifying it too closely with a single narrative moment. In any commentary on the so-called 'Arrest' image in Kells, this principle of multivalence is vital. Paradoxically, much modern scholarship has tried to eliminate this sense of multivalence, attempting to reduce the scene to a single narrative moment rather than recognising that the fascination of the scene lies precisely in the rich variety and ambiguity of the associations it exploits. The two flanking figures, whether they themselves are good or evil, bring about good for mankind. They initiate and support Christ's gesture of prayer, his *orans* posture; this *orans* posture is itself a prefigurement of the gesture by which Christ, stretching out his hands on

---

note 45 above, p 222). The *primicerius defensorum* was the chief legal advocate of the city. His headquarters were in the Lateran, and he was always a cleric by this period, sometimes a deacon, although frequently in minor orders and often married (Noble, 223).

[58]Andrieu, *Ordo* I, no 113, II, 104.

[59]Alexander, '*Illumination*', 282.

[60]For a discussion of the 'principle of multivalence' as a central principle behind liturgically-inspired monastic art and literature, see Ó Carragáin, 'Christ over the beasts and the Agnus Dei: two multivalent panels on the Ruthwell and Bewcastle crosses' in *Sources of Anglo-Saxon culture*, ed Paul E Szarmach, Studies in Medieval Culture 20, (Kalamazoo, Michigan 1986) 377-403; and Ó Carragáin, 'The Ruthwell Cross and the Irish high crosses: some points of comparison and contrast', in Ryan, 118-28 (pp 122-23). See also the discussion in Häussling (note 16 above) 98-100, 107-10, 172-73.

the cross, was seen to draw to himself all human history (*Qui expansis in cruce manibus traxisti omnia ad te secula*).[61]

An anonymous seventh-century Irish computistical tract, *De ratione conputandi*, contains a very brief summary of the Passion, which emphasizes the idea of the procession to the Mount of Olivet to which the Book of Kells devotes such artistry:

> *Primo uero azymorum die dominus noster Iesus Christus, cenans cum discipulis, postquam sui corporis et sanguinis sacramentum patefecit, ad montem Oliueti, sicut euangelia sancta testantur, progressus ibique detentus est a Iudeis, tradente discipulo. Dehinc, .vi. feria subsequente, id est .vii. Kl Aprelis, crucifixus est et sepultus tertiaque die, hoc est .v. Kl Aprelis, dominico, resurrexit a mortuis.*[62]

I by no means want to argue for any influence of this passage on the Book of Kells. The passage is interesting precisely because it provides independent testimony of what was probably a common tendency. The summary, through its very brevity, indicates how Christ's solemn *introit* to Mount Olivet could become imaginatively important to *any* monk familiar with liturgical ceremonies. The anonymous author emphasized the *ad montem Oliveti ... progressus* because it enabled him to stress the link between Christ's revelation at the Last Supper of the sacrament of his body and blood, and his subsequent sacrificial death on the Cross. To emphasize such a link was theologically and liturgically important: through the Eucharist the Church, the body of Christ, could until his return in glory participate in the life his death had won.[63] The mass involved a progressive series of three processions or 'entrances'; this series provides one relevant context for the Book of Kells 'Arrest' page. The first procession was the *introit*, the solemn entrance of the celebrant at the beginning of mass. In the *Ordo Romanus primus*, the solemn procession of the bishop up the nave, supported by deacons and preceded by seven lighted candles, itself suggested that the advancing bishop represented Christ ('who walks among the seven golden

---

[61]*Versus* sung on Holy Thursday and Holy Saturday. For its early medieval uses, see René-Jean Hesbert, 'Le graduel *Christus* à l'office des trois jours saints', *Ephemerides liturgicae* 97 (1983) 241-61. For the biblical reminiscences used in the chant, see Ó Carragáin, 'Ruthwell Crucifixion poem' (note 8 above) 45-46. For the motif of Christ stretching out his hands in prayer on the Cross, see Victor Saxer, '"Il étendit les mains à l'heure de sa Passion". Le thème de l'orant(e) dans la littérature chrétienne des IIe et IIIe siècles', *Augustinianum* 20 (1980) 335-65; also Jungmann, I, 107. For a full survey of earlier interpretations of the page, see Carol Farr, 'Lection', 218-26; see also her discussion of the *orans* pose, 227-36.

[62]Ó Cróinín and Walsh (note 27 above) 196, lines 11-17: 'On the first day of unleavened bread our Lord Jesus Christ, dining with his disciples, after he had revealed to them the sacrament of his body and blood, and proceeded to the Mount of Olivet, as the holy gospels testify, was arrested there by the Jews, his disciple betraying him. On the following Friday, that is on the 7th Kalends of April, he was crucified and buried and on the third day, that is, on the 5th Kalends of April, Sunday, he rose from the dead'.

[63]For the theological importance of the relationship between Christ's offering of his body and blood *in mysterio* in the Eucharist and his subsequent self-offering on Calvary, see De Lubac (note 4 above) 65-87.

lamp-stands': Apocalypse 2:1). The second procession or 'entrance' was the presentation of the gifts; as we have seen, the pope, advancing to receive these gifts, was supported by two senior officials.[64] The third 'procession', a metaphoric one, took place at the beginning of the canon of the mass. The *Ordo Romanus primus* describes how all the priests and bishops surrounding the pope at the altar stood upright during the Preface, until they began to recite with the pope 'the angelic hymn, that is *Sanctus, Sanctus, Sanctus*'. All bowed for the angelic hymn. When they had finished, the *ordo* specifies that all the other clerics around the altar remained bowed for the canon prayers. At this point, the two manuscripts which contain the first version of the *Ordo* read *Ut autem expleverint, surgit pontifex solus in canone*: 'as they finish [the angelic hymn] the pope alone rises [ie stands upright] for the Canon'. But all the other manuscripts read *surgit pontifex solus et intrat in canonem*: 'the pope alone rises and enters into the Canon'.[65] The alteration of the *ordo* reflects the increased sense north of the Alps, from the mid-eighth century, that during the canon the celebrant entered a metaphoric Holy of Holies to re-enact Christ's sacrifice.[66] For the canon prayers, the celebrant would have stood alone, unsupported by junior clerics; but he would have stood in the *orans* posture, with hands raised to either side of his body.[67] The *introit*, offertory and canon provided a series of advances towards, entrances into, the enactment of the eucharistic mystery. This series was central to the symbolic structure of the mass. The question, which of the three 'entrances' is most relevant to Kells folio 114r, is of secondary importance. More important is to realise that, not only were solemn advances by the celebrant towards the eucharistic mystery a central feature of the mass-ritual, but that, taken together, such advances provided a unified metaphor for the way in which in eucharistic action all christians entered with Christ into the divine mystery. This metaphor is beautifully and concisely expanded in a collect prayer widely used in the early middle ages on Holy Thursday (the 'procession' of Christ and his apostles to the Mount of Olives took place after nightfall on that evening). The collect was assigned in various sacramentaries either to the mass for the reconciliation of penitents on Holy Thursday morning, or to the ceremony of reconciliation itself (the reference to rebirth in the collect refers to the approaching baptism of the catechumens on Holy Saturday, the vigil of Easter, as well as to the

---

[64]In the Byzantine liturgy, the presentation of the gifts was known as the 'great entrance', to distinguish it from the earlier 'little entrance' at the *introit*. See Robert Taft, *The great entrance: a history of the transfer of gifts and other pre-anaphoral rites of the liturgy of St Chrysostom*, Orientalia christiana analecta 200, 2nd edn (Rome 1978). The Eastern and Western offertory processions are compared in Jungmann, II, 1-16. The ancient Gallican liturgy had a fully-developed 'great entrance' rite corresponding to the Byzantine rite: Jungmann, II, 5 and *Expositio antiquae liturgiae gallicanae*, ed E C Ratcliff, HBS 98 (London 1971) 10-11. It is not impossible that such a 'great entrance' might have been known in some Irish monasteries.

[65]Andrieu, *Ordo* I, no 88; Andrieu, II, 95-96.

[66]Discussions of the various versions of this passage in Andrieu, II, 95-96, note; Jungmann, I, 72 and II, 104-105, 138-42; Batiffol (note 9 above) 89. The sense that at this point of the mass the priest entered an inner sanctum must have been increased by the tendency, from the late eighth century onwards, for the celebrant to recite the canon prayers silently: Jungmann, II, 104.

[67]Jungmann, II, 141-42.

reconciliation of the penitents on Holy Thursday). This collect presents Christ's resurrection as confirming the glory of all those reborn in Christ, and sees this as the heart of the Paschal mystery into which all the christian community can, by God's grace, enter forthwith. The collect asks God 'to grant to all your servants more fully and perfectly to enter into all the mysteries of the Paschal feast, so that faithful hearts may come immediately to know how much they should rejoice in the glory granted to those born to new life, [a glory] confirmed in Christ': *Omnipotens sempiterne deus, da, quaesumus, uniuersis famulis tuis plenius adque perfectius omnia festi paschalis introire mysteria, ut incunctanter pia corda cognoscant, quantum debeant de confirmata in Christo renascentium glorificatione gaudere: per.*[68]

Through the liturgy all of the church participated in the glorious entry of Christ, their high priest, into the holy of holies (cf Heb. 9:11-28) where they shared with him in the life of the Trinity. On folio 114r of the Book of Kells the text and illustration encouraged contemplation of the way in which Christ, through his Passion, his death (when 'tradidit Spiritum': John 19:30) and resurrection (when his Father raised him up: Phil.2:9) enacted this entry in human form, revealing the heart of the mystery of the Trinity. Such contemplation was important for each monk who looked at the book because they believed that, in union with Christ its head, the church his body participated in this mystery and drew its life from it: that through the rites of initiation and the Eucharist, each christian participated in Christ's priesthood as in his sacrifice. 'The Arrest of Christ' is too limiting a title for the Kells page precisely because it misses the symbolic, mystical and communal dimensions of the text and image on folio 114r. The later text of *Ordo Romanus primus* provides the model for a simpler and better title: '*Christus intrat in Passionem*', 'Christ enters into the Passion'.

---

[68]The beautifully balanced final clause of the collect can be read in two complementary ways: 'how, in Christ, the glorification of the reborn has been confirmed' or 'how the glorification of those reborn in Christ has been confirmed [by the paschal mysteries]'. The collect appears for Holy Thursday in the Old Gelasian sacramentary, the sacramentaries of Gellone (CCSL 159, p 76, par. 589), Angoulême (CCSL 159C, p 81, par. 599) and St Gall, and in the Bobbio Missal. Text quoted from Leo Cunibert Mohlberg, Peter Siffrin and Ludwig Eisenhöfer, *Liber sacramentorum Romanae eclesiae ordinis anni circuli (Cod. Vat. Reg. lat. 316 / Paris Bib. Nat. 7193, 41/56 (Sacramentarium Gelasianum),* Rerum Ecclesiastarum Documenta, Series maior, Fontes, 4, 3rd ed (Rome 1981) 55, no 349; see also *The Bobbio Missal, a Gallican mass-Book (MS Paris. Lat. 13246),* ed E A Lowe, HBS 53 (facsimile), 58 (text) and 61 (Notes and Studies), 3 vols (London 1917-24) II, 62, no 196 (text), III, 124 (notes). On the theological background of the concept ('*introire mysteria*') central to the collect, see De Lubac (note 4 above) 267. The Preface of the Gregorian Mass for the ordination of a priest explicitly states that offering the mass involves 'entering into the mysteries'. See the Hadrianum text: *Le sacramentaire grégorien. Ses principales formes d'après les manuscrits les plus anciens,* ed Jean Deshusses (Fribourg-en-Suisse 1971) I, 307, no 199, par. 830: '*da nobis quaesumus ut ad sacrosancta mysteria immolando sacrificia cum beneplacitis mentibus facias introire*' ('we ask you to grant and allow us to enter into the most holy mysteries, and to the sacrifices that must be offered, with minds well pleasing to you'). On the metaphoric dimensions of the Kells page itself, see Jennifer O'Reilly, 'The Book of Kells, folio 114r: a mystery revealed yet concealed' in *The age of migrating ideas: early medieval art in Northern Britain and Ireland,* ed R Michael Spearman and John Higgitt (Edinburgh and Stroud 1993) 106-14 (pp 113-14).

Evidence that the symbolic possibilities of the *sustentatio* tableau and visually related images were widely appreciated in the early medieval West can be found in other early medieval liturgical ceremonies and in early medieval Irish sculpture. The sung liturgical chant which most clearly suggests the tableau is a phrase from the Old Latin version of the Canticle of Habakkuk. In the Roman rite, this canticle was sung every Friday at lauds; but it was also used weekly in those Celtic monasteries of which we have evidence. At Rome, and thus in Northumbria, an extract from the canticle, including the verse we shall examine, was sung as a responsory after the first Old Testament reading at the adoration of the Cross on Good Friday.[69] It contains the words *in medio duorum animalium innotesceris* ('you will be known in the midst of two animals'). Early christian commentary related the 'two animals' phrase to a variety of ways in which Christ was revealed between two figures. Jerome, who was writing a commentary on the whole Book of Habakkuk as one of the prophetic books of the Old Testament, sees vast ecclesiological and historical import in the phrase. He relates the phrase to the way 'the Saviour is to be understood and believed in the primitive church, which was brought together both from the circumcised and from the uncircumcised — the Saviour surrounding himself, on the one side and on the other, by two peoples'. Jerome's interest in the ecclesiological import of phrase is again to be seen in his second level of interpretation: 'there are those who interpret the two animals as the two Testaments, Old and New, which can be said to be truly life-giving and full of life, to breathe [the Spirit: there is a clear pun in Jerome's verb *quae spirent*], and in the midst of which the Lord may be known'.[70] Jerome emphasizes that the phrase is reminiscent of the statement in Exodus (25:22) that in the temple Yahweh would speak to Israel from the midst of the two cherubim of beaten gold on top of the Ark of the Covenant (*de medio duorum cherubim*): Yahweh would speak seated on the wings of the cherubim, with the Ark for his footstool. Jerome sees this reminiscence of the Book of Exodus as implying the most profound possible interpretation of *in medio duorum animalium*: the life of the Trinity, in which the Father is made known through the Son and the Holy Spirit.[71] Bede approaches the phrase in a different way. Unlike Jerome, Bede did not write a commentary on the Book

---

[69]The liturgical use of the canticle, and patristic commentary on the text, are discussed in three studies by Ó Carragáin (1986, note 60 above) 383-88, (1987, note 60 above) 118-19 and 'The meeting of St Paul and St Anthony: visual and literary uses of a eucharistic motif' in *Keimelia: studies in archaeology and history in memory of Tom Delaney*, ed Gearóid Mac Niocaill, Patrick Wallace (Galway 1988) 1-58 and pls I-XII (pp 4-6 and passim: Irish liturgical uses of the canticle are discussed at p 20, note 2). A T Lucas independently argued for the relevance of the *in medio duorum animalium* phrase to early Irish sculpture in '"In the middle of two living things". Daniel or Christ?' in *Figures from the past: studies in figurative art in christian Ireland in honour of Helen M Roe*, ed Etienne Rynne (Dublin 1987) 92-97. Lucas did not examine the liturgical uses of the canticle, but convincingly related the phrase to the ancient and widespread Gilgamesh motif (a king or warrior flanked by animals) in the visual arts.

[70]Jerome, *Commentarium in Abacuc Prophetam ad Chromatium*, in his *Commentarii in prophetas minores*, ed M Adriaen, CCSL 76A (Turnhout 1970) 618-54 (p 621). See Ó Carragáin (1986, note 60 above) 385-86; (1988, note 69 above) 11.

[71]Adriaen (note 70 above) 620-21. See Ó Carragáin (1988, note 69 above) 28.

of Habakkuk, but wrote on the canticle as an independent liturgical text. He was writing for an unnamed nun, who like himself sang the canticle every Friday at lauds (and thus sang it twice on Good Friday, at lauds and at the adoration of the Cross). Bede therefore begins his commentary by emphasizing the significance of the weekly liturgical use of the canticle:

> The canticle of the prophet Habakkuk, which you asked me to interpret for you, beloved sister in Christ, above all prophesies the sacred mysteries of the Lord's Passion (*sacramenta dominicae passionis maximo pronuntiat*). Therefore, by the custom of the holy, universal and apostolic church it is customary to repeat it solemnly each week on Friday, on which that same Passion was brought to completion. But it also mystically describes the course of his incarnation, resurrection, and ascension into heaven, the faith of the nations and the lack of faith of the Jews. In contemplation, the prophet saw the state of the present age, the peace in which sinners live and the afflictions of the just ...[72]

Faithful to the programme sketched in these opening lines, Bede relates the *in medio duorum animalium* phrase to two moments in Christ's life: to the Transfiguration, in which Christ was made known between Moses and Elijah, and to the Crucifixion in which he was revealed between the two thieves.[73] It is clear from both Jerome's and Bede's commentaries that the flanking *animalia* could, for a monastic audience, take on a vast variety of human, animal, inanimate, abstract or angelic forms. The relevance of the phrase was determined, not by the nature (good or evil or neutral) of the flanking 'animals' but by the fact that, in the midst of these figures or through these events, the divine and human natures of Christ could be recognised. The likelihood that in the Book of Kells 'Arrest of Christ' the flanking men refer to the *in medio duorum animalium* phrase is greatly strengthened by a visual pun. The artist established a visual link between these flanking men and the large symmetrical biting animal heads which arch and meet above Christ's head. As Jonathan Alexander has pointed out, these two animals mirror the action of the pair of red-haired men who grasp the arms of Christ; the appearance of two animals in the scene directly suggests the words (and perhaps, to a monastic onlooker, the music) of the canticle. It may be that the biting animals, as Alexander suggests, underline the 'aggressive purpose' of the flanking human figures.[74] Whether the biting animal heads represent good or evil (or are ethically neutral), the Kells artist establishes a clear visual parallel between them and the flanking human figures. This technique is analogous to the way in which the Pictish sculptors of the Nigg stone establish a visual parallel between a pair of symmetrical human figures (Saints Paul and Anthony) and the pair of

---

[72]*Expositio Bedae presbyteri in Canticum Abacuc Prophetae*, ed J E Hudson, CCSL 119B (Turnhout 1983) 381, lines 1-9.
[73]Hudson (note 72 above) 383-84, lines 60-77. Bede's lemma reads *IN MEDIO DVORVM ANIMALIVM INNOTESCES*; the Vespasian Psalter (London, BL, Cotton MS Vespasian, A.I, southern English, cAD 700) reads *innotesceris*: see Ó Carragáin (1986, note 60 above) 384-86.
[74]Alexander, 'Illumination', 283.

symmetrical animals (lions or dogs? good, evil, or just animal-like?) who crouch at their feet and contemplate, like the saints, the heavenly bread and the chalice through which Christ is known.[75] In the Kells 'Arrest' page, whether the flanking men are good or evil, even if they know not what they do, they assist Christ in carrying out his supreme prayer to his Father. The central, dominant figure is the figure of Christ, whose eyes gaze so searchingly at the viewer, and on whom the flanking men gaze while they grasp his arms. The two pairs of flanking figures, men and animals, direct the viewer's contemplation to Christ: they powerfully remind the onlooker, who has recognised the liturgical chant to which they refer, to recognise Christ as both king and priest.[76]

The 'Arrest' page is not the only evidence that the Kells artists were interested in the visual possibilities of the *in medio duorum animalium* chant. When, ten folios later, St Matthew's Passion narrative reaches its climax, two great animal heads flank the capital *T* of *Tunc crucifixerant XPI cum eo duos latrones* (folio 124r): for anyone familiar with the canticle and the long tradition of its Good Friday use, the association between the animal heads and the *latrones* is impossible to miss.[77] There is also a clear reminiscence of the canticle at the top of the canon table on folio 2v (pl 2). Here the bearded head-and-shoulders figure at the top of the page, at the summit of the major arch, is identified as Christ by three small golden crosses with their bases at the head of the bearded man and their tops at the golden halo he wears. Jonathan Alexander sees a reference to 'God as Trinity' in these three small crosses,[78] and this identification could be defended, for example by comparing them to the three crosses within the halo of the eagle symbol in the Matthaean Four Symbols page, folio 27v. But the three crosses within the halo at the top of folio 2v are arranged differently. One of the crosses is placed centrally, directly over the central parting in the bearded man's flowing hair. It is slightly larger than the flanking crosses, and has decorative touches (tiny dark triangles at top and bottom of the upright)

---

[75]Ó Carragáin (1988, note 69 above) 7-14. See also the visual parallel established between the paired saints and paired beasts on the Pictish Dunfallandy slab (ibid, p 7) and between the seated saints on the high cross at Moone and the high-backed chairs with dog-like animal heads behind the head of each saint (pp 20-22). The standard analyses of the relationships between the Book of Kells and Pictish art are those by Isabel Henderson, 'Pictish art and the Book of Kells' in *Ireland in early medieval Europe*, ed D Whitelock, R McKitterick and D Dumville (Cambridge 1982) 79-105; and 'The Book of Kells and the snake-boss motif on Pictish cross-slabs and the Iona crosses' in Ryan, 56-65.

[76]It is clear that a reference to the *sustentatio* image, and to the related idea that Christ is to be known between two animals, are only two elements among a much more subtle complex of associations which the 'Arrest' image is designed to attract. For a comprehensive commentary on the image and its manuscript context, see O'Reilly (note 68 above); she also lists Ottonian examples of references in the visual arts to the 'sustentatio' tableau (p 113), usefully updating and supplementing Jungmann, I, 69, n10. For further visual references to 'in medio duorum animalium' in early medieval art, see now Michael Ryan, 'The menagerie of the Derrynaflan chalice' in Spearman and Higgitt (note 68 above) 151-61 (pp 158-60); and O'Reilly (note 68 above) 109-10.

[77]On this image, and its relation to the missing Crucifixion page opposite to it, see O'Reilly (note 68 above) 108-09.

[78]Alexander, 'Illumination', 306.

which they lack. The flanking crosses are tilted outwards from the central cross, and this increases the sense that they are subordinate to it. The artist does not seem to have intended a direct theological reference to 'God as Trinity', but rather an historical reference to Calvary, where Christ was crucified between two thieves. By including in the halo references, not only to Christ's own cross on Calvary, but also to the flanking crosses of the thieves, the Kells artists have encouraged a reminiscence of the Canticle of Habakkuk. For Jerome, the idea that *in medio duorum animalium innotesceris* referred to Christ crucified between two thieves was already a commonly accepted idea (this fact suggests that the Canticle of Habakkuk was already sung on Good Friday at Rome in the late fourth century). As we have seen, Jerome preferred more far-reaching interpretations of the phrase, but Bede made the Good Friday reference central to his explanation of the verse. It would seem that on folio 2v the Kells artist was thinking in similar terms. A number of additional details reinforce the likelihood that we have here a reference to Calvary. Jonathan Alexander refers to the bearded man as 'naked' and this observation may be correct.[79] However, underneath the thick black wisps of the man's beard a brown circular collar is clearly visible. It may have been intended as a metal torque; but it may also have been intended as the collar of a garment. Below the brown circular collar, two small double circles may simply mark out the man's chest, but they could conceivably be ornaments on a tight garment. On the man's right arm, the hatching may represent flesh and muscles, but instead looks like folds of a fairly tight sleeve. However, the 'sleeves' are not marked off clearly from the heels of the man's hands. Even if the man is clad in a garment which stretches to his wrists, it clings so tightly to his skin that the shapes of his arms and of his chest are clearly visible. It seems clear that the artist first drew a naked torso. Whether he then provided it with a torque, or with some additional sketching to suggest a skin-tight, long-sleeved colobium with a brown circular neck, the effect is to reveal the body of the bearded man. Either the man's upper body is naked, or it is as good as naked. The garment, if it exists, is see-through. The arms of the man are slightly bent, but stretched out in a position reminiscent both of the *orans* posture and of the posture of crucifixion (they are stretched out far more widely and gracefully than the arms of the Christ in the 'Arrest' page, folio 114r). Two lion-like animal-heads emerge from the interlaced upper borders of the canon table. Each beast encircles the nearest outstretched arm of the bearded man with its long tongue, entangling it loosely in a simple knot. At the same time, the bearded man firmly grasps the tongue of each beast where it emerges from its mouth. The emphasis on the shape and physical reality of the bearded man's upper body, his outstretched arms, and the animal-heads which pinion him and which he grasps, all combine to make it extremely likely that the artist was thinking of the liturgical uses of the Canticle of Habakkuk when designing this part of the canon table. The three crosses of the halo do not occur in isolation. The significance of the two flanking crosses is suggested by the symmetrical relations between these crosses and the flanking animals, who provide a direct reminiscence of the

---

[79]ibid, 306.

phrase *in medio duorum animalium* in the Good Friday canticle. The bearded man, with his outstretched arms, seems to represent Christ in the hour of his Passion. The image of Christ refers at once to his divinity (symbolised, as Jonathan Alexander saw, by the large halo) and to his humanity (symbolised by the crosses, by the finely realised, perhaps naked, physical body, and the palpable human courage with which he grasps the tongues of the beasts). But Bede, in his commentary on *in medio duorum animalium* emphasizes precisely that at the Crucifixion both the divinity and the humanity of Christ were revealed:

> Indeed, [the phrase 'you are known in the midst of two animals'] can be not unsuitably taken as 'in the midst of two thieves'; for by dying on the Cross between these, he made known that he was a man. However, by the darkening of the sun, the earthquake, and the other miracles which the Gospel narrates as being performed about the Cross, he made known that he was God. He made known how merciful he was, when he himself interceded with his Father for his executioners. From his example the prophet, who foresaw this in the spirit, exhorted us not only to bear patiently the oppressions of evil ones, but to beg for these very persecutors the grace of his mercy.[80]

The relationship between the animals and the central Christ-figure is ambiguous. Their long looped tongues wrap round and imprison his arms; yet he seems firmly and willingly to grasp these tongues. The artists have created a small but powerful image which at once suggests the reality of Christ's Passion, and his willing acceptance of it. The emphasis on the beasts' tongues is a witty touch. Knotted around the man's arms and firmly grasped by his hands, these beast tongues never could speak; but, no matter how silent and immobile they seem on the page, no matter how caught and entangled, the paired long-tongued animals proclaim the bearded man in their midst as Christ.

The artists of the canon tables usually designed the two pages of each opening as a unity. The frame of the opposite page of this opening, folio 3r (pl 3), provides a significant contrast with the frame of folio 2v. The artists presumably felt that visual and symbolic unity was particularly important in this opening, as Canon II (the gospel passages common to Matthew, Mark and Luke) begins on folio 2v, and is continued on folio 3r (it ends overleaf, on folio 3v; and on folio 3v all of Canon III, the sections common to Matthew, Luke and John, is also recorded). On folio 3r the squared-off spandrels of the upper frame again turn into biting animal masks with extended, knotted tongues. But on folio 3r the human figure at the summit of the main arch is significantly different from the Christ-figure on folio 2v. He is not haloed, but is instead enclosed in a golden circular band which is

---

[80]Hudson (note 72 above) lines 69-77, pp 383-84, trans Ó Carragáin (1986, note 60 above) 386. On the early reception of Bede by Irish exegetes, see Joseph F T Kelly, 'The Venerable Bede and Hiberno-Latin exegesis' in *Sources of Anglo-Saxon culture*, Studies in Medieval Culture 20 (Kalamazoo 1986) 65-75.

interrupted by the inhabited interlace in front of the animal heads. He is not bearded, and his golden hair is considerably shorter than is the hair of the Christ-figure on the opposite page. His shoulders are swathed in a voluminous brown garment, in striking contrast to the palpable emphasis on Christ's physical body on folio 2v. The figure on folio 3r is much smaller than the Christ of 2v, and his small body is enclosed by the golden circular band, so that the animal-heads flank, not so much this human figure, but rather the 'cup or chalice form in front of him, from which extends foliage'[81] and on which he gazes. The chalice-and-foliage motif is similar to that found at the foot of folio 202r, at the end of the Lucan genealogy. Five interlaced strands of foliage sprout from the chalice on folio 3r. Each ends in a trefoil (references to the Trinity or to the Cross as the Tree of Life?). The foliage interlace is inhabited by two small but ornate birds, one on each side of the chalice. Each bird has its tail in the air, so that the two golden tails come between the snouts of the two biting animal heads and the golden circle which encloses the small human figure. Each bird lowers its beak to peck at the knotted extended tongues of one of the beasts (again the emphasis on tongues). At the centre of the foliage sprouting from the cup, one sprout stands upright and culminates in a trefoil, so that the sprout as a whole clearly resembles a tiny cross.

Early eighth-century Northumbrian sculpture provides an analogue for this combination of iconographic motifs. On the narrow sides of the Ruthwell Cross two columns of foliage interlace, each inhabited by a variety of animals and birds, together contrast with the broad north side, on which a number of figural panels refer to the eucharistic bread. At Ruthwell, the inhabited foliage scrolls recall both the vine and the Tree of Life. Inhabited by feeding animals and birds, the foliage provides scenes of the harmony of a renewed Paradise, with particular reference to Apocalypse 2:7: 'to him that overcometh I will give to eat of the tree of life which is in the Paradise of my God'. The similarity of the Ruthwell foliage interlace to vinescroll interlace, and the structural balance between the narrow sides and broad sides of the cross, suggest that (as the broad north side is filled with references to the eucharistic bread) these narrow sides may refer to the blood of Christ in the Eucharist. A similar foliage scroll, combining references to the vine, the Tree of Life and the Eucharist, occurs on the Bewcastle Cross.[82] On folio 3r of Kells, the chalice from which inhabited foliage sprouts demands to be seen in eucharistic terms. One key to the unity of the opening, folios 2v-3r, seems to be the continuity and contrast between historical event and liturgical enactment of that event. On folio 2v, there is a direct representation of Christ, revealed in his Passion as God and man. This is matched on folio 3r by a representation of the life offered to men by the glorified Christ, the true vine (John 15:1) who offers life from the eucharistic cup. On folio 3r, as on folio 2v, the large lion-like animal heads are vital to the meaning of the scene. They mutely proclaim Christ, here

---

[81]Alexander, 'Illumination', 306.
[82]See Ó Carragáin (note 8 above) 'Ruthwell crucifixion poem', 34-35; 'Bewcastle cross', 30-33, 36-40.

(folio 3r) known *in medio duorum animalium* in the Eucharist, as he was once made known between thieves on the Cross (folio 2v). The brown-clothed man in folio 3r may stand for a priest celebrating mass; or he may be a generalised figure standing for the christian community: in the eighth century, theologians stressed that the whole community offered the eucharistic sacrifice.[83] Nor is the balanced contrast between the naked Christ on folio 2v and the chalice with its foliage on folio 3r simply one between the historical event of Calvary and its eucharistic re-enactment in the mass. The Christ figure on folio 2v incorporates a visual reminiscence of a central text of the mass itself. His widely spread arms, grasping the animals' tongues, combine with his upper body to recall the cross-bar of a roman capital or uncial letter 'T'. The rest of Christ's body is concealed behind the arch, so that the upright of the 'T' is only implied. However, the implication is strengthened by the golden cross in the halo over Christ's head: the fully presented cross implies the full body of the crucified Christ. But the first words of the canon of the mass, *Te igitur*, also began with the letter 'T'; and in continental sacramentaries from the eighth century onwards that letter was increasingly elaborated to recall Christ's sacrifice and his priestly prayer on the Cross.[84] The iconographic structure of the Ruthwell Cross and the iconographic structure of the Kells opening 2v-3r are clearly analogous: both balance eucharistic images of Christ's body (Kells folio 2v) against images of his blood (Kells folio 3r). But the human figures and animal heads at the summit of the main arches on folios 2v-3r are not to be seen in isolation. All the major elements of these two balanced pages were planned as a unity. As we have seen both pages were devoted to the same canon table, Canon II (the passages common to Matthew, Mark and Luke). On each page of the opening, the relevant evangelist symbols crowd between the canon tables and the main arch. Each page of the opening suggests that Christ is announced both through the evangelist symbols and, in historical action and liturgical enactment, *in medio duorum animalium*: it was natural for the artists to make witty play between the symbolic animals of the evangelist symbols and the symbolic animals which recall the Canticle of Habakkuk. Moving upwards from the canon tables to the column-capitals and the great arches, the eye first encounters the *bona adnuntiatio* of the evangelist symbols, then moves to the culminating

---

[83]See Raphael Schulte, *Die Messe als Opfer der Kirche: die Lehre frühmittelalterlicher Authoren über das Eucharistische Opfer*, Liturgiewissenschaftliche Quellen und Forschungen 35 (Münster, Westfalen 1959) 12-118; and Rupert Berger, *Die Wendung 'Offerre pro' in der römischen Liturgie*, Liturgiegeschichtliche Quellen und Forschungen 41 (Münster, Westfalen 1964). It is in the context of this communal understanding of the eucharistic sacrifice that a wide variety of insular sculptors could consistently present the figures of Saints Paul and Anthony, who were monks but not ordained priests (but who broke bread miraculously sent from heaven) as symbols of the Church's eucharistic sacrifice. See also Häussling (note 16 above) 155-56, 246-55.

[84]See Rudolf Suntrup, '*Te igitur* — Initialen und Kanonbilder in mittelalterlichen Sakramentarhandschriften' in *Text und Bild* (note 49 above) 278-382. See also O'Reilly (note 68 above) 108-110. On the importance in early christian art of bearded portrait-busts of Christ, see Rainer Warland, *Das Brustbild Christi: Studien zur spätantiken und frühbyzantinischen Bildgeschichte, Römische Quartalschrift* 41. Supplementheft (Rome, Freiburg, Vienna 1986) which has a fine analytic catalogue of surviving examples, pp 193-267.

images, Christ's body (folio 2v) and the chalice of his blood (folio 3r). On each page of the Kells opening we move from an image of how Christ is announced by the word of the gospels (the evangelist symbols) to a culminating image, at the head of the page and the apex of the major arch, of how his body (2v) and blood (3r) are made present as *bona gratia* in the Eucharist.[85] As the eye of the onlooker moves from the canon tables to their architectural frames, it experiences the dramatic sequence, from word to sacramental action, common to the *Apertio aurium* ceremony and to the mass. The essential function of canon tables was to act as a reference guide to the harmony of the gospel texts which follow. It was appropriate that the rich variety of evangelist symbols in the canon table pages (folios 1r-5r) should prepare the viewer for the great four symbols pages later in the book. Similarly, the two small vignettes on folios 2v-3r, full of dramatic and symbolic life, prepare the viewer of the book for the great image of Christ *in medio duorum animalium* in St Matthew's account of the Passion (folio 114r), and for the two animals of the *Tunc crucifixerant XPI cum eo duos latrones* page (folio 124r).

The unity of this opening, folios 2v-3r, depends on significant contrast as much as on similarity. Fundamental to this unity is the twice-repeated visual pun of the long-tongued flanking animal heads, which seem designed to recall the Good Friday chant *in medio duorum animalium innotesceris*. To remember the music of its liturgy, early monasticism relied on oral tradition: musical notation is very unlikely to have reached Iona or Ireland before the Book of Kells was written.[86] In an oral musical tradition, the way to remember music was to recall the words traditionally chanted, and the liturgical actions which accompanied these chants. The visual pun of the two animal heads may have been intended to remind the onlooker, not just of the words *in medio duorum animalium* but of the music and

---

[85] The phrase *bona gratia* comes from the classic expression of the early medieval understanding of the Eucharist as theophany in *Isidori Hispalensis episcopi Etymologiarvm sive originvm Libri XX*, ed W M Lindsay (Oxford 1911) VI, pp xix, 38: *Sacrificium dictum quasi sacrum factum, quia prece mystica consecratur in memoriam pro nobis Dominicae passionis; unde hoc eo iubente corpus Christi et sanguinem dicimus. Quod dum sit ex fructibus terrae, sanctificatur et fit sacramentum, operante invisibiliter Spiritu Dei; cuius panis et calicis sacramentum Graeci Eucharistian dicunt, quod Latine bona gratia interpretatur. Et quid melius sanguine et corpore Christi?* The best modern account of how the Eucharist was understood in early medieval devotion and theology is still J A Jungmann's major study, 'Die Abwehr des germanischen Arianismus und der Umbruch der religiösen Kultur im frühen Mittelalter', *Zeitschrift für katholische Theologie* 69 (1947) 36-99, translated (neither elegantly nor accurately) as 'The defeat of teutonic Arianism and the revolution in religious culture in the early middle ages', in Jungmann, *Pastoral liturgy* (London and New York 1962) 1-101. In a later article, 'Von der *Eucharistia* zur "Messe"', *Zeitschrift für katholische Theologie* 89 (1967) 29-40, Jungmann provided another fine account of the fundamental devotional change of direction in the early middle ages from stressing eucharistic thanks and prayer ascending to God, to seeing the mass in terms of descent from heaven to earth: a theophany in which the holy substances of Christ's flesh and blood were made present as *bona gratia* to the participants (p 37). On this shift in devotional perspective, see also Jungmann, I, 82-85; Häussling (note 16 above) 251-55; Nathan Mitchell (note 28 above) 61-120; and Arnold Angenendt, 'Sühne durch Blut', *Frühmittelalterliche Studien* 18 (1984) 437-67 (p 452).

[86] On the oral transmission of chant, see the discussion of the *Vita prima* of St Brigit, above, pp 410-11.

liturgical actions which accompanied these words. These mute-tongued monsters may have sent onlookers away humming, or at least thinking of, chants and ceremonies they performed each week or each year.

In early medieval Irish sculpture the west sides of the two great crosses at Monasterboice provide a remarkable analogue for the principle of multivalence built into the single 'Arrest' page in the Book of Kells (pls 85-86). The Monasterboice crosses unmistakably refer, like Kells, to the *sustentatio* image. But while the Kells 'Arrest' page works by embodying a variety of associations in a single image of Christ, the Monasterboice crosses articulate various levels of association in a whole series of separate but related images of Christ between two creatures. In the Kells image, Christ's Crucifixion is implied; on the Monasterboice crosses, it is explicitly presented, as the central image of each west side. In the Kells image, different levels of meaning are fused, so that the image can be interpreted in a variety of different ways. In contrast, on the west sides of both Monasterboice crosses, the themes of human suffering and divine triumph, expressed in the central Crucifixion scenes, are also separately articulated in a series of small panels below and above the Crucifixion scenes. Each of the panels presents an image of Christ flanked by two men. Each therefore is visually related to the Crucifixion scenes, in which Christ is flanked by Longinus and Stephaton. The small flanking panels lead the eye of the onlooker away from, and back towards, the central image of each west side, the Crucifixion. They encourage the onlooker to see a variety of visual, and thus thematic, links between the Crucifixion and these scenes of suffering and recognition.

On the shaft of Muiredach's Cross (pl 87), three small panels occur below the crossing. The lowest of these has explicit, and apparently ironic, references to *sustentatio*: its central theme seems to be Christ's kingship, ironically revealed in his Passion. In his right hand Christ holds a vertical staff or reed as though he were a king. But a soldier grasps Christ's raised left forearm; and this soldier holds a sword in his left hand, with its point at Christ's navel. On the left side of the panel, the second soldier holds his sword over his right shoulder, and pulls at Christ's cloak with his left hand. The panel seems to summarise the early stages of the Passion, and to combine elements of an 'Arrest' scene with the representation of the Mocking of Christ as King.[87] In the small panel directly above, Christ, facing frontally, is flanked by two other frontal figures. All three hold books; Christ holds the book in his left hand, and his right hand is raised, with two fingers extended in a gesture of blessing. The left hand figure points towards Christ's right side in an attitude of recognition. Harbison has found a convincing parallel between this gesture and that of St Peter in the now-lost apse of Sant'Andrea in Catabarbara in Rome, and convincingly interprets the scene as a representation of the raised Christ, recognised as king and priest by, and between, Saints Peter and Paul. This panel therefore

---

[87]Peter Harbison, I, 144 (Panel W 1), 270-72; II, fig 482; III, figs 875-80.

reverses the theme of the Arrest-Mocking below.[88] The ubiquity of books in scenes in which the triumph of Christ is recognised is noteworthy. It may be explained by the copying of ancient artistic models; but it is likely to have been reinforced by, and to have itself encouraged, the use of precious gospel books for display purposes in liturgical processions like those we have examined in the *Apertio aurium* and *Ordo Romanus primus*. The third small panel, just below the transom, represents the *traditio clavium*.[89] It complements the scene of the raised Christ directly below: Christ the King now hands on the keys (his power to bind and loose) to St Peter, and the New Testament to St Paul. The two saints, as they receive the symbols of their ecclesiastical offices, bow courteously to Christ in gestures which recall the solemn transferrals of liturgical books and objects in the *Apertio aurium* and *Ordo Romanus primus*. Christ no longer stands: in this scene he sits enthroned, and demonstrates his kingly power by generously transmitting it to his two most eminent officers. As the eye travels upwards along the shaft of Muiredach's Cross it encounters one scene of suffering in which Christ is paradoxically revealed as *Rex Iudaeorum*, and two scenes in which Christ is progressively revealed as the risen king and the source of the church's authority. At the foot of the shaft the dedicatory inscription, a request for prayers for abbot Muiredach (*OR DO MUIREDACH LASNDERN ... RO*: 'prayer for Muiredach who had the cross erected') forms the background to two cats in high relief. The cats exemplify, respectively, kindness and aggression: 'The cat on the left licks its kittens which it holds in its front paws, while the other cat is about to devour a bird which it grasps in front of it'.[90] In a fine stroke of monastic wit, a playful counterpoint to the serious scenes above in which Christ is three times made known *in medio duorum*, Muiredach's need for prayers is still made known to the patient reader who peers among his two vigorous cats.

The three small panels, by reiterated variations on the *sustentatio* tableau, encourage the viewer to read the great Crucifixion scene as likewise a theophany, in which Christ is revealed as God and man. If the viewer is aware of the association between the *sustentatio* tableau and the *in medio duorum animalium innotesceris* chant, the small panels encourage him to seek reminiscences of that chant in the Crucifixion scene. Reminiscences are not hard to find, as the sculptors seem to have used all their ingenuity to present Christ crucified between a variety of flanking figures. The largest of these, Longinus and Stephaton, are much smaller in scale than the figure of Christ, and are thus clearly subordinated to him. Two round knobs or heads on either side of Christ's knees are likely to represent the sun and moon (*sol et luna*).[91] Two angels, hovering above Christ's shoulders, support his head. At the beginnings of the crossing to left and right, outside the figures of Longinus and Stephaton, are two small figures which have been identified by Harbison as the earth (*Gaia*) and the ocean or water (*Tellus*). Harbison's

---

[88]Harbison, I, 144 (Panel W 2), 293-94; II, figs 480-81; III, figs 919-26.
[89]Harbison, I, 144 (Panel W 3) and 294-95; II, figs 480-481; III, figs 925-29.
[90]Harbison, I, 143.
[91]Harbison, I, 144.

suggestion is attractive, as it would add earth and water to the cosmic symbols of *sol et luna*.[92] Even 'two animals' themselves are present. Immediately below the feet of the crucified Christ, a small bird with outstretched wings stands on the ground. Below the line representing the ground, animal interlace winds around four bosses. Another four bosses linked by animal interlace occur just above the two angels who support the head of Christ, and between the bosses and the housecap 'two birds interlock their necks so that their heads face back towards their tails' (pl 88).[93] Whatever about the interpretation of individual details, the intention of the sculptors is clear: to multiply references to flanking figures (angelic, allegorical, human and animal) so as to encourage the onlooker to view the Crucifixion scene as an epiphany of Christ as man, and a theophany of Christ as God.

As analogues for the 'Arrest' scene in Kells, the west faces of the Monasterboice crosses therefore provide significant contrasts as well as similarities. To a certain extent, different artistic principles are at work in the book and in the sculpture. The book compels a recognition of multivalence by fusing a number of associations in a single image. The sculpture openly demonstrates that the Crucifixion is a multivalent image by visually relating it to a number of smaller scenes, some of arrest and suffering, others of recognition and glory.[94] Nevertheless, a number of these smaller scenes are themselves complex in design and in meaning, as the variety of modern interpretations of them indicates.[95] The best example of a truly multivalent image in these monuments is perhaps the panel at the top of the west side of Muiredach's Cross (pl 88). In its use of the *sustentatio* tableau this panel itself provides a striking analogue of the multivalence embodied in the Kells 'Arrest' image. In the panel the central figure, Christ, has his arms raised towards heaven. His hands are clearly displayed, palms facing outwards. On each palm, in slanting light, slight protuberances can still be seen. They seem to denote the marks of nails. The gesture therefore serves to display the wounds in his hands; it also establishes in the panel a sense of upward movement. But the gesture is also clearly a gesture of prayer, reminiscent of an *orans* gesture. The outstretched hands of Christ in this panel are clearly related visually to his outstretched hands in the great central Crucifixion scene: this visual reminiscence of the Crucifixion tableau

---

[92]Harbison, I, 145, 279; II, figs 480-81; III, figs 892-94.

[93]Harbison, I, 145; II, fig 481.

[94]Yves Christe, *La vision de Matthieu (Matth. XXIV-XXV). Origines et développement d'une image de la Seconde Parousie*, Bibliothèque des Cahiers Archéologiques X (Paris 1973), argues that in christian iconography a gradual shift took place between the eighth and tenth centuries from ahistorical, theophanic, triumphal images of Christ, modelled on ancient imperial iconography, to an increasing emphasis on the representation of particular historical events in Christ's life; he argues that the Carolingian period was decisive in this shift towards historical particularism (pp 50-54).

[95]Harbison's great study is particularly valuable, not only for its minute descriptions and excellent photographs of the crosses and intelligent analyses of them, but because it carefully documents the various modern interpretations of individual panels. On the two great Monasterboice crosses, see Harbison, I, 139-53; II, figs 472-99.

in the *orans* posture (above it) implies that the Crucifixion was, like this upper panel, an act of prayer.

How then are we to interpret this panel? What meaning or meanings are we to attach to it? As the marks of nails are still visible in Christ's hands, the panel is primarily a picture of Christ made known, after the resurrection, between two angels. It carries one stage further the tableaux of Christ's kingship in the three small panels directly below the Crucifixion. As the panel occurs at the top of this side of the cross, and as Christ's raised hands reach towards the sky, the panel clearly refers to the Ascension.[96] However, the angels support the raised hands of Christ, so that his hands form a gesture clearly reminiscent of the *orans* posture. It would I think be a mistake to refuse to see in such a gesture a visual reminiscence of the great Old Testament example of the *orans* gesture, when at the battle of Rephidim the hands of Moses raised in prayer were supported by Aaron and Hur (Exodus 17:11-12).[97] As Christ stands between two angels, and as the scene is placed on a house-cap which is clearly designed to recall the design of a church building, it is reasonable also to see in the scene a reference to the Temple, in which God was known between two cherubim.[98] But the abstract shadows of the Old Testament are here seen as fulfilled in the physical reality of the New: the angels no longer conceal God's body with their wings (as they do in the Vulgate text of Isaiah's vision, Is. 6:1-3); they reveal it, and turn to the onlookers as though to invite them to recognise in Christ's wounded but glorified body God 'revealed between two cherubim'.[99] The emphasis on the wounds in Christ's hands may be intended to remind the onlookers of the Parousia, in which Christ is to display his wounds to those who pierced him.[100] Apart from the various subsidiary associations, the central originality of the panel has been to fuse two narrative moments into

---

[96]As demonstrated convincingly by Roger Stalley, 'European art and the Irish high crosses', *PRIA* 90C (1990) 135-58 (pp 138-41); Harbison, I, 145; III, figs 915-16. I find the arguments of Stalley and Harbison persuasive; but I wish to emphasize the other dimensions of meaning which the sculptors at Monasterboice have incorporated into their image, dimensions which I do not find in the analogues adduced by Stalley and Harbison.

[97]R A S MacAlister, *Monasterboice, Co Louth* (Dundalk 1946) 43; but see Harbison, I, 290-91.

[98]Ó Carragáin (1988, note 69 above) 29. A similar reference to Christ 'between two cherubim' may have been intended in the inner pair of angels who physically support Christ in the Porte Miégeville at Toulouse: Stalley (note 96 above) 140, pl II.

[99]Ó Carragáin (1988, note 69 above) 27-29.

[100]As was recognised by Helen Roe, *Monasterboice and its monuments* (Dundalk 1981) 33-34, who saw in the scene a reminiscence of Zechariah 12:10-11 'and they shall look upon me, whom they have pierced', a prophecy quoted in St John's gospel at the moment of Christ's death (John 19:37). John's gospel was read, in most European liturgies, on Good Friday; and Zechariah's prophecy was cited at the beginning of St John's Apocalypse: 'Behold, he cometh with the clouds, and every eye shall see him: and they also that pierced him' (Apocalypse 1:7-8). The aspect of the panel which looks forward to the parousia of Christ is 'fulfilled' in the central images of the opposite, east side of Muiredach's cross, both in the small *Majestas domini* scene in which Christ reappears between two angels, and in the great tableau of the Last Judgement: see Harbison II, fig 490. See now the fine analysis of references to these scriptural texts in early medieval art in Jennifer O'Reilly, 'Early medieval text and image: the wounded and exalted Christ', *Peritia* 6-7 (1987-88) 72-118 (pp 94-100).

a single triumphal image of Christ. One moment, the Ascension, is an historical event which took place in the past (but which, as a theophany of Christ, was continually made present in the liturgy); the other, Christ's display of his wounds on the Last Day, is to take place 'any moment', at an unknown day or hour: it is an urgent eschatological image, encouraging the onlooker to swift repentance. The sculptors have created an image which expresses the full force of the prophecy, which Luke in the Acts of the Apostles placed in the mouths of the two men in white. These appear after Christ has disappeared, and say to the apostles 'Why are you Galileans standing here looking into the sky? This Jesus who has been taken up from you into heaven will come back in the same way as you have seen him go to heaven' (1:11). At Monasterboice the 'men in white' appear as winged angels holding books: they appear, not after Christ has disappeared, but honouring him and making him known in a *sustentatio* tableau. Their books imply that in this *sustentatio* the Old Testament as well as the New has been fulfilled.[101] The Monasterboice artist has created a truly multivalent image. The ability to create images rich in association, as in this panel and in the 'Arrest' page of the Book of Kells, was one of the great glories of early medieval monastic culture.

Such rich multivalence is alien to our own scholarly traditions, much influenced by nineteenth-century positivism; thus it was natural that most of the scholarly effort on the Monasterboice iconography has been expended in identifying the precise narrative content of the individual panels, in eliminating the uncertainty implied in multivalence. This scholarly effort has by no means been misdirected. It is a necessary field of enquiry, and the variety of interpretations advanced for each panel by a variety of scholars has great value. Some identifications may indeed be unconvincing or mistaken; but many are only apparently contradictory: they are intelligent scholarly responses to the multivalence of association built into some of the panels. But the efforts to tie down individual panels to particular narrative moments need to be complemented by a recognition that, in high crosses, the *fundamental* image is the cross as a whole (as, in the Book of Kells, the fundamental image is the book itself, not any page within it). Individual sides of each cross tend to form subordinate unities, and meaningful relationships are often established between opposite sides of crosses.[102] Individual panels should be seen in the context of the greater images provided by the monument as a whole. Panels should be seen as it were as individual words in the complex sentence which is expressed only by the overall design of the cross, primarily through the complex relationships established between the various parts of the monument.

---

[101]See Jerome's reference to *in medio duorum animalium* as referring to the way in which both Old and New Testaments reveal Christ, quoted above, pp 422-23.
[102]Some of the relationships between opposite sides of crosses are explored in Ó Carragáin (1988, note 69 above) 16-20 (South Cross, Kells), 20-22 (Moone); 'Bewcastle Cross' (note 8 above) 30-33; and 'Ruthwell Crucifixion poem' (note 8 above) 15-29, 50-2.

The Monasterboice crosses are particularly interesting in this regard. It is clear that the designers composed each side as a visual unity, made up of visually related panels, so that each side provides a series of variations on a single visual theme. The west side of each cross is dominated by a Crucifixion scene, and the small panels above and below the Crucifixion scene provide an ordered visual commentary on the implications of the Crucifixion. In a series of variations on the theme that 'Christ is to be known between two creatures', they set forth the various levels of association, from suffering to triumph and from Passion to Parousia, which Christ's act of Atonement involves. Central to the design of the west sides of the Monasterboice crosses, but not much featured on the east sides,[103] is the 'figure of three' design in which the status of the central figure is revealed by placing that figure between two other figures. To see these west sides we have to face east, towards the rising sun. There was an early christian tradition, well known both in England and in Ireland, that Christ faced west on the Cross.[104] In the early medieval period, the congregation and the celebrant faced east to celebrate mass. Could mass, or other stational processions, have been celebrated before the Monasterboice crosses in the early middle ages?[105] If so, the *sustentatio* tableau might have been enacted while the celebrant was standing near or passing before the monuments, either at the *introit*, offertory, Preface or communion of the mass, or during a stational procession within the monastic enclosure. Such a liturgical tableau would have expressed through dramatic action the idea which unifies the west sides of these monuments: that the liturgical celebration (in which the celebrant like Christ on the Cross was honoured between two creatures) was a participation by mankind in Christ's sacrificial prayer to his Father when, raised up on the Cross, he sent forth the Spirit which drew all ages to him.

---

[103]Note the almost complete absence of the 'figure of three' tableau on the east side of Muiredach's Cross (Harbison, II, fig 473). There the only occurrence of the tableau is the seated figure (of Christ?) between two angels, directly above the Last Judgement scene. Harbison (I, 142) identifies this tableau as a *majestas domini*. If his identification is correct, then this small tableau can be seen as the fulfilment of the prophecy implied in the multivalent 'Ascension — display of wounds' panel at the top of the west face. The east side of the Tall Cross at Monasterboice (Harbison, II, figs 488-90) is similarly lacking in 'figure of three' tableaux, except for the single example, on the arm of the cross to the left of the large central scene, which Harbison (I, 148) identifies as the temptation of St Anthony.

[104]See Ó Carragáin (1987, note 60 above) 120; (1988, note 69 above) 9.

[105]As suggested by Otto Nussbaum, *Der Standort des Liturgen am christlichen Altar vor dem Jahre 1000: eine archäologische und liturgiegeschichtliche Untersuchung*, Theophaneia, Beiträge zur Religions - und Kirchengeschichte des Altertums 18, 2 vols (Bonn 1965) I, 372. On Nussbaum's general thesis, see now Marcel Metzger, 'La place des liturges à l'autel', *Revue des sciences religieuses* 45 (1971) 113-45. On the importance of orientation in medieval liturgy, see above all Cyrille Vogel, '*Versus ad Orientem*. L'Orientation dans les *Ordines Romani* du haut moyen âge', *La Maison-Dieu* 70 (1962) 67-99; Vogel, '*Sol Aequinoctialis*. Problèmes et technique de l'Orientation dans le culte chrétien', *Revue des sciences religieuses* 36 (1962) 175-211; and Barbara Maurmann, *Die Himmelrichtungen im Weltbild des Mittelalters*, Münstersche Mittelalterschriften 33 (Munich 1976). The various uses to which crosses were put are surveyed by Ann Hamlin, 'Crosses in early Ireland: the evidence from written sources' in Ryan, 138-40.

In interpreting such images as the four evangelist pages or the 'Arrest' page
in the Book of Kells we should keep in mind, not only the images which
survive in the visual art of the period, but also the vanished visual images
of early medieval liturgical action. The performance of a developed liturgy
was, certainly by the eighth century, central to European monastic life. The
Book of Kells probably stems from such a liturgically aware monastic
culture. Such lost dramatic images as we can reconstruct through the
surviving liturgical documents provide us with *one* important context
(among many) within which the images of the Book of Kells may be
interpreted.

Textual structure, decoration, and interpretive images in the Book of Kells

The Book of Kells presents the earliest surviving examples of full-page illustrations inserted within the text of a gospel manuscript: the Temptation of Christ (pl 42) and the depiction called the 'Arrest of Christ' (pl 28). Their uniqueness makes them difficult to place as links in a tradition of bible and gospel book illustration or to explain iconographically by established methods of art history. Nevertheless, their positions within the text relate them to insular gospel book decoration in one striking way.

As Patrick McGurk[1] noticed in his studies of the textual structuring of early gospel manuscripts, they are inserted at two points sometimes emphasised in insular manuscripts with enlarged, often decorated initial letters. Some of the largest and most elaborate mark off major divisions organizing the text, while smaller ones usually articulate minor divisions equivalent to paragraphs, sentences, and phrases. According to Malcolm Parkes,[2] decoration in insular manuscripts forms an equivalent to punctuation, the two graphic forms having been developed side-by-side in Ireland. Their equivalence can be seen in the text of the temptation according to Luke, presented in block format in an eighth- or ninth-century Irish manuscript, Bodleian, Rawlinson G.167[3] (pl 129). Enlarged letters and *et* signs are embellished with dotted contours and their interior spaces filled with colour. A few of these decorated letters correspond to beginnings of Eusebian sections,[4] others roughly to verse beginnings. In contrast with this block format, the columned format of a manuscript articulating the text *per cola et commata*, with each verse beginning on a new line, such as the Lindisfarne Gospels, would place each of these letters at the beginning of a verse line. Each verse represents a sense unit, set off by a pause when read aloud, which was the normal way of reading in antiquity and the early

---

[1]P McGurk, 'Two notes on the Book of Kells and its relation to other insular gospel books', *Scriptorium* 9 (1955) 105-07; McGurk, *Gospel books*. I am indebted to the librarians, colleagues, and staffs of institutions who assisted in obtaining access to manuscripts and libraries. I am particularly grateful to Bernard Meehan and the staff of Trinity College Library, Patricia Stirnemann, Michelle and Cecil Brown, Julian Plante of the Hill Monastic Library, Joan Williams of Hereford Cathedral Library, and Henry Mayr-Harting. The Research Institute and the Humanities Center of the University of Alabama in Huntsville provided funds for travel and photographs.

[2]M Parkes, 'The contribution of insular scribes of the seventh and eighth centuries to the "grammar of legibility"' in *Grafia e interpunzione del latino nel medioevo*, ed A Maierù, Lessico intellettuale europeo 41 (Rome 1987) 15-31 (p 23).

[3]Folios 10v-11v; P McGurk, 'The gospel book in Celtic lands before AD 850: contents and arrangement', in *Irland und die Christenheit: Bibelstudien und Mission*, ed P Ní Chatháin and M Richter (Stuttgart 1987) 166-89 (pp 170, 172-173).

[4]At *Ihs autem* (incipit verse 1) and *et nihil manducavit* (in middle of 2).

middle ages.[5]

Structuring, especially minor structuring, varies, however, from manuscript to manuscript, just as modern punctuation is subjective. In this way, graphic articulation of a text is interpretive: its purpose is to make the meaning of text accessible and to remove ambiguity from the meaning of written text, an especially important consideration when its language is secondary for its audience, as Parkes,[6] Jean Vezin,[7] and David Ganz[8] have pointed out. The importance of the interpretive aspects of textual articulation is magnified by the fact that large format gospel manuscripts like this were made for public reading during the liturgy,[9] a context which was itself interpretive and authoritative. In other words, meaning of scripture was expanded but it could not be ambiguous, and presentation of the text had to be controlled in order that its meaning should not be subverted.[10]

In the Bodleian manuscript one can also see the upper end of the textual structure in the conspicuously enlarged abbreviation of *Iesus* at the upper left. It rebegins the gospel narrative after the lists of the genealogy of Christ, visible above it. Thus, as graphic articulation of the narrative structure of the gospel text, it parallels the famous Chi Rho initials, which stand in the corresponding point in the Gospel of Matthew. The incipit at Luke 4:1 and the Chi Rho represent a kind of second beginning of their books. McGurk,[11] Jonathan Alexander,[12] and Julian Brown[13] have suggested that the two illustrations in the Book of Kells arose from the insular tradition of emphasising certain points in the textual structure with full-page, elaborately decorated initials such as the Chi Rho. The Temptation illustration stands at this point, facing the first words of the story at Luke 4:1, expanded in the Book of Kells to a full-page, floridly decorated incipit. The emphasized incipits at Luke 4:1 can be explained from a structural standpoint, but this does not explain the reasons for selecting this point, and that at which the 'Arrest' stands, for placement of full-page illustrations, nor

---

[5]J Vezin, 'Les divisions du texte dans les évangiles jusqu'à l'apparition de l'imprimerie' in Maierù (note 2 above) 53-68 (pp 54, 56-57); B Bischoff, *Latin palaeography: antiquity to the middle ages*, trans D Ó Cróinín and D Ganz (Cambridge 1990) 169.

[6]Parkes (note 2 above) 15-16, 20-21, 28-29.

[7]Vezin (note 5 above) 58-59.

[8]D Ganz, 'The preconditions for caroline minuscule', *Viator* 18 (1987) 23-43 (pp 38-43).

[9]Henry, 153; Vezin (note 5 above) 64. H Gneuss, 'Liturgical books in Anglo-Saxon England and their Old English terminology' in *Learning and literature in Anglo-Saxon England: Studies presented to Peter Clemoes on the occasion of his sixty-fifth birthday*, ed M Lapidge and H Gneuss (Cambridge 1985) 91-141 (pp 94, 106-09). Of course, whether the Book of Kells itself was ever actually read from during the liturgy cannot be proved.

[10]M Banniard, 'Le lecteur en Espagne wisigothique d'après Isidore de Séville: de ses fonctions à l'état de la langue', *Revue des études augustiniennes* 21 (1975) 112-44 (pp 131-33).

[11]McGurk (1955, note 1 above) 106-07.

[12]Alexander, *Insular manuscripts*, 73-74.

[13]T J Brown, 'The Latin text' in *Evangeliorum quattuor codex Lindisfarnensis*, ed T D Kendrick *et al*, 2 vols (Olten and Lausanne 1956-60) II, 34, 38, 40.

does it explain the unusual iconography of the two.

Perhaps the answers lie in the nature of the whole system of graphic structuring: the Irish and Anglo-Saxon monastic intelligentsia who developed these systems quite clearly envisioned it as a member of a comprehensive system of understanding the meaning of scripture and communicating it to the body of the church.[14] Furthermore, the illustrations probably were viewed in specific liturgical contexts.[15] Many of the full-page initials and the illustrations perhaps marked the beginnings of important passages for lection during Lent and Holy Week, corresponding to the pericopes of early, non-Roman lection systems, such as those recorded in the margins or capitularies of the Valerianus Gospels,[16] Rabula Gospels,[17] Gospels of St Kilian,[18] and Burchard Gospels.[19] The Temptation illustration was probably viewed on the first Sunday in Lent, when the account according to Luke is known to have been read in two seventh- and eighth-century North Italian liturgies[20] and in the late sixth-century liturgy represented by the notations in the Syriac Rabula Gospels.[21] The illustration shows Christ tempted on the roof of the Temple, not as a full-length figure but as a giant bust atop the building which is packed with rows of figures. This does not literally depict the gospel text, but rather interprets it using a standard tool of western exegesis, the figure of the Head (Christ) unified with the Body (the church). This very useful interpretive figure was first written up in a fourth-century exegete's manual, the *Liber Regularum*, by the renegade Donatist, Tyconius.[22] Augustine made certain its acceptance and widespread use by including it in his *De doctrina christiana*,[23] and using it throughout his work,[24] including his *Enarratio* on Psalm 90,[25] the

---

[14]M Irvine, 'Bede the grammarian and the scope of grammatical studies in eighth-century Northumbria', *Anglo-Saxon England* 15 (1986) 15-44; Vezin (note 5 above) 58-59; Parkes (note 2 above) 17-21, 24-25, 28-29.

[15]Farr, 'Liturgical influences', 127-41.

[16]H White, *The four gospels from the Munich manuscript now numbered lat. 6224 in the Royal Library at Munich*, Old Latin Biblical Texts 3 (Oxford 1888); G Morin, 'Un nouveau type liturgique', *Revue bénédictine* 10 (1893) 246-56; G Godu, 'Évangiles', *DACL*, 5/1, cols 852-923, at table of North Italian lections following col 882.

[17]A Merk, 'Das älteste Perikopensystem des Rabbulakodex', *Zeitschrift für katholische Theologie* 37 (1912) 202-16.

[18]P Salmon, 'Le système des lectures liturgiques contenu dans les notes marginales du MS Mp.th.q.I^a de Würzbourg', *Revue bénédictine* 61 (1951) 38-53; P Salmon, '... additions et corrections', *Revue bénédictine* 62 (1952) 294-96.

[19]G Morin, 'Les notes liturgiques de l'Evangélaire de Burchard', *Revue bénédictine* 10 (1893) 113-26.

[20]The lection systems presented in the *Codex Forojuliensis* and the Valerianus Gospels. D de Bruyne, 'Les notes liturgiques du *Codex Forojuliensis*', *Revue bénédictine* 30 (1913) 208-18 (p 212); White (note 16 above) liii, 78; Morin (note 16 above) 250.

[21]Merk (note 17 above) 207, 213.

[22]Tyconius, *Liber regularum*, ed F C Burkitt, in *Texts and studies, contributions to biblical and patristic literature* 3/1 (Cambridge 1895) 1-85 (pp 1-11); P Bright, *The Book of Rules of Tyconius: its purpose and inner logic*, Christianity and Judaism in antiquity 2 (Notre Dame, Indiana 1988).

[23]III.92-134, edition in CSEL 80, 104-107.

[24]Burkitt, 'Introduction' (note 22 above) xxiv.

[25]Augustine, *Enarratio in Psalmum XC* CCSL 39, 1254-78. See also Farr, 'Liturgical influences', 133-34; Farr, 'Lection', 81-96.

Quadragesimal psalm. In the *Enarratio*, Augustine interprets the Temptation of Christ by creating with words in the mind of the hearer a multi-leveled animate image of the church as the Body of Christ, the Head, resembling the visual depiction in the Book of Kells. A similar verbal figure in abbreviated version appears in a series of insular psalm titles,[26] which were written for interpretation often taking into account the liturgical context of the feast with which a psalm may be associated.[27] Bede drew upon the same image in his exegeses of the Tabernacle[28] and the Temple,[29] interpreted as equivalent figures,[30] and explained historical, allegorical, tropological, and anagogical figures using the Temple as an example in his work *De schematibus et tropis*.[31] Thus, with the Temptation illustration an interpretive figure is inserted into the graphic structure of the gospel text. Presented at opportune points in the text and in the liturgical year, the two illustrations put before the reader, and perhaps before a larger audience, complex, multi-leveled images which express both the means of interpretation and the past, present, and future sense of this interpretation.

Compared with the position of the Temptation illustration, placement of the other illustration at folio 114 seems more arbitrary in terms of graphic structure. It is literally set within the text of Matthew, facing the institution of the Eucharist, at 26:26-29. The words of verse 30, *Et ymno dicto exierunt in montem oliveti* ('And having said the hymn, they went out onto Mount Olivet'), are inscribed within the arch enframing the three human figures. On its verso, the ornamented incipit of verse 31 enlarges to cover the page with the words *Tunc dicit illis iesus: omnes vos scan(dalum ...)* ('Then Jesus said to them, "You will all fall away because of me tonight"').

This emphasis at verse 31 probably results from an early series of chapter divisions. A close study of continental and insular gospel manuscripts

---

[26]For example, the seventh-century *Breviarium in Psalmos*, edition in PL 26, col 116D: 'Iste psalmus ... de capite, vel membris cantatur. Caput in coelo, membra in terra. Et proprie intelligitur de jejunio, et illa tentatio eremi. Praevidebat propheta, quod venturus erat Christum in carne, ut tentaretur a diabolo'. Its influence may be apparent as well in the St Columba series, in P Salmon, *Les 'Tituli psalmorum' des manuscrits latins* (Paris 1959) 67; and the Pseudo-Bedan series, in PL 93, 970B; on their relationship to the figure of the Church, see L Scheffczyk, '*Vox Christi ad Patrem — Vox Ecclesiae ad Christum*: christologische Hintergründe der beiden Grundtypen christlichen Psalmenbetens und ihre spirituellen Konsequenzen' in *Liturgie und Dichtung, ein interdisziplinäres Kompendium*, ed J Becker and R Kaczynski, Pietas liturgica 1, 2 (St Ottilien 1983) II, 579-614 (pp 607-10).
[27]Salmon (note 26 above) 9, 30; M McNamara, 'Psalter text and psalter study in the early Irish church', *PRIA* 73C (1973) 201-98 (pp 214-15).
[28]Bede, *De tabernaculo et vasis eius ac vestibus sacerdotum*, ed D Hurst, CCSL 119A, 1-139 (pp 42-43, lines 1-70).
[29]Bede, *De templo libri II*, ed D Hurst, CCSL 119A, 140-234 (p 147, lines 1-35; pp 172-73, lines 1023-63).
[30]Farr, 'Liturgical influences', 131-34; Farr, 'Lection', 53-60.
[31]Bede, *Concerning figures and tropes*, trans G H Tannenhaus, in *Readings in medieval rhetoric*, ed J M Miller, M H Prosser, and T W Benson (Bloomington, Indiana 1973) 96-122 (pp 120-121); Irvine (note 14 above) 37-38. Other examples of the influence or translation of these verbal interpretive figures into figural images in insular manuscripts may be seen in the diagram of the Tabernacle in the *Codex Amiatinus* and the diagram of the Temple in the Book of Armagh.

suggests that early Irish manuscript production adopted this particular textual division. For example, the *Codex Corbeiensis* (Paris, BN, lat. 17225, folio 33r), a fifth-century column-formatted copy of a pre-Jeromian gospel text from Italy,[32] presents verse 31 with chapter number and with its first words in red letters (**pl 76**). In the early Irish gospel manuscript, *codex Usserianus primus* (TCD, MS 55, folio 25v),[33] this division is articulated within the block layout of the text with a series of red commas from the end of verse 30 at midline (**pl 67**). Verse 31 is written in red lead. This archaic way of articulating the division survives in the Durham A.II.17 gospels[34] where textual break and incipit *Tunc Iesus ...* are now dramatically emphasized by decorative 'punctuation' and kinetic letter shapes. In contrast, the Echternach Gospels (Paris, BN, lat. 9389, folio 65v),[35] even though closely related palaeographically and artistically to Durham A.II.17,[36] abandons the earlier type of text break and decorative emphasis with its advanced romanizing two column layout and *per cola et commata* articulation, as do other surviving insular gospel books presenting the meticulously organized layouts of Italianate articulation.[37] Nevertheless, this archaic feature of textual structuring, a conspicuously punctuated or decorated break between verses 30 and 31 and an emphasis on the incipit of verse 31, survives in the Book of Kells and other eighth- and ninth-century gospel books presenting text in block format and preserving other archaic features of structure. The pocket gospel books[38] (**pl 113**), for example, and the Breton manuscript called the 'Gospels of St Gatian'[39] (**pl 130**) are

[32]Vezin (note 5 above) 55-56; McGurk, *Gospel books*, 62-63; McGurk, 'Texts', 42-43; *CLA* (1950) v, no 666.

[33]McGurk, *Gospel books*, 79; McGurk (note 3 above) 172; *CLA* (1972) II, no 271.

[34]*The Durham Gospels; together with fragments of a gospel book in uncial: Durham, Cathedral Library, MS. A.II.17*, ed C Verey, T J Brown, E Coatsworth, and R Powell, (Copenhagen 1980) 20-21, folio 38 (2)v; McGurk, *Gospel books*, 29, 118.

[35]McGurk, *Gospel books*, 60-62; *CLA* (1950) v, no 578.

[36]T J Brown, 'The Irish element in the insular system of scripts to circa AD 850' in *Die Iren und Europa im früheren Mittelalter*, ed H Löwe, Veröffentlichungen des Europa Zentrums Tübingen: Kulturwissenschaftliche Reihe, 2 vols (Stuttgart 1982) I, 101-19 (p 111); Bischoff, (note 5 above) 91; *CLA* (1950) v, no 578; R McKitterick, 'The diffusion of insular culture in Neustria between 650 and 850: the implications of the manuscript evidence', in *La Neustrie: les pays au nord de la Loire de 650 à 850: colloque historique internationale*, ed H Atsma, Beihefte der Francia 16, 2 vols (Sigmaringen 1989) II, 395-432 (pp 423-27).

[37]For example, the Lindisfarne Gospels (folio 82r), the Royal Gospels (BL, Royal I.B. vii, folio 47r), and the *Codex Bigotianus* (Paris, BN, lat. 281, folio 68v). On romanizing layouts and articulation in insular manuscripts, see Brown (note 36 above) 108-09; Parkes (note 2 above) 24-29. On attribution of *Bigotianus* to eighth-century southern England, see McGurk, *Gospel books*, 59-60; *CLA* (1950) v, no 526, Alexander, *Insular manuscripts*, 60; Bischoff (note 36 above) 59-60.

[38]Dublin, TCD, MS 60 (Book of Mulling), folio 47v; TCD, MS 59 (Book of Dimma), folio 26; P McGurk, 'The Irish pocket gospel book', *Sacris erudiri* 8 (1956) 249-70; McGurk (note 3 above) 165-70; T J Brown (note 36 above) 113.

[39]Paris, BN, nouv. acq. lat. 1587, folio 28r; McGurk, *Gospel books*, 64; McGurk (note 3 above) 176; *CLA* (1950) v, no 684; Alexander, *Insular manuscripts*, 78-79; Bischoff (note 5 above) 90. On the other hand, the early ninth-century Book of Armagh (TCD, MS 52, folio 49v) places no special emphasis on either verse, even though the manuscript, presenting the gospels in a relatively small, block format, shares some of the features of the pocket gospel books, according to McGurk (note 3 above) 165-167, 173; however, Brown (note 36 above) 113, points out its relationships with the Echternach Gospels and Durham A.II.17. Also, the Hereford Gospels, usually given

included in this group. The reason for its survival, even in books connected with the romanizing phase of manuscript production of the late seventh and eighth centuries, may be because these manuscripts were made for use in some connection with a non-Roman liturgy in which this break in the text of the Passion in Matthew had acquired some sort of significance when read publicly, probably on Holy (Maundy) Thursday. The Passion is known to have been read from Matthew in non-Roman liturgies represented by seventh- through ninth-century pericopes and notations in the Lectionary of Luxeuil,[40] Valerianus Gospels,[41] *Codex Rehdigeranus*,[42] and other manuscripts.[43]

The importance of such a liturgical context to the questions at hand may be supported by a glance at two eighth-century continental manuscripts presenting texts for reading in non-Roman liturgies. The Bobbio Missal[44] presents the text of the institution of the Eucharist with verses 30-31 as part of the gospel pericope for Holy Thursday mass. Five lines down from the top of folio 97r, one sees a cross inserted into the text, between *montem oliveti* and *Tunc dicit*, at exactly the same point as the illustration in the Book of Kells. Furthermore, on the preceding folio a cross was added in the right margin, with indication in the text at the beginning of the institution of the Eucharist. In the Book of Kells this is the exact text facing the illustration, and that arrangement in Kells results from careful spacing on the preceding folio.[45] Whether the cross between verses 30 and 31 signifies a cue for some

a date of late eighth century and origin in Wales or western England (Alexander, *Insular manuscripts*, 63-64; McGurk (note 3 above) 174), presents its text in block format, but articulates Matthew 26: 30-31 by centring the end of verse 29 over verse 30, which is written out on a single line extending into the left margin. A small cross indicates the enlarged beginning of the verse (*Et ymno dicto*) written with an emphatic diminuendo. Verse 31 is clearly subordinated, with an incipit matched in size by many other initials of Eusebian sections. The beginning of the institution of the Eucharist, at verse 26, stands in midline and is marked with a heavy round point.

[40]Paris, BN, lat. 9427; *Le Lectionnaire de Luxeuil*, ed P Salmon, Collectanea biblica latina 7 and 9, 2 vols (Rome 1944, 1953), I, 87-88.

[41]Munich, Bayerische Staatsbibliothek, Clm 6224; Morin (note 16 above) 250; Godu (note 16 above) no 20 in table following col 882.

[42]Wroclaw, Stadbibliothek, Rehdig. 169 (destroyed 1945); G Morin, 'L'année liturgique à Aquilée antérieurement à l'époque carolingienne', *Revue bénédictine* 19 (1902) 1-12 (pp 2, 7). According to Lowe, 'a small correction on folio 120v is possibly insular, saec. viii', *CLA* (1959) VIII, p 16.

[43]Rabula Gospels, see Merk (note 17 above) 206, 213; 'Gospels of St Kilian' (Würzburg, Universitätsbibliothek MS Mp.th.q.1a), see Salmon (note 18 above) 43; Milan, Bibl. Ambros., MS C 39 inf., see G Morin, 'Un système inédit de lectures liturgiques en usage au VIIe/VIIIe siècle dans une église inconnue de la haute Italie', *Revue bénédictine* 20 (1903) 375-88 (p 378); Bobbio Missal (Paris, BN, lat. 13246), discussed below. See also Farr, 'Lection', 271-79, for further references and discussion.

[44]Paris, BN, lat. 13246, folios 96r-96v; reproduced in facsimile in *The Bobbio Missal*, ed E A Lowe, HBS 53 (London 1917); see also the edition of the text, with notes and studies by A Wilmart, E A Lowe, and H A Wilson, *The Bobbio Missal: a gallican mass book (MS Paris Lat. 13246)*, HBS 58, 61, (London 1920, 1924, repr in one volume, Woodbridge 1991) II, 61.

[45]*Kells facsimile*, folio 113r, presenting the text of Matthew 26:21-25. The block format was modified with centred verse endings to fill out the page so that verses 26-29 could be placed as a block on the following page.

visual or verbal feature of liturgy cannot be known, but it clearly indicates the importance of the point between the two verses in a liturgical reading and not simply a division to organize the text graphically. The second manuscript is a gospel book (Paris, BN, lat. 256) made in the neighbourhood of Paris around 700, with various lection notations added during the eighth century.[46] In this uncial manuscript, Matthew 26:31 (**pl 131**) is written in red lead, indicating a textual division. The first letter *T*, however, is drawn in black and set upon a 'platform', giving it the appearance of a cross on an altar or stand. The *figura* or shape[47] of the uncial *T*, like the Greek *Tau*, easily transforms into a sign with liturgical and textual significance: the Eucharist, Passion, Crucifixion, and salvation.[48]

The *figura* of the insular half-uncial *T*, for all its expressive and kinetic potential, cannot so easily take on this multiple sense, unless historiated in some way.[49] Possibly this is why an image of Christ depicted in the prayer pose called by insular monks the 'cross vigil' is placed at this point: to interpret and unify the texts of Eucharist and Passion (**pls 27-28**). Interpretive imagery united with liturgical text appears in eighth-century continental manuscripts, sometimes in gospel books, but also in other liturgical books. In the Gellone Sacramentary, the incipit *Te igitur* in the canon of the mass visually connects Eucharist, Crucifixion, and prophecy, as Jennifer O'Reilly[50] has shown. The Kells illustration resembles an efflorescence of punctuation, rather than the form of a letter. Nonetheless, this inflated punctuation becomes like the Gellone letter a *figura* articulating and linking the eucharistic text facing it, into a whole with the story of the sacrifice and martyrdom of Christ that follows, as Suzanne Lewis has suggested.[51] But also it expands the meaning of the events to include past,

---

[46]McGurk, *Gospel books*, 57-58; *CLA* (1950) v, no 524; F Mütherich, 'Les manuscrits enluminés en Neustrie' in Atsma (note 36 above) II, 319-338 (pp 320-21); T Klauser, *Das römische Capitulare evangeliorum, Texte und Untersuchungen zu seiner ältesten Geschichte*, Liturgiewissenschaftliche Quellen und Forschungen 28, 2nd edn (Munster 1972) xxxiii; G Morin, 'Le lectionnaire de l'Église de Paris au VIIe siècle', *Revue bénédictine* 10 (1893) 438-441.

[47]On the importance of the shapes of letters in ancient rhetoric and early medieval exegesis, see Parkes (note 2 above) 16-19, 28; Irvine (note 14 above) 16-17, 21-22; on the importance of the letters of the alphabet in the context of early Irish politics, see J Stevenson, 'Literacy in Ireland: the evidence of the Patrick dossier in the Book of Armagh', in *The uses of literacy in early medieval Europe*, ed R McKitterick (Cambridge 1990) pp 11-35 (pp 21-22).

[48]J O'Reilly, 'The Book of Kells, folio 114r: a mystery revealed yet concealed' in *The age of migrating ideas: early medieval art in northern Britain and Ireland*, ed R M Spearman and J Higgitt (Edinburgh 1993) 106-14 (pp 108-10); idem, 'The rough-hewn cross in Anglo-Saxon art' in Ryan, 153-58 (p 154).

[49]On the preference of uncial letters for gospel incipits, see C Nordenfalk, *Die spätantiken Zierbuchstaben*, Die Bücherornamentik der Spätantike 2 (Stockholm 1970) 122; J A Harmon, *Codicology of the Court School of Charlemagne: gospel book production, illumination, and emphasized script*, European University Studies Series 28, History of Art 21 (Frankfurt am Main 1984) 107-08.

[50]In the version of her lecture delivered at 'The Book of Kells Conference', 7 September 1992; also, B Raw, *Anglo-Saxon crucifixion iconography and the art of the monastic revival*, Cambridge studies in Anglo-Saxon England 1 (Cambridge 1990) 80-81, 116.

[51]S Lewis, 'Sacred calligraphy: the Chi Rho page in the Book of Kells', *Traditio* 36 (1980) 139-59 (p 155).

present, and future significance.

Harbison[52] and others[53] have pointed out the rich field of meaning associated with the cross pose assumed by Christ in the illustration. It is the early christian *orans* pose of prayer often signifying martyrdom.[54] As a typological figure of the cross, it is a well-known triumphal sign because of its prominence in the Old Testament story of the victory over Amalech.[55] Fifth- and sixth-century exegetes continue to connect the pose with the Passion and salvation,[56] but writers such as Maximus of Turin[57] and Gregory[58] put less emphasis on the association with literal martyrdom and more on its power as a weapon for the present-day believer who continues the struggle against evil by daily prayer. In an insular monastic context, the cross vigil's association with the passions of Christ and the martyrs and its connection with daily struggle against evil became a part of the holy man's identity of martyr in the expanded concept of martyrdom developed by the Irish, in which the ascetic experienced daily 'white martyrdom'.[59] In the illustration, Christ stands in the posture of the christian hero, the martyr, of which he is the first of all, the one imitated by the holy warriors carrying on the martyrdom in the sense of daily battle against the devil, who torments the church of the present from the time of the Passion up to the defeat of the Antichrist and Last Judgement.[60]

---

[52]P Harbison, 'Three miniatures in the Book of Kells', *PRIA* 85C (1985) 181-94 (pp 185-86).

[53]See Farr, 'Lection', 227-36.

[54]T Klauser, 'Studien zur Entstehungsgeschichte der christlichen Kunst', *Jahrbuch für Antike und Christentum* 3 (1960) 112-33; M-L Thérel, *Les symboles de l''Ecclesia' dans la création iconographique de l'art chrétien du IIIe au VIe siècle* (Rome 1973) 125-33; E Kleinbauer, 'The orants in the mosaic decoration of the rotunda at Thessaloniki: martyr saints or donors?', *Cahiers archéologiques* 30 (1982) 25-45; J Lindblom, 'Altchristliche Kreuzessymbolik', *Studia orientalia* 1 (1925) 102-13 (pp 109-11); Eusebius, *History of the Church from Christ to Constantine*, trans G A Williamson (New York 1965) 336.

[55]A K Porter, *The crosses and culture of Ireland* (London 1931) 52-53; M Schapiro, *Words and pictures, on the literal and the symbolic in the illustration of a text*, Approaches to semiotics, paperback series 11 (Paris 1973) 18.

[56]L Gougaud, *Devotional and ascetic practices in the middle ages*, trans G C Bateman (London 1927) 6-10.

[57]Maximus of Turin, *De cruce et resurrectione domini*, Sermo 38.3, in CCSL 23, 149-50, lines 32-41.

[58]Gregory the Great, *In primum regum expositiones* 6.3-4, in PL 79, 409B-410A.

[59]Gougaud (note 56 above) 10-12; J T McNeill and H Gamber, *Medieval handbooks of penance* (New York 1938) 31-32; W Godel, 'Irisches Beten im frühen Mittelalter', *Zeitschrift für katholische Theologie* 85 (1963) 261-381, 389-439 (314-15); P O'Dwyer, *Céli Dé: spiritual reform in Ireland 750-900* (Dublin 1981) 108-10, 120; C Stancliffe, "Red, white, and blue martyrdom' in *Ireland in early medieval Europe: studies in memory of Kathleen Hughes*, ed D Whitelock, R McKitterick, D Dumville (Cambridge 1982) 21-46 (pp 21-27, 29-45); D O Laoghaire, 'Irish elements in the *Catechesis celtica*' in P Ní Chatháin and M Richter (note 3 above) 146-64 (p 148).

[60]J Jeremias, *The unknown sayings of Jesus* (London 1957) 57-58; S Raponi, 'Christo tentato e il cristiano. La lezione dei Padri', *Studia moralia* 21 (1983) 209-38 (pp 210-11, 225-27); K Baltzer, 'The meaning of the Temple in the Lucan writings', *Harvard theological review* 58 (1965) 263-77 (pp 263-74). Also, the reference to the constant temptation of the Church in the anonymous eighth-century Irish commentary, on Luke 22:3, in CCSL 108C, 34, lines 219-23: '*Usque ad tempus*. Id, crucis usque ad bellum Antichristi in fine mundi, vel, *usque ad tempus* definitum prophetaturi, id,

In addition to the cross pose's references to the Passion and Crucifixion, it presents a eucharistic image in specific relation to the text facing it. Suzanne Lewis has already suggested that the chiastic *figura* of Christ's body grasped on either side may depict the *cofractio panis* of Iona's eucharistic rite.[61] The unique text of the institution of the Eucharist presented in Kells supports her suggestion. To the end of verse 26 ('This is my body ...'), the text of Kells adds *quod confringitur pro seculi vita*,[62] 'which is broken in pieces for the life of the world', using the verb, *confringo*, from which derives the term for the shared breaking of the host.[63] Thus, the book presents to the reader/viewer a deliberate verbal and visual play on the text of the institution of the Eucharist. The liturgical reenactment of passion and martyrdom is placed within the spiritual history of the world where it serves as the manifestation of the promise of salvation during the time of the present church until the end of the world. This connection is expressed verbally in the eucharistic formula of the Stowe Missal[64] and in the hymn 'Quando communicant sacerdotes' (or 'Sancti venite') in the Antiphonary of Bangor,[65] with their apocalyptic reference to the Last Judgement and Second Coming, as pointed out by Fritz Säxl.[66]

But the *figura* of eucharistic crucified body is further embellished in a way that links it to the words of verse 30 in the arch above it. Plant tendrils ascend from the heads of the two figures flanking Christ to enframe the words '... they went out to Mount Olivet'. As Carl Nordenfalk suggested these plants probably serve as cues to evoke the *locus sanctus*, Mount Olivet.[67] But also the gnarled branches of the plants appearing to grow from the heads of the two figures and the 'bracketed' *in montem oliveti* possibly were meant to identify the two figures as the two witnesses appearing in John's vision, described in Apocalypse (11:3-13): the two olive trees who 'stand in the presence of the Lord of the Earth'. A similar image appears in the Old Testament, in one of Zechariah's visions, in which the prophet sees a stone with seven eyes and the two olive trees appear on either side of a

usque ad iudicium veniat'. Warnings for constant vigilance against the devil's temptations appear also in connection with the celebration of Holy Thursday in the *Navagatio sancti Brendani abbatis*, ed C Selmer (Notre Dame, Indiana 1959, repr Dublin 1989) chs 6-7, 15, pp 12-16, 40-45. See Farr, 'Lection', 240-42.

[61]Lewis (note 51 above) 155.

[62]McGurk, 'Gospel text', 59-152 (pp 65, 97); also J O'Reilly's discussion in this volume, p 371, and in Spearman and Higgitt (note 48 above) 112-13.

[63]I am most grateful to P Meyvaert for bringing this point to my attention, in his personal communication, July 1989.

[64]*The Stowe Missal MS D.II. 3 in the Library of the Royal Irish Academy, Dublin*, ed G F Warner, HBS 31 (facsimile), 32 (text), 2 vols (London 1906, 1915, reprinted in one volume 1989) I, folios 36r-36v, II, p 18.

[65]*The Antiphonary of Bangor*, ed F E Warren, HBS 4, 10, 2 vols (London 1893, 1895) II, 10-11; F E Warren, *The liturgy and ritual of the Celtic church* (Oxford 1881) 187-89; M Curran, *The Antiphonary of Bangor and the early Irish monastic liturgy* (Dublin 1984) 47-49.

[66]F Säxl, 'The Ruthwell Cross', *Journal of the Warburg and Courtauld Institutes* 6 (1943) 1-19 (p 4).

[67]C Nordenfalk, 'Another look at the Book of Kells' in *Festschrift Wolfgang Braunfels*, ed F Piel and J Träger (Tübingen 1977) 275-79 (pp 275-76); C Nordenfalk, *Celtic and Anglo-Saxon painting* (New York) 124.

lamp with seven lights.[68] As prophets they bear witness against the Antichrist, whom they will fight against as warriors at the end of the world. The Antichrist will kill them, making them the last martyrs. In insular exegesis and apocrypha, the pair are identified as the Old Testament holy men, Enoch and Elias, who because of their spiritual perfection were taken bodily to heaven.[69] Insular literature pictures them in the landscape of paradise where they remain preaching and prophesying in the present time, awaiting the end of the world.

Their earliest mention in an insular context occurs in the mid-seventh century Irish exegetical work, De mirabilibus sacrae scripturae,[70] and continues in insular writings through the eighth century, including those of Aldhelm,[71] Blathmac,[72] Bede,[73] and the anonymous Irish authors of commentaries on the Apocalypse,[74] and onward into middle Irish apocrypha[75] and the homilies of Aelfric.[76] They are often associated with the

[68]Zechariah 4:2-14.

[69]M McNamara, The Apocrypha in the Irish Church (Dublin 1975) 1-3, 6, 26, 139. This identification originates as early as the second century in the association in early Hebrew, Greek, and Coptic apocryphal texts of Elias with prophecy about the physical appearance of the Antichrist, based on Malachi 3:23. B McGinn, 'Portraying Antichrist in the middle ages' in The use and abuse of eschatology in the middle ages, ed W Verbeke, D Verhelst, A Welkenhuysen (Leuven, Belgium 1988) 1-48 (pp 5-6).

[70]Augustinus Hibernicus, De Mirabilibus Sacrae Scripturae, 22, PL 35, col 2184: ... jamjamque Elias igneo curru receptus velut ad coelum, considerante Elisaeo, rapitur. Et hactenus ipse, sicut et Enoch in testimonium novissimi temporis, adhuc sine morte servatur, ut scilicet horum in ore duorum testium, novissimi testimonii sermo consistat, in extremo tempore, paulo antequam damnetur satanas, qui humanum genus aperto bello deprimat.
[... at that moment Elias was carried away in a fiery chariot into heaven, while Elisha watched attentively. And thus far, also like Enoch for the testimony at the end of time, he is kept in that place without death, as the word of final testimony stands in the mouth of these two witnesses at the end of time, shortly before Satan, who oppresses the human race with open war, is condemned.]

[71]Aldhelm, 'De virginitate, Carmen', in Aldhelmi Opera, Monumenta Germaniae Historica Scriptores, series 1, vol 15, ed R Ehwald, 350-471 (lines 248-82, pp 363-65); 'The Carmen de virginitate', in Aldhelm: the poetic works, ed and trans M Lapidge and J Rosier (Cambridge 1985) 97-259 (pp 108-09).

[72]Blathmac, 'Poem to Our Lady', quatrains 256-59, in Poems of Blathmac, son of Cú Brettan, together with the Irish Gospel of Thomas and a poem on the Virgin Mary, Irish Texts Society 47, ed and trans J Carney (Dublin 1964) 1-88 (pp 87-88).

[73]Explanatio apocalypsis, PL 93, 162B-D, 164C-D.

[74]The Pseudo-Isidoran commentary published by K Hartung, Ein Tractat zur Apokalypse des Apostels Johannes (Bamberg 1904) and more recently by G Rapisarda, Incerti Auctoris Commentarius in Apocalypsin (Catania 1967), reprinted in Patrologia Latinae Supplementum 4, ed A Hamman (Paris 1958-71) cols 1850-63 (col 1859); in the unpublished 'Reference Bible', passage cited by M McNamara, 'Plan and source analysis of Das Bibelwerk, Old Testament' in P Ní Chatháin, M Richter (note 3 above) 84-112 (p 99).

[75]McNamara (note 69 above) 1-3, 6, 26, 139; The two sorrows of the kingdom of heaven, Descensus ad inferos, Vision of Adamnan, and Antichrist, in Irish biblical apocrypha: selected texts in translation, ed and trans M McNamara and M Herbert (Edinburgh 1989) 19-21, 77-86 (p 86), 137-48 (p 147), 149-50 (p 150).

[76]Aelfric, Dominica I in Quadragesima, B Thorpe, The homilies of the Anglo-Saxon Church. The first part, containing the Sermones Catholici or Homilies of Aelfric, 2 vols (London 1844-46, reprinted New York 1971) II, 100-01; see also E Green, 'Enoch, Lent, and the Ascension of Christ' in De ore domini: preacher and word in the middle ages, ed T Amos, Studies in medieval culture (Kalamazoo, Michigan 1989) 13-25 (pp 13-19).

structuring of the history of the world, as in *De schematibus et tropis* where Bede explains a reference in Ecclesiasticus (44.16), 'Enoch, the seventh descendant of Adam ... carried out of the world', as an anagogical figure of the 'future bliss of the elect', reserved for them to enjoy at the end of the world, the seventh age.[77]

Moreover, in the Middle Irish story 'Settling of the manor of Tara', Fintan mac Bóchna, who came to Ireland before the Flood and survived into christian times, was eventually taken away, 'people think ... in his physical body ... to some secret divine place as Elijah and Enoch were taken to paradise, so that they are awaiting the resurrection of that aged patriarch'.[78] Kim McCone[79] has recently pointed out how the story of Fintan, in which the hero is asked by the Irish to lay out 'the foundations of chronology of the hearth of Tara itself with the four quarters of Ireland around it', assimilates pre-christian Irish past and Old Testament history with post-Patrician Irish and New Testament world order to enhance and maintain the authority of the Irish aristocratic *literati* and the church, whose interests and identity were thoroughly merged. The equation of Fintan with the two Old Testament heroes most certainly serves to reinforce this historical assimilation.[80]

Furthermore, McCone[81] suggests that the five-ridged stone set by Fintan at the site of the meeting of the fifths in Uisnech to signify Ireland, and the place of the Uisnech and Tara within it, is meant to imitate the Old Testament stones set up by Samuel and Josua, associated in the Bible accounts with kingship and witness to divine truth. If McCone is correct, this connection may be important in an Old Irish context because Isidore, a favourite source of insular exegetes, identifies the stone upon which Moses sat, arms raised, during the battle with Amelech as the *Lapis Adiutorii* of Samuel. Isidore also identifies it as the stone with seven eyes seen by Zechariah in his vision of the seven-light candelabrum fuelled by the two olive trees.[82] This passage from the *Quaestiones in vetus testamentum* was almost certainly known in Ireland and possibly in Northumbria by the eighth century.[83] The stone (as well as the candelabrum) presents an

[77]Bede (note 31 above) 120.
[78]Cited in K McCone, *Pagan past and Christian present in early Irish literature*, Maynooth Monographs (Maynooth 1989) 76; D Ó Corráin, 'Irish vernacular law and the Old Testament' in P Ní Chatháin, M Richter (note 3 above) 284-307 (p 294).
[79]McCone (note 78 above) 75-76.
[80]Ó Corráin (note 78 above) 293-94.
[81]McCone (note 78 above) 76.
[82]Isidore, *Quaestiones in vetus testamentum*, PL 83, col 299D: '... sedet Moyses super lapidem qui in Zacharia septem habebat oculos et in Samuelis volumine appellatur Lapis adjutorii et utramque manum ejus, Aaron et Hur, quasi duo populi aut duo Testamenta sustenant.'
('... Moses sat upon the stone which in Zechariah had seven eyes and in the Book of Samuel is called the Stone of Help, and Aaron and Hur, just as the two people or the two testaments, held each hand of his.')
[83]J N Hillgarth, 'Ireland and Spain in the seventh century, *Peritia* 3 (1984) 1-16 (pp 7-8); B Bischoff, 'Die europäische Verbreitung der Werke Isidors von Sevilla', *Mittelalterliche Studien* 1 (1966) 171-94 (pp 181, 183); M L W Laistner, 'The library of

eschatological and Christological figure, referred to in the Apocalyptic vision of the lamb with seven eyes. Further, the olive trees (Enoch and Elias, and also, by implication in the Tara story, Fintan) connect Old Testament and Apocalyptic visions. These powerful visionary images linked by the respected and up-to-date exegesis of Isidore to authoritative christian history, past and future, may have presented considerable appeal to a still-dynamic aristocracy surviving from a pre-christian age, who were, therefore, extremely interested in merging themselves with the past, present and future authority of the church. Allusions by literature about the history of history, such as the 'Founding of the Manor of Tara', to the identification of indigenous past with historical 'markers' like the boundary stones and Old Testament heroes that are going to reappear at the end of the world make use of a framework of spiritual history, enabling the social elite of the insular world to maintain and reinforce its authority and prestige within a new christian society. The authority carried by such imagery may have brought about visual images intended to resonate with the significance of this framework of spiritual history.

As the Temple in Jerusalem evoked the multilayered image of the body of the church of past, present, and future, so Mount Olivet evoked a layering of spiritual history: the Passion, the Ascension, and the end of the world. The Passion begins with the going out to Mount Olivet: Christ ascended into heaven from Mount Olivet, and he will return 'in the same way',[84] which was assumed to mean in the same place, and he is to appear not only as he appeared ascending but also as he appeared during his passion.[85] Mere mention of Mount Olivet often triggers an exposition of this time-sandwich of Passion, Ascension, and Apocalypse. The image of the two witnesses is carried in its layers, for they signify ascension and are associated with the final triumph over the Antichrist, who, according to some sources, will be killed by the Archangel Michael on Mount Olivet. Apocalypse writings of the tenth and eleventh centuries mention the location,[86] but the eschatological associations of Enoch, Elias, and Mount Olivet may be alluded to in the 'Reference Bible'.[87]

Because of the special resonances of 'Mount Olivet' and because of the division in textual structure at this point, punctuation becomes here a way

---

the Venerable Bede' in *Bede, his life, times, and writings*, ed A H Thompson (Oxford 1935) 237-66 (p 265).

[84] Acts 1:11-12.

[85] J Vaesen, 'Sulpice Sévère et la fin des temps' in Verbeke et al (note 69 above) 49-71 (p 55).

[86] Adso, *De ortu et tempore Antichristo*, PL 40, col 1134; Corpus christianorum continuatio mediaevalis 45, ed D Verhelst (Turnhout 1976) 28-29; cited in Green (note 76 above) 20-21. See also Green's discussion of later Enoch imagery, in the *Old English Genesis*, and iconography, in Anglo-Saxon manuscripts, ibid, 19-20. See also the association of Enoch and Elias with post-Resurrection sightings of Christ on Mount Olivet prior to his Ascension in the *Gospel of Nicodemus*, in McNamara and Herbert (note 75 above) 73-77.

[87] Cited by McNamara (note 74 above) 99: 'Id est residuum populi Israhel sub Helia et Enoch fugiens persecutionem Antichristi ascendet in montem benedictionis fidei Patris et Filii et Spiritus Sancti.'

of articulating, in the sense of dividing two sections of narrative content, and also a *figura*, unifying their meaning within an important liturgical lection.

Embedded into the Book of Kells' two *figurae*, the illustrations, is a complex symbolic ordering of time, imparting to history a spiritual significance, the stages of the presence of God on earth and in heaven. Although the exact context in which the two images would have been viewed remains unknown, it is surely important that they were placed into a book that served as an expression of authority, both of God and of the spiritual élite — priests and deacons — who actually presented the gospel book — the word of God — publicly by displaying it, reading from it, and verbally interpreting it to the broader audience of monks and laity.[88] Above them were bishops who controlled the things necessary to administering the sacraments,[89] the tangible signs of the presence of Christ, emphatically expressed in the two illustrations. Professor Ó Corráin[90] has made clear the importance of political background in understanding the Book of Kells. The political importance of control of the gospel text should not be overlooked. The systems of rhetoric and grammar which were fundamental to interpretation in the insular world were part of aristocratic cultural forms.[91] It is not surprising, therefore, that the illustrations may present an expansion of gospel events into a layering of time, a concept basic to christian theology and liturgy, but also a powerful tool for an élite to use to maintain and justify their position by placing themselves in connection with the truly important historical structures. While undoubtedly the illustrations served an exclusive audience on some personal level as objects of contemplation to impart revelation, this function itself was part of a larger process of interpreting and communicating.[92] The spiritually privileged served within a hierarchy functioning as a controlling interface between the presence of God and the people, a role of which Isidore,[93] Bede[94] and other exegetes wrote at length. Images in the Book of Kells may present *figurae* which reveal not only the truth of divine presence to the 'spiritually rational' but also paradigms of the process by which that truth was seen and passed on.

---

[88]Isidore, *De ecclesiasticis officiis* II, vii, ed C Lawson, CCSL 113, 64-69; Bede, *In Ezram et Neemiam* I, ed D Hurst, CCSL 119A, 235-392 (p 277, lines 1446-63); Farr, 'Liturgical influences', 135-37; R Reynolds, *The ordinals of Christ from their origins to the twelfth century*, Beiträge zur Geschichte und Quellenkunde des Mittelalters 7 (Berlin 1978) 56-68.

[89]H Mayr-Harting, *The coming of christianity to Anglo-Saxon England*, 3rd edition (University Park, Pennsylvania 1991) 135; Reynolds (note 88 above) 56-57, 60, 63.

[90]In this volume, pp 1-32.

[91]Parkes (note 2 above); Irvine (note 14 above).

[92]Irvine (note 14 above).

[93]Banniard (note 10 above); Irvine (note 14 above) 26-27.

[94]Mayr-Harting (note 89 above) 218-19; Irvine (note 14 above).

Crucifixi, Sepulti, Suscitati:
remarks on the decoration of the Book of Kells

Martin Werner

The Book of Kells has been the subject of much analysis directed at revealing its birthplace and date and the origin of its text, script and decoration.[1] Far fewer have been attempts to discover the existence of an iconologic, iconographic or liturgical impulse dictating the selection and arrangement of picture pages and/or ornament.[2] Of these Susan Lewis' examination of the Chi Rho page and related folios and especially Carol Farr's dissertation and paper on the liturgical background of two illustrations have been most important.[3] Although Lewis' general theory and her pioneering identification of the liturgical character of certain of the full-page miniatures must be recognised, her conclusions on several important points of meaning cannot be accepted. Farr's more comprehensive account of the influence of a lections system on the choice and placement of full-page illustrations and accompanying ornamented text pages is generally convincing, but she directs varying and sometimes little attention to programmatic aspects of the decoration of the preliminaries, the gospel incipits, the several isolated but lavishly ornamented incipit pages, the evangelist portraits and the 'ornament'. Including scrutiny of these large decorated pages and aspects of the repertoire of ornament in a study acknowledging Farr's substantial contribution will, I believe, yield a more precise and comprehensive picture of the elaborate plan followed for the embellishment of the manuscript.

Three factors necessarily restrict the scope of any inquiry into the programme: the incomplete nature of the book, the possibility that some of the impressively decorated pages have been incorrectly bound into the manuscript, and the existence of the thousands of figural, animal, foliate

---

[1] For discussion see *Kells commentary*.

[2] O K Werckmeister, *Irisch-northumbrische Buchmalerei des 8. Jahrhunderts und monastische Spiritualität* (Berlin 1967), interpreted four insular miniatures, including two in the Book of Kells, as reflecting an historic change in insular spirituality, a turning away from an earlier ascetic outlook derived from Cassian toward a contemplative theology centered on the *imago Dei* and preserved in the writings of Bede. In their reviews A Grabar, *Cahiers archeologiques* 17 (1968) 254-56, and P Meyvaert, *Speculum* 46 (1971) 408-11 were highly critical of this thesis. See also P McGurk's studies on the 'architecture' of early gospel books. These suggest the possibility that enlarged and ornamented initials were employed to set off important gospel lections: 'Two notes on the Book of Kells and its relation to other insular gospel books', *Scriptorium* 9 (1955) 105-08; idem, 'The Irish pocket gospel book', *Sacris Erudiri* 8 (1956) 249-70; idem, *Gospel books*. Henderson also comments on the question.

[3] S Lewis, 'Sacred calligraphy: the Chi Rho Page in the Book of Kells', *Traditio* 36 (1980) 139-59; Farr, 'Lection'; eadem, 'Liturgical influences', 127-41.

and geometrical details that both imply and challenge unequivocal meaning. In addressing the first, let us take note of various lacunae. At least ten leaves of text are missing at the opening. Folio 26v in the preliminaries is incomplete as are folios 177 in Mark, 229 in Luke and 330 in John — indications of the disappearance of text equalling that on about six leaves. Of greatest consequence is the disappearance at the end of John of twelve or thirteen leaves, the last four chapters on the Passion. Today, of the three hundred and seventy leaves that can be specified as once belonging to the book, only three hundred and forty remain.[4]

Controversy attends attempts at reconstructing the initial plan of decoration, but it seems likely that each gospel was prefaced by a page with the four evangelist symbols and a portrait of the gospel author, and begun with an elaborately ornamented incipit. If so, the codex has lost its portrait of Mark and its four symbols and portrait pages in Luke. John retains its author portrait but lacks illustrations. Given the importance of John's account of the Passion and the employment of illustrations in Matthew and Luke, it is very likely John once had one or two full-page illustrations.

Many of the most richly ornamented pages in the Book of Kells are on single leaves, the backs of which are (or originally were) blank. Before its last rebinding in 1953, the manuscript is known to have been rebound at least five times. What probably was its original binding was removed when the gospel book was stolen in 1007.[5] Its replacement is unrecorded. Then in 1742 the codex was rebound at which time bifolia 336/335, reported lost in the sixteenth century, was replaced in the wrong order.[6] Later in 1826, in the course of a disastrous rebinding, the surfaces of many leaves were damaged and leaves were cut off an inch at their margins obliterating valuable details of decoration and a number of then recent entries pertinent to pagination.[7] By 1892 a number of leaves had separated from the 1826 binding, some being exhibited in the Library. 1895 witnessed the penultimate rebinding,[8] again an unsuccessful attempt, for Françoise Henry tells us that in the 1920s 'twenty-two folios at the beginning were kept under separate cover'.[9] By 1952 another leaf had become loose.[10] Thus, before 1953, picture pages not directly or unequivocally connected to a particular text may have been moved from their initially intended positions.[11]

---

[4] B Meehan, 'Dimensions and original number of leaves' in *Kells commentary*, 175-76.
[5] The leaves missing from the beginning and end have usually been ascribed to the damage done when the binding was removed during the 1007 theft, but as Meehan (note 4 above, 175) points out there may have been other reasons for such lacunae. Not only are the first leaf of the first gathering and the last of the final gathering especially exposed but they may have been employed as board linings.
[6] B Meehan, 'Collation' in *Kells Commentary*, 185-92 (p 185).
[7] William O'Sullivan, 'Binding memories of Trinity Library' in *Decantations: a tribute to Maurice Craig*, ed A Bernelle (Dublin 1992) 168-76 (p 173).
[8] idem, 'Bindings: documentary evidence' in *Kells commentary*, 193-95 (pp 193-94).
[9] Henry, 152.
[10] Meehan (note 7 above) 194.
[11] When the manuscript was disbound in 1953, it included one hundred and forty leaves which were singles or had become nearly separated from their pair. See R Powell, 'Report on the repair and rebinding of the Book of Kells', *Annual Bulletin of*

As regards the issue of analysis of ornament for iconographic meaning, there are those who believe symbolic interpretation to be pointless because unprovable,[12] yet for the reason that so much of the decoration of the Book of Kells is clearly symbolic, there is need to scrutinise ornament for such expression.[13]

Nevertheless, because most of our attention will be directed to the portraits, illustrations and large figurative groupings, in only a few instances will more than cursory attention be given to details of ornament.

Despite its missing, incompleted, projected and possibly misplaced picture pages and the ambiguity surrounding the minutiae of decoration, the codex reveals much through its codicological divisions, placement and elaboration of incipits, and types of illustrations. The preliminaries consist of lists of Hebrew names (incomplete and beginning in the middle of a list on folio 1r), architectural canon tables, *Breves causae* and *Argumenta*. Then come the four gospels, each of which, as noted, probably began with an evangelist symbols page, an evangelist portrait, and an intricately ornamented initial page. Besides these gospels openings, Matthew 1:18, the beginning of the Nativity story which follows the royal descent of Jesus in the genealogy, is treated like the beginning of a gospel. Here the monogram of the Greek form of Christ's name (Chi Rho) fills the page, leaving room for only a small line of text at the bottom. Two miniatures, each on a single leaf, are inserted before the Chi Rho page (folio 34r), Christ Enthroned (folio 32v), and the cross-carpet page (folio 33r). We shall take up the issue of whether these miniatures were always intended as part of a *Christi autem generatio* sequence in Matthew and whether they had a prescriptive liturgical function in due course. In any event, however interpreted, they now function as constituents of an introductory series and this same introductory role is performed by the Madonna and Child on folio 7v. Painted on a single leaf, the portrait faces a page of richly ornamented text, the opening initial of the *Breves causae* of Matthew (*Natiuitas Christi in Bethlem Iudeae*) in the preliminaries. It consequently introduces an important section of text but, again, questions have been raised concerning its original position.

Tentative acceptance of the Madonna and Child and Christ Enthroned miniatures as introductory portrait pages sets them apart from another picture page category, that of full-page illustrations introduced within the body of the manuscript and accompanied by a page of enlarged and decorated text. The Temptation of Christ (folio 202v) and Arrest of Christ

---

the Friends of Trinity College Dublin (1953) 11-12; A Cains, 'Bindings: technical description' in *Kells commentary*, 197-207.

[12]See for example, C Nordenfalk, 'Katz und Maus und andere Tiere im Book of Kells' in *Zum Problem der Deutung frühmittelalterlicher Bildeinhalte: Akten des 1. internationalen Kolloquiums in Marburg a.d. Lahn 15. bis 19. Februar 1983*, ed H Roth (Sigmaringen 1986) 211-19.

[13]For a strong argument in favour of symbolic meaning for ornament, see I Henderson, 'The Book of Kells and the snake-boss motif on Pictish cross-slabs and the Iona crosses' in Ryan, 56-65 (p 65).

(folio 114r) fall under this rubric. They are painted on bifolia with no blank side and their material connection to the gospel text in which they are introduced can easily be shown. Without doubt they are in their originally intended places.

The Temptation of Christ illustration faces the opening of Luke 4:1 on folio 203r, the beginning of the Temptation narrative. The Arrest of Christ precedes Matthew 26:31, folio 114v, part of the narrative of Christ on the Mount of Olives. Neither miniature precisely illustrates its text, but Farr has identified the first illustration as facing a lection for Quadragesima Sunday in Lent following a non-Roman liturgical system,[14] and the second as coming before an initial likely to have been intended as a lection for Holy Thursday, again reflecting non-Roman usage.[15] Quite possibly a third illustration was meant for the manuscript. Henry suggested folio 123v in Matthew, a blank page, to have been reserved for a Crucifixion facing the enlarged and ornamented initials of Matthew 21:38,[16] the text of the Crucifixion which according to Farr was a Good Friday lection possibly modelled on a cento used in a liturgy of non-Roman type.[17]

The likelihood that a Crucifixion was planned for folio 123v removes folio 124r from the next category, that of isolated ornamented initial pages that do not face or follow full-page illustrations, a category imperfectly appreciated and scarcely studied. Folios 183r and 285r belong to this division. Each is elaborately decorated, is part of a bifolium, in its original

---

[14]Farr's dissertation first came to my attention in the summer of 1990. By then my article on the cross-carpet page in the Book of Durrow had been published and I had nearly completed a study of the iconography of the miniatures in the Book of Kells. This study, like the Durrow piece much concerned with liturgical reference, was presented in abbreviated form at the Maynooth Conference that same summer. Although our perspectives differ, it would appear that Farr and I had come to some of the same general conclusions concerning the importance of Easter pericopes for the imagery in Kells. However, her scholarship on non-Roman lection systems was considerably more comprehensive than mine. So as to clearly credit her contribution, I shall refer to her references when citing these systems.

[15]Farr, 'Liturgical influences', 131, notes that three extant lection systems use Luke as the source for the Quadragesimal lection. They appear in notations in the Syriac Rabula Gospels and in two north Italian systems found in the *Codex Forojuliensis* and the Valerianus Gospels; ibid, 131, nn 49-51. Henderson, 168-75, however, connects the reading to Holy Saturday. Pericopes for Matthew 26 read on Maundy Thursday are recorded in eight early manuscripts preserving non-Roman liturgies. Again, as with the Quadragesima lection, the earliest is in the Rabula Gospels. The Latin manuscripts include the Lectionary of Luxeuil, *Codex Valerianus*, Gospels of St Kilian, Milan, Biblioteca Ambrosiana, MS C.39, Milan, Biblioteca Ambrosiana, MS n. 28, Part inf., *Codex Rehdigeranus*, and the Bobbio Missal. Most employ north Italian lection systems; two preserve Gallican liturgies; Farr, 'Lection', 271-75; Lewis (note 3 above) 155. Farr, 'Lection', 216-17, also cites a Visigothic liturgy preserved in the eleventh-century Spanish *Liber Comicus*, wherein there are readings for a Passion cento for Matthew 26:30.

[16]Henry, 173.

[17]For non-Roman liturgies preserving Matthew's account of the Crucifixion as a Good Friday lection, cf Milan, Bibl. Ambros., MS n. 28, Part inf; *Codex Rehdigeranus*; *Codex Forojuliensis*; Gospels of St Kilian, Trier Gospels. The *Liber Comicus* contains a Good Friday Passion cento which begins the narrative of the Crucifixion at Matthew 27:38; Farr, 'Lection and interpretation', 128-29, nn 17-23.

position and meant to stand alone.[18] Folio 183r begins the Crucifixion with
Mark 15:24-25 (pl 32). Farr cites a Good Friday reading in the sixth-century
Syriac Rabula Gospels as part of the only lections system known to include
such a pericope.[19] Folio 285r displays initials for Luke 24:1, the description
of the women at Christ's tomb, a reading for Easter in several non-Roman
lections (pl 50).[20]

To this group of ornately decorated and framed text pages in the body of
one or another of the gospels — or perhaps belonging to a sub-division —
may be added folio 127v, Matthew 28:1-5. Here *Vespere h (autem)* begins a
second account of Easter morning marked by enlarged incipits. But unlike
the capitals in Luke or those of other of the major decorated incipits, only
the opening initials are emphatically singled out: a large *V* comprised of
interlaced snakes is followed by a framed line of initials set against a yellow
ground. It is unusual to find such a row of decorated initials along a full line
of text in the Book of Kells. Appearing as introductory *Argumenta* and *Breves
causae*, apart from folio 127v it is not found in the gospel texts. Yet Matthew
28:15 being a popular Easter Vigil reading the Kells initials were probably
intended as marking a pericope.[21]

Despite the fact that the emphasized incipits in the Book of Kells do not
conform precisely to any single early lections system, it has become obvious
that they must have marked lections. And as Farr concludes:

> Such comparisons of Kells full-page incipits with lection systems
> suggest the decoration of the manuscript's text may have been
> influenced by a non-Roman liturgy retaining a very early type of
> lections system ... These systems present elaborate cycles of readings
> for Lent and Holy Week, some with passion centos or distribution of
> passion text over the offices and masses of Holy Week. In contrast,
> Roman systems present much more elaborate cycles of readings from
> Advent and the weeks following the Nativity than do these non-Roman
> systems give for the same liturgical season.[22]

---

[18]Alexander, 'Illumination', *Kells commentary*, 268, n 12, misquotes Henry, 173, in
stating that she proposed folio 285r to have once accompanied, or have been
intended to accompany, a Resurrection miniature. She actually wrote 'It is not likely
to have faced an illustration, as that would have some text on the back and no text is
missing'.

[19]Farr, 'Lection', 333-34.

[20]Among others: Gospels of St Kilian; Lectionary of Luxeuil; Trier Gospels; Rabula
Gospels; Farr, 'Liturgical influences', 129, nn 26, 27.

[21]That the Book of Kells should have more than one lection marked for the Easter
Vigil is not unprecedented. Other feasts had more than one reading for vigils, mass
and offices; Farr, 'Lection', 131, n 282. Then too, Kells, which follows insular
tradition in its greater emphasis on Luke 24 over Matthew 28, may reflect a practice
suggested by the notes in the Rabula Gospels and a few liturgies in Gaul that the
Luke Resurrection text was read on Easter Sunday. Farr, 'Lection', 338-59.

[22]Farr, 'Liturgical influences', 130. For Roman system, see T Klauser, *Das römische
Capitulare Evangeliorum: Texte und Untersuchungen zu seiner ältesten Geschichte*,
Liturgewissenschaftliche Quellen und Forschungen 28, 2nd ed (Münster 1972).

Speculating that the early lections system influencing the distribution of incipits in Kells may have been a western fourth or fifth-century system resembling that in the Rabula Gospels or perhaps later western lections influenced by eastern practice, and touching on aspects of insular monastic practice encouraging to the adaptation of such a system,[23] Farr does not deal with the possibility of specific historic circumstance favouring the decorative and iconographic enhancement of this system. Yet we shall find Columban history to yield valuable insight on the matter of such inspiration.

An excellent place to engage this issue is the sequence of miniatures at Matthew 1:18. The series includes the magnificently detailed eight-circles cross on folio 33r (pl 21). Unique as the only carpet page in the manuscript, the folio is also unusual because its central emblem is composed of circles connected so as to form the outlines of a double-barred cross whose transoms are equidistant from its centre. Filled with Celtic pelta, trumpet and spiral patterns in grey against a black ground, the cross is outlined in yellow and enframed by the red border of the interspace compartments and outer frame. Embedded in this ornate setting and denied a supporting base, the central form acts as a lying or recumbent cross. Insular illumination yields but one earlier example of a double-barred cross-carpet page, that opening the Book of Durrow. Once again a large yellow cross is built up of eight foci, but they are now squares to which meander-like patterns are attached, the whole embedded in a compact field of interlace. As in the Kells miniature, the two transoms of the cross are of equal length and equidistant from the centre and again the emblem has no supporting base.

In a recent inquiry into the iconographic character of the Durrow cross-carpet page, I presented substantial textual and archaeological evidence in support of the possibility that the central form on the Durrow folio was conceived as a patriarchal cross, the double-barred emblem of the True Cross, the Cross of Crucifixion.[24] For our purposes, the most pertinent primary document is De Locis Sanctis, a report on the holy places of the East by Adomnán, ninth abbot of Iona.[25] Written c683 and based on the direct testimony of the Gallic pilgrim Arculf, its description of the Holy Sepulchre, Jerusalem, and of the Easter rites at Hagia Sophia, Constantinople, support an interpretation of the Durrow cross-carpet page as a highly abstract representation of the fragments and titulus of the True Cross displayed on the altar of the church of Golgotha in the Holy Sepulchre complex for the solemn Good Friday Adoratio Crucis ceremony. Folio 2r, the facing Majestas Crucis in the early insular codex, is dominated by an interlaced cross whose placement and distinctive ornamented base points to its identity as the Cross of Golgotha, the jewelled cross once standing on the site of the Crucifixion and representing the Crucifixion cross. The four evangelist

---

[23]Farr, 'Liturgical influences', 136; eadem, 'Lection', 341-48.

[24]M Werner, 'The cross-carpet page in the Book of Durrow: the cult of the True Cross, Adomnán and Iona', Art Bulletin 72 (2) (1990) 174-223.

[25]Text, translation and study by D Meehan, Adamnan's De locis sanctis (Dublin 1958).

symbols in the interstices of the Durrow cross become identified with the four rivers of Paradise where the Tree of Life - Crucifixion Cross grew. Together with complementary cosmological and christological ideas and associated dogma, the folios 1v-2r scheme seems meant to call to mind images of adjacent *loca sancta* the relic of the True Cross on the altar of Golgotha church and the great commemorative cross surmounting Golgotha hill. Within the context of *loca sancta* and early Easter liturgy, the eight linked crosslets of the Durrow patriarchal cross may symbolise the 'eighth day', the day of Christ's Resurrection. There is good reason to claim the *loca sancta* reference of the Durrow introductory sequence for Adomnán and to propose the creation of the manuscript at Iona during the years the great scholar prepared his pilgrimage text, that is, between 682 and 686.

The Durrow and Kells Gospels have long been shown to have significant textual elements in common. But in his recent detailed analysis of the Kells preliminaries Patrick McGurk revealed an even more intimate relation than had been suspected. He concluded that 'Durrow was the direct ancestor of Kells via one or two intermediaries ...'.[26] Aware of McGurk's findings J J G Alexander had this to say about the Kells eight-circles cross page:

> It seems clear that here the artist of the Book of Kells was able to draw on an insular, and perhaps, if the Book of Durrow was made at Iona or in the Irish ambit as some scholars think, a specifically Celtic tradition. In view of the link to the Canon Tables ... the Book of Durrow may even have been itself the model.[27]

Although the Durrow-Kells relationship has been given significant new substantiality and the dependence of the Kells cross-carpet page on that in Durrow recognised, because Durrow folio 1v and Kells folio 33v have been judged as essentially ornamental compositions the importance of their typological congruity has not been appreciated: quite clearly the Kells emblem must carry the same meaning as the earlier insular example. It is a patriarchal cross, the symbol of the True Cross.

The eight-circles cross page now occupies a position opposite the miniature of Christ Enthroned on folio 32v and before the XPI monogram on folio 34r. Before its iconographic function within the manuscript can be elucidated, it is, of course, necessary to inquire as to whether it was originally intended for this placement. More precisely, were the Christ Enthroned and cross-carpet pages meant to be complementary and to preface the Chi Rho miniature? Each is a singleton and conceivably could have been created for other locations, a possibility recently proposed for the Enthroned Christ.[28] Thus, for example, one or both miniatures might have been conceived for

---

[26]McGurk, 'Texts', 58.
[27]Alexander, 'Illumination', 274.
[28]Indeed, Farr, 'Lection', 321-30; eadem, 'Liturgical influences', 130, postulates both the Enthroned Christ and Madonna and Child pages as 'portrait pages' perhaps originally intended for other than present placement and to be distinguished from the 'illustrations' by stylistic and compositional differences.

insertion after the canon tables and before the Madonna and Child page and
Matthew *Breves causae*, the most ornate and complex of initial pages
introducing the *Breves causae* and *Argumenta* of the preliminaries. Is this
likely?

Two pages, originally blank, intervene between the canon tables and the
Virgin and Child miniature. Copies of Irish charters (more properly *notitiae*),
assigned by Gearóid Mac Niocaill to the third quarter of the twelfth century,
appear on the last two pages of the canon tables, on the back of a leaf
carrying the last table, and on the vacant folio backing the Virgin and Child
page.[29] This must mean that the Virgin and Child miniature was in its
present position at the end of the twelfth century.[30] Because the
overspreading of the charters does not allow for intervening leaves, it also
means that after the twelfth century the Christ Enthroned and cross-carpet
pages could not have been introduced to folios following the canon tables.
Arguably, single leaves could have gone astray between the time of the theft
of the Book of Kells in 1007 and the introduction of the charter copies.[31]
However, Kells remained the dominant Columban monastery in Ireland
through the mid-twelfth century so that it is unlikely that the correct
sequence of leaves would not be understood and maintained there.[32]

Alternately, placement before Matthew, that is before the folio 27v four
symbols page, is conceivable for the two miniatures now prefacing the Chi
Rho. A Christ in Majesty appears as frontispiece to Matthew in a continental
gospel book of the eighth century and in another of the early ninth

---

[29]Copies of Irish 'charters', more properly *notitiae*, appear on folios 5v-7r and 27r.
They record land transactions concerning the monastery of Kells. No 1 begins on
folio 6r and was completed on folio 5v; nos 2 to 5 are on folios 6v-7r, and nos 6 and 7
on folio 27r. Other such texts apparently were entered in the manuscript, on leaf or
leaves now lost, after folio 330r; Mac Niocaill, 'Charters'.

[30]Moreover, there is a verdigris green employed for elements of the Madonna and
Child page matched by similar use in the *Breves causae* page opposite. This
complementary utilisation is not found elsewhere in the Book and tends to support
the probability that folio 7v was intended to face the folio 8r incipit.

[31]The earliest reference to the Book of Kells occurs in 1007, when its theft was
recorded in the *Annals of Ulster* and the *Chronicon Scotorum*. This reference has been
translated and interpreted in many ways. Most recently P Meyvaert, 'The Book of
Kells and Iona', *Art Bulletin* 71 (1989) 11, n 22, translated the *Chronicon Scotorum*
entry which reads:

    Soiscélae mór Coluim chille do dubgait isin aidche asind erdum in doim liacc
    móir Chenannsa. In soscéla sin do fogbáil dia fichet adaig ar díb mísaib, iar
    ngait de a óir ⁊ fót tairis.

    The wicked theft of the great Gospel of Colum cille by night from the airdam of
    the great stone church of Kells. The same Gospel was found after two months
    and twenty days, its gold stripped from it and a sod covering it.

Meyvaert explains 'airdam' as probably a chapel attached to the church in which the
relics of St Columba were kept. As Meehan, 'The history of the manuscript' in *Kells
commentary*, 317-29 (p 317), observes, we cannot tell whether the passage was meant
to mean the manuscript was stolen for its ornamentation, its binding or its box
shrine, although, most likely, it was a valuable box shrine that attracted the attention
of thieves. See also G Mac Niocaill, 'The background to the Book of Kells' in *Kells
commentary*, 27-33 (pp 31-32).

[32]Mac Niocaill (note 31 above) 32-33; also Herbert.

century.[33]

Of course, using the Christ Enthroned and cross-carpet folios to introduce Matthew would create two sequences of miniatures before a gospel incipit, an awkward and unprecedented arrangement. Moreover, for the reason that the original programme of decoration seems to have called for a four symbols page before each of the gospels rather than a carpet page such as occurs in the Durrow and Lindisfarne Gospels, introduction of its one splendid carpet page proximate to the Matthew four symbols miniature would likewise appear to be inappropriate.

This said, it remains that there are some vague suggestions of placement intention for the Matthew 1:18 sequence. In St Gall, Stiftsbibliothek, MS 51, an Irish gospel book of the second half of the eighth century, a cross-carpet page precedes the enlarged XPI in Matthew.[34] Interesting too is Alexander's observation that the Christ Enthroned miniature in our codex is inserted after the first three pages of text of Matthew's gospel, folios 29v to 31v, which following the initial *L* on folio 29r lists the names of the ancestors of Christ coming to an end with the words *usque ad Christum generationes XIIII.* The next page is blank but for Alexander 'the image is linked to the specific words of the Gospel text' referring to the Saviour.[35]

In truth, the most compelling evidence for the authenticity of the Matthew 1:18 sequence is the character of folio 34r itself. The large monogram page elaborates an insular tradition of emphasizing the *Christi autem generatio* proclaiming the mystery of the Incarnation so as to effect, as it were, a second opening in the gospel of Matthew.[36] In Kells this seems to have encouraged the addition of complementary 'introductory' miniatures so that

---

[33]The Gospels of Saint Croix of Poitiers, a manuscript from the Amiens region, most likely of the second half of the eight century; the early ninth-century Lorsch Gospels, a product of the Court School of Charlemagne; M Werner, 'The *Madonna and Child* miniature in the Book of Kells, Part I', *Art Bulletin* 54 (1972) 14, n 59.

[34]Alexander, *Insular manuscripts*, 66-67, pls 200, 201. McGurk (note 2 above) 257, discussing the growth of the XPI initials in insular gospel books, surmises that 'the development of the XPI monogram into a fully decorated page led to a break in the manuscript which called for some sort of preface or frontispiece; this is the case in the Irish St Gall 51, it may also be the case in Kells'. It is also worth noting that in the ninth-century Irish Macdurnan Gospels (London, Lambeth Palace, MS 1370) the St Matthew portrait (folio 4v) precedes the Chi Rho page in Matthew (folio 5); Alexander, *Insular manuscripts*, 86-87, pls 322, 326; Henry, 173.

[35]Alexander, 'Illumination', 281. And, of course, the miniature is introduced before the XPI mongram, the name of Christ.

[36]Since the gospel of St Matthew begins with a genealogical history of Christ, the actual narration of the Nativity, or Incarnation, does not begin until Matthew 1:18. It comes to be given more elaborate treatment than the actual incipit of Matthew: Henry, 173; McGurk (note 2 above) 257-258. For the history of the chrism as an iconographic symbol, see E Kirschbaum, *Lexikon der christlichen Ikonographie* (Rome 1968) I, 456-58. Worthy of attention is the fragmentary Irish gospels of probably early seventh-century date, the *codex Usserianus primus* (TCD, MS 55; Alexander, *Insular manuscripts*, 27, pl 1) which has an XPI monogram cross at the end of St Luke (folio 149) with the explicit of Luke and incipit of Mark written on either side. Here the Chi marks the end of one gospel and the beginning of another and suggests a related *raison d'être* for the Kells Matthew 1:18 initial.

there seems little reason to doubt that the *Christi autem generatio* series was intended. In other words, besides beginning the narrative after the enumeration of names of Christ's genealogy, the Chi Rho initials are to be understood as a constituent of a complex iconographic concatenation. We are already aware of the importance of the influence of a lections system on the distribution of enlarged and ornamented incipits in our manuscript and, hence, must give serious attention to Lewis' interpretation of folio 34r as marking the beginning of a pericope read for the Nativity vigil.[37] From this liturgical vantage point she postulates that Christ Enthroned, the eight-circles cross and the initials and decoration of the *Christi autem* pages to set forth the tripartite dogma of nativity, death and resurrection.

But there are serious problems with this reading. Farr has observed the only known systems designating lections beginning *XPI autem* to be north Italian, and yet in insular gospels dependent on the Roman system and displaying an enlarged and ornamented Chi Rho, the second part of the verse, the *Cum esset desponsata* which opens all recognised Roman lections of Matthew 1:18 (instead of the *XPI autem* which is, in fact, part of the conclusion of Matthew's genealogy), is not accented.[38] And that is not all. In Kells the richly decorated lections are of two types. Pericopes are marked by two page demonstrations of full-page illustration and facing or following elaborated incipits (Temptation, folios 202v-203r; Arrest, folios 114r-114v; Crucifixion, folios 123v (?) - 124r) or by single ornate incipits (folios 183r, 285r). All the incipits are Easter season pericopes. While it is undeniable that a great deal is novel and sometimes illogical in the makeup of the Book of Kells, it nevertheless seems strange that if folio 34 was meant as a lections reading it would not follow internal precedent and either be accompanied by a single picture page or stand alone. A cycle of miniatures before a lections incipit — and one that does not mark a reading for the Easter liturgy — is surely an anomaly. The plausibility of Lewis' theory is further compromised by the presence of the Madonna and Child page in the preliminaries. Not a Nativity scene and, as observed, almost certainly in its proper place, we must suppose it was chosen for its location opposite the beginning of the *Breves causae* of Matthew because of the latter's prominent reference to the birth of Christ at Bethlehem. Yet one must wonder why if Matthew 1:18 is meant to be a Nativity vigil reading, the Madonna and Child miniature was not placed there where it would surely perform a valuable liturgical function and strengthen the doctrinal emphasis Lewis argues for as well. From this brief review it becomes apparent that a hypothesis built on an interpretation of Matthew 1:18 in Kells as a reading for the Nativity vigil cannot go unchallenged.

This is not to say Lewis is entirely incorrect. Though her identification of folio 32v as carrying a representation of the Logos Incarnate is unconvincing

---

[37]Lewis (note 3 above) 141, n 6.

[38]Farr, 'Liturgical influences', 129, n 33. She also notes, ibid, 129, n 34, that Bede's homily for the vigil of the Nativity begins with the Roman lection incipit *Cum esset desponsata*.

she characterises the eight-circles cross page as symbolising the True Cross
and the monogram page, the *nomen sacrum*, as alluding to the Eucharist,
Crucifixion and Resurrection. But because of her stipulation of the primary
function of the sequence as elaborating a liturgical reading she insists on
overly emphasising the Incarnation in relation to the Christmas liturgy.
Interpreting Matthew 1:18 as if it were the opening of a gospel permits a
more balanced understanding of the folios 32v-34r series and also serves to
clarify our Easter hypothesis.[39] It permits the Enthroned Christ, flanked by
four angels and framed by two peacocks enmeshed in vines on either side of
a golden cross, to be viewed as a rare type of *Majestas Domini*, the Second
Person at the end of time perpetually worshipped by the heavenly
creatures, the Christ of the Resurrection, Second Coming and Last
Judgement.[40] The great double-barred cross on folio 33r, the facing page, is
the True Cross. It refers to the Crucifixion and alludes to the Incarnation
and Resurrection within a christological framework. Introduced between
the Christ Enthroned and *Christi autem* miniatures, its sequential
arrangement and the symbolic character of the accompanying pages recall
the demonstration brought forward by the juxtaposed folios 1v-2r in the
Book of Durrow. As for the third miniature, carrying the *nomen sacrum*, the
page refers to Incarnation and Resurrection, perhaps within the framework
of the Fall and Redemption.[41]

---

[39]Something of an anomaly within the system of gospel incipits is folio 188v. It
follows the elaborate *quoniam* for Luke 1:1, folio 188r and enlarges and ornaments
the words *Fuit in diebus hero*, beginning Luke 1:5 after the prologue. Emphasized in
other insular gospel books, it was read in numerous western liturgies for the vigil of
the Feast of St John the Baptist; Farr, 'Lection', 339.

[40]However, P Harbison, 'Three miniatures in the Book of Kells', PRIA 85C (1985)
181-94 (181-84) sees the origin of the page in a representation of the *Raised Christ* in
which Christ is accompanied by angels and Peter and Paul. Conversely, Farr,
'Lection', 326-30, speculates the portrait to be an Apocalyptic Christ, or Christ
enthroned in the heavenly tabernacle.

[41]Werckmeister (note 2 above) 147-70, concentrates on the Chi of folio 34r (ignoring
the Rho, the Iota and other possible symbols). He interprets it as a cosmological
salvific symbol, elucidating its meaning through an explication of Irenaeus,
particularly of his allegorical framework for the dialectic between the Incarnation of
the Logos and salvation made possible by Christ's death on the Cross. Examining
the symbolism of the Chi form and that of the rhombus at its junction, Werckmeister
proposes the doctrinal thrust of the miniature to flow from the interconnected ideas
of the Creation and re-Creation of the cosmos. The cross shape of the Chi signifies
the axis of the 'mundus'; its four arms indicate the four directions of the compass
(*forma quadrata mundi*). Representing time the rhomboid is filled with the three
animal types described in Genesis: the quadrupeds of the earth, the birds of the air
and the reptiles of the water; humans are present at the corners as *imago Dei*. All are
elements of an *allegoria mundi* referring to the Creation and the Fall. Referring to
history, the Chi recalls the Resurrection and the possibility of Redemption, for it is
both the Saviour's initial and the sign of the Cross through which mankind will be
redeemed; it is the *nomen sacrum* and the Incarnate word, revealing the cosmic order
through the theory of Salvation.
Lewis (note 3 above) though she embraces much of Werckmeister's interpretation,
emphasizes her thesis that the miniature marks a Nativity Vigil lection. For her the
shape of the Chi, corresponding to the *Crux decussata*, refers to Salvation through
Crucifixion and extends throughout creation to embrace the animals representing
earth (cats and mice), water (fish and otter), and air (moths, angels) that populate the
page. Moreover, the moth, because of its metamorphosis, speaks of the Resurrection.
The fish signifies the body of Christ, his death and resurrection. The otter is 'a sacred
servant bringing the fish - Eucharist to the holy hearts' of the observers. The cats are

Intended to bring to mind the True Cross relic displayed for the Good Friday *Adoratio crucis*,[42] the emblem on folio 33r possesses complex eschatological meanings important in assessing its relation to the Christ Enthroned representation. The Fathers believed that those parts of the Cross touched by Christ's body miraculously ascended to heaven to become the Cross of the Second Coming (Matthew 24:30). Similarly, the intimate connection between the Crucifixion Cross and the Second Advent is emphasized in the early Anglo-Saxon poem *The Dream of the Rood*, and in Bede.[43]

Soteriological expression is also of great interest. In Venantius Fortunatus' hymns on the True Cross (which became part of the Good Friday *Adoratio crucis* rite), redemption is the central theme: the Cross is the Tree of Salvation, the Incarnation (Nativity) and Passion (Crucifixion) are the supreme moments of the Redemption. Christian thought fostered an intimate connection between the Incarnation and Redemption doctrines. Gregory, for example, viewed Christ's suffering and death as a sacrificial offering and referred to Christ's death in terms of conflict and triumph; often the church Fathers attempted to assimilate concepts of divine victory

---

defenders of spiritual nourishment because they chase mice who nibble at a disc-shaped host, the latter also to be regarded as the moon, yet another symbol of Resurrection. Together the animals refer to the Logos Incarnate and underline the tripartite dogma of birth, death and resurrection. For S Mussetter, 'An animal miniature on the monogram page of the Book of Kells', *Mediaevalia* 3 (1977) 119-30, the creatures at the base of the Chi are cats signifying the devil. The mice they chase hold the wafer of the Eucharist which carries the potential of their redemption. Henderson, 161, believes the Chi Rho to reveal the mystery of Incarnation; its four arms represent the four rivers of the virtues flowing out of Paradise, symbolising the world and making reference to earth, water, and air. Nordenfalk (note 11 above) 211-19, however, questions these interpretations, especially those assigning symbolic meaning to the animals and humans in the miniature. Animals, birds and humans, he notes, appear throughout the manuscript including text pages where they mostly seem devoid of iconographic reference. Alexander, 'Illumination', 276, also emphasizes the decorative role of the animals, etc.

[42]Almost certainly, like the eight squares of the Durrow double-barred cross on folio 1v, the eight circles of the Kells patriarchal cross were intended as symbols of the Resurrection. As I demonstrated earlier (note 24 above) 215, n 202, Augustine examined the meaning of Easter by means of the symbolism of the sacred numbers 6, 7 and 8. For Augustine six designates Good Friday, seven Holy Saturday and eight Easter Sunday. Closer in time to the creation of the Book of Kells, John Scottus Erigena, *Periphyseon - on the division of nature*, trans by M Uhlfelder (Indianapolis 1974) v, 358, wrote of the number 8 as symbolising the Resurrection. Inspired by Pseudo-Dionysius, Maximus the Confessor and Boethius, he referred to its properties:

> The resurrection of the Lord too occurred on the eighth day for the very purpose of signifying mystically that blessed life which will come after the sevenfold revolution of this life through seven days, after the consummation of the world, since human nature, as we have said, will return to its beginning by an eightfold ascent: five parts within the bounds of nature, three supernaturally and superessentially within God Himself, for the pentad of creation will be united with the triad of the Creator, so that God alone appears in everything just as only light shines bright in the clearest air.

For an interpretation of the decoration of the Ardagh chalice according to Erigena's number symbolism, especially his Resurrection ascription to the number 8, see H Richardson, 'Number and symbol in early christian Irish art', *JRSAI* 114 (1984) 1-30.

[43]Werner (note 24 above) n 207.

and sacrificial offering with the idea of Redemption.[44]

All this is indicative of the christological and soteriological thrust of the
Christi autem cycle and suggests the juxtaposition of folios 32v and 33r as
intended to convey the relation between the patriarchal cross, the paradigm
of Christ's humanity, and his pain and suffering in the temporal sphere (the
orthodox idea of the Incarnation necessitates the complete humanity and
divinity of the Son of God and from an early date the material, yet
imperishable, wood of the Crucifixion Cross was perceived as proof of both,
and indeed, the relics of the True Cross became one of the major arguments
for Christ's mortal existence, suffering, death and rebirth) and Christ in
Majesty, the Son dwelling eternally in heaven with the Father. Together the
two pages enunciate the principle of Christ as a single entity with two
distinct natures, one human, the other divine. With its evocation of the
Incarnate Word and Resurrection and joined to folios 32v and 33r, the
Christi autem page restates and extends this essential christology while
coinstantaneously recapitulating a dialectic of divinity and triumph and
humanity and forebearance, the framework for Redemption. We have
observed that although the Kells cross-carpet page does not mark an Easter
lection, it was intended to be identified with the Good Friday *Adoratio
crucis*. Given the fact that the ceremony encouraged a sacramental
participation in the mystery of the Redemption and bearing in mind the
eucharistic references for the Matthew 1:18 sequence briefly mentioned (and
to which we shall return), it seems reasonable to suppose the series, among
others, to have been meant to remind the viewer of the masses conducted
during the Easter season, especially those of the Easter triduum. Quite
clearly, therefore, the *Christi autem* sequence was conceived as part of an
Easter scheme centred on the illustrations and pericopes marking readings
for Quadragesima Sunday, Holy Thursday, Good Friday and the Easter
Vigil. Our reading of the complex symbolism of the Kells carpet page also
reveals another significant point. Because of its putative reliance on the
example of the patriarchal cross page in the Book of Durrow, itself seen as
dependent on Adomnán's *De locis sanctis*, the pilgrims guide takes on a
special importance. More precisely, it seems possible that the creation of
Adomnán's text and the introductory pages in the Book of Durrow, so
suggestive of a profound interest in the Easter rites and the True Cross cult,
may have provided the impetus for the iconographic elaboration of the non-
Roman lections system employed for the Book of Kells.

As stated, at the heart of the Kells Easter programme are the Temptation
and Arrest illustrations, their incipits, the unfinished Crucifixion sequence
and the isolated richly ornamented incipits. We need not linger long on the
intact sequential groups. It is true they offer great difficulties of
interpretation but their essential liturgical reference and function seem
assured. Facing a decorated incipit with the text of Luke 4:1 describing
Christ's first temptation, the folio 202v illustration, itself depicting the third
temptation wherein the Devil takes Christ onto the Temple in Jerusalem and

---

[44]ibid.

suggests he jump to prove he is the Son of God, is quite rare before the Romanesque period and, in fact, the Kells miniature is the first extant example. Its initial page marks a lection for Quadragesima Sunday, the first Sunday in Lent and Farr depends upon this lenten context to explain much of the picture's unusual iconography.[45] Worth noting is the insular interest in forty-day fasts; the Fathers and insular exegetes equate the forty-day fast of Lent with the fasts of Moses, Elias, Christ, etc and with other forty-day or forty-year periods mentioned in scripture. Lent also had eschatological significance. It symbolised the struggle of the church anticipating the Second Coming, with Easter bringing rejoicing and spiritual awakening.[46]

The miniature on folio 114r is preceded by a page carrying the text of Matthew 26:26-29 (the Last Supper and the institution of the Eucharist) and itself is inscribed with lines from Matthew (26:30, the beginning of the story of the disciples going out to the Mount of Olives and Gethsemane after the Last Supper). An initial page with Matthew 26:31 follows, but the Arrest is described sixteen verses later at Matthew 26:47. Even more than the Temptation illustration, the picture is difficult to relate to its immediate gospel text. It shows Christ standing frontally with arms outstretched. Two smaller figures grasping his arms are on either side. The scene is framed by an arch with lion heads at the top. Directly above the heads of the smaller figures are plants emerging from bulbous chalices. The miniature has been variously identified, but no one has yet presented a case strong enough to disallow the traditional designation of the scene as the Arrest of Christ.[47] It marks an important point in a lection for Holy Thursday, the Thursday before Easter Sunday, the day commencing the Easter triduum and which by the early middle ages came to include the rite sanctifying the host for the Mass of the Praesanctified on Good Friday.

Both Henderson and Farr discount Carl Nordenfalk's identification of the two plant tendrils framing Christ's head as referring to the Mount of Olives but Nordenfalk must be correct, for the plants twine round and underline the words *in montem oliveti* of Matthew 26:30 inscribed under the arch. This is a point of some importance as it, again, concerns Adomnán's *De locis sanctis*. That those responsible for the Book of Kells directly consulted Adomnán's traveller's guide is supported by Nordenfalk's explanation of the tendrils of the Arrest as based on Arculf's report to the abbot of Iona that it is rare to find trees on the Mount of Olives save vines and olives.[48] In

---

[45]Farr, 'Lection', 19-191.

[46]Farr, 'Liturgical influences', 131-35, nn 82-84. Henderson, 168-75, understands the Temptation scene, and its incipit, as referring not to Quadragesima Sunday but to Holy Saturday.

[47]For interpretations of the scenes as an Arrest of Christ, see M Schapiro, 'The miniatures of the Florence Diatessaron: their place in late medieval art and supposed connection with early christian and insular art', *Art Bulletin* 55 (1973) 494-531; Lewis, (note 3 above) 155; C Nordenfalk, *Celtic and Anglo-Saxon painting: book illumination in the British Isles, 600-800* (New York 1976) 124; Henderson, 162-163; Alexander, 'Illumination', 282-83; Farr, 'Lection', 244-96; Henry, 188. Harbison (note 40 above) 181-94, however, proposes the scene to be Christ on the Mount of Olives.

[48]Henderson, 162-63, believe the vines to be symbolic of the newly instituted

other words, the Arrest tendrils are based on an eye witness description of vines on the Mount of Olives. To the degree that they generally identify, or are identified with, the church or shrine at a holy site, and hence the reading of the mass at that place, *loca sancta* images have a liturgical meaning.[49] In this instance the reference serves to enhance the Maundy Thursday reading.

There remains, of course, folio 124r, perhaps once part of a lection sequence such as are the Temptation and Arrest initials. Matthew 27:28, the *Tunc crucifixerant*, follows a most unusual page, folio 123r, which contains only fifteen lines of text instead of the usual seventeen — lines deliberately spaced so as to close with the *Titulum*. In turn 124r faces a blank page, folio 123v, whose placement between the singular *Titulum* and *Tunc crucifixerant* incipit suggests it to have been reserved for a full-page Crucifixion scene, [50] a possibility enhanced by the tiny figures in three small compartments of folio 124r who face left as if to witness the death of the Saviour.[51] Completed, the folios 123v-124r sequence would have resembled the nearby Arrest set and the Temptation series in Luke in the sense that in each series the incipit is lavishly decorated but undisturbed by individual figures or figural groupings introduced above, below, or to either side of the initials. This is in sharp contrast to the isolated ornamented incipits — one in Mark and one in Luke — displaying prominent human figures in intimate alliance with initials.

The folio 183r miniature pictures a book-carrying angel seated to the left of the central row of the enlarged and embellished *Erat autem* of Mark 15:24-25, the Crucifixion account. Above the framing element at the right looms a purple clad figure. Undoubtedly it is the feet of this same purple clad figure we see extending below the framing device at the left. The singularity of this assemblage is equalled by that of folio 285r, where four angels are symmetrically dispersed around the *Una* of the *Una autem sabbati ualde de lu[culo]* of Luke 24:1, the beginning of the story of the Resurrection. Never meant to accompany a full-page illustration, the two incipits, as we have observed, are noticeably unlike the incipits that perform this function. Is it

Eucharist. Lewis (note 3 above) 155, has a similar interpretation of the vines as referring to the wine of the sacrament. Farr, 'Lection', 245, proposes the plants to be two olive trees inspired by references in the Apocalypse and Zachariah. C Nordenfalk, 'Another look at the Book of Kells' in *Festschrift Wolfgang Braunfels*, ed F Piel and J Träger (Tübingen 1977) 275-79, cites Adomnán's reference in *De locis sanctis* (note 25 above, 64-65) (As the holy Arculf relates, it is rare to find any other trees on Mount Olivet except vines and olives ...) as indicating the rinceaux vines of the Arrest as representing the plants on the Mount of Olives.

[49]For discussion of Palestinian *loca sancta* imagery with its specific topographical details and liturgical reference, see K Weitzmann, '*Loca Sancta* and the representational arts of Palestine', *Dumbarton Oaks Papers* 28 (1974) 31-51; G Vikan, *Byzantine pilgrimage art*, Dumbarton Oaks Byzantine Collection Publication 5 (Washington, DC 1982).

[50]Henry, 173; Alexander, *Insular manuscripts*, 72.

[51]The five bust figures also act as a device to bring text and putative illustration into intimate relation. This arrangement resembles that on folio 7v, where the tiny busts in a rectangular compartment in the border surrounding the Madonna and Child face toward the *Breves causae* similarly facilitating contiguity; Werner (note 33 above) 13, n 54.

possible that with their lections reference and figural groups these monadic incipits constitute an insular invention, a kind of conflated illustration-incipit, wherein text is both setting and explanation for the figures within? Folio 285r speaks most eloquently to this prospect.

On the page the uprights of the large dominant *U* frame an interlace field with two confronted peacocks and begin the topmost row of three tiers of capitals. To the left of the *U* is a standing angel holding a book; another book-carrying angel is seated on the *na* to the right. Just below the first figure, holding what appears to be a flabellum, an angel reclines on the second row of initials. Completing the heavenly quartet, a winged figure with a flowering staff is perched on the right end of the same initial row. A green ground sets off the *na* of the *Una*, left and right segments of the central initial tier and the midmost section of the lower initial band. Enclosing the initials is an intricately detailed border filled with rinceaux vines growing from vases on each of the four axes and enlivened by running quadrupeds; a large lion's head dominates the upper right hand corner.

We must not neglect one important detail — the initial *M* in the central row of initials. By introducing a vertical bar and two horizontal bars completed by rectangular terminals between its two outer verticals, its creator has transformed the capital into a framed patriarchal cross typologically similar to the monumental emblem on folio 33r. Patriarchal cross-shaped *M's* occasionally appear in insular incipits.[52] Besides the one before us, two such initials are employed for the Kells frontispieces.[53] They are small, peripherally placed, not proximate to figural groupings, and lack the distinctive 'architectural' terminals of the *Una autem* initial. In contrast, set off against the vellum ground and apart from the surrounding letters and placed between the angels and on the main vertical axis below the right stem of the opening *U*, the latter has a singular prominence. While Matthew's account of the visit of the Marys to Christ's tomb on Easter morning has received greatest liturgical prominence, Luke 24:1-3 is listed as a lection for the Easter Vigil in a number of seventh and eighth-century continental books, and, because we cannot doubt the same intent for the *Una autem* page, there is good reason to presume the *M*- patriarchal cross to stand in symbolic relation to the angel tetrad.

In attempting to reconstruct the objective of the author of the folio 285r locution, we may benefit from our understanding of the Kells cross-carpet page, folio 33r, as alluding to the triduum sacrum rites. The True Cross is the central theme and symbol of the Easter commemoration. Originating in the East, by the close of the seventh century the Good Friday *Adoratio* was

---

[52]See, for example, XPI pages to St Matthew in Lichfield, Cathedral Library, Gospels (St Chad), p 15; St Gall, Stiftsbibliothek, Cod. 51, p 7; opening of St John, Oxford, Bodleian Library, MS Auct D.2.19, folio 129; opening of Mark, TCD, MS 56, folio 22; Alexander, *Insular manuscripts*, pls 76, 201, 269, 275.

[53]Matthew 26:30, folio 114v and Mark 1:1, folio 130r.

beginning to appear in the Latin service.[54] There is evidence of the knowledge of the rite in early eighth-century Northumbria,[55] and we have earlier referred to the testimony provided by Adomnán's *De locis sanctis*, where the Easter triduum with its display of the primary relic of the Crucifixion Cross on the altar of Hagia Sophia, Constantinople, is described.[56] Implicit in the Durrow and Kells cross-carpet pages this declaration seems similarly intended for our *M* initial. The text of the *Una autem* page is the lesson for the Easter Vigil. Together the lesson and the *M*-patriarchal cross strongly suggest an intent to convey a sense of the unfolding ceremonial of Holy Week.

We have seen that folio 114v, the *Tunc dicit illis* in Matthew, was meant to mark a lection for Maundy Thursday, the first day of the Easter triduum. The church did not permit the consecration of the host on Good Friday. Instead, consecration took place on Maundy Thursday with the host reserved for the Good Friday mass which was called in consequence the Mass of the Praesanctified.[57] As it evolved, the Good Friday *Adoratio crucis* acquired strongly representational and dramatic elements. In the Roman rite, by 700, it employed two deacons standing behind the covered cross who regard the cross not as an object of meditation but rather as the original Cross on which Christ died. They introduce responses supposedly spoken by the dying Jesus to the unmerciful Jews. Priest and chorus answer with antiphons as a sort of tragic chorus. The cross, transported through the choir, is returned to a place near or on the altar symbolising Christ's tomb, a 'sepulchrum' which first became part of the Easter liturgy on Maundy Thursday.[58]

There is written testimony from the mid-tenth century to the effect that after the mass on Good Friday morning another dramatic representational ceremony followed. This was the *Depositio*, a burial service involving the host.[59] Once again highly developed ideographic constituents are employed including the internment of the host in a receptacle with a covering rock in imitation of the tomb of Christ. Another deposition rite, perhaps a variant, was sometimes introduced between the *Adoratio crucis* and the Mass of the Praesanctified. Like the 'Burial of the Host', this entombment deposits the cross in a 'sepulchrum' and the congregation, already intensely engaged, is

---

[54]Werner (note 24 above) 189-90.

[55]ibid, 199-200.

[56]Meehan (note 25 above) III, 3, pp 109-11; Werner (note 24 above) 203-08.

[57]See O B Hardison, *Christian rite and christian drama in the middle ages* (Baltimore 1965) 116-28 and passim.

[58]L A Molien, *La prière de l'Église* (Paris 1924) II, 392-98; P Gueranger, *Liturgical year*, 15 vols (1901-1918) VI, 438-46.

[59]The earliest description of the Good Friday burial is found in a tenth-century life of St Ulrich — apparently a traditional practice in the Cathedral of Augsburg, *c*950; *Acta Sanctorum*, Julii (Paris and Rome 1867) II, 103; K Young, *The drama of the medieval church* (New York 1933) I, 553; J N Dalton, *The Collegiate Church of Ottery St Mary* (Cambridge 1917) 252-53, suggested a seventh-century date for the earliest use of the *Depositio*. See also Hardison (note 57 above) 130 ff.

further drawn into the Easter ceremonial.[60] The worshippers have stood, as it were, beneath the cross, kissed its base and obeyed Christ's *improperia*. Now they are witness to the Redeemer's brief interlude in the tomb. After the closing and sealing of the simple enclosure or portion of the altar representing the sepulchre, a response was sung. Its dramatic element is remarkably realistic: 'rolling a stone to the door ... setting soldiers to watch it'.[61] The *Elevatio* follows with host or cross taken up from the 'sepulchre' to commemorate Christ's departure from the tomb. Usually this occurred just before the beginning of the Easter nocturn.[62]

These theatrical representations of the death and resurrection of the Saviour contain the seeds of a more fully developed resurrection ceremony — a brief play — to follow, the *Visitatio Sepulchri*, the visit of the women to the tomb on Easter morning. Its first extant appearance complete with directions for staging is in the *Regularis concordia*, the code of English monastic observance approved at the Synod of Winchester, *c*970. Here it follows the *Adoratio Crucis* and *Depositio* (once again the earliest circumstantial accounts). Introduced at the end of matins on Easter morning, it is composed of detailed instructions to the clergy and the dialogue called the *quem quaeritis*,[63] which dramatizes 'the moment when humanity, represented by the holy women visiting the tomb of Christ, first recognise the full significance of the Incarnation':

> While the third lesson is being read, four of the brethren shall vest, one of whom, wearing an alb as though for some different purpose, shall enter and go stealthily to the place of the 'sepulchre' and sit there quietly, holding a palm in his hand. Then, while the third respond is being sung, the other three brethren, vested in copes and holding thuribles in their hands, shall enter in their turn and go to the place of the 'sepulchre', step by step, as though searching for something. Now these things are done in imitation of the angel seated on the tomb and of the women coming with perfumes, he that is seated shall see these three draw nigh, wandering about as it were and seeking something, he shall

---

[60]K Young, *The dramatic associations of the Easter Sepulchre* (Madison 1920) 1-9; N C Brooks, *The Sepulchre of Christ in art and liturgy* (Urbana 1921) 33-36 and passim.

[61]J G Davies, *Holy Week: a short history* (Richmond 1963) 52-53; Brooks (note 60 above) 168 ff.

[62]As prescribed in several tenth-century texts; Brooks (note 60 above) 112 ff; Hardison, (note 57 above) 136-37.

[63]*Quem quaeritis* is the exchange between the three Marys and the Angel at the tomb:
    Interrogatio: *quem quaeritis in sepulchro Christicolae?*
    Responsio: *Jhesum Nazarenum crucifixum o caelicolae. Non est hic; surrexit sicut praedixerat. Ite nunciate quia surrexit de sepulchro.*
In its simpler versions, this dialogue was employed as a trope to *Resurrexi*, the *Introit* for Easter Day. Sometimes it became part of the festal procession before the mass. Most often, it was placed at the end of Easter matins; given dramatic development it became the *Visitatio Sepulchri*; D A Bjork, 'On the dissemination of the *quem quaeritis* and the *Visitatio sepulchri* and the chronology of their early sources' in *The drama of the middle ages*, ed C Davidson, et al (New York 1982) 1-24; D Berger, *Le Drame liturgique de Pâques. Liturgie et théâtre* (Paris 1976) 149; A McGee, 'The liturgical placement of the *quem quaeritis* Dialogue', *Journal of the American Musicological Society* 29 (1976) 1-29.

begin to sing softly and sweetly, *quem quaeritis*. As soon as this has been sung right through, the three shall answer together, *Ihesum Nazarenum*. Then he that is seated shall say *Non est hic. Surrexit sicut praedixerat. Ite, nuntiate quia surrexit a mortuis*. At this command the three shall turn to the choir saying *Alleluia. Resurrexit Dominus*. When this has been sung he that is seated, as though calling them back, shall say the antiphon *Venite et videte locum*, and then, rising and lifting up the veil, he shall show them the place void of the Cross and with only the linen in which the Cross has been wrapped. Seeing this the three shall lay down their thuribles in that same 'sepulchre' and taking the linen, shall hold it up before the clergy; and, as though showing that the Lord was risen and was no longer wrapped in it, they shall sing this antiphon: *Surrexit Dominus de sepulchro*. They shall then lay the linen on the altar.[64]

Viewed in relation to the lenten and Easter triduum references articulated by the lection sequences and the *Christi autem* cycle and the role of folio 285r as a reading for the Easter Vigil from Luke's account of the Resurrection, the *Regularis concordia's Visitatio* would seem to provide the key to an interpretation of the four angels and patriarchal cross on the page. It becomes possible to understand the True Cross emblem as the cross of the triduum rites that culminate in the *Visitatio Sepulchri* — the cross in the 'sepulchre' during the *Adoratio* and *Depositio* — and the four angels as the four 'brethren' who 'go to the place of the sepulchre' in imitation of the angel at the tomb and the women who carry perfumes to anoint the body of Christ.

Arguably, on our page, the letters comprising the *autem sabbati* and enclosing the *M*-patriarchal cross on which two angels sit are meant to represent the altar where the rite is performed.

To be sure, the *Regularis concordia* (and related texts) is younger by a century or more than the Book of Kells and cannot be quoted as a direct textual

---

[64]Cambridge, Corpus Christi College, MS 190; *Regularis Concordia*, trans and ed by T Symons (London 1953) 49-50:

Dum tertia recitatur lectio, quattuor fratres induant se, quorum unus, alba indutus ac si ad aliud agendum, ingrediatur atque latenter sepulcri locum adeat ibique, manu tenens palmam, quietus sedeat. Dumque tertium percelebratur responsorium residui tres succedant, omnes quidem cappis induti, turibula cum incensu manibus gestantes ac, pedetemptim ad similitudinem quaerentium quid, ueniant ante locum sepulcri. Aguntur enim haec ad imitationem angeli sedentis in monumento, atque mulierum cum aromatibus uenientium ut ungerent corpus Ihesu. Cum ergo ille residens tres, uelut erraneos ac aliquid quaerentes, uiderit sibi approximare, incipiat mediocre uoce dulcisone cantare *Quem quaeritis*? Quo decantato finetenus, respondeant hi tres, uno ore, *Ihesum Nazarenum*. Quibus ille: *Non est hic. Surrexit sicut praedixerat. Ite, nuntiate quia surrexit a mortuis*. Cuius iussionis uoce uertant se illi tres ad chorum, dicentes *Alleluia. Resurrexit Dominus*. Dicto hoc, rursus ille residens, uelut reuocans illos, dicat antiphonam: *Venite et uidete locum*. Haec uero dicens, surgat et erigat uelum ostendatque eis locum, cruce nudatum sed tantum linteamina posita quibus crux inuoluta erat; quo uiso deponant turibula quae gestauerant in eodem sepulcro, sumantque linteum et extendant contra clerum ac, ueluti ostendentes quod surrexerit Dominus et iam non sit illo inuolutus, hanc canant antiphonam: *Surrexit Dominus de sepulcro*, superponantque linteum altari.

source for its iconographic expressions. It has been argued, however, that the *Visitatio* has significant early antecedents and even that it was in existence in the ninth century.[65] O B Hardison, for example, finds it difficult to believe that a climactic Resurrection rite would not have existed at a time when the other major ceremonies of the Easter triduum (and even of the Passion beginning with Palm Sunday) were in place: ceremonies which had representational elements of linear, chronological time and devices of verisimilitude including pantomime, stage props, costume and dialogue.[66]

The venerable Vigil Mass, a source of ideas drawn upon for the Resurrection rite,[67] has more extra-liturgical, representational and mimetic characteristics than any other service of the year[68] so that it is of special interest that the Venerable Bede in *Homilia evangelii de pascha* and *In Lucae evangelium expositio* explained the visit to the tomb as an allegory on the Vigil Mass and emphasized the parallels between the two: angels are present at the sacrifice; the altar is the tomb; the sacrament is the *corpus Domini*; the clergy and congregation are the women and the prayers and virtues are the *aromata*; the corporal and altar cloths are the sindon in which Christ was shrouded by Joseph of Arimathea.[69] Bede was one of the major sources consulted by the great Frankish exegete Amalarius of Metz (c780-850) who devoted a lifetime to liturgical symbolism.[70] It is not surprising

---

[65]Bjork (note 63 above) 1-24.

[66]Hardison (note 57 above) 84, 157, 176.

[67]The question of the possible liberation of the *quem quaeritis* trope from its liturgical context or the development of more dramatic components within the liturgy is complex and difficult. Berger (note 63 above) 149, has proposed the dramatic dialogue of the trope to originate in a ceremony employed for the Vigil of Easter Day which later was included in the ceremony before Easter mass. J Drumbl, 'Dramaturgia medievale (II): ricostruire la tradizione' in *Biblioteca Tiatrale* 10-11 (Milan 1974) 44, 58 and passim, finds no transference from the liturgical rite to the sacred drama, ie from the *quem quaeritis* dialogue to the *Visitatio* play. Instead, he believes, the dramatic aspects of the dialogue were expanded later by means of stage elements and the use of the 'Holy Sepulchre' at the altar or in the church. See also W A Smolden, 'The origins of the *quem quaeritis* trope and the Easter Sepulchre music-dramas, as demonstrated by their musical settings' in *The medieval drama*, ed S Sticea (Albany 1972) 121-54. Drumbl *op. cit.*, 55 ff, also points out that Matthew 28:9 was central to the Easter liturgy of Jerusalem observed by Egeria in the late fourth or early fifth century and found in documents of the fifth century including the Armenian lectionary of c460; A Franceschini and R Weber, 'Itinerarium Egeriae' in *Itineraria et alia geographica*, CCSL 175-76 (Turnhout 1965) 27-90; A Renoux, *Le Codex Arménien Jerusalem 121*, Patrologica Orientalis 25, I and 26, II (Turnhout 1969-71). The liturgy in Jerusalem helped shape the Roman rite and the development of the liturgical Ordines in the seventh and eighth centuries; E G Martimort, *L'Église en prière - introduction à la liturgie* (Tournai and Paris 1965). Furthermore, the similarities between the orthos of the Easter matutin in Jerusalem and the later monastic form of the Latin *quem quaeritis* trope (ninth century) have been noted; M Huglo, 'L'Office du dimanche de Paques dans les monastères bénédictins', *Revue grégorienne* 30 (1951) 191-203; Drumbl *op. cit.*, 56; G Pochat, 'Liturgical aspects of the *Visitatio Sepulchri* scene' in *Riforma Riligiosa e Arti nell' Epoca Carolingia*, ed A A Schmid (Bologna 1979) 151-56 (p 152). See further Werner (note 24 above) 188-89.

[68]Hardison (note 57 above) 162-63.

[69]*Homilia evangelii de pascha*, PL 129, 1433; *In Lucae evangelium expositio*, PL 92, 622-24.

[70]Amalarius appears to have been the first Carolingian scholar to undertake a wide-ranging and methodical study of the liturgy. He produced two allegorical interpretations of the mass: *Eclogae de Ordine Romano* (814) and his major work, *Liber Officialis* (c820-822); *Amalarii Episcopi Opera Liturgica Omnia*, ed J M Hanssens, 3 vols,

that Amalarius would allegorically interpret the Vigil Mass as a reenactment of the Passion. For him subdeacons become the disciples at the foot of the cross; they witness the deposition and mourn Christ's Holy Saturday stay in the tomb. Most important, they are seen as the holy women who anoint him at the deposition and burial; at the tomb on Sunday morning they are told by an angel 'He is not here'.[71] There are striking similarities between Amalarius' allegory and the *Regularis concordia's Visitatio*. As Hardison specifies, though Amalarius' comments do not in themselves constitute an Easter play, they do describe the deacons, the thuribles, the albs and the tomb motif; and they contain dialogue-like elements and phrases later found in the visitation play.[72]

Amalarius' first allegorical interpretation of the mass, the *Eclogae* appeared in 814, but Carol Heitz credits Angilbert, abbot of St Riquier (Centula), (750/755-c814) with comparable liturgical innovation. For Heitz, the church of St Riquier was designed to symbolise the Holy Sepulchre,[73] and Angilbert's *Institutio*, in a manner similar to that of Amalarius in his commentary on the Vigil Mass in *Liber officialis*, contained antecedents of the *Depositio, Elevatio* and *Visitatio*.[74] It was, however, at Amalarius' Metz that the liturgy increasingly came to resemble sacred drama. Recently Robert Calkins, in a study of the Drogo Sacramentary of c840, pointed to Amalarius' influence on that work and found the scholar's allegorical references to the deacons at the altar during the mass as the holy women at

---

Studi e Testi 138-140 (Vatican City 1948-1950) II, III. See also A Cabinis, *Amalarius of Metz* (Amsterdam 1954); R McKitterick *The Frankish church and the Carolingian reforms, 789-895* (London 1977) 148-53. For discussion of Amalarius' interpretation of the ceremonies of the mass and Holy Week as reenactments of Christ's Passion, see C M Chazelle, 'The Cross, the Image and the Passion in Carolingian thought and art' (unpub. PhD diss., Yale University 1985) 207-08, 285 ff.

[71]*Liber Officialis*, III, 9-13 and *Eclogae de ordine romano*, XXII, 2-6, in Hanssens (note 70 above) II, 259-61, III, 252-54.

[72]Hardison (note 57 above) 72 ff, 160 ff, 171-72, 194-95. Significantly, Cabinis (note 70 above) 62-64, observes:

It was Amalarius who associated the idea of the holy women with deacons or subdeacons in the symbolism of the Resurrection story in connection with the liturgy. Before there could be the 'quem quaeritis'-trope, someone had to connect all those details — and Amalarius did ... It is highly significant in regard to this that a ninth-century manuscript was presumably present and presumably used in the library of Saint Gall where also the first manuscript (tenth century) of the 'quem quaeritis'-trope was found.

See further, Andrieu, III, 343, 347 ff; G Roemer, 'Die Liturgie des Karfreitags', *Zeitschrift für katholische Theologie* 77 (1955) 56; R Haussherr, *Der tote Christus am Kreuz: Zur Ikonographie des Gerokreuzes* (Bonn 1963) 215 ff.

[73]C Heitz, *Recherches sur les rapports entre architecture et liturgie à l'époque carolingienne* (Paris 1963) 75 ff; also, E Lehmann, 'Die Anordnung der Altäre in der karolingischen Klosterkirche zu Centula', ibid, 377 ff.

[74]The *Institutio de diversitate officiorum* which details the liturgical ceremonial of Angilbert is contained in the *Libellus Angilberti* in Vatican City, Cod. Reginenses MS lat. 235, the second part of which dates to the early eleventh century. It appears with the *Chronicon Centulense*, an account of the history of the abbey from the fifth century to 1088 by Hariulf, a monk of St Riquier (died 1143), *Hariulf, Chronique de l'abbaye de saint-Riquier (Ve siècle - 1104)*, ed F Lot (Paris 1894). See V H Elbern, 'Liturgisches Gerät in edlen Materialien zur Zeit Karls des Grossen' in *Karl der Grosse, Lebenswerke und Nachleben*, III, *Karolingische Kunst*, ed W Braunfels (Dusseldorf 1965) 115-67.

the tomb to be a direct source for the decoration of the text.[75] This same artistic and intellectual milieu produced a curious example of the scene of the Marys approaching the tomb of the Resurrected Lord carved on a Metz school ivory of c860, now in Paris. It features a simple basilican structure in place of earlier or contemporary types of the Holy Sepulchre which Heitz ascribes to a wish to refer to the small basilica of S. Pierre-le-Majeur in Metz where the Easter liturgy was performed. The three women have coarse features and odd hairstyles. Heitz suggests them to be depicted as monks, draped as women in their albs as mentioned in later didascalic rubrics. For Heitz, the ivory supports the possibility that the *Visitatio* rite was in existence by the mid-ninth century.[76] But, of course, no texts of an elaborated liturgical play are extant from this time. Still, at the very least, all this textual and archaeological evidence is strongly suggestive of the possibility that key elements of the *Visitatio* rite were being developed in Latin centres by 800,[77] and permits the use of the *Regularis concordia* text as a point of departure for an interpretation of the Kells *Una autem* incipit as a highly abstract depiction of the *Visitatio* ceremony.

An analysis of the tomb motif tends to support this reading. In one of the apocryphal gospels, the protoevangelium of Peter, the moment of Christ's rising from the dead is described as accompanied by a great cross issuing from the grave and reaching to the stars.[78] This association of monumental cross and tomb is recorded in certain Irish representations of the guards at the tomb including reliefs on the tenth-century (?) Market Cross, Kells (with two of the women) and West Cross, Monasterboice.[79] Besides symmetrically placed guards and an angel to the right both reliefs display a large, slender cross at the centre rising above a recumbent Saviour. Quite possibly, the M-patriarchal cross on folio 285r was similarly intended to call to mind the emblem ascending from the tomb at the moment of the Saviour's Resurrection.

---

[75]Drogo Sacramentary (Paris, BN, MS lat. 9428). R C Calkins, 'Liturgical sequence and decorative crescendo in the Drogo Sacramentary', *Gesta* 25 (1986) 17-23, describes 'an elaborate sequential orchestration of decoration and hierarchy of script in concert with an awareness of the ceremonial opening of the Mass' in the manuscript of c840. He finds this likely to be strongly indebted to Amalarius' influence — probably following his return to Metz in 838.

[76]The ivory is Paris, BN, lat. 9390; Heitz (note 73 above) 102 ff, 152-53, 214. See also C Heitz, 'L'Architecture carolingienne à la lumière de la réforme religieuse' in *Riforma Religiosa e Arti nell'Epoca Carolingia*, ed Alfred A Schmid, Atti del XXIV Congresso C.I.H.A. (Bologna 1979) 5-14; eadem, 'Architecture et liturgie processionelle à l'époque préromane', *Revue de l'Art* 24 (1974) 30-47; eadem, 'The iconography of architectural form' in *The Anglo-Saxon church: papers on history, architecture, and archaeology in honour of Dr H M Taylor*, ed L A S Butler and R K Morris (London 1986) 90-100.

[77]For additional arguments in favour of a date before the tenth century, see A Wilmert, 'Le Samedi-Saint monastique', *Revue bénédictine* 24 (1922) 161-62; Hardison (note 57 above) 171-72, 187; Bjork (note 63 above) 19; P Weber, *Geistliches Schauspiel und kirckliche Kunst* (Stuttgart 1894) 32.

[78]M R James, *The Apocryphal New Testament* (Oxford 1924) 92-93; E Hennecke, *The Apocryphal Books of the New Testament* (Philadelphia 1963) I, 142.

[79]A K Porter, *The crosses and culture of Ireland* (New Haven 1931) figs 61, 62.

Concomitantly, its identification as the altar cross of the Easter triduum would define it as a *locus sanctus* symbol, a fact of no small consequence, for Kurt Weitzmann, in his analysis of the painted lid of the famous early christian Palestinian *Sancta Sanctorum* reliquary box in the Vatican, has identified the small cube-like object within the ciborium in the scene of the Marys at the tomb as an altar covered with a purple cloth decorated with central cross and *gamandine*. The altar motif defines the ciborium not as Christ's tomb of the gospel narrative but as it existed as a pilgrimage site in the Anastasis of the Holy Sepulchre before being destroyed by the Persians in 614, ie, as a real historical structure recognised as invoking the idea of the mass at the holy site.[80] Accordingly, the *Una autem* patriarchal cross so closely identified with the *Adoratio Crucis* of Good Friday is also to be understood as the cross displayed on the altar for the Easter Vigil *Visitatio Sepulchri*.

For the present, leaving aside the details of the portrayal of the four angels, let us now turn to the question of symbolic intent for certain of the 'decorative' motifs and patterns on the page. Certainly, as the nebulous line separating iconographic meaning from ornamental convention is approached, over-analysis must be carefully avoided, especially because so many elements of design are found in diverse settings throughout the book. However that may be, contextual coincidence which speaks of a desire to heighten the meaning of text, cross and angel quartet must also be acknowledged. There is the example of the lion's head in the upper right corner of the frame. Henry has proposed it and other lions' heads (and complete animals) in the manuscript to be Resurrection symbols. We shall take up this issue again, but suffice to say that such a view is consistent with a thesis advocating a *Visitatio* explication for folio 285r. Also of interest are the peacocks confined within the opening *U* of the *Una*. Traditionally, peacocks are symbols of the Resurrection and functioning as such here permits the creatures to enhance the gravity of the Easter theme.[81] Then there are the vines issuing from chalices decorating the frame. As in the Christ Enthroned miniature, they may be eucharistic symbols and as such necessarily referring to the sacrifice of Christ.[82] Finally, there are the snakes

---

[80]Weitzmann (note 49 above) 41, fig 43. But see Vikan (note 49 above) 19, who interprets the cross design within the ciborium as a gold embroidered drapery hanging from a tie rod over the entrance. It may be of some interest that the stone which was rolled to the door of the *Monumentum* is described by Adomnán (Meehan (note 25 above) I, 3, pp 46-47) as forming a quadrangular altar covered by linen in the eastern part of the church'.

[81]In the Christ Enthroned miniature this symbolism is enhanced by the host emblems on the wings of the peacocks. For peacock symbolism, see Werner (note 33 above) 132; H Lother, *Der Pfau in der altchristlichen Kunst* (Leipzig 1929).

[82]H Richardson, 'Derrynaflan and other early church treasures', *JRSAI* 110 (1980) 92-115 (p 93) indicates an early use of glass for chalices and suggests the chalices in the Christ Enthroned and Luke genealogy tailpiece are of blue glass. In the *Una autem* initial a chalice issuing vines occupies each side of the frame. This quaternity is interesting in light of Amalarius' interpretation of four silver chalices as representing the four quarters of the earth to which news of the Resurrection will penetrate; *Liber officialis*, in Hanssens (note 70 above) II, 362. See also Werner (note 24 above) 183, n 33.

— the four that cover the top of the strokes of the *U*, another pair that swirl about the peacocks in the curve of the initial, and a single creature at the base of the right stem — which Isabel Henderson has convincingly proposed as emblematic of Resurrection.[83] As far as one can judge, therefore, there is reason to allow for the possibility of symbolic meaning for certain ornamental motifs on the *Una autem* page. At most, such reference would simply underscore the fundamental signification of the miniature as expositing on the *Visitatio Sepulchri* and the plausibility of a thesis crediting the Kells artists as creating here a kind of figured gloss.

That the figural and other elements on folio 183r, our second isolated ornamented text page, are similarly intended to illustrate a lections reading seems very likely.[84] But here the imagery is difficult to relate to the Mark 15:24-25 Good Friday reading. While the purple clad frame figure bears some affinity to a figure on folio 202r at the end of the Luke genealogy and to a figure above the frame in the portrait of St John (both of which we shall propose as symbolising the Crucified Christ), it lacks identifying attributes. As for the seated angel at the left, the figure resembles the angel on the *na* of the *Una autem* page and thus, perhaps, may have been meant to allude to the Resurrection.

There are two figures in our miniature and two deacons mentioned for the *Depositio* rite in the *Regularis concordia* who place the cross in the 'sepulchre' in 'imitation' of the burial of Christ. Perhaps an early version of the Good Friday *Depositio* or *Elevatio* with its commemoration of Christ's departure from the tomb served to inspire the artist of the *Erat autem* initials just as a presumptive version of the *Visitatio* served as a point of departure for the *Una autem* miniature.[85] Acceptance of such a possibility would allow us to

---

[83]Henry, 208, observing that because the snake sheds its skin yet does not die, it can be employed as a symbol of eternity or resurrection. Because of the emphatic use of the motif in the most prominent settings, she suspected its Resurrection reference in the Book of Kells. I Henderson (note 13 above) 64-65, supports this reading, pointing to the Iona sculptors' placement of snake imagery in the most conspicuous parts of their crosses, and to the association of snake-boss ornament with the Crucifixion and other Passion imagery on the Cross of Muiredach, Monasterboice. Similarly in Kells it is used to emphasize the text of the Passion: folios 27v, 29r, 34r, 114r, 124r, 127v, 183r, 184v, 188r, 202v, 273v, 274v, 276v, 282v, 285r, 291v, 292r, 337v.

[84]The richly marked lections for Good Friday in Matthew (folio 114v) and Mark (folio 183r) may possibly reflect the tendency of insular gospel books to emphasize parallel readings from two or more gospels. Farr, 'Liturgical influences', points to the elaborate cycles for Lent and Holy Week in non-Roman lections systems as partial explanation. See also note 21.

[85]In the *Regularis Concordia* (note 64 above) 42, the Good Friday night office has two deacons 'as it were like thieves' stripping the altar of its cloth; two deacons carry the Cross to the altar. Then during the *Depositio* (ibid, 44-45):

> ... on that part of the altar where there is space for it there shall be a representation as it were of a sepulchre, hung about with a curtain, in which the holy Cross, when it has been venerated, shall be placed in the following manner: the deacons who carried the Cross before shall come forward and, having wrapped the Cross in a napkin there where it was venerated, they shall bear it thence, singing the antiphons *In pace in idipsum, Habitabit* and *Caro mea requiescet in spe*, to the place of the sepulchre. When they have laid the Cross therein, in imitation as it were of the burial of the Body of our Lord Jesus Christ, they shall sing the antiphon ...

view the book-carrying angel at the left as the angel at the tomb on Easter
morning and the lozenge-shaped form on which he sits as the capstone of
the tomb (or sarcophagus lid as in many early depictions). The purple clad
frame figure would then become the Risen Christ, a Resurrection
presentation (perhaps) intensified by the lozenge repeated in the framing
element and by the lion's head and snake motif completing the E of the
opening *Erat*. Clearly, this would mean a shift in emphasis from the Good
Friday Crucifixion text on the page toward a Resurrection reference in a
Good Friday liturgical rite, a possibility not altogether unlikely given the far
from direct correlation between the Arrest and Temptation miniatures and
their accompanying texts.

In attempting to determine whether and how the Kells full-page miniatures
express their function and purpose, Farr has proposed that many of the
large and small figures found throughout the manuscript and previously
resisting identification stand for deacons. These include the figures holding
books with hand extended from the right side of an enveloping mantle,
resembling a chausible, which covers the left hand. The deacon prepared
the altar and read the gospel at mass; he was the churchman most familiar
with the gospel text.[86] In the light of our analysis of the two isolated
ornamented incipits, Farr's thesis is remarkably felicitous for it helps
explain the appearance of the angels in the miniatures. Two of the angels
we have identified as 'brethren' on folio 285r, and the angel of Resurrection
on folio 183r (as well as the 'Angel of the Lord' on folio 187v) are draped
and posed with books in similar fashion to the wingless figures with
chasubles and books seen elsewhere. Recalling Amalarius' allegorical
interpretation of the Vigil Mass where deacons 'become' the women at the
tomb, etc, the clergy of the *Visitatio* on the Metz ivory in Paris, and the
deacons of the *Adoratio Crucis*, *Depositio* and *Visitatio* described in the

---

(… sit autem in una parte altaris, qua uacuum fuerit, quaedam assimilatio
sepulcri uelamenque quoddam in gyro tensum quo, dum sancta crux adorata
fuerit, deponatur hoc ordine. Veniant diaconi qui prius portauerunt eam et
inuoluant eam sindone in loco ubi adorata est; tunc reportent eam canentes
antiphonas *In pace in idipsum*, alia: *Habitabit*; item: *Caro mea requiescet in spe*,
donec ueniant ad locum monumenti; depositaque cruce, ac si Domini Nostri
Ihesu Christi corpore sepulto, dicant antiphonam …)

[86]The eighth-century insular *Collectanea* (PL 94, 555) describes the liturgical garment
worn by the deacon when he read the gospel as a chasuble open on the right side
'because the author of the gospel, whom the deacon shall imitate was pierced on the
right side'. It also characterises the office of deacon as that of guardian and custodian
of the altar and reader of the gospel. The deacon was of the sixth of seven orders just
behind that of priest; Farr, 'Lection', 344-45; eadem, 'Liturgical influences', 135, nn
85-87. As regards this matter, Kathleen Szpila has called to my attention the
possibility that at the top centre above the *Liber* on folio 29r the book-carrying figure
appears to be wearing a yellow stole. In the middle ages, the stole was generally
worn by bishops, presbyters and deacons. By the sixth century Gallican and Spanish
councils decreed the use of the *oraria* or stole to distinguish rank. In 675, the second
Council of Braga ordered priests to wear their *oraria* crossed over the chest as is
usual today. However, the custom does not seem to have taken hold until much
later; D Rock, *The church of our fathers*, 4 vols (London 1905) I, 342-43. Amalarius of
Metz, *De ecclesiasticis officiis*, I, xx, PL 105, 1096, wrote that the deacon receives the
stola at his ordination by the bishop; C E Pocknee, *Liturgical vesture* (Westminster,
Maryland 1961) 22.

Regularis concordia, Farr's hypothesis serves to suggest the angels in the Kells miniatures are deacons with added wings.[87] In the Book of Kells, it would appear, deacons are presented in their liturgical roles as readers (wingless) and as performers of sacred drama (winged).

To this point (and with the exception of the *Christi autem* cycle in Matthew) we have concentrated our attention on those full-page illustrations and display pages that bear witness to a definite liturgical scheme and choice of subjects. It will be useful to turn to other pages in the manuscript less directly implicated in a lections system but which nonetheless appear to take up the Easter theme. Of these, the portrait of St John on folio 291v is most important (**pl 51**). Even within its own evangelist portrait class, the miniature is unique. The evangelist is depicted as bearded and seated on a draped cushion within what may be a draped high-backed throne. A closed gospel codex is in his left hand. In his right is a large pen held above an ink pot close by his right foot. Behind John's head is a large circular device variously interpreted as his nimbus or the upper part of the throne.[88] A heavy, elaborately panelled frame, with large crosses at its compass points, encloses the author portrait. Making an already idiosyncratic scheme even more extraordinary is the bearded head with draped shoulders and nimbus looming above the centre of the upper part of the border. On the same axis below are the figure's draped feet. His clenched hands extend from behind the frame at the sides.

The extruded figural elements of the St John portrait are absent from the

---

[87]In her analysis of the Marys at the tomb depicted on three sixth-century (?) pyxides, A St Clair, 'The Visit to the Tomb: narrative and liturgy on three early christian pyxides', *Gesta* 18 (1979) 27-35, interprets the boxes as eucharistic containers whose imagery 'incorporated references to the eucharistic liturgy within the framework of events from Christ's life'. She points to a similar combination expressive of 'the liturgical re-enactment of the Passion' on a sixth-century glass chalice in the Dumbarton Oaks Collection: M Ross, *Catalogue of the Byzantine and early medieval antiquities in the Dumbarton Oaks Collection, I: metalwork, ceramics, glass, glyptics, painting* (Washington 1962) no 96, pl LIV. Here two angels carrying codices flank a baldachin enclosing a cross on steps. Significantly, St Clair suggests a connection between the two angels and the two deacons in the guise of angels at the altar in the account of the eucharistic liturgy by the fifth-century Nestorian scholar Narsai: *The liturgical homilies of Narsai*, trans R H Connolly (Cambridge 1909) XXIII, XXIV, 4, 12, 56, 77. Depicting the brethren or deacons as winged angels may also reflect some confusion as to the identification of the figures at the Easter morning tomb. From as early as the fourth century, a fusion had taken place in depictions of these figures. Thus, in the late fourth-century ivory panel in the Castello Sforcesco, Milan, of the Marys at the Sepulchre (J Beckwith, *Early christian and Byzantine Art* (Harmondsworth 1970) pl 36) one sees the 'young man' with a halo and carrying a scroll sitting on a rock as described by St Mark. But instead of three women, there are only two. Matthew describes an angel dressed in white, sitting on a rock and speaking with the two Marys, while Luke speaks of the three Marys encountering two men in shining robes. Clearly, a combination of Matthew 28:1-7 and Luke 24:5 has occurred.

[88]A M Friend, 'The canon tables of the Book of Kells' in *Medieval studies in memory of Arthur Kingsley Porter*, ed W R W Koehler (Cambridge, Mass. 1939) II, 611-40 (p 635), identifies the design as 'a great scalloped nimbi'; Henry, 183, agrees; Werckmeister (note 2 above, 101 ff) believes the device to be part of the saint's throne. Together with the four crosses at the compass points of the frame it suggests to him a kind of baldachin symbolising the vault of heaven.

other two male portraits in the Book of Kells, the Matthew (folio 28v) and Christ Enthroned (folio 32v), and the miniature omits their use of an inner arcade. Some of these inconsistencies may have to do with the way the Fathers view John in relation to the other evangelists and the distinctions drawn between his gospel and the synoptic gospels. John (21:20-24) identifies himself as the disciple Christ most loved; his is the gospel most mystically conceived.[89] Augustine and Bede testify to John being the evangelist who most emphatically emphasizes the deity of Christ and his equality with the Father.[90] In the British Isles, John's special status is manifested in the Anglo-Saxon use of John 1:1-5 as a charm against sickness,[91] and the copying of the gospel as a book separate from and detached from the synoptic gospels;[92] and Bede chose John to translate into Anglo-Saxon.[93]

It is obvious that John had a singular prestige, but perhaps of greater relevance is John's characterisation of himself as the evangelist who witnessed the Crucifixion and later visited the sepulchre on Easter morning (John 18:25, 35; 20:1-10), the employment of John's Passion narrative during Holy Week, and most especially the use of his account of the Crucifixion on Good Friday.[94] The portrait of John faces the *In principio* which begins the

---

[89]John's sublimity as an evangelist was an important concern of ninth-century exegetes; John Scottus Erigena, *Homilia ... Joannem*, cap. 1, 1-4, PL 122, 283-85; Alcuin, *Commentariorum in Joannem Liber Primus*, PL 100, 743-72. Almost from the first a distinction was drawn between the Fourth Gospel and the preceding three 'Synoptics'. Besides its emphasis on Christ's divinity, John's gospel does not include important events detailed in the Synoptics such as the institution of the Eucharist at the Last Supper, while introducing others such as the story of John and Peter at the Sepulchre on Easter morning. See M Schapiro, 'Two Romanesque drawings in Auxerre and some iconographic problems' in *Studies in Art and Literature for Belle Da Costa Greene*, ed D Minor (Princeton 1954) 333-37; C H Dodd, *The interpretation of the fourth gospel* (Cambridge 1953); R Bultmann, *The gospel of John* (Oxford 1971).

[90]Augustine, *De consensu evangelistorum*, I, 4, PL 34, 1045, and preface to *Tractatus in Joannis evangelium*, PL 24, 1377. Bede, *Homilia*, VII, PL 94, 38 ff and *Homilia*, VIII, ibid, 46.

[91]Passages from the gospels, and especially John 1:15, from early christian times were worn as a charm to ward off sickness. Evidence of magical use of the verses survives from Anglo-Saxon England; T J Brown, *The Stonyhurst Gospel of St John* (Oxford 1969) 30-32. R Powell, 'The Books of Kells and Durrow: comments on the vellum, the make-up and other aspects', *Scriptorium* 10 (1956) 3-21 (pp 14-15), referring to the use of the Book of Durrow as a cure for sick cattle, observed that the condition of the leaves of the manuscript shows that it was a portion of John (6:63 to 12:4) used for immersion.

[92]See Brown (note 91 above) for a detailed study of the seventh-century codex found among the relics of St Cuthbert. Then there is the Stowe Missal. Between 1045 and 1052 it was enshrined in a *cumdach* with a gospel of St John. Even if once part of an Irish pocket gospels, as has been suggested, the placement of the gospel of John in the same shrine as the Missal is significant. Brown, ibid, 34, sees it as reflecting early medieval practice of placing the fourth gospel in a shrine for prophylactic reasons. For Stowe Gospel: see Alexander, *Insular manuscripts*, 68-69. St Gall, Stiftsbibliothek, MS 60 of probable early ninth-century Irish origin is also a gospel of John; ibid, 80.

[93]At the time of his death Bede was said to be translating John into English; Charles Plummer, *Venerabilis Bedae opera historica*, I, (Oxford 1896) I, CLXIII. G B Brown, *The arts in early England* (London 1930) VI (1), 9-10, suggested that Bede used the Stonyhurst Gospel as the basis of his translation.

[94]See J A Jungmann, *The early liturgy* (Notre Dame 1959) 253-65. Moreover, according to the Rule of Tallaght, along with St Paul's epistles, it was read at night

canonic gospel text and was almost certainly meant to introduce the entirety of that text, as was the image of the author itself. Yet the portrait also seems to be a visual essay on the meaning of the Resurrection. Two aspects of the composition signal this reading: the strange circular design behind John's head and the figural elements projecting from behind the frame.

Whether recognised as a kind of throne-back baldachin as Otto Werckmeister has suggested, or as a nimbus as generally assumed, the circular arrangement framing the evangelist's head is both large and puzzling. It is certainly without precedent in evangelist portrait iconography. Earlier we briefly engaged the issue of consultation of Adomnán's *De locis sanctis*. It would seem that a strong case can be made for the influence of the text on the form of John's nimbus design, or more specifically the influence of one of Arculf's *loca sancta* schemes on the circular device. In the pilgrims guide the Anastasis of the Holy Sepulchre is described:

> We questioned the holy Arculf concerning [the place of the cross and resurrection] especially concerning the sepulchre of the Lord and the church built over it, the shape of which Arculf himself depicted for me on a waxed tablet.

> Well this extremely large church, all of stone and shaped to wondrous roundness on every side, rises up from foundations in three walls. Between each wall there is a broad passage and three altars too in these three skilfully constructed places of the centre wall. Twelve stone columns of wondrous magnitude support this round and lofty church, where are the altars mentioned, one looks south, the second north and the third toward the west ...[95]

Adomnán goes on:

> Now in this sepulchre according to the number of the twelve holy apostles, twelve burning lamps shine always day and night. Four of them are placed low down at the bottom of the sepulchral bed: the other eight are placed higher up above the margin toward the right hand side.[96]

Folio 4v in Vienna, Nationalbibliothek, Cod. 458 is thought to be the most accurate of surviving copies of the Holy Sepulchre plan 'Arculf depicted ... on a waxed tablet' (**pl 61**).[97] The Anastasis with its three niches and circular

---

on alternate weeks: E J Gwynn, 'The Rule of Tallaght', *Hermathena* 44 (1927) second supplemental volume, p 13. See also J F Kelly, 'Hiberno-Latin theology' in *Die Iren und Europa im frühen Mittelalter*, ed H Lowe (Stuttgart 1982) II, 558-59.
[95]Meehan (note 25 above) I, 2, pp 42-45.
[96]ibid, I, 3, pp 46-47.
[97]Arculf's plans have survived in several forms and some have been presented together for comparison by A Heissenberg, *Grabeskirche und Apostelkirche* (Leipzig 1908) 75-77, pls IX, X, and J Wilkinson, *Jerusalem pilgrims before the crusades*

corridors dominates the drawing. Significantly, when the central niche of
the Vienna Anastasis diagram is aligned with the upper circle of the three
affixed to the circular nimbus framing John's head (the circle partially
hidden by the blue-bordered interlaced cross), a striking parallel is effected
between ground plan and framing device. That this near identity is more
than coincidence seems validated not only by the Palestinian *loca sancta*
references discovered elsewhere in the decoration of the codex, but by
details of the nimbus. Particularly interesting are the twelve half circles
enclosing step patterns bisected by a central line (two of these are partially
concealed by the saint's shoulders) and the arrow-shaped figures projecting
from them toward John's head. The half circles conform to Adomnán's
description of twelve supporting columns in the sepulchre and a search for
counterparts in Kells yields but one similar configuration, that employed for
the base of the outer left column of the canon table on folio 4v (**pl 6**) —
perhaps confirmation of the architectural exemplification intended for the
motif in St John's nimbus. For the reason that in the Vienna plan the twelve
lamps recorded as surrounding the 'sepulchral bed' are presented as twelve
arrow-shaped figures, it is also possible to speculate on the meaning of the
red arrowlike forms attached to the nimbus half circles. Ten are visible, but
twelve are implied because the arrows spring from the clearly visible twelve
half circles.

These details and the introduction of important symbolic imagery around
the Saviour's head in the Christ Enthroned miniature and around Matthew's
head in his portrait page prompts a search for symbolic statement in other
of the nimbus parts.[98] The three discs overlapping the purple banding of the
outer circle of the nimbus are of interest in this regard. Proposed as inspired
by the three niches of Arculf's Anastasis plan, they suggest an inventive
variant of the niche idea. They are filled with eight pointed star-shaped
designs. Already in the early christian period such signs were used as
versions of Christ's chrism and inscribed on eucharistic cakes.[99] It is difficult

---

(Warminster 1977) 193-97. Most copies of Adomnán's pilgrimage text do not contain
plans, but there are still a number from which to choose. With respect to the
Anastasis, the plan of the Holy Sepulchre with the Anastasis is found in the ninth-
century Vienna, Nationalbibliothek, MS 458; Paris, BN, MS lat. 13048; Zurich,
Rhenau, MS 74; and Karlsruhe, Landesbibliothek, MS Aug. 129 (the last three in
Wilkinson, ibid, pl V). All display slight variations; in the Vienna plan the altar
niches are rounded and are identified as *altare in accodentali rotunda*. Vienna,
Nationalbibliothek, MS 458, was written by a certain Baldo, a teacher in the
cathedral school of Salzburg, *c*850, who had connections with Ireland: an Irishman
named Dungal was his friend and pupil; Meehan (note 25 above) 30. Versions of the
plan also appear in several copies of Bede's *De locis sanctis*; Wilkinson, ibid, 193.
[98]See note 118.
[99]'Chrisme', *DACL*, III, 1482-1534, figs 2839, 2840, 2853, 2882, 2883, 2894, 2904; W
Kellner, 'Christusmonogram', *Lexikon der christlichen Ikonographie* (Rome 1968) I, 456-
58; Werckmeister (note 2 above) figs 8c, 9a-9d. G Galavaris, *Bread and the liturgy*
(Madison 1978) 37-38, figs 18, 19, illustrates two sixth-century bread stamps from
Egypt which he believes carry cross emblems. Composed of eight pointed
compartments the designs resemble the Kells circular devices. Galavaris interprets
the diagonals of his stamps as rays of light most likely dependent on the legend of St
Helena's discovery of the three Golgotha crosses — the Cross of Christ miraculously
radiating light to reveal itself as the True Cross. The use of azymes or unleavened
bread for the Eucharist should also be noted. The Sixteenth Council of Toledo in 692

to imagine more evocative emblems of the rituals performed at the altars in the niches of the Anastasis.[100]

John, we recall, came to the tomb, the principal *locus sanctus* of Resurrection, on Easter morning. Earlier he was witness to the Crucifixion and this brings us to a consideration of the fragmented nimbed figure set on the compass points of the frame enclosing the enthroned author. Werckmeister proposed it to be primarily representative of the Creator embracing the cosmos.[101] Helen Roe related it to a small group of Irish seventh and eighth-century monuments mainly characterised by the display of a disembodied head placed above a 'breastplate' motif — formulations she believed to be crucifixions dependent upon the example of a type of symbolic crucifixion depicted on certain of the early christian Holy Land ampules where the nimbed bust of the Saviour is set immediately above the Cross of Golgotha-Tree of Life.[102] Roe's arguments are not consistently convincing,[103] but her insistence on an interpretation of the Kells frame figure as the Crucified Christ seems correct. Attention has hitherto centred on that portion of the fragmentary figure above St John, but, plainly, the extremities are of equal importance. By way of demonstration, let us note that although John's feet

---

ruled that eucharistic bread should be *ex studio praeparatus*, that is, not ordinary bread but *modica tantum oblata* or small obleys (The Book of Kells Chi Rho page may show one of these held by mice; another may be depicted on folio 48r). Alcuin, *Ep.* LIX, PL 100, 289, explains this as because 'the bread which is consecrated into the Body of Christ should be more pure, without the leavening of an alien corruption'. See J H Creehan, 'The liturgical trade route: east to west', *Studies* 65 (1976) 87-99 (p 92).

[100]Reference to Arculf's plan may possibly occur elsewhere in our codex. As Carol Kline has pointed out to me, folio 203r, the Temptation incipit *Jesus autem plenus spiritus sancto* (Now Jesus, full of the Holy Spirit) for Luke 4:1 ornamentally treats the *u* of *Jesus* as a circle which can be read as replicating Arculf's three walls with three niches. I would add that the central interlaced leaf-like figure has a series of twelve dots, again reminiscent of the twelve columns of the Holy Sepulchre.

[101]Werckmeister (note 2 above) 122 ff. A Heimann, 'Three illustrations from the Bury St Edmunds Psalter and their prototypes', *Journal of the Warburg and Courtauld Institutes* 39 (1966) 39-59, also interprets the Kells frame figure as the Creator embracing the cosmos. Henry, 194, and Lewis (note 3 above) 151, n 52, have argued for an interpretation of the figure as the *Verbum*, the Logos Incarnate. Henderson, 175-76, believes it may possibly represent God the Father, also recognised in the figure at the top of the facing *In Principio*. He tentatively proposes the central figure on folio 291v as St John resting on the bosom of Christ or, alternately, as God the Son accompanied by God the Father (above).

[102]H Roe, 'A stone cross at Clogher, Co Tyrone', *JRSAI* 90 (1960) 191-206, associates a small stone cross at Clogher with several Irish slabs, crosses and metalwork objects and the Kells St John frame figure. All, she asserts, display a symbolic Crucifixion and are ultimately dependent on the inspiration of an iconography created in early christian Palestine. See also A K Porter (note 79 above) 51.

[103]In the symbolic Crucifixion scenes on the ampules the nimbed bust of Christ is set immediately above the Cross of Golgotha - Tree of Life; A Grabar, *Ampoules de Terre Sainte* (Paris 1958) pls XI-XIV, XVI-XVIII, XXXVII-XXXIX, XLVII, XLIX; see also R Grigg, 'The Cross-and-Bust image: some tests of a recent explanation', *Byzantinische Zeitschrift* 77 (1979) 16-33. Such scenes do serve to lend credence to the idea of a Crucifixion comprised in part of a bust of the Saviour as being above the frame in the Kells portrait page. However, apart from our miniature, none of the Irish examples listed by Roe presents Christ's feet; and only one other shows Christ's hands. It must also be observed that the Kells arrangement seems remote from an iconography in which the figural elements are arranged around a central circular 'breastplate' motif.

and those of the figure below the frame have little circles at the heels, these heels sets are not quite alike. The type used for the enthroned evangelist is one of two frequently employed in the manuscript: either heels bear small and unfilled circles as for the seated author or they display equally diminutive but borderless red dots.[104] In contrast, our frame figure's heels have circles of greater radius neither left colourless nor filled with red but containing the same purple hue as the robe which descends between the feet. The detail, in other words, is without exact parallel in the Book of Kells and calls for an explanation detached from that applied to the other circle types. As the circles signifying the nails driven into Christ's feet are pictured in Crucifixion scenes of earlier or contemporary date[105] (and later appear on Christ's horizontally positioned feet in the Crucifixion in the Irish eleventh-century (?) Southampton Psalter),[106] there can be little doubt that, despite the sandal straps worn by the frame figure, the circles on his feet record a like Crucifixion reference.

The sleeved hands at the sides of the frame are also worth studying. Both hands are clenched. There is a thin red object in the hand to John's right. Most of the vellum has been cut away from around the hand to John's left making details difficult to decipher. In 1908, S F H Robinson was certain he saw an object in each fist.[107] Given the small size and delicate dimensions of the object in the clenched hand to John's right and the depiction of Christ's nail wounds in innumerable early Crucifixions, an explanation of the portrait page as displaying one of the Crucifixion nails (and once possibly two) seems reasonable and adds to the weight of evidence in support of our iconographic hypothesis.[108] Before leaving this matter and placing no undue

---

[104]The unfilled circles type appears on folios 7v, 8r, 202r, 291v (St John). The small red dot type is seen on folios 2v, 27v and 280r. See also C Nordenfalk, 'An illustrated Diatessaron', *Art Bulletin* 50 (1968) 129, for a discussion of an 'ankle rings' motif in Kells.

[105]Folio 383v, Durham, Cathedral Library, MS A.II.17; p 266, St Gall, Stiftsbibliothek, MS 51; Alexander, *Insular manuscripts*, 40-42, fig 202; pp 66-67, fig 203; Werner (note 24 above) 197, nn 108-110.

[106]Folio 38v, Cambridge St John's College, MS C. 9 (59); Alexander, *Insular manuscripts*, 88-89, fig 351.

[107]S F H Robinson, *Celtic illuminative art in the Gospel Books of Durrow, Lindisfarne and Kells* (Dublin 1908) page facing pl XIV. Werckmeister (note 2 above) 127, identifies the object as a plant.

[108]If, originally, each hand held a red object, an alternative explanation is possible if (because of size) less plausible than the nail thesis. In Meehan (note 25 above) I, 50-51) Adomnán writes:

> Arculf saw the soldier's lance ... with which he pierced the side of the Lord when he was hanging on the cross. The lance is in the porch of the basilica of Constantine, inserted in a wooden cross, and its shaft is split into two parts.

The reference, then, may be to the two lance parts. Or, perhaps, because Longinus with his lance and Stephaton with his sponge-tipped staff are nearly ubiquitous in insular Crucifixion scenes, folio 291v may once have represented lance and staff. Roe (note 102 above) 203, has taken note of the constant appearance of the two soldiers in Crucifixion scenes carved on the Irish high crosses. The pair figure in the Durham A.II.17 Crucifixion (see note 105) and in Irish metal work; for an illuminating discussion of the latter, see R N Bailly, 'A Crucifixion plaque from Cumbria' in *Early medieval sculpture in Britain and Ireland*, ed John Higgitt, British Archaeological Reports, British series (Oxford 1986) 125-52. Both Roe and Werckmeister identify the source for the Crucifixion with soldiers imagery as originating in early christian

emphasis on the point, it should also be noted that the parts of the frame figure are set behind four large interlaced crosses introduced at the compass points, again perhaps to signify the death of Christ.

Examination of the portrait of St John thus invites its recognition as combining a plan of the Anastasis of the Holy Sepulchre and an image of Christ on the Cross. The holiest sites in early christian Jerusalem were the Martyrium, the Anastasis and between them the monumental Golgotha Cross. This being so, we are not surprised to discover expressions of these last two *loca sancta* in the juxtaposed Crucifixion/women at the tomb images on many of the early Palestinian ampules and related works.[109] And, of course, we have proposed an abstract Crucifixion-Resurrection conjunction in the eight-circles cross page and a complex association of tomb and True Cross emblem on the *Una autem* page in our insular codex. It goes without saying that facing the *In principio* incipit the portrait of John is not an illustration or gloss on an Easter lection. It seems intended to bring to mind, nevertheless, an abundance of Easter associations including thoughts of the evangelist's unique witness to the Crucifixion, his presence later at Christ's tomb, and the profound importance of his gospel for the Easter service; perhaps, most important, it serves to echo and recapitulate the meaning of the triduum brought forward in the Maundy Thursday, Good Friday and Easter Sunday lection sequences and single folios.[110]

Besides the Kells St John portrait, another display page seems to stand apart from the system of lections incipits yet speaks of the wider programme. This is folio 187v containing the concluding words of St Mark's Gospel, Mark 16:19-20, describing the Ascension (**pl 33**). As Alexander has pointed out, the text in black ink is formed into two triangles conforming to a scribal tradition which fashions the last lines of text into an ornamental

---

Palestine. G Schiller, *Iconography of christian art* (Greenwich, Conn. 1972) II, 91-92, finds such Holy Land arrangements to have a christological thrust, symbolising the opposition between life and death and underlining the double identity of God and man in Christ. Additionally, the two soldiers allude to the idea of Redemption. John 19:34 informs us that one of the pair pierced the Saviour's side with a spear and water ran from the wound. Let us further observe that in a late eighth-century copy of St Paul's Epistle written in or near Würzburg (Würzburg, Univ., Cod. M. p. th. f. 69) folio 7v displays a Crucifixion — perhaps based on an Irish model — wherein the lance and rod are crossed over Christ's chest but the soldiers themselves are not present; Alexander, *Insular manuscripts*, 78, pl 265.

[109] For ampules see Grabar (note 103 above) pls XI-XIV, XVI, XVIII, XXII, XXIV, XXVIII, XXXIV-XXXVIII. For related material see G Schiller, *Ikonographie des Christlichen Kunst* (Gutersloh 1971) III, 18-30. Recently, P Harbison, 'A group of early christian carved stone monuments in County Donegal' in Higgitt (note 108 above) 50, suggested the group of robed figures beneath the Crucifixion on the east face of the Carndonagh Cross to be the 'Three Holy Women coming to the Tomb'. He finds the same three figures below a fragmentary Crucifixion from Perthshire, ie on a stone labelled Abernathy No 4, National Museum of Antiquities in Edinburgh.

[110] Here, too, notice should be made of the snake ornament which occupies all four corners of the frame on folio 291v as well as the panels on the right side of the facing *In Principio* page. Significantly, on folio 337r (John 16:7-14) the last word is framed by a single snake, while, on the verso, Christ alludes to his approaching death and resurrection.

configuration.[111] Within a saltire design framed by the limbs of two large beasts are, at the left, an angel holding a book and labelled *Angelus* in orange; at the right is a winged lion beside whom is the word *dni* (*domini*) again in orange. The page is directly followed by the gospel of Luke. For this reason and despite the fact that if they were intended as evangelist symbols they would presumably have stood for Matthew and Mark rather than Mark and Luke (ie the evangelist whose gospel is ending and the evangelist whose gospel is about to begin), the angel and lion have been construed as together constituting an evangelist symbols page for Luke.[112] However, some years ago Henry argued for interpreting the page as an unfinished Ascension.[113] In light of our analysis of folios 183r and 285r, it seems more likely that it is a complete albeit highly abstract and abbreviated version of the Saviour 'taken up into heaven and set down at the right hand of God', with the 'Angel of the Lord' at the left rehearsing the event and the lion at the right, turning to look at the angel, symbolising St Mark, who was present when Christ rose and recorded the event in his gospel, a gospel here coming to a close in the Book of Kells.

Not marked as a pericope for Ascension Day, the page may yet allude to one of the chief feasts of the christian year and Easter season.[114] Following Easter Sunday by forty days and marking the solemn end of the post-Resurrection appearances and the exaltation of Christ to heaven, it forms a counterpart to Quadragesima Sunday, the beginning of the forty-day lenten fast in preparation for Easter marked by the folio 114v incipit.

In our discussion of the *Una autem* and John portrait pages we fleetingly touched on the issue of the symbolic interpretation of ornament. Quite troubling as to purpose are the elaborate and diversified combinations of figural, animal, vegetable and geometric elements decorating large and small initials, or filling gaps and indicating 'turns' in the text. This ornamentation seems mostly not to have iconographic connection to the text, but there are some obvious exceptions. The snakes of the *Vespere* of Matthew 28:1-5 on folio 127v — the beginning of the description of the Marys at the sepulchre, an Easter pericope — proposed as Resurrection symbols, unambiguously appear to perform this function here. Then there is a text section concluding with an odd conjunction of motifs likely to have symbolic intent: the tailpiece of the Luke genealogy on folio 202r displays a bust of a figure above, and his legs below, a frieze-like rectangular frame

---

[111] J J G Alexander, 'Descriptions of illuminated pages' in *Kells commentary*, 312.

[112] Most recently by W O'Sullivan as reported by B Meehan, 'Dimensions and original number of leaves' in *Kells commentary*, 176, n 9. See also Alexander, *Insular manuscripts*, 72.

[113] Henry, 173, pointed to the possibility that the page was intended to display an Ascension similar to that in the Turin Gospels (Turin, Biblioteca Nazionale, Cod. O. IV. 20, folio 1a) an Irish gospels fragment of perhaps the first half of the ninth century; Alexander, *Insular manuscripts*, 80-81, pl 279.

[114] H Frere, *Studies in the early Roman liturgy*, II, *The Roman gospel lectionary* (London 1934) 42, lists Mark 16:14-20 as a reading for Ascension Day in the 'Standard Series' representing models brought forward by Charlemagne at the end of the eighth century.

enclosing two compartments respectively containing a pair of affronted peacocks and a vase with two symmetrical interlaced vine scrolls (**pl 41**). 'The Lord' is mentioned in the genealogy just above the frame figure and would seem to identify him as Christ. With its lack of nimbus, its centrally parted hair, forked beard, curvilinear stylisations and downward pointing feet (each foot displaying a circle), this Christ figure is surprisingly similar to the Crucified Christ carved on the eighth century(?) Calf of Man Crucifix,[115] and quite possibly has the same identity. With regard to the peacocks and vine scrolls, they are motifs conjoined in the Christ Enthroned on folio 32v, where they make obvious eucharistic reference to Resurrection and Redemption. Manifestly, there is good reason to understand the tailpiece as a symbolic Crucifixion meant to call up thoughts of the Easter triduum rites, and perhaps, in part, added to introduce or complement the Temptation illustration and incipit (folios 202v-203r) which immediately succeed the Luke genealogy.

Elsewhere it is often difficult to make clear distinction between ornament and symbol. Vines and vine scrolls are quite commonplace. Lions' heads or complete creatures decorate all four introductory gospel incipits, and earlier we had reason to cite the lion's head in the *Una autem* miniature and Henry's suggestion of the lion as a recurrent Resurrection symbol in the codex.[116] Similarly, there are the several appearances of snakes, again suspected of Resurrection reference. The cross, of course, is the primary symbol of Christ's removal to heaven, but it is not always certain when it is functioning simply as a compositional or ornamental motif or in its emblematic mode. Yet we must not fail to note its extraordinary ubiquity within the scheme of decoration. In company with crosses, implied or otherwise, around which the symbols of the four evangelists alternate, the Andrews cross-shaped Chi of the *Christi autem* page (and X-shaped arrangements elsewhere) and the double-barred crosses on folios 33r, 130r, and 285r, there are numerous other cross designs. For example, there is an interesting variant of the patriarchal cross type to be seen in the compartment below the figure in the jaws of a lion in the upper right hand corner of folio 130r — an interlaced emblem topped by a titulus composed of two V shapes. Large and small single-barred crosses figure within nimbi, etc in figural scenes, and in initials of varying size and complexity; they appear as marginal designs on text pages as well. Last, let us mention folios 30v and 31r in Matthew where the text is divided into two vertical columns and marked horizontally by lozenges, circles, etc, so as to clearly outline the form of a cross. The cross on the altar recalls Christ's death which the mass mystically renews. Obviously when symbolically intended (and whatever else it may signify in specific settings),[117] a central purpose in the Book of Kells must surely have been to act as a reminder of the Easter festivals given

[115]L M Angus-Butterworth, 'The Calf of Man Crucifix', *Transactions of the Ancient Monuments Society*, ns 117 (1970) 31-37; B R S Megaw, 'The Calf of Man Crucifixion', *Journal of the Manx Museum* 6 (75) (1958) 55-58.
[116]On lion symbolism, see Schiller (note 109 above) II, 122.
[117]For cross symbolism, see Werner (note 24 above).

emphasis in the incipits and illustrations.

The omnipresent cross and cross patterns, the many lions' heads and complete lions, the snakes, vases and vines may in numerous instances have been purely ornamental and not set down in accord with an iconographic master plan. Yet together with the pages we may call the core display (the Arrest and Temptation sequences, the two isolated 'illustrated' incipits and the modestly decorated Good Friday incipit in Matthew) and those pages we shall designate as 'supporting' (the Matthew 1:18 cycle, the proposed Ascension in Luke, the Crucifixion tailpiece in the same gospel and the portrait of John) — pages either marking gospel readings for the first Sunday of Lent, Maundy Thursday, Good Friday and Easter Sunday or recapitulating the meaning of the Easter festivals — many of these scattered motifs, suggestive as they are of a recurrent Resurrection leitmotif, should perhaps be perceived as elaborating a large scale, but clearly focused, programme.

Combined with a traditional insular system of preliminaries with canon tables, a system also emphasizing the opening of the four gospels with four symbols, carpet, evangelist portrait and ornate incipit pages, the Easter programme could sometimes emphatically embrace this tradition as in the cross-carpet and John portrait miniatures.[118] From this perspective the

---

[118]To this point focus has been directed to the full-page illustrations and display pages which have either a direct liturgical function as regards the Easter rites or appear to elaborate Easter reference and doctrine. To be sure, though not employed as part of the lections system, the text of the preliminaries are decorated and this scheme is not lacking in iconographic intent. Of particular interest are the evangelist symbols in the beast canon tables. These, sometimes grouped below a mysterious figure at the top of the frame to form 'an illusive *Majestas Domini*', have a further symbolic dimension adumbrated by the Luke symbol on folio 1v. Despite its head and hoofs, the composite creature is not especially calf-like. With its body of an eagle and calf's head the folio 2v Luke symbol is equally strange. This hybridism may have its basis in the writings of the Fathers; by the end of the fourth century as Gregory demonstrates, the four beasts were interpreted as representing the four stages of the life of Christ: birth, death, resurrection, and ascension. Christ was a man in his birth, a calf in his death, a lion in his resurrection and an eagle in his ascent to heaven; Gregory, *Homilia in Ezechielem*, IV, PL 94, 815. Significantly, this fourfold symbolism is employed in a seventh- to eighth-century Irish gospel commentary, the *Expositio quatuor evangeliorum* of Pseudo-Jerome, published under the names Jerome and Walafrid Strabo, PL 30, 531-90 and PL 94, 861-916. See R E McNally, 'The evangelists in the Hiberno-Latin tradition' in *Festschrift Bernhard Bischoff zu seinem 65*, ed Johanne Autenrieth and Franz Brunhölzl (Stuttgart 1971) 116. If, as seems to be the case, the composite beings have the same meaning, they constitute image-signs of the Passion clearly in accord with the variety of Easter significations in the gospel texts; on evangelist symbols, see Henry, 199. Besides in the preliminaries the evangelist symbols appear together introducing Matthew, Mark and John. With each of its symbols framed within a rectangular compartment folio 27v opening Matthew's gospel is simplest. That for Mark, folio 129v, is considerably more complex. Again it is divided into four rectangular cells but now flabella-carrying symbols are framed by circles, above or below which are one or two additional evangelist symbols. Perhaps juxtaposed are the creatures in their apocalyptic-evangelistic and allegorical (birth, death, resurrection and ascension) roles — a contrivance analogous to that employed for the composite symbols in the canon tables. However that may be, of the full-page evangelist symbols compositions, that for St John, folio 290v, is most unusual. The page is divided into four triangular spaces by a saltire cross ending in lions' heads. As noted elsewhere

Virgin and Child miniature remains anomalous. It is dedicated to the mystery of Incarnation. Yet it is not lacking in reference to Resurrection,[119] and it is placed in the preliminaries where it does not elaborate a lections reading. Clearly, however perceived, it should not detract from a conclusion that the decorators of the Book gave greatest emphasis to a celebration of

---

this cross and its diamond-shaped crossing may carry cosmic allusions similar to those of the Chi on folio 34r. Of course, since the interior frames of the first two four-symbols miniatures suggest a cross, or have a cross-shaped central motif, these pages as well as folio 290v can be viewed as *Majestas Crucis* compositions. The cosmic cross around which the symbols are distributed in these presentations carries much the same meaning as the Chi of the great Chi Rho miniature, including that of harmonising the universe through the form of Christ's death on the cross. For cosmic cross iconography, see Werner (note 24 above) 211. Finally, there is the remarkable employment of the evangelist symbols in the portrait of Matthew, folio 28v. Here the throne sides end in lion-headed finials, and the heads of the Luke and John symbols appear above the throne bolster respectively at left and right. Henderson, 155-59, interprets the page as a kind of *Majestas Domini*, and Alexander, 'Illumination', 280, suggests the seated figure at the centre to be 'the Man symbol of St Matthew, rather than the Evangelist himself'. However, the figure is not winged and the page follows a four-symbols miniature. Most likely, the central figure is St Matthew and the page, like the St John portrait page, a complex variant of a traditional portrait miniature.

[119] The Virgin and Child are surrounded by four winged angels which I have identified as probably the archangels Michael, Gabriel, Raphael and Uriel, a quartet with significant eucharistic reference; Werner (note 33 above) 11, n 41. Their attributes are similarly symbolic. Three of the angels carry wands or sceptres with circular tops, the fourth, at the lower right, holds a stem upside down terminating in leaves. The first three attributes appear to be flabella, the fans used in the early christian period during mass to drive off flies. Representations of these fans appear often in early medieval art in the West, including the British Isles. In the Book of Kells, besides on the Madonna and Child page, they appear on folios 5r and 129v. The fourth angel on folio 7v may also be holding a flabellum. D McRoberts, 'The ecclesiastical significance of the St Ninian's Isle treasure', *Proceedings of the Society of Antiquaries of Scotland* 94 (1960/1) 301-14 (pp 310-11), suggests the object to be a floriated flabellum, coloured yellow to represent gilded wood or metal. This flabellum type, comprised of leaves or feathers, he believes appears on the Molaise book shrine and on a cross-slab from St Vigeans. Possibly, as I have suggested (note 33 above, 12, n 49), the attribute may refer to the palm, the palm blessed before the principal mass on Palm Sunday and given the status of a sacramental object. It is the symbol of Christ's Resurrection in the *Dominica in Palmis*. Farr, 'Lection', 324, however, suggests the object to be a branch of hysop, a plant used in the purification of sanctuaries; and Alexander (note 111 above) 307, believes it may refer to the stem of Jesse in Isaiah 2:1. In the Book of Kells the angel quartet always seems to figure in a significant iconographic context. The group frames the Madonna and Christ Child on folio 7v, it flanks the Enthroned Christ on folio 32v, it appears above Christ in the Temptation on folio 202v and frames the *U* of the folio 285r *Una autem*. Yet the angels of these quartets carry varying attributes and although there is never more than one flowering staff-bearing angel or more than two book-bearing angels on the same page, this pattern, or lack of one, defies interpretation. Be that as it may, in the Madonna and Child miniature, the Virgin wears a lozenge-shaped brooch. Werckmeister, we recall (note 41 above), viewed the rhomboid of the XPI page's Chi as alluding to the Creation, Fall, Resurrection and Redemption. Richardson (note 42 above) 5, noting the many occurrences of the lozenge in the manuscript's decoration, sees it as a symbol of the Saviour; see also V H Elbern, 'Zierseiten in Handschriften des frühen Mittelalters als Zeichen sakraler Abgrenzung' in *Der Begriff der Repraesentatio im Mittelalter*, ed A Zimmermann (Berlin 1971) 340-56 (pp 353-54). Of particular interest are the analogies between the Kells Chi diamond form and *carmen figuratum* by Alcuin and other Carolingian exegetes discovered by Chazelle (note 70 above) 29-51. Alcuin's panegyric to the Cross creates an acrostic similar to that employed by Venantius Fortunatus for his *carmen figuratum*, where the diamond shape signifies the shape of the world. As a final observation on folio 7v, let us note that the Virgin's throne is capped by a lion-headed finial — again a detail very likely signifying Resurrection.

the meaning of the Easter rites.

In part this must originate in the medieval view of Easter as the 'queen of festivals'. As Leo the Great observed, even Christmas is celebrated as preparation for the *festum festorum*.[120] Easter is not simply the feast of Christ's Resurrection; it is the feast of the Redemption accomplished by the Saviour's death and rebirth, the redemption that is the very basis for the life of the church. And there is much in Irish monasticism to encourage the acquisition of a non-Roman lections system with 'elaborate cycles of readings for Lent and Holy Week'. At the same time, the development of the Easter theme in the Book of Kells is far more ambitious and idiosyncratic than in any other insular gospel book, and it seems likely, as was earlier suggested, that much of the impetus for the Kells programme and perhaps even the procurement of non-Roman lections systems grew out of the events surrounding Arculf's sojourn at Iona, the recording of his travels in Adomnán's *De locis sanctis* and the creation of the Book of Durrow.

This raises the formidable question of the date of the Book and the place of its origin. *De locis sanctis* was written on Iona; very likely so too was the Book of Durrow. Books are portable and conceivably both manuscripts, copies or close variants could have affected the Kells iconographic programme in a centre other than Iona. But considering the probability that together Durrow and *De locis sanctis* are more likely to have been available in the place of their creation than elsewhere, their testimony adds weight to the hypothesis — growing in recent years — that the Book of Kells was begun in the Iona scriptorium.[121] George Henderson and Meyvaert have

---

[120]Leo, *Sermo*, XLII, PL 54, 294-97.

[121]For support for the Iona origin thesis, see Henry, 205-10, 218; I Henderson, 'Pictish art and the Book of Kells' in *Ireland in early medieval Europe: studies in memory of Kathleen Hughes*, ed D Whitelock, R McKitterick and D Dumville (Cambridge 1982) 79-105; eadem (note 13 above); eadem, 'Pictish vine-scroll ornament' in *From the Stone Age to the 'Forty-Five': studies presented to R B K Stevenson*, ed A O'Connor and D V Clarke (Edinburgh 1983) 243-68; Royal Commission on the Ancient and Historical Monuments of Scotland, *Argyll: an inventory of the monuments*, IV, *Iona* (1982) 17 ff, 47; D MacLean, 'The Kells Cross in Knapdale: the Iona School and the Book of Kells' in Higgitt (note 108 above) 175-91; J A Calvert, 'The early development of the Irish high crosses and their relationship to Scottish sculpture in the ninth and tenth centuries' (unpub. PhD diss., University of California, Berkeley 1978) 92 ff, RCAHMS, *Argyll: an inventory of the monuments*, V, *Islay, Jura, Colonsay and Oronsay* (1984) 210; McGurk, 'Gospel text', 60-69. Of special interest is folio 201r in the Kells Lucan genealogy. Lewis (note 3 above) 139, n 1, noted that after an initial error Nordenfalk observed that a figure between the columns of the genealogy appears to be emphasizing the name of one of the ancestors of Christ *Iona*, which can mean dove or Columba and thus that the manuscript may be associated with the saint and Iona. Meyvaert (note 31 above) 6-9, further shows that Jerome in his interpretation of Hebrew names translated Iona as Columba and that this interpretation was employed by Adomnán in his life of St Columba of *c*700. Meyvaert uses the genealogy detail as one of several arguments that the Book of Kells was a product of the Iona scriptorium. He turns, for example, to the *De locis sanctis*/Book of Kells relationship, proposing that Arculf's presence on Iona accounts for some elements of ornament in the gospel book. Arculf had been to Egypt and Meyvaert finding Coptic influence on the form of vegetable and animal decoration points to Arculf as initiating this development. Arculf has become something of a *deus ex machina* for the introduction of eastern elements to insular centres, especially to Iona. An event in the life of Dicuil demonstrates other such contacts. Dicuil was

suggested mid-eighth-century creation on Iona for the manuscript.[122] There are difficulties with this conclusion for there remains the possibility that a late-eighth-century gospel book of the Court School of Charlemagne inspired aspects of the canon table designs and particular decorative motifs elsewhere in the Book.[123] And similarities have been recognised between initials in a series of northern French manuscripts of c800 and those in Kells. Significantly, they have been interpreted as the consequence of close contacts between Corbie, Centula & Perrone and Anglo-Saxon and Irish foundations during the Carolingian Age.[124] If our analysis of the two isolated ornamented Kells incipits is correct, such communication may have included the transmission of new dramatic-representational Easter rites.

All this tends to recommend the plausibility of Friend's 1939 thesis, reiterated by Henry in 1974, that the Book of Kells was begun in the Iona scriptorium in the late eighth century.[125] Whether its completion was interrupted by Viking raids of the early ninth century and the manuscript sent to Kells at that time, or as some have advanced recently, that the codex was kept with St Columba's relics, which were not sent to Kells until 877, remains an intriguing but open question.[126]

More important, perhaps, is the iconographic contiguity between the Durrow and Kells Gospels. That both manuscripts place great and unusual weight on a rich iconographic celebration and contemplation of Easter is obvious. So too is the unprecedented complexity and breadth the authors of the Kells programme brought to their celebration of the Easter theme, an

---

an Irish monk at Iona during the lifetime of Scribne and was present when the latter received a monk who had visited the Holy Land sometime before Scribne's death in 772; J F Kenney, *The sources of the early history of Ireland*, I, *ecclesiastical* (New York 1929) 545. In any event, Meyvaert cites my conclusion of a Coptic model for the Kells Madonna and Child miniature (Werner, note 33 above) to reinforce his argument. I would add that in a recent study of Coptic Madonna and Child imagery, R Bergman, 'The earliest Eleousa: a coptic ivory in the Walters Art Gallery', *Journal of the Walters Art Gallery* 48 (1990) 37-56 (p 51), would seem to endorse my thesis.
[122] Henderson, 178-98; Meyvaert, 10-13.
[123] On this, see C Nordenfalk, 'One hundred and fifty years of varying views on early insular gospel books' in Ryan, 4, n 8; McGurk, 'Texts', 57; Alexander, 'Illumination', 269-70, 272.
[124] Henry, 213-21, draws attention to resemblances between Kells initials and those in the Psalter of Corbie (Amiens, BM, MS 18). Among the other manuscripts associated with the north French group are the Stuttgart Psalter (Stuttgart, MS Bibl. Fol. 23), and the Sacramentary of Gellone (Paris, BN, MS lat. 12048). For studies of insular elements in the Amiens Psalter, see G L Micheli, *L'Enluminure du haut Moyen Âge et les influences irlandaises* (Brussels 1939) 86-87; J Porcher, 'L'Évangelaire de Charlemagne et le Psautier d'Amiens', *Revue des Arts* (1957) 51 ff; idem, 'Aux origines de la lettre ornee médiévale', *Melanges Eugène Tisserant* (Vatican City 1964) II, 273-276. L Traube, 'Persona Scottorum', *Sitzungsberichte der Bayerischen Akademie* (Munich 1900), has detailed a close relationship between Corbie, Centula (St Riquier), and Pérrone and English and Irish monasteries. Let us note on this point that Alcuin numbered Amalarius among his pupils, knew the abbot of Corbie and was a friend of Angilbert of Centula; L Wallach, *Alcuin and Charlemagne*, repr of 1959 ed (New York 1968); Chazelle (note 70 above) 316.
[125] See Alexander, 'Illumination', 289. Harbison (note 40 above) conjectures, however that the manuscript was created at Kells in the 820s or 830s.
[126] Henderson, 178-98; Meyvaert (note 31 above)

amplification that came to include the pictorial cultivation of rites of the entire Easter triduum, Lent and possibly Ascension Day. The light this casts on Columban monasticism and the interest of the Iona community deserves further study, as does the role Arculf and Adomnán may have played in all this.

Pl 1 Book of Kells, folio 1v: Canon I 1

Plates

Pl 2 Book of Kells, folio 2v, detail showing top of canon table: evangelist symbols and Christ between two animals

Pl 3 Book of Kells, folio 3r, detail showing top of canon table: evangelist symbols and eucharistic cup between two animals

Pl 4 Book of Kells, folio 3v: Canons II 3-III

Pl 5 Book of Kells, folio 4r: Canon IV

Pl 6 Book of Kells, folio 4v: Canon V

Plates

Pl 7 Book of Kells, folio 6v: twelfth-century copy of charter in Irish relating to the monastery at Kells

Pl 8 Book of Kells, folio 7r: twelfth-century copy of charter in Irish relating to the monastery at Kells

Pl 9 Book of Kells, folio 7v: Virgin and Child

Pl 10 Book of Kells, folio 8r: opening of *Breves causae* of Matthew

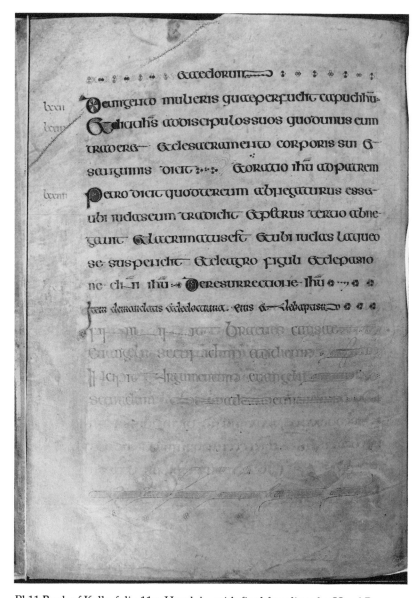

Pl 11 Book of Kells, folio 11v: Hand A , with final four lines by Hand B

Pl 12 Book of Kells, folio 12r, detail: beginning of *argumentum* of Matthew

Pl 13 Book of Kells, folio 188v, detail: *Fuit in diebus Hero/dis*

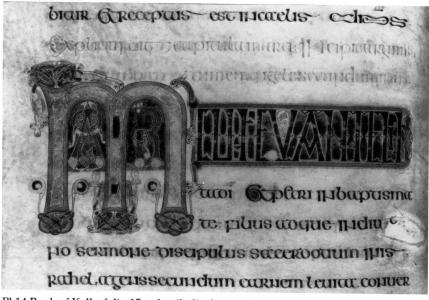

Pl 14 Book of Kells, folio 15v, detail: display panel

Pl 15 Book of Kells, folio 19v, detail: display panel

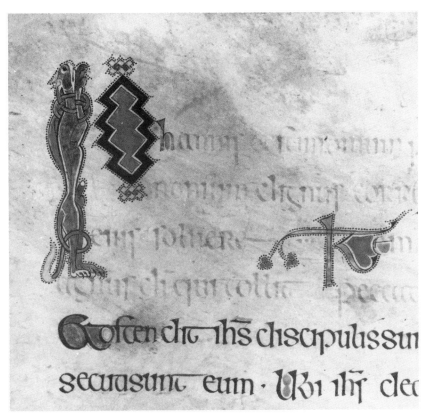

Pl 16 Book of Kells, folio 24r, detail

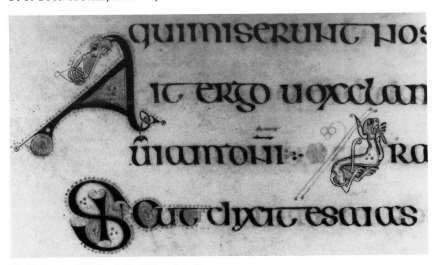

Pl 17 Book of Kells, folio 293v, detail

Pl 18 Book of Kells, folio 28v: St Matthew

Pl 19 Book of Kells, folio 29r: *Liber generationis*

Pl 20 Book of Kells, folio 32v: the Christ figure

Pl 21 Book of Kells, folio 33r: eight-circle cross

Pl 22 Book of Kells, folio 34r: Chi Rho page

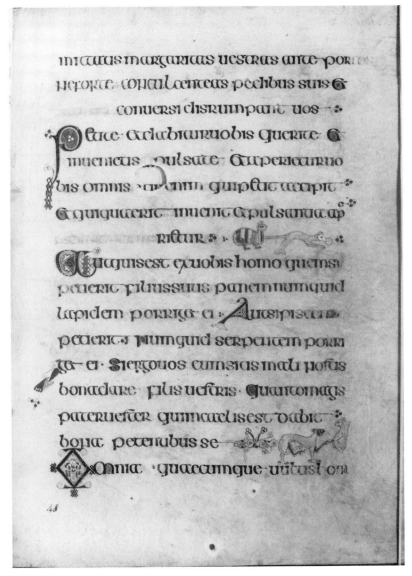

Pl 23 Book of Kells, folio 48r: Matthew 7:6-12

Pl 24 Book of Kells, folio 83v, detail

Pl 25 Book of Kells, folio 99v, detail

ⲟⲁⲥⲥⲉⲩⲇⲓⲧ ⲓⲏ̄ⲥ ⲏⲓⲉⲣⲩⲥⲟⲗⲓⲙⲓⲥ ⲉⲥⲧⲁⲩⲧⲉⲙ ⲏⲓⲉ·
ⲣⲩⲥⲟⲗⲅⲙⲓⲥ ⲥⲩⲡⲉⲣⲡⲣⲟⲃⲁⲧⲓⲟⲁ ⲡⲓⲥⲁⲓⲁ ⲅⲩⲁⲉ·
ⲟⲟⲅⲩⲟⲙⲓⲩⲁⲧⲩⲣ. ⲏⲉⲃⲣⲁ ⲉⲓⲟⲁⲉ· ⲃⲉⲑⲥⲁⲓⲇⲁ· ⲓⲩ·
ⲡⲟⲣⲧⲓⲟⲟⲥ ⲏⲁⲃⲉⲩⲥ·]ⲁⲏⲓⲓⲥ ⲓⲁⲟⲉⲃⲁⲧ ⲙⲩⲗⲧⲓⲁ
ⲟⲟ ⲙⲁⲅⲩⲁ ⲗⲁⲩⲅⲩⲉⲩⲁⲩⲙ ⲟⲁⲉⲗⲟⲣⲩⲙ ⲟⲗⲁⲓ
ⲇⲟⲣⲩⲙ ⲁⲣⲓⲟⲟⲣⲩⲙ ⲉ̄ⲭⲥⲡⲉⲟⲟⲁⲩⲟⲩ ⲡⲁⲣⲁ
ⲗⲓⲁⲟⲟⲣⲩⲙ ⲁⲅⲩⲁⲟⲟⲙⲟⲩⲙ̄ꝯ ꞉ Aⲩⲅⲉⲗⲩⲥ
ⲁⲩⲧⲉⲙ ⲟⲏⲓ ⲥⲉⲟⲩⲩⲇⲩⲙ ⲧⲉⲙⲡⲩⲥ ⲇⲓⲥⲟⲟⲩⲇⲉ·
ⲃⲁⲧ ⲓⲩⲡⲓⲥⲟⲁⲩⲁⲙ ⲉ̄ ⲙⲟⲩⲉⲃⲁ ⲟⲁⲣ ⲁ ⲅⲩⲁⲟ ⲅⲩⲓ·

Pl 26 Book of Kells, folio 303r, detail

Cenantibus autem eis accipit
ihs panem & benedixit ac
fregit deditquediscapulis suis
dicens accipite edite exhocomnis
hocest enim corpus meum quod
confrinigitur proseculi uitae
Accapens calicenigratias
agit &dedit illis dicens
bibite exhocompnes hicest enim
sanguis meus pout testamenti
quieffundetur pronobis & pro
multas inremisionem peccatoris·
Dico autem uobis quianonbi
bam amodo dehoc genime uitas
usque indiem illum quo illud
bibam uobiscum nouum inregno
patris

Pl 27 Book of Kells, folio 113v: Matthew 26:26-29

Pl 28 Book of Kells, folio 114r: 'Arrest of Christ'

Pl 29 Book of Kells, folio 124r: Matthew 27:38

uenit ihs ingalileam————⁖ cens quoni
Praedicans euangelium regni di dicens
cam inpletum est tempus & adpropin
quauit regnum di ⁖ penitemini & credite
euangelio & praeteriens secus mare
galilee uidit symonem & andream
fratrem eius mittentes retia in mare
erant enim piscatores ⁖⁓⁓⁓⁓⁓
& dixit eis ihs uenite postme & fac
iam uos fieri piscatores hominum————
& protinus relictis retibus secuti sunt eum⁖
& progressus indepussillum uidit
iacobum zebedei · & iohannem fratrem
eius · & ipsos in naui componentes retia⁖
& statim uocauit eos & relicto patre
suo zebedeo in naui cum mercinariis se
cuti sunt eum ⁖ & ingrediuntur————

Pl 30 Book of Kells, folio 131v: Hand A

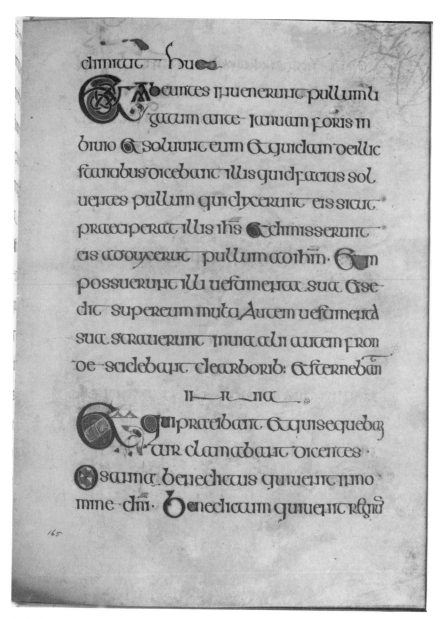

Pl 31 Book of Kells, folio 165r: Hand D

Pl 32 Book of Kells, folio 183r: Crucifixion narrative (Mark 15:24-25)

Pl 33 Book of Kells, folio 187v: end of St Mark's gospel (Mark 16:19-20)

Pl 34 Book of Kells, folio 188r: *Quoniam*

Pl 35 Book of Kells, folio 188r, detail: beard-pullers

&superomnia monta·ina iudae divul
gabantur omnia uerba haec & possu
erunt omnes quiaudiebant incordesuo
dicentes quidputas puer iste erit &
enim manus dni erat cumillo &zacha
rias pater eius impletusest spu sco
&profetauit dicens
Dicais dns ds israhel quiauisi
tauit & fecit redemptionem
plebis suae & erexit cornu salutis
nobis indomu dauid pueri sui Sicut lo
cutusest peros scorum profetarum
suorum quiabinosunt & liberauitnos
abinimicis noftris & demanu omnium
quinos oderunt & adfaciendam miseri
cordiam cumpatribus noftris & memoratu
rari testamenta sui sci Iusiurandum

Pl 36 Book of Kells, folio 193r: Hand C

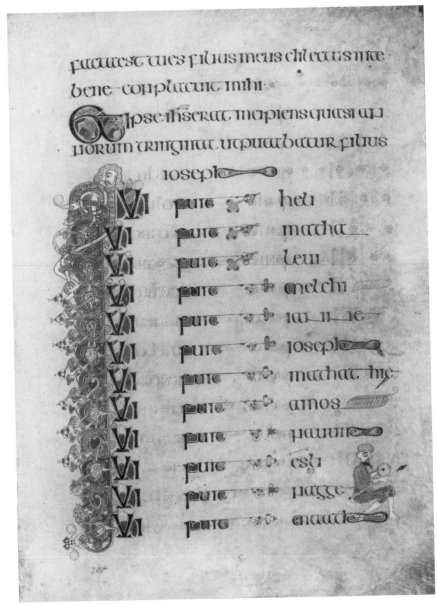

Pl 37 Book of Kells, folio 200r: genealogy of Christ

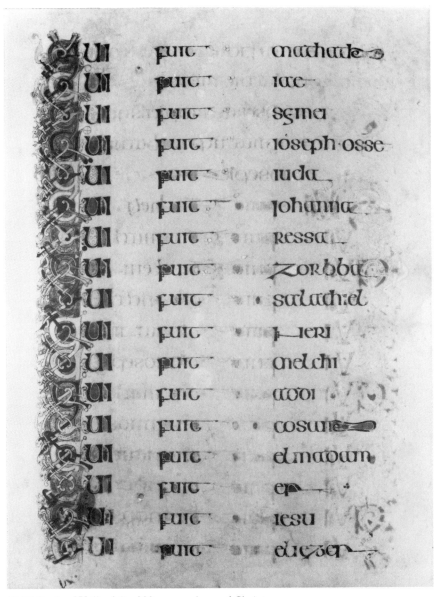

Pl 38 Book of Kells, folio 200v: genealogy of Christ

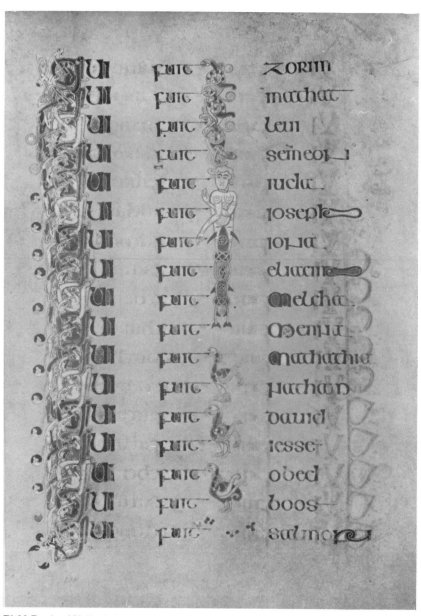

Pl 39 Book of Kells, folio 201r: genealogy of Christ

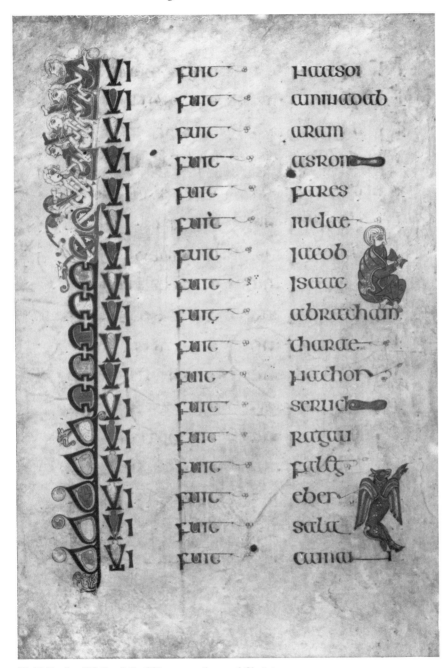

Pl 40 Book of Kells, folio 201v: genealogy of Christ

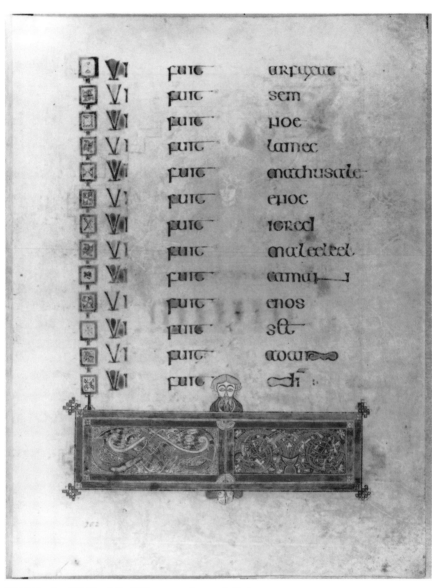

Pl 41 Book of Kells, folio 202r: genealogy of Christ

Pl 42 Book of Kells, folio 202v: Temptation of Christ

Pl 43 Book of Kells, folio 203r: *Iesus / Autem / Plenus / Spiritus / Sancto*

mam suam nonpotest meus esse disa
pulus & quinonbaiulat crucem suam
& uenit post me nonpotest meus esse
disapulus ꝰ Quis enim exuobisuo
lens turrem aedificare nonprius
sedens conputat sumptus quae ne
cessarisunt si habet adperficiendum
nepost quam ω posuerit fundamen
tum & nonpotuerit perficere omnes
quiuident incipiant inludere ei dicen
tes quiahic homo coepit aedificare &
nonpotuit consummare Aut quis
rexiturus committere bellum adui
susalium regem nonsedens prius co
gitat si possit cumdecem milibꝰ oc
currere ei quiainuiginti milibus
uenit aduersumse alioquin adhuc

249

Pl 44 Book of Kells, folio 249r: Hand D

Pl 45 Book of Kells, folio 250r: detail Hand D

Pl 46 Book of Kells, folio 253v, detail

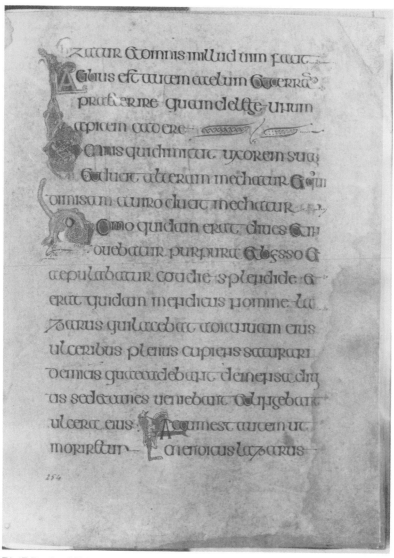

Pl 47 Book of Kells, folio 254r: Luke 16:16-22

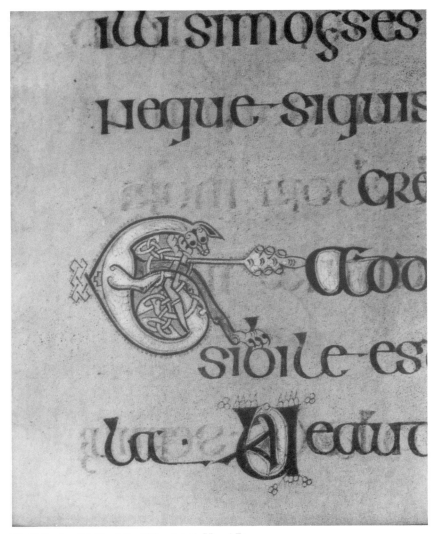

Pl 48 Book of Kells, folio 255r, detail: Hand D

Pl 49 Book of Kells, folio 283r, detail

Pl 50 Book of Kells, folio 285r: *Una autem sabbati ualde delu[culo]* (Luke 24:1)

Pl 51 Book of Kells, folio 291v: St John

Pl 52 Book of Kells, folio 292r: opening of St John's gospel

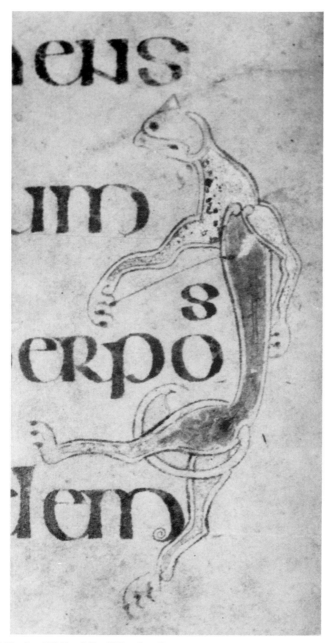

Pl 53 Book of Kells, folio 327r, detail

Pls 54a-b Book of Kells: samples of textlines written by Hands A and B

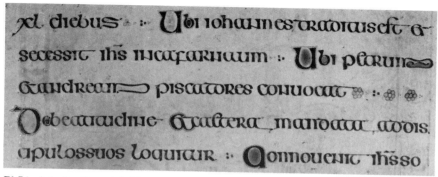

Pl 54a folio 8v, lines 4-8: Hand A

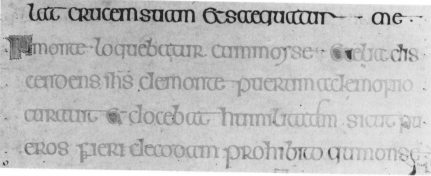

Pl 54b folio 21r, lines 9-13: Hand B

Plates

Pls 55a-b Book of Kells: samples of textlines written by Hands C and D

Pl 55a folio 85r, lines 1-5: Hand C

Pl 55b folio 94r, lines 1-5: Hand D

Pl 56 Book of Kells: samples of spelling and writing *Jerusalem*

no 1	folio	11r	Hand A
no 2	folio	11r	Hand A
no 3	folio	78r	Hand C
no 4	folio	91r	Hand D
no 5	folio	167v	Hand D
no 6	folio	167v	Hand D
no 7	folio	246v	Hand D
no 8	folio	246v	Hand D
no 9	folio	246v	Hand D
no 10	folio	256r	Hand D
no 11	folio	282r	Hand D

Pls 57a-b Book of Kells: samples of ligatured *st* and elongated *e* over *g* or *t*

Pl 57a: ligatured *st*

no 1	folio 8v	Hand A
no 2	folio 11r	Hand A
no 3	folio 20v	Hand B
no 4	folio 81v	Hand C
no 5	folio 94v	Hand D
no 6	folio 105r	Hand D
no 7	folio 138r	Hand A
no 8	folio 138r	Hand A
no 9	folio 246r	Hand D
no 10	folio 253v	Hand D
no 11	folio 255v	Hand D
no 12	folio 304r	Hand A
no 13	folio 309v	Hand A

Pl 57b: elongated *e*

no 1	folio 8v	Hand A
no 2	folio 11r	Hand A
no 3	folio 21r	Hand B
no 4	folio 78r	Hand C
no 5	folio 81v	Hand C
no 6	folio 81v	Hand C
no 7	folio 138r	Hand A
no 8	folio 139v	Hand A
no 9	folio 246r	Hand D
no 10	folio 257r	Hand D
no 11	folio 260r	Hand D
no 12	folio 304r	Hand A
no 13	folio 311r	Hand A

Pls 58a-b Book of Kells: samples of vertical and suprascript *m*

1	mửoceʒ	1	habepꝛꞇ	
2	uiaʒ	2	ꞃꞇoeꞁꞁaꞃꞇ	
3	conceꞃ̃eụʒ	3	supeꞃꞃegꞁꞇ	
4	cꞃibulꞇꞇꞇoꞇeʒ	4	ꞁꞇquꞇꞇꞇꞇaꞇꞇ	
5	muꞇꞇaʒ	5	seꝺꞇꞇ	
6	hoc scꞇꞇʒ	6	cuꞇꞇꞇꞇaꞇꞇꞇe	
7	guʒ	7	ꞇꞇoeꞇꞇ	
8	cꞇꞇꞇeꝺꞇꞇʒ	8	cꞇꞇ homꞁꞁe	
9	cꞇꞇopꞇꞇꞇꞇaʒ	9	cꞇꞇfuꞁꞇoꞁꞇꞇ	
10	quoꝺꞁꞇꞇꞇaʒ			
11	secꞇꞇꞁꞇꞇꞇʒ			
12	pꞇꞇꞇꞇeʒ			

Pl 58a: vertical *m*

no 1	folio 15v	Hand A
no 2	folio 90r	Hand D
no 3	folio 94r	Hand D
no 4	folio 104v	Hand D
no 5	folio 142r	Hand C
no 6	folio 189v	Hand C
no 7	folio 244r	Hand D
no 8	folio 262r	Hand D
no 9	folio 284r	Hand D
no 10	folio 297v	Hand A
no 11	folio 302v	Hand A
no 12	folio 304r	Hand A

Pl 58b: suprascript *m*

no 1	folio 82r	Hand C
no 2	folio 96r	Hand D
no 3	folio 172r	Hand D
no 4	folio 245v	Hand D
no 5	folio 247v	Hand D
no 6	folio 251r	Hand D
no 7	folio 262r	Hand D
no 8	folio 262r	Hand D
no 9	folio 297v	Hand A

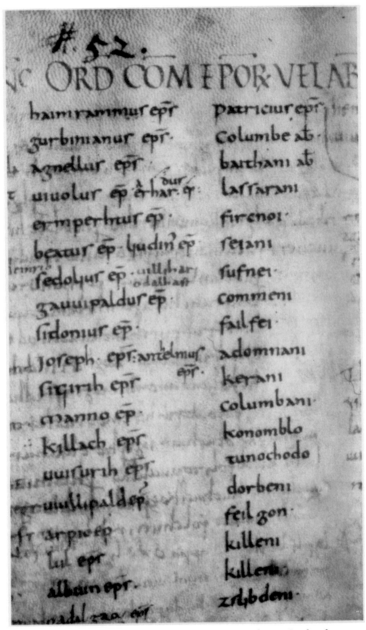

Pl 59 Abbots of Iona and other Irish saints in confraternity-book of St Peter's, Salzburg, Erzabtei St Peter, MS A.1., p 52

Pl 60 Iona, vallum and monastic area from north-east (*RCAHMS AG 11,999*)

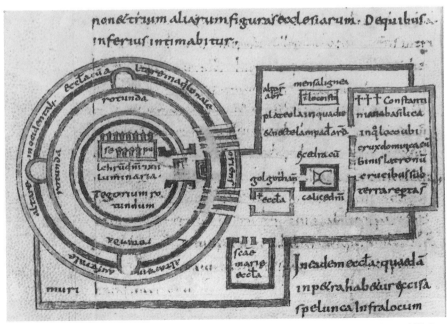

Pl 61 Vienna, Österreichische Nationalbibliothek, Cod. 458, folio 4v: plan of Holy Sepulchre

Pl 62 Iona, clay moulds excavated 1974 (*scale* 2:1) (*RCAHMS AG 10,704*)

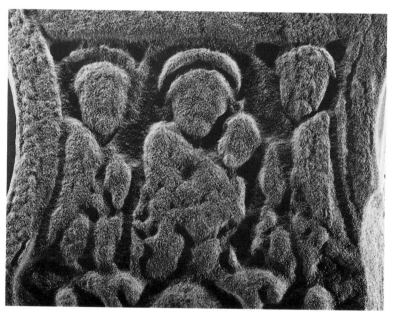

Pl 63 Iona, St Oran's Cross, Virgin and Child with angels (*RCAHMS AG 5028*)

Pl 64 Iona, St John's Cross (west face) as re-erected in Abbey Museum, 1990 (*RCAHMS* B 64010)

Pl 65 Tara: Rath na Riogh (*aerial photo, D L Swan*)

Pl 66 Kells from the north (*aerial photo, D L Swan*)

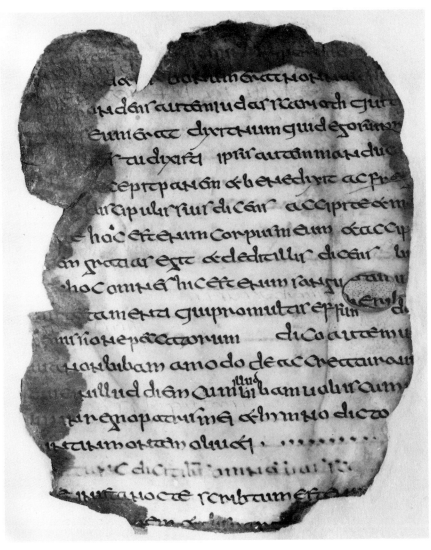

Pl 67 TCD, MS 55 (*codex Usserianus primus*), folio 25v: Matthew 26:30-31

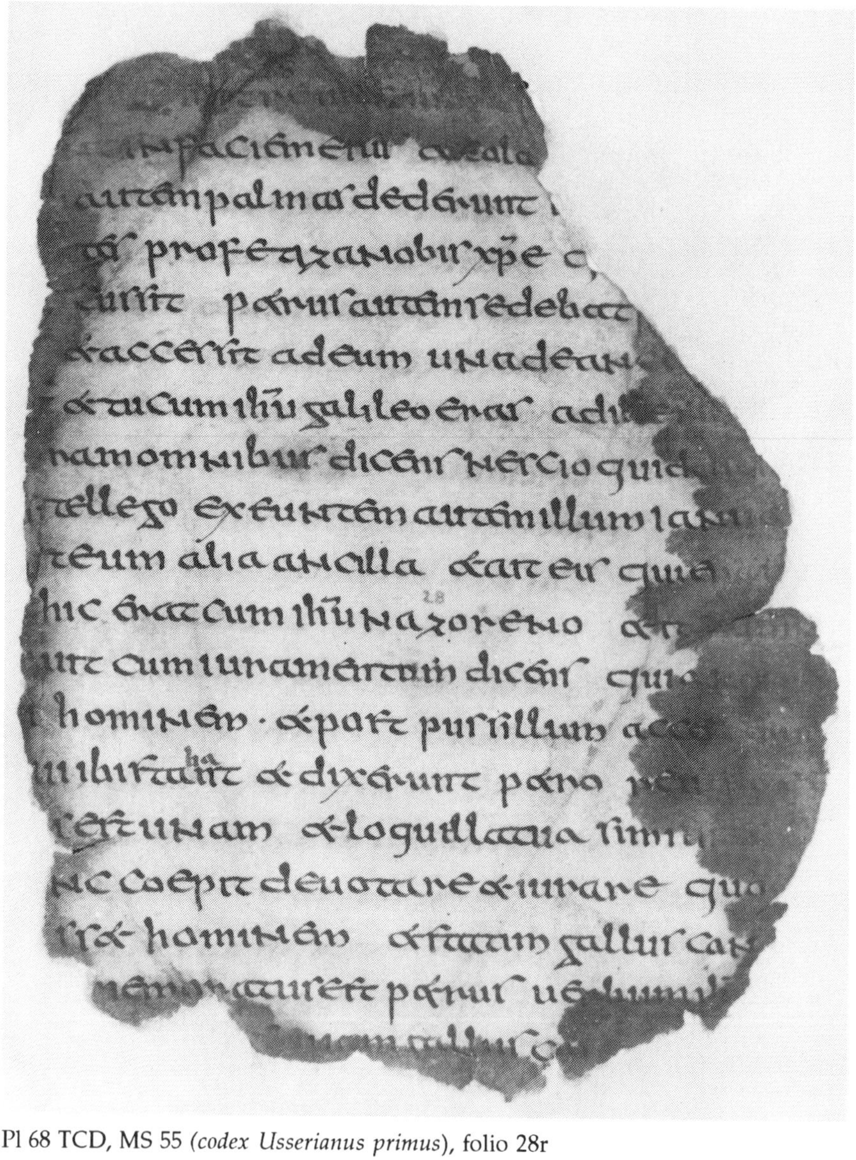

Pl 68 TCD, MS 55 *(codex Usserianus primus)*, folio 28r

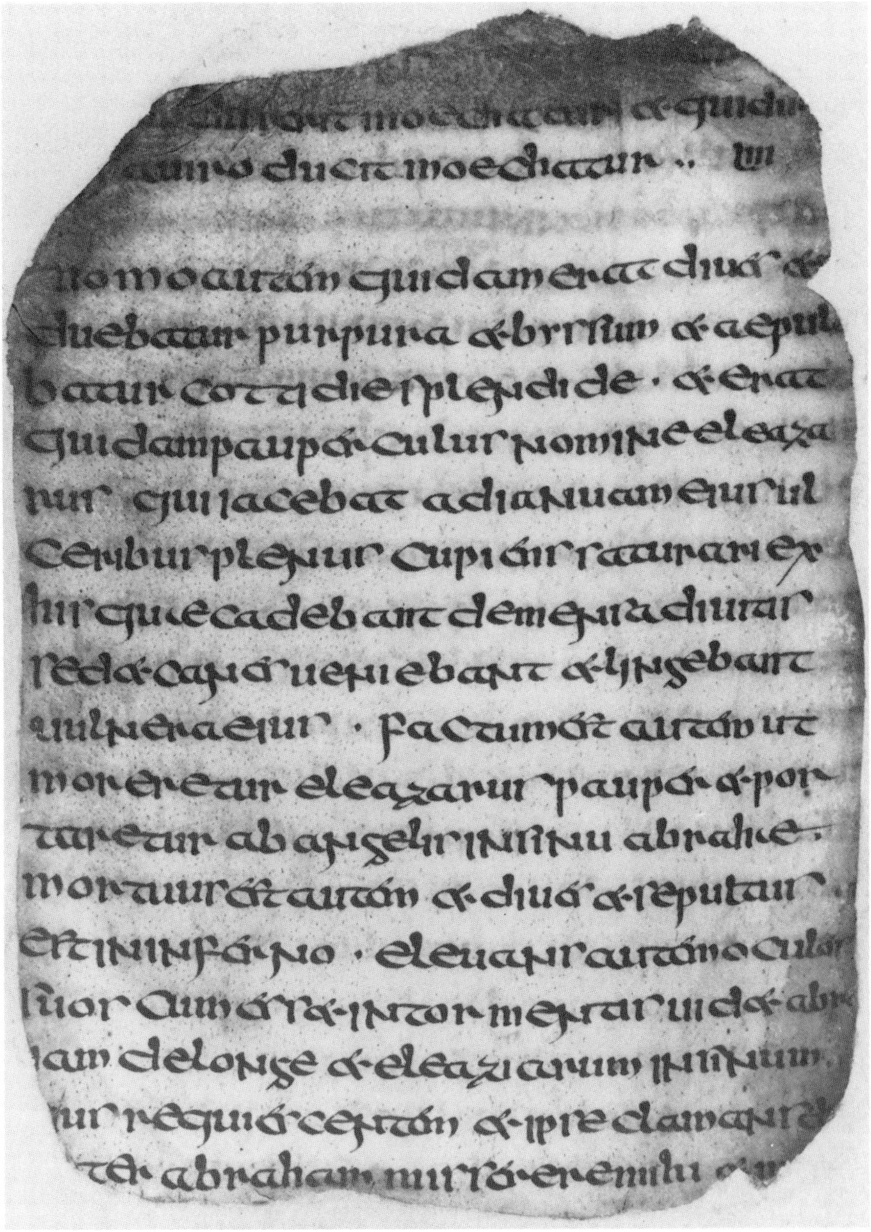

Pl 69 TCD, MS 55 (*Codex Usserianus primus*), folio 126v

Pl 70 Biblioteca Apostolica Vaticana, Barb. Pal. lat. 235, folio 13v

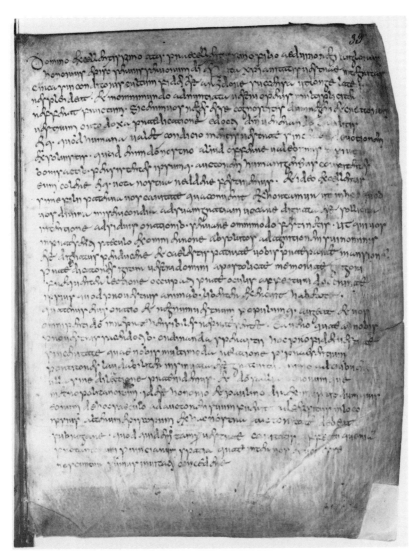

Pl 71 Paris, Bibliothèque Nationale, MS lat. 10837, folio 33r

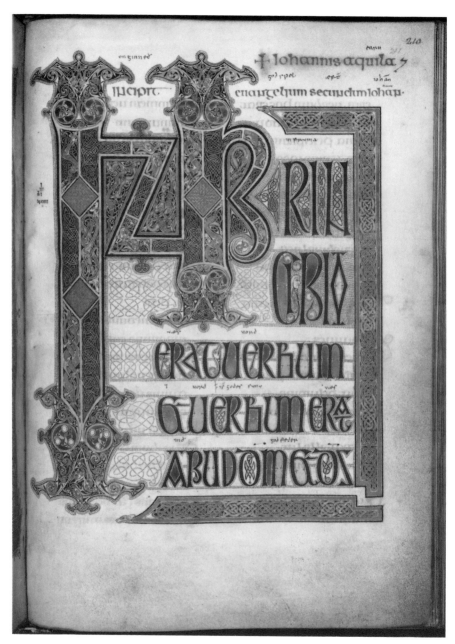

Pl 72 London, British Library, Cotton Nero D. IV (Lindisfarne Gospels), folio 211r: opening of St John's gospel

Pl 73 TCD, MS 52 (Book of Armagh), folio 32v, detail: *imago hominis*

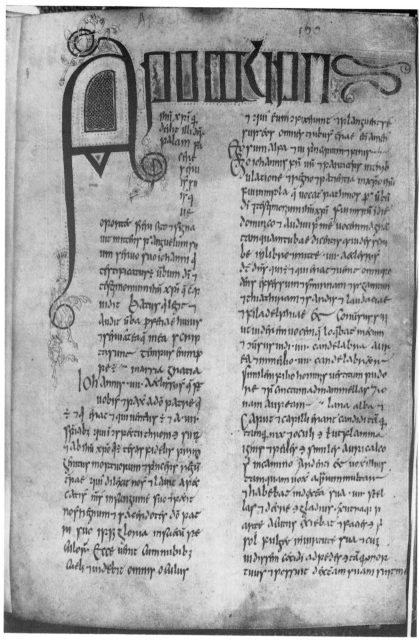

Pl 74 TCD, MS 52 (Book of Armagh), folio 160r: *Apocalypsis*

Pl 75 Paris, Bibliothèque Nationale, lat. 9389, folio 75v (Echternach Gospels):
Lion of St Mark

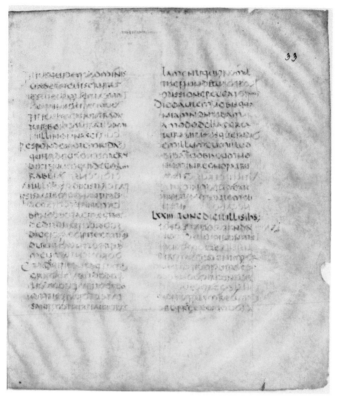

Pl 76 Paris, Bibliothèque Nationale, lat. 17225 (*Codex Corbeiensis*),
folio 33r: Matthew 26:24-31

Pl 77 Durham, Dean and Chapter Library, MS A.II.17, folio 38⁴r detail:
unfinished spiral disks inside the *D* of *DEIOHANNE BAPTISTA* showing
the compass prick left by the artist during layout (*The Dean and Chapter of Durham*)

Pl 78 TCD, MS 57, Book of Durrow, folio 124v: Calf symbol of Luke

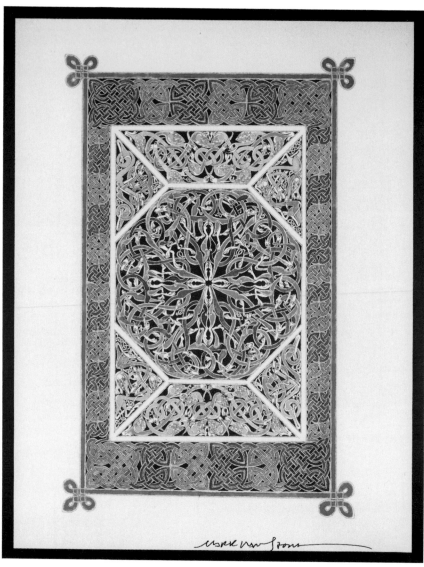

Pl 79 Imitation insular carpet-page (*Mark Van Stone, 1978*)

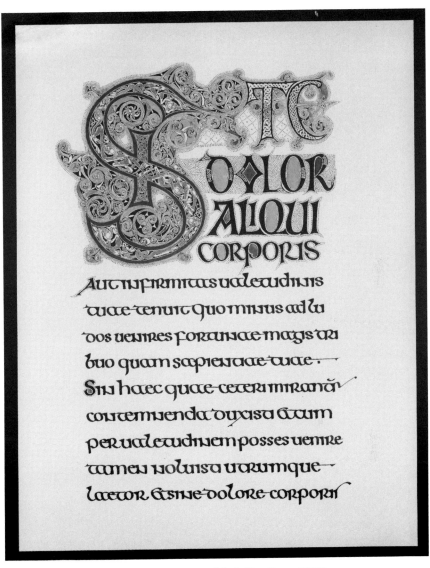

Pl 80 Imitation initial, text quill-written (*Mark Van Stone, 1978*)

Pl 81 Pictish cross-slab at Nigg (Ross and Cromarty) (*photo: Roger Stalley*)

Pl 82 Tower Cross at Kells, east face (*photo: Roger Stalley*)

Pl 83 Tower Cross at Kells, west face: Crucifxion (*photo: Roger Stalley*)

Pl 84 Tower Cross at Kells, west face: Last Judgement/*Majestas Domini*
(*photo: Roger Stalley*)

Pl 85 Monasterboice, Tall Cross, west face (*Green Studio, Dublin*)

Pl 86 Monasterboice, Muiredach's Cross, west face (*Green Studio, Dublin*)

Pl 87 Monasterboice, Muiredach's Cross, west face, shaft (*Green Studio, Dublin*)

Pl 88 Monasterboice, Muiredach's Cross, west face, panel at head of cross (*Green Studio, Dublin*)

Pl 89 The possible Mocking of Christ scene on the west face of the shaft of the high cross at Drumcliff, county Sligo (*photo: Peter Harbison*)

Pl 90 Tower cross at Kells, east face, detail showing Adam and Eve together with Cain and Abel (*photo: Roger Stalley*)

Pl 91 The Raised Christ flanked by apostles and angels on the east face of the cross at Durrow, county Offaly (*Commissioners of Public Works in Ireland*)

Pl 93 Spiral scrolls and animal interlace on the south side of the shaft of the cross at Drumcliff, county Sligo
(*photos: Peter Harbsion*)

Pl 92 The Virgin and Child on the end of the south arm of the high cross at Drumcliff, county Sligo

Pl 94 Beard-pulling men on the top of the side-panels of the underside of the ring on the present west side of the Market Cross at Kells, county Meath — from a cast in the National Museum of Ireland (*photo: Peter Harbison*)

Pl 95 Beard-pullers at the bottom of the shaft on the north side of Muiredach's Cross at Monasterboice, county Louth (*photo: Peter Harbison*)

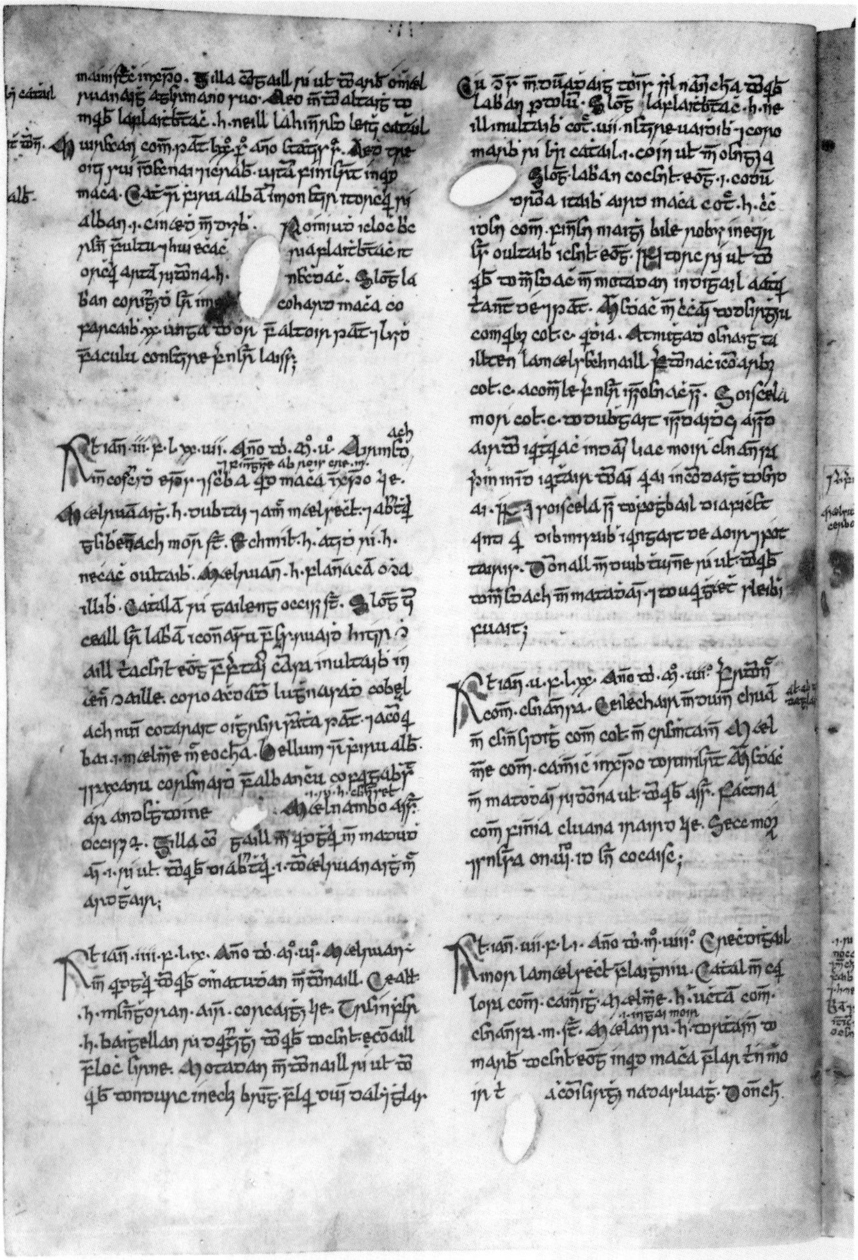

Pl 96 Oxford, Bodleian Library, MS Rawlinson B 489, folio 35v: the entry relating to Kells is to be seen on the right hand column about half way down

Pl 97 The Derrynaflan Paten, eighth century AD (*National Museum of Ireland*)

Pl 98 The Ardagh Chalice, eighth century AD (*National Museum of Ireland*)

Pl 99 The cover of the Lough Kinale book shrine shortly after its discovery (*National Museum of Ireland*)

Pl 100 Detail of the border along the edge of the cover of the Lough Kinale book shrine showing the openwork spiral ornament (*National Museum of Ireland*)

Pl 101 View of the most intact fragment from the side of the Lough Kinale book shrine.
The large central medallion and one of the smaller flanking medallions are present
(*National Museum of Ireland*)

Pl 102 View of the two attachments which were fitted to the ends of the Lough Kinale
book shrine and which held a carrying-strap (*National Museum of Ireland*)

Pl 103 Amiens, Bibliothèque Municipale, MS 18 (Psautier de Corbie), folio 73, detail

Pl 104 Paris, Bibliothèque Nationale, lat. 13392 (Homélies de saint Grégoire), folio 27, detail

Pl 105 Paris, Bibliothèque Nationale, lat. 11685 (Raban Maur, *De laudibus sancte Crucis*), folio 25v

Pl 106 Paris, Bibliothèque Nationale, lat. 11685 (Raban Maur, *De laudibus sancte Crucis*) folio 25v, detail

Pl 107 Paris, Bibliothèque Nationale, lat. 8878 (*Beatus* de Saint-Sever), p 184

Pl 108 Paris, Bibliothèque Nationale, lat. 8878 (*Beatus* de Saint-Sever) p 184, detail

Pl 109 Chapiteau, Église Saint-Hilaire de Poitiers: principal face (*Musée des Monuments Français*)

Pl 110 Chapiteau, Église Saint-Hilaire de Poitiers: detail (*Musée des Monuments Français*)

Pl 111 Paris, Bibliothèque Nationale, nouv. acq. lat. 1390 (*Vie de saint Aubin*), folio 4

Pl 112 Amiens, Bibliothèque Municipale, MS 18 (Psautier de Corbie), folio 92v, detail

Pl 113 TCD, MS 60 (Book of Mulling), folio 47v: Matthew 26:30-31

Pl 114 TCD, MS 60 (Book of Mulling), folio 81v: St John

Pl 115 London, British Library, MS Harley 2788, folio 6v: Canon I 1

Pl 116 Maaseik, Church of St Catherine, Trésor (Maaseik Gospels), folio 5v:
Canon II 3 (*Copyright ACL Bruxelles*)

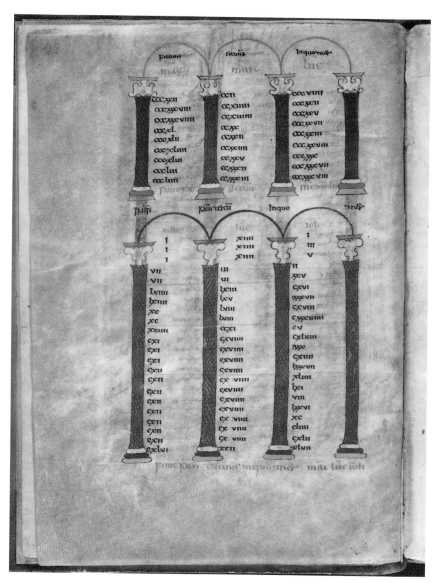

Pl 117 Augsburg, Universitätsbibliothek, Cod. I.2.4°2 (Augsburg Gospels), folio 9v:
Canon II 4-III

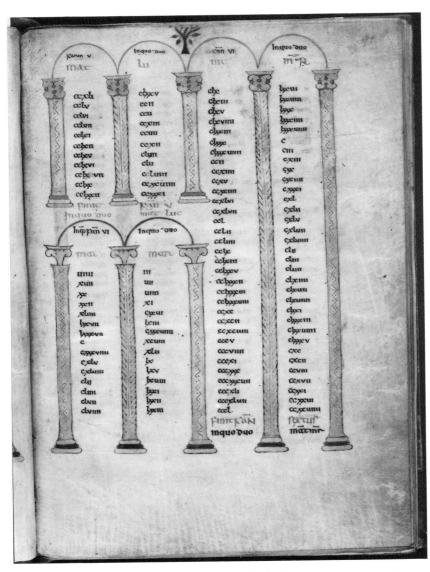

Pl 118 Augsburg, Universitätsbibliothek, Cod. I.2.4°2 (Augsburg Gospels), folio 11r:
Canon V 2-VI

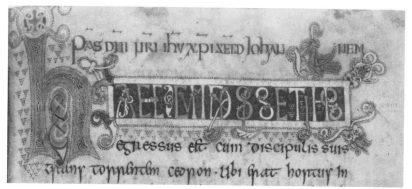

Pl 119 Cambridge University Library, MS Ll.I.10 (Book of Cerne), folio 32, detail:
display panel (*by permission of the Syndics of Cambridge University Library*)

Pl 120 Cambridge University Library, MS Ll.I.10 (Book of Cerne), folio 43, detail:
display panel (*by permission of the Syndics of Cambridge University Library*)

Pl 121 London, British Library, Cotton Vespasian A.I. (Vespasian Psalter), folio 110,
detail: display panel

Pl 122 Cambridge, University Library, MS Ll.I.10 (Book of Cerne), folio 88v, detail (*by permission of the Syndics of Cambridge University Library*)

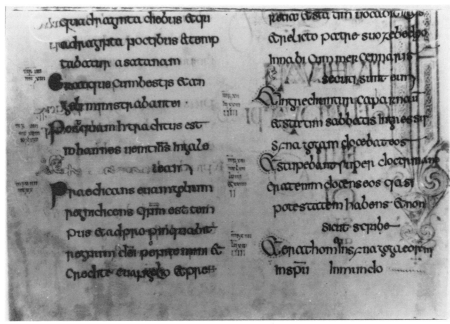

Pl 123 Vatican City, Biblioteca Apostolica Vaticana, Barb. lat. 570 (Barberini Gospels), folio 51v

Pl 124 Vatican City, Biblioteca Apostolica Vaticana, Barb. lat. 570 (Barberini Gospels), folio 125: *In principio*

Pl 125 London, British Library, Harley 2965 (Book of Nunnaminster), folio 4v

Pl 126 Cambridge, University Library, MS Ll.I.10 (Book of Cerne), folio 2v:
Matthew portrait (*by permission of the Syndics of Cambridge University Library*)

Pl 127 London, British Library, Add MS 17738 (Mosan Floreffe Bible), folio 187

Pl 128 St Catherine's monastery, Mount Sinai: icon, 'Scala paradisi' by John Climacus

Luke

qui fuit enos · qui fuit adam
qui fuit seth · qui fuit di ·

Ihs autem plenus spu sco regresus
est iordane agebatur inspu in desertum
diebus xl & noctibus xl & temptabatur adiabu
lo · & nihil manducauit indiebus illis & con
summatis illis essuriunt · Dixit autem illi dia
bulus si filius di es dic lapidi huic ut panis
fiat · & respondit ad illum ihs scriptum est
quia non in pane solo uiuit homo sed inomni
in uerbo di · & duxit illum diabulus & osten
dit illi omnia regna orbis terrae inmomento
temporis · & ait ei tibi dabo potestatem hunc
uniuersam & gloriam illorum quia mihi tra
dita sunt & cui uoluero do illa · tu ergo si
adoraueris coram me erunt tua omnia ·
& respondens ihs dixit illi scriptum est
dnm dm tuum adorabis & illi soli seruies ·
& duxit illum inhirusalem & statuit eum su
pra pinnam templi & dixit illi si filius dies
mitte te deorsum hinc · scriptum est enim

Pl 129 Oxford, Bodleian Library, Rawlinson G.167, folio 10v: Luke 3:38-4:10

Pl 130 Paris, Bibliothèque Nationale, nouv. acq. lat. 1587 (Gospels of St Gatian of Tours), folio 28r: Matthew 26:14-31

NON ẽuıs setho
mo ılle
Respondensau
tem ıudas quıtra
dıdıt eum dıxıt
Numquıd egosú
rabbı aũll,tudı
xıstı·
Caenantıb:aute
eıs accepıt ıhs
panem etbene
dıxıt acr̄regıt·
dedıtq: dıscıpulıs
suıs etaıt accıpı
te etcomedıte hoc
est corpusmeum
Et accıpıenscalı
cem gratıase
gıt etdedıt ıllıs
dıcens bebıte
exhocomnes
hıceste nımsan
cmsmeus nouıtes
tamentı quıpro
multıs effunde
tur ınremıssıo
neampeccatorú
dıco autem uobıs
non bıbam amo
do dehoc genı

mıne uıtıs usque
ındıē ıllú cumıl,
ludbıbam uobıs
cum nouum ın
regno patrısmeı
Et ẽmno dıcto
exıerunt ınmon
tem oleum
ıhs omnes uos
scandalum patı
emını ınmeınıs
tanocte
Scrıptum estenım
per cutıã pasto
rem etdıspergen
tur oues gregıs
postquam autem
resurrexero prae
cedam uosıncalı
leam
Respondensau
tem petrusaıt
ıllı etsıomnes
scandalızatıpue
rıntınte egonú
quam scandalıza
bor amllıhs a
mendıcotı bıquıa
ınhacnocteante·

Pl 131 Paris, Bibliothèque Nationale, lat. 256, folio 60v: Matthew 26:24-34

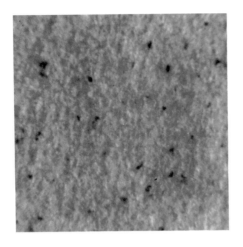

Pl 132 Book of Kells, folio 24v, hair side.
Follicle pocket pigment or dark hair fragments. This pattern is frequently found in the Book of Kells.
(Pls 132-46 are taken at the same magnification of x10)

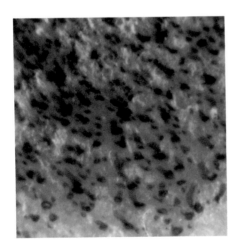

Pl 133 Calf slunk by William Cowley — an area left as witness to gauge the amount removed by scraping. The dense area of follicle pigment or hair is 0.58 mm thick down to 0.21 mm and with a sparse residue down to 0.17 mm seen in pl 134.

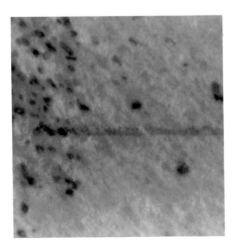

Pl 134 Calf slunk by William Cowley shows the transition from 0.21 mm down to 0.17 mm.

Pl 135 Book of Kells, folio 27v, hair side. The photo-micrograph illustrates an area of the eagle symbol of John. White hair and/or follicle pockets without pigment. It has been suggested that this is goatskin.

Pl 136 Calf slunk by Benjamin Vorst. Dark brown hair fragments remain in the follicle pockets. Some epidermal debris from rough dry scraping. Spine neck area.

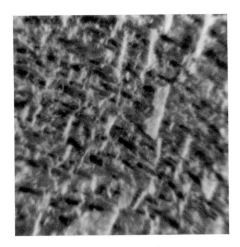

Pl 137 Calf slunk by Benjamin Vorst. This shows the transition zone between the fully haired and unhaired portion from the head right flank edge. Hair white, compare to pl 135.

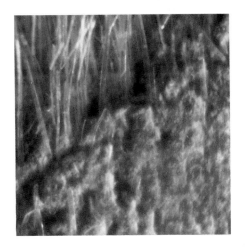

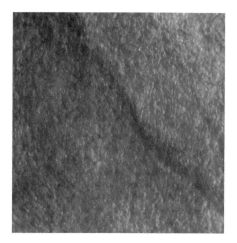

Pl 138 Book of Kells, folio 31r: vein tissue from the flesh side.

Pl 139 Calf slunk by William Cowley. Flesh side of pl 133 showing vein tissue. A particular feature of calf is the overall network that survives; in goat it is present, but rarely in sheep.

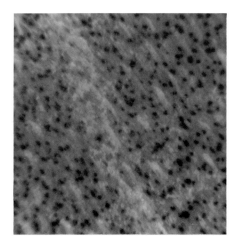

Pl 140 Calf slunk by Benjamin Vorst. Hair side with hair fragments or follicle epidermal pigment and vein with clear follicle pockets. Compare to pl 132. Slunk skin samples are about 4 square feet.

Pl 141 Lambskin by La Pergamena. Head left flank, near the axilla.

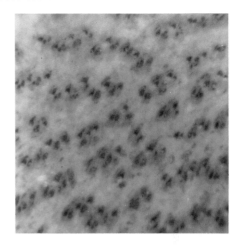

Pl 142 Lambskin, 3 square feet. Head left axilla. Note the relatively larger grain pattern, compared to pl 141.

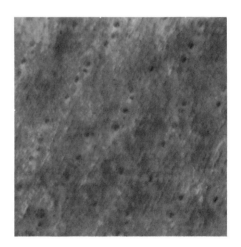

Pl 143 Lambskin. Head left axilla. Compare with pl 141. This contrast between the soft belly grain of the axilla and the main body of the skin is not so marked in goat and kidskin. The axilla grain area of the sheep is the most reliable clue to its identity. No comparable pattern is to be seen in calfskin.

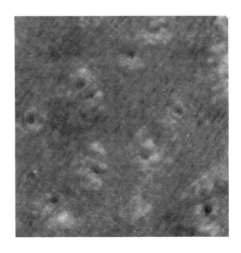

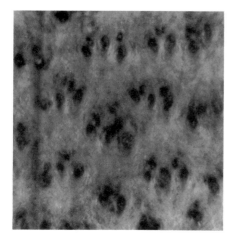

Pl 144 Goatskin (for covering) by William Cowley. The skin is 6.75 square feet and has a 0.35 mm thick flank with clouding of residual epidermal layer.

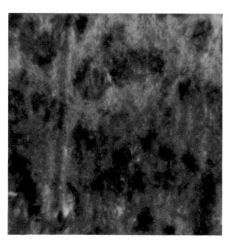

Pl 145 Goatskin. Transition between the residual epidermal layer and the corium layer.

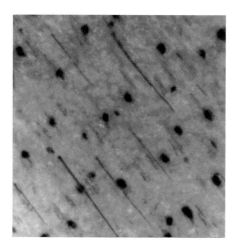

Pl 146 Goatskin by William Cowley. A generally whiter skin, with an area near the axilla that is relatively featureless, lacking deep follicle pockets; but this constitutes only a small area. It could be confused possibly with pl 132, except the follicle pattern and spacing are different.

COLOUR SECTION: KEY TO PLATES 147-191

Pl 147 Analysis of the Book of Kells with the stereomicroscope, August 1991.

Pl 148 Analysis of the Book of Kells with the colour spectrometer, August 1991.

Pl 149 Book of Kells, folio 7v (Virgin and Child). Christ's tunic is painted with copper green pigment.

Pl 150 Book of Kells, folio 24r. Filling of initial with orpiment. Text written with mauve and red lead.

Pl 151 Book of Kells, folio 28v (Matthew). The hair is painted with orpiment, the beard with yellow ochre; the coloristic appearance is disturbed by a layer of dirt.

Pl 152 Book of Kells, folio 5r (canon table). Hair and mouth of the beast painted with green *vergaut* and with two different shades of the blue mixture.

Pl 153 Book of Kells, folio 291v (John). The tunic is painted with a mixture of yellow ochre and sap green; the folds are made with pure sap green and red lead.

Pl 154 Book of Kells, folio 114r (Arrest of Christ). Red lead overpainted over copper green (*pentimento*).

Pl 155 Book of Kells, folio 114r (Arrest of Christ). Red brown ochre in the hairs with drawing in dark brown ochre and iron gall ink.

Pl 156 Book of Kells, folio 27v (Symbols). Cross held by the angel (detail); orpiment glazed with honey-coloured ochre, the orpiment can be seen clearly where the colour layer has partly flaked off.

Pl 157 Book of Kells, folio 291v. Brown ochre as filling of interlace.

Pl 158 Book of Kells, folio 114v. Purple dye, pink and mauve mixture used in the ornamentation.

Pl 159 Book of Kells, folio 183. Brownish and red purple in the garment of the angel.

Pl 160 Book of Kells, folio 7v (Virgin and Child). The angel's tunic is painted with the blue mixture (lapis lazuli, indigo and purple dye), the mantle with greenish indigo.

Pl 161 Book of Kells, folio 114r (Arrest of Christ). Garment painted with translucent brown ochre.

Pl 162 Book of Kells, folio 202v (Temptation). The devil is painted with *vergaut* mixed with carbon, the wings with black ink.

Pl 163 Book of Kells, folio 34r (Chi Rho page). Brown-black iron gall ink used for the drawing; coloured with red lead and orpiment.

Pl 164 Book of Kells, folio 5r (canon table). The angel's wings are painted with the light blue mixture, the dots with dark blue mixture. The fan is painted with greenish indigo.

Pl 165 Book of Kells, folio 183r. Filling with azure blue mixture.

Pl 166 Book of Kells, folio 27v (Symbols). The white face of the angel shows no sign of corrosion and is thus most probably chalk.

Pl 167 Book of Kells, folio 2v (canon table). The small purple columns were clearly painted after the text.

Pl 168 Book of Kells, folio 2v (canon table). The small purple column was clearly painted after the text. Detail.

Pl 169 Book of Kells, folio 3r (canon table). Different shades of brownish and red purple as filling in the capitals, in the background of the angel and in the heads of the beasts.

Pl 170 Stockholm, *Codex Aureus*, folio 6v (canon table). The background of the angel is painted with the same purple dye as in the Book of Kells. The white face is here painted with lead white which shows black corrosion.

Pl 171 Book of Kells, folio 114r (Arrest of Christ). Purple garment of Christ.

Pl 172 Vatican Library, Barberini Gospels, folio 50v (Mark). The purple mantle and the pink tunic are prepared with the same purple dye as that used in the Book of Kells.

Pl 173 Durham, Cathedral Library, MS A.II.10., folio 3v. Blue mixture made from lapis and indigo; *vergaut*, red lead and orpiment.

Pl 174 St Gall Gospels, p 78 (Crucifixion). Blue mixture from lapis and indigo; purple dye and brown ochre.

Pl 175 Book of Kells, folio 32v (Christ).

Pl 176 Book of Kells, folio 32v (Christ). Modelling of vases with purple dye; pseudo-chrysography with orpiment.

Pl 177 Book of Kells, folio 32v (Christ). Peacock (left): the *pentimento* in the wing (red lead over copper green) can be seen where the red lead has flaked off; the legs are modelled differently.

Pl 178 Book of Kells, folio 32v (Christ). Peacock (right): the *pentimento* in the body (dark blue mixture over copper green) can be seen where the blue has flaked off; the legs are modelled differently.

Pl 179 Book of Kells, folio 32v (Christ). Modelling and pseudo-chrysography in the angel's garment.

Pl 180 Book of Kells, folio 32v (Christ). Where the pink frame is heavily cracked, the first layer in orpiment can be detected (*pentimento*).

Pl 181 Book of Kells, folio 7v (Virgin and Child). Multicoloured spots on the angel's wing.

Pl 182 Book of Kells, folio 7v (Virgin and Child). Multicoloured spots on the angel's wing (detail).

Pl 183 Book of Kells, folio 32v (Christ). Snakes in the margin: the blue overpainting leaves a small green margin.

Pl 184 Book of Kells, folio 4v (canon table). Light blue mixture partly glazed with thin purple dye.

Pl 185 Book of Kells, folio 188 (*Quoniam quidem*). Blue border unevenly glazed with pink mixture and ornamented with red lead. The perfect state of conservation proves that the marbling-like appearance of the glaze was intended.

Pl 186 Book of Kells, folio 291v (John). The different blue shades are produced by mixtures (lapis, indigo and white, lapis and white, indigo, white and purple dye).

Pl 187 Book of Kells, folio 292 (*In principio*). The different blue shades are produced by glazing the light blue mixture with purple dye.

Pl 188 Sutton Hoo, enamel of hanging bowl. (*London, British Museum*).

Pl 189 Book of Kells, folio 290v (Symbols). Calf: iridescent effects of pink glaze over copper green.

Pl 190 Book of Kells, folio 290v (Symbols). Angel: multicoloured spots on the wing.

Pl 191 Seventh-century beads from Eichstätten (Baden Württemberg). (From B Sasse, *Leben am Kaiserstuhl im Frühmittelalter* (Stuttgart 1989) front cover).

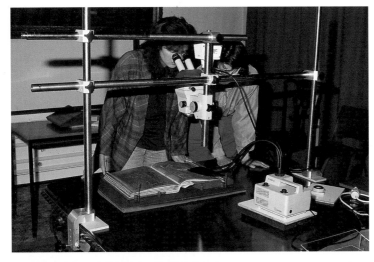

Pl 147

Pl 148

Pl 149

Pl 150

Pl 151

Pl 152

Pl 153

Pl 154

Pl 155

Pl 156

Pl 157

Pl 158

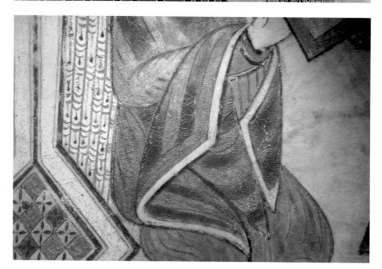

Pl 159

Pl 160

Pl 161

Pl 162

Pl 163

Pl 164

Pl 165

Pl 166

Pl 167

Pl 168

Pl 169

Pl 170

Pl 171

Pl 172

Pl 173

Pl 174

Pl 175

Pl 176

Pl 177

Pl 178

Pl 179

Pl 180

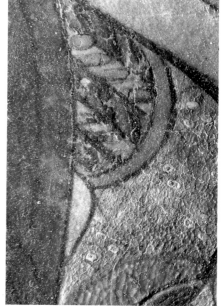

Pl 181

Pl 182

Pl 183

Pl 184

Pl 185

Pl 186

Pl 187

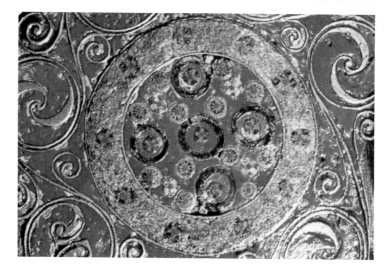

Pl 188

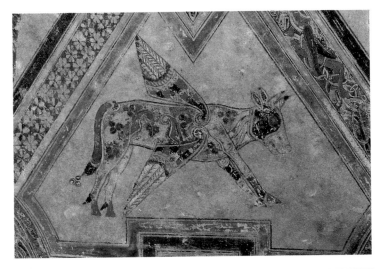

Pl 189

Pl 190

Pl 191